KEY INDICATORS OF CHILD AND YOUTH WELL-BEING

Completing the Picture

KEY INDICATORS OF CHILD AND YOUTH WELL-BEING

Completing the Picture

Edited by

Brett V. Brown

LEA Lawrence Erlbaum Associates
Taylor & Francis Group

New York   London

Lawrence Erlbaum Associates
Taylor & Francis Group
270 Madison Avenue
New York, NY 10016

Lawrence Erlbaum Associates
Taylor & Francis Group
2 Park Square
Milton Park, Abingdon
Oxon OX14 4RN

© 2008 by Taylor & Francis Group, LLC
Lawrence Erlbaum Associates is an imprint of Taylor & Francis Group, an Informa business

Printed in the United States of America on acid-free paper
10 9 8 7 6 5 4 3 2 1

International Standard Book Number-13: 978-0-8058-6313-0 (Softcover) 978-0-8058-4809-0 (Hardcover)

Library of Congress Cataloging-in-Publication Data

Key indicators of child and youth well-being : completing the picture / edited by Brett V. Brown.
   p. cm.
  Includes index.
  ISBN-13: 978-0-8058-4809-0 (cloth : alk. paper)
  ISBN-10: 0-8058-4809-6 (cloth : alk. paper)
  ISBN-13: 978-0-8058-6313-0 (pbk. : alk. paper)
  ISBN-10: 0-8058-6313-3 (pbk. : alk. paper)
   1. Children--Social conditions--Statistics. 2. Youth--Social conditions--Statistics.
  3. Children--Health and hygiene--Statistics. 4. Youth--Health and hygiene--Statistics.
  5. Social indicators. 6. Health status indicators. I. Brown, Brett V.

HQ767.9.K49 2007
305.23021--dc22   2006032810

Visit the Taylor & Francis Web site at
http://www.taylorandfrancis.com

Contents

PART V: CHILD AND YOUTH INDICATORS IN PRACTICE

PART VI: SOCIAL INDEXES OF CHILD WELL-BEING

Preface

In the early 1990s, researchers and policymakers focusing on children's well-being stood at the dawn of a social indicators revival. There were strong signs that social indicators were coming to play an increasingly important role in many aspects of governance, including needs assessment and planning, goal-setting, and accountability (Brown & Corbett, 2003). Forces that appeared to encourage this incipient revival included a shift toward performance-based management techniques (Stagner, 1997); the devolution of political power to the state and local levels; and the revolution in information technology, which substantially lowered the cost of data collection and access (Kingsley, 1998).

While the forces driving the use of child and youth indicators were clear and growing stronger, the tools themselves, the indicators, were in important respects inadequate to the task. Many important dimensions of well-being, such as child mental health, lacked any adequate measures appropriate for large-scale surveys; the research base on which many indicator measures were grounded was often thin; and data for even strong measures were often not available except at the national level (Hauser, Brown, & Prosser, 1997). Those involved in the field were concerned that unless the tools were upgraded in short order, the revival might falter.

In 1994, researchers met to assess the current status of child and youth indicators in the United States and to make recommendations for their future development. Papers from this conference appeared several years later in the book *Indicators of Children's Well-Being* (Hauser et al., 1997). The work represented in that volume helped lay the foundation for several important developments at the federal level. These included the establishment of the Federal Interagency Forum on Child and Family

Statistics (a consortium of more than 20 federal agencies that collect data on children) and several periodic reports to the nation on the condition of children and youth, including the seminal *America's Children: Key National Indicators of Well-Being,* and *Trends in the Well-Being of America's Children and Youth.*

During the following decade, the social indicators revival did not sputter out but instead gained strength in every dimension, including more and better measures; vastly expanding amounts of data collected at all levels of geography (national, state, and local); greater accessibility of data through reports, Web-based databases, and community GIS data systems; a steadily growing research base; and tremendous growth in the use of indicators as tools for planning and governance at the national, state, and local levels (Brown & Moore, 2003).

Today, indicators of child and youth well-being have become indispensable tools supporting public and private efforts to improve the lives of America's children and youth. With growth come new challenges and new needs for better measures, more data, and the research to back them all up. In response, Child Trends and the National Institute for Child Health and Human Development's Family and Child Research Network once again brought together many of the nation's leading researchers in child and youth development to identify the progress that had been made since the 1994 conference in the development, collection, dissemination, and use of key social indicators of child and youth well-being and to identify key opportunities for new indicators development and application in the coming decade. Several years later, the updated papers from that 2001 conference are offered to a broader audience in the present book.

The collection begins with a series of chapters covering key indicators in the areas of health, education, and social and emotional development. Because both the constructs and the appropriate measures within these broad areas can vary dramatically by age, each chapter tends to focus on one or two developmental stages (e.g., early childhood, middle childhood, adolescence). A second set of chapters focuses on indicators of the social contexts influencing child and youth development, including the family, peers, the school, and the community. A third set addresses the use of indicators as policy tools at the state and community levels. The collection finishes with a discussion of broad, summary indexes of child well-being.

Each chapter in this collection offers the reader a focused discussion of key indicators within its respective topic area as well as summaries on the status of existing research to back up those indicators, the available measures and data to track them, and recommendations for development in the coming decade. A number of larger recurring themes run through the chapters that address the status and needs for the child and youth indicators field as a whole, which are discussed below.

WHO SHOULD READ THIS BOOK?

The practical nature of the social indicators field is such that policy-makers, practitioners, researchers, and data collectors are dependent on one another for the advancement of their own areas of concern. Advancement for the field as a whole requires ongoing communication and mutual understanding among all these groups. This book is written for professionals within all these groups who focus on child and youth issues. It is intended as a tool for building that common understanding and a common framework. The intended readership includes professionals working at the national level and in the community, in state agencies and private foundations, in universities and in local service programs. The book is also well suited for students of public policy and the social sciences as a broad introduction to the field of social indicators of child and youth well-being.

AREAS OF PROGRESS AND CHANGE

Data Collection

Data collected at the state and local levels to support local decision making has expanded substantially. The American Communities Survey, fully implemented in 2005, allows states, communities and, eventually, neighborhoods to get annually updated estimates on key sociodemographic characteristics of children and their families across the country (see chap. 13). In addition, the State and Local Area Integrated Telephone Survey system provides a flexible and cost-efficient mechanism for the collection of state-level health data, with recent products including the National Survey of Children with Special Health Care Needs and the National Survey of Children's Health (see chap. 1). Finally, when important measures are not available through existing data collection mechanisms, local communities are finding innovative ways to collect their own data using instruments such as the Search Institute's Profiles of Student Life: Attitudes and Behaviors Survey, which focuses on youth assets (see chap. 7).

In addition, several major national longitudinal studies have been launched, some of which are already yielding important new insights into key factors influencing well-being from early childhood through the transition to adulthood. Such research serves as the foundation for identifying and developing key indicators of well-being. Examples include the National Longitudinal Study of Adolescent Health, featured in chapter 9 of this volume, and the National Longitudinal Survey of Youth 1997, which is following adolescents ages 12 through 16 on an annual basis into adulthood. At the other end of the age spectrum are the Early Child Longitudinal Studies, both the Kindergarten Cohort and the Birth Cohort, which promise to yield valuable insights into the important milestones of and influences affecting early development and school readiness (see chap. 3).

Dissemination

The availability of child social indicator data at all levels of geography has increased exponentially over the last decade, and the variety of indicators offered has also expanded. As discussed in chapter 2 by Stagner and Zweig, federal agencies, foundations, and national research organizations have been very active in developing new indicators reports and increasing ease of access to reports and indicators data over the Internet. Examples include *America's Children: Key National Indicators of Well-Being* (http://www.childstats.gov), an annually updated report produced by the Federal Interagency Forum on Child and Family Statistics; Fedstats (http://www.fedstats.gov), a one-stop shop for access to federal statistics, including data on children and youth; and the *Child Trends DataBank* (http://www.childtrendsdatabank.org), a continuously updated Web-based source for the latest data and research on more than 100 indicators of child and youth well-being. In addition, KIDS COUNT, a project of the Annie E. Casey Foundation that started in 1990 with its first annual report on state-level indicators of child well-being, the *KIDS COUNT Data Book*, has constantly expanded its reach and now supports regular reports in each of the 50 states, the District of Columbia, Puerto Rico, and the U.S. Virgin Islands. In addition, KIDS COUNT provides a great deal of state and local data on children and youth from the decennial census, the American Communities Survey, vital statistics, and other sources on its Web site (http://www.kidscount.org).

Research

The chapters in this volume demonstrate that in the last decade the research base supporting child and youth indicators has expanded in many domains and for previously neglected age groups. Areas that have seen particular growth in the last decade include early development and school readiness (chap. 3), neighborhood influences (chap. 11), and socioemotional development in middle childhood (chap. 5). This growth is at least partly the result of new databases such as those described earlier. It also results, in part, from a shift in focus in the programs and services affecting children and youth away from a sole concern with the prevention of negative outcomes and toward the promotion of positive development as well as a greater awareness of the importance of social contextual influences on development (chaps. 5 and 13).

Finally, research on summary indices of child well-being has also advanced in recent years. The conference began with a presentation by Ken Land on his work in developing the Child Well-Being Index (CWI), a composite measure based on 28 individual measures of well-being that is now published by the Foundation for Child Development (see chap. 14).[1] As with the Index of Leading Economic Indicators, the CWI, and others like it (O'Hare & Bramstedt, 2003; Moore & Vandivere, 2004), attempts to capture the overall state of well-being rather than any particular aspect. The CWI seeks to answer a critical question: "Overall, are things getting better or worse for children?" As Land himself agrees, there is much work that can and should be done to strengthen these indices over time.

Application

In the last decade, the use of social indicators as tools to guide child, youth, and family policy has expanded rapidly. Applications include monitoring and needs assessment; goal-setting and tracking; accountability; reflective practice; and, on rare occasions, evaluation (Brown & Corbett, 2003; Moore, Brown, & Scarupa, 2003). In addition to individual efforts in states such as Vermont, which has embraced the use of indicators to guide state and community decisions in many areas (see chap. 13), states have begun to form consortia around the use of social indicators in particular areas, including early child development (chap. 3), and welfare reform (chap. 12). These consortia allow states to share experiences and combine resources and thinking in ways that strengthen their work.

BROAD RECOMMENDATIONS FOR THE FUTURE

The chapters in this book make many concrete recommendations for future research, measure development, and data collection within the specific topic areas each chapter addresses. In addition, these chapters make a number of broader recommendations, which were reinforced in the conference discussion, that warrant highlighting here.

Develop a Common Framework

The social indicators field is incredibly diverse, involving researchers from many disciplines and requiring ongoing discussion and coordination among researchers, practitioners, and the broader community to function well. These groups have their own frameworks and terminologies for talking about child and youth well-being. Translation and communication across the frameworks are often difficult. This situation creates barriers that can prevent researchers from working together effectively on common problems, that may prevent practitioners from applying the fruits of existing indicators research in their own work, and that can prevent academics from pursuing research of the greatest practical importance to those wanting to use social indicators to produce positive results for children.

Future progress in the field will depend in part on the ability of these diverse groups to develop a common framework and a common language. This point was made forcefully at the conference by Magda Peck, then president of City Match, a member organization of city and county maternal and child health programs around the country. Richard Murphy of the Academy for Educational Development, who was a discussant at the conference, argued that indicators should resonate with the people who are going to use them in the field, meaning that they should be understood as important in the context of their own work. Peter Benson, president of the Search Institute, went further, arguing that researchers and data collectors should be guided in their work in part by what people at the community level regard as important, because these were the things most likely to be acted on at the local level.

Chapter 7, by Eccles, Brown, and Templeton, provides an example of an attempt by academics (in this case, members of the Committee on Community-Level Programs for Youth, organized by the National Research Council and the Institute of Medicine) to synthesize the various frameworks being used in youth development research and practice into a single common frame.

Promote a System of Continuous Improvement

Many of the chapters in this collection note the need for closer coordination between the social indicators that we track and the research that supports them. Addressing this need means that researchers should make efforts to advance the research base for important indicators where research and measurement development are weak. It also means that data collection efforts need to incorporate new indicators and new measures, and to drop old ones, in response to research advances. In chapter 2, Stagner and Zweig, discussing indicators of youth health and development, speak in terms of a "system of continuous improvement" in which research and indicator-tracking systems continuously inform each other. Organizations such as the Federal Interagency Forum on Child and Family Statistics can help with the necessary coordination between federally funded research and data collection to make this a reality.

Expand Indicator Data Available at the State and Local Levels

As noted earlier, the last decade has seen substantial expansion of child and youth well-being indicator data available at the state and local levels. Federal agencies have played a strong role in this development, and many states and communities have also been working systematically to increase available data by collecting new data and mining existing administrative data sources. These points are made strongly in the chapters that focus on the use of indicators for planning and other policy purposes (chaps. 3, 12, & 13) and were echoed by many discussants at the conference. As long as responsibility for promoting the well-being of children and youth continues to devolve to the state and local levels, the need for more and better indicator data will also increase.

Develop More Measures of Positive Development

Many of the child and youth indicators that we track in the United States focus on negative outcomes and negative environments. In part, this is the result of government program funding, which has historically tended to focus on the prevention and remediation of problems rather than the promotion of strengths. However, a greater emphasis on community-level action has led to more of a focus on the positive, as it appears to be a greater motivating and sustaining factor than a narrow focus on preventing problems (chap. 13).

A stronger focus over the last decade on positive development in youth and early childhood programs has led to a period of research and measurement development on positive traits such as caring, confidence, compassion, and resilience (see chaps. 3 & 5–7). Such work is still in its infancy, however, as researchers and practitioners struggle to turn general constructs (e.g., happiness, courage) into more precise concepts and measures (see Moore & Lippman, 2005).

Develop More Culturally Sensitive and Culturally Robust Indicators

Social indicators need to be culturally sensitive in two respects. First, they should reflect both existing research and cultural values of what is desirable or undesirable. Although cross-cultural agreement on many negative outcomes, such as drug use, is common, it is more difficult to find agreement on the most desirable positive outcomes. Ripke and colleagues provide the example of independence from parents as a commonly discussed developmental milestone for adolescents, something that may not be true for Hispanics. Evidence indicates that Hispanics report greater closeness to parents as they reach adolescence (see chap. 5).

Second, even where there is cross-cultural agreement on a broad construct there can still be important cultural differences in the ways those values are expressed. Conference discussant Deborah Coates cited the example of civic engagement, a commonly held value that may have significantly different expressions across cultural and socioeconomic groups.

The authors of several of the chapters in this volume express the concern that many existing measures have not been adequately analyzed for cross-cultural validity and cultural sensitivity, arguing that such tasks should be systematically incorporated into social indicators research and development in the coming decade.

CONCLUSION

The chapters in this book provide compelling evidence that the field of child and youth indicators has made substantial advances in the last decade in all areas, including measure development, data collection, supporting research, and the use of indicators as instruments of policy and planning. These chapters also make clear that there is a lot of work to be done before we "complete the picture," to use words from the title of this collection, and they provide clear direction for that future development.

Although the work of the last decade has not harvested all of the low-hanging fruit, continued advances in the coming decade will require greater levels of planning and coordination among researchers, data collectors, and those who use social indicator data to better the lives of America's children and youth. We hope that this collection of chapters will help build a common language, framework, and set of goals across these professional groups that will be needed to meet the remaining challenges before us and that the coming decade may be as fruitful as the last.

ACKNOWLEDGMENTS

I would like to thank the sponsors who provided the support for the 2001 conference "Key Indicators of Child Well-Being: Completing the Picture" and for the subsequent preparation of the conference papers for publication.

Foundation for Child Development
The Annie E. Casey Foundation
Edna McConnell Clark Foundation
MacArthur Network on Successful Pathways Through Middle
    Childhood
National Institute of Child Health and Human Development
National Institute of Child Health and Human Development Family
    and Child Research Network
Office of the Assistant Secretary for Planning and Evaluation, U.S.
    Department of Health and Human Services

I also extend thanks to the discussants at the conference for their insights and suggestions: Peter Benson, Baron Holmes, Deborah Coates, Tom Kingsley, Judith Erickson, Laura Lippman, Robert Granger, Kristin Moore, Melissa Healy, Richard Murphy, Donald Hernandez, Magda Peck, Con Hogan, and Rafael Valdivieso.

Hsien-Hen Lu, coauthor of Chapter 15, passed away before the publication of this volume. We will always be grateful for his methodological contributions to the development of indices of child well-being.

Finally, a special thanks is extended to Dena Aufseeser for her tireless and expert assistance in the preparation of the manuscript, and to Pilar Marin and Kyleen Hashim.

NOTES

1. For current information on the CWI, visit http://www.fcd-us.org/ourwork/k-index.html

REFERENCES

Brown, B., & Corbett, T. (2003). Social indicators and public policy in the age of devolution. In R. Weissberg, L. Weiss, O. Reyes, & H. Walberg, (Eds.) *Trends in the well-being of children and youth* (pp. 27–52). Washington, DC: Child Welfare League of America.

Brown, B., & Moore, K. (2003). Child and youth well-being: The social indicators field. In R. Lerner, F. Jacobs, & D. Wertlieb (Eds.), *Handbook of applied developmental science: Promoting positive child, adolescent, and family development through research, policies, and programs* (pp. 437–468). Thousand Oaks: Sage.

Hauser, R., Brown, B., & Prosser, W. (Eds.). (1997). *Indicators of children's well-being.* New York: Russell Sage Foundation.

Kingsley, T. (1998). *Neighborhood indicators: Taking advantage of the new potential.* Chicago: American Planning Association.

Moore, K., Brown, B., & Scarupa, H. (2003). *The uses and misuses of social indicators: Implications for public policy.* Washington, DC: Child Trends.

Moore, K. A., & Lippman, L. (Eds.). (2005). *Conceptualizing and measuring indicators of positive development: What do children need to flourish?* New York: Kluwer Academic/Plenum.

Moore, K., & Vandivere, S. (2004) Turbulence: The effects of change. In A. Cosby, R. Greenberg, L. Southward, & M. Weitzman (Eds.), *About children: An authoritative resource on the state of childhood today* (pp. 56–59). Washington, DC: American Association of Pediatrics.

O'Hare, W., & Bramstedt, N. (2003). *Assessing the KIDS COUNT Composite Index.* Baltimore: Annie E. Casey Foundation.

Stagner, M. (1997). Preface. In R. Hauser, B. Brown, & W. Prosser (Eds.), *Indicators of children's well-being* (pp. xxiii–xxiv). New York: Russell Sage Foundation.

List of Contributors

Neil G. Bennett
Baruch College
New York, New York

Christina J. Borbely
Columbia University
New York, New York

Jeanne Brooks-Gunn
National Center for Children
*   and Families*
New York, New York

Brett V. Brown
Child Trends, Inc.
Washington, D.C.

Julia Calkins
Elementary School Teacher
Seattle, Washington

Shannon E. Cavanagh
University of Texas
Austin, Texas

Thomas J. Corbett
University of Wisconsin
Madison, Wisconsin

Ayonda Dent
U.S. Census Bureau
Washington, D.C.

Jacquelynne Eccles
University of Michigan
Ann Arbor, Michigan

Ann Flanagan
University of Virginia
Charlottesville, Virginia

David Grissmer
University of Virginia
Charlottesville, Virginia

Tamara Halle
Child Trends, Inc.
Washington, D.C.

Kathleen Mullan Harris
University of North Carolina
Chapel Hill, North Carolina

Dennis P. Hogan
Brown University
Providence, Rhode Island

Aletha C. Huston
University of Texas
Austin, Texas

Vicki L. Lamb
Duke University
Durham, North Carolina

Kenneth C. Land
Duke University
Durham, North Carolina

Hsien-Hen Lu
Columbia University
New York, New York

Nancy Geyelin Margie
University of Maryland
College Park, Maryland

Daniel Mayer
Maynard Public Schools
Maynard, Massachusetts

Ann Meier
University of Minnesota
Minneapolis, Minnesota

Martha Moorehouse
U.S. Department of Health
and Human Services
Washington, D.C.

Jeffrey D. Morenoff
University of Michigan
Ann Arbor, Michigan

Michael Msall
University of Chicago
Chicago, Illinois

David Murphey
State of Vermont, Agency
of Human Services
Waterbury, Vermont

Sarah Kahler Mustillo
Duke University
Durham, North Carolina

John Ralph
National Center for Education
Statistics
Washington, D.C.

Mairead Reidy
Chapin Hall Center for Children
Chicago, Illinois

Marika Ripke
University of Hawaii at Manoa
Honolulu, Hawaii

Jodie Roth-Herbst
Columbia University
New York, New York

Robert J. Sampson
Harvard University
Boston, Massachusetts

Gary D. Sandefur
University of Wisconsin
Madison, Wisconsin

Matthew W. Stagner
The Urban Institute
Washington, D.C.

Janice Templeton
University of Michigan
Ann Arbor, Michigan

Catherine Walsh
Rhode Island KIDS COUNT
Providence, Rhode Island

Martha Zaslow
Child Trends, Inc.
Washington, D.C.

Janine M. Zwieg
The Urban Institute
Washington, D.C.

Introduction: About the Chapters

Brett V. Brown

This volume contains 15 chapters by top researchers in the field of child and youth well-being in the areas of health, education, social and emotional development, the social context of development, practical application, and the construction of summary indices. In this Introduction, I offer brief descriptions of the content of each chapter as a preview of what is to come.

PART I: HEALTH INDICATORS

Chapter 1: Key Indicators of Health and Safety: Infancy, Preschool, and Middle Childhood (Hogan and Msall)

This chapter provides an excellent overview of available health indicator data from more than 20 national data sources covering the years 1995 through 2003. Drawing on several existing child health frameworks, Hogan and Msall identify indicators across five areas: (a) prenatal and birth information; (b) overall health status; (c) medical care utilization; (d) medical conditions; and (e) environmentally related conditions, including injury, accidents, and safety. They review the strengths and limitations of available data sources, identify which indicators are available in each data source, and give priority to a more limited set of key indicators across the five categories.

Chapter 2: Indicators of Youth Health and Well-Being: Taking the Long View (Stagner and Zweig)

Stagner and Zweig review advances in data collection and dissemination on youth health and well-being since the early 1990s, including key national publications and data resources as well as improved interagency coordination in these areas through the Federal Interagency Forum on Child and Family Statistics. They call on the research and data collection communities to develop a "system of continuous improvement," a comprehensive, self-correcting youth health surveillance system in which basic research informs indicator measurement and data collection on an ongoing basis. This effort would require greater coordination between the content of longitudinal data sources, which support research, and cross-sectional data collection, which is the backbone of social indicator surveillance systems. In particular, the authors call for new research to identify the most important risk factors affecting youth health overall as well as the most important health measures considered in terms of both current well-being and long-term functioning.

PART II: EDUCATION INDICATORS

Chapter 3: Progress in the Development of Indicators of School Readiness (Halle, Reidy, Moorehouse, Zaslow, Walsh, Calkins, Margie, and Dent)

This is a well-integrated review of contemporary early school readiness indicators research, and data collection and use, with particular attention to activities at the state level. The chapter begins with a literature review on early school readiness, taking a multifaceted view that includes the readiness of children for school and the readiness of schools for children, as well as family and community supports known to support school readiness. The authors review national and state data sources and presents their relevant indicators content in well-organized summary tables. They also describe the activities and experience of several multistate consortia focusing on early school readiness indicators and the data sources that states have developed to track school readiness. The chapter highlights the experiences of Vermont and Rhode Island, both state pioneers in this area. The authors conclude with recommendations that include the periodic launching of fresh cohorts of existing longitudinal surveys, like the Early Childhood Longitudinal Studies (kindergarten and birth cohorts), and adding more measures to existing national surveys in the areas of mathematical knowledge, transition practices from early child care and education settings to kindergarten, supports related to perinatal health, and later health screening and care (as contributors to school readiness).

Chapter 4: What Do the National and State National Assessment of Educational Progress Scores Tell Us About the Achievement of American K-12 Students? (Flanagan and Grissmer)

This chapter begins with a discussion of the relative merits of the Scholastic Aptitude Test and National Assessment of Educational Progress (NAEP) educational assessment scores as indicators for tracking trends in academic achievement in the United States. Preferring the NAEP, the authors proceed with a creative use of national and state math and reading assessment results, combined with data on family and school characteristics, to explore alternative explanations for the different patterns of gains between Black students and White students between 1970 and the mid-1990s. Further exploration examines the potential role of particular school characteristics that may influence assessment scores, including desegregation levels, reductions in pupil–teacher ratios, and expanded kindergarten and prekindergarten programs. (N.B.: Since the time this Introduction was written, the NAEP assessments have taken on even greater significance as indicators, because they are now one of the principal tools for monitoring state improvement under the Federal No Child Left Behind initiative.)

PART III: SOCIAL AND EMOTIONAL DEVELOPMENT INDICATORS

Chapter 5: The Assessment of Psychological, Emotional, and Social Development Indicators in Middle Childhood (Ripke, Huston, Eccles, and Templeton)

These chapter authors, members of the MacArthur Research Network on Successful Pathways Through Middle Childhood, provide readers with a strong introduction to the understudied world of development in middle childhood, covering roughly ages 5–6 through 11–12. After a general discussion of the core developmental tasks at this stage, the authors identify seven core domains of development and discuss key indicators within each domain, as well as the current status of measurement of those indicators. The seven areas are (a) motivation and goals for the future, (b) psychological well-being and distress, (c) activities and time use, (d) self-regulation and control, (e) social competence, (f) relationships with peers and adults, and (g) ability and attitudes concerning multiculturalism and diversity. The authors make specific recommendations for indicators requiring development in the coming decade (e.g., civic competency) and for the modification of existing measures for inclusion in national surveys. In addition, they make more general recommendations, such as: focusing on the creation of indicators that are applicable across different cultural groups; using multiple informants in multiple contexts to strengthen indicators measurement; and extending assessments of middle childhood development to the community level.

Chapter 6: Developing Indicators of Confidence, Character, and Caring in Adolescence (Roth, Borbely, and Brooks-Gunn)

This chapter focuses on indicators of positive adolescent psychological and emotional development captured in the three domains of (a) confidence, (b) character, and (c) caring, part of a larger framework of youth development often referred to as "the five Cs" that also includes competence and connection (Lerner, Fisher, & Weinberg, 2000). The chapter begins with a discussion of the key constructs within each of those three domains (e.g., self-efficacy, self-esteem, and identity within the confidence domain) and how they relate to well-being. The authors then discuss how the measurement and data collection in these domains have progressed in the last decade, identifying relevant measures, scales, and survey instruments. The authors end with a set of recommendations for future indicator development, identifying four in which only a modest amount of additional work is needed (self-esteem, volunteering, scholastic identity, and leadership) and four additional areas in which more substantial research and measurement development is required (self-efficacy, self-control, responsiveness, and attentiveness).

Chapter 7: A Developmental Framework for Selecting Indicators of Well-Being During Adolescent and Young Adult Years (Eccles, Brown, and Templeton)

This chapter draws heavily on the work of the Committee on Community-Level Programs for Youth, organized under the National Research Council/Institute of Medicine and chaired by the lead author, Jacquelynne Eccles. The chapter begins with a review of what is known about psychological and social assets of adolescence and early adulthood based on theory, empirical research, and practical wisdom from the field. That is followed with a review of existing indicators to reflect the key constructs identified in the literature review, focusing on survey and administrative data sources at the community, state, and national levels. The authors also discuss measures developed in various regional studies. In addition, the chapter focuses on individual psychological and social assets and on characteristics of the social environment known to promote positive development in these areas. Personal assets include such constructs as emotional self-regulation, mastery, personal efficacy, planfulness, strong moral character, connectedness, and commitment to civic engagement. Key dimensions of social context include opportunities for skill building and efficacy; emotional and instrumental support; safety; appropriate structure; opportunities to belong; and integration across the contextual environments of family, school, and community.

PART IV: SOCIAL CONTEXT OF DEVELOPMENT INDICATORS

Chapter 8: The Family Environment: Structure, Material Resources, and Child Care (Sandefur and Meier)

This chapter examines indicators of three aspects of the family environment that influence the lives of children: (a) family structure, (b) poverty and material resources, and (c) child care. It begins with a brief review of the research relating these dimensions of family context to child outcomes. Then the authors review the recommendations for indicator development in these areas from the 1994 conference on child indicators, noting where and to what extent these recommendations have been implemented in national indicators publications. The chapter ends with recommendations for additional indicator development in the three areas for the coming decade. Among these recommendations are adopting recommendations for the measurement of poverty made by the National Research Council report on poverty measurement (Citro and Michael, 1995); developing family consumption measures that go beyond existing measures, such as housing, health insurance, and food security; developing family structure indicators that reflect cohabitation, blended families, and same-sex parents; and developing additional measures of father involvement in the lives of children.

Chapter 9: Indicators of the Peer Environment in Adolescence (Harris and Cavanagh)

The authors begin this chapter with a brief review of the literature on the importance of peer influences for youth outcomes. A weakness of much of the existing literature is that data on peer characteristics are often based on youth report about their peers rather than reports directly from peers. The potential selection biases that result can be difficult to overcome. In the National Longitudinal Survey of Adolescent Health, by contrast, peer data were collected from the peers themselves. The authors use this data source to explore measures of friendship presence, composition, and quality. They recommend that future research supporting indicators of the peer environment rely on data collected directly from peers and that additional research should be done on aspects of the peer influence that positively influence youth development.

Chapter 10: Key Indicators of School Quality (Mayer and Ralph)

This chapter, which was adapted from a major national report from the National Center for Education Statistics (Mayer, Mullens, & Moore, 2000), reviews the research literature relating school characteristics to student learning. On the basis of that review, the authors identify 13 characteristics and discuss in more detail the five with the strongest research base: (a) teacher academic skills, (b) teacher experience, (c) class size, (d) course content, and (e) technology. The chapter addresses available measures and data quality issues for each. The authors stress the need for a well-rounded set of school quality indicators to guide education policy decisions, particularly as a context for understanding differences and trends in standardized student test results.

Chapter 11: Constructing Community Indicators of Child Well-Being (Morenoff and Sampson)

This chapter provides a review of the burgeoning research literature on neighborhood effects on child and youth development during the 1990s and into the present. Some research has focused on that the authors call *structural differentiation*, especially spatial concentration by socioeconomic status, race, and family structure, and the poor child outcomes associated with concentrated structural disadvantage. Other research has focused more on the neighborhood social mechanisms that may affect child and youth well-being directly, including institutional resources, relationships and social ties, and norms/collective efficacy. The authors then highlight several reliable and empirically validated measures of social mechanisms in each of those three areas based on data from the Project on Human Development in Chicago Neighborhoods study. The authors conclude the chapter by recommending that more research be conducted to develop neighborhood indicators that also take into account the qualities of the surrounding neighborhoods and that additional work be done to define neighborhood boundaries in ways that relate more directly to children's experiences. They also recommend that future data collection efforts in neighborhood research use a data collection technique used in the Project on Human Development in Chicago Neighborhoods study, systematic social observation, to capture qualities not measurable through standard respondent survey techniques. Neighborhood indicators that should receive more attention and development in the coming decade include an index of concentrated extremes (based on structural differences as described earlier); indicators of social cohesion and child-centered social control; and observational-based indicators reflecting disorder, housing quality, and alcohol advertisement and sales.

PART V: CHILD AND YOUTH INDICATORS IN PRACTICE

Chapter 12: Social Indicators as Policy Tool: Welfare Reform as a Case Study (Corbett)

In this chapter, Corbett provides an introduction to the policy uses of social indicators, including a brief history of their use in the United States, a discussion of the different types of indicator measures, discussion of the standards for their development based on earlier work by Kristin Moore (1997), and a typology of uses originally developed by Brown and Corbett (2003).

Corbett then offers an instructive case study of the use of social indicators under welfare reform by a group of states called the *Welfare Peer Assistance Network*, which included the midwestern states Illinois, Indiana, Iowa, Michigan, Minnesota, Ohio, and Wisconsin. Corbett's basic premise is that the devolution of authority under welfare reform has resulted in a tremendous diversity of programs at the state and local levels, with a corresponding change of focus in accountability from one of inputs and process to one of social outcomes. The chapter discusses how the group and its members grappled with these changes and provides instructive examples of major social indicators efforts to support planning and accountability in Iowa, Ohio, and Wisconsin.

Chapter 13: Creating Community Capacity to Use Social Indicators (Murphey)

This chapter brings together research-based knowledge and practical tips for readers interested in using social indicators at the community level. It is based on the author's years of working with communities in Vermont, long a leader among states in the use of social indicators for planning and accountability. The discussion considers how communities can use social indicators to pursue consensus goals, using a theory of change to relate actions to goals, criteria and considerations for choosing social indicators, sources of data for community-level indicators, and effectively communicating indicator data to stakeholders and the media. Tasks of priority for the coming decade recommended by the author include developing better tools for small-area data analysis; developing more indicators of positive development (which are particularly important in sustaining community involvement); conducting research to identify how different indicators are related, and which are the most important ones on which to focus; and working to develop social forecasting models.

PART VI: SOCIAL INDEXES OF CHILD WELL-BEING

Chapter 14: Child and Youth Well-Being in the United States, 1975-1998: Some Findings From a New Index (Land, Lamb, and Mustillo)

Although the indicators discussed in other sections of this book provide insights into how children are doing in any particular area of life, they do not allow us to assess how children are doing overall and whether life in general is getting better or worse for them. To fill this need, Land and colleagues have developed a single composite index called the *Child Well-Being Index* (CWI).[1] The index is constructed using information from 28 measures across seven domains of well-being. These domains were originally developed in the adult quality-of-life literature and adapted by the authors to apply to the lives of children and youth. They include: (a) material well-being, (b) social relationships, (c) health, (d) safety/behavioral concerns, (e) productive activity, (f) place in the community, and (g) emotional/spiritual well-being. Measures for the 28-item index were limited to national estimates that have been taken on a regular basis since 1985. A second version was also constructed that uses 25 measures that have been available since 1975. The index is calculated by creating subindexes for each of the seven domains, then combining them into a single index with each domain receiving equal weighting.

The chapter examines historical trends in the overall index and for each of the subindexes. It also uses various forms of the index to compare across different racial-ethnic and age groups. The index is also calculated with reference to "best practices standards" that compares current well-being to an optimal index value based on the highest levels of well-being in the component indicators recorded in other countries rather than to national values in some base year.

At the conference and elsewhere, reviewers of the CWI have praised Land and colleagues for their thorough and thoughtful work in developing the index, but some have questioned whether the measures and the data underlying the index are currently of sufficient breadth and quality to provide an index that fully reflects overall child and youth well-being. Conference discussant Kristin Moore, for example, was concerned that several of the seven domains comprising the CWI had generally weak measures (e.g., emotional and spiritual relationships), whereas other domains had stronger measures but were missing critical elements (e.g., a measure of mental health in the health domain). Such holes in the index would make it problematic as a reliable measure of overall child well-being and trends in well-being, although subindexes representing those domains where the measures were strong overall would be very useful. Others were concerned with a more general issue of how such indexes could be responsibly used for comparisons across states of social groups when key demographic characteristics were not controlled for (see, e.g., chap. 15, this volume).

The authors acknowledge problems with the adequacy of the measures used in certain areas, particularly in the domains of social relationships and emotional/spiritual well-being. They argue, however, that the index is a valuable lens from which to gauge how well our social indicators system is doing in covering the essential dimensions of child well-being and in helping to identify gaps that can be filled over time through better research and data collection that will strengthen the index over time.

To that end, the Foundation for Child Development has made a commitment to support the development and dissemination of the CWI through at least the year 2011. In 2004, the index was introduced to the broad public and policymakers to build awareness of its value as a measure for summarizing the condition of children. The Foundation for Child Development intends for the index to be updated on an annual basis.[2]

Chapter 15: Methodological Issues Surrounding the Construction of an Index of Child Well-Being (Bennett and Lu)

This chapter explores the sensitivity of summary indexes of child well-being to alternative weighting schemes and to controlling for selected demographic background characteristics. The authors used a simple, three-variable index based on timely progress in school, health status, and poverty status. Alternative weighting of the index components had little effect on the ranking of states based on the index. However, when controls for the immigration status and racial composition of the child population were applied, the state rankings changed substantially. The findings indicate that researchers who would use state rankings based on such indexes to shed light on how states are doing in promoting child well-being ought to consider using controls for characteristics over which the states have little or no influence before making comparisons.

NOTES

1. In the chapter, it is referred to as the *Index of Child and Youth Well-Being*, but it is currently called the *Child Well-Being Index* or the *Foundation for Child Development Child Well-Being Index*.
2. To learn more about recent work on the CWI, visit http://www.fcd-us.org

REFERENCES

Brown, B., & Corbett, T. (2003). Social indicators as tools of public policy. In R. Weissberg, H. Wallberg, M. O'Brien, & C. Kenter (Eds.), *Long-term trends in the well-being of children and families* (pp. 27–52). Washington, DC: Child Welfare League of America Press.

Citro, C. F., & Michael, R. T. (1995). *Measuring poverty: A new approach.* Washington, DC: National Academy Press.

Lerner, R. M., Fisher, C. B., & Weinberg, R. A. (2000). Toward a science for and of the people: Promoting the civil society through the application of developmental science. *Child Development, 71,* 11–20.

Mayer, D. P., Mullens, J. V., & Moore, M. T. (2000). *Monitoring school quality: An indicators report.* Washington, DC: U.S. Department of Education

Moore, K. (1997). Criteria for indicators of child well-being. In R. Hauser, B. Brown, & W. Prosser (Eds.), *Indicators of children's well-being* (pp. 36–44). New York: Russell Sage Foundation.

Part I

Health Indicators

Chapter **1**

Key Indicators of Health and Safety: Infancy, Preschool, and Middle Childhood

Dennis P. Hogan
Brown University
Michael E. Msall
University of Chicago

In any study of child well-being, health is a necessary and major component. The acute and chronic medical conditions of children are important, as are accidental injuries and other injuries resulting from neglect or abuse. In addition, measures of health status, medical care access and utilization, and the health environments in which children live are all important for understanding the diverse health situations of children with medical conditions and for differentiating the ways in which appropriate preventive and well-child care are being provided to U.S. children and youth. In this sense, measures of child health are indicators of health outcomes that assess the well-being of children. However, these indicators of health are also important for understanding the cognitive, behavioral, and emotional development of children, in so far as health conditions may limit children in their developmental trajectories.

This chapter highlights recent innovations in the measurement of child health, considering only those studies that collected data in 1995 to 2003. We emphasize data sources that are nationally representative of the entire population of children (rather than, e.g., a clinical or client population). Finally, we consider only those studies that measure the family ecology of children so that health disparities can be documented and understood.

This chapter highlights the diverse ways in which health is now measured for children through age 11 years, and the sources of those measurements. Because indicators of child health depend on the physical and physiological maturation of children as well as age-graded developmental trajectories, this chapter distinguishes measures that are appro-

1

priate for children during the prenatal period and the first year of life, for children of preschool ages 1 through 4, and young school-age children ages 5 through 11.

We first review four common perspectives on the measurement of child health, examining their conceptual bases, emphasis, and use, followed by a brief discussion of our own perspective on the measurement of child health. This is followed by a presentation of information on 22 major surveys relevant to child health and a discussion of the surveys we consider the most useful for the measurement of child health. The measurement of particular aspects of child health by these 22 surveys is considered for several dimensions of health: prenatal and birth information; overall health status; medical care utilization; medical conditions; and environmental factors, including injury, accidents, and safety. Before describing each of these in full, we make recommendations about the best and most appropriate indicators of child health for use by scientists and policy advocates.

ASSESSING STUDIES OF CHILD HEALTH

Often, the operationalization of a health concept varies across data sources, and these variations are analyzed (Berry, 1992). These variations commonly relate to the time interval over which a behavior is measured, whether a health indicator is simply present or includes a consideration of intensity and duration, and whether the measurement is for one point in time or at different points in time over the early life course. In the case of the latter, the analyst must determine whether these age-related patterns are indicative of underlying developmental processes or simply indicative of changing situations over time.

For the infants and children through age 11 considered in this chapter, a parent or other person in the household typically provides information in health surveys. A concern with the validity of information from proxy respondents is paramount in the study of adolescent behavior but is not a critical consideration for any but the oldest of the children considered here (e.g., those age 10 or 11 in regard to safety habits, tobacco and alcohol use, or health knowledge). Research has shown that information on child health collected from mothers is far more complete, valid, and reliable than that provided by fathers or others in the household. This particularly is the case regarding information about medical conditions, health care utilization, and adult assessments of overall child health (e.g., health status). Data on child health from across these various sources is judged to be of better quality to the extent that it is usually or always provided by the mother.

Some studies go a step further and verify information on child health with reference to medical records or school records, or they use direct observation, including medical examination and developmental assessments. In general, such expert information is more valid than mothers' reports and provides a substantial improvement in measures of child health (Berry, 1992). However, variations in record keeping, coding, and the retrieval of medical and other official records can lessen this apparent advantage. The cost of these additional kinds of data collection often limit the sample sizes that are affordable, creating other sources of imprecision into measures of child health.

A source of imprecision generally found in studies of child health is their restriction to the noninstitutionalized population of children. Although relatively few in number (0.3% of all children), these excluded children are selective of children with severe and multiple health problems. Although a study of the noninstitutionalized population is satisfactory for studying the health, health care needs, and access of children served by a variety of government programs, this omission can produce bias when a researcher wishes to estimate the number of children with particularly severe physical and mental disabilities or to estimate the total costs of medical services for children (Hogan, Msall, Rogers, & Avery, 1997). In these cases, research using the sources cited here must be supplemented by specialized studies of children in institutions.

Given the complexities of child health and its measurement, it is clear that any treatment of the topic must necessarily be selective. This chapter draws on several criteria for indicators of child well-being discussed by Moore (1997). These include attention to the multidimensional character of child health; the inclusion of measures of child health appropriate to children in the three age groups; and clarity, consistency, and methodological rigor. In *Indicators of Child Well-Being*, Hauser, Brown, and Prosser (1997) devoted three separate chapters to the measurement of child health at three different ages: (a) prenatal and infant (Lantz & Partin, 1997), (b) preschool (Wolfe & Sears, 1997), and (c) preadolescent school-age children (Starfield, 1997). As such, these chapters provided a much more detailed treatment of their topics than is possible in this chapter. They included substantial attention to the histories of measures, the indexes that can be constructed from multiple indicators or batteries of items for a single construct, and the construction of rates from vital registry systems using direct and indirect methods. They also reported the scores on health indicators available at the national, state, and local levels. This information remains current and is a good starting point for the understanding of preferred constructs and issues. Thus this chapter does not focus on issues of scale and index construction. An excellent discussion of this topic for persons of all ages is found in McDowell and Newell (1996).[1]

CONCEPTUAL APPROACHES TO INFANT HEALTH

Major neonatal and genetic advances have resulted in the increased survival of children with complex health impairments (Lester & Miller-Loncar, 2000; Msall & Tremont, 1999, 2000). In addition, there is increased recognition of the complexity of developmental and behavioral consequences associated with prenatal exposure to tobacco, alcohol, cocaine, opiates, marijuana, and both illicit and legal substances (Lagasse et al., 1999). Lastly, major family and community-level challenges in the form of teen parenting, single parenting, and preschool children living in poverty have highlighted the importance of measuring children's health status, health access, developmental and behavioral processes, and adverse factors (e.g., exposure to lead, homelessness, violence) occurring in early childhood (Shonkoff & Phillips, 2000).

Key measures of infant health include somatic growth; self-regulatory processes in feeding; sleep; child-caregiver interactions; and emergence of core competencies in gross and fine motor skills, prelingusitic communicative skills, play, social interaction, and adaptive skills. Five key questions emerge in the study of infant health:

1. Is growth in body size and proportions occurring?
2. Are there major neurological challenges (e.g., epilepsy, parenchymal brain injury, or abnormalities of tone)?
3. Are there major sensory challenges (vision or hearing)?
4. Are there specific organ system impairments (pulmonary, cardiac, gastrointestinal) requiring specific health intervention?
5. Are the child's developmental skills progressing in communication, adaptive, and behavioral-learning domains?

Over the past three decades in the United Status, there has been rapid implementation of perinatal management strategies, as well as early childhood disorders that are life threatening resulting in a marked increase in survival among babies born prematurely. In the United States in the year 2000, 44,592 infants with birth weight less than 1,500 grams (3 lbs, 4 oz) out of 58,967 births survived because of advances in neonatal care (Lorenz, 2000; Stevenson et al. 1998; Vohr & Msall, 2000;). In 2000, 94% of very low birth weight infants (1,001g–1,500g), 85% of extremely low birth weight infants (751g–1,000g), and 52% of micropreemie infants (501g–750g) survived (NCHS, 1999; Maternal and Child Health Bureau [MCHB], 2000, p. 21; see http://www.cdc.gov/nchs). Additional medical and surgical advances in the management of term infants with cardiopulmonary, genetic, neurological, or gastrointestinal impairments have also resulted in increased survival. The five parameters of child health are particularly salient for both very low birthweight survivors and pre-term children.

Major advances in immunization have substantially decreased the number of children with neurological, developmental and behavioral impairments because of hemophilus influenza, streptococcal pneumonia, measles, mumps, and rubella (MCHB, 2000, p. 27) during the first 2 years of life. This points to the need for studies of the health of infants and preschool-age children to collect data on immunization (Centers for Disease Control and Prevention, 1998).

In the aggregate, early childhood survival is at an all-time high (Guyer et al. 1999; MCHB, 2000, p. 23). In 2000, 99.2% of infants survived 1 year, and 99.9% survived from their 1st to their 5th birthdays (see http://www.cdc.gov/nchs). This does not suggest, however, that societal concerns about child health have lessened. The overall status of children's health in terms of growth, respiratory disorders, developmental skills, and family resources are of concern given the family and societal investments that are needed to produce adults who will be equipped to deal with the rigors of adulthood and the improvements in human capital necessary to keep our nation productive (Hauser et al., 1997; Hogan, Rogers, & Msall, 2000). The prevalence in the United States of early childhood poverty; single-parent child birth; and parental struggles with jobs, education, and mental health reveals major gaps in maximizing family social capital and optimizing health and development (Annie E. Casey Foundation, 2003).

Four causes account for more than half of all infant deaths: (a) birth defects, (b) premature birth, (c) sudden infant death syndrome, and (d) respiratory distress syndrome (http://www.cdc.gov/nchs; MCHB, 2000, p. 24). Complex chronic conditions account for nearly 40% of all infant deaths (Feudtner, Christakis, & Connell, 2000). The use of alcohol, tobacco, and illegal substances during pregnancy is a major risk factor for low birthweight and other detrimental outcomes (LaGasse, Seifer, & Lester, 1999; Lester, Lagasse, & Seifer, 1998). Finally, breastfeeding is an important contributor to improved infant health. Trends show that breastfeeding rates have increased during the past 10 years from early infancy during the first 6 months of life, but beyond these ages rates of breastfeeding drop dramatically (MCHB, 2000, p. 18). Thus, infant health can best be understood with reference to both risk factors and medical conditions in the context of the family ecology and caregiver behaviors (Shiono & Behrman, 1995).

CONCEPTUAL APPROACHES TO CHILD HEALTH

The concept of children's health ranges from describing measures of the following 10 areas:

1. *Birthweight status* (normal birthweight [> 2.5 kg], moderate low birthweight [1.5–2.49 kg], very low birthweight [1.0 kg–1.49 kg], extremely low birthweight [0.75 kg–0.99 kg], and micropreemies [< 750 g]).
2. *Small for gestational age* (birthweight < 10th percentile for gestation), somatic growth (height, weight, and head circumference).
3. *Genetic impairments* (Trisomy 21 [Down syndrome], phenylketonurea, cystic fibrosis, spina bifida, sickle cell anemia).

4. *Neurological and sensory impairments* (seizure disorders, cerebral palsy, microcephaly, blindness, deafness), developmental disabilities (degrees of mental retardation, autistic spectrum disorders, and communicative disorders).
5. *Complex physical impairments* requiring medical/technological intervention (tracheostomy, gastrostomy, ventilator supports, central venous access).
6. *Chronic health impairments* (asthma, diabetes mellitus, HIV/AIDS, inflammatory bowel disease).
7. *Learning and attention disorders* (specific learning disabilities in reading, mathematics, or written language, impulsivity, hyperactivity, inattention).
8. *Injuries* (fractures, lacerations, drowning, motor vehicle trauma).
9. *Behavior and mental health disorders* (self-regulation, externalizing, internalizing, depression, anxiety).
10. *Risk-taking behaviors* (tobacco, alcohol, cocaine, opiate use, unsafe sexual practices).

A variety of frameworks have been used to address the complexity of children's health and well-being. One builds on a framework of medical diagnosis of impairments (pathophysiological processes that affect organ system performance; International Classification of Disease-9 [ICD-9]; World Health Organization [WHO], 2000). This framework is best applied in comprehensive clinical investigations for impairments that affect a child's daily health functioning (Starfield, 1997). A classical example of a life-threatening impairment is appendicitis. On the basis of certain child symptoms, recurrent physical examinations, and supportive laboratory data, a child undergoes timely surgery and avoids the complication of peritonitis and septic shock. This clinical medical tradition aims for accurate diagnosis, critical analysis of laboratory indicators, and intense medical cohort studies designed to reveal optimal management strategies. This tradition does not easily lead to describing the prevalence of a variety of chronic disorders in the population or those disorders that may influence developmental or behavioral status.

Except for the most common childhood medical conditions (e.g., asthma and attention deficit disorder), the incidence of medical conditions critical to health (e.g., cerebral palsy, autism, Down syndrome, spina bifida, and muscular dystrophy) occur with individual rates of less than 2/1,000 (Newacheck & Halfon, 1998). Even with the population surveys that include 25,000 children, the occurrence of these medical conditions is too small to provide a stable basis for population estimates or detailed analysis. The collection of medical condition data for population studies of children allows investigators to look at groups of major categories of medical conditions (e.g., all neurodevelopmental disorders, all major genetic malformations) and permits, on a case-by-case basis, the assessment of access and utilization of appropriate medical care and the extent to which a potentially disabling medical condition becomes functionally limiting (Newacheck, Strickland, Shonkoff, & Perrin, 1998).

The second framework arises from developmental and behavior disorders (American Psychiatric Association, 1994; Wolraich, Felice, & Drotar, 1996). It includes detailed assessments that detect discrepancies between an individual child's performance and that of his or her peers. This process quantifies delays in development or intensity of clusters of behavioral states and establishes criteria for mental retardation, autism, communicative impairments, specific learning disabilities, attention deficit hyperactivity disorders, or attachment disorders. The strength of this model is intense performance evaluation of developmental and behavioral processes, often involving several hours of standardized interviewing and structured observation. One problem with this approach is the difficulty setting cutpoints that distinguish serious developmental and behavioral variations from milder forms of the impairment.

One weakness of the developmental disability model is that a large number of children do not receive comprehensive assessments that are informed by current best practice. In addition, the disorders themselves do not necessarily mean that a child will not develop certain skills in the future despite having some school or vocational challenges. Neither the medical impairment nor the developmental disability model describes a child's performance at home or in the community on tasks relating to skills in essential daily activities (Msall & Tremont, 1999). For example, to state that a child has the medical impairment of spina bifida does not allow for a statement that the child is able to walk, dress, and maintain continence despite having lumbo-sacral level spinal cord dysfunction. Similarly, describing the child as having a paraplegic motor impairment because the child does not perform the running task quickly enough on the Peabody Developmental Motor Scales does not take into account how the child negotiates stairs or participates in outdoor activities with peers after school or whether he or she requires a brace, orthopedic shoes, or other equipment to stabilize ankle and foot alignment.

The third perspective on a child's health status takes into account medical use, compensatory services (physical therapy, occupational therapy, speech-language therapies, special education services, early intervention enrollment), or behavior supports (counseling, medication; Stein & Silver, 1999; Stein, Westbrook, & Bauman, 1997). The strength of this model is that it can identify a heterogeneous population of children with chronic medical, developmental, or behavioral impairments. The weakness of this model is that it does not describe the severity of the conditions, and that some of the endpoints rely on services not directly linked to traditional medical care. That is, the use of services in the absence of reported health limitations is taken as an indication of a chronic health condition (certainly a reasonable assumption). Bias (e.g., socioeconomic class, poverty status) in the identification of children with chronic medical conditions may occur when some groups in the population are better able to seek treatment and rehabilitation services than others.

A fourth perspective promulgated by the WHO (1980, 1997) is that health is multidimensional and requires analyses on several dimensions. Within the United States, the Institute of Medicine (1997), the National Center for Medical Rehabilitation Research (NCMRR; in the National Institute of Child Health and Human Development), and the Centers for Disease Control and Prevention extended this model (Butler, Chambers, & Goldstein, 1999; Lollar, Simeonson, & Nando, 2000; NCMRR National Advisory Board, 1993).

The goals of the WHO model are to have an understanding of the level of analysis (e.g., molecular, cellular, organs, body systems person performance), the social and cultural context, and the environmental adaptations and constraints that support the individual's participation in their community roles. An important contribution of this model is that it does not assume a linear progression among impairment, functional limitations, disability status, and community participation. An example would be a girl with a bilateral congenital limb reduction disorder that produced below-the-knee amputation. This girl, with prostheses, walks in all community settings, wears dresses that cannot distinguish her skin texture from typical peers, skis, and goes to college. Her overall adapted function and community participation would be classified as a success but could not be described in traditional impairment and developmental performance assessments. This perspective is further specified in the *ICD-9* classification of disability recently adopted by the WHO.

The key dimension that bridges the gap between this girl's complicated impairment and her health state is the ability to describe the contribution of her impairment to her overall health status; specify her functional skills and challenges; describe her developmental, educational, and vocational competencies; and specify the context of fulfilled or challenge roles in her daily self-maintenance and community participation in an age-specific developmental timeframe as modified by assistive technology. Each of these dimensions lends themselves to key survey queries that are able to describe her health status in a way that encompasses physical health; developmental, behavioral, and mental health; assistive technology; family and community supports; and social roles.

These disease- and medical-based frameworks of child health include, but do not highlight, the key role of injuries in child health. Although not a distinct perspective, public health builds on these perspectives by placing central emphasis that among children (beyond infancy) injuries are the leading cause of death and disability (Graiter, 1992; Lewit & Baker, 1995). Many of these accidents are preventable through public health measures (lead abatement, school safety, emphasis on sports that less often result in injury) and safety in the home, car, or community (no or secured firearms, smoke detectors, seat belt use, helmet use).

Perspective 4 is the basis for our development of a multidisciplinary perspective on infant and child health that is appropriate for describing population parameters of health indicators, recognizes the uniqueness of and the relationships between various dimensions of child health, and permits an examination of disparities in health ("Disability and Perinatal Care," 1995; Hack & Fanaroff, 1999; Hack, Taylor, Klein, & Mercuri-Minich, 2000; Hogan & Msall, 2002; McCormick, 1999; McCormick, Workman-Daniels, & Brooks-Gunn, 1996; Shonkoff & Meisels, 2000). Attention to body systems can lead to recognition of a complex ongoing medical impairment ranging from life-threatening, recurrent-episodic disorders (e.g., identified by allergies, asthma, diabetes mellitus, cystic fibrosis), chronic infections (HIV/AIDS), accidental or intentional injuries, neurosensory disorders (cerebral palsy, epilepsy, deafness, blindness), developmental disabilities (mental retardation, communication disabilities, and autism) and learning and behavior disorders (attention, impulsivity, hyperactivity, learning and emotional disorders).

We outline here the major criteria that are used to develop our suggestions for preferred measures of infant and child health and injuries. Drawing on the NCMRR framework for multiple dimensions of health, and the WHO framework of functional activity and community participation, our recommended instrument recognizes that there are a variety of dimensions of child health that are unique conceptually even though they may be interrelated. Based on the *ICD-9*, we include medical impairments (medical conditions) including mental health disorders (WHO, 2000). Based on the WHO and NCMRR frameworks, and the research of developmentalists, we expand attention beyond medical conditions to include limitations in ability to perform developmentally appropriate everyday tasks (mobility; self-care; communication, including sensory skills to receive and provide information; and behavioral skills and learning ability). We expand the consideration of risk factors and injuries consistent with the public health perspective.

The approach we advocate for the assessment of infant and child health thus recognizes that some children are more at risk than other children for poor health because of maternal behaviors, aspects of the family environment, and the child's own safety behaviors. Our approach goes beyond simply ascertaining risks, conditions, and limitations to consider whether the child receives medical care and rehabilitation, and the forms of this assistance. Finally, our approach measures the ways in which all of these factors define the overall health of a child and their implications for the child's ability to participate fully in the society.[2]

RECOMMENDED INDICATORS FOR THE STUDY OF CHILD HEALTH

This new and recommended instrument to assess infant and child health leads to the discussion of the types of health indicators that are essential for comprehensive and sound measurement of infant and child health and safety. On the basis of the detailed review of the major data sources and the questions asked in each that we provide later, this new perspective provides an analytic framework to recommend key indicators of health during infancy, preschool, and middle childhood years.

The study of prenatal health factors should include a consideration of major risk and protective factors for pregnancy and information about the timing of prenatal medical care. These are indicators of whether the mother used tobacco and alcohol during the pregnancy, whether and when she saw a health professional during her pregnancy, and whether the mother took vitamins to prevent anemia and neural tube defects. These items directly capture the major risk factors during pregnancy. We avoid lengthening the instrument by asking detailed questions about each habit. Survey design experience has shown that such detailed questions are more subject to unreliability and reporting bias and often create analytic problems because of missing data. In practice, sample sizes usually force researchers to ignore the details of use and use a summary measure that characterize whether mothers did or did not engage in a behavior. Recall in clinical settings indicates that the ability of a mother to provide prenatal health information deteriorates rapidly as the child ages. We recommend these indicators for studies of infants and children under age 5.

The study of infant health needs to include demographic information about the child at birth, an indication of high risk (length of gestation and birthweight), the circumstances of delivery, and the presence of birth defects or complications. Whether a baby is breastfed and the duration of the breastfeeding are key behavioral indicators that tap infants' nutritional adequacy and protection from disease. In addition to these objective measures, information is quite useful on the mother's (or caregiver's) perception of the health situation of a child relative to other children of similar ages. Such measures have proven quite useful as predictors of negative health outcomes (hospitalization, disability) and provide an indication of the stresses poor child health creates for families. These prenatal and infant indicators are essential for the study of infant health but also should be gathered in studies of older children to capture the early origins of their current health.

In infancy and preschool years, safety risks include accidental injuries (falls, burns, drowning), inadequate physical resources (food, housing, safe water), and availability of developmental supports (parenting, extended family, mentoring, child care). In middle childhood, as children near adolescence, risk-taking behaviors (tobacco, alcohol, sexuality, illicit drugs) and community risks (domestic violence, adult unemployment, underresourced schools, minority status [discrimination]) are key determinants of adolescent adaptation and transition to adult roles (higher education, employment, family formation).

A simple-to-obtain but important indicator of child health requires measures of the size of infants and children (height, weight, and head circumference). These ideally are obtained by interviewers trained in standardized measurement procedures. However, even the more approximate estimates of mothers can provide a rough indication of stunting and inadequate growth. Children whose height is below the 5th percentile may have a normal variant (i.e., constitutional short status); a genetic disorder (chromosomopathy, inborn error of metabolism, inborn error of morphogenesis [i.e., chondrodysplasia]); or a complex, chronic condition (congenital heart disease, celiac disease, renal tubular acidosis). Children whose weight is below the 5th percentile may be undernourished because of difficulty accessing calories, or because complex neurological-genetic disorders may interfere with coordinated sustained efficient suck and swallow. Another cause of low weight is because complex cardiopulmonary conditions result in caloric intake not exceeding metabolic needs. Excess weight for height may reflect the aggregate impact of easy access to high-calorie foods, decreased physical activity opportunity (outside play; being on an athletic team; physical work contribution, such as farm work), and sedentary behaviors (e.g., TV watching).

Varieties of other questions are not appropriate for infants but can be appropriate for children beyond infancy. We suggest a checklist designed to capture the major medical conditions of childhood disorders. This procedure is preferable to obtaining information about medical conditions only when a particular limitation or health service is indicated, because it allows the identification of a population at risk and can then ask about rates of health outcomes to these risk groups.

Information on impairments is an appropriate complement to data on medical conditions because it represents the social, behavioral, and emotional realities of the lives of individual children. Many studies neglect emotional, behavioral, and psychological health, and we argue that any picture of child health is incomplete without this information. We prefer questions that ask about the presence of impairments because they are not biased by the utilization of specialized health services. In practice, these must be supplemented by questions about the use of medical services; research on parental responses to child health questions shows that the use of services is a critical indicator of the presence of impairments, identifying children who would otherwise not be recorded as having impairments.

Indicators of activity limitations relate the child's medical health and to the ability of children to operate in their everyday worlds. Children who cannot perform age-appropriate physical functions, or who cannot play with peers or go to school, face special challenges in everyday life and in making developmental progress. We include a question on continence as an indicator of family stress.

Compared with these more specific measures of child health, the health status dimension includes items that indicate the health situation of the child relative to other children and changes in the child's situations over his or her lifetime. These items can be objective (as with anthropometric measurements) or subjective. Experience has shown that subjective measures, such as the child's health status, are excellent predictors of future utilization of medical services and worsening health situations. If a study has room for only a few measures of child health, it should concentrate on the collection of these items measuring child health status.

We recommend attention to a child's performance in activities or roles that can be described in terms of strengths and challenges. Examples include play with peers; self-care competencies in eating, dressing, bathing, and maintaining continence; changing positions; mobility; negotiating stairs and the outdoor environment; communicative skills involving understanding and use of one's family language; learning (preschool developmental skills, learning to read, calculate, and compose written language); and behavior (self-regulation, social interaction, judgment and maturity).

A key indicator of a child's health is provided by items that encompass the child's functioning within a developmental framework. Attention to specific infancy, preschool, and middle childhood biopsychosocial themes can enable researchers to examine cumulative risk and protection factors in settings of resiliency and abnormal trajectories given various contextual supports of human, social, cultural, and neighborhood factors. Such indicators are only now becoming widespread in population studies such as the Early Childhood Longitudinal Study-Kindergarten Cohort (ECLS-K), and often require information that cannot be obtained in an interview format. Because of this, we have refrained from recommending precise objective indicators of development, relying instead on parental assessment of the pace of a child's development.

Table 1.1 lists the items that are needed for a reasonably quick survey assessment of the multiple and complex dimensions of child health. It does not indicate preferred wording for each indicator because this will depend upon the purpose for which the data are collected and thus may vary from study to study. What we emphasize here are the necessary indicators of child health, grouped into categories corresponding to the multiple dimensions of child health. These key indicators are intended to serve as a reference for studies that plan to use secondary sources of data for child health and safety and for primary data collection efforts in which the comprehensive survey measurement of child health is important.

Table 1.1

Indicators of Family Ecology

Description	Source
Race/ethnicity	CPS, ECLS-B, ECLS-K, LBID, MEPS, NAMCS, NAS, NHANES, NHDS, NHES, NHIS, NIS, NLSY, NSCH, NSECH, NSFH, PSID, SIPP, SLAITS, SPCU3, SPD,
Parents' educational attainment	CPS, ECLS-B, ECLS-K, LBID, MEPS, NAS, NHES, NHIS, NIS, NLSY, NSCH, NSECH, NSFH, PSID, SIPP, SLAITS, SPCU3, SPD,
Labor force participation	CPS, ECLS-B, ECLS-K, NHANES, NHES, NHIS, NLSY, NSCH, NSECH, MEPS, PSID, SIPP, SLAITS, SPD
Family income/Poverty	CPS, ECLS-B, NAS, NHANES, NHIS, NHES, NIS, NLSY, NSECH, NSFH, MEPS, PSID, SIPP, SLAITS, SPCU3, SPD
Receipt of welfare benefits	CPS, ECLS-B, ECLS-K,MEPS, NHANES, NHES, NHIS, NIS, NSECH, NSFH, PSID, SIPP, SLAITS, SPD
Parents' marital status	CPS, ECLS-B, ECLS-K, LBID, NHANES, NHDS, NHES, NHIS, NIS, NLSY, NSCH, NSECH, NSFH, PSID, SIPP, SLAITS, SPCU3, SPD
Presence of or relationship with father or "father figure"	ECLS-B, ECLS-K, NLSY, NSFH, PSID, SPD
Family-child engagement in literary/educational activities	ECLS-B, ECLS-K, NHES, NLSY, NSECH, NSFH, PSID, SLAITS, SPCU3, SPD
Childcare	NSECH, NSCH

DATA SOURCES FOR THE STUDY OF CHILD HEALTH

Data sources for the study of child health can be characterized as:

- measuring child health at one point in time or longitudinally as the child ages;
- based on samples of populations of children developed in the screening of random samples of households or from lists of children (school enrollment, hospitalization records, birth and death certificates, or medical registries);
- collecting general information on child health or more specialized and detailed measures of particular aspects of child health; and
- involving a one-time or recurrent cross–sectional design.

Table 1.2 provides basic information about purpose, periodicity, and target population of each of the 22 data sources we have identified un-

Table 1.2.

Survey Instrument List

Abbreviation	Survey Name	Supplements & Topical Modules	Purpose	Periodicity	Target population	Internet references
CPS	Current Population Survey	Food Security Supplement	To provide estimates of employment, unemployment, other characteristics of general labor force, population as a whole, various subgroups of the population	Monthly since 1942	Civilian, non-institutional and off-base Armed Forces households	www.ers.usda.gov/ DatFoodSecurity/ CPS
ECLS-B	Early Childhood Longitudinal Survey-Birth Cohort		To provide a comprehensive and reliable longitudinal data set that describes the growth of America's children from birth through first grade	Began in 2000	Approximately 15,000 births in year 2000—large number of blacks, Hispanics, Asians, low birth weight, twins	http://nces.ed.gov/ ecls
ECLS-K	Early Childhood Longitudinal Survey-Kindergarten		To gather information on the knowledge and skills of young children as they enter kindergarten and move through the primary grades	Ongoing since 1998	Nationally representative sample of children from kindergarten to fifth grade	http://nces.ed.gov/ ecls
LBID	Linked Birth and Infant Death Data File		To link birth and death certificates in order to monitor and explore the complex interrelationships between infant death and risk factors present at birth	Annually since 1983	All infants born in U.S. who died before reaching one year of age	http://www.cdc.gov /nchs/products/ elec_prods/subject /linkedbd.htm
MEPS	Medical Expenditures Panel Survey		To continually provide policymakers, health care administrators, businesses and others with timely, comprehensive information about health care use and costs and to improve the accuracy of economic projections	Ongoing since 1996	Nationally representative subsample of households that participated in prior year's NHIS	www.meps.ahcpr. gov/survey.htm
NAMCS	National Ambulatory Medical Care Survey		To meet need for objective, reliable information about provision and use of ambulatory medical care services in US; data collected from physician rather than patient	Annually since 1989	Random sample of patient visits to non-federally employed office-based physicians primarily engaged in direct patient care	http://www.cdc. gov/nchs/about/ major/ahcd/U.S. /nhamcsds.ht

NAS	National Asthma Survey		Examines the health, socioeconomic, behavioral, and environmental predictors that relate to better control of asthma.			
NHANES	National Health and Nutrition Examination Survey		To obtain nationally representative information on health and nutritional status of U.S. population through interviews and direct examinations.	NHANES III: 1988-1994; became annual survey in 1999	Noninstitutionalized persons age 2 months and older	ww.cdc.gov/nchs/nhanes.htm
NHDS	National Hospital Discharge Survey		To meet the need for information on characteristics of inpatients discharged from non-federal short-stay hospitals in U.S.	Annually since 1965	National sample of inpatients in short-stay, general or children's general hospitals	www.cdc.gov/nchs/aboutmajor/i/hdasd/nhds.htm
NHES	National Household Education Survey	Early Childhood Readiness Supplement; School Safety and Discipline Supplement	To collect detailed information on educational issues from relatively large and targeted sample of households in a timely fashion; to monitor participation in adult education, childcare arrangements and educational experiences of young children.	Annually since 1993; topical components repeated on 3-4 year cycle	Noninstitutionalized population; supplement—children ages 3 to 7	http://nces.ed.gov/nhes/
NHIS	National Health Interview Survey	Disability Supplement; Immunization; Health Insurance; Access to Care	To provide a continuing picture of health status based on self-reports of personal experiences and attributes.	Annually since 1957; redesigned 1997	Civilian, noninstitutionalized households, randomly selected children under 18	www.cdc.gov/nchs/nhis.htm
NIS	National Immunization Survey		To collect information on immunization coverage and health care of children.	Annually since 1994	Children 19-35 months of age	http://www.cdc.gov/nis/
NLSY79–child	Children of the National Longitudinal Survey of Youth 1979	Child Supplement; Mother Supplement	To collect child development data on children born to female respondents in NLSY to create large national data resource for study of child outcomes.	Biennially since 1986	Children of NLSY females only; children of male respondents from NLSY not included	http://www.bls.gov/nls/nlsy79ch.htm

(continued)

Table 1.2 *(continued)*

Abbreviation	Survey Name	Supplements & Topical Modules	Purpose	Periodicity	Target population	Internet references
NMES	National Medical Survey Expenditures		To document how Americans use health care services and to Survey determine amount and pattern of health expenditures (previous in series to MEPS—data is comparable).	Last study conducted 1987	Civilian, noninstitutionalized households	
NSECH	National Survey of Early Childhood Health		To collect national baseline data on pediatric care and its impact from the parent's perspective. Questions focus on the delivery of pediatric care to families with children under 3 years of age and the promotion of young children's health by families in their homes.		Households with children ages 4 to 35 months.	
NSCH	National Survey of Children's Health		Examines the physical and emotional health of children age 0–17		Households with children ages 0 to 17	
NSFH	National Survey of Families and Households		To look at causes and consequences of changes in American family and household structure such as patterns of fertility, marriage, mortality, migration, family composition, household structure	1987-88 wave; 1992–94 followup wave; 3rd wave planned	Noninstitutionalized U.S. families and households	www.ssc.wisc.edu/nsfh/
PedNSS	Pediatric Nutrition Surveillance Survey		To continuously monitor the nutritional status of low-income children participating in federally funded maternal and child health and nutrition programs; includes 44 states, District of Columbia, 5 tribal governments.	Ongoing since 1973	Low-income children in federally funded nutrition programs	www.cdc.gov/pednss/index.htm

			Purpose	Timing	Population	URL
PSID	Panel Survey of Income Dynamics	Child Development Supplement	To provide researchers with a comprehensive, nationally representative, longitudinal database of children and families with which to study dynamic process of early human capital formation	Ongoing since 1997	Parents and their 0- to 12-year-old children	http://psidonline.isr.umich.edu/
SIPP	Survey of Income and Program Participation	Medical Expenses & Utilization; Child Care; Children's Well-Being; Child Disability; Functional Limitations	To collect source and amount of income, labor force information, program participation, eligibility data, general demographic characteristics to measure the effectiveness of existing federal, state, and local programs; to estimate future costs and coverage for government programs; to provide improved statistics on income distribution of income in U.S.	Continuing survey with monthly interviewing; 4 year panel introduced 1996	Civilian, noninstitutionalized households	www.sipp.census.gov/sipp
SLAITS	State and Local Area Integrated Telephone Survey	Children with Special Health Care Needs	To collect important health care data at State and local levels in order to supplement current national collection strategies and help meet various program and policy needs	Annually since 1997	Households with children 19-35 months; subgroups such as persons with specific health conditions or low-income households	www.cdc.gov/nchs/slaits.htm
SPCU3	Survey of Parents with Children Under 3		To collect data on pressures and concerns faced by parents during the first 3 years of their children's lives.	One time survey, 1995–96	Parents with children under 3	www.cmwf.org
SPD	Survey of Program Dynamics		To collect data necessary to evaluate impact of Person Responsibility and Work Opportunity Reconciliation Act of from 1996.	Annually from 1996–2001	Sample households interviewed in 1992-94 or 1993-95 SIPP; includes children <18	www.sipp.census.gov/spd

Sources: Zill, N. Researching the Family, 1993. Centers for Disease Control and Prevention, National Center for Health Statistics. National Institute of Child Health & Human Development. US Department of Education, National Center for Education Statistics. Agency for Healthcare Research and Quality. US Census Bureau. Commonwealth Fund.

der the criteria noted earlier. The table is a compendium of information that should assist researchers in identifying the methods for measuring various dimensions of child health, information about the studies that have used these methods, and references to Internet sites from which one can obtain more detailed information. (Our information on these surveys is drawn from these Internet sources.) We now describe in more detail selected studies that are most relevant to the measurement of child health.

Intensive Description of Child Health

The National Health Interview Survey (NHIS) is the most comprehensive general population survey representing child health. The NHIS began in 1957 and was extensively redesigned in 1996 and further refined in 1997. It is an annual household-based sample of the population that collects health information for persons of all ages, including children. The survey includes approximately 43,000 households and 106,000 persons of all ages (approximately 25,000 children under age 18).[3] The NHIS is representative of the United States and its major regions, as well as the more populous states. The NHIS includes a larger sample of children than any other study and is thus especially valuable for the study of relatively rare medical conditions; by pooling several annual surveys, it is possible to further increase the number of children available for the study of relatively rare populations (e.g., the very poor; specific types of minority families; or children with specific medical conditions, such as asthma).

In its 1996/97 redesign the NHIS continued to ask core questions about the health of all individuals in households but added supplemental adult and child surveys (children under age 18) that were administered to 1 randomly selected adult and child per household (approximately 13,600 children). Information collected in the NHIS for children include reports on sicknesses, medical conditions, impairments, accidents and injuries, medical care and service utilization, health care access, and the ability to participate in age-appropriate activities (see Tables 1.3-1.5 and Table 1.6). The child supplement provides specific information about a broad spectrum of issues relating to child health and uses data collection methods designed to enhance the quality of the health information collected. The redesign greatly improved the collection of medical conditions information, permitting unprecedented and reliable measurement of the incidence of specific medical conditions (see Table 1.7) and the ways in which these relate to medical care utilization, impairments, functional limitations, and participation. Before the 1996/97 redesign, the 1994/95 NHIS used a special design to measure disability and describe the utilization of specialized medical services for children with disability and other chronic health needs. The NHIS also is an excellent source of information about accidents, injuries, and the safety of children.

Table 1.3

Health Status Indicators

Measure	Description	Source	Infant	Age 1-4	Age 5-11
Health Status	Health is: Excellent, good, fair, poor (respondent's impression)	NHANES III, NHIS-family core, NLSY children, ECLS-B, ECLS-K, SLATS, SIPP, PSID, MEPS-CE, NHES, SPD, SPCU3, NSECH, NSCH	X	X	X
	Mental health is: Excellent, good, fair, poor (respondent's impression)	MEPS-CE			X
	Current health compared with 12 months ago (better, worse, about the same)	NHANES III		X	X
	Resists illness very well (definitely F, mostly F, mostly T, definitely T) (T or F)	MEPS-HE	X	X	X
	Catches things "going around"/gets sick easily (definitely F, mostly F, mostly T, definitely T) (T or F)	MEPS-HE	X	X	X
	Less healthy than other children (T or F)	MEPS-HE	X	X	X
	Illness that required medical attention (past year)	NLSY-child	X	X	X
	Regularly taking prescription medications (not vitamins) (past year)	NHIS-child, SLAITS-special needs, SLAITS, SIPP, NLSY-child, NSECH, NSCH, NAS	X	X	X
	Needs or uses more medical care, mental health or educational services than usual for most children of the same age	SLAITS-special needs, SLAITS		X	X
	Needs special therapy, such as physical, occupation or speech therapy	SLAITS-special needs, NSECH,		X	X
	Condition or impairment expected to last 12 months or longer	NHANES III, SLAITS -special needs, SLAITS, NSCH	X	X	X
	Regularly receives shots or injections at home	NHIS-disability		X	X
	Ever had menstrual cycle (females age 8+)	NLSY-child			X
	Severe diarrhea, enough to limit daily activity for > 1/2 day (past year) —age < 6	NHIS-child prevention	X	X	<6
	Ever had chicken pox (age?)	NIS, NHANES III	X	X	X
	Ever had asthma?	NSECH, NSCH, NAS			

(continued)

19

Table 1.3 (continued)

Measure	Description	Source	Infant	Age 1-4	Age 5-11
	Ever had eczema, skin allergies, food allergies?	NSECH, NSCH			
	Ever had more than three ear infections?	NSECH, NSCH			
	Gets enough sleep?	NSCH			
	Good teeth?	NSCH			
Activity Limitations	Able to take part at all in usual play activities (current)	NHANES III	X	X	
	Has condition that limits play activities	NHES:96, NLSY-child, MEPS, PSID, NAS	X	X	
	Kind or amount of play activities limited by impairment or health problem (current)	NHIS family, NHANES III, MEPS	X	X	
	Limited in ability to crawl, walk, run, play	SIPP-topical module, NHANES, NHIS-child, NHIS disability	X	X	
	Has emotional or mental condition that makes it difficult to play with or get along with children of the same age	SIPP-topical module,NSCH (other people)			X
	Limited in attendance or unable to attend school because of impairment or physical or mental health problem	MEPS, NLSY-child, PSID			X
	Limited in ability to do regular school work	SIPP-topical module, NLSY-child, PSID, SPD, NAS			X
	Kind or amount of ordinary play limited by health	MEPS	X	X	
	Needs more help than usual for age in everyday activities due to impairment or condition (eating, dressing, bathing or using toilet)	NHANES III, SLAITS -special needs, MEPS, SIPP topical module, NHIS-disability, SPD			X
	Needs constant supervision because of physical, mental, emotional problem	NHIS-disability		X	X
	Limited in any way by impairment or health problem (physical, mental, developmental)	NHANES III, MEPS,SIPP -topical module, SLAIT-Sspecial needs, ECLS-B	X	X	X
	Difficulty walking, climbing stairs, grasping objects, reaching overhead, lifting, bending, stooping, standing for long periods of time	MEPS			X
	Medical, behavioral, emotional, or other health conditions affect ability to do things usual for age (past 12 months)	SLAITS - special needs			X

Category	Measure	Source			
	Duration of limitation in years	NLSY-child		X	X
	Rank severity of condition from 0 to 10	SLAITS -special needs		X	X
	Receives services from Early Intervention or Special Education Services	SLAITS -special needs, MEPS, NHANES III, SIPP topical module, SPD, ECLS-B	X	X	X
	Special equipment required (cane, crutch, walker, etc) (past year)	SIPP-topical module, NHANES, NHIS-child, ECLS-K, MEPS, NLSY-child, NHIS-disability, SLAITS-special needs, SPD		X	X
	Takes medication regularly to help control activity level or behavior	NLSY-child, NSCH (ADD)		X	X
	Difficulty sleeping because of asthma	NAS			
	Limited in abilities because of condition	NSCH			
	Limited or prevented in doing things most children of the same age can do	NSCH			
Missed School/ Bed days	Missed school days because of illness, injury, poisoning (past 12 months)	PSID, MEPS-DD, NHIS-family, NHANES, SLAITSspecial needs, NAS (from asthma)			X
	Days in bed >1/2 day due to illness or injury (past 2 weeks and year)—AGE 1-3	MEPS-DD		X	
Anthropometric measure	Height and weight without shoes, age	MEPS-HE, NHIS-child, NLSY-child, SIPP, PSID, NSCH	X	X	X
	Low (5th percentile) height-for-age, low weight-for-height, and high (95th percentile) weight-for-height	Pediatric Nutrition Surveillance System	X	X	X
Parental Health and Character	Mother's nervous	NSECH			
	Mother's calm	NSECH			
	Mother's down in the dumps	NSECH			
	Mother's depressed	NSECH			
	Difficulty coping with parenthood	NSECH			
	Someone to turn to for help, support	NSECH, NSCH			
	Types of parental concern for child	NSECH, NSCH			
	Parents' physical health	NSCH			
	Parents' emotional health	NSCH			
	Attend parenting class after birth	NSECH			
	Health difficulties been burden to family	NSCH			
	Parents safety proofed house	NSECH			
	Parents smoke	NSCH			

**Age categories may not correspond to each listed source, see Survey Instrument descriptions

Table 1.4
Indicators of Medical Care Utilization

Measure	Description	Source	Infant	Age 1-4	Age 5-11
Access to Care	Seen or talked to medical doctor about child (past 2 weeks)	NHIS-family	X	X	X
	Seen or talked to medical doctor or assistant about child (past year)	NHIS-child, NHANES III, NHES, SIPP, PSID, NLSYchild, SLAITS, NHIS-disability, SPD, NSECH, NSCH	X	X	X
	Seen or talked to mental health professional—psychologist, psychiatrist, clinical social worker (past year)	NHANES III, SLAITS-special needs, NHIS-disability, NHIS-child, NLSY-child, PSID, NSCH	X		X
	Is there a usual place (doctor's office, clinic, etc.) where child goes for routine care?	NHIS-child, MEPS-AC, SLAITS, SLAITS -special needs, SPCU3, ECLS-B, NSECH, NSCH	X	X	X
	Is there a usual place where child goes when sick or injured?	NHIS-child, MEPS-AC, SLAITS, NHANES III, SLAITS-special needs, NHES, SPD, NSECH	X	X	X
	Is there a usual place where child goes for advice about health?	NHIS-child, NHANES III, MEPS-AC, SLAITS, SLAITS -special needs, SPD	X	X	X
	Reasons for not having usual source of health care	MEPS-AC	X	X	X
	Time since seen or talked to medical doctor or assistant about child —sick or injured (past year)	PSID, NHANES III		X	X
	Time since last routine care visit (<6 mo., 6 mo - 1 yr., 1 -2 yrs., ...)	NHES, NLSY-child, PSID, SLAITS-special needs, SLAITS	X	X	X
	Time since last saw or talked to health professional about health (<6 mo., 6 mo - 1 yr., 1 -2 yrs.,)	NHES, NHIS-child, NHANES III	X	X	X
	How many well-baby checkups (#, never, don't know)	ECLS-B	X		
	Phone calls to medical doctor about child (since previous interview)	SLAITS, NHIS-family (past 2 weeks), NSECH	X	X	X
	Rate of visits by diagnosis category	NAMCS	X	X	X
	Satisfaction with health care provider (length of visits, information provided, listening to concerns)	SLAITS, MEPS-AC, SLAITS-special needs, SPCU3, NSECH, NSCH	X	X	X

Category	Item	Source			
	Referred to specialist	NSECH			X
	Had problems getting health care	NSECH			
	Had depression	NSCH			
	ADHD	NSCH			
	Behavioral problems	NSCH			
	Bone, jt problems	NSCH			
	Diabetes	NSCH			
	Autism	NSCH			
	Developmental delay	NSCH			
	Physical impairment	NSCH			
	Fever, allergies, migraines	NSCH			
	During the past twelve months injured or required medical care	NSCH			
	Need interpreter when speaking with dr.	NSCH			
	Went to dr. for preventative care	NSCH			
Dental Care	Time since last dentist visit (<6mo., 6 mo.-1 yr., 1-2 yrs.)	NHANES III, SIPP, NLSY-child, NHIS-child, MEPS, NHES, SLAITS-special needs, SPD		X	X
	Dental sealants	SIPP, NHIS-child prevention			>6
Hospitalization	Outpatient (mental health/substance abuse) services (past year)	NHIS-disability	X		X
	Inpatient (mental health/substance abuse) services (past year)	NHIS-disability	X		X
	Emergency room visits (past year)	NHIS-disability, SLAITS, NHIS-child, NSCH, NSECH, NAS (asthma)	X	X	X
	Different times overnight in hospital in past year	SLAITS, SIPP, NHANES III, NHIS-family, SPD, NSCH, NSECH, NAS (asthma)	X	X	X
	Different times overnight in hospital since birth	PSID, NAS (asthma)	X	X	X

(continued)

Table 1.4 (continued)

Measure	Description	Source	Infant	Age 1-4	Age 5-11
	Rate of hospitalization by diagnosis	National Hospital Discharge Survey	X	X	X
	Inpatient/outpatient surgery (past year)	NHIS-child		X	X
Insurance	Medicaid	PSID, NLSY-child, NAMCS, NHANES III, SLAITS special needs, NHIS-disability, NHIS-family, SPCU3, SPD, ECLS-B, NSECH, NSCH, NAS	X	X	X
	Medicare	PSID, NAMCS, NHANES III, NHIS-family, SPD, NAS	X	X	X
	Title V	SLAITS-special needs, NSECH	X	X	X
	State Children's Health Insurance Program—	SCHIP NHANES III, SLAITS-special needs, SPD, ECLS-B,	X	X	X
	State sponsored health plan	PSID, NHIS-family	X	X	X
	Medigap	PSID, NHANES III, SLAITS-special needs, NHISfamily, SPD, NSECH	X	X	X
	Military—VA	PSID, NHANES III, SLAITS-special needs, NHISdisability, NHIS-family, NSECH	X	X	X
	CHAMPUS/TRICARE/CHAMP-VA	PSID, NHANES III, SLAITS-special needs, NHISdisability, NHIS-family, SPD, ECLS-B, NSECH	X	X	X
	Indian Health Service	PSID, NHANES III,SLAITS-special needs, NHISdisability, NHIS-family, SPD, ECLS-B, NSECH	X	X	X
	Private Insurance	PSID, NAMCS, NHANES III, SLAITS-special needs, NHIS-disability, NHIS-family, ECLS-B, NSECH	X	X	X
	Employer based insurance	PSID, NLSY-child, NHANES III, SLAITS-special needs, NHIS-disability, NHIS-family, SPCU3, SPD, NSECH	X	X	X
	Union provided plan	SPD, NSECH	X	X	X
	Other government program (specify)	PSID, NHANES III, NHIS-family, SPCU3, SPD, ECLS-B	X	X	X
	Other source	SPCU3, NSECH	X	X	X
	Single service plan (dental, vision, prescriptions)	NHANES III, SLAITS-special needs, NSECH	X	X	X
	Time spent without health/medical insurance	SLAITS, SLAITS -special needs, NHANES, NHISfamily, MEPS, NSECH, NSCH, NAS	X	X	X

Currently or ever uninsured (how long?)	SPCU3, SPD, ECLS-B	X	X	X
Months of coverage in past year?	PSID, SLAITS-special needs	X	X	X
Is child covered by health insurance now?	PSID, SLAITS, SPD, NSECH, NSCH	X	X	X
WIC Benefits	NSECH			
Dental Insurance	NSCH			
Did child receive all the care needed? Why?	NSCH			
Trouble paying for child's birth, health, medical expenses, formula, food, childcare	NSECH			
Vaccinations				
Whether vaccination card is available	NHIS- immunization, NIS	X		
Vaccination up-to-date for age	PSID	X		
Diptheria-Tetanus-Pertussis (DPT)—number of shots	NIS,MEPS, NHIS- immunization	X		
Polio (by mouth, pink drops)—number of vaccines	NIS,MEPS, NHIS- immunization	X		
Measles-Mumps-Rubella (MMR)—number of shots	NIS,MEPS, NHIS- immunization	X		
Haemophilus Influenza (HIB)—number of shots	NIS, NHIS- immunization	X		
Chicken Pox/Varicella—number of shots	NIS, NHIS- immunization	X		
Rotavirus—number of shots	NIS	X		
Pneumococcal/Prevnar—number of shots	NIS, NHIS- immunization	X		
Hepatitis A	NSCH, NHIS- immunization	X		
Hepatitis B	NHIS- immunization	X		
Tetanus-Diptheria	NHIS- immunization	X		
Tetramune	NHIS- immunization	X		
ACTHib shot	NHIS- immunization	X		
Influenza	NHIS- immunization	X		
Received other immunizations listed on shot records	NIS, NHIS- immunization	X		

**Age categories may not correspond to each listed source, see Survey Instrument descriptions

Table 1.5
Indicators of Impairment

Measure	Description	Source	Infant	Age 1-4	Age 5-11
Sight	Blindness	NHIS-child, NHANES III, PSID, NLSY-child, MEPS, ECLS-B	X	X	X
	Correctable, improvable, not correctable with glasses	ECLS-K			X
	Wears glasses or contact lenses	NHIS-child, NHANES III, SPD		>2	X
	Difficulty seeing even with glasses	NHIS-child, NHANES III, MEPS, ECLS-K, SIPP topical module, SPD, NSCH		X	X
	Needed eyeglasses or vision care (past year)	SLAITS-special needs		X	X
	Recognizes familiar people at 2 or 3 feet with glasses	MEPS		X	X
	Serious difficulty seeing	ECLS-B, ECLS-K, NLSY-child	X	X	X
	Ever had vision tested (age?)	ECLS-K			X
Hearing	Hearing status: good, a little trouble, a lot of trouble, deaf	NHANES III	X	X	X
	Deafness	NHIS-child, NHANES III, PSID, NLSY-child, MEPS, ECLS-B		X	X
	Deafness in one or both ears	ECLS-K			X
	Hard of hearing	ECLS-K			X
	Wears hearing aid	MEPS, ECLS-K, SPD		X	X
	Cochlear implants	ECLS-K			X
	Difficulty hearing even with hearing aid	MEPS, ECLS-K, SIPP-topical module, SPD			X
	Hears some things with hearing aid	ECLS-K, MEPS		X	X
	Serious hearing difficulty	ECLS-B, ECLS-K, NLSY-child	X	X	X
	Needed hearing aid or hearing care (past year)	SLAITS-special needs		X	X
	Ever had hearing tested (age?)	ECLS-B, ECLS-K			X
Speech	Difficulty having speech understood	SIPP-topical module			X
	Ever evaluated on ability to communicate	ECLS-K			X

Category	Item	Source			
	Pronounces words, communicates with and understands others	ECLS-K			X
	Stuttering, stammering or speech problems	NSCH		X	X
Development	Delay in growth or development (When? Seen doctor? Taken medicine?)	NHIS-child, NHES, PSID, ECLS-B	X		X
	Emotional or behavioral problem (lasting more than 3 months) (When? Seen doctor? Taken medicine?)	SLAITS, SPD		X	X
	Compared with other children, child is independent and takes care of him/herself (better than, as well as, slightly less well, much less well, don't know)	ECLS-K	X		X
	Ever evaluated by professional in response to ability to pay attention or learn (age?)	ECLS-K			X
	Learning disability (When? Seen doctor? Taken medicine?)	NHIS-child, ECLS-K, NHES, PSID, NHANES III, SPD, NSCH		X	X
	Seen doctor/counselor for any emotional, developmental or behavioral problem (When was last time?)	NHIS-child, NSECH, NSCH			X
	Learning disability, minimal brain dysfunction, hyperkinesis or hyperactivity, serious emotional disturbance, mental retardation	NLSY-child			X
	Learning disability or mental retardation	NHES, NLSY-child, NSCH		X	X
	Doctor said mentally retarded	NHIS-child, PSID, NSCH		X	X
	Respondent feels child is fast, slow, or about on time in development	SLAITS, ECLS-K	X	X	X
Physical Impairments	Condition that limits ability to move arms and legs	SIPP-topical module, ECLS-B	X	X	X
	Crippled, orthopedic handicap	NHES, PSID	X	X	X
	Deformity of arm, hand, finger	SIPP-topical module	X	X	X
	Missing legs, feet, arms, hands, or fingers	SIPP-topical module	X	X	X
	Head or spinal cord injury	SIPP-topical module	X	X	X
	Coordination in moving arms and legs compared to other children (better than, as well, slightly less well, much less well, don't know)	ECLS-K		X	X

**Age categories may not correspond to each listed source, see Survey Instrument descriptions

27

Table 1.6

Indicators of Injuries and Safety

Measure	Description	Source	Infant	Age 1-4	Age 5-11
Accidental Injuries	Accidents or injuries that required medical attention (past year)	MEPS-CN, NLSY-child, ECLS-B	X	X	X
	Injury or poisoning that required medical attention	NAMCS	X	X	X
	Poisonings as cause of accident/injury	NLSY-child, NHIS-family	X	X	X
	Most recent accidents that required medical attention (past 3 months)	NHIS-family, ECLS-B	X	X	X
	Causes of recorded accidents	NAMCS, NHIS-family, NLSY-child	X	X	X
	Receiving medication or treatment for conditions since accident or injury	MEPS-CN	X	X	X
	Resulting conditions (e.g.. Broken bones, burns, poisoning)	NHIS-family, NLSY-child	X	X	X
	Place where accident occurred (e.g.. Home, day care, street)	NAMCS, MEPS-CN, NHIS-family, NLSY-child, ECLS-B	X	X	X
	Whether any disabling condition is the result of an accident	MEPS-CN, NHIS-family	X	X	X
	Injury due to motor vehicle accident specifically	NHIS-family	X	X	X
	Whether ever hospitalized due to accident or injury	NLSY-child, NHIS-family, ECLS-B	X	X	X
	Use of child safety seats, seat belts (most of time, sometimes,occasionally, never)	NHIS-child prevention	X	X	
Safety	Ipecac syrup in home	SLAITS	X	X	X
	Phone number to poison control center readily available	NHIS-family	X	X	X
	Use of baby gates, window guards, other barriers	SLAITS	X	X	
	Use safety latches on cabinets	SLAITS	X	X	
	Put stoppers or plugs in electrical outlets	SLAITS	X	X	
	Put padding on hard surfaces or sharp edges	SLAITS	X	X	
	Use of protective sports gear	NHIS-child prevention			X
	Lead paint in house—analyzed?	NHIS-adult prevention	X	X	X
	Lead poisoning/elevated lead levels in blood	NHANES III, PSID	X	X	X
	Household air tested for radon gas	NHIS-adult prevention	X	X	X
	Number of working smoke detectors in home	NHIS-adult prevention	X	X	X
	Ammunition in home (with firearm, locked up)	NHIS-adult prevention	X	X	X
	Special features installed in house (ramps, railings, elevators, automatic doors, etc)	NHIS-disability	X	X	X

**Age categories may not correspond to each listed source, see Survey Instrument descriptions

Table 1.7

Indicators of Other Medical Conditions

Measure	Description	Source	Infant	Age 1-4	Age 5-11
Conditions Lists	3+ ear infections	NHIS-child, SLAITS, PSID, NLSY-child, NHANES III, SIPP, ECLS-B, ECLS-K	X	X	X
	Allergic conditions	NLSY-child	X	X	X
	Anemia	NHIS-child, NHANES, PSID	X	X	X
	Asthma	NHIS-child, SLAITS, PSID, NLSY-child, NHANES III, SIPP, ECLS-B	X	X	X
	Autism	NHIS-child, PSID, SIPP	X	X	X
	Birth defect	NHIS-family	X	X	X
	Cancer	SIPP	X	X	X
	Cerebral Palsy	NHIS-child, SIPP	X	X	X
	Chronic nervous disorder	NLSY-child		X	X
	Congenital heart condition/heart trouble	NHIS-child,SIPP, NLSY-child, ECLS-B	X	X	X
	Cystic Fibrosis	NHIS-child	X	X	X
	Diabetes	NHIS-child, PSID	X	X	X
	Down Syndrome	NHIS-child, ECLS-B	X	X	X
	Dyslexia	ECLS-K			X
	Eczema/skin allergy	NHIS-child, SLAITS	X	X	X
	Food/digestive allergy	NHIS-child, SLAITS	X	X	X
	Frequent diarrhea or colitis	NHIS-child, ECLS-B	X	X	X
	Frequent/severe headaches	NHIS-child, NHANES III		>2	X
	Hearing difficulty/deafness	SIPP, PSID, NLSY-child, NHES	X	X	X
	Hyperactivity	(ADHD, ADD) PSID, SIPP, NLSY-child, NHES, ECLS-K, NHANES III		>2	X
	Learning disability (specify)	PSID, SIPP, NLSY-child, NHES, ECLS-K, NHANES III		>3	X
	Mental retardation	SIPP, PSID, NLSY-child, NHES, ECLS-K	X	X	X
	Muscular Dystrophy	NHIS-child	X	X	X
	Orthopedic impairment	PSID, NLSY-child, NHES	X	X	X

(continued)

29

Table 1.7   *(continued)*

Measure	Description	Source	Infant	Age 1-4	Age 5-11
	Overweight	NHANES III			X
	Respiratory Allergy/ hay fever	NHIS-child, NLSY-child, SIPP, NHANES III	X	X	X
	Seeing difficulty/blindness	SIPP, PSID, NLSY-child, NHES	X	X	X
	Serious emotional disturbance	SIPP, PSID, NLSY-child, NHES		X	X
	Seizures/Epileptic fit or convulsion	NHIS-child, PSID, NLSY-child, SIPP, NHIS-child	X	X	X
	Sickle Cell Anemia/blood disorder	NHIS-child, NLSY-child	X	X	X
	Speech impairment or delay	PSID, SIPP, NLSY-child, NHES			X
	Spina bifida	ECLS-B	X	X	X
	Stuttering/stammering	NHANES III		>2	X
	Turner's Syndrome	ECLS-B	X	X	X
	Other conditions (specify)	NHIS-child, PSID, NLSY-child, ECLS-K, NHES, SLAITS	X	X	X
Information about each condition	Taken medication for condition (past 12 months)	MEPS	X	X	X
	Receiving services for condition	NHES	X	X	X
	Limitations due to condition	NHIS, NHANES, NHES, MEPS, NLSY, SIPP, SLAITS	X	X	X
	How long ago condition was first noticed	NHIS-family	X	X	X
	Saw doctor for condition (30 days acute, 12 months chronic)	MEPS	X	X	X
	Affect on overall health	MEPS	X	X	X

**Age categories may not correspond to each listed source, see Survey Instrument descriptions

The strengths of the current NHIS are its large sample sizes, with a capacity to represent major geographic areas and specific population subgroups. The data quality of the NHIS generally is very high with, in the case of many measures, a long time series available. However, specific medical indicators (e.g., parent reports of medical condition or birthweight) are subject to unreliability and are of uncertain validity at the individual level (these problems are much greater for children who are older and/or for whom the mother is not the respondent). The NHIS provides major indicators of the family ecology, but it lacks information on changes in the family ecology over time and on the complex dynamics of child health. The NHIS is thus most appropriate for estimating population parameters for indicators of child health and health disparities and relatively weak for causal analysis. An exception is the 1996 Medical Expenditure Panel Survey, which is a prospective study (seven interviews over 2.5 years) that provides comprehensive information about health care use and costs for a 25% subsample of 1995 NHIS households.

Prenatal and Infant Health and Survival

Birth certificates provide the best data available on circumstances of a child's birth because it is provided directly by medical attendants at the time of birth. The 2003 revised birth certificate standard form includes the demographics for mothers and their infants (age of mother, mother's prenatal care and risky behaviors, gestation period, the infant's number of older siblings, birthweight, and length), the Apgar score representing the infant's status at birth, abnormal and congenital medical conditions, and breastfeeding plans/initial behaviors.

These data are generally of good quality; however, recent research has suggested that the record on congenital medical conditions is less valid. In the past decade, tremendous strides have been made in designing birth certificates to collect usable data on the multiple dimensions of risk (discussed previously) that affect infant survival and infant health. This includes information on tobacco, drug, and alcohol use during pregnancy; the timing of prenatal care and adequacy of care; and participation in the Women, Infants, and Children program (see Table 1.8). The exact form of data collected varies by state, but in recent years there has been a trend toward the adoption of uniform birth certificate information. Strides have also been made in connecting infant death records to infant births, greatly facilitating the study of infant mortality.

The introduction of machine-readable birth and matched infant death files (the Linked Birth and Infant Death Files) has made these registration systems much more useful for calculating indicators of child survival, prenatal and infant health, and health disparities. A very specific advantage of this data source is that it includes the full population of births (approximately 3.9 million) for each year and deaths of those

Table 1.8
Prenatal and Birth Indicators

Measure	Description	Source	Infant	Age 1-4	Age 5-11
Parents' characteristics	Age of mother and father	LBID, SPCU3, NSECH	X		
	Education of mother	CPS, ECLS-B, ECLS-K, LBID, MEPS, NHES, NHIS, NIS, NLSY, NSFH, PSID, SIPP, SLAITS, SPCU3, SPD, NSECH	X		
	Race and ethnicity	CPS, ECLS-B, ECLS-K, LBID, MEPS, NAMCS, NHANES, NHDS, NHES, NHIS, NIS, NLSY, NSFH, PSID, SIPP, SLAITS, SPCU3, SPD, NSECH	X		
	Marital status	CPS, ECLS-B, ECLS-K, LBID, NHDS, NHES, NHIS, NIS, NLSY, NSFH, PSID, SIPP, SLAITS, SPCU3, SPD, NSECH	X		
	Medical risk factors	LBID	X		
	Nativity of mother	LBID	X		
Pregnancy information	Did mother smoke during pregnancy? How many cigarettes or packs?	NHANES III, ECLS-B, LBID			
	What month of pregnancy did mother quit smoking?	NHANES III	X		
	Did mother drink during pregnancy? How many drinks?	ECLS-B, LBID	X		
	Did mother take vitamins before and/or during pregnancy?	ECLS-B	X		
	Received assistance from private health insurance, Medicaid, WIC, food stamps, AFDC	PSID	X	X	X
	What month of pregnancy did mother first see a doctor or other health care professional	SPCU3, LBID	X	<3	
	How many weeks of prenatal care during pregnancy?	ECLS-B, LBID	X		
	Trouble paying for prenatal care	NSECH			
	Attend childbirth class before birth	NSECH			
	Infant Birth Information Apgar score (5 minutes)	LBID	X		
	Interval since last live birth	LBID	X		
	Gestation period	LBID	X		
	Total birth order	LBID	X		
	Child's sex	LBID, NSECH, NSCH	X		
	Abnormal conditions of newborn	LBID	X		
	Child's weight at birth (>5 1/2 lbs.; >3 lbs.;>9 lbs.)	NHES, SLAITS, NHANES III, PSID, ECLS-K, NHIS, MEPS, SPCU3, LBID, NSECH	X	X	X
	Was it a multiple birth?	ECLS-K		X	X

Category	Item	Source(s)					
	Place of delivery	LBID	X				
	Method of delivery	LBID, SPCU3	X				
	Preterm birth (> 2 weeks early)	ECLS-K, PSID, SPCU3	X	X	X	X	X
	Received newborn care in intensive care unit, premature nursery, other special care facility (how long?)	NHANES III, NHES, PSID, ECLS-B	X	X	X		X
	Any handicapping conditions at birth/congenital anomalies	NHES, LBID	X	X			
	Health at birth better/worse/same as other babies	PSID	X	X			
	Was child breastfed? How long?	PSID, SLAITS, Pediatric Nutrition Surveillance System, SPCU3, ECLS-B, NSECH	X	<3			
	Infant weight gain	LBID	X	X			
	Any medical problems in 2 weeks after discharge from hospital that required medical attention	SPCU3	X	<3			
	Age of child when introduced to solid foods	NSECH					
	Attended parenting class after birth	NSECH					
Infant Death Information	Age at death	LBID	X				
	Place of accident	LBID	X				
	Cause of death	LBID	X				
Infant Behavior	During feedings, kicks and squirms (almost never, < 1/2 time, about 1/2 time, > 1/2 time, almost always)	PSID, NLSY-mother, ECLS-B	X				
	During sleep, moves around crib	PSID, NLSY-mother	X				
	Gets sleepy about same time each evening	PSID, NLSY-mother, ECLS-B	X				
	Gets hungry about same time each day	PSID, NLSY-mother, ECLS-B	X				
	Same mood when child wakes up each morning	PSID, NLSY-mother	X				
	Turns away or cries as if afraid when sees stranger	PSID, NLSY-mother, ECLS-B	X				
	Turns away or cries as if afraid when sees unfamiliar dog or cat	PSID, NLSY-mother, ECLS-B	X				
	Turns away or cries as if afraid when taken to doctor, dentist, nurse	PSID, NLSY-mother	X				
	Becomes upset when parent leaves him/her alone in room	PSID, NLSY-mother	X				
	Laughs or smiles during play with parent	PSID, NLSY-mother	X				
	Laughs or smiles when playing alone	PSID, NLSY-mother	X				
	Laughs or smiles in bath	NLSY-mother	X				
	Cries or becomes upset at unexpected loud sounds	PSID, NLSY-mother, ECLS-B	X				
	Trouble soothing when he/she is upset	PSID, NLSY-mother, ECLS-B	X				
	Gets fussy or irritable during day	PSID, NLSY-mother	X				
	Compared with other infants, how often does he/she cry or fuss?	PSID, NLSY-mother	X				
	Bedtime/naptime/mealtime at same time everyday	NSECH					

**Age categories may not correspond to each listed source, see Survey Instrument descriptions

33

infants (approximately 28,000) during their first year of life, enabling researchers to address infant health and health disparities for relatively rare risk groups (Guyer et al., 1999). Because the Early Childhood Longitudinal Study-Birth Cohort (ECLS-B) is based on sample frame of birth certificates, the sampled cases for that study also include this prenatal and child health data from birth certificates.

Population-Based Studies of Child Health and Development

The Panel Study of Income Dynamics (PSID) and the National Longitudinal Study of Youth (NLSY) are two longitudinal studies of households and families that provide panel data on household economic resources and expenditures and on human capital formation and employment (http://psidonline.isr.umich.edu, http://www.bls.gov/nls). Because these two nationally representative surveys provide extensive information on the household and family ecology of children, and changes in that ecology over time, they have creatively been adapted to provide corresponding panel data on child health and development. The PSID has a special Child Development Supplement that collects information on the health history and current status and the development of children ages 0 through 12 in 1997 (see Tables 1.3 and 1.4). The supplement also collected detailed information about the cognitive and emotional family environments of children as well as characteristics of their neighborhoods and schools. The PSID Child Development Supplement is among the highest quality data sets available for the analysis of child health, but it lacks the large number of sample children ($N = 3,563$) needed to study key, relatively small, population groups.

The NLSY-Child Survey has extensive information on the household and family environments of children, especially data on the mother's marriage and birth history, her labor force and employment history, and child care arrangements (http://www.bls.gov/nls). This study collected biennially, beginning in 1986, extensive information on child health, cognition, socioemotional development/behavior, and home environment. The original study design included children under age 18; in 1994, the assessments were done only for children age 14 or younger. The sample design allows investigators to use sibling models to assess the maximum effects of family ecology on child outcomes.

Information collected in a special survey of the children of NLSY respondents (NLSY-Child), collected longitudinal information on child development and its linkages to the life situations and events of their mothers. A major limitation of the NLSY-Child survey arises in potential bias rooted in its research design. The basic NLSY sample of women began in 1979 and was age restricted to include women aged 14 through 21. For example, by 1994, any children under age 5 were born to mothers 24 or older. This study thus omits children of the older cohort of young women who were born when their mothers were teens and overrepresents births to mothers who were relatively old at first birth; on a period basis, this means the annual sample of births in recent years is restricted to older mothers. This may bias our understanding of the problems children currently encounter in child health and development by omitting these children with the highest risk family ecology profile.

Although the PSID Child Development Supplement has a much smaller sample of children than the NLYS-Child, we believe it provides a stronger basis for studies of child health statuses and trends. The sample is unbiased and represents a contemporary cohort of children. The measurement of the family ecology is more extensive, and there are better measures of child development over the early life course. In addition, supplemental questions about family food security and child nutrition offer an important perspective on children in exceptionally high-risk families. Finally, the PSID generally provides somewhat better quality information on household and family income and on the receipt of welfare by program.

Studies of Child Health and Cognitive and Emotional Development

In response to the need for more dynamic, process-related information that can be used for causal, policy-relevant analyses of child health and development, the U.S. Department of Education has recently launched two major panel studies that are destined to become major sources of data for the study of child health. The ECLS-K began in 1998. It involves a national sample of 22,000 children in kindergarten who will be followed annually through the fifth grade. The goal of the study is to gather information on the school readiness of children (knowledge and skills of children as they enter kindergarten) and the ways these influence cognitive development and other developmental outcomes over the primary grades. The study is extraordinary in the multidimensionality and depth of the data collected. Schools and teachers provide information, as do parents and primary day care providers. Information about children is obtained directly and through the direct study of children (whose interactions and actions with parents are videotaped). The entire thrust of this study is to measure complexities in the family ecology and the school ecology of children and the diverse mechanisms that connect these environments to health and developmental outcomes. The health emphasis of the ECLS-K is directed toward the measurement of impairments that might influence educational outcomes (see Tables 1.6 and 1.7), but the ECLS-K has little information on other aspects of health and health care utilization.

The ECLS-B began in 2001. It involves a national sample of approximately 15,000 children drawn from birth certificates who will be followed at key intervals during infancy and early childhood. The ECLS-B is unique in its focus on the health and development of children from birth until first grade. Developmental theories, particularly those related to cognitive competencies, typically begin with children who are preschool age (as in ECLS-K), missing much salient information that could identify the early origins of differences among children at this age. However, the ECLS-B recognizes that the pathways by which children acquire different levels of school competencies and other age-appropriate skills originates in the circumstances of birth and is greatly influenced by early life child interactions with parents and the kinds of home environments those parents or other guardians provide. The ECLS-B also recognizes that any effective approach to the study of child health, development, and school readiness must be multidimensional. It draws on expertise from a broad array of social, medical, psychological, and education scientists, incorporating needed information for each disciplinary perspective.

The ECLS-K and ECLS-B are uniquely valuable to researchers because they will provide detailed and comprehensive information for the study of the family ecology and its association with child health and developmental competencies for children from birth to first grade and from kindergarten to Grade 5, thus covering the periods infancy, preschool, and young school-age children that are the subject of this chapter. The ECLS-B provides more indicators of infant health, medical conditions, accidents and injuries, and medical services utilization than the ECLS-K. It also includes more detail about the family ecology. Therefore ECLS-B is of somewhat greater value for the study of child health, but the needed time series are only now becoming available to researchers. The ECLS-K captures a critical period of a child's life-entry into school-and has excellent measures relating to developmental competencies for children now in the early years of primary school.

Both data sources have the advantages and disadvantages of longitudinal studies: they currently provide only a partial picture of the early life trajectories of children and will provide a more complete picture only by the later part of this decade. By beginning 2 years earlier and at a later age, the kindergarten cohort will provide longitudinal data somewhat earlier than the birth cohort study. Extraordinary efforts are being made in both studies to assure that full data for a child is provided by all informants and that loss to follow-up will be minimized. However, these are difficult problems to resolve, and experience suggests that it is likely that analysts using the data will need to have a strategy for dealing with case-missing and variable-missing issues.

The ECLS-B and ECLS-K are the most exciting new studies of children undertaken during the past decade. Any analyst interested in a dynamic picture of child health and development in a changing family ecology should turn first to these innovative studies.

Dynamics of Family and Household Ecology

Beginning in 1996, the Survey of Income and Program Participation (SIPP) followed a panel of 36,000 households, interviewing them 12 times over 48 months, collecting information about each month. SIPP is designed to capture the complexities of household structures, families, and subgroups as this change with birth and death and the movement of persons into and out of the household (http://www.sipp.census.gov/sipp). For these people, SIPP collects monthly employment and income data. SIPP provides uniquely comprehensive data on the dynamics of welfare, insurance, and other social supports for each household member, including children. SIPP collects information on impairment and health utilization for at least one point in time for each panel. Thus, SIPP provides static information for the study of child health but complements this with the best information available on family, economic, and welfare dynamics.

The 1996 and later SIPP panels enroll about 24,000 children under age 18 (of whom approximately 16,300 are ages 6-14, for whom child health data are collected); by pooling panels, it is possible to study very detailed population groups (e.g., children in households with a biological mother and cohabiting partner, children living in a household headed by a sister). Comparisons of panels before and after the 1996 welfare reform permit investigations of how this dramatic change in public policy has affected overall child health and the well-being of children with chronic health problems or disabilities. SIPP is designed to capture state-to-state variations in these processes.

SIPP provides the data of choice for researchers interested in how the dynamics of household structure and income relate to child health. SIPP also provides the best data for analyses that seek to understand how welfare and program participation and health insurance relate to child health. Investigations using SIPP will need to deal with data-missing and case-missing (loss to follow-up) issues, but these are not insurmountable. Of the various data sources reviewed in this chapter, SIPP is by far the most complex. Great investments of time and consultations with experts on SIPP are essential for an investigator to use these data.

The Survey of Program Dynamics (SPD) began with a SIPP/SPD bridge survey in 1996 and then subsampled 17,500 households that included children under 18 who were in the 1992-94 or the 1993-95 panels for subsequent study in the SPD. The purpose of the SPD was to collect longitudinal data to provide a dynamic perspective on the Person Responsibility and Work Reconciliation Act of 1996 (i.e., welfare reform). The design for this study is that SIPP would provide data for the baseline and early period of the Person Responsibility and Work Reconciliation Act. The SPD follows families, children, and adolescents to assess the postimplementation results of welfare reform. This has the potential to be an especially valuable source of data on the relationship of public policy programs to the health of children.

The initial efforts yielded data with loss to follow-up that were unacceptable to many researchers. The U.S. Census Bureau convened an expert panel on this problem and has gone back into the field to improve rates of participation in SPD by SIPP respondents and to hold them in the annual SPD survey waves. Early reports indicate that these efforts have met with some success. If so, the SIPP/SPD data will be especially valuable for research on child health concerned with dynamics in the family ecology and social program environment.

State and Local Area Integrated Telephone Survey

The State and Local Area Integrated Telephone Survey (SLAITS) offers a way of collecting important health care data nationally and at the state and local levels. SLAITS uses a random digit dial telephone design approach and is based on the sampling frame for the National Immunization Survey (NIS), an ongoing telephone survey that screens nearly 1 million households per year to produce estimates of vaccination coverage of children aged 19 through 35 and, through screener information, provides data for a sampling frame of children under 18 years of age. SLAITS focuses on a different topical module each year. The National Survey of Early Childhood Health in 1992, the National Survey of Children's Health in 2003, and the National Asthma Survey in 2003 were each the result of a topical model in SLAITS. In 2000/01, SLAITS was devoted to the National Study of Children with Special Health Care Needs, which collected data on a national sample of children under age 18 years with regard to appropriate medical homes, adequate health insurance, access to needed services, and coordination of care. In each state and the District of Columbia, more than 3,000 households are screened to identify about 750 children under age 18 with special health care needs.[4]

SLAITS and its special survey modules are the preferred source of data for researchers and policymakers interested in the health of children, the appropriateness and adequacy of the care received, and the family and health care environment of children, particularly those with special needs. These are the only surveys of child health representative at the national level that also can include (depending on the module and financing) samples that are representative at the state level.

The review of data sources in this chapter illustrates the tremendous variation in design and instruments used to assess child health. Some of the health indicators are drawn from validated measures that have been shortened for survey use. Many other measures were formulated by the researchers conducting the study and have face validity but have not been assessed for reliability or validity. Each is useful for the study of child health, but they would be far more useful if there were an agreement on common instruments to test child health. We have developed an instrument for the concise measure of child health that is appropriate for a comprehensive study of the multiple dimensions of infant and child health (see Table 1.1). This instrument is only a stopgap solution. The next step for researchers and policymakers is to develop, pilot, and pretest new indicators suitable for the sample survey study of infant and child health. Measurement standards used in all major surveys would provide data to dramatically increase knowledge of infant and child health and safety and provide a more solid basis for effective policies.

Table 1.9
Indicators of Food Security and Nutrition

Measure	Description	Source	Infant	Age 1-4	Age 5-11
Food security	Household has enough of and the kinds of food wanted; enough of but not always the kinds of food wanted; sometimes not enough food; often not enough food	PSID, CPS, NHANES III, SPD, ECLS-B	X	X	X
	Worried about whether food would run out	PSID, CPS, NHANES III, SPD, ECLS-B	X	X	X
	Food didn't last/ not enough money to buy more food	PSID, CPS, NHANES III, SPD, ECLS-B	X	X	X
	Couldn't afford to prepare balanced meals	PSID, CPS, NHANES III, SPD, ECLS-B	X	X	X
	Ever cut size of child's meals (past year)	PSID, CPS, NHANES III, SPD, ECLS-B	X	X	X
	Child skipped meal because there was not enough food—how often? (past year)	PSID, CPS, NHANES III, SPD, ECLS-B	X	X	X
	Child ever hungry because family couldn't afford food (past year)	PSID, CPS, NHANES III, SPD, ECLS-B	X	X	X
	Child ever not eat for 1/2 day or more (past year)	PSID, CPS, NHANES III, NHES, SPD, ECLS-B	X	X	X
Nutrition	Does child eat breakfast regularly (how often, past week)	PSID, NHES	X	X	X
	Ever received WIC or food stamps	NIS, ECLS-B, ECLS-K, NHES, NHANES III, PSID, SLAITS, CPS, SPCU3	X	X	X

**Age categories may not correspond to each listed source, see Survey Instrument descriptions

Table 1.10

Indicators Recommended for the Study of Infant and Child Health

Measure	Description
Pregnancy information	Did mother smoke during pregnancy? How many cigarettes or packs per day?
	Did mother have any serious illness during pregnancy?
	Did mother drink during pregnancy? How many drinks per week?
	Did mother take vitamins before and/or during pregnancy?
	Did mother take any medications during pregnancy?
	What month of pregnancy did mother first see a doctor or other health care professional?
Birth information	Child's weight at birth (>9 lbs, 5.5–8.99 lbs, 3.51–5.49 lbs, 2.2–3.5 lbs, <2.2 lbs)
	Was it a multiple birth—twins, triplets, other? (yes/no)
	Preterm birth (2–4 weeks early, 5–8 weeks early, 9–12 weeks early, 13–16 weeks early)
	Received newborn care in intensive care unit, premature nursery, other special care facility (how long?)
	Health at birth better/worse/same as other babies
	Was child breastfed? How long?
	Did child have a birth defect requiring surgery?
Conditions	Asthma
	Autism
	Birth defect requiring surgery
	Cancer
	Cerebral palsy
	Cystic fibrosis
	Dental visit in last year
	Diabetes
	Down's syndrome
	Emergency room visit in past year
	Heart disease requiring surgery
	Hyperactivity (ADHD, ADD)
	HIV/AIDS
	Injuries (fracture, laceration, poisoning, automobile trauma, gunshot/knife wound)
	Language or speech disorder
	Learning disability (specify)
	Mental retardation
	Muscular dystrophy
	Phenylketonuria
	Seizures/epileptic fit or convulsion
	Sickle cell anemia/blood disorder
	Spina bifida
	Sight is: (1) blindness, (2) difficulty seeing even with glasses, (3) needed eyeglasses or vision care past year, (4) no correction necessary

Measure	Description
Impairments	Hearing is: (1) deafness, (2) hard of hearing, (3) wears hearing aid, (4) difficulty hearing even with hearing aid, (5) no hearing problems
	Speech is: (1) difficulty having speech understood, (2) unable to talk in sentences after age 5
	Development is: (1) delay in development (When? Seen by doctor? Taken medication?); (2) emotional or behavioral problem lasting more than 3 months (When? Seen by doctor? Taken medication?); (3) learning disability (When? Seen by doctor? Taken medication?); (4) seen doctor/counselor for any emotional, developmental or behavioral problem (When was last time?)
Activity Limitations	Has condition that limits play activities
	Has behavioral or emotional condition that makes it difficult to play with or get along with children of the same age
	Needs more help than usual for age in everyday activities due to impairment or condition (eating, dressing, bathing or using toilet)
	Needs diaper during the day or night (yes/no)
	Difficulty walking, climbing stairs, grasping objects, reaching overhead, lifting, bending, stooping, standing for long periods of time
	Receives services from Early Intervention or Special Education Services
	Takes medication regularly to help control activity level or behavior
	Missed more than 10 school days (past 12 months)
	Has a condition that limits schooling
Health Status	Health is: Excellent, good, fair, poor (respondent's impression)
	Mental health is: Excellent, good, fair, poor (respondent's impression)
	Current health compared with 12 months ago (better, worse, about the same)
	Needs or uses more medical care, mental health or educational services than usual for most children of the same age
	Needs special therapy, such as physical, occupation or speech therapy
	Condition or impairment expected to last 12 months or longer
	Development compared to other children your child's age: very slow, slow, a little slow, above average, advanced
	Low (less than 5th percentile) height-for-age, low weight-for-height (less than 5th percentile), and high (95th percentile) weight-for-height and body mass index

**Age categories may not correspond to each listed source, see Survey Instrument descriptions

ACKNOWLEDGMENTS

This research was supported by the National Institute of Child Health and Human Development Network on Family and Child Well-Being and by research and conference supplements from the National Center for Medical Rehabilitation Research and the Assistant Secretary for Planning and Evaluation. Michael E. Msall's efforts were also supported in part by MCH Grant MC J-449505-02-0. We thank Kelley Holder for her excellent research assistance in the preparation of the complex tables in this chapter and Michelle Tremont for her contributions to the medical measurement sections of this chapter.

NOTES

1. This survey was fielded again in 2005–06. For additional information, visit http://www.cdc.gov/nchs/about/major/slaits/cshcn_05_05.htm
2. An excellent review of survey-based data for developmental research, including some studies that are not nationally representative but of excellent quality, is available in Brooks-Gunn, Berlin, Leventhal, and Fuligni (2002). Measures that assess the disability outcomes of children are found in Lollar, Simeonsson, and Nanda (2000).
3. Nearly all aspects of social life in America, including the lives of children, are social and culturally constructed. For preadolescent children of all ages, these cultural and social constructions occur largely at the level of family, and the effects of these on the family's capacity to nurture, protect, and promote the life chances of their children (Bronfenbrenner & Evans, 2000). Certain variables—measures of race–ethnicity, family structure, and family socioeconomic status—are essential for any meaningful discussion of disparities in child health. In addition, on the basis of the literature showing that other adults in the household may ameliorate the challenges commonly associated with single parents, several studies measure the presence and type of other adults in the household. Measures of family poverty and welfare receipt are also important to understand how poverty itself and the various dimensions of government support modify the family ecology. Other population surveys measure the family learning environment (family reading and learning activities and opportunities for children to develop cognitive skills).
4. For additional information on the NHIS, visit http://www.cdc.gov/nchs/about/major/nhis/hisdesc.htm

REFERENCES

American Psychiatric Association. (1994). *Diagnostic and statistical manual of mental disorders* (4th ed.). Washington, DC: Author.

Annie E. Casey Foundation. (2003). *KIDS COUNT data book: State profiles of child well-being.* Baltimore: Author.

Berry, S. H. (1992). Methods of collecting health data. In A. L. Stewart & J. E. Ware, Jr. (Eds.), *Measuring functioning and well-being* (pp. 48–85). Durham, NC: Duke University Press.

Bronfenbrenner, U., & Evans, G. W. (2000). Developmental science in the 21st century: Emerging questions, theoretical models, research designs, and empirical findings. *Social Development, 9,* 115–125.

Brooks-Gunn, J., Berlin, L. J., Leventhal, T., & Sidle Fuligni, A. (2000). Depending on the kindness of others: Current national data initiatives and developmental research. *Child Development, 71,* 257–268.

Butler, C., Chambers, H., & Goldstein, M. (1999). Evaluating research in developmental disabilities: A conceptual framework for reviewing treatment outcomes. *Developmental Medicine & Child Neurology, 41,* 55–59.

Centers for Disease Control and Prevention. (1998). National, state, and urban area vaccination coverage levels among children aged 19-35 months-United States, July 1996 to June 1997. *Morbidity Mortality Weekly Report, 47,* 108–116.

Disability and perinatal care: Measurement of health status at two years. (1995). Oxford, England: National Perinatal Epidemiology Unit.

Feudtner, C., Christakis, D. A., & Connell, F. A. (2000). Pediatric deaths attributable to complex chronic conditions: A population-based study of Washington state, 1980-1997. *Pediatrics, 106,* 205–209.

Graiter, P. L. (1992). Injury surveillance. In W. Halpern, E. L. Baker, & R. R. Manson (Eds.), *Public health surveillance* (pp. 1412–156). New York: Von Nostrand Reinhold.

Guyer, B., Hoyert, D. L., Martin, J. A., Ventura, S. J., MacDorman, M. F., & Strobino, D. M. (1999). Annual summary of vital statistics–1998. *Pediatrics, 104,* 1229–1246.

Hack, M., & Fanaroff, A. (1999). Outcomes of children of extremely low birth-weight and gestational age in the 1990's. *Early Human Development, 53,* 193–218.

Hack, M., Taylor, G., Klein, N., & Mercuri-Minich, N. (2000). Functional limitations and special health care needs of 10- to 14-year-old children weighing less than 750 grams at birth. *Pediatrics, 106,* 554–560.

Hauser, R. M., Brown, B. V., & Prosser, W. R. (Eds.). (1997). *Indicators of child well-being.* New York: Russell Sage Foundation.

Hogan, D. P., & Msall, M. E. (2002). In *Parenting and the child's world: Multiple influences on intellectual and social-emotional development* (pp. 311–327). Fairfax, VA: Techbooks.

Hogan, D. P., Msall, M. E., Rogers, M., & Avery, R. (1997). Improved disability population estimates of functional limitation among American children age 5–17. *Maternal and Child Journal, 1,* 203–216.

Hogan, D. P., Rogers, M. L., & Msall, M. E. (2000). Functional limitations and key indicators of well-being in children with disability. *Archives of Pediatric and Adolescent Medicine, 154,* 1042–1048.

Institute of Medicine. (1997). *Enabling America: Assessing the role of rehabilitation science and engineering* (E. N. Brandt & A. M. Pope, Eds.). Washington, DC: National Academy Press.

Lantz, P., & Partin, M. (1997). Population indicators of prenatal and infant health. In R. M. Hauser, B. V. Brown, & W. R. Prosser (Eds.), *Indicators of child well-being* (pp. 47–75). New York: Russell Sage Foundation.

Lester, B. M., LaGasse, L. L., & Seifer, R. (1998). Interpreting research on prenatal substance exposure in the context of multiple confounding factors. *Clinics in Perinatology, 26,* 39–54.

Lester, B. M., & Miller-Loncar, C. L. (2000). Biology versus environment in the extremely low-birth weight infant. *Clinics in Perinatology, 27,* 461–482.

Lewit, E. M., & Schuurmann Baker, L. (1995). Unintentional injuries. *The Future of Children, 5*(1), 5–30.

Lollar, D. J., Simeonsson, R. J., & Nanda, U. (2000). Measures of outcomes for children and youth. *Archives of Physical Medicine and Rehabilitation, 81*(12, Suppl. 2), S46–S52.

Lorenz, J. M. (2000). Survival of the extremely preterm infants in North America in the 1990's. *Clinics in Perinatology, 27,* 255–262.

McCormick, M. C. (1999). Conceptualizing child health status: Observations from studies of very premature infants. *Perspectives in Biology & Medicine, 42,* 372–386.

McCormick, M. C., Workman-Daniels, K., & Brooks-Gunn, J. (1996). The behavioral and emotional well-being of school-age children with different birth weights. *Pediatrics, 97,* 18–25.

McDowell, I., & Newell, C. (1996). *Measuring health* (2nd ed.). Oxford, England: Oxford University Press.

Moore, K. A. (1997). Criteria for indicators of child well-being. In R. M. Hauser, B. V. Brown, & W. R. Prosser (Eds.), *Indicators of child well-being* (pp. 36–44). New York: Russell Sage Foundation.

Msall, M. E., & Tremont, M. R. (1999). Measuring functional status in children with genetic impairments. *American Journal of Medical Genetics, 89,* 62–74.

Msall, M. E., & Tremont, M. R. (2000). Functional outcomes in self-care, mobility, communication, and learning in extremely low birthweight infants. *Clinics in Perinatology, 27,* 381–401.

Maternal and Child Health Bureau. (2000). *Child health USA 2000.* Washington, DC: U.S. Government Printing Office.

National Center for Medical Rehabilitation Research National Advisory Board. (1993). Medical rehabilitation research: Report and plan for medical rehabilitation research (NIH Publication No. 93–3509). Bethesda, MD: National Center for Medical Rehabilitation Research.

Newacheck, P. W., & Halfon, N. (1998). Prevalence and impact of disabling childhood chronic conditions. *American Journal of Public Health, 88,* 610–617.

Newacheck, P. W, Strickland, B., Shonkoff, J. P., & Perrin, J. M. (1998). An epidemiologic profile of children with special health care needs. *Pediatrics, 102,* 107–123.

Shiono, P. H., & Behrman, R. E. (1995). Low birth weight-Analysis and recommendations. *The Future of Children, 5*(1), 1–4.

Shonkoff, J. P., & Meisels, S. J. (Eds.). (2000). *Handbook of early childhood intervention* (2nd ed.). Cambridge, England: Cambridge University Press.

Shonkoff, J. P., & Phillips, D. A. (Eds.). (2000). *From neurons to neighborhoods.* Washington, DC: National Academy Press.

Starfield, B. (1997). Health indicators for preadolescent school-age children. In R. M. Hauser, B. V. Brown, & W. R. Prosser (Eds.), *Indicators of child well-being* (pp. 95–111). New York: Russell Sage Foundation.

Stein, R., & Silver, E. J. (1999). Operationalizing a conceptually-based noncategorical definition: A first look at US children with chronic conditions. *Archives of Pediatrics & Adolescent Medicine, 153,* 68–74.

Stein, R., Westbrook, L. E., & Bauman, L. J. (1997). The questionnaire for identifying children with chronic conditions: A measure based on a noncategorical approach. *Pediatrics, 99,* 53–521.

Stevenson, D. K., Wright, L. L., Lemmons, J. A., Oh, W., Korones, S. B., Papile, L. A., et al. (1998). Very low birthweight outcomes of the National Institute of Child Health and Human Development Neonatal Research Network, January 1993 through December 1994. *American Journal of Obstetrics & Gynecology, 179*(6, Pt. 1), 1632–1639.

Vohr, B. R., & Msall, M. E. (2000). Neuropsychological and functional outcomes of very low birth weight infants. *Seminars in Perinatology, 21,* 202–220.

Wolfe, B. L., & Sears, J. (1997). Health indicators for preschool children, ages one to four. In R. M. Hauser, B. V. Brown, & W. R. Prosser (Eds.), *Indicators of child well-being* (pp. 76–94). New York: Russell Sage Foundation.

Wolraich, M. L., Felice, M. E., & Drotar, D. (1996). The classification of child and adolescent mental diagnoses in primary care: *Diagnostic and Statistical Manual for Primary Care (DSM-PC),* Child and Adolescent version. Elk Grove Village, IL: American Academy of Pediatrics.

World Health Organization. (1980). *International classification of impairment, disability, and handicap.* Geneva, Switzerland: Author.

World Health Organization. (1997). *International classification of functioning, disability and health.* Geneva, Switzerland: Author.

World Health Organization. (2000). *International classification of disease-9.* Geneva, Switzerland: Author.

Chapter 2

Indicators of Youth Health and Well-Being: Taking the Long View

Matthew W. Stagner
Janine M. Zweig
The Urban Institute

Adolescence is a time of tremendous change, growth, risk, and reward. Adolescents themselves worry about whether they are succeeding at current tasks and whether they will make a smooth transition to adulthood. Parents worry about the risks their adolescents may take and whether they are investing enough time and other resources in their children. Policymakers, educators, and program operators worry, too, that many adolescents struggle-at home, at school, and in their communities. They worry as well that too few adolescents achieve their full potential and that the investments our society makes in adolescents are insufficient or ill timed.

Indicators of adolescent well-being can help policymakers, service providers, and concerned community members track the condition of adolescents. They can highlight changes in problems, note progress or lost ground, and call attention to relative risks. Despite this, indicators rarely point directly to the causes or solutions of problems-and measuring the right set of indicators for adolescents is a challenge. For instance, should we measure the condition of adolescents directly, or through the conditions of their families, schools, and communities? How should we capture the wide range of risks and the variety of possible positive activities in which adolescents engage? Because adolescence is a period of rapid change and transition, how can we best capture the ways current activities and conditions in youths' lives affect their developmental pathways?

In this chapter, we assess the state of health and social indicators for adolescents (aged 12–17) in the early 21st century. We document progress over the last few years and suggest some ways to continue to improve our understanding of how youth are faring. We first examine the progress in the development of systems for measuring youth well-being. Second, we describe new data sources that can help us build on recent successes to measure youth well-being more fully. Third, we look forward and provide a framework for thinking about a more comprehensive set of youth indicators within a self-correcting surveillance system. We argue that if we can better understand the connections between current activities or conditions and developmental pathways, then we can better define and monitor key elements of adolescent life. We challenge the research community to create a surveillance system of continuous improvement in youth indicators, with updated measurement of what really matters in adolescence based on ongoing empirical evidence of what most affects the successful transition to adulthood.

PROGRESS IN SYSTEMS FOR MEASURING YOUTH WELL-BEING

Since 1994, there has been tremendous growth in the use and dissemination of indicators of youth well-being. In the following sections, we look back to the National Institute of Child Health and Human Development's November 1994 conference, entitled "Indicators of Children's Well-Being," and note progress toward several recommendations made during that conference (Elster, 1997; Kennedy & Prothrow-Stith, 1997). Elster (1997) suggested that youth indicators should focus on the individual adolescent and not the larger family or community context, be justified on the basis of the degree of burden or suffering experienced by the adolescent or society, be measurable and easily understood by society, and be amenable to reporting based on distinctions that are consistent developmentally (e.g., gender, racial-ethnic group). Building on Healthy People 2000's (HP 2000) National Health Promotion and Disease Prevention Objectives, he suggested six indicators of adolescent health and well-being under three broad categories. For *Health Status*, he recommended the number of teens seen in emergency rooms with an intentional or unintentional injury. For *Risk Reduction and Health Promotion*, he recommended the rate of teens who drink alcohol daily, the rate of teens who drove a motor vehicle after drinking during the past month, and the rate of teens who carry a weapon to school. For *Health Services*, he recommended the rate of teens with completed immunizations and the rate of teens who have a primary health care provider.

Kennedy and Prothrow-Stith (1997) recommended measurement of problem behaviors, specifically, alcohol and drug use, risky driving practices, violence, and risky sexual behavior and correlates of such behaviors to make more informed decisions. They also suggested that the indicator system should allow us to link correlates with myriad problem behaviors, not just one. More specifically, they reflected on the utility of adding family-level and community-level indicators to existing individual-level monitoring systems such as the Youth Risk Behavior Survey (YRBS). A final recommendation was to implement a National Longitudinal Survey of Youth (NLSY) every decade so surveillance of adolescent health is current and causal links between indicators and outcomes can be drawn. We echo this recommendation, because we believe it corrects what we see as a major limitation of the current surveillance system.

Both Elster (1997) and Kennedy and Prothrow-Stith (1997) acknowledged that many of the recommended indicators of adolescent health could already be monitored by surveillance systems in place at the time the recommendations were made. Each of the six indicators Elster identified as important were already being monitored regularly, and continue to be, using data from the National Ambulatory Medical Care Survey, the YRBS, Monitoring the Future, and the National Health Interview Survey. The indicators of adolescent health recommended by Kennedy and Prothrow-Stith were then, and remain to be, measured by some surveys mentioned earlier as well as the National Household Survey of Drug Abuse (NHSDA),[1] the Fatal Accident Reporting System, the Uniform Crime Reports, the National Crime Victimization Survey, the National Survey of Family Growth, and the Vital Statistics.

Progress has been made toward meeting these recommendations by improving the systems for summarizing and disseminating youth indicators. One major contributor has been the Federal Interagency Forum on Child and Family Statistics. The forum was created in 1994 by the chief statistician at the Office of Management and Budget and includes partners from many government agencies as well as private research organizations.[2] It promotes the integration of data collection and reporting of child and family issues. The partners work together to identify data collection priorities and increase the dissemination of information on the status of children, youth, and families to policymakers and community members. This interagency collaboration has produced *America's Children: Key National Indicators of Well-Being*, which summarizes current key indicators of health and well-being for children and youth. These annual reports document an array of indicators of problem behaviors and conditions. They provide current information to policymakers and program planners about issues facing youth today.

These volumes also identify key indicators that are missing from current surveillance mechanisms. In 2005, like in previous years, *America's Children* identified three health indicators that are lacking (disability, mental health, and child abuse and neglect), two behavior and social environment indicators that are lacking (positive behaviors and youth violence), and three population and family characteristics that are missing (children's use of time, family interactions, and environmental conditions). The Interagency Forum provides an ongoing mechanism to reassess the adequacy of indicators and to apply new research knowledge to the production and reporting of indicators. Given the broad range of concerns facing youth, such interagency and interdisciplinary work is essential.

In addition, the reporting of indicators from individual federal agencies is also more comprehensive than in the early 1990s. For example, *Trends in the Well-Being of America's Children and Youth*, published by the U.S. Department of Health and Human Services, presents a summary of a broad range of youth indicators. These include child population; family structure; neighborhoods; poverty and income; financial support; parental and youth employment; consumption and food security; mortality, health conditions, and health care; social development; physical health and safety; substance use, sexual activity, and fertility; school enrollment and attendance; achievement and proficiency in reading, science, mathematics, and the arts; and family literacy.

Trends in the Well-Being of America's Children and Youth makes it possible to see a wide array of federal statistics in one volume. It presents far more indicators than just the "key" indicators reported by the interagency forum. Between its inception in 1996 and 2003, several indicators relevant to youth were added, including reading habits, student computer use, abuse of alcohol or other controlled substances, sufficient hours of sleep, closeness with parents, activities with parents, firearm-related deaths, serious violent victimization of teens, numbers of "detached" youth (not in school or working), physical fighting, life goals of high school seniors, religious attendance, voting behaviors, employment behaviors, seat belt use, and television viewing habits. The regular reporting of such varied indicators is a true accomplishment.

The Internet has also brought advances. In particular, the FedStats web site (http://www.fedstats.gov) has provided a new and easily accessible way to track the well-being of adolescents through government statistics. FedStats provides access to official statistics collected and published by more than 70 federal agencies without having to know in advance which agency produces them, including all agencies reporting expenditures of at least $500,000 per year in statistical activities. The Interagency Forum's web site (http://www.childstats.gov) links to FedStats and provides access to the forum's annual report, *America's Children*, and to other information produced by member agencies. One important feature is a list of contacts that provide further information on particular indicators. It has never been so easy for citizens, policymakers, and researchers to access information on the condition of youth and to understand the sources of that information.

Other Internet resources include the Child Trends DataBank and the KIDS COUNT web site. The Child Trends DataBank (http://www.childtrendsdatabank.org) is a one-stop shop for users to review over 100 indicators of child and youth health and well-being. The DataBank is continually updated to reflect the most current estimates of indicators and results are documented in easily accessible language for multiple types of users. Indicators include local, state, national, and international data.

The KIDS COUNT web site (http://www.aecf.org/kidscount/) is supported by the Annie E. Casey Foundation. KIDS COUNT tracks the status of children and youth at the state and national levels. It provides indicators of health and well-being to inform policy debates at the local, state, and national levels. The most recent *KIDS COUNT Data Book*, the 17th annual edition, was released in June 2006.

PROGRESS IN DATA SOURCES FOR MEASURING YOUTH WELL-BEING

As systems of indicators reporting have progressed, new longitudinal data sets have been developed that can help us understand, over several years, how conditions and activities in youth are related to successful transition to adulthood. Two important research developments occurred during the 1990s that can meaningfully inform the work of identifying adolescent indicators: (a) the National Survey of Adolescent Health (Add Health) and (b) the second cohort of the NLSY (NLSY 97). Through these nationally representative longitudinal projects we will be able to link adolescent behaviors, and combinations of behaviors, to young adult outcomes. In addition, adolescent problem behaviors can be linked to risk and protective factors in multiple domains, such as individual, peer, family, school, and community domains. Such data will help shed light on what the most important indicators are for inclusion in surveillance systems. In the following sections, we outline the information incorporated in the two longitudinal studies and note advancement in one cross-sectional study.

NATIONAL LONGITUDINAL STUDY OF ADOLESCENT HEALTH

Add Health (http://www.cpc.unc.edu/addhealth) was designed to examine adolescent physical, mental, emotional, and reproductive health. Add Health's first wave of data collection was completed in 1994-95. That year, 90,000 youth completed in-school surveys about their background, friends, school life, school work and activities, and general health status. Of these youth, 21,000 also participated in an in-home survey about family and peer relationships, school environment, health risk behaviors (including sexual activity, violence, substance use, etc.), psychosocial adjustment, physical health, and perceptions of risk. Wave II was completed in 1996 1 year after Wave I. Wave III was collected in 2001 and 2002, when the respondents were young adults approximately between the ages of 18 and 26. Wave III focuses on the transition to adulthood and on young adult well-being related to health and health behaviors, employment, higher education, relationships, parenting, and community involvement. The Add Health data allow researchers to link risk and protective factors to indicators of adolescent and young adult health and well-being. In addition, the Wave III data are an excellent resource for us to understand the shorter term outcomes related to adolescent behavior and other pre-existing indicators.

NATIONAL LONGITUDINAL SURVEY OF YOUTH

The NLSY (http://www.bls.gov/nls) is a set of related studies. The first began in 1979 to examine labor force participation and related activities of youth. Approximately 13,000 youth, ages 14 through 22, were surveyed at the time and have participated in up to 20 waves of data collection. Youth were interviewed annually from 1979 through 1994 and biennially since then. Participants have been asked about their educational and employment histories, income and assets, use of public programs, insurance coverage, child care, health conditions, substance use, sexual activity, marriage, and fertility. Since 1986, children of the women in the 1979 NLSY study have been surveyed biennially as well. Data are collected on all children, but the information collected varies on the basis of the developmental level of the children: children under age 10, children aged 10 and under 15, and children age 15 and older. The youngest children's surveys include demographic and family background and assessments of cognitive, socioemotional, and physiological well-being. Children 10 and older are assessed about family interaction, schooling, dating and peer relationships, health, religious attendance, substance use, and home responsibilities. Surveys for youth 15 and over include further assessments of training, employment, fertility, marriage, delinquent and criminal activities, and future expectations.

In addition, in 1997, a second NLSY cohort of 9,000 youth ages 12 to 16 years began. Youth are interviewed annually, and seven waves of data collection have been completed to date. Waves 1 through 8 are publicly available. The information being collected is similar to that of the 1979 cohort, but enhancements have been made. Wave 1 contains a parent questionnaire about family background and history. Two sets of school surveys are also connected to the cohort. In 1996 and 2000, surveys were conducted in all schools with a 12th grade in the same sampling area as the original respondents.

The original sample of youth (NLSY 1979) and the new sample of youth (NLSY 1997) are excellent resources for understanding both the short- and long-term outcomes related to indicators of adolescent health and well-being. The new sample provides us with current longitudinal data on these issues. Recent work by Michael and colleagues (2001) suggests how valuable this data set will be for understanding the long-term consequences of adolescent activities and conditions. Explorations of the role of family environment in sexual debut (M. R. Moore, 2001) and role of parental regulation in time use decisions (Tepper, 2001) are examples of this value.

NATIONAL HOUSEHOLD SURVEY ON DRUG ABUSE

In addition to progress made in longitudinal data, advances have been made in one cross-sectional data set that helps link risk and protective factors with youth behaviors. Kennedy and Prothrow-Stith's (1997) suggestions regarding the monitoring of community- and family-level indicators has been addressed by the Substance Abuse and Mental Health Services Administration, the agency that conducts NHSDA (http://www.oas.samhsa.gov/nhsda.htm). NHSDA has been conducted periodically since 1972 and annually since 1981. In 1997, the agency added a new section to NHSDA to assess risk and protective factors related to substance use in six domains: (a) community (e.g., availability, marketing), (b) family (e.g., family conflict, family communication), (c) peer (e.g., friends' use), (d) individual (e.g., perceived risk), (e) school (e.g., grades, antidrug education programs), and (f) general (e.g., participation in activities, religious beliefs). The survey also oversamples youth ages 12 to 17 years and young adults 18 to 25 years. Data summaries through 2005 are now available online and cover illicit drug use; alcohol use; tobacco use; trends in initiation of substance use; prevention-related measures (the risk and protective factors described earlier); substance dependence, abuse, and treatment; and the prevalence and treatment of mental health problems. Although the additions to NHSDA are useful in understanding adolescent risk and protection and indicators of adolescent health and well-being, they do not allow us to correlate these risk and protective factors with other problem behaviors beyond substance abuse.

PROGRESS IN POSITIVE INDICATORS OF ADOLESCENT WELL-BEING

To date, much of the focus of indicator research is on identifying how "bad off" U.S. youth are. Misbehaving or nonconforming youth represent an undue burden on society, and programs and policies should address such concerns. Yet the indicators research field should continue to move from a perspective of burden and risk to one of including asset and positivity. Some movement has occurred in recent years toward a perspective that balances monitoring both adolescent problems and adolescent assets. K. A. Moore (1999) noted that we should monitor not just what we do not want for our youth but also what we do want for them. By doing this, we will be able to do two tasks. First, monitoring problem behaviors allows decision makers and program designers to craft policy and interventions to reduce risks for youth, essentially bringing risky youth up to a "normal" level of risk. Second, monitoring positive indicators allows policymakers and program designers to be alerted to ways of moving youth from zero to beyond and to enhance their development in meaningful ways.

The utility of the second task has already been demonstrated by a recent National Research Council and Institute of Medicine (NRC/IOM) report (2002). The report first identifies personal and social assets and then links these adolescent developmental assets to program features that can promote them. Specifically, eight program features are identified as aspects of positive developmental settings: (a) physical and psychological safety; (b) appropriate structure; (c) supportive relationships; (d) opportunities to belong; (e) positive social norms; (f) support for efficacy and mattering; (g) opportunities for skill building; and (h) integration of family, school, and community efforts.

Efforts are being made to identify important positive indicators of adolescent health and well-being. For instance, in 2003, Child Trends brought together national experts to participate in the "Indicators of Positive Development Conference."[3] The group identified a number of important positive indicators of adolescent health and well-being and analyzed how to measure such features including character, spirituality, life satisfaction, hope, positive behaviors, positive relationships (with parents and siblings), time use, healthy habits, mastery motivation, achievement task values, school self-regulation, school connectedness and engagement, connection to community, civic engagement, social identity, and economic behavior. Also, reports from the Federal Interagency Forum on Child and Family Statistics (2000, 2003) call to our attention the need to monitor positive indicators of adolescent health and well-being. Specifically, the forum has identified participation in positive activities; the formation of close attachments to family, school, and community; and higher level course-taking as positive indicators.

Current surveillance system surveys are beginning to include such positive indicators.

MONITORING THE FUTURE

The MTF survey (http://www.monitoringthefuture.org), conducted annually on repeated cross-sections of youth, includes a number of positive indicators as well as indicators of adolescent health and well-being, as stated previously. The indicators include attitudes toward marriage, understanding the relationship of good grades and status in school, the importance and value of hard work, expectations of working in adulthood, and volunteering (Brown, 2001).

YOUTH RISK BEHAVIOR SURVEY

The YRBS (http://www.cdc.gov/HealthyYouth/yrbs/index.htm) mostly contains indicators of problem behavior during adolescence but also contains some positive indicators of adolescent health. Participation in physical exercise, team sports, and HIV education courses may be considered positive indicators of adolescent health. Also, the YRBS contains questions about healthy eating habits. Although some progress has been made toward this end, greater work must be done to include a wider variety of positive indicators and those specifically identified in *America's Children* (2003).

FRAMEWORKS FOR THINKING ABOUT A COMPREHENSIVE SET OF YOUTH INDICATORS

Although the advances in systems of indicators and new data have been impressive, further progress in indicator research requires a conceptual framework to guide development. Without such a framework we cannot easily answer questions such as which indicators are important and why. Applying a conceptual framework to indicator research allows for clear direction and purpose in the work.

HEALTHY PEOPLE 2010 CRITICAL OBJECTIVES AS A FRAMEWORK FOR INDICATORS

During the 1994 conference, Elster (1997) suggested that the Department of Health and Human Services' HP 2000 objectives are useful in formulating a conceptual framework for identifying adolescent indicators of health and well-being. He used these objectives as a starting point to identify the specific indicators he recommended be monitored. The HP 2010 (U.S. Department of Health and Human Services, 2000) objectives are somewhat different than those posed for HP 2000. For HP 2000, there were 39 objectives specific to youth with a number of additional objectives that apply to youth. They range from behavioral objectives in substance use, violence, and preventive health behaviors to mental health objectives, such as depression. For HP 2010, there are only 21 specific youth objectives, with a number of additional objectives related to youth. Fifteen of the 21 objectives mirror those posed for 2000; however, there are six new objectives that are specific to youth: (a) increase the use of safety belts; (b) reduce the proportion of youth who rode with a driver under the influence of alcohol; (c) reduce weapon carrying on school property;[4] (d) reduce the proportion of adolescents with disabilities who are reported to be sad, unhappy, or depressed;[5] (e) reduce the number of youth with HIV infection; and (f) reduce the proportion of adolescents with chlamydia trachomatis.

    HP 2010 objectives can be measured using many of the current surveillance data sets with adolescent indicators. For example, the rationale for including most of the questions in the 2001 YRBS is that they measure and monitor progress toward HP 2010 objectives (Centers for Disease Control and Prevention, 2001). Some new measures and/or new oversampling strategies of particular youth may need to be added to the surveys to capture the full range of the HP 2010 objectives (e.g., disabled youth feeling unhappy, sad, or depressed). There currently is not a one-to-one correspondence between the HP 2010 objectives and the indicators in the monitoring system.

Whereas HP 2010 sets goals for the nation, other frameworks may serve as more useful starting points when thinking about indicators. HP 2010 presents a comprehensive list of objectives to meet regarding adolescent health without identifying why these particular objectives are important for youth, the relative importance of the objectives, or why we may want to focus on one more than another. A framework that allows us to understand objectives in relation to the types of harm or potential dangers it exposes youth to (as well as the potential benefits for youth) may be more useful.

NATIONAL RESEARCH COUNCIL AND INSTITUTE OF MEDICINE REPORT

In 2002, the NRC/IOM released a report (referred to previously) called *Community Programs to Promote Youth Development*. The NRC/IOM brought together experts on adolescent health and development to examine what the field knows about promising adolescent development. As part of this process, the group identified a set of personal and social assets that facilitate positive youth development. This asset list might be another useful conceptual framework within which we can identify indicators of adolescent health and well-being.

The NRC/IOM (2002) outlined four categories of personal and social assets: (a) physical development, (b) intellectual development, (c) psychological and emotional development, and (d) social development. For example, physical development assets include good health habits and good health risk management skills. Intellectual development includes assets such as knowledge of essential life skills, vocational skills, and cultural contexts; school success; and good decision-making skills. Psychological and emotional development includes assets such as good mental health, emotional self-regulation and coping skills, confidence in personal efficacy, strong moral character, and a commitment to good use of time. Finally, social development includes assets such as connectedness to parents, peers, and other adults; attachment to prosocial institutions; and commitment to civic engagement.

The NRC/IOM report presents a comprehensive list of assets important to healthy development. However, like the HP 2010 objectives, the assets are listed without identifying the relative importance of the assets or why we may want to focus on one more than another. Again, a framework that allows us to understand assets in relation to the potential benefits for youth may be more useful.

ROLE OF OUTCOMES AS A FRAMEWORK FOR INDICATORS

Adolescent health indicators may be useful for understanding the current situation of youth, but they should also identify and monitor situations and activities, both positive and negative, that significantly affect the transition to adulthood. For example, monitoring sexual activity and pregnancy is important because a teen pregnancy and birth may dramatically affect the likelihood a teen mother will attend college or even finish high school. As a consequence, she may be a much more likely candidate than her peers who are not mothers to need public assistance and to encounter other negative outcomes.

It seems that one important question to consider is "why are we interested in indicators of adolescent health to begin with?" Indicators help us identify levels of risk to which youth are currently exposed or in which they are participating to inform decision makers and program planners about how best to help youth. But why are we interested in knowing this information? Perhaps it is because we believe that these indicators of health have implications for individual development and social adaptation. However, to date, little research on indicators has looked to how outcomes of particular youth behaviors or health circumstances can guide the field. An example of the utility of indicators predicting outcomes was demonstrated by Barber and Stone (2003) at the "Indicators for Positive Development" conference. They found that youth involved in prosocial activities reported less participation in health risk behaviors and more involvement in civic organizations. Also, youth in school involvement activities showed better academic outcomes and occupational outcomes by age 29.

Identifying indicators of adolescent health is complicated and knowing if we have identified meaningful indicators of health is even more complex. Elster (1997) recommended that indicators should be chosen on the basis of the degree to which they burden both the adolescent and society and the extent to which they can be targeted and changed through intervention. However, we do not know for certain what the most critical adolescent indicators are for young adult development and functioning. Intuitively and intellectually, many of us think that levels of substance use, sexual intercourse, and violent behavior are important to monitor and address for youth. However, to be sure we are identifying and monitoring the most crucial indicators we need a greater scientific understanding of what makes a difference for adolescent developmental outcomes. We need to more fully explore the connection between adolescent indicators and outcomes and find answers to questions such as "Is it one behavior or vulnerability alone that affects outcomes, or is it combinations of behaviors and vulnerabilities that put youth at particular risk for negative outcomes?" Because some degree of normal behavioral experimentation is expected during adolescence (Elster, 1997), it is critical to identify the most important markers of negative outcomes for youth and consider this information when identifying the indicators of adolescent health. Next, we explore the value of two existing frameworks that incorporate outcomes.

PSYCHOSOCIAL MODELS OF ADOLESCENT DEVELOPMENT

Jessor (1992) and Blum, McNeely, and Nonnemaker (2001) have developed psychosocial models of adolescent development from an ecological perspective that may be useful as conceptual frameworks for indicator research. The models link risk and protective factors from multiple domains of life to health risk behaviors and lifestyles during adolescence (indicators) and to health and life-compromising outcomes in adolescence and young adulthood (see Table 2.1). Jessor (1992) described the importance of including outcomes in such a model capturing adolescent health:

> What is at risk from engaging in risk behavior includes but far transcends physical health and physical growth. Risk behaviors can jeopardize the accomplishment of normal developmental tasks, the fulfillment of expected social roles, the acquisition of essential skills, the achievement of a sense of adequacy and competence, and the appropriate preparation for transition to the next stage in the life trajectory-young adulthood. (p. 22)

Either of the two models presented in Table 2.1, or a combination of the two models, may be useful conceptual frameworks for understanding indicators of health risk. Researchers can use a right-to-left approach to identify important indicators of adolescent health by first sorting out which outcomes we are most concerned with and then tracking indicators that lead to those poorer developmental outcomes. Thus, understanding outcomes of adolescent behavior and health statuses could be an important guide to identifying the most useful indicators of adolescent health to monitor.

RECOMMENDATIONS

The major limitation of the current surveillance system is that we are unable to link indicators to future outcomes. Each of the surveys in the current surveillance system is a repeated cross-section of nationally representative samples. Although this method allows us to examine trends of adolescent health indicators over time, we lack the ability to examine developmental pathways over time, and we are unable to link indicators to young adult functioning and outcomes. Kennedy and Prothrow-Stith (1997) stressed the importance of assessing indicators longitudinally during the initial 1994 conference. We echo this recommendation and believe that investing in longitudinal data of youth and

Table 2.1
Summary of Elements of Jessor's (1992) and Blum et al.'s (2001) Models of Adolescent Development

Domains of risk and protection	Adolescent risk behaviors/ lifestyles (indicators)	Health and Life-Compromising Outcomes
Jessor:		
• Biology/genetics • Social environment • Perceived environment • Personality • Behavior	• Problem behavior (e.g., substance use, delinquency, drunk driving) • Health-related behavior (e.g., unhealthy eating, tobacco use, sedentariness, nonuse of seat belts) • School Behavior (e.g., truancy, dropout, drug useat school)	• Health outcomes (e.g.,disease/illness, lowered fitness) • Social roles outcomes (e.g., school failure, social isolation, legal trouble, early childbearing) • Personal developmental outcomes (e.g., inadequate self-concept, depression/suicide) • Preparation for adulthood outcomes (e.g., limited work skills, unemployability, amotivation)
Blum et al.		
• Macrolevel environment • Social environment • School • Family • Peers • Individual	• Substance use (e.g., tobacco, alcohol, marijuana, and other drug use) • Diet and exercise (e.g., inactivity, unhealthy eating, eating disorders, overconsumption) • Injury/violence (e.g., weapon carrying, interpersonal violence, seat belt non-use, helmet non-use, motorcycle use, drinking and driving,sexual assault) • Sexual/reproductive (e.g., non-contraception,condom avoidance, early sexual debut, multiple sexual partners)	• Physical health outcomes (e.g., appropriate pubertal development, normotensive,age-appropriate cholesterol,LDL, perception of self as healthy, physically fit, injury free, not obese or over fat, no STDs/HIV, no unintended pregnancies) • Emotional health outcomes (e.g., perception of self as happy, no clinical evidence of depression, no history of suicide attempts, no mental or emotional health disorders) • Social health outcomes (e.g., contributing to the community, positive family relationships, prosocial values,relationships with healthy peers)

analyzing it on the basis of the conceptual frameworks by Jessor (1992) and/or Blum et al. (2001). Recent developments in longitudinal data— Add Health and the 1997 NLSY—make this type of analysis possible.

We challenge the research community to create a system of continuous improvement in which developmental outcomes research informs the indicator surveillance systems. By doing this type of analysis, a comprehensive, self-correcting surveillance system can be built using the current resources available in tandem. We could continue to use the nationally representative surveillance surveys that are conducted on repeated cross-sectional samples, such as the YRBS and the NHSDA, to monitor recent trends in indicators of adolescent health and well-being.

This line of indicator research will continue to be somewhat simplistic and straightforward to answer epidemiological questions regarding adolescent health. At the same time, we can conduct more complex analysis on nationally representative longitudinal samples to further illumine what the most important health indicators are for adolescent and young adult development and functioning.

Such longitudinal analysis would have two focuses. First, it would identify longitudinally the risk and protective factors from multiple domains related to indicators. Second, and perhaps more important, the analysis would examine the outcomes of particular behaviors and statuses over time to help us understand what the most critical indicators of adolescent health are in terms of both short- and long-term functioning. This approach addresses directly one of Elster's (1997) criteria for identifying indicators. He posited that indicators must be justifiable based on the burden they ultimately place on the adolescent him- or herself and on society. We are adding to Elster's criteria by arguing the burden should be assessed in relation both to the here-and-now of youth circumstances and in relation to future transitions. *Burden* can be defined in the latter case as the lack of successful transition to adulthood. And we cannot really know how current behavior affects future transitions without comprehensive, current, longitudinal research focusing specifically on outcomes. The outcome approach allows us to examine how meaningful particular indicators of behaviors and health statuses are to the lives of adolescents and their loved ones. Using this comprehensive approach, the results from the longitudinal analyses can then inform adaptations to the cross-sectional surveillance system on which we currently rely, therefore allowing for self-correction of the system.

ROLE OF OUTCOMES AND POSITIVE INDICATORS

The role of outcomes research in enhancing our surveillance system is relevant for both problem behaviors as well as indicators of positive youth development. Just as we are interested in understanding how a particular indicator relates to the burden it places on youth and society, we are also interested in learning the extent to which positive indicators relate to successful transition to adulthood, positive developmental pathways, and enhancement of youths' lives. For example, it may be useful to monitor adolescent involvement in volunteer activities in their communities. Participation in such activities may indicate the likelihood of youth developing into adults who take responsibility and leadership roles in their community, continue to participate in volunteering, and work for the betterment of their community in general.

Specific and important questions about positive indicators, such as "What does higher level course-taking and close attachments to school mean for adolescent development into adult members of society?," must be addressed. Answering questions about outcomes are just as crucial for positive indicators as they are for negative or risk indicators. Without such links between indicators and outcomes, we would not be able to correct the current surveillance system and capture the most useful positive measures of adolescent health and well-being.

LOOKING FORWARD: CONCLUDING THOUGHTS

Social scientists made impressive gains in the 1990s in describing the well-being of adolescents and in reporting regularly on their condition. Thanks to these gains, we are poised to do more. Using extant and developing measures—and the data resources now available and planned—it may be possible to create a system of tracking the impact that conditions and behaviors in adolescence have on the successful transition to adulthood. Such information on long-term consequences can further improve measures and highlight those measures that capture best what contributes to early adult success or failure. This work should focus both on the risks adolescents take as well as the factors (behaviors, contexts, and conditions) that may protect them from harm. We are ready for a more subtle and flexible view of adolescent well-being that captures not only current benefit and harm but also how current activities, behaviors, and contexts may affect later life courses.

ACKNOWLEDGMENTS

The nonpartisan Urban Institute publishes studies, reports, and books on timely topics worthy of public consideration. The views expressed should not be attributed to The Urban Institute, its trustees, or its funders.

NOTES

1. Editor's note: The name of the NHSDA has been changed to the *National Survey on Drug Use and Health*.
2. For more information, see http://www.childstats.gov/whatisit.asp
3. For papers from this conference, see Moore and Lippman (2005).
4. In 2000, the objective regarding weapon carrying was a general category and was not specific to school property.
5. In 2000, the objective regarding mental health issues was a general category and was not specific to youth with disabilities.

REFERENCES

Barber, B., & Stone, M. (2003, March). *Adolescent activity participation*. Paper presented at the Indicators of Positive Development Conference, Washington, DC.

Blum, R. W., McNeely, C., & Nonnemaker, J. (2001, March). *Vulnerability, risk and protection*. Paper presented at the Workshop on Adolescent Risk and Vulnerability: Setting Priorities, Washington, DC.

Brown, B. V. (2001). *Youth attitudes on family, work, and community service: Implications for welfare reform*. Washington, DC: Urban Institute.

Centers for Disease Control and Prevention. (2001). *2001 Youth Risk Behavior Survey: Item rationale for the 2001 questionnaire*. Atlanta, GA: U.S. Department of Health and Human Services, Centers for Disease Control and Prevention, Center for Chronic Disease Prevention and Health Promotion, Division of Adolescent and School Health.

Elster, A. B. (1997). Adolescent health indicators. In R. M. Hauser, B. V. Brown, & W. R. Prosser (Eds.), *Indicators of children's well-being* (pp. 112–121). New York: Russell Sage Foundation.

Federal Interagency Forum on Child and Family Statistics. (2005). *America's children: Key national indicators of well-being 2005*. Washington, DC: U.S. Government Printing Office.

Federal Interagency Forum on Child and Family Statistics. (2000). *America's children: Key national indicators of well-being 2000*. Washington, DC: U.S. Government Printing Office.

Federal Interagency Forum on Child and Family Statistics. (1997). *America's children: Key national indicators of well-being*. Washington, DC: Office of Management and Budget.

Jessor, R. (1992). Risk behavior in adolescence: A psychosocial framework for understanding action. In D. E. Rogers & E. Ginzberg (Eds.), *Adolescents at risk: Medical and social perspectives* (pp. 19–34). Boulder, CO: Westview.

Kennedy, B. P., & Prothrow-Stith, D. (1997). The status of adolescent problem behavior indicators. In R. M. Hauser, B. V. Brown, & W. R. Prosser (Eds.), *Indicators of children's well-being* (pp. 442–454). New York: Russell Sage Foundation.

Michael, R. T. (Ed.). (2001). *Social awakening: Adolescent behavior as adulthood approaches*. New York: Russell Sage Foundation.

Moore, K. A. (1999, September). *Indicators of child and family well-being: The good, the bad, and the ugly*. Paper presented at the National Institutes of Health, Office of Behavioral and Social Sciences Research, Bethesda, MD.

Moore, K. A., & Lippman, L. (Eds.). (2005). *Conceptualizing and measuring indicators of positive development: What do children need to flourish?* New York: Kluwer Academic/Plenum.

Moore, M. R. (2001). Family environment and adolescent sexual debut in alternative household structures. In R. T. Michael (Ed.), *Social awakening: Adolescent behavior as adulthood approaches* (pp. 109–136). New York: Russell Sage Foundation.

National Research Council and Institute of Medicine. (2002). *Community programs to promote youth development* (J. Eccles & J. A. Gootman, Eds.). Washington, DC: National Research Council and Institute of Medicine.

Tepper, R. L. (2001). Parental regulation and adolescent discretionary time-use decisions: Findings from the NLSY97. In R. T. Michael (Ed.), *Social awakening: Adolescent behavior as adulthood approaches* (pp. 79–106). New York: Russell Sage Foundation.

U.S. Department of Health and Human Services. (2000). *Healthy People 2010: Objectives for improving health* (Vol. 1). Washington, DC: U.S. Government Printing Office.

U.S. Department of Health and Human Services. (1990). *Healthy People 2000: National health promotion and disease prevention objectives*. Washington, DC: U.S. Government Printing Office.

U.S. Department of Health and Human Services, Office of the Assistant Secretary for Planning and Evaluation. (1997). *Trends in the well-being of America's children and youth 1996*. Washington, DC: U.S. Government Printing Office.

U.S. Department of Health and Human Services, Office of the Assistant Secretary for Planning and Evaluation. (2000). *Trends in the well-being of America's children and youth 2000*. Washington, DC: U.S. Government Printing Office.

Part II

Education Indicators

Chapter 3

Progress in the Development of Indicators of School Readiness

Tamara Halle
Child Trends

Mairead Reidy
Chapin Hall Center for Children

Martha Moorehouse
U.S. Department of Health and Human Services

Martha Zaslow
Child Trends

Catherine Walsh
*Rhode Island KIDS COUNT
and the 17-State School Readiness Indicators Initiative*

Julia Calkins
Elementary School Teacher

Nancy Geyelin Margie
University of Maryland

Ayonda Dent
U.S. Census Bureau

In their review of school readiness indicators, Phillips and Love (1997) anticipated major data collection efforts that would increase the depth and breadth of measures of school readiness available at the national level and that might be used for monitoring of progress toward school readiness at a more local level. Substantial progress has been made in the measurement of school readiness in the last 10 years, and we are now at the point of beginning to harvest the results of such efforts.

This chapter is organized to provide an overview of the conceptualization of school readiness and a review of major recent developments in the measurement of school readiness at the national and state levels. In addition to reviewing progress, it notes gaps and issues to address in further work.

CONCEPTUALIZATION OF SCHOOL READINESS
AS A FRAMEWORK FOR MEASUREMENT

Recent comprehensive reviews of the research on children's early development underscore that children's readiness for school is multifaceted (Halle, Zaff, Calkins, & Margie, 2000; Huffman, Mehlinger, & Kerivan, 2000; National Research Council & Institute of Medicine, 2000). Early language and literacy skills are central (Snow, Burns, & Griffin, 1998; Whitehurst & Lonigan, 2002). Children's language and prereading skills at school entry predict later academic outcomes, and children who enter school behind in these skills may have difficulty catching up (Hair et al., 2006; Kurdek & Sinclair, 2000; La Paro & Pianta, 2000; Reynolds & Bezruczko, 1993). In acknowledgment of the central role of early language and literacy development, current federal policy initiatives seek to strengthen early learning opportunities across the range of early childhood care and education settings.

In addition to the central role of early language and literacy development for school readiness, children's social and emotional development during the early years are emphasized by recent comprehensive reviews of the research, including those by the Committee on Integrating the Science of Early Childhood Development (National Research Council & Institute of Medicine, 2000) and the Committee on Early Childhood Pedagogy (National Research Council, 2001). These reviews have found cognitive and socioemotional development in early childhood to be closely linked. For example, the reviews indicate that children who can regulate their emotions are better able to concentrate and focus on tasks, an extremely important ability in school.

Literature reviews commissioned by the Child Mental Health Foundations and Agencies Network (Cavanaugh, Lippitt, & Moyo, 2000; Huffman et al., 2000; with an overview provided by Peth-Pierce, 2000) also affirm the importance of a multifaceted view of children's readiness and underscore the particular importance of social and emotional development. These reviews conclude that "children who are socially and emotionally ready for school generally have improved school outcomes, better odds of later school and vocational success, better later social and emotional development and an easier time developing relationships with peers" (Peth-Pierce, 2000, p. 2). Recent research confirms these conclusions (Blair, 2002; Raver, 2002). Huffman and colleagues (2006) identified as risk factors for difficulty in transitioning to kindergarten which include children's experience of poor parenting practices, a history of poor peer relationships, early behavior and adjustment problems, and parental psychological problems. In addition to social-emotional and cognitive factors, physical health continues to be widely acknowledged as a basic component of school readiness (National Research Council & Institute of Medicine, 2000).

According to Forgione (1998) and Love, Aber, and Brooks-Gunn (1999), a literature review by Kagan, Moore, and Bredekamp (1995) for the National Education Goals Panel (NEGP) Goal 1 Working Group has been critical in creating a bridge from the conceptualization to the measurement of school readiness. The major national surveys that we discuss in this chapter build on the conceptualization of school readiness outlined by Kagan et al.; some state and community efforts are guided by it as well.

Kagan and colleagues (1995) identified five dimensions of children's development as contributing to their ability to participate in and learn from school: (a) physical well-being and motor development (including appropriate growth, fitness, health/ill-health, gross and fine motor skills, and ability to integrate information from multiple senses); (b) language development (including aspects of emergent literacy, such as ability to recall familiar stories, awareness of the function of print, and awareness of sequence in stories; emergent writing skills such as ordered scribbling; vocabulary; awareness of social conventions in speech; and ability to follow directions given orally); (c) cognition and general knowledge (including mastery of specific knowledge such as names of letters and shapes, knowledge about the properties of objects, and mathematical concepts); (d) social and emotional development (including the formation of positive relationships with teachers and peers, the ability to cooperate with peers, positive self-concept, ability to comprehend others' emotions and respond appropriately to them, and ability to interpret and express one's own feelings); and (e) approaches toward learning (including curiosity about new tasks, persistence and attentiveness with tasks, ability to draw out lessons from experiences, and imagination and creativity).

Updates to this work have focused on early mathematic concepts (part of the cognition and general knowledge area of school readiness). Among the issues raised at a workshop on school readiness measures sponsored by the U.S. Department of Health and Human Services was the need to reflect new scientific advances in the measurement of school readiness in mathematics and all other domains (U.S. Department of Health and Human Services, 2002).

In addition to providing a detailed description of five dimensions of readiness for school in children, the NEGP Goal 1 Working Group's conceptualization identified two further components to school readiness: (a) readiness of the schools themselves and (b) family and community supports for children in the early years that lay the groundwork for children's readiness.

Some of the key components of ready schools include creating linkages between children's schools and their early education and care environments, evaluating and using strong curricula, supporting the ongoing professional development of teachers, responding to the needs of children from differing backgrounds, carrying out assessments both to plan instruction and for purposes of program planning and accountability, and helping to assure that children and families have access to key services in their communities (NEGP, 1998).

Multiple types of family and community supports could be important to children's readiness for school. From among the range of potential early supports, the NEGP identified three as of particular importance: (a) parents functioning as their children's first teachers, devoting time every day to help their preschool-age children learn, and having access to supports for their parenting; (b) children's access to high-quality early care and education programs to help them prepare for school; and (c) children's access to health care, nutrition, and physical activity to help them arrive at school alert and open to learning experiences.

We turn now to an examination of the types of school readiness measures that are available in national surveys and state data sources, and we give examples of some of the measures that have been developed and are in use across a selection of states. At both the national and state levels, we examine in turn the three key components of school readiness noted in the conceptualization presented earlier: (a) readiness in children, (b) readiness of schools, and (c) family and community supports.

ADVANCES IN THE DEVELOPMENT AND USE OF SCHOOL READINESS INDICATORS AT THE NATIONAL LEVEL

Overview of National Databases

To better understand the national efforts to measure school readiness, we first briefly describe our sources of data. The five national databases that have the most substantial and most current content related to school readiness are: (a) the Early Childhood Longitudinal Study-Kindergarten class of 1998–99 (ECLS-K), (b) the National Household Education Surveys Program (NHES), (c) the Head Start Family and Child Experiences Survey (FACES), (d) the Head Start Impact Study (HSIS), and (e) the Early Head Start Research and Evaluation Project (EHSRE).[1]

Each of these data sets has particular strengths (see Table 3.1 for a summary of key features). For example, the ECLS-K is distinguished by being a nationally representative sample of over 22,000 children who entered kindergarten in 1998. The children come from over 1,000 classrooms (representing both public and private, part-day and full-day kindergarten programs) and are followed throughout their elementary school years and into high school.

FACES is representative of all Head Start programs, centers, classrooms, children, and parents (see descriptions in Tarullo & McKey, 2001; see also the FACES web page at http://www.acf.hhs.gov/programs/opre/hs/faces/index.html). Like the ECLS-K, FACES is longitudinal in design, so that it follows the same children into the early years of elementary school (i.e., kindergarten and first grade). Both 3-year-olds and 4-year-olds participate, so that it is possible to measure between having one versus two years of Head Start. FACES has recurrent waves of data collection; multiple cohorts are followed longitudinally for each data wave. The first wave of data collection began in 1997 (FACES 1997), the

Table 3.1

Key Features of the National Data Sets with Major School Readiness Measures

Feature	ECLS-K[1]	NHES[2]	FACES[3]	HSIS[4]	EHSRE[5]
Sponsoring Agencies	U.S. Department of Education, National Center for Education Statistics	U.S. Department of Education, National Center for Education Statistics	Commissioner's Office of Research and Evaluation of the Administration on Children, Youth, and Families	Commissioner's Office of Research and Evaluation of the Administration on Children, Youth, and Families	Commissioner's Office of Research and Evaluation of the Administration on Children, Youth, and Families
Population Sample	Over 22,000 kindergartners from over 1,000 kindergartens, representing both public and private schools	The population varies by survey and administration year. In 1993, a School Readiness Survey was administered, which included information on almost 11,000 children and supplemental school readiness items in the 1999 parent interview (sample size nearly 3,600)	FACES 1997: A national probability sample of 3,200 children (including cohorts of three-year-olds and four-year-olds) in 40 Head Start centers FACES 2000: A national probability sample of 2,800 children (including cohorts of three-year-olds and four-year-olds) entering Head Start in 43 new Head Start programs FACES 2003: A national probability sample of 2,400 children (three-year-olds and four-year-olds) entering 63 Head Start programs FACES 2006: A national probability sample of approximately 3,500 children (three-year-olds and four-year-olds) entering 60 Head Start Programs	Approximately 6,000 children (including a cohort of three-year-olds and a cohort of four-year-olds) from 425 centers (Head Start and non-Head Start centers)	Random assignment of 3,001 children from zero to age three conducted at 17 research sites

(continued)

Table 3.1 (continued)

Feature	ECLS-K[1]	NHES[2]	FACES[3]	HSIS[4]	EHSRE[5]
Study Design	Longitudinal	Cross-Sectional	Longitudinal	Longitudinal	Longitudinal
Data Collection Schedule (Periodicity)	Fall and Spring of 1998-1999 (Kindergarten); Fall of 1999 (first grade – for only 25% of original sample); Spring of 2000 (first grade – for the full sample); Spring of 2002 (third grade); and Spring of 2004 (fifth grade).	Spring of 1991, 1993, 1995, 1996, 1999, 2001, 2003, 2005	FACES 1997: Spring 1997, Fall 1997, Spring 1998, Spring 1999, Spring 2000. FACES 2000: Fall 2000, Spring 2001, Spring 2002, Spring 2003 FACES 2003: Fall 2003, Spring 2004, Spring 2005, Spring 2006 FACES 2006: Fall 2006, Spring 2007, Spring 2008, Spring 2009	Three-year-old cohort: Fall and Spring of 2002-2003 (Head Start), Fall and Spring of 2003–2004 (Head Start), Spring of 2005 (kindergarten), and Spring of 2006 (first grade) Four-year-old cohort: Fall and Spring of 2002-2003 (Head Start), Spring of 2004 (kindergarten), and Spring of 2005 (first grade), Spring 2006 (second grade), Spring 2007 (third grade	Birth to Three Phase (1996-2001); Pre-Kindergarten Follow-Up Phase (2001–2004)
Sources of Information	Parent, teacher, and school administrator interviews, as well as direct child assessment.	An adult respondent for an entire household can give information for up to three children.	Data collection methods for the main samples include parent interviews, teacher and administrator interviews (both Head Start staff and elementary school staff), direct child assessment, and direct observation of the classroom. Data collection methods for the validation sub-study include home visit parent interviews, home and neighborhood observations, monthly telephone contacts with the family, and community agency telephone interviews.	Parent, teacher, and school administrator interviews, as well as direct child assessment.	Parent interview, parent-child videotape, father interview, father-child videotape, child care center staff interview, and child-caregiver observation.

Other Key Features	The study over-sampled Asian and private school kindergartners in Fall 1998 to permit separate estimates of different groups.	Random digit-dialed phone surveys are administered. The 1993 administration contained a specific school readiness survey. Another school readiness survey is planned for 2007.	Cohorts of three- and four-year-olds are followed longitudinally through the end of kindergarten or first grade. Allows measurement of having 1 or 2 years of Head Start. FACES is administered recurrently. The first wave was begun in 1997, the second in 2000, the third wave in Fall 2003, the fourth wave in Fall 2006.	This study was based on measures selected for the ECLS-K and FACES, to maximize comparability across studies.	The Birth to Three Phase included an evaluation of the impact of Early Head Start on child/family outcomes, an implementation study, and local research projects to address positive child and family development in Early Head Start programs. The Pre-Kindergarten Follow-Up Phase addresses the experiences of children after Early Head Start.

[1] Early Childhood Longitudinal Study, Kindergarten Class of 1998 – 99
[2] National Household Education Surveys Program
[3] Family and Child Experiences Survey
[4] Head Start Impact Study
[5] Early Head Start Research Evaluation Study

second in 2000 (FACES 2000), the third in fall 2003 (FACES 2003) and the fourth in fall 2006 (FACES 2006).

HSIS is a random-assignment study of the effects of Head Start. It compares children enrolled in Head Start to comparable children not enrolled in Head Start. In total, approximately 6,000 children from 425 centers participated, including a cohort of 3-year-olds and a cohort of 4-year-olds. Participants who were randomly assigned to be in the control group did not receive Head Start services, but could enroll in other services in the community. Data collection for HSIS began in 2002. Children in the HSIS study were followed longitudinally through their first grade year (Spring 2006). In 2006 the U.S. Department of Health and Human Services awarded a contract to follow the HSIS children through their third grade year. Data collection will occur in Spring 2007 and Spring 2008.

EHSRE is a multifaceted, random-assignment study of 3,001 children and families across 17 research sites that support improvement to the Early Head Start program. Early Head Start programs offer families options of weekly home visits by child development staff (home-based option), child development services administered in a child care center (center-based option), or a combination of the two (mixed approach). Also longitudinal in design, EHSRE was implemented in two waves. Random assignment was conducted within the 17 sites in 1996 and again in 1999. During the Birth to Three Phase (which included an implementation study, impact study, and local research projects), data were gathered through direct assessments of the children and caregivers when children were 14, 24, and 36 months old. Parents were interviewed at approximately 7, 16, and 28 months after enrolling in the Early Head Start program. As a part of the Pre-Kindergarten Follow-Up Phase, tracking interviews were conducted when children were 42 months of age and continued every 6 months until the spring before the children entered kindergarten. There are plans for an Elementary School Follow-Up Phase as well.

NHES, although not longitudinal in design, still allows monitoring of indicators over time for national samples of young children. NHES is a series of random digit dialed household surveys conducted throughout the United States. One adult responds for the entire household and gives information on up to three children in the household. Thus far, NHES has been administered in the spring of 1991, 1993, 1995, 1996, 1999, 2001, 2003, and 2005. A special School Readiness survey was conducted as part of the NHES in 1993 with additional school readiness items in the 1999 parent interview; almost 15,000 children are represented in the 1993 survey. A similar School Readiness survey is planned for 2007. In addition, the NHES Early Childhood Program Participation survey was included in 1991, 1995, with a subset of questions also asked in 1999. The most recent fielding of the Early Childhood Program Participation survey was in 2005.

We now examine the measures available for indicators of children's readiness for school in these national databases, followed by an examination of indicators of schools' readiness for children, and then family and community supports.

Measures of the Readiness of Children

Table 3.2 summarizes the coverage of the five dimensions of children's readiness for school by indicators in the five national databases described earlier. As we can see from Table 3.2, the ECLS-K, FACES, HSIS, and EHSRE all have extensive coverage of indicators of readiness in children across all five domains of school readiness. With the exception of the 1993 School Readiness survey, NHES is noticeably lacking coverage of indicators of approaches to learning and has minimal coverage in the area of cognition and general knowledge. Below, we provide information on the types of measures used to gather these indicators for each data set.

ECLS-K. Information on children's physical well-being and motor development is gathered from the parent interview (for children's general health and potential developmental difficulties) and from direct child assessment (e.g., height and weight, and fine and gross motor skills). Both parents and teachers report on children's ability to sit still and pay attention; according to the literature, the lack of these abilities is considered a potential developmental difficulty.

Children's language development, including language comprehension and production (for non-language-minority children only),[2] and children's emergent literacy skills, are gathered from direct assessments of the child and from teacher report. The kindergarten and first grade direct child assessment provides information on letter recognition, understanding of letter-sound relationships at the beginning and ending of words, sight word recognition, and understanding of words in context (West, Denton, & Reaney, 2000). The teacher reports on several of these abilities, as well as children's interest in reading and writing and awareness of conventions regarding print. Parents report on only a few of these skills.

Children's cognitive development in the areas of mathematics, scientific knowledge and thinking, and general knowledge are gathered through a combination of direct child assessment and teacher report. The kindergarten and first grade direct child assessment provides information on recognizing single-digit numbers and basic shapes, counting beyond 10, recognizing two-digit numbers, identifying the next number in a sequence, identifying the ordinal position of objects, recognizing sequences and patterns, comparing relative size, estimating, interest in common instruments for measurements, and performing simple addition and subtraction as well as basic multiplication and division (West, Denton, & Reaney, 2000). Teachers report on several of these abilities. They also report on children's observational and problem-solving skills and their knowledge of living and nonliving things. Parents report on only a few cognitive development items in the areas of cognition, mathematics, and general knowledge.

Children's social and behavioral development is reported by both the parent and the teacher using the Social Rating Scale (an instrument adapted from the Social Skills Rating Scale; Gresham & Elliot, 1990).

Table 3.2

Indicators of Children's School Readiness in National Data Sets

Domains of Readiness	ECLS–K[1]	NHES[2,3]	NHES 1993 School Readiness survey[4]	FACES 2000[5]	HSIS[6]	EHSRE[7]
Physical Well-being and Motor Development						
Physical Well-being	X	X	X	X	X	X
Motor Development	X	X*	X	X	X	X
Language Development						
Language Comprehension	X			X*	X*	X*
Language Production	X	X*	X*	X	X*	X*
Emergent Literacy	X	X	X	X	X	X
Cognition and General Knowledge						
Mathematical Knowledge	X	X*	X*	X*	X*	X*
Scientific Thinking	X			X*		
Scientific Knowledge	X			X*		
General Knowledge		X*	X*	X*	X*	X*
Social and Emotional Development						
Social Development	X		X	X	X	X
Emotional Development	X	X*	X	X	X	X
Approaches Toward Learning	X		X	X	X	X

[1] Early Childhood Longitudinal Study, Kindergarten Class of 1998–99
[2] National Household Education Surveys Program
[3] This includes all years and all iterations of the NHES, except the 1993 School Readiness Survey
[4] This was a special survey given in 1993 to measure the constructs of school readiness
[5] Family and Child Experiences Survey
[6] Head Start Impact Study
[7] Early Head Start Research Evaluation Study
*This construct or domain has been covered in at least one iteration of the survey; however, in general, it has not been covered extensively, either over time, or in terms of particular constructs. Extensiveness is a judgment, as determined by Child Trends, to identify where coverage is limited.

Likewise, information on children's approaches to learning is also gathered from parents and teachers using the Social Rating Scale.

NHES. Information on disabilities, one major construct related to children's readiness, was collected in all years of the NHES. Parents were asked what diagnoses their children had received, including learning disabilities, speech impairments, deafness, blindness, and orthopedic impairments.

In 1993, the questionnaire contained many more detailed questions about children's readiness. It included several questions on motor, social, and emotional development as well as approaches toward learning; however, only two questions in the area of cognition and general knowledge were asked (the ability to count and the ability to identify colors). Another major category was language, with one item on language production (the ability to be understood clearly by others) and several on emergent literacy, such as an interest in reading, an understanding of the structure of stories, and the ability of the focal child to write his or her name. Some, but not all, of the children's readiness items from NHES 1993 were repeated in 1999 and 2001; the majority of those that were repeated assessed emergent literacy abilities, such as familiarity with some letters of the alphabet, interest in reading-related activities, awareness of the conventions of reading books, and emerging writing skills.

FACES. Many of the measures collected in FACES 2000 are similar to or the same as measures used in FACES 1997; comparability was sought with the ECLS-K as well. In the interest of space, we describe in this chapter only data available in FACES 2000. The FACES 2000 surveys and direct child assessments during the kindergarten year cover all five dimensions of children's readiness for school (see Table 3.2). Direct assessments of the children's cognitive development include measures of children's receptive vocabulary; letter-word identification, applied problem solving, and dictation; story and print concepts; analysis of letter sounds, syllables, and words; and ability of the child to write his or her name.[3] Measures of the children's social and emotional development are based on three informants (teachers, parents, and the FACES interviewer), assuring that multiple perspectives are included in the overall picture. Note, however, that teachers report on children's social behavior in the school context, whereas parents report on children's behavior in general. Measures of the child's health are based mostly on parent report and include items concerning chronic health conditions, disabilities, overall health, and motor development. Parents also report on approaches to learning, with interviewer ratings also providing information on task persistence and following directions during the assessment process. The measures of cognitive development focus heavily on language and literacy, and information regarding some of the further aspects of cognitive development are not as extensively covered.

HSIS. The measures used in HSIS were based on measures selected for FACES and ECLS-K to maximize comparability across studies, although some updated versions of measures (e.g., the Woodcock–Johnson III Tests of Achievement; Woodcock & Johnson, 2001) and some new measures were used. Consequently, there is similarity in the indicators available across these data sources. Direct assessments of the child yield indicators of all five dimensions of children's readiness, including vocabulary development, emerging literacy, early mathematical skills, perceptual-motor development, and social and communicative competence. However, the direct assessment focuses most heavily on language and literacy development. Parents are asked about children's health and physical well-being, including developmental delays and chronic health conditions. Both parents and teachers report on children's social skills and problem behaviors, response to directions, and task persistence. Many of these items are gathered at the end of the year, rather than at the beginning. Parents are asked only three questions about their child's cognition and general knowledge: whether their child can (a) count by rote and (b) identify shapes and (c) colors.

EHSRE.   Information on children's health and motor development is based on parent responses. Parents report any accidents, hospitalizations of the child, child safety in the home, and immunizations.

Measures of cognitive and language development are gathered through two types of direct child assessments: (a) the Mental Development Index from the Bayley Scales of Infant Development (Bayley, 1993) and (b) the Peabody Picture Vocabulary Test (Dunn & Dunn, 1997).

Children's social-emotional development, comprising rudiments of attentiveness and children's aggressive behavior, are examined by observational measures from videotaped parent-child interactions and parent interviews. Parents were videotaped with their children in a semistructured play assignment. Parents were given three bags of toys (the "three bag task") and asked to play with the child in whatever manner the child wished, but the parent was instructed on the order in which to play with the bags (U.S. Department of Health and Human Services, 2002). Instructions were vague so that the interactions between the parent and child would be natural. The parent interview also included a section of questions on school readiness. Parents reported on the child's ability to complete and start new tasks, the child's ability to regulate his or her emotions and thinking, and whether the child liked to be involved in activities such as pretend play.

Measures of the Readiness of Schools

A summary of the categories of indicators of the readiness of schools gathered in each of the four national data sets is noted in Table 3.3. In the following sections, we review the measures used to gather this information in each of the data sets.

ECLS-K.   Data on schools' readiness in the ECLS-K are gathered through teacher and school administrator reports. Teachers report on their own level of education, professional development activities, and characteristics of their classroom. Both teachers and administrators report on practices that foster communication with the parents, especially practices that help children and families transition to kindergarten (e.g., whether there are orientation sessions or "open houses" for parents before school starts). However, very little information is gathered about transitional practices between early care and education programs and schools (see Table 3.3). School administrators report on their own level of education and characteristics of the school, such as whether the school provides before- and after-school care.

NHES.   NHES currently contains very few items on schools' readiness. Each year, parents were asked about communication with their child's teacher. In 1999 and 2001, questions on the provision of before- and after-school care were included. The most recent survey, in 2005, includes a few new questions related to schools' readiness, such as whether the school holds routine meetings with parents or informs parents on how the child is doing between progress reports, makes the parent aware of volunteer opportunities at the school, provides tutoring for children falling behind academically, or provides access to community

Table 3.3
Indicators of Schools' Readiness for Children in National Data Sets

Domains of Readiness	ECLS-K[1]	NHES[2,3]	NHES 1993 School Readiness survey[4]	FACES 2000[5]	HSIS[6]	EHSRE[7]
Characteristics of Schools	X	X*				
Take Responsibility for Results	X*					
Serve Children in Communities		X*			X*	
Characteristics of Principals	X					
Characteristics of Teachers	X	X*			X*	
Characteristics of Classrooms	X	X*	X*		X*	
Transitional Practices						
Home to School	X	X	X*		X*	
Early Care and Education Settings to School	X*					X

[1] Early Childhood Longitudinal Study, Kindergarten Class of 1998–99
[2] National Household Education Surveys Program
[3] This includes all years and all iterations of the NHES, except the 1993 School Readiness Survey
[4] This was a special survey given in 1993 to measure the constructs of school readiness
[5] Family and Child Experiences Survey
[6] Head Start Impact Study
[7] Early Head Start Research Evaluation Study

*This construct or domain has been covered in at least one iteration of the survey; however, in general, it has not been covered extensively, either over time, or in terms of particular constructs. Extensiveness is a judgment, as determined by Child Trends, to identify where coverage is limited.

supports such as health care or nutrition services. The 2003 NHES Parent and Family Involvement in Education survey asks whether the school assesses children's learning using age-appropriate methods, a factor of particular importance for accurate measurement of children's progress.

FACES. There is extensive data collection in the FACES 2000 surveys regarding Head Start classrooms, teachers, directors, and programs. However, indicators of the readiness of schools are generally seen as referring to the quality of kindergarten classrooms and the schools in which they reside. FACES 2000 does collect information on kindergartens and schools, but the information is not as extensive as for Head Start classrooms and programs.

Information on the readiness of schools is collected from both parents and kindergarten teachers. Teachers report on their education, training, experience, and ongoing professional development. Parents report on participation in the classroom. Teachers report on whether the program is full- or half-day, whether a teaching assistant is present, class size, and frequency of classroom activities (e.g., math, social studies, reading, art, music, physical education), and availability and quality of learning center materials in the classroom. Parents provide further information regarding the readiness of schools, including whether tutoring is provided for a child falling behind, whether help is provided that accesses community supports such as health care and nutrition programs, and whether the classroom is open to parent involvement.

The FACES 2000 surveys do not focus strongly on such aspects of schools' readiness as principal qualifications or school facilities. This reflects both the emphasis in this survey on earlier program, classroom, and facility characteristics (i.e., during the Head Start year[s]), as appropriate to the nature and goals of this survey, and perhaps the state of measures development in these areas.

HSIS. HSIS assesses the quality of Head Start classrooms and programs. As mentioned earlier, many of the HSIS measures are similar to, or the same as, the measures used in FACES and the ECLS-K.

However, a limited set of measures of school quality were collected once children reach elementary school. For instance, in the kindergarten and first-grade years, secondary sources, such as attendance and immunization records, average test scores, number of children receiving free or reduced lunch, and teacher:student ratios were used to measure and track the school environment. The school principal or other staff completes an interview to obtain information about the overall operation and quality of the program setting. Finally, kindergarten teachers were asked to report on the kindergarten program and provisions for children's transition to kindergarten, including whether the teacher obtained any information from the Head Start program or alternative care provider about the child's developmental status or special needs.[4]

EHSRE.   The first two phases of data collection in EHSRE surveys do not encompass information on kindergarten and schools, but an Elementary School Follow-Up phase is in the planning stages. Parents are asked if they know what school their child will attend for kindergarten, the name of the school, and the school district. A forthcoming Elementary School Follow-Up phase may provide additional items related to the transition to school and schools' readiness to receive children.

Measures of Family and Community Supports for School Readiness

The indicators gathered in each of several major areas of family and community supports for all four national data sets are noted in Table 3.4.

ECLS-K.   All information on family and community supports in the ECLS-K is based on parent report. Information on a variety of parent-child literacy and other activities are available from the ECLS-K (see Table 3.4). The information on children's health that is gathered from parents in the ECLS-K is about birthweight, vision, behavior, hearing, activity level, speaking, and overall rating of health. For information on preschool experience, parents report on how many days a week, and hours a week, children spent in various types of care, ranging from relative care to center-based care, during the year prior to kindergarten entry. The surveys also ask about current child care situations. More detailed information on the quality of those care environments may be better obtained from interviews with care providers or center administrators. Indeed, another longitudinal study of young children sponsored by the NCES, the Early Childhood Longitudinal Study-Birth Cohort (ECLS-B), which began collecting data in 2001, will be able to provide this more detailed information because it includes interviews of care providers and administrators.

NHES.   The main focus of the school readiness components of NHES seems to be family and community supports, with a strong emphasis on preschool participation. In every year (excluding the 2003 survey), parents were asked about their children's participation in relative care, non-relative care, Head Start, and center-based care (with some minor variations). Questions included the amount of time spent in each type of care and the number of children and adults in each setting.

Another strong emphasis is on literacy practices in the home. All administrations contained questions on how much parents or other family members read to children and how often they visited libraries. In addition, the surveys contained varying items on other parent-child and family-child activities, such as singing songs together, going to museums or concerts, and directly teaching children.

Other family and community supports related to health, dental, and mental health services and parent support activities were addressed by

Table 3.4

Indicators of Family and Community Supports for School Readiness in National Data Sets

Domains of readiness	ECLS-K[1]	NHES[2,3]	NHES 1993 School Readiness survey[4]	FACES 2000[5]	HSIS[6]	EHSRE[7]
Health						
Prenatal care						
Infant birthweight	X	X	X	X	X	
Health care	X	X	X	X*	X*	X*
Family-Child Activities						
Family-Child Language and Literacy Activities	X	X	X	X	X*	X*
Other Family-Child Activities	X	X	X	X	X	X
Support for Families of Preschoolers	X	X*		X*	X*	X*
Parent Well-being	X			X	X	X
Preschool Experience						
Preschool Participation	X	X	X	X	X	
Quality of Preschool Centers	X*	X*	X*	X	X	
Quality of Home-based Preschool Settings	X*	X*		X*	X	
Teacher-Child Activities				X	X	

[1] Early Childhood Longitudinal Study, Kindergarten Class of 1998–99
[2] National Household Education Surveys Program
[3] This includes all years and all iterations of the NHES, except the 1993 School Readiness Survey.
[4] This was a special survey given in 1993 to measure the constructs of school readiness.
[5] Family and Child Experiences Survey.
[6] Head Start Impact Study.
[7] Early Head Start Research Evaluation Study.

*This construct or domain has been covered in at least one iteration of the survey; however, in general, it has not been covered extensively, either over time, or in terms of particular constructs. Extensiveness is a judgment, as determined by Child Trends, to identify where coverage is limited.

NHES at different time points. To obtain details about which questions were addressed at which time points.

FACES.   With its first wave(s) of data collection during the Head Start year or years, and with detailed surveys of parents and Head Start staff members, and direct observation of the classroom environments, the FACES 2000 surveys provide a great deal of information about fam–

ily and community supports prior to school entry. Regarding family supports for children's school readiness, the parent interview provides information about parent-child literacy activities as well as other cognitively stimulating activities with the child. There are direct observations of the Head Start classroom, including completion of the Early Childhood Environment Rating Scale (ECERS; Harms & Clifford, 1980) and the Arnett Scale of Caregiver Behavior (Arnett, 1989) for both the lead and assistant teachers. Profiles of classroom scheduling and learning activities, as well as counts of adult:child ratios, are also based on direct observation. Parents report on children's participation in other forms of early childhood care and education. A limited set of interview items address the child's health and health care as well as parent participation in parenting education and support programs.

HSIS.   Much of the information on family and community supports is gathered through parent report. Parents are interviewed to obtain parental beliefs toward, and their participation in, their child's learning as well as information on demographic characteristics. There are also extensive teacher questionnaires for Head Start teachers to obtain biographical information as well as information on their beliefs about working with children and the quality of the program. Classroom observations are also made using the Early Childhood Environment Rating Scale-Revised (ECERS-R; Harms et al., 1998) and the Arnett Scale of Teacher/Caregiver Behavior (Arnett, 1989). The quality of home-based care arrangements is assessed using the Family Day Care Rating Scale (Harms & Clifford, 1989) and the Arnett Scale of Teacher/Caregiver Behavior (Arnett, 1989). The center director and other staff complete an interview to obtain information about the overall operation and quality of the program setting.

EHSRE.   The current surveys for EHSRE focus on child care settings, gathering information on professional development activities of Early Head Start teachers, child care providers, and interactions with children. Child care staff is assessed using the Arnett Scale of Teacher/Caregiver Behavior (Arnett, 1989) and the ECERS-R (Harms et al., 1998). To assess the parents' support for preparing children for school, parents are asked if they read to the child, teach him or her songs, play games, teach him or her the alphabet, or involve the child in chores. In addition, parents are asked to complete a Family Support Scale (Dunst, Jenkins, & Trivette, 1984) to measure their contentment with the support (help from family, relatives, organizations) they receive in raising a young child. Data are also gathered through observations of the home using the Home Observation for Measurement of the Environment measure (Caldwell & Bradley, 2001), which assesses the organization of the home as well as the stimuli available to a child in the home environment. There was also a separate interview designed specifically for fathers to assess how Early Head Start programs support fathers' relationships with their children and the children's mothers.

Uses of National School Readiness Indicators in Policy

Given the current interest in school readiness at the national policy level, data analysis using nationally representative samples of young children and their families and schools has the potential to inform early education policies. Because of the relatively recent availability of data from these five national databases, initial findings have only recently been released. For example, analyses of the 1997 and 2000 FACES data indicate that Head Start children begin the Head Start year at a great disadvantage compared with other children (based on national norms on standardized tests of cognitive development). They show significant gains over the Head Start year in aspects of social and cognitive development, including increases in social skills, decreases in hyperactive behavior, and increases in vocabulary and early writing skills. Children assessed in the 2000–01 year showed greater gains in knowledge of book and print conventions than children assessed in the 1997–98 year. Letter knowledge declined over the 1997-98 year but remained steady over the 2000–01 year. Nevertheless, these children's scores on cognitive measures of school readiness are still well below the national average (Child Outcomes Research and Evaluation & the Head Start Bureau, 2003).

Recent findings from EHRSE show small to moderate impacts on child outcomes at age 3 (Love et al., 2005). Early Head Start children scored higher on average than the control group in the cognitive and language development assessments, although both groups scored below the national norms. The Early Head Start three-year-olds were less likely to score in the "at-risk" range (lower than 85) on the Mental Development Index than the control children. In addition, the Early Head Start children had lower levels of aggressive behavior and higher attention spans than the control children. In addition to measures of children's school readiness, Love et al. (2005) reported on measures of family and community supports for school readiness. Specifically, their study revealed positive impacts on parental emotional support to the child and on parental support for children's language and learning. Mixed-approach programs (i.e., those that combined home-based and school-based Early Head Start models) and programs that fully implemented their performance standards showed the greatest impacts across multiple outcomes.

First-year findings of the HSIS study show small to moderate impacts on children's development in multiple developmental domains for children three and four years of age who have received nine months of Head Start (U.S. Department of Health and Human Services, Administration for Children, Youth, and Families, 2005). Within the cognitive domain, Head Start had significant impacts on three- and four-year-olds' prereading and prewriting skills as well as parent-reported literacy skills. Head Start three-year-olds also had significantly better vocabulary skills than control respondents. However, no significant impacts were found for oral comprehension skills or phonological awareness (i.e., the ability to distinguish the component sounds within words), or early math skills for either age group. Within the social-emotional domain, the results indicated that Head Start reduced three-year-olds' problem behaviors but had no effect on social skills or measures of approaches to learning. No significant impacts in the social-emotional domain were found for children entering Head Start as four-year-olds. Within the health domain, impacts were found for improved dental care for both three-year-olds and four-year-olds and improved overall health for three-year-olds. Within the parenting domain, positive impacts were found for three-year-olds on parents' educational activities (e.g., reading to the child and taking child to cultural events) and parents' discipline strategies (specifically, reduced frequency of spanking). For four-year-olds, there was a significant impact on parents' educational activities but no impact on parents' discipline strategies. There were no significant impacts on child safety practices for either age group. In general, there was a larger number of statistically significant, positive effects on three-year-olds than on four-year-olds. HSIS is still in progress, with data collection planned through third grade. Future reports will follow children through the end of first grade, examine additional areas of possible impact, and assess variation in impact by program characteristics (e.g., classroom quality, full-day vs. half-day programs) and community characteristics.

These findings collectively have been influential in the current policy emphasis on building the literacy skills of children within early childhood care and education settings and promoting family and community supports for school readiness. Further attention could be paid in future work within both the research and policy arenas to addressing the readiness of schools.

STATE ADVANCES IN THE DEVELOPMENT AND USE OF SCHOOL READINESS INDICATORS

We turn now from national data collection to state-level efforts, noting that many states identify school readiness as an important goal for children entering elementary school and seek measures of how children are progressing toward that goal at state and community levels. Much of this work has been accomplished as part of a number of state indicator initiatives, and in this section we highlight some of the measures of readiness in children, the readiness of schools, and family and community supports that have been developed in the context of these initiatives.[5]

First, the Child Indicators Project provided a context between 1998 and 2001 in which 14 states worked to strengthen their states' child indicators and to institutionalize the use of indicators in state and local policymaking.[6] This initiative, sponsored by the Office of the Assistant Secretary for Planning and Evaluation of the U.S. Department of Health and Human Services,with additional support from the Administration for Children and Families and the David and Lucile Packard Foundation, encouraged states to develop a series of goals for children. School readiness was a central goal for many of these states, and state teams, frequently formed through partnerships among state government agencies that had lead responsibility for addressing children's issues, working to build a series of indicators to track progress toward this goal. The objective of the Child Indicators Project was to support states' efforts to advance their work given their own local situations and their sets of goals and interests.

Second, 17 states participated in the three-year National School Readiness Indicators Initiative, "School Readiness Indicators: Making Progress for Young Children."[7] Launched in 2001, this initiative was sponsored by the David and Lucile Packard Foundation, the Ewing Marion Kauffman Foundation, and the Ford Foundation. It brought together 17 states to develop and use indicators as a tool for policy and communications on critical school readiness issues. States worked individually and collectively to create a set of measurable indicators of school readiness. State teams worked within each state to adopt a set of indicators related to school readiness, track data over time and at state and local levels, and report findings to policymakers and the general public. The goal was to use the indicators to stimulate policy, program, and other actions to improve children's readiness at kindergarten entry and to improve the ability of all children to read at grade level by third grade.

The experience in states and communities across the nation shows that indicators of child well-being can be important tools for bringing government and community leaders together to make strategic investments in children and families. In the experience of the state indicators initiatives, the most powerful sets of indicators span the ages from birth through age eight; address all domains of child development; and include information on ready children, ready schools, ready services, ready families, and ready communities.

State Data Sources

States use a range of data sources to build indicators of readiness in children, readiness in schools, and family and community supports. These include administrative data; vital statistics; census data; surveys at the child, family, and community levels; and direct assessment data. National data sets, described earlier, can also be important sources of benchmarking for states.

It is not surprising that states often seek to maximize existing administrative data sources given the tremendous cost associated with new data collection strategies. Some states have employed staff members, sometimes called *data quality technicians*, to assess the quality and usefulness of existing administrative data sources. Many states have made effective use of data from administrative records on health, education, child care and early education, income support program participation, child welfare, and other service systems. Administrative data are used most effectively when partnerships are developed among state agencies with lead responsibility for addressing children's issues and implementing programs, including children's health, education, social services, and child welfare. Not only are these partnerships critical to the identification of shared goals, but they also facilitate the sharing of data across agencies and, at times, the development of new indicators based on linked individual-level administrative data.

Although many states, particularly in the early stages of indicator development, eschew expensive, large-scale surveys, many have successfully used existing survey data or strategically added questions to existing surveys. Examples of the latter include market rate surveys of child care providers and health interview surveys. Despite the costs, some states have developed and implemented new surveys that can incorporate multiple perspectives and include the voices of children, parents, teachers, and health care professionals in indicator development. Cross-agency collaboration is again seen as critical to amassing the support and expenditures necessary for such new data collection. Because school readiness is multidimensional, and no one agency can be held solely responsible for developing indicators—or indeed, making changes that could be reflected in the indicator measures—many agencies can rally around a school readiness outcome. This has contributed to successful shared responsibility for both outcomes and data expenditures.

A wide range of states conduct screenings or assessment programs for kindergartners (see, e.g., Saluja, Scott-Little & Clifford, 2000). These can potentially provide states with important measures of children's skills and characteristics. In a few states, especially those collecting Work Sampling data[8] throughout the kindergarten year, assessments are conducted primarily for the instruction of individual children. In most instances, the goal of the recent wave of state-level assessments appears to be program evaluation and monitoring. States and researchers caution against using assessments to make inappropriate (grade placement or retention) decisions for young children. The guidelines provided by the Goal 1 Early Childhood Assessments Resource Group assert that different purposes of assessment need to be carefully distinguished and, furthermore, that the strategy of assessment in a particular circumstance needs to be chosen in keeping with the underlying purpose (NEGP, 1998). This is especially important given that technical requirements and the nature of the information obtained differ for assessments with different purposes.[9] When universal assessments are carried out and reported for purposes of program monitoring and tracking of children statewide, special steps need to be taken against use of the information for other purposes. To protect against misuse (e.g., data collected for program monitoring used instead for individual placement or retention decisions), data can be stored in such a way that individual or classroom identifiers are not available, and data can be reported only at an aggregate level. It should be noted that some states have found poor interrater reliability in the ratings completed for Work Sampling and caution against using the ratings for aggregate reporting purposes when they were originally designed for informing instruction of individual children; further direct examinations of this issue are needed (Zaslow & Halle, 2003). As an alternative to aggregate data on all kindergartners, a representative sample for the state can be collected (Clifford 2000).[10]

Finally, national data sets can be an important data source for states and can be used for benchmarking purposes. North Carolina is an example of a state that benchmarks its data on readiness in children and readiness in schools against data from the national surveys (especially ECLS-K and FACES). This makes it possible to assess the readiness of children and schools in North Carolina relative to national norms (see Maxwell, Bryant, Ridley & Keyes-Elstein, 2001).

State-Level School Readiness Measures

Significant progress has been made by many states in the development of school readiness measures. To illustrate this progress, we begin by summarizing some key principles underlying the early stages of school readiness indicator development in the states. We then focus in particular on the work of Rhode Island and Vermont, two states that led the early work on school readiness indicators through the Child Indicators Initiative and continue to advance the work in the field. Rhode Island and Vermont are examples of two different approaches to the development of a set of indicators that effectively capture the multifaceted nature of school readiness outlined earlier.[11] Finally, in recognition of the significant body of work that is emerging in many states to measure and benchmark progress in school readiness, we highlight some interesting indicators currently in place across a range of states.

In the early stages of school readiness indicator development, states have concentrated their efforts on the health and family conditions that surround children and the prevalence of community supports. They do this because family and community supports—including the availability and quality of child and family services, such as health care, early education, and child care—are critical to achieving positive child outcomes (e.g., Institute of Medicine, 2001; Piesner-Feinberg et al., 1999). Additionally, in most states, administrative data are readily available to develop such measures. Measures of children's health and physical safety from birth through school entry include the extent to which children are immunized, the prevalence of exposure to lead in the environment, and the rates of injuries and hospitalizations experienced by children. Measures of the extent of community-level support include the extent to which children participate in early intervention programs; have access to quality, affordable, and accessible child care; and have access to health insurance and nutritious breakfast programs. Measures of parent involvement in early education programs are used to assess the family's support for school readiness.

States are increasingly also devoting considerable attention to appropriate methods to assess what children know and can do. Although many states have indicators in place that reflect test score achievement and grade retention, very few have yet found appropriate data sources for child outcome indicators across the domains of early child development (e.g., language and literacy, social-emotional development, cognition, and approaches to learning). To get a sense of some of the advances made in these areas, we turn to the work of two states that were early leaders in school readiness indicator development: Rhode Island and Vermont.

Rhode Island.   Rhode Island has taken an incremental and pragmatic approach to developing school readiness indicators, where the desire for a holistic view of school readiness was integrated with a need for immediate measures to inform state policy and state investments in young children. In Rhode Island, the impetus for school readiness indicators came from a governor's cabinet on children's issues, which endorsed three outcomes to guide the work of all child-serving agencies. One outcome is that all children enter school ready to learn. Rhode Island began to work on indicators to assess progress toward this goal and recognized that access to quality early care and education would be an investment of potential importance to children. The governor and the legislature supported increased investments in child care, especially as welfare reform took hold. It became critical to put school readiness indicator development on the fast track when legislative leaders asked whether these child care investments were linked to improvements in children arriving at school ready to succeed.

Because the Rhode Island legislature wanted immediate signals as to whether things were moving in the right direction, the state took a practical, multipronged approach to indicator development. First, the significant components of school readiness were conceptualized by working with other states and with experts across the country and, from this, a logical set of indicators that provided a good reflection of a young child's school readiness was selected. Second, the indicators already in place were refined with available data. Third, instead of waiting for the perfect set of measures before beginning, indicators were built incrementally, adding each year to their indicators. Fourth, existing surveys were extended to gather new data. In particular, school readiness questions were added to the School Accountability for Learning and Teaching survey, which was administered to teachers and students in all Rhode Island schools. Underlying all of these strategies was a clear sense and articulation of the reasons for collection and use of indicators.

The Rhode Island indicators, both existing and planned, place a strong emphasis on the health of children from birth through kindergarten; reflect the roles of families, communities, and the early care and education systems; and acknowledge the importance of measuring critical aspects of what children know and can do. Although continually changing as data sources evolve, examples of indicators in place as of July 2003 are shown in Table 3.5. A series of indicators reflects whether infants are born healthy, whether they have access to health services (access in the early years to health care, well-child care and vision/dental care, etc.), and the extent of health problems (vision, lead exposure, asthma, etc.) children exhibit at kindergarten entry. The extent to which children live in safe and stable families, and whether the family environment supports early learning, reflect family conditions that support school readiness. A strong emphasis is placed on the prevalence and patterns of early childhood care and education, and efforts are made to measure the extent to which children have access to early care and education programs, children who are at high developmental or social risk receive early intervention, and early care and education programs are of high quality. The extent to which schools are ready for all children further reflects the level of community support for school readiness and, as can be seen in Table 3.5, indicators have been developed to capture important dimensions of ready schools.

Vermont. Vermont has focused on the design of a novel set of surveys intended to capture the multidimensionality of school readiness at the community level. Both Vermont's Agency of Human Services and its Department of Education have adopted the goal of children being ready for school. There is a strong history of developing and using community-level indicators across the state and thus a need for good measures of how well communities are ensuring that all children are prepared to make the most of their school experience.

Vermont's measurement strategy does not assess children directly; instead, it relies on a series of surveys that capture the multiple perspectives of kindergarten teachers and school principals to create a "snapshot" of key areas of school and community supports critical to ensuring that young children start school on the right foot. In the Ready Schools' Principal Questionnaire, school principals report on schools' transition-to-kindergarten practices, quality of schools, opportunities for parental involvement in schools, and preschool opportunities and other school-community partnerships and supports. The Ready Kindergartners Questionnaire collects information on teachers' assessment of children's developmental competence. It captures the five interrelated

Table 3.5

Rhode Island School Readiness Indicators of Ready Children, Ready Schools, and Family and Community Supports

Domains of Readiness	Construct	Indicator
Physical Well-being and Motor Development	Physical Well-being	% of children under age 6 with elevated lead levels
	Motor Development	% of children with undetected disability or developmental problem at K entry that requires special education services
Language Development	Language Comprehension	% of children in grades K-3 who are at or above grade level in reading / language arts
	Language Production	% of children with untreated dental problems at kindergarten entry
	Emergent Literacy	% of kindergarten students who represent sounds and words with print
Cognition and General Knowledge	Mathematical Knowledge	% of children in grades K-3 who are at or above grade level in mathematics
	Scientific Knowledge	% of fourth graders who are at or above proficiency levels on the health knowledge standards
	General Knowledge	% of kindergarten children with difficulty learning academic subjects
Social and Emotional Development	Social Development	% of kindergarten children with difficulty working with other students
	Emotional Development	% of kindergarten children who are overly aggressive to peers
Approaches Toward Learning		% of kindergarten children with poor concentration or limited attention
Characteristics of Schools	Take Responsibility for Results	% of elementary schools classified as improving schools (based on % of children meeting proficiency levels on state standards)
	Serve Children in Communities	% of low-income children in schools serving the School Breakfast Program
	Characteristics of Principals	% of elementary principals with a degree in early childhood or elementary education
	Characteristics of Teachers	% of kindergarten teachers with a degree in early childhood education
	Characteristics of Classrooms	% of kindergarten children who are enrolled in a full-day K program

(continued)

TABLE 3.5   (*continued*)

Domains of Readiness	Construct	Indicator
Transitional Practices	Home to School	% of schools that have formal process for family-child visit to school before the start of the kindergarten year
	Early Care and Education Settings to School	% of kindergarten teachers who know child's early care setting
	Emotional Development	% of kindergarten children who are overly aggressive to peers
Health	Prenatal Care	% of women with delayed prenatal care (beginning after the first trimester) or no prenatal care
	Infant Birthweight	% of infants born low birth weight (less than 5.5 pounds)
	Health Care	% of children under age 6 with health insurance
Family-Child Activities	Family-Child Language and Literacy Activities	% of families with preschool children that read to their preschool child every day
	Other Family-Child Activities	% of parents who often took their child to special places and events in the community
	Support for Families of Preschoolers	% of eligible children enrolled in comprehensive programs (Early Head Start, Early Start, Head Start)
	Parent Well-being	% of births to teens
Preschool Experience	Preschool Participation	% of children enrolled in early care and education program the year prior to kindergarten entry
	Quality of Preschool Centers	% of child care slots in accredited programs
	Quality of Home-based Preschool Settings	% of family child care slots in accredited programs
	Teacher-Child Activities	% of child care and early education programs that are implementing the Rhode Island Early Learning Standards

dimensions of early development and learning identified by the NEGP as aspects of children's readiness for school. Teachers are asked to consider a range of student skills and to rate whether the skill is not observed in the classroom, whether the student is beginning to demonstrate the skill, whether the student demonstrates the skill but does not use it consistently, or whether the student has mastered the skill and can perform it independently.[12] The Ready Schools Teacher Questionnaire focuses on the extent to which support from a variety of personnel, including the principal, school psychologist or social worker, special education teacher, speech and language therapist, behavior specialist, curriculum specialist, and others are available to teachers when needed.

Vermont's approach was developed with the extensive input of parents, preschool and kindergarten teachers, principals, academic researchers, a range of regional early childhood organizations, and Agency of Human Services and Department of Education personnel. When developing the questionnaires, Vermont looked widely at and borrowed heavily from other instruments to choose items that the group felt fit with Vermont's early childhood emphases. A selection of the indicators developed by Vermont under Children's School Readiness and Schools' Readiness for Children is provided in Table 3.6.

Indicator Progress Across States

Many other states are in the process of developing sets of school readiness measures that reflect all domains of child development from birth to age eight. Although continually changing as state teams prioritize issues and as data sources evolve, we highlight in Table 3.7 some of the indicators in place as of May 2003 that are not reflected in the work of Rhode Island and Vermont as just summarized.

Use of State-Level Indicators in Policy and Practice

Indicators of school readiness have many uses. They can be used to describe child, family, and community conditions; to inform state and local community planning and policymaking; to measure progress in improving child outcomes; and to monitor the impact of investments and policy choices. School readiness indicators can guide policy decisions in state government both administratively and legislatively and can be used to render government agencies more accountable to their constituencies.

To illustrate the effect indicators can have on policy development and improved child outcomes, we give the example of the use of an indicator of childhood lead poisoning. In 1995, the Rhode Island Department of Health, in partnership with Rhode Island KIDS COUNT, developed the state's first indicator of childhood lead poisoning. Instead of reporting overall blood lead levels, the indicator zeroed in on the specific number of children entering kindergarten with a history of elevated lead levels (greater than 10 micrograms of lead per deciliter of blood). The data for this indicator were published in the *1996 Rhode Island KIDS COUNT Factbook*. That year, more than 1 in 3 children entering kindergarten had elevated lead levels, increasing to almost 1 in 2 children in the cities with the highest child poverty rates. As a result of the ensuing lead poisoning prevention, abatement, and treatment programs, dramatic progress was made. By 2003, the percentage of lead poisoned kindergartners had decreased from 36 percent to 12 percent.

Table 3.6
A Selection of Vermont's Measures of Ready Children and Ready Schools

Domains of Readiness	Construct	Indicator
Language Development	Language Comprehension	% of students who Understands simple directions, requests and information
	Language Production	% of students who Communicate needs, wants, and thoughts in primary language
		% of students who engage in conversation (e.g., completes sentences, turn-taking, etc.)
Cognition and General Knowledge		% of students who understand the purpose of books
		% of students who can recall and explain sequence of events
		% of students who recognize his/her name in print
		% of students who use pencils, crayons and brushes to express ideas
		% of students who engages in imaginative play
		% of students who can meet and play with different children appropriately for his/her age
		% of students who use problem-solving skills to address social dilemmas with peers
		% of students who interacts positively with adults in the classroom
		% of students who separates easily from caregiver
Social and Emotional Development		% of students who appropriately expresses a range of emotions (happy, sad, angry, frustrated) in the school day
		% of students who adapt to transitions
Approaches Toward Learning		% of students who follow simple rules and instructions in the classroom
		% of students who persist with self-selected activity (approx 15 minutes) with intermittent teacher attention
		% of students who sit still and pay attention during group activities
		% of students who appear enthusiastic, and interested in classroom activities
		% of students who use a variety of strategies to problem-solve in the classroom
		% of students who pay attention during teacher-directed group activities (approx 15 minutes)
		% of students who know when and how to use adults as a resource
		% of students who initiate activities in the classroom
		% of students who are curious (asks questions, probes, tries new things, etc.)

Domains of Readiness	Construct	Indicator
Characteristics of Schools	Serve children in communities	School-Community Partnerships and Supports % of standard met by community schools (where the standard is: Action Planning includes pre-K and K; all listed school-sponsored activities that are offered, with at least "medium-level" participation; all listed community-based activities are at least co-sponsored by the school; and parent involvement is at a "medium" level)
	Characteristics of Teachers	% of kindergarten teachers who have early childhood educational qualifications
		% of standard met by community school(s) (where the standard is: 13 of the listed supports must be "available" or "available with a wait"; and one of these must be a counselor, behavioral specialist, school psychologist, or school social worker)
	Characteristics of Classrooms	% of standard met by community school (s) (where standard is based on classroom size, the extent to which teachers have early childhood education endorsements, and the derivation of classroom instruction (for example teacher observations , statewide standards, and school district curriculum)
Transitional Practices	Home to School	% of standard met by community school(s) (where the standard is at least 10 of a series of practices including whether the school has open houses for parent and children; whether new students receive home visits; whether parents receive information packets describing kindergarten; and whether the school offers practice or half-day school introductions or practice bus rides)
	Early Care and Education Settings to School	Does teacher visit preschool(s) or parent-child center(s)

In addition to specific policy initiatives, such as the lead poisoning prevention example, states also use these data to give relevant actors a more informed view of the environment in which they work. For example, in Vermont the focus has been primarily on providing communities with an aggregate measure of their children's school readiness. Communities receive their own reports that detail readiness indicators of kindergarten children (in the aggregate) and of schools in multiple areas, such as children's early literacy, social skills, and general knowledge, and school-sponsored transition activities. The Agency of Human Services' *Community Profiles* (http://humanservices.vermont.gov/), annual compilations of a number of indicators across 10 outcomes, incorporate summary indicators from the assessments to create an overview of community status on the outcome "Children Are Ready for School." This information provides a baseline for communities to assess their progress toward achieving this important outcome. Schools find these data particularly valuable as they develop action plans. The infor-

Table 3.7
Examples of States' School Readiness Indicators*

Domain of readiness	Construct	Indicator
Ready Children		
Physical Well-being and Motor Development	Physical Well-being	% of children entering kindergarten with undetected vision or hearing problems: CT, ME, NH, RI, VA
	Motor Development	% of infants born with neural tube defects (e.g. spina bifida): KY
Language Development	Language Comprehension	% of students who meet reading proficiency standards in fourth grade: MOST STATES
	Emergent Literacy	% of kindergarten students who demonstrate age-appropriate pre-literacy skills: MA, NH
Cognition and General Knowledge	Mathematical Knowledge	% of students who meet mathematics reading proficiency standards in fourth grade: MOST STATES
Social and Emotional Development	Social Development	% of kindergarten children who appropriately establish and maintain relationships with peers and adults: KS, ME
Approaches Toward Learning		% of 1st graders retained: AZ, AR, CO
Ready schools		
Characteristics of Schools	Serve Children in Communities	% of school districts offering before and after-school programs: AR, MA, NH, WI
Transitional Practices		
Family and Community Supports	Early Care and Education Settings to School	% of districts requiring a transition plan between kindergarten and early education programs : KS, MA, WI
Health	Health Care	% of 2-year-olds with up-to-date immunizations: MOST STATES
Family-Child Activities	Support for Families of Preschoolers	% of children enrolled in public health programs who have a developmental screening by age 3: CA, MA, WI
Preschool Experience	Quality of Preschool Centers	Turnover rate for head teachers (or lead teachers) in child care centers: ME, KS, WI

*For a complete list of up-to-date indicators for each of the 17 states participating in the National School Readiness Indicators Initiative, visit the initiative website at www.gettingready.org. Additional information on use of indicators in the states can be found at http://aspe.hhs.gov and at www.childtrends.org.

mation is not being used to identify individual children or teachers. The focus is on aggregate (group) data that suggest how well the community is providing the opportunities and experiences essential for school readiness. Vermont officials hope that the availability of community-level data will act as a catalyst to foster discussion of whose responsibility it is that children arrive in school ready to learn and to encourage conversation at the community level of what it means to be ready for school and of what families and communities can do to support their children's readiness.

FUTURE DIRECTIONS

This review suggests that the period since the 1994 conference and the 1997 publication *Indicators of Children's Well-Being* (Hauser, Brown, & Prosser, 1997) has been one of a virtual growth spurt in terms of the development of indicators of school readiness. We see major progress in the development of measures as well as in the collection of new data, in both national and state data collection efforts. It is particularly exciting to see a more complex conceptualization of school readiness, grounded in reviews of research and practice, reflected in recent data collection efforts at both the national and state levels. Data are being collected on children's readiness, schools' readiness, and family and community supports for children's readiness, albeit with different surveys and data collection efforts giving different emphases to these components.

With the availability of major new data resources on school readiness at the national level as well as the deepening work at the state level, we are also seeing the multiple uses of school readiness indicators. In recent efforts, school readiness indicators have been used to do the following:

- provide a broad description of the condition of children and of schools, both overall, and for key subgroups;[13]
- provide a portrayal of how earlier development leads to children's school readiness, and how subsequent development builds from readiness at school entry;[14]
- provide a source of national data for benchmarking in state surveys;
- examine changes over time in measures of children's readiness as part of efforts to monitor state and community investments in early childhood;
- Identify patterns of concern and to begin to put in place policies and programs to address the patterns (see, e.g., Tarullo & McKey, 2001); and
- Provide a picture of where supports for children's school readiness are strong, and where they could be strengthened.

We expect that the coming decade will be a period of continued growth in the development and use of indicators of school readiness. As the work in this area continues to grow and mature, we see a number of possibilities for future focus. In particular, at the national level, we see that it would make a substantial contribution if the ECLS-K and Early Childhood Longitudinal Study-Birth Cohort data were collected on a recurrent basis, with new cohorts launched periodically. Although it would clearly be a major undertaking to complement these very substantial and important data collection efforts with recurrent data collection, to do so would permit indicators of school readiness to be tracked over time for successive cohorts of nationally representative samples of preschoolers and kindergartners. Similarly, it is important that the FACES survey continues to be collected for new cohorts of Head Start children over time so that indicators of school readiness can be tracked for this important group of children and families. It would be an important contribution if the NHES would establish a core of school readiness measures to collect in each subsequent year of data collection with a school readiness module. We look forward to the results of the school readiness survey planned for NHES 2007.

In addition, some school readiness constructs are not as well covered as others in the national data sets, and a review of measures to strengthen certain areas would be valuable. It is notable that across all of the national surveys, coverage of children's mathematical knowledge and other areas of cognitive development are much less systematic than coverage of children's language and literacy development. As noted earlier, recent efforts are focusing on developing measures for early mathematic concepts (Bridges, Berry, & Zaslow, 2003; U.S. Department of Health and Human Services, 2002). In addition, there has been limited focus on transition practices from early childhood care and education settings into kindergarten. Finally, relatively little attention has been given to supports related to perinatal health and health supports, or later health screening or care, as contributors to school readiness. These areas could be foci for further measures development.

At the state level, it will be important to monitor the extent to which states have a balanced set of indicators that reflect child outcomes as well as schools' readiness and family and community supports. It will also be important to monitor whether strategies involving direct child assessments continue to follow the principles that have been articulated for the assessment of young children. It will be especially important for states to identify the purpose of their state assessments and to match the data collection efforts to the purpose. Finally, it will be interesting to see whether, over time, there is convergence of the indicators of school readiness that states collect. This could be a powerful way to move, as a nation, toward a set of benchmarks to measure the progress of children from birth to school entry, even as individual states continue to measure additional benchmarks based on their own priorities and investments.

ACKNOWLEDGMENTS

The contributors from Child Trends gratefully acknowledge the John S. and James L. Knight Foundation for their support in preparing a literature review entitled *Background for Community-Level Work on School Readiness* (2000) that provided essential background for this chapter. We thank Kelly Maxwell, Donna Bryant, and Stephanie Ridley of North Carolina's Smart Start; and Baron Holmes of South Carolina's First Steps to School Readiness for insight into the design of school readiness efforts in their respective states; Sharon Lynn Kagan and Dick Clifford for first-hand information on the work of the National Education Goals Panel Goal 1 working groups; Kristin Moore and Brett Brown of Child Trends for their comments on this chapter; and Lindsay Pitzer, Stephanie Cochran, Thomson Ling, and Kevin Cleveland of Child Trends for assistance in preparing this chapter for publication.

The contributors from Chapin Hall and Assistant Secretary for Planning and Evaluation, U.S. Department of Health and Human Services, gratefully acknowledge all of the participants in the Child Indicators Project for the information and input they have provided through this collaborative project. They especially thank David Murphey of Vermont's Agency of Human Services. We are grateful to Harold Richman of Chapin Hall for his comments and support of the Initiative. Catherine Walsh of Rhode Island KIDS COUNT thanks the 17 state teams participating in the National School Readiness Indicators Initiative.

NOTES

1. Other contemporary data sets, such as the National Survey of America's Families, contain some measures pertaining to school readiness. However, the five data sets highlighted here are the most relevant in terms of target population and detail in measurement of school readiness.
2. In both kindergarten and first grade, language-minority children were administered an English language screening test. If they did not pass the screener in a given year, and their home language was Spanish, they were administered a math assessment in Spanish, as well as a psychomotor assessment in Spanish (kindergarten only). Therefore, language-minority children with limited English proficiency did not participate in the reading or general knowledge assessments.
3. Specific measurement instruments included the Peabody Picture Vocabulary Test-III (Dunn & Dunn, 1997), subtests of the Woodcock-Johnson Psycho-Educational Battery-Revised (Woodcock & Johnson, 1990), Phonemic Analysis Task from the Test of Language Development-III (Hammill & Newomer, 1996), and a modified version of the CAP Early Childhood Diagnostic Instrument (Mason & Stewart, 1989).
4. This information is based on the HSIS OMB package documentation (Section A.2). Because the kindergarten surveys are not yet available for review, the indicators are not noted in Table 3.2.
5. Although we recognize that significant advances have also been made by many states that are not participants in these initiatives, our focus here is on the progress made through these initiatives.
6. Fourteen states participated in the Child Indicators Project: Alaska, California, Delaware, Florida, Georgia, Hawaii, Maine, Maryland, Minnesota, New York, Rhode Island, Utah, Vermont, and West Virginia. States were selected on the basis of the readiness to make advancements and have a range of experience in this area. (More information is available on the Assistant Secretary for Planning and Evaluation web site: http://www.aspe.hhs.gov)
7. The "School Readiness Indicators Initiative: Making Progress for Young Children" involves 17 states, including Arizona, Arkansas, California, Colorado, Connecticut, Kansas, Kentucky, Maine, Massachusetts, Missouri, New

Hamphsire, New Jersey, Ohio, Rhode Island, Vermont, Virginia, and Wisconsin. More information on the 17-state project, coordinated by Rhode Island KIDS COUNT, is available at http://www.gettingready.org

8. Work Sampling is a method developed by Sam Meisels and colleagues that enables early child care and education providers to collect individual-level assessment data across the domains of child development through documentation of school projects and ongoing observations of progress within the classroom.

9. The four purposes of assessment are (a) to inform the course of instruction and support individual children's learning; (b) to identify special needs; (c) to perform program evaluation and monitoring of trends; and (d) to make decisions about individual students, teachers, classrooms, and programs ("high stakes" assessments).

10. A report from North Carolina exemplifies the use of representative samples to present an overview of children's progress statewide (see Maxwell et al., 2001).

11. We recognize that many other states aim to develop sets of indicators that reflect the multifaceted nature of school readiness, and are guided by the NEGP framework. For example, evaluations of North Carolina's early childhood initiative, Smart Start, used the NEGP framework for school readiness to guide measurement and analyses (Maxwell et al., 2001), as did the statewide evaluation of South Carolina's early childhood initiative, "First Steps to School Readiness" (Zaslow et al., 2003).

12. Schools also provide data on children's health insurance status, usual source of care, and screening for hearing and vision problems.

13. See, for example, recent ECLS-K reports (Denton & West, 2002; West, Denton, & Germino-Hauskin, 2000; West, Denton, & Reany, 2000).

14. See, for example, analyses of the ECLS-K by Hair, Halle, Terry-Humen, Lavelle, and Calkins (2006), and analyses of FACES by Resnick and Zill (2000).

REFERENCES

Arnett, J. (1989). Caregivers in day-care centers: Does training matter? *Journal of Applied Developmental Psychology, 10*, 541–552.

Bayley, N. (1993). *Bayley Scales of Infant Development, second edition: Manual.* San Antonio, TX: Psychological Corporation.

Blair, C. (2002). School readiness: Integrating cognition and emotion in a neurobiological conceptualization of children's functioning at school entry. *American Psychologist, 57*, 111–127.

Berry, D. J., Bridges, L. J., & Zaslow, M. J. (2003). *Early childhood measures profiles* (pp. 1–404). Washington, DC: Child Trends.

Caldwell, B. M., & Bradley, R. H. (2001). *Home inventory administration manual* (3rd ed.). Little Rock: University of Arkansas.

Calkins, J., Zaslow, M., Halle, T., & Margie, N. G. (2001). *School readiness in St. Paul* (Report prepared for the John S. and James L. Knight Foundation). Washington, DC: Child Trends.

Cavanaugh, D. A., Lippitt, J., & Moyo, O. (2000). Resource guide to federal policies affecting children's emotional and social development and readiness for school. *Off to a good start: Risk factors for academic and behavioral problems at the beginning of school and selected federal policies affecting children's social and emotional development and their readiness for school* (pp. 95–221). Chapel Hill, NC: University of North Carolina; FPG Child Development Center.

Child Outcomes Research and Evaluation and the Head Start Bureau Administration for Children and Families. (2003). *Head Start FACES 2000: A whole-
child perspective on program Performance* (fourth progress report). Washington, DC: U.S. Department of Health and Human Services.

Clifford, D. (2000, February). Comments made at the Workshop on Getting Positive Outcomes for Children in Child Care, Washington, DC.

Denton, K., & West, J. (2002). *Children's reading and mathematics achievement in
kindergarten and first grade* (NCES 2002-125). Washington, DC: U.S. Department of Education, National Center for Education Statistics.

Dunn, L. M., & Dunn, L. M. (1997). *Peabody Picture Vocabulary Test-Third edition.*
Circle Pines, MN: American Guidance Service.

Dunst, C., Jenkins, V., & Trivette, C. (1984). Family Support Scale: Reliability
and validity. *Journal of Individual, Family, and Community Wellness, 1,* 45–52.

Florida Partnership Board, School Readiness Performance Standards Work-
group. (2000). *Proposal for the assessment of children's school readiness.* Unpublished manuscript.

Forgione, P. D. (1998). *Early childhood education: Critical data needs for a critical
period in child development.* Paper prepared for hearing on "Are Our Children
Ready to Learn?" U.S. Senate, Committee on Labor and Human Resources.
Available: http://nces.ed.gov/pressrelease/senhrtest.html

Gresham, F. M., & Elliot, S. N. (1990). *Social Skills Rating System manual.* Circle
Pines, MN: American Guidance Service.

Hair, E., Halle, T., Terry-Humen, E., & Calkins, J. (2003). Children's school readiness in the ECLS-K: Predictions to academic, health, and social outcomes in
first grade. *Early Childhood Research Quarterly, 21,* 431–454.

Halle, T., Zaff, J., Calkins, J., & Margie, N. G. (2000). *Background for community-
level work on school readiness: A review of definitions, assessments, and investment
strategies. Part II: Reviewing the literature on contributing factors to school readiness.* Paper prepared for the John S. and James L. Knight Foundation.

Hammill, D. D., & Newomer, P. L. (1996). *Test of Language Development-Pri-
mary-Third edition.* Circle Pines, MN: American Guidance Service.

Harms, T., & Clifford, R. M. (1980). *Early Childhood Environment Rating Scale.*
New York: Teachers College Press.

Harms, T., & Clifford, R. M. (1989). *Family Day Care Rating Scale.* New York:
Teachers College Press.

Harms, T., Clifford, R. M., & Cryer, D. (1998). *Early Childhood Environment Rating Scale-Revised.* New York: Teachers College Press.

Hauser, R., Brown, B., & Prosser, W. (Eds.). (1997). *Indicators of child well-being.*
New York: Russell Sage Foundation.

Huffman, L. C., Mehlinger, S. L., & Kerivan, A. S. (2000). Risk factors for academic and behavioral problems at the beginning of school. *Off to a good start:
Risk factors for academic and behavioral problems at the beginning of school and
selected federal policies affecting children's social and emotional development
and their readiness for school.* Chapel Hill, NC: University of North Carolina;
FPG Child Development Center, 1–94.

Institute of Medicine. (2001). *Coverage matters: Insurance and health care* (M. S.
Coleman & A. Kellermann, Eds.). Washington, DC: National Academy Press.

Kagan, S. L., Moore, E., & Bredekamp, S. (1995). *Reconsidering children's
early development and learning: Toward common views and vocabulary.*
Washington, DC: National Education Goals Panel, Goal 1 Technical Planning Group.

Kurdek, L. A., & Sinclair, R. J. (2000). Psychological, family, and peer predictors of academic outcomes in first- through fifth-grade children. *Journal of Educational Psychology, 92*, 44–457.

La Paro, K. M., & Pianta, R. C. (2000). Predicting children's competence in the early school years: A meta-analytic review. *Review of Educational Research, 70*, 443–484.

Love, J. M., Aber, J. L., & Brooks-Gunn, J. (1994). *Strategies for assessing community progress toward achieving the first national educational goal* (MPR Reference No. 8113-110). Princeton, NJ: Mathematica Policy Research.

Love, J. M., Aber, J. L., & Brooks-Gunn, J. (1999). *Ready or not, here they come: Strategies for achieving school success for all Kansas City children.* Unpublished manuscript.

Love, J. M., Kisker, E. E., Ross, C., Raikes, H., Constantine, J., Boller, K., et al.. (2005). The effectiveness of Early Head Start for 3-year-old children and their parents: Lessons for policy and programs. *Developmental Psychology, 41*, 885–901.

Mason, J. M., & Stewart, J. (1989). *The CAP Early Childhood Diagnostic Instrument* (prepublication edition). American Testronics.

Margie, N. G., Halle, T., Zaslow, M., & Calkins, J. (2001). *School readiness in Charlotte* (Report prepared for the John S. and James L. Knight Foundation). Washington, DC: Child Trends.

Maxwell, K. L., Bryant, D. M., Ridley, S. M., & Keyes-Elstein, L. (2001). *North Carolina's kindergartners and schools: Summary report.* Chapel Hill: University of North Carolina, Frank Porter Graham Child Development Center. Retrieved July 3, 2001. Available http://www.fpg.unc.edu/~SchoolReadiness/.

National Education Goals Panel. (1997). *Getting a good start in school.* Washington, DC: Author.

National Education Goals Panel. (1998). *Principles and recommendations for early childhood assessments.* Washington, DC: Author.

National Research Council. (2001). *Eager to learn: Educating our preschoolers* (B.T. Bowman, M. S. Donovan, & M. S. Burns, Eds.). Washington, DC: National Academy Press.

National Research Council & Institute of Medicine. (2000). *From neurons to neighborhoods: The science of early childhood development* (J. P. Shonkoff & D. A. Phillips, Eds.). Washington, DC: National Academy Press.

Peisner-Feinberg, E. S., Burchinal, M. R., Clifford, R. M., Culkin, M. L., Howes, C., Kagan, S. L., et al. (1999). *The children of the Cost, Quality, and Outcomes Study go to school: Executive summary.* Chapel Hill: University of North Carolina at Chapel Hill, Frank Porter Graham Child Development Center.

Peth-Pierce, R. (2000). *A good beginning: Sending America's children to school with the social and emotional competence they need to succeed.* Bethesda, MD: Child Mental Health Foundations and Agencies Network.

Phillips, D. A., & Love, J. M. (1997). Indicators for school readiness, schooling, and child care in early to middle childhood. In R. M. Hauser, B. V. Brown, & W. R. Prosser (Eds.), *Indicators of children's well-being* (pp. 125–151). New York: Russell Sage Foundation.

Raver, C. C. (2002). Emotions matter: Making the case for the role of young children's emotional development for early school readiness. *Social Policy Report, 16*. Society for Research in Child Development.

Resnick, G., & Zill, N. (2001, April). *Unpacking quality in Head Start classrooms: Relationships among dimensions of quality at different levels of analysis.* Poster session presented at the Biennial Meeting of the Society for Research in Child Development, Minneapolis, MN.

Reynolds, A. J., & Bezruczko, N. (1993). School adjustment of children at risk through fourth grade. *Merrill-Palmer Quarterly, 39*, 457–480.

Saluja, G., Scott-Little, C., & Clifford, R. M. (2000). Readiness for school: A survey of state policies and definitions. *Early Childhood Research and Practice* [On-line serial], *2*(2). Retrieved July 3, 2001 from http://ecrp.uiuc.edu/v2n2/saluja.html

Shepard, L. A., Taylor, G. A., & Kagan, S. L. (1996). *Trends in early childhood assessment policies and practices.* Unpublished manuscript.

Snow, C. E., Burns, M. S., & Griffin, P. (Eds.). (1998). *Preventing reading difficulties in young children.* Washington, DC: National Academy Press.

Tarullo, L. B., & McKey, R. H. (2001, April). *Design and implications of the Head Start Family and Child Experiences Survey (FACES).* Paper presented at the Biennial Meeting of the Society for Research in Child Development, Minneapolis, MN.

U.S. Department of Health and Human Services. (2002). *Early childhood education and school readiness: Conceptual models, constructs, and measures* (Workshop summary). Retrieved September 5, 2003 from http://www.nichd.nih.gov/crmc/cdb/Kyle-workshop.pdf

U.S. Department of Health and Human Services Administration on Children, Youth, and Families. (2002). *Making a difference in the lives of infants, toddlers, and their families: The impacts of early Head Start, Vol. III.* Retrieved March 7, 2006 from http://www.acf.hhs.gov/programs/opre/ehs/ehs_resrch/reports/impacts_vol3/impacts_vol3.pdf

U.S. Department of Health and Human Services, Administration for Children Youth, and Families (2005). *Head Start impact study: First year findings.* Retrieved September 9, 2003 from http://www.acf.hhs.gov/programs/opre/hs/impact_study/reports/first_yr_finds/first_yr_finds.pdf

West, J., Denton, K., & Germino-Hausken, E. (2000). *America's kindergartners: Findings from the Early Childhood Longitudinal Study, Kindergarten Class of 1998-99, Fall 1998* (NCES 2000-070). Washington, DC: U.S. Department of Education, National Center for Education Statistics.

West, J., Denton, K., & Reaney, L. M. (2000). *The kindergarten year: Findings from the Early Childhood Longitudinal Study, Kindergarten Class of 1998-99* (NCES 2001-023). Washington, DC: U.S. Department of Education, National Center for Education Statistics.

Whitehurst, G. J., & Lonigan, C. J. (2002). Emergent literacy: Development from prereaders to readers. In S. B. Neuman & D. K. Dickinson (Eds.), *Handbook of early literacy research* (pp. 11–29). New York: Guilford.

Woodcock, R. W., & Johnson, M. B. (1990). *Woodcock-Johnson Psycho-Educational Battery-Revised.* Chicago: Riverside.

Woodcock, R. W., & Johnson, M. B. (2001). *Woodcock-Johnson III Tests of Achievement.* Itasca, IL: Riverside.

Zaslow, M., Calkins, J., & Halle, T. (2000). *Background for community-level work on school readiness: A review of definitions, assessments, and investment strategies. Part I: Defining and assessing school readiness-Building on the foundation of NEGP work* (Report prepared for the John S. and James L. Knight Foundation). Washington, DC: Child Trends.

Zaslow, M., & Halle, T. (2003). Statewide school readiness assessments: Challenges and next steps. In C. Scott-Little, S. L. Kagan, & R. M. Clifford (Eds.), *Assessing the state of state assessments: Perspectives on assessing young children* (pp. 57–65). Greensboro, NC: SERVE.

Zaslow, M., Halle, T., Calkins, J., & Margie, N. G. (2000). *School readiness in Miami* (Report prepared for the John S. and James L. Knight Foundation). Washington, DC: Child Trends.

Zaslow, M., Halle, T., Johnson, R., Bridges, L., Guzman, L., Pitzer, L., & Calkins, J. (2003). *First Steps and Further Steps: Early outcomes and lessons learned from South Carolina's school readiness initiative: 1999–2002 program evaluation report* (Report prepared for the State of South Carolina). Washington, DC: Child Trends.

What Do National and State National Assessment of Educational Progress Scores Tell Us About the Achievement of American K-12 Students?

Ann Flanagan
David Grissmer
University of Virginia

Achievement scores are a particularly good measure of the changing environment for our children, because research has linked achievement to the combined influence of families, communities, and schools. Changes in achievement scores over time must inevitably be traced to changes in the quality of the student's families, schools, or their communities. The link between achievement and the quality of families, communities, and schools must be interpreted to include the child's environment long before school entry—in fact, from conception—and to a broad definition of *community* that includes media and cultural influences and the quality of health, nutrition, and social support systems.

Changes in scores over time are one source of information about children's well-being, but achievement scores also vary dramatically among racial-ethnic groups, between advantaged and disadvantaged children, and across states. These differences also must be traced to differences in the characteristics of families, schools, and communities. A consistent explanation is needed based on empirical research that attempts to explain both changing achievement patterns over time and differences among racial-ethnic groups and differences across states and school districts.

Public policies seek to improve achievement directly through their influence on the quality of schools, families, and communities or indirectly through legislative and judicial intervention directed toward creating more equitable access to quality schools and communities. In the last 30 years, we have witnessed dramatic changes in our families, schools, and communities and in our social and educational policies. An important question is whether these changes have left an imprint on achievement scores. These changes include the following:

- *National efforts to equalize opportunity and reduce poverty that began in the mid-1960s and continued or expanded in subsequent decades.* These efforts included federally funded preschools (e.g., Head Start), compensatory funding of elementary schools with large numbers of poor students, desegregation of schools, affirmative action in college and professional school admissions, and expanded social welfare programs for poor families.
- *Changes in school attendance and school-related changes that were not primarily designed to equalize opportunity.* These changes include increased early schooling, greater per-pupil expenditures, smaller classes, significant changes in the characteristics of teachers, and systemic reform initiatives.
- *Changes in families and communities that may have been somewhat influenced by efforts to equalize opportunity and reduce poverty but that occurred mainly for other reasons.* Specifically, parents acquired more formal education, more children lived with only one parent, more children had only one or two siblings, and the proportion of children living in poverty rose. At the same time, poor Blacks concentrated more in inner cities, while the more affluent Blacks moved to the suburbs.

Seeking explanations for changing achievement trends and differences in achievement between groups is important for several reasons. In 1995, federal, state, and local governments spend approximately $500 billion per year in social, educational, and criminal justice expenditures on U.S. children and youth (Office of Science and Technology Policy, 1997).[1] About two thirds of these expenditures were directly for education, but most of the remaining expenditures would be expected to affect school performance through their influence on family and community quality.

The amount spent on children appears to have increased substantially over time (Fuchs & Rekliss, 1992), although there is debate about the magnitude of the real increase in spending (Rothstein & Miles, 1995; Grissmer, Flanagan, Kawata, & Williamson, 2000). Thus, an important set of public policy questions is associated with how effective this increased spending has been at improving the well-being of our children.

Achievement scores are also a key predictor of years of schooling, and together these indicators are key predictors of labor market performance; future health status; welfare utilization; drug, alcohol, and tobacco use; teen pregnancy; and criminal behavior (Institute of Medicine, 1994, 2001; National Research Council, 2001; National Research Council & Institute of Medicine, 1999, 2001). Thus, doing poorly in school provides an early indicator of important later behavior, and solving these problems independent of improving schooling outcomes seems problematic.

Achievement gaps may also be at the heart of racial divides in the country. In their landmark volume on the Black-White achievement gap, Jencks and Phillips (1998) suggested that reducing the gap in scores between Black and White students would do more to move America toward racial equality than any other alternative. They argued that eliminating the gap might eventually solve many of the others issues that separate the races: the need for affirmative action policies in colleges and jobs, the gap in wages, and perhaps even segregated communities.

Achievement scores in elementary and middle schools also fill an important gap in indicators of children's well-being. Most long-term measures of children's well-being are collected at birth or during the teen years. Nationally representative achievement scores in reading and math have been collected at fourth and eighth grades since 1971 and provide one of the few consistent measures of well-being between birth and adolescence.

Finally, improving schools and educational outcomes has been near the top of the issues concerning Americans and its elected representatives since the mid-1980s. These concerns were triggered by the *Nation At Risk* report (National Commission on Excellence in Education, 1983), making achievement scores one of the more visible and watched measures of child well-being by the American public. The quality of educational outcomes is perceived to be linked to the future success of our economy and our international competitiveness. Current perceptions based on international achievement comparisons place the quality of American K-12 education at the middle or below the quality of that in other countries. According to this view, maintaining competitiveness will require a better educated workforce. Because the future labor force will increasingly be made up of racial-ethnic minorities, improving educational outcomes for these groups would seem to be important to our country's future.

There are also very mixed perceptions of whether American K–12 educational outcomes are declining or improving and of the efficacy of investing additional money in public schools to improve outcomes (Greenwald, Hedges, & Laine, 1996; Grissmer et al., 2000; Hanushek, 1996; Hedges, Laine, & Greenwald, 1994; Krueger, 1998). Unfortunately, there are widespread misperceptions about achievement trends and comparisons partly due to the high visibility of perverse measures of achievement (SAT scores) and to naive interpretations arising from achievement trends and differences (Grissmer, 2000).

The most highly visible "indicator" of achievement for the American public is the SAT score, and Americans appear to judge the quality of K-12 education partly by SAT scores. Figure 4.1 shows the results of

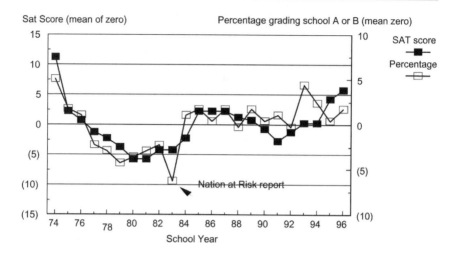

Figure 4.1. Comparison of the trends in SAT scores with percentage of adults giving schools a grade of A or B.

annual public opinion poll that asked adults to grade U.S. schools. The percentage of adults who gave schools an A or a B is graphed against changes in annual average SAT scores.[2] The data show that public opinion appears to follow the SAT trends.

The well-known flaws in the SAT scores for monitoring national achievement trends partly result from the self-selected sample (Advisory Group on the Scholastic Aptitude Test Score Decline, 1977; Grissmer, Kirby, Berends, & Williamson, 1994; Koretz, 1986, 1987; Rock, 1987). The scores are biased downward because of an increasing percentage of students taking the test and the changing composition of test-takers. However, another source of bias arises because the students making the largest achievement gains from 1970 to 1990-minority and disadvantaged students-are largely missed by the SAT because they do not go to college. Ironically, if K–12 education improves, allowing more children to attend college, then SAT scores will decline. Thus, SAT scores are probably a perverse indicator of K–12 school quality. Because of their visibility, SAT scores have caused serious misconceptions about student performance and the quality of schools.

In this chapter, we examine data from the results of the National Assessment of Educational Progress (NAEP), given to a nationally representative sample of 9-, 13-, and 17-year-old students since the early 1970s and to representative samples of students within states since 1990. It is the only data on the basis of which statistically valid trends and state comparisons can be made. We first describe the NAEP data and review the major national trends in reading and math achievement and provide current explanations for these trends based on empirical research. Next, we focus on the pattern of score differences across states and provide the current explanations for these differences based on the empirical literature. Finally, we provide recommendations on improving NAEP data to monitor the well-being of children and summarize what the achievement scores tell us about children's well-being.

NATIONAL ASSESSMENT OF EDUCATIONAL PROGRESS ACHIEVEMENT TESTS

The NAEP are the only tests using nationally representative samples of U.S. students that can be used to track long-term national trends and accurately measure differences between states (Campbell, Hombo, & Mazzeo, 2000). The tests have been given to national samples of 9-, 13-, and 17-year-old students since 1969. The early tests were in science, math, and reading and were administered approximately every 4 years through 1988 and more frequently after 1988. Writing tests were started in 1984, and geography, history, civics, and the arts have been tested more recently.

There are two national NAEP samples, called the *Long Term Trend* and the *Main Assessment*. The Long Term Trend is a set of questions that have remained relatively stable over the course of the tests and are used to measure the long-term trends. Because the set of stable questions were begun in the 1970s, these questions tend to measure more basic skills of students. The Main Assessment is a test that changes in response to changing curricula and educational practices and reflects more critical thinking skills through constructed response questions requiring sentences to a few paragraphs. Because this test periodically changes the content of what is tested, it can reliably measure short-term trends, but it cannot be used to track long-term trends. The state NAEP tests begun in 1990 are based on the redesign of the national Main Assessment in 1990, but the testing framework has remained the same since 1990, allowing reliable trends through 1998. In this chapter, we use data from all three tests.

NAEP data collection takes students approximately 90 min to complete for a given subject. Matrix sampling of questions is used to allow testing a broad range of knowledge while limiting the time each student is tested. Bib spiraling of questions ensures that effects from the placement of questions within booklets and grouping of questions are minimized. The sampling is based on a multistage design that first chooses a geographical area (county, group of counties, or Metropolitan Statistical Area), then schools within geographical areas, and then students within schools. Public school samples are stratified to achieve increased racial-ethnic minority representation. The NAEP samples are stratified to allow the reporting of scores for three mutually exclusive location types: (a) central city, (b) urban fringe/large town, and (c) rural/small town. National samples were over 25,000 in the 1970s but declined to 5,000 to 6,000 in the 1990s.[3]

The national NAEP samples are insufficient to measure achievement at the state level. The absence of comparable state achievement measures stymied efforts to determine which states and localities were performing better than others and to identify the reasons for better performance. In 1990, representative samples of students in participating states were tested to allow valid comparison of achievement performance across states.[4] Nine state tests have been given between 1990 and 1998 in fourth- and eighth-grade reading and math.

Although the primary purpose of NAEP has been to simply monitor the achievement of American students, the scores are increasingly being used to evaluate the effects on youth from the dramatic changes in families, communities, and schools and from our nation's educational and social policies. The 17-year-olds tested by the NAEP in 1971 would have grown up in families and communities and attended schools largely unaffected by the changes cited earlier; however, those recently tested would have lived their entire lives in families, communities, and schools reshaped by these policies. It would be hard to take a position about the quality of our families, communities, and schools and the effectiveness of social and educational policies that would be inconsistent with the trends in the NAEP data.

LONG-TERM NATIONAL ASSESSMENT OF EDUCATIONAL PROGRESS TRENDS

Overall NAEP scores show small to modest gains from 1971 to 1996 for all three age groups and in both reading and math. The gains in reading were small-approximately 0.10 standard deviations (3 percentile points) or less for all age groups. However, math gains were larger for 9- and 13-year-old students-between 0.15 and 0.30 standard deviations. However, these aggregate results mask important differences by racial-ethnic groups.

Across ages and subjects, the largest gains in scores occurred for Black students, but significant gains were also registered by Hispanic and lower scoring White students, with small or no gains registered by average and higher scoring White students (Grissmer et al., 1994; Grissmer, Flanagan, & Williamson, 1998a, 1998b; Hauser, 1998; Hedges & Nowell, 1998).[5] Figure 4.2 shows Black and White seventeen-year-olds' reading and math scores between 1971 and 1996.[6] Figures 4.3 and 4.4 show the same data for 13- and 9-year-olds. A difference between Black and White scores at a given year represents a change in the Black-White gap. The following points stand out:

- The Black-White gap narrowed for all ages in both subjects due to substantial gains in Black students' scores while White students registered much smaller gains.

Standard Deviation Units

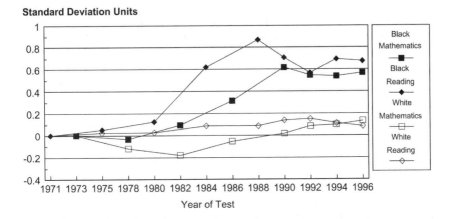

Figure 4.2. National Assessment of Educational Progress mathematics and reading scores for age 17 students by race.

Standard Deviation Units

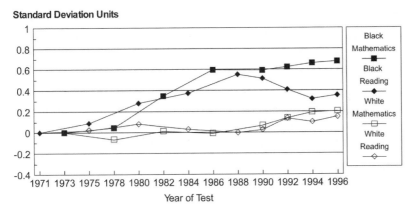

Figure 4.3. National Assessment of Educational Progress mathematics and reading scores for age 13 students by race.

• The Black-White gap narrowed the most for 13- and 17-year-olds due to dramatic increases in Black scores from the late 1970s to the late 1980s whereby Black gains were 0.6 to 0.7 standard deviations above White gains.

• For 13- and 17-year-olds, the gap stabilized or widened in the 1990s due to significant declines in Black reading scores and stable Black math scores while White math scores were increasing. By 1996, Black students' gains were between 0.2 and 0.6 standard deviations greater than White students' gains.

• The Black–White gap for 9-year-olds narrowed by 0.25 to 0.35 standard deviations by 1996. The pattern of gains among Black 9-year-olds is quite different from the pattern among Black adolescents, and the pattern is somewhat different for reading and math. Black 9-year-olds gained more than older Blacks during the 1970s and gained less than older Blacks during the 1980s. Although Black 9-year-old reading scores also show declines after 1988, unlike adolescent reading scores, they later returned to 1988 levels. Black 9-year-olds' math scores continued increasing after 1988.

We ordinarily think of learning both reading and math as a cumulative process where the level of early achievement partially affects the level of later achievement. So, achievement gains at 9 years old might be expected to translate into gains at 13 and 17, and gains at 13 translate into gains at 17. However, other patterns by age are also possible. Many early interventions appear to boost achievement scores only in the early grades and have little effect on achievement at older ages (Barnett, 1995). So, this pattern would show gains at age 9, but much smaller or no gains at older ages. A third possibility would be gains at older ages without gains at younger ages. These might be caused, for instance, by tougher curricula in middle and high school with no changes in K–3 curriculum.

Charting scores by entering school cohorts tests which of these patterns are present (see Figures 4.5 and 4.6). We characterize cohorts by the year in which they would normally have been in first grade, namely, the year in which they were 6 years old.[7] Each entering school cohorts could have taken three tests in their school career-at ages 9, 13, and 17. For instance, Figure 4.5 shows that the 1977 entering school cohort scored 0.44, 0.38, and 0.84 standard deviations above the earliest cohort measured at ages 9, 13, and 17, respectively. Because NAEP tests

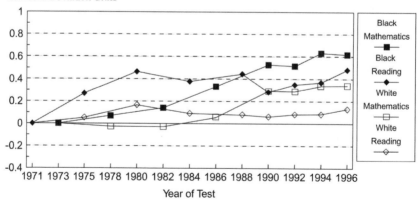

Figure 4.4.   National Assessment of Educational Progress mathematics and reading scores for age 9 students by race.

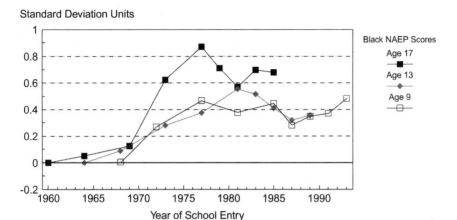

Figure 4.5.   National Assessment of Educational Progress (NAEP) reading scores for Black students by year of school entry.

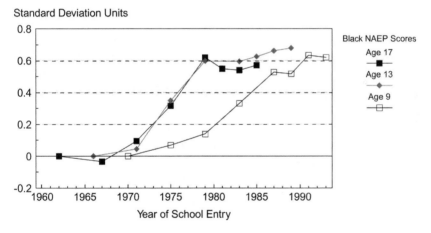

Figure 4.6.   National Assessment of Educational Progress (NAEP) mathematics scores for black students by year of school entry.

have not been given at regular intervals, few cohorts have all three scores. However, we connect the scores for each age group so that the pattern within each cohort can more easily be detected.

The data show that Black gains were largely confined to a group of about 10 cohorts born in the mid-1960s to mid-1970s and entering school around 1970 to 1980. For later cohorts, Black scores and the Black-White achievement gap have-for most age groups and subjects-remained stable or declined.

The cohort data show little evidence of the pattern of early gains that fade by later grades. Instead, the data show evidence that gains at age 9 are usually followed by equal or larger gains at older ages. For reading, 9- and 13-year-old scores show similar gains within cohorts, whereas 17-year-old scores show additional gains over those of younger ages. For math, it indicates that much of the early gains for the 1970–80 cohorts occurred after age 9, although later gains at age 9 were not matched by gains at older ages. Thus, the data show evidence for some cohort effects that appear to lift scores for all age groups, but it also shows evidence for age specific effects that differ for reading and math.

Even when Black gains were largest, they never came close to eliminating the Black-White gap. The largest reduction in the gap was for 17-year-olds' reading scores between 1971 and 1988. In 1971, the median Black student scored between the 10th and 12th percentiles of the White distribution. By 1988, the median Black student scored between the 26th and 28th percentiles of the White distribution. For the other age groups, the gap did not narrow as much.

The most striking feature of the NAEP results for Blacks is the size of adolescents' gains for cohorts entering from 1968-72 to 1976-80. These gains were 0.6 standard deviations averaged across reading and math. Such large gains for very large national populations over such short time periods are rare, if not unprecedented. Scores on IQ tests given to national populations seem to have increased gradually and persistently throughout the 20th century, both in the United States and elsewhere (Flynn, 1987; Neisser, 1998). However, no evidence exists in these data involving large populations showing gains even close to the magnitude of the gains made by Black student cohorts over a 10-year period.

Even in intensive programs explicitly aimed at raising test scores, it is unusual to obtain gains of this magnitude. Early childhood interventions are widely thought to have the largest potential effect on academic achievement. Yet only a handful of "model" programs have reported gains as large as one half a standard deviation (Barnett, 1995). These programs were very small-scale programs with intensive levels of intervention. Even when early childhood programs did produce large initial gains, the effects usually faded at later ages. Among Blacks who entered school between roughly 1968 and 1978, in contrast, the gains were very large among older students and were not confined to small samples but occurred nationwide.

EXPLAINING THE PATTERN OF NATIONAL ASSESSMENT OF EDUCATIONAL PROGRESS TRENDS

Beginning in the mid-1990s, research was directed toward explaining the pattern of differential gains by race and for low and higher scoring White students. Hypotheses focused on changes in the families, schools, and communities and the impact of social and educational policies emanating from civil rights legislation and War on Poverty programs (Grissmer, Flanagan, & Williamson, 1998b). The large gains for minority and disadvantaged students, as well as the smaller gains (or lack of gain) among average and higher scoring White students, posed a challenge to the thesis that additional spending in education, especially for compensatory programs, and social programs was ineffective. The timing of the Black gains by age coincides with the broad-scale implementation of such efforts if one assumes that most of the effects would occur only if students experienced these changes from the early grades forward.

Two studies have made estimates of the net impact of changes in family characteristics during this period (Cook & Evans, 2000; Grissmer et al., 1994). Surprising some, both studies predicted gains in achievement between 1970 and 1990 based on changing family characteristics. The predicted gains mainly occurred because of higher parental education levels and smaller family size. Higher gains were predicted for Black students due to much larger increases in parental education levels and larger reductions in family size. However, these gains could account for the smaller score gains among all Whites but could explain only about one quarter of the Black gains.

Jencks and Phillips (1998) reported three analyses that focused on the convergence of the Black-White gap in the 1970s and early 1980s and the subsequent stabilization or divergence beginning in 1988 (Grissmer, Flanagan, & Williamson, 1998b; Hedges & Nowell, 1998; Phillips, Crouse, & Ralph, 1998). Two of the studies used NAEP data as well as achievement and survey data from other studies. All agree that significant narrowing occurred for cohorts born before about 1978—but no further narrowing occurred for later cohorts. Although the Black-White gap for reading actually widened beginning in 1988, Phillips et al. (1998) concluded that the widening was not statistically significant.

Furthermore, Grissmer, Flanagan, and Williamson (1998b) suggested that the timing of the Black gains by age group and region suggested two major hypotheses for the gains. The first hypothesis was based on changes in schooling: changing pupil:teacher ratios and class sizes, changing teacher characteristics, and changing curricula. Per-pupil spending increased during this period, and the increase was disproportionately spent on compensatory programs directed toward minority and lower income students or to programs that might have disproportionate effects on their scores. Pupil:teacher ratios fell nationally in this period of rising minority NAEP scores by approximately 8 students per teacher-similar to reductions in the Tennessee experiment.[8] Experimental evidence now suggests that minority and low-income students have much larger effects on achievement from such reductions (Finn & Achilles, 1999; Krueger, 1999; Nye, Hedges, & Konstantopoulos, 1999a, 1999b). The national Black score gains that would be predicted by the Tennessee experimental results are not inconsistent with explaining part of these national gains (Ferguson, 1998; Finn & Achilles, 1999; Grissmer et al., 1998; Krueger, 1998). So, increased resources and the differential direction of resources to minority and disadvantaged children remain as viable explanations in accounting for Black and low-scoring White achievement gains.

A second explanation emerged, more closely related to the changes engendered by the civil rights movement and the War on Poverty. De-segregation could explain only part of such gains, because desegrega-tion only occurred in the South in this period, whereas Black score gains occurred in all regions (see Figure 4.7). Other suggested effects were a possible shift in the motivation for and attitudes toward education of Black parents and students stemming from better opportunities for fu-ture schooling and jobs. An additional possible shift from these efforts could have occurred in the behavior and attitudes of teachers of Black students that resulted in increased attention and resources.

Analysis of NAEP scores appears to be central to the debates about changes in American families and schools and the effectiveness of social and educational policies. The effective absence of these scores from these national debates has allowed many widespread beliefs to proliferate that seem to be at odds with the NAEP results. The NAEP data do not suggest that families have deteriorated since 1970. Neither do they suggest that schools have squandered money or that social and educational policies aimed at helping minorities have failed. Instead, they suggest that family environments changed in positive ways from 1970 to 1996, that the im-plementation of the policies associated with the civil rights movement and the War on Poverty may be a viable explanation for large gains in Black scores and that certain changes in U.S. schools and curriculum are consistent with NAEP score gains. Although this evidence alone cannot reject the hypotheses about deteriorating families and schools and the in-effectiveness of social and educational policies, the advocates of such be-

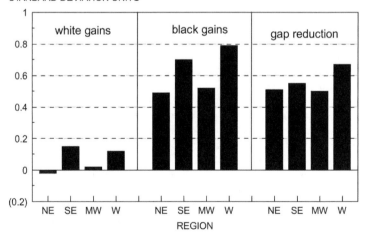

Figure 4.7.   Change in NAEP scores for 13- and 17-year-old students averaged across math and reading tests between the 1970s and 1992. MW = Midwest, NE = Northeast, SE = Southeast, W = West.

liefs must provide an explanation for NAEP scores consistent with their positions. The NAEP scores from 1971 through 1988 generally support a more positive picture of our families, schools, and public policies; however, trends in Black achievement since 1988-90 have been more discouraging, and it is critical to understand why the gains have stalled.

STATE ACHIEVEMENT PATTERNS

Descriptive characteristics of the 11 state reading and math tests given from 1990 to 2000 are shown in Table 4.1 (Campbell, Donahue, Reese, & Phillips, 1996; Miller, Nelson, & Naifeh, 1995; Reese, Miller, Mazzeo, & Dossey, 1997; Shaughnessy, Nelson, & Norris, 1998). Because state participation was voluntary, the sample of states changes from test to test. A total of 46 states have taken at least one test, with about 35 states participating in most tests. Two types of exclusions from testing are allowed: (a) limited English proficiency and (b) individualized education plan/disabled. Approximately 1% to 2% of students nationally are excluded for limited English proficiency and about 4% to 6% for individualized education plan/disabled.[9]

The results of seven reading and math test given at either the fourth- or eighth-grade level across states between 1990 and 1996 are characterized in Figure 4.8 (Campbell et al., 1996; Miller et al., 1995; Reese et al., 1997; Shaughnessy et al., 1998). The scores are averaged across all tests in which each state participated. The pattern of scores shows that smaller, more rural northern states are disproportionately in the upper part of the distribution, whereas southern states disproportionately appear in the lower half of the rankings. Highly urban eastern, midwestern, and western states tend to be closer to the middle of the distribution. However, exceptions are present in nearly all categories.

Table 4.1

Description of Eleven State NAEP Reading and Math Tests Given Between 1990–2000

Year	Subject	Grade Level	States Tested	Range-Student samples	Range-School samples
1990	Math	8	38	1,900-2,900	30 – 108
1992	Math	4	42	1,900-2,900	44 – 143
1992	Reading	4	42	1,800-2,800	44 – 148
1992	Math	8	42	2,000-2,800	28 – 112
1994	Reading	4	39	2,000-2,800	51 – 117
1996	Math	4	44	1,800-2,700	51 – 132
1996	Math	8	41	1,800-2,700	30-116
1998	Reading	4	39	1,700-2,700	65-117
1998	Reading	8	35	1,700-2,500	31-110

Source: NAEP Trial State Assessment Program 1990, 1992, 1994, 1996, and 1998.

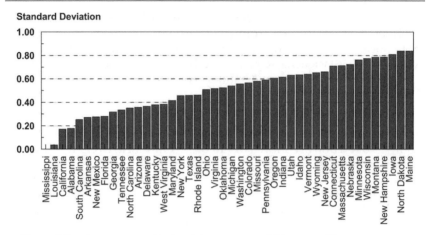

Figure 4.8.   Average state National Assessment of Educational Progress scores across seven tests.

The difference between the scores for the highest and lowest states is 0.75 to 1 standard deviation across tests. Average scores in the highest ranked state would be approximately between the 62nd and 67th percentiles nationally, whereas average scores from the lowest state would be around the 33nd to 38th percentile. This represents a significant variation in test scores among students from different states.

EXPLAINING THE PATTERN ACROSS STATES

Family Effects

Research that attempts to explain the variance in test scores across populations of diverse groups of students shows that family and demographic variables explain the largest part of total explained variance (Grissmer et al., 2000). Among commonly collected family characteristics, the strongest associations with test scores are parental education levels, family income, and race-ethnicity. Secondary predictors are family size, the age of mother at child's birth, and family mobility. Other variables, such as being in a single-parent family and having a working mother, are sometimes significant after controlling for other variables.[10] Because the states differ significantly in the racial-ethnic composition of students and in the characteristics of the families of students, one would expect that a significant part of the differences in the NAEP test scores might be accounted for by these differences.

The differences among states in our sample for eight family/demographic measures for families with children 8 through 10 years old are summarized in Table 4.2. The racial/demographic composition of states varies dramatically, with less than 1% of students being Black in many small northern states to almost 50% in Mississippi. The Hispanic student population is less than 5% in most states but rises to almost 50% in

Table 4.2

Range of Variation in Family Characteristics Across States In Our Analysis

Characteristic	Mean	Min.	Max.
Black (%)[a]	12.5	0.2	48.4
Hispanic (%)[a]	9.6	1.7	49.8
Parents' highest education, college degree (%)[a]	25.9	17.5	40.0
Parents' highest education, less than high school diploma (%)[a]	14.5	5.9	25.9
Family income (000)[a]	35.0	25.1	49.0
Teen births (%)[b]	12.8	7.2	21.3
Single parent (%)[a]	18.9	10.1	31.6
Working mothers (%)[a]	69.4	53.9	78.5
Family mobility (%)[c]	64.8	50.0	75.9

[a]*Source*: 1990 Census, Characteristics are for families with children 8–10 years old.
[b]*Source*: Statistical Abstract, 1993, Table 102.
[c]*Source*: 1992 4th Grade NAEP test (family did not move in last two years).

New Mexico. States also vary considerably in the average levels of parental education and family income and the proportion of births to teen parents and single parent families. A measure of family mobility—the percentage of families who did not move in the last 2 years—also varies, from less than 55% in Texas, Arizona, California, and Florida to over 74% in Vermont, New Hampshire, and North Dakota.

Not surprisingly, over two thirds of the variance in achievement scores across states is accounted for by differing family characteristics. The northern rural states have a very small proportion of minority students, single-parent families and births to teen mothers, better than average parental education and income, and low family mobility. These characteristics, independent of school characteristics, explain their high scores. The northern urban states generally have similar family characteristics to the northern rural states in their rural and suburban areas, but opposite characteristics in their central cities. This combination places their overall state scores near the middle of the state distribution. Southern states have the lowest scores because of their high proportion of minority students, low parental education and family income, high teen birth and single-parent family rates, and high family mobility.

The pattern of scores across the nation can be more easily characterized by region and locality (Grissmer & Flanagan, 2001). The average scores based on eight national Main Assessment NAEP reading and math tests given between 1990 and 1998 are shown in Figure 4.9.[11] Students in the rural and suburban areas of the Northeast and Midwest—approximately one third of students nationally—score significantly higher than nearly every other region and locality. The scores of these students would place them near the top of international comparisons. White stu-

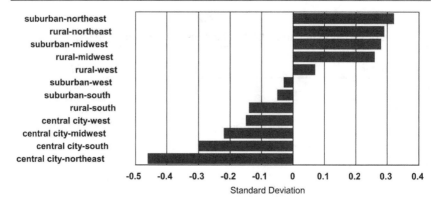

Figure 4.9.   Average scores across eight National Assessment of Educational Progress Main Assessments given from 1990 through 1998 in math and reading at fourth and eighth grade.

dents in these areas-almost 30% of students nationally-would very likely place first in international competition.

However, central city students in these two regions are among the lowest scoring in the nation. Black and White students in central cities in these two regions have among the lowest scores compared with Black and White students in other regions or localities. The gap between central city and suburban scores are largest in these two regions. The states with the largest Black-White score gap are Minnesota, Connecticut, Wisconsin, and Michigan-all relatively high-spending states in the Northeast or Midwest. The rural and suburban students in the South and West score near the national average, whereas central city students, regardless of region, score the lowest.

The location of the students in the lowest 20th percentile of achievement from these tests are identified in Figure 4.10, which shows that approximately 42% of low-scoring students are in the South, and two thirds of low-scoring students are either in the South or central cities. White students constitute 37.6% of those in the lowest quintile, whereas Black students constitute 32.8% and Hispanics 29.6%. These data suggest that child well-being differs markedly across region and locality. Although family characteristics account for a large part of this variance, the question is whether school characteristics also play a role.

School Effects

The variance across states in the level of expenditure per pupil and how that money is spent is very large. There are several sources of nonfamily influence on state education policies and characteristics. Because educational funding and policymaking is inherently a political process, differences in political persuasion and leadership at all levels of policymaking

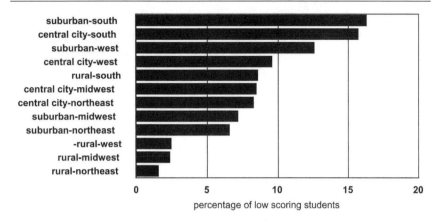

Figure 4.10.   The location of students scoring in the lowest quintile of scores across eight National Assessment of Educational Progress Main Assessments given from 1990 through 1998 in math and reading at fourth and eighth grade.

can produce differences that do not reflect the characteristics of families. The courts have also influenced school policies through enforcement of policies designed to produce equity and adequacy in educational opportunity. The states also differ widely in their historical reliance on various sources of taxation for education and on funding reliance from local, state, and national sources. Thus, states and communities will have different vulnerability to economic cycles that can influence educational spending.

We illustrate the differences using six common measures: (a) per-pupil spending, (b) pupil:teacher ratio, (c) teacher salary, (d) teacher degree levels, (d) teacher experience, and (e) proportion of children in public prekindergarten (see Table 4.3).

One method to estimate the effect of state-specific social and educational policies independent of family characteristics is to estimate random effect models (Grissmer et al., 2000). These estimates essentially provide measures of the difference in scores across states for students with similar family background. Such estimates will tell us whether the score differences for similar students among state are statistically significant and, if so, identify states at each extreme.

The results in Table 4.4 show that the estimated range of score differences for students from similar families is, at most, about one third of a standard deviation, or 11 to 12 percentile points on a national scale.[12] In general, the results show three bands of states within which differences cannot be statistically distinguished with present scores. The results show that 8 to 12 states have statistically significant, higher random effects than average states, whereas 10 to 12 states have statistically significant, lower random effects than the average state. There is a broad range of states near the middle that cannot be statistically distinguished.

Table 4.3

Range of Variation in State Education Characteristics Among States in Our Analysis

Characteristic	M	Min.	Max.
Pupil: teacher ratio	18.1	14.2	26.4
Per pupil expenditure (000)[a,b]	5.96	4.00	9.20
Teacher salary (000)[a,b]	34.4	28.3	44.0
% Teachers without advanced degree[a]	57.3	15.0	88.0
% Teachers with 0-3 years of experience[a]	9.6	3.3	14.0
% Teachers with 20 plus years of experience[a]	24.0	15.2	37.9
% Students in public pre-kindergarten[a]	6.8	0.2	30.8
% Teachers reporting inadequate resources[c]	40.1	17.0	57.0

[a]*Source*: Digests of Educational Statistics (1980-1998).
[b]Constant 1993-94 dollars adjusted for Cost of Living Differences Across States.
[c]NAEP teacher survey for 4th grade teachers in 1992.

Unlike raw scores, the results show some southern states in the top ranks and some northern states in the lower ranks. States with high family income and education appear throughout the table, as do states with high and low percentages of minorities. Some states, such as Montana, Iowa, North Dakota, and Maine, have high raw scores as well as high value-added scores. States with similar raw scores in the same regions can appear with wide separations. In particular, Minnesota and Wisconsin have similar raw scores (and family characteristics) but statistically different scores for similar students. Other examples are Georgia and Tennessee; Maine, Vermont, and New Hampshire; and Montana, North Dakota, and Nebraska.

Perhaps the most striking difference is between Texas and California, two states that have similar demographic characteristics. Research also identifies some of the educational characteristics that account for these differences. Other things equal, states with higher per-pupil spending have higher scores. However, how the money is spent appears to be as important. States that have lower pupil:teacher ratios in lower grades, higher participation in public prekindergarten, teachers who report better resources, and lower teacher turnover rates have higher scores for students from similar families. The research suggests that these effects are generally observed with greater frequency in states with high scores for students from similar families. For instance, California had the largest pupil:teacher ratio in the nation, teachers who reported very inadequate resources, and no public prekindergarten program. Texas, on the other hand, had pupil:teacher ratios below the national average, the largest

Table 4.4
A value-added measures from a random effect model (Standard Deviation units)

State	SES	State	SES
Texas	0.200***	Florida	−0.002
Wisconsin	0.1401***	Ohio	−0.007
Montana	0.1081***	Massachusetts	−0.013
Iowa	0.1031***	Colorado	−0.018
Maine	0.0841***	Idaho	−0.022
Indiana	0.0831***	Washington	−0.027
Georgia	0.0791***	New York	−0.029
Missouri	0.0645**	New Hampshire	−0.033
Oklahoma	0.05510*	Arkansas	−0.039
North Dakota	0.05310*	Delaware	−0.051***
New Jersey	0.05210*	Maryland	−0.051***
Nebraska	0.04510*	Tennessee	−0.051*
New Mexico	0.039	Oregon	−0.054
Virginia	0.036	Kentucky	−0.063***
Arizona	0.029	Mississippi	−0.067*
Wyoming	0.029	Louisiana	−0.089***
Connecticut	0.024	Alabama	−0.090***
South Carolina	0.024	Utah	−0.092***
Michigan	0.017	West Virginia	−0.109***
North Carolina	0.016	Vermont	−0.121***
Pennsylvania	0.015	Rhode Island	−0.128***
Minnesota	0.010	California	−0.153***

Note: Significant levels are indicated by *, **, and *** respectively.

share of children in public prekindergarten of any state, and teachers who reported high levels of resources.

IMPROVING THE NATIONAL ASSESSMENT OF EDUCATIONAL PROGRESS DATA

The NAEP data provide important indicators for assessing children's well-being and are becoming central to evaluating the impact of educational and social policies. Improving these measures can be done in several ways (Grissmer & Flanagan, 2000). Here we address two issues: (a) a redesign of the sample to be district rather than school based and (b) improving family variables.

A SCHOOL DISTRICT NATIONAL ASSESSMENT OF EDUCATIONAL PROGRESS SAMPLE

If NAEP could become a school district sample rather than a school sample, then historical data from school districts (not available at the school level of aggregation) could be used in the formulation of variables. A district-level sample would also result in improved family variables in NAEP data, because census data would be available for most school districts. At present, family variables in NAEP cannot be improved with census data at the school level, because privacy concerns prohibit their use within school areas. A school district sample would also address another NAEP deficiency–namely, the absence of several educational policy variables not available at the school level, such as per-pupil spending. A much wider and better defined set of educational policy variables is readily available at the school district level and is already being collected. Thus a school district, rather than school level, NAEP sample would be desirable from the standpoint of improving family controls and educational policy variables.

Another advantage of moving to a district sample is that comparisons of scores could be made for major urban and suburban area school districts. It is the urban school systems that pose the largest challenge to improving student achievement, and being able to develop models of NAEP scores across the major urban school districts could provide critical information in evaluating effective policies across urban districts.

IMPROVING FAMILY-LEVEL VARIABLES

The primary objective of NAEP has always been seen as monitoring trends in achievement rather than explaining those trends. One result of this philosophy is that few family variables have been collected with NAEP. Compared with family data collected with other national achievement data, or on other government surveys dealing with children's issues, NAEP collects very few family variables. In addition, the quality of the family variables collected has always been questioned, because they are reported by the students tested. The perception of weak family variables may partially explain why NAEP scores have not been used more frequently in research on educational and social policies.

A comparison of NAEP family data with census data at the state level finds that NAEP variables for race and family type (single parent or two parent) match census data well (Grissmer et al., 1998). However, students substantially inflate their parents' education level at the college level. Fourth-graders report that 58% of their families include a college graduate, compared to 26% in the census; comparable figures for eighth-graders are 42% compared to 25% in the census. However, reports of "high school only" and "not a high school graduate" are much more accurate. Students appear to be unable to distinguish between "some college" and "college graduate," and individuals using NAEP data should combine these two categories when using the data.

There are several ways that the family variables can be improved in the NAEP data collection. Although there may be ways of improving children's responses, and some additional information may be gathered from teacher surveys administered with the NAEP, there may be no substitute for initiating a parent survey with NAEP.

SUMMARY

Achievement scores are an important indicator of children's well-being, because they reflect the joint influence of families, schools, and communities. Significant changes or differences in the quality of a child's home, school, or community environment should leave an imprint on achievement scores. Achievement scores are also one of the few indicators available that have monitored the well-being of preteen children for over 30 years. Finally, achievement scores are one of the most visible and politically important measures of child well-being.

Achievement scores reveal that students at ages 9, 13, and 17 are scoring higher in the 1990s than in the 1970s in reading and math. The overall gains are modest, with gains in math being somewhat larger than gains in reading. However, there are dramatic differences in the magnitude of gains by racial-ethnic groups. The largest gains were made by Black students, followed by Hispanic and lower scoring White students. Higher scoring White students made the smallest gains. These trends would imply that the well-being of children has improved, with the largest change in well-being occurring for minority and more disadvantaged White students. The differential gains also are responsible for a significant reduction in the gap between White and minority students. However, most of the gains by minority and disadvantaged students occurred for those entering school in the 1970s and early 1980s. Since that time, no further reduction in the score gap has occurred, with some evidence that it may have widened in reading.

Research suggests that this pattern of achievement trends is linked to positive changes in the family environment and the quality of schools. Net changes in the characteristics of families would predict higher achievement mainly on the basis of increases in parental education levels and smaller family size. The net influence of these two factors offsets other changes in the family, such as increased single-parent families and more births to younger mothers. Changes in parental education levels and family size were much more dramatic for minority families.

However, changes in the family seem to account for much of the White score gains, but only a small portion of the larger gains in minority scores. The pattern and timing of minority and lower scoring White student gains are consistent with changes in their schooling environment. The impact of civil rights legislation, the War on Poverty programs, and compensatory school funding seems to have changed the schooling environment for minority, particularly Black, children, beginning in the late 1960s and early 1970s. The pattern of score gains is consistent with the timing of these changes. If we assume that the full impact of these programs occurred only for students who experienced the changed school environment over their entire school career, then cohorts entering school in the late 1960s and early 1970s would be expected to show the largest score gains. Because many of these changes slowed or stopped during the 1980s, one would expect that differential gains would also slow or stop.

The schooling changes that seem most consistent with the pattern of achievement would be desegregation of schools, reductions in pupil:teacher ratios, and expanded kindergarten and prekindergarten programs. More research is needed to make compelling cases for the relative effects of these or other changes.

Achievement scores to measure the comparable well-being of children in each state have been available since 1990. Research on these indicators provides important evidence that tend to support the picture emerging from the national trend data. There exist significant differences in the characteristics of families, schools, and communities across states, and these characteristics have also changed in remarkably different ways across states.

ACKNOWLEDGMENTS

The research underlying this study has been supported by grants from the Department of Education in the National Assessment of Educational Progress Secondary Analysis program, the Center for Research on Educational Diversity and Excellence, and the Office of Policy and Evaluation Services, and by the Exxon-Mobil Education foundation.

NOTES

1. This estimate does not include the foregone taxes for deductions for children and day care. Besides public sector spending on children, approximately $560 billion is spent in the private sector on children, bringing the average public and private spending per child to approximately $15,000 annually. This amount is estimated on the basis of the assumption that the cost of raising a child to age 18 to be approximately $150,000, with approximately 70 million individuals between the ages of 0 and 18. Thus, annual expenditures are $150,000 − 70,000,000/18 = $560 billion. (See U.S. Department of Agriculture, 1997, for estimates of the cost of raising children.)
2. The graph normalizes both variables to a mean of 0. The regression fit for the following equation: school grade = $a + b$ (average SAT score) gives $b = .79$ ($t = 5.2$), $R^2 = .56$.

3. See NAEP documentation for a discussion of survey design and sampling techniques used.
4. Beginning in 2004, all 50 states began to participate in the NAEP.
5. Hispanic scores were not separated until 1975 and thereafter. For this analysis, we have not included these scores.
6. The scores have been converted to relative scores by assuming that the earliest test score for each race is zero. Thus, the difference in scores reflects changes in the Black-White gap from the earliest test. The scores are converted to standard deviation units by taking the mean score difference from the earliest test and dividing by a metric that remains constant over the period: the standard deviations of all students for the earliest year. Another common practice is to measure the gap with respect to the standard deviation in the same year. Because the standard deviation for all students declines for mathematics scores, but increases for reading scores, this method changes the metric over time and would result in a somewhat different measure of gap reduction.

   The 1973 and 1971 scores for non-Hispanic White students were estimated, because the only published scores are for combined Hispanic and non-Hispanic White students in those years. Tests after 1973 have separate data for Hispanic and non-Hispanic White students. We make a small correction in the 1971 and 1973 data for White students by determining the proportion by age group of students who were Hispanic and assuming that the difference between Hispanic and non-Hispanic White scores were the same in 1971 and 1973 as for the 1975 reading and 1978 math tests.

   Also, the 17-year-old NAEP scores reflect only students rather than all 17-year-olds, so the 17-year-old scores will be biased with respect to 9- and 13-year-old scores. We make a correction for 17-year-old scores using the proportion of 17-year-olds in school by race in 1971–73 and 1996. We assume that those not tested would have scored 0.5 standard deviations below the mean score for their respective race-probably a conservative assumption. School enrollment data from the October Current Population Survey show that approximately 88% of White 17-year-olds and 83% of Black 17-year-olds were in school in 1970, versus 89% and 90% in 1988 (Cook & Evans, forthcoming).
7. See Koretz (1986, 1987) for earlier applications of this technique to NAEP and other data sets. Grissmer et al. (in press) also presented and interpreted this cohort data.
8. There is some evidence, however, that actual class size may not have declined in proportion with pupil:teacher ratio (Boozer, Krueger, & Wolkon, 1992). We also do not know whether class size differentially changed for Black and White students.
9. The definitions and patterns of exclusions changed as of the 2000 NAEP administration.
10. See Grissmer et al. (1994, Appendix E) for estimates of the relationships between national achievement scores and family characteristics for a national sample of eighth-graders of almost 25,000 students. The family characteristics commonly available for analysis are often proxies for other variables that actually measure different behavior within families. When variables such as reading time with children, home environment, parenting styles, and measures of the characteristics of the relationships within families are available, these variables usually replace part of the effects from the more commonly available variables.

11. NAEP tests (Main Assessments) were given from 1990 to 1998 (see Table 4.1). These tests were given to representative national samples, including public and private school students. Our analysis only includes public school students in the fourth and eighth grades. The public school sample size per test varied from around 3,000 to 9,000, with the total combined sample being approximately 52,000. The nine tests include 3 fourth-grade reading tests, 3 eighth-grade math tests, 2 fourth-grade math tests, and 1 eighth-grade reading test. So, the combined sample includes a composite picture of reading and math achievement at fourth and eighth grade during the 1990s.

12. See Grissmer et al. (2000, Table H.1) for these and related results and the method used for estimation.

REFERENCES

Advisory Group on the Scholastic Aptitude Test Score Decline. (1977). *On further examination*. New York: College Entrance Examination Board.

Barnett, W. S. (1995). Long-term effects of early childhood programs on cognitive and school outcomes. *The Future of Children, 5*(3), 25–50.

Boozer, M. A., Krueger, A., & Wolkon, S. (1992). Race and school quality since *Brown v. Board of Education. Brookings Papers on Economic Activity, Microeconomics*, 269–326.

Burtless, G. (1996). *Does money matter? The effect of school resources on student achievement and adult success*. Washington, DC: Brookings Institution.

Campbell, J. R., Donahue, P. L., Reese, C. M., & Phillips, G. W. (1996). *NAEP 1994 reading report card for the nations and the states: Findings from the National Assessment of Educational Progress and Trail State Assessment*. Washington, DC: National Center for Education Statistics.

Campbell, J. R., Hombo, C., & Mazzeo, J. (2000). *Trends in academic achievement* (NCES-2000-469). Washington, DC: U.S. Department of Education.

Coleman, J. S., Campbell, E. Q., Hobson, C. J., McPartland, J., Mood, A. M., Weinfeld, F. D., & York, R. L. (1966). *Equality of educational opportunity*. Washington, DC: U.S. Government Printing Office.

Cook, M., & Evans, W.N. (2000). Families or schools? Explaining the convergence in White and Black academic performance. *Journal of Labor Economics, 18*, 729–754.

Digest of Educational Statistics. (1980-1998). *National Center for Educational Statistics* (NCES 1999-036). Washington, DC: U.S. Department of Education.

Ferguson, R. F. (1998). Can schools narrow the Black-White score gap? In Jencks & M. Phillips (Eds.), *The Black-White score gap* (pp. 318–374). Washington DC: Brookings Institution.

Finn, J., & Achilles, C. (1999). Tennessee's class size study: Findings, implications and misconceptions. *Educational Evaluation and Policy Analysis, 20*(2), 97–109.

Flynn, J. R. (1987). Massive IQ gains in 14 nations: What IQ tests really measure. *Psychological Bulletin, 101*, 171–191.

Fuchs, V. R., & Reklis, D. M. (1992). America's children: Economic perspectives and policy options. *Science, 255*, 41–45.

Greenwald, R., Hedges, L. V., & Laine, R. (1996). The effect of school resources on student achievement. *Review of Educational Research, 66*, 361–396.

Grissmer, D. (2000). The use and misuse of SAT scores. *Journal of Psychology, Public Policy, and Law, 6*, 223–232.

Grissmer, D. W., & Flanagan, A. (2000). Moving educational research toward scientific consensus. In D. Grissmer & M. Ross (Eds.), *Analytic issues in the assessment of student achievement* (pp. 43–90). Washington, DC: National Center for Educational Statistics.

Grissmer, D. W., & Flanagan, A. (2002). In J. E. Chubb and T. Loveless (Eds.), Bridging the achievement gap (NCES-2000-050). Washington, DC: The Brookings Institution.

Grissmer, D. W., Flanagan, A., & Kawata, J. (1998). *Assessing and improving the family characteristics collected with the national assessment of educational progress* (DRR-1914-IET). Santa Monica, CA: RAND.

Grissmer, D. W., Flanagan, A., Kawata, J., & Williamson S. (2000). *Improving student achievement: What state NAEP scores tell us* (MR-924-EDU). Santa Monica, CA: RAND.

Grissmer, D., Flanagan, A., & Williamson, S. (1998b). Why did Black test scores rise rapidly in the 1970s and 1980s? In C. Jencks & M. Phillips (Eds.), *The Black- White test score gap* (pp. 182–226). Washington, DC: Brookings Institution.

Grissmer, D., Flanagan, A., & Williamson, S. (1998a). Does money matter for minority and disadvantaged students: Assessing the new empirical evidence. In W. Fowler (Ed.), *Developments in school finance* (NCES 98-212, pp. 98–212). Washington, DC: U.S. Department of Education.

Grissmer, D. W., Kirby, S. N., Berends, M., & Williamson, S. (1994). *Student achievement and the changing American family.* Santa Monica, CA: RAND.

Grissmer, D., Williamson, S., Kirby, S. N., & Berends, M. (1998). Exploring the rapid rise in Black achievement scores in the United States (1970-1990). In U. Neisser (Ed.), *The rising curve: Long-term changes in IQ and related measures* (pp. 251–286). Washington, DC: American Psychological Association.

Hanushek, E. A. (1996). School resources and student performance. In G. Burtless (Ed.), *Does money matter? The effect of school resources on student achievement and adult success* (pp. 43–73). Washington, DC: Brookings Institution.

Hauser, R. M. (1998). Trends in Black-White test score differentials: Uses and misuses of NAEP/SAT data. In U. Neisser (Ed.), *The rising curve: Long-term changes in IQ and related measures* (pp. 219–250). Washington, DC: American Psychological Association.

Hedges, L. V., Laine, R. D., & Greenwald, R. (1994). Does Monday matter: Meta-analysis of studies of the effects of differential school inputs on student outcomes. *Educational Researcher, 23*(3), 5–14.

Hedges, L. V., & Nowell, A. (1998). Black–White Test Score Convergence Since 1965. In C. S. Jencks & M. Phillips (Eds.), *The Black-White test score gap* (pp. 149–181). Washington, DC: Brookings Institution.

Institute of Medicine. (1994). *Growing up tobacco free: Preventing nicotine addiction in children and youths.* Washington, DC: National Academy Press.

Institute of Medicine. (2001). *Promoting health: Intervention strategies from social and behavioral research.* Washington, DC: National Academy Press.

Jencks, C., & Phillips, M. (1998). *The Black-White test score gap.* Washington, DC: Brookings Institution.

Koretz, D. (1986). *Trends in educational achievement.* Washington, DC: Congressional Budget Office.

Koretz, D. (1987). *Educational achievement, explanations and implications of recent trends.* Washington, DC: Congressional Budget Office.

Krueger, A. B. (1998). Reassessing the view that American schools are broken. *Economic Policy Review*, **xx**, 29–43.

Krueger, A. B. (1999). Experimental estimates of education production functions. *Quarterly Journal of Economics, 114*, 497–532.

Krueger, A. B. (2000). *An economist view of class size reductions*. Princeton, NJ: Mimeo.

Ladd, H. F. (Ed.). (1996). *Holding schools accountable*. Washington, DC: Brookings Institution.

Miller, K. E., Nelson, J. E., & Naifeh, M. (1995). *Cross-state data compendium for the NAEP 1994 grade 4 reading assessment*. Washington, DC: National Center for Education Statistics.

Moore, K. A., Miller, B. C., Glei, D., & Morrison D. R. (1995). *Adolescent sex, contraception, and childbearing: A review of recent research*. Washington, DC: Child Trends.

Mullis, I. V. S., Dossey, J. A., Owen, E. H., & Phillips, G. W. (1993). *NAEP 1992 mathematics report card for the nation and the states: Data from the National and Trail State Assessments*. Washington, DC: National Center for Education Statistics.

National Commission on Excellence in Education. (1983). *A nation at risk: The imperative for educational reform: A report to the nation and the Secretary of Education*. Washington, DC: U.S. Department of Education.

National Research Council. (2001). *Understanding dropouts: Statistics, strategies, and high-stakes testing*. Washington, DC: National Academy Press.

National Research Council and Institute of Medicine. (1999). *Risks and opportunities: Synthesis of studies on adolescence*. Washington, DC: National Academy Press.

National Research Council and Institute of Medicine. (2001). *Juvenile crime, juvenile justice*. Washington, DC: National Academy Press.

Neisser, U. (Ed.). (1998). *The rising curve: Long-term changes in IQ and related measures*. Washington, DC: American Psychological Association.

Nye, B. A., Hedges, L., & Konstantopoulos, S. (1999a). *The effects of small class size on academic achievement: The results of the Tennessee class size experiment*. Manuscript submitted for publication.

Nye, B. A., Hedges, L., & Konstantopoulos, S. (1999b). The long term effects of small classes: A five-year follow-up of the Tennessee class size experiment. *Educational Evaluation and Policy Analysis, 20*(2), 127–142.

Office of Science and Technology Policy. (1997). *Investing in our future: A national research initiative for America's children for the 21st century*. Washington, DC: The White House.

Phillips, M., Crouse, J., & Ralph, J. (1998). Does the Black-White score gap widen after school entry? In C. Jencks & M. Phillips (Eds.), *The Black-White Test score gap* (pp. 229–272). Washington, DC: Brookings Institution.

Reese, C. M., Miller, K. E., Mazzeo, J., & Dossey, J. A. (1997). *NAEP 1996 mathematics report card for the nation and the states*. Washington, DC: National Center for Education Statistics.

Rock, D. A. (1987). The score decline from 1972 to 1980: What went wrong, youth and society, *18*, 239–254.

Rothstein, R., & Miles, K. H. (1995). *Where's the money gone? Changes in the level and composition of education spending*. Washington, DC: Economic Policy Institute.

Shaughnessy, C. A., Nelson, J., & Norris, N. (1998). *NAEP 1996 mathematics cross state data compendium for the grade 4 and grade 8 assessment* (NCES-98-481). Washington, DC: U.S. Department of Education.
U.S. Department of Agriculture. (1997). *Estimates of the costs of raising children.* Washington, DC: Author.

Part III

Social and Emotional Development Indicators

The Assessment of Psychological, Emotional, and Social Development Indicators in Middle Childhood

Marika Ripke
University of Hawaii at Manoa
Aletha C. Huston
University of Texas at Austin
Jacquelynne Eccles
Janice Templeton
University of Michigan

Our charge in this chapter is to consider indicators of psychological, social, and emotional development in middle childhood. *Middle childhood* is the period from about age 5 or 6 to age 11 or 12. Over a century ago, Freud relegated middle childhood to the status of an uninteresting "latency" period between the psychosexual developments of the early years and the emergence of adult sexuality at puberty. In recent years, both scholars and policymakers have rekindled interest in middle childhood as a period in which children develop or fail to develop the foundations for adult competence, responsibility, and independence. That change is reflected in the editor's decision to commission chapters for this volume that focus specifically on middle childhood-a change from the last volume on child indicators (Hauser, Brown, & Prosser, 1997), in which the age span was divided into early childhood and adolescence.

We begin with a discussion of the important developmental tasks or changes in middle childhood; then we present some basic assumptions that guided our selection of constructs. Next, we identify the seven constructs or domains that we believe comprise central features of psychological, emotional, and social development in middle childhood. Within each construct, we identify and evaluate current status indicators, including how these indicators are measured, and provide suggestions for future indicators in domains where they are especially lacking or underdeveloped. We end with a discussion of the domains

131

and indicators that are most underdeveloped and make recommendations for future assessment.

DEVELOPMENTAL TASKS OF MIDDLE CHILDHOOD

Many classic developmental theories define stages or qualitative
changes in development, the most widely influential perhaps being
Erikson's (1950) theory of psychosocial development. Erikson's theory
described the crucial developmental task in middle childhood as developing a sense of *industry*-mastering the basic tools and skills needed for
adult life in one's culture. The hazard during this period is a sense of inferiority if children's abilities and tools are inadequate or if they despair
of becoming productive in ways that are valued in their society. Other
developmentalists (e.g., Aber & Jones, 1997) have proposed the ability
to regulate behavior and emotions, skills in negotiating conflicts and
solving interpersonal problems, and a sense of competence in both social
and academic domains as salient tasks in this age period. Using these
ideas, we organize the tasks of middle childhood according to the four
rubrics discussed below, keeping in mind the important role that the
contexts to which children are exposed (e.g., schools, home environment) play in mastering these developmental tasks.

Self-Concept, Motivation, and Well-Being

The concepts of industry and inferiority are metaphors for positive and
negative aspects of self-concept, motivation, and well-being. For most
children, entry into formal schooling between ages 5 and 7 marks the
beginning of new experiences of evaluation and comparison to others.
In the subsequent years, children learn to evaluate themselves in ways
that reflect the standards of the society around them, making judgments about whether they are fulfilling their own or others' expectations for competency. Although academic achievement is central for
many children, feelings of competence can result from acquiring the
fundamentals of many skills, including sports, playing musical instruments, visual arts, social and leadership skills, computer-based activities, and languages. Perceived competence composes part of a network
of motivations and beliefs that include values for attainment of goals,
an orientation to the future, attributions about the reasons for success
and failure, and a sense of self-efficacy-all of which are positive indicators (Eccles, Wigfield, & Schiefele, 1997).

Children who fail to attain at least some of the competencies they and
others consider important are vulnerable to low feelings of self-worth,
high levels of anxiety (particularly about failure), and depression. Although there may be precursors of these aspects of psychological
well-being in the preschool years, middle childhood is the period in
which they are first manifested in ways that can be reliably observed
and measured.

Self-Regulation

During middle childhood, children gain a great deal of independence, become increasingly involved in activities and relationships outside the home, and take on increasing responsibility for their actions. By the end of this age period, most children can be safely left alone without adult supervision. With increasing freedom, children need to develop skills in regulating their own behavior.

One often-ignored feature of increasing independence is children' control over the their own environments. For example, parents have considerably less influence on children's use of television and computer games in middle childhood than in the preschool years (Bickham et al., 2003). Scarr and McCartney (1983) argued that children actively influence their environments by "niche-building," that is, by choosing places, people, and activities. Bandura (1976) described a process of *reciprocal determinism* by which children choose settings; settings encourage children to practice particular behaviors; practice affects skills and preferences; and skills and preferences influence subsequent choices of environments. For example, a child who chooses to go to a recreation center on the weekends might be exposed to several different sporting activities. After practicing each sport, she may realize that she is most skillful and/or most enjoys playing basketball, and thus in turn joins the basketball team at her school. We argue, therefore, that children's time use and activities are indictors of child attributes as well as context.

Social Competence

Social competence includes skills at initiating and maintaining social interactions and at dealing with and resolving conflicts. Changes in social and moral reasoning in middle childhood form one basis for developing social skills. Social reasoning includes the ability to reflect on oneself, the accurate perception of others' intentions; thoughts, and feelings; and the ability to generate alternative ways of dealing with social situations.

Because the United States is increasingly multicultural, competence in relating across cultures, languages, and ethnic groups is important for the well-being of individuals and of the larger society. Some years ago, Harrison, Wilson, Pine, Chan, and Buriel (1990) proposed that minority children needed to develop cognitive flexibility and skills at recognizing that different contexts require different behavior. We argue that such abilities are important for all children in a multicultural society.

Relationships

Most developmentalists agree that relationships with one or both parents form an early base for emotional well-being. Relationships are different from social skills. A child can be charming but have no close friends. Adult preoccupation with potential negative influences of peers may lead to undervaluing the positive contribution of peer relationships to well-being. The failure to form friendships can portend more serious problems in adolescence and later life. Hence, it is important to measure children's friendships.

With those cautions, we also note that peer influences increase dramatically during middle childhood; conformity to peers reaches its peak around age 12 or 13. Children in middle childhood also spend increasing amounts of time with peers and friends. Hence, the values and behaviors of a child's peers are one important context and, at the same time, an indicator of the child's own values and behavior.

Last, children's relationships with adults outside their families become increasingly important during middle childhood. Children spend less time under their parents' supervision during this time and become increasingly under the supervision of-and form relationships with-other adults, such as teachers, coaches, church leaders, and activity instructors. These relationships are important to assess.

ASSUMPTIONS ABOUT THE GOALS OF DEVELOPMENT

The choice of indicators rests on assumptions about the goals we as a society hold for our children. What do we consider important? What do we want for our children now and in the future? In this section, we identify some of the assumptions guiding our selection, drawing on some of the criteria for indicators proposed by Moore (1997). We recommend that indicators should: include positive as well as negative outcomes; strike a balance between emphasizing the child's present well-being and future as an adult (*well-becoming*); recognize that social behavior is context specific, allowing for assessment in multiple contexts and from multiple informants; be appropriate for a multicultural population; and be comprehensive across several domains of development.

Balance of Positive and Negative Outcomes

Childhood indicators assess negative behavior more frequently than positive, in part because there is less agreement regarding the behavior and characteristics that make up positive development (Moore, 1997). However, the absence of problems does not necessarily mean that children are doing well. There is abundant evidence that negative attributes (e.g., aggressiveness) are not simply the opposite of positive attributes (e.g., skill at resolving conflicts). A child who is not causing trouble in school is not necessarily one who has friends or who feels a sense of competence and efficacy. Program and policy efforts designed to reduce negative outcomes are not necessarily those that are most effective for increasing positive outcomes (see Aber & Jones, 1997, for an extensive discussion of this issue). As we attempt to develop new indicators, we need to put special effort into identifying good and broadly accepted indices of positive developmental outcomes.

Focus on Present Versus Future Well-Being

In many policy discussions about children there is a tension between considering the child as a person in the present and the child as a nascent adult. Many indicators are selected because they predict to future adult poverty, unemployment, teen pregnancy, and crime. The well-being of a child at any age has value for its own sake, and indicators should be selected to reflect both current and future outcomes. It is important to gather information not only on children's characteristics but also on how they perceive their future. Children's own perceptions of their future can influence current behavior, motivation, and choices that have long-term consequences.

Social Behavior is Context Specific

Unlike cognitive skills, which are relatively stable across contexts and time, social behavior varies by the social context in which the child is observed. In a recent meta-analysis of longitudinal studies predicting early school adjustment, for example, social behavior observed in preschool or kindergarten was very modestly related to behavior in first or second grade (La Paro & Pianta, 2001). In the New Hope study, with a sample of over 600 children from low-income families, parents' and teachers' ratings of children's positive and problem behaviors (using the Social Rating Scale System; Gresham & Elliott, 1990) had an average correlation of about .20 (Bos et al., 1999). The reasons for low consistency across situations and time probably lie partly in measurement problems, but we believe they also indicate true variability across contexts. Children (and adults) can be socially skilled in some situations and inept in others, assertive in some contexts and obsequious in others.

Whatever the reasons for inconsistencies, it is clear that indicators of social and emotional development should include multiple respondents (e.g., parent, teacher, child, peer) and multiple contexts (e.g., school, home) in which children spend time. We stress the importance of including self-reports of children. In the New Hope study, children's responses on measures of well-being had very low correlations with reports of positive or negative behavior by parents or teachers. In many national surveys parents are the only source of information about children; such data have serious limitations.

Multiculturalism

The American population is becoming increasingly diverse, and that is especially true for children. The proportion of non-White children ages 5 to 14 has increased from approximately one quarter to one third since 1980 and is expected to reach one half by 2020 (U.S. Department of Commerce, Bureau of the Census, 1993, 1996). The 2000 census reflects fast-growing Hispanic and Asian populations. Cultural variations raise fundamental questions about the generality and appropriateness of indicators, particularly in the domain of social and emotional development. Do different groups hold the same values about what is healthy and desirable? Even if the constructs are similar, the measures may have different meanings or different levels of validity for children from different cultural groups.

We need research to establish instances in which generalization is appropriate or in which patterns differ. For example, as non-Latinos reach adolescence, they report becoming less close to their parents, but Latino adolescents report greater closeness to parents (Lerner, 1998). Independence from parents may signify positive development for non-Latinos, but not for Latinos. In addition, much more work is needed to establish the extent to which other assets may need to be added for different cultural groups.

Biases in measurement represent another problem. Adults' ratings of problem behavior and social skills reflect their own sets of values and expectations. Teachers, who are predominantly middle class and often White, may perceive behavior of children of color as defiant or aggressive because it does not match their concepts of appropriate behavior, and they may not recognize social skills that are outside their frame of reference (e.g., Harrison et al., 1990).

Thus, we need to take seriously ethnic diversity (both within and between ethnic groups) and devise assessments that tap into both commonalities and diversities, including what we consider healthy development and whether the meaning of *healthy development* is interpreted the same by various cultures.

Comprehensive Coverage

Children have different areas of strength and weakness, so indicators should span a wide array of outcomes and behaviors. We offer suggestions in the following section for outcomes that we consider particularly important to assess during middle childhood.

CURRENT SOURCES OF DATA COLLECTION OF MIDDLE CHILDHOOD INDICATORS

The following eight national surveys collect data on some aspect of the psychological, emotional, and social development of children in middle childhood: (a) the National Household Education Survey, (b) the National Longitudinal Study of Youth 1979, (c) the National Assessment of Educational Progress (NAEP), (d) the National Institute of Child Health and Human Development (NICHD) study of Early Child Care and Youth Development, (e) Progress of Canadian Children, (f) the Panel Study of Income Dynamics, (g) the Early Childhood Longitudinal Study-Kindergarten Cohort, and (e) the National Survey of America's Families.

These surveys differ in the comprehensiveness of their assessment of indicators in middle childhood. For example, the National Longitudinal Study of Youth gathers only social development indicators from mothers about their children under the age of 10, thus missing out on the child's self-report. The Early Childhood Longitudinal Study-Kindergarten Cohort, on the other hand, gathers a wide range of data on children's social and emotional development, including children's self-report as well as parental and teacher report. Of course, time and financial constraints often limit the amount and extent of information collected. At the end of this chapter, we provide some suggestions for alleviating these constraints.

Various regional surveys have also collected fairly comprehensive data on middle childhood indicators, such as the Project of Human Development in Chicago Neighborhoods, the Los Angeles Family and Neighborhood Study, the Childhood and Beyond Study (CAB), and the 3-Cities Study. The John D. and Catherine T. MacArthur Foundation's Research Network on Successful Pathways Through Middle Childhood has resulted in several projects assessing indicators in middle childhood, including: the New Hope Project (see Brock, Doolittle, Fellerath, & Wiseman, 1997; http://www.mdrc.org/project_16_30.html), the MacArthur School Engagement Project (see http://childhood.isr.umich.edu/current/engage.html), the MacArthur School Transition Study (see http://childhood.isr.umich.edu/current/macar.html), the Children of Immigrants Project (see http://childhood.isr.umich.edu/current/children.html), and the California Childhood Project http://childhood.isr.umich.edu/current/calif.html).

These national and regional surveys use many of the same (or modified versions of) well-validated and standardized instruments shown in Table 5.1. More detailed information on these surveys, including constructs assessed and specific measures used, can be found in the Appendix.[1]

A valuable resource for information regarding child indicators is the Children, Youth, and Families at Risk Initiative and Evaluation Collaboration Project, National Outcomes Work Group for Children. Their web site (http://www.ag.arizona.edu/fcs/cyfernet/nowg) contains suggestions of outcomes and specific measures, some of which we touched on in this chapter.

IMPORTANT DEVELOPMENTAL DOMAINS
IN MIDDLE CHILDHOOD

We consider the following seven domains as key to children's social and emotional development in middle childhood: (a) motivation and goals for the future, (b) psychological well-being and distress, (c) activities and time use, (d) self-regulation and control, (e) social competence, (f) relationships with peers and adults, and (g) ability and attitudes concerning multiculturalism and diversity. These domains overlap with

TABLE 5.1

Current Measures Available to Assess Children's Psychological, Emotional, and Social Development

Age/Grade	Construct	Measure name	References
		Motivation	
Grades 4-8	Intrinsic Motivation	Children's Academic Intrinsic Motivation Inventory (CAIMI)	Gottfried, (1985)
Ages 6-14	Self Concept	Self Concept of Ability	Eccles, (1999)
		Psychological well-being and distress	
Ages 6-18	Anxiety	Revised-Child Manifest Anxiety Scale	Pela & Reynolds, (1982)
Ages 6-18	Worry/Anxiety	Penn State Worry Questionnaire-Children	Corpita et al., (1997)
Ages 9-18	Anxiety	Social Anxiety Scale for Children	La Greca, Kraslow-Dandes, Wisk, Shaw, & Stone, (1988)
Ages 8-13	Anxiety	Screen for Child Anxiety Related Emotional Disorders (SCARED)	Birmaher et al., (1997)
Grade K & up	Social Distress	Loneliness and Social Dissatisfaction	Cassidy, J., & Asher, S.R. (1992)
Ages 8-13	Depression	CES-D	Radloff, L.S., (1977)
Grade 1 & up	Depression	My Feelings (modified CES-D)	Radloff, L.S., (1977)
Ages 7-13	Depression	Self-Rating Scale of Depression	Birleson, (1981)
Ages 8-13	Depression	Children's Depression Inventory	Kovacs, (1985)
Grades 11-12	Self-Esteem	Rosenberg Self-Esteem Scale	Rosenberg, (1965)
Grades 2-9	Self Esteem	Culture-Free Self-Esteem Inventories	J. Battle, (1992, 2nd ed.)
Ages 8 & up	Self Concept	Self-Description Questionnaire	H. W. Marsh, (1988)
		Self Regulation and Control	
Ages 9-14	Self Control	Perceived Self-Control Scale	Humphrey, (1982)

Social Competence

Age	Category	Instrument	Citation
Ages 3-18	Social Skills SSRS	(Social Skills Rating System)	Grensham, F.M., & Elliot, S.N. (1990)
Ages 2-12	Pos./Neg. Behavior	Positive Behavior Scale	Quint, Bos, & Polit, (1997)
Ages 3 & up	Problem Behavior	Behavior Problem Index (BPI)	Peterson & Zill, (1986)
Ages 2-16		Child Behavior Checklist (CBCL)	Achenbach & Edlebrock, (1981)
Grades 3-6		Response Decision Instrument	Crick & Werner, (1998)
Ages 8 & up		Perceived Competence Scale for Children	S. Harter, (1982)
Pre- and Primary school		Pictorial Scale of Perceived Competence and Social Acceptance for Young Children	S. Harter & R. Pike, (1984)

Relationships with peers and adults

Age	Category	Instrument	Citation
Grade 1 & up	Peers/Friends	Friends or Foes	Ladd, (1983); Vandell, (1995)
Grade 1	Peers	Playmate Questionnaire	Clark, K.E. & Ladd, G.W., (2000); Vandell, (1995)
Preschool– Grade 3	Teacher	Student-Teacher Relationship Scale (STRS)	Pianta, (1992)
Grades 1-12		Patterns of Adaptive Learning Survey (PALS)	Midgley et al., (1996)
Grades 3-6		Teacher as Social Context (TASC)	Belmont, Skinner, Wellborn, & Connell, (1992)

Abilities and attitudes about multiculturalism/diversity

Age	Category	Instrument	Citation
Grades 1, 4, & 7	Empathy	Empathy in Children	B.K. Bryant, (1982)
Grade 1	Ethnic identity	Ethnic Preference and Identity Measure	Johnson & Castillo, (1984)
Ages 6-12		Perceived Racial Stress & Coping Test	Johnson , (1996)

what others researchers consider to be important indicators of well-being in middle childhood (Benson, 1997; Lerner, 1998; Moore, Evans, Brooks-Gunn, & Roth, 2001). As stated earlier, approaches to the use of childhood indicators assesses negative behavior more frequently than positive behavior, mostly because there is little agreement regarding the behavior and characteristics that make up positive development (Moore, 1997). We will discuss what we consider, and what existing research suggests as being, indicators of healthy, positive development within each of these seven domains. Specific measures that we consider to be strong candidates for assessing constructs within these domains are presented in Table 5.1.

MOTIVATION AND GOALS FOR THE FUTURE

This is an area that is especially important to children in middle childhood, particularly because the decisions children make during this period affect their future outcomes, such as educational and occupational attainment. In the past, researchers have described early and middle childhood as a period of fantasy aspirations for career development, claiming that up to age 11, children aspire widely and impulsively to occupations and that it is only during the shift from adolescence to adulthood that there is a change from fantasy choices to realistic choices (Cosby, 1974; Ginzberg, 1952).

However, more recent research has shown that childhood plays a very important role in career development and that the process of occupational choice during childhood is more complex than previously theorized. Gottfredson (1981) argued that childhood is a period in which important career decisions are made, including the elimination of some career options—something that may obviously affect future career outcomes.

For the most part, children enter middle childhood with a very optimistic outlook on their abilities and future expectancies (Eccles, 1999). However, research suggests there are dramatic declines in children's academic motivation, interests, values, and competence beliefs with the transition to junior high (see Eccles et al., 1997). This makes the identification of positive motivation indicators in middle childhood even more crucial, and it may be particularly important for certain groups, such as Latinos, who have much higher dropout rates than other ethnic groups.

In addition to educational and occupational goals, various other personal goals should be assessed in middle childhood. However, as Burnett and Meisells (2001) pointed out, there are no age-appropriate measures of goals for children in early elementary school. Existing measures usually begin assessments with children in fourth or fifth grade. This may be in part because there is an absence of research on the ability of younger children to report personal goals. In addition to needing more research investigating children's capacity to identify their goals, we suggest that more longitudinal studies be conducted to gain a better understanding of what positive indicators of motivation in middle childhood look like in relation to later successful outcomes (e.g., in academic and work domains) so that programs designed to promote positive development in particular areas can make adjustments accordingly.

We propose that being hopeful and having positive expectations regarding their personal future are important indicators for children in this domain. This includes having high academic and occupational motivation (aspirations, expectations, interests, and values); positive expectancies for future mental and physical health, including life expectancy; positive social goals (e.g., family, friendships, relationships); and prosocial and responsibility goals (e.g., to help others, be a productive citizen of society).

Both the Michigan Childhood Development Study (Eccles, Wigfield, Harold, & Blumenfeld, 1993) and the CAB assess children's self-concepts, expectations for successes, and achievement-related values and beliefs in various domains (e.g., math, reading, music, English, sports). The Children's Academic Intrinsic Motivation Inventory (Gottfried, 1985) is a widely used measure of children's motivation, as are Eccles's measures of children's self-concept of ability.

PSYCHOLOGICAL WELL-BEING AND DISTRESS

This is perhaps the most researched area with children of this age group. We consider positive indicators of middle childhood to encompass positive psychological well-being and low feelings of distress. We suggest the following as specific positive indicators within this domain: low anxiety, a positive self-image, a positive and realistic level of self-esteem, and a lack of depression.

Self-image and *self-concept* refer to one's ideas about his or her skills, personality, and other characteristics, whereas *self-esteem* is the part of self-concept or self-image that deals with one's feelings (i.e., positive or negative) about one's values and competence as a person (Berndt, 1997; Harter, 1985). Children develop their self-esteem and individuality during middle childhood, as they begin comparing themselves with peers. In the last decade, promoting children's self-esteem has become a high priority for educational and community programs because of research demonstrating links between positive self-esteem and the confidence and motivation necessary for other desirable outcomes, such as achievement and the ability to interact positively with other people. Children who do not perceive themselves as competent during middle childhood may be at risk for undesirable outcomes later in life, such as social isolation, anger, and depression (Cole, 1991; Parkhurst & Asher, 1992).

Harter (1982) stressed the importance of promoting a realistic sense of competence as a goal, rather than just increasing self-esteem or perceived competence. Following from this, an important indicator in this domain that should be given more attention is children's ability to self-identify their areas of strength, skills, and areas requiring improvement, instead of just assessing their competence in a few, preselected domains. It is important to assess children's skills in a way that taps a comprehensive range of areas, because not all children possess competence in such specific domains. For example, many children may not feel competent in math or sports but instead feel good about their knowledge of science or their ability to paint, facilitate and lead activities with peers, or maintain friendships. Many current measures do assess children's perceived competence in various domains (e.g., Eccles's self-concept of ability scales), with sports, math, and English being among the most common. We suggest assessing an even wider variety of domains (e.g., computer skills, taking care of pets, listening skills, ability to make friends), with one method of measurement allowing children to self-identify their areas of strengths and weaknesses.

Of the most widely used and well-validated measures of self-concept are Harter's (1982, 1984) measures, which are self-report and cover and variety of domains, and Marsh's (1988) Self-Description Questionnaire, which contains eight self-concept scales, including the assessment of peer and parent relationships. Many consider the Self-Description Questionnaire-I (Marsh, 1990) to be the best measure of self-concept because of its multidimensionality and high validity with preadolescent children (Burnett & Meisells, 2001; Byrne, 1996).

The most widely used depression measures include the Center for Epidemiologic Studies Depression Scale (L. S. Radloff, 1977), the Self-Rating Scale of Depression (Birleson, 1981) and the Children's Depression Inventory (Kovacs, 1985). It may be desirable-for instance, in the interest of time-to gather information about children's psychological well-being overall with one measure instead of administering separate scales of depression, self-concept, anxiety, and so on. There are a few such measures that tap multiple aspects of children's psychological well-being, such as the Loneliness and Social Dissatisfaction Questionnaire (Asher, Hymel, & Renshaw, 1984; Asher & Wheeler, 1985; Cassidy & Asher, 1992), which assesses children's feeling of social adequacy, loneliness, and perceptions of peer status.

ACTIVITIES AND TIME USE

There is a growing concern about children's use of free time. Middle childhood is a period when children begin gaining a great deal of independence and become increasingly involved in activities (Canadian Council on Social Development, 2001). Participation in activities can have important effects on children's social and academic development, although the outcomes are dependent on type of arrangement (e.g., structured, adult-supervised vs. unstructured, not adult supervised) and type of activity (e.g., sports vs. academic enrichment), as well as child's socioeconomic status (e.g., how much family income is allocated or available for enrolling children in extracurricular activities, what activities does the neighborhood or community offer?).

We believe that children's constructive use of time and participation in positive activities are indicators of healthy positive development in middle childhood, particularly in the attainment and development of skills. Structured, out-of-school activities often provide children with adult-supervised, constructive time use, aiding in the development of prosocial skills and reducing the likelihood of involvement in deviant behavior (Carnegie Corporation, 1992). On the other hand, children's involvement in "self-care" time use may have different outcomes. Although some researchers have found that time spent in self-care is related to difficulties in behavior, such as lower social competence (Pettit et al., 1997; Pettit, Bates, Dodge, & Meece, 1999), externalizing behavior problems, and participation in deviant behavior (Posner & Vandell, 1999; Richardson et. al., 1989; Steinberg, 1986; U.S. Department of Education and U.S. Department of Justice, 2000), others have found no overall differences in self-perceived social ability, behavior problems, or social adjustment (Galambos & Maggs, 1991; Lovko & Ullman, 1989; Rodman, Pratto, & Nelson, 1985).

The relationships between children's activity participation and social behavioral outcomes may differ for children according to family income levels. Studies have shown negative effects of self-care on children living in low-income neighborhoods (Pettit et al., 1999; Posner & Vandell, 1994), whereas the social development of children in middle-class communities does not differ according to the type of care (Steinberg, 1986; Vandell & Corasaniti, 1988). Positive effects of formal after-school arrangements on low-income children's social conduct, such as social competence (Posner & Vandell, 1994) and lower levels of internalizing behavior problems (Marshall et al., 1997; Pettit et al, 1997), have been found. Moreover, youth who participate in activities that are structured or approved by adults have better school performance and less deviant behavior than do those who spend after-school time in unsupervised activities with peers. This difference is especially apparent for youth in low-income families and neighborhoods (Carnegie Corporation, 1994; Catalano, Berglund, Ryan, Lonczak, & Hawkins, 1999; Pettit, Bates, & Dodge, 1997). Thus, when deciding on what specific indicators we consider to be positive, it is important to keep in mind that it may differ according to socioeconomic status.

We suggest that leisure time use should be given special attention, because little is known about the contribution of different types of activities (and the circumstances surrounding them) to children's behavior. Children today are less likely to be responsible for household chores than were children in the early part of the century, thus giving them more free time (Capella & Lerner, 1999). Moreover, because more parents are working, children are spending increasing amounts of out-of-school time without adult supervision.

Indicators in this area should include both the amounts and types of activities in which children participate. Moreover, when gathering data on children's time use, it is very important to make distinctions between time of year (e.g., summer vs. school year) as well as time of week (weekday vs. weekend), because activities may vary considerably under these various circumstances. It is also important to collect information on the specific circumstances surrounding each activity, including who else was engaged in the activity with the child (e.g., friends, peers), and whether the child was being supervised by an adult. The New Hope and CAB projects gather these type of information in detail, assessing things such as the type of activity, frequency and duration of the activity, the presence or lack of supervision or company, and whether the activity occurred on a weekday or weekend.

Advances in technology (e.g., computers, video games, digital cable) have opened up a wider range of possible activities in which children may be engaged during their free time; thus, data on media usage–including television, computers, movies, and video games–should also be assessed. Last, there appears to be more interest in assessing children's participation in civic, community, prosocial, and leadership activities over the last two decades, although measures assessing participation in these activities are still underdeveloped.

SELF-REGULATION AND CONTROL

Central to the definition of *self-regulation* is the ability to manage/control one's impulses. This is an area that is underdeveloped with children in middle childhood.

We include self-regulation separate from social competence because a certain degree of self-regulation is necessary for children's development of more advanced social competence, such as the negotiation of conflicts and social problem solving, especially with peers (Aber & Jones, 1997). We believe the following to be important indicators of children's ability to self-regulate their behavior: hyperactivity and impulsivity; responsibility and independence; and leadership, contribution, and citizenship.

Responsibility and Independence

Responsibility and independence are related characteristics that are important to being successful adults, because they are requirements for managing one's day-to-day life and schedule, the completion of tasks in a timely manner, and the ability to admit and correct mistakes (Shaffer, 1999). The development of independence and responsibility is a process that begins in infancy and continues into adulthood. Independent and responsible children are more apt to be successful in school, careers, and social relationships (Dubow, Huesmann, & Eron, 1987; Shaffer, 1999).

Indicators of responsibility and independence are especially sensitive to age. The following are indicators that we feel are appropriate for children in middle childhood; some of them were guided by suggestions from the National Outcomes Work Group for Children: the ability to initiate and follow through on activities, accept responsibility for mistakes and actions, feed oneself and act appropriately during mealtime activities, dress oneself appropriately, attend to one's own personal hygiene needs, and take care of personal belongings.

Leadership, Contribution, and Citizenship

Studies of peer relationships have shown that the qualities children like in their peers include behaviors and skills related to contribution and citizenship, such as altruism, kindness, and helpfulness (Cartledge & Milburn, 1995; Dygdon, Conger, Conger, Wallanda, & Keane, 1980), whereas teachers cite desired qualities in their students such as cooperation, following rules, and basic self-help behavior (Milburn, 1972). We add the following two to this list of positive indicators: (a) participating in and volunteering for school-related tasks and (b) following established rules, guidelines, and limits in various contexts.

Related to this topic, and an area that is underdeveloped, are children's connections and contributions to larger society. Indicators of this domain should include both children's perceived and real measures of connections and contributions to society. We suggest the following three indicators: (a) children's sense of belonging to community and society; (b) involvement in school, neighborhood, community; and (c) a demonstrated interest in improving their community and society.

The U.S. Department of Education (National Center for Education Statistics) has established the following educational objective for our nation's children: "To be well educated means to possess skills and civic dispositions necessary for effective participation in government and society." This goal is thought to be accomplished through the development of *civic competency*, which includes civic knowledge (e.g., identifying and explaining meaning of citizenship), participatory skills (e.g., evaluating, taking, and defending positions), and civic dispositions (e.g., becoming an independent member of society and assuming the responsibilities of a citizen). The 1998 NAEP is the only national survey that gathers information on these indicators through the administration of both closed- and open-ended items.

SOCIAL COMPETENCE

The ability to interact effectively with others is an important skill for life success, particularly because it spans many aspects of one's life. Competence in social situations is demonstrated by many indicators, including the ability to cooperate with others; manage aggression; engage in conflict resolution; and demonstrate social problem-solving, social reasoning, and coping skills.

The development of social competence is ongoing. Children in middle childhood are constantly refining their social skills. Well-developed social skills prepare children for successful interpersonal relationships, aid them in making healthy decisions, and sharpen their problem-solving skills (Leffert, Benson, & Roehlkepartain, 1997), whereas deficits in interpersonal skills are often associated with later delinquency, substance abuse, school dropout, and poor self-concept (Bukowski & Hoza, 1989). Unfortunately, educators report that more and more children are entering kindergarten lacking adequate social skills and behavior controls (Marshall, Temple, Montes, & Russell, 1996).

Although there is a consensus that promoting children's social competence is an important objective, measuring it reliably in children has been challenging. This is in part because many aspects of social competence involve subjective judgments and are context specific. Thus, multimethod assessments (including multiple informants) are highly recommended for assessing children's social competence.

Social problem solving involves the strategies children use to evaluate social situations, identify their own and others' feelings, develop solutions and understand the consequences of these solutions, and make choices (Marshall et al., 1996). Coping skills are part of social problem solving. Because children often lack control over situations in which they may find themselves that they perceive as stressful, and the resources available vary considerably from situation to situation, when evaluating and measuring indicators of coping it is important to assess not only whether children's efforts are successful but also what their repertoire of effort and strategies consist of. Thus, having both a range of strategies in one's repertoire and the ability to use them flexibly when the situation deems necessary may be considered the most important indicators of children's ability to be effective copers (Compas, 1987; Ryan-Wenger, 1992).

Additional indicators of positive coping and problem-solving skills with children in middle childhood are the ability to do the following: gather information, devise a plan of action, identify more than one solution for a problem, and possess the knowledge and acceptance of consequences of behavior. Indicators of more general social competence include the ability to appropriately express needs to other children and adults, interact appropriately with adults and other children, engage in productive group work, possess interaction and decision-making skills, have friends of a similar age, and be part of a social network (National Outcomes Work Group for Children).

Achenbach's Child Behavior Checklist is the most commonly administered screening instrument for tracking emergence of behavior problems in children, and it is appropriate for children ages 4 through 18. It has been standardized on children in the United States and abroad. The Social Rating Scale System is also very commonly used and is especially good for comparing behavior in multiple settings because it has both a parent and teacher report (Grensham & Elliot, 1990).

RELATIONSHIPS WITH PEERS AND ADULTS

Middle childhood is a time when children become increasingly involved in relationships outside the home. It also is a time when outside influences take on greater importance in influencing what children do and the choices they make (Canadian Council on Social Development, 2001). Positive relationships are important to children's social and emotional well-being, including relationships with parents, other family members (e.g., uncles, aunts, grandparents, siblings, cousins), other adults (e.g., teacher, coach, school counselor, family friend), peers, and friends. Although there are many widely used measures assessing parent-child relationships, there is a need for more measures of peer, sibling, teacher, and other adult relationships, particularly child self-report measures.

Parents

Compared with cognitive and academic outcomes, children's social behavior and emotional well-being are more strongly related to the social and affective features of parents' interactions with them, including the quality of discipline provided, and less strongly related to the cognitive environment. Children and youth who manifest positive social behavior and low levels of psychological distress perceive their relations with parents positively, and they tend to have mothers who are warm and who eschew harsh punishment (see McLoyd, 1998, for a review). Young people who engage in deviant and delinquent behavior also have parents who provide low levels of supervision, monitoring, and control (McLoyd, 1998; Sampson & Laub, 1994).

Other Adults and Family Members

Urie Bronfenbrenner, an important scholar and child advocate, asserts that every child needs one adult who thinks he or she is absolutely wonderful. Other family members or adults may serve as this person. Unfortunately, there are few measures of children's perceptions of social support. Reid, Landesman, Treder, and Jaccard (1989) developed a scale that examines children's (ages 6–12) perceptions of social support. This is the only measure for children of this age, and there is limited research on the validity of this measure. Gathering information on only parent-child relationships may yield an incomplete picture of important relationships in children's lives.

Siblings

Over the last decade, research has shown that siblings play important roles in each other's lives, both in early and middle childhood (Bryant,

1982; Dunn & Kendrick, 1982; Dunn & Munn, 1986) as well as later in life (Cicirelli, 1982). Older siblings have been found to provide important support to younger siblings, often acting as a teacher and a caregiver (Daniels, Dunn, Furstenberg, & Plomin, 1985). Moreover, the influence of older siblings has been shown to be particularly important for certain ethnic groups (Henderson, 1997; Steinberg, Dornbusch, & Brown, 1992). For instance, in Latino families older siblings often serve as important mentors and role models because they may be more able than parents to assist with homework and demonstrate positive school behavior. Moreover, older siblings in Latino families often serve as important sources of emotional support and companionship because of the valuation of close family ties found in many Latino families (Cooper, Denner, & Lopez, 1999).

Teachers

Relationships with teachers are important for many reasons. As Wigfield, Eccles, and Rodriguez (1998) pointed out, positive relationships with teachers are crucial to children's motivation. For instance, children seek help from their teachers when they perceive the teachers as warm and supportive (Newman, 1994).

There are a few existing measures that tap into student-teacher relationships. The Patterns of Adaptive Learning Survey (Midgley et al, 1996) includes both a student and teacher form. The child report assesses children's perceptions of the motivational and instructional techniques of their teacher, and teachers assesses their own motivational and instructional techniques. However, this measure is not intended for students below fourth grade. The Health Behavior of School Aged-Children Survey includes a few items measuring student-teacher relationships, including children's report of teacher support (see http://www.hbsc.org/publications/research_protocols.html).

The Teacher as Social Context (TASC) instrument (Belmont et al., 1992) assesses both teacher and student report of child-teacher interactions and measures both positive and negative outcomes. A short form is also available (TASC-Short Form). The Student-Teacher Relationship Scale, used in the NICHD Study of Early Child Care, measures teachers' perceptions of the student-teacher relationship (see http://www.nichd.nih.gov/od/secc/index.htm).

Peers/Friendships

Relationships with peers are powerful indicators of both current and future adaptive functions (Coie, Lochman, Terry, & Hyman, 1992; Hymel, Rubin, Rowden, & Lemare, 1990). The influence of peers in engagement in of positive and negative behavior is well documented, with close and best friends having the greatest influence (Berndt, 1996). Friendships aid in the promotion of coping skills and strategies, moral development, and positive self-esteem (Hartup & Stevens, 1999, Piaget, 1965). Familiarity and understanding of social norms, initiation and maintenance of social bonds, and defining and sharing leadership roles are all learned through peer relationships (Gottman & Parker, 1987).

A common measurement of peer relationships is asking children to nominate or rate their peers on various qualities. It is important to gather information on both the number and quality of friendships, as well as whether or not their friends are their same age, sex, and race. A measure used in the NICHD study ("Friends or Foes?") gathers sociometric ratings of children from their caregiver/teacher about their friends, including their friends' age, ethnicity, and gender, and makes distinctions between playmates and close friends. The NICHD study also uses a questionnaire in which mothers report the age, sex, and ethnicity of their child's playmates as well as the frequency and location of play, and harmony, balance, and conflict of play interaction (see http://www.nichd.nih.gov/od/secc/index.htm). Other studies that include measures of peer relationships and influence include the Progress of Canadian Children Study, the Los Angeles Family and Neighborhood Study, and the Profile of Student Life: Attitudes and Behaviors. More information on these studies can be found in the Appendix.

ABILITY AND ATTITUDES CONCERNING MULTICULTURALISM AND DIVERSITY

The United States is becoming more culturally diverse. In middle childhood, children develop the ability to take other people's perspectives and to understand that others may have different viewpoints. Respect for cultural and individual differences are important indicators of children's personal and social adjustment. This domain includes children's responses to other people who may differ from them on both an individual and group level, such as gender, social class, immigration status, culture, ethnicity, or in other ways. Suggested indicators of children's positive attitudes toward multiculturalism and diversity (i.e. cultural competence) include interacting with people different from them; recognizing and respecting similarities and differences between themselves and others; demonstrating respect and concern for others; acknowledging differences in culture, race, gender, socioeconomic status, ability, and family; participating in making school and community welcoming and inclusive of diversity; and demonstrating an awareness of and comfort with people different than them.

Existing measures in this domain are extremely limited. Measures used in the past to tap into this domain assess children's empathy, such as Bryant's (1982) Empathy in Children scale for children in Grades 1 through 8. However, as Berndt (1997) pointed out, children generally have more empathy toward people they perceive as similar to themselves; thus, solely assessing empathy as a measure of children's attitudes toward diversity becomes problematic.

Children of immigrants and children of color face distinct challenges in their development. These challenges naturally make issues of identity particularly salient to these children; thus, it is important that we gain a better understanding of ethnic identity and its links to children's socioemotional development. In the past, researchers have focused mostly on negative psychological effects of immigration on psychiatric and behavioral problems.

Fortunately, there has been a recent call to examine these issues in the last decade, in part as a response to the fast-growing number of various racial and ethnic minority groups, whose development and well-being will have important ramifications to the well-being of society as a whole. There have been several recent developments of studies designed to address these issues, such as the California Childhood Project and the Children of Immigrants Study. In fact, because of the lack of research and existing measures in this area, the first step of researchers in the Children of Immigrants Study was to pilot measures that were created to tap into constructs such as racial-ethnic identity and esteem and discrimination during middle childhood. They also adapted measures from other work, such as Deborah Johnson's (1996) Racial Stories and Perceived Racial Stress and Coping Apperception Test. Another existing measure in this area is the Ethnic Preference and Identity Measure (Johnson & Castillo, 1994), which assesses ethnic preference and salience. A modified version of this measure was used in the NICHD Study of Early Child Care and Youth Development (see http://secc.rti.org/).

RECOMMENDATIONS FOR THE FUTURE

The following five brief recommendations outline the areas that we feel need most improving in the coming decade.

1. *In recognition that behavior is context specific, data should be gathered from multiple informants (including the child when possible) and across multiple contexts.* A starting point for gathering data from multiple informants is to adapt items from existing measures (e.g., parent report of child's behavior) for use in other contexts or with other informants (e.g., teachers, grandparents, church minister, coaches). This relates to the next recommendation.

2. *Modify existing measures.* Aber and Jones (1997) discussed the difficulty of using labor- (and financially) intensive data gathering in national surveys. However, in recent years we have seen more and more modification of measures for the purpose of inclusion in national surveys. For example, Vandell and her colleagues modified the Center for Epidemiologic Studies Depression Scale (L. S. Radloff, 1977) for use in the NICHD Study of Early Childhood. The ethnic

identity task used in the NICHD Study of Early Child Care and Youth Development (see http://secc.rti.org/display.cfm?t=f&i=FH13) was also a modification to the Ethnic Preference and Identity Measure (Johnson & Castillo, 1994). We suggest more research on the appropriateness of modifying existing measures/scales that are established with older children for use with children in middle childhood.

A suggestion for the alleviation of time constraints is to add or combine items from existing measures with similar formats. For instance, Burnett and Meisells (2001) recommend adding and adapting items from the TASC (Belmont et al., 1992) to the Self-Description Questionnaire-I (Marsh, 1990). Doing this would not add much time to the administration of the measure, and the benefit would be the collection of information about various different people in children's lives. Last, using reduced versions of existing measures often saves time without jeopardizing the quality of information obtained. For example, the Chicago Neighborhood Study used a reduced version of Child Behavior Checklist (Achenbach, 1991), as have many other regional and national surveys.

3. *Create indicators applicable to different cultural groups.* More work is especially needed on the role of constructs linked to cultural and ethnicity, including cultural knowledge, ethnic identities, coping skills for dealing with experiences of discrimination and racism, and management skills for living in an ethnically and culturally diverse world.

4. *Extend assessments of middle childhood to community and local levels.* We strongly suggest that more work be conducted that will assess children's well-being at the community level. A great example of this, accomplished with adolescents, is through the administration of the Profiles of Student Life: Attitudes and Behaviors survey. This survey was developed by the Search Institute and has been administered in over 1,000 communities since 1989. It is designed for youth in Grades 6 through 12; however, modifications could be made to assess children in middle childhood.

The questions used in the survey were culled primarily from national surveys. The primary goal of the Search Institute in the development and administration of this survey was to inform social action by providing communities with a common language, a unified and complete vision of positive youth development, and the means to identify and strengthen the developmental processes within their community. The survey is very comprehensive and includes multiple measures in many domains of youth development, including areas that we have identified in this chapter as being particularly underdeveloped in middle childhood, such as moral character, capacities to take responsibility for one's actions, planning ahead, and making choices. The survey is particularly strong in social development measures, including participation in various activities both in and out of school, volunteering in the community, capacity for empathy and sensitivity, friendship skills, and respect for cultural diversity, all of which are domains that are fairly underdeveloped in middle childhood. The coverage in the social context domains is also comprehensive, including the assessment of supportive relationships in the family, as well as adults outside the family, in the school and in the community. Thus, the adaptation and implementation of this survey for use with children in middle childhood would be a great asset for measuring these important domains at the community level.

5. *Develop and expand civic competency measures.* The 1998 National Assessment of Educational Progress and the National Household Education Survey are the only national surveys that assess civic competency and knowledge. An easy way to gather data on children's civic activity participation is to add questions to existing measures of out of school time that assess children's involvement in prosocial, civic, and community activities.

NOTES

[1]The Appendix is not necessarily comprehensive.

APPENDIX

NATIONAL SURVEYS

1. National Household Education Survey (NHES)

Ages: Four populations: (a) 3 and older not in kindergarten, (b) K-5, (c) 6-12, and (d) homeschooled.

Social-emotional constructs assessed: The Parent and Family Involvement Component of the NHES focuses on children's schooling, children's homework and behavior, civic knowledge, and involvement and activities with children outside of school.

Web site: http://nces.ed.gov/nhes/

2. National Longitudinal Study of Youth (NLSY) and Children of NLSY 79

The NLSY is a nationally representative sample of men and women with an oversampling of Black, Hispanic, and economically disadvantaged White youth. Beginning in 1986, interviewers administered an extensive set of assessment instruments to the children of all the female respondents. These assessments include information about cognitive, socioemotional, and psychological aspects of the child's development as well as about the quality of the home environment.

Ages: Begins with children ages 6 through 7 and tracks them through graduation to middle school.

Social-emotional constructs assessed: Achievement and ability, behavior problems, and home environment, child-parent interaction, friendships, religious attendance. The achievement and ability measures are drawn from assessments administered by the survey interviewer. The behavior problems and home environment measures are drawn from maternal reports.

Measures used: HOME, BPI, Harter Self-Perception Profile for Children.

Web site: http://nces.ed.gov/nhes/

3. National Assessment of Educational Progress, a.k.a. "The Nation's Report Card"

Ages: Grades 4, 8, and 12.

Social-emotional constructs assessed: Civic competence.

Web site: http://nces.ed.gov/nationsreportcard/

4. NICHD study of Early Child Care and Youth Development

Ages: First visited at 1 month to first grade.

Social-emotional constructs assessed: Social competence, behavior problems, psychological well-being, friendships, peer relationships, student-teacher relationships.

Measures used: Loneliness and Dissatisfaction Questionnaire, Depression ("My Feelings" i.e., modified Center for Epidemiologic Studies Depression Scale [L. S. Radloff, 1977]), Child Behavior Checklist (CBCL; Achenbach, xxxx), Child Evaluation-Social Skills with Peers subscale, Friends or Foes, Playmate Questionnaire, Social Skills Rating System (Gresham & Elliott, 1990), Student-Teacher Relationship Scale, Teacher as Social Context (Belmont et al., 1992), Ethnic Preference and Identity Measure (Johnson & Castillo, 1994).

Web site: http://secc.rti.org/

5. Progress of Canadian Children

Ages: School-aged.

Social-emotional constructs assessed: Social Engagement (family, peer, community, and societal relationships), Socioemotional States (anxiety, hyperactivity, emotional disorders, indirect aggression, inattention), Civic Vitality, Skill Development (sports, lessons, community groups, activities, summer camp, computer, video, chores), Prosocial Behavior.

Web site: http://www.ccsd.ca/pubs/2002/pcc02/

6. Early Childhood Longitudinal Study-Kindergarten Cohort

Longitudinal study of children in 1998-99 kindergarten class, the first national data available on children in public and private kindergarten.

Ages: Kindergarten.

Social-emotional constructs assessed: Social and emotional development that contributes to social competence, including social skills (cooperation, assertion, responsibility, and self-control) and problem behaviors (impulsive reactions, verbal and physical aggression).

Web site: http://nces.ed.gov/ecls/

7. National Survey of America's Families (1997 and 1999)

The National Survey of America's Families provides a comprehensive look at the well-being of adults and children 13 states: Alabama, California, Colorado, Florida, Massachusetts, Michigan, Minnesota, Mississippi, New Jersey, New York, Texas, Washington, and Wisconsin. The survey incorporates ways of measuring changes in child well-being designed by Child Trends. The 1999 National Survey of America's Families, like its 1997 counterpart, is a survey of the economic, health, and social characteristics of children, adults under the age of 65, and their families.

Ages: 18 and under.

Social-emotional constructs assessed: Children's social and positive development (participation in training programs and recreational activities-teams, clubs, scouts), religious problems, and behavior problems.

Measures used: Behavior Problem Index.

Web site: http://newfederalism.urban.org/nsaf/methodology.html

8. Panel Study of Income Dynamics: Child Development Supplement (PSID-CDS)

Ages: 0-12 years.

Social-emotional constructs assessed: Cognitive, behavioral, and health status of children assessed by mother, a second caregiver, an absent parent, the teacher, the school administrator, and the child. Parental and caregiver time with children, other ways children spend their time out of school time, and teacher-reported time use. Assessment of other resources, including learning environment in the home, teacher and administrator reports of school resources, and decennial-census-based measurement of neighborhood resources.

Measures used: See http://psidonline.isr. umich. edu/CDS/ quescodetable.html.umich.edu/src/child-development/instruments.html for a full list of measures.

Web site: http://psidonline.isr. umich. edu/CDS

REGIONAL SURVEYS:

9. Project of Human Development in Chicago Neighborhoods

Ages: Begins with nine different age groups, from prenatal to age 18, and follows them for 8 years.

Social-emotional constructs assessed: Antisocial behavior, emotional factors/mental health, school factors, social network, personality/attitudes/personal identity, use of time/activities.

Measures used: CBCL (Achenbach, 1991), "Jobs and Routine Activities" measure

Web site: http://www.hms.harvard.edu/dsm/workfiles/html/research/phden/phdcn.htm

10. New Hope Project (24- and 60-month surveys)

New Hope is a antipoverty demonstration program operating in two neighborhoods in Milwaukee, Wisconsin. The New Hope program makes a simple offer to participating households: If there is a household member working full time, the program will assure that household income rises above the poverty line and that household members have access to child care and medical services. As such, it represents a work-based alternative to welfare and a new way to address the income needs of the working poor. Eligibility for the program is restricted to households in the two neighborhoods with income below 150% of the poverty line and that includes an adult who is willing to work full time (i.e. 30 hours/week).

Ages: 3-12 years at 24-month assessment.

Social-emotional constructs assessed: Anxiety (Revised Child Manifest Anxiety Scale), depression, social competence/behavior, academic motivation and achievement, occupational aspirations and expectations, social problem-solving skills, activity participation, friendships, delinquent behavior, parent-child relationships.

Measures used: Loneliness and Dissatisfaction Questionnaire, Response Decision Instrument, Perceived Competence Scale for Children.

Web site: http://www.mdrc.org/project_8_30.html

11. Los Angeles Family and Neighborhood Study

Ages: 3 through 17.

Social-emotional constructs assessed: Neighborhood, family, and peer effects on children's development.

Measures used: CBCL (Achenbach, 1991), modified HOME.

Web site: http://www.lasurvey.rand.org/

12. 3 Cities Study

This study focuses on the effects of welfare reform on children's and adolescent's well-being, including health, cognitive development, school achievement, and emotional and behavioral development. Sites include San Antonio, Boston, and Chicago.

Ages: Two cohorts: birth to age 4, and 10 through 14.

Social-emotional constructs assessed: Social, emotional, and behavioral development and well-being.

Measures used: New Chance Positive Behaviors Scale, CBCL (Achenbach, 1991), Brief Symptom Inventory (BSI-18) using the ACASI, Behavior Problem Index.

Web site: http://www.bgsu.edu/organizations/cfdr/about/pdf/Lein_Summary.pdf

13. Childhood and Beyond

Ages: Grades K-4.

Social-emotional constructs assessed: The development of self and task beliefs within and across domains; the role of these beliefs in shaping children's behavioral choices across the domains; the antecedents of parents' and teachers' beliefs about their children in each of these domains; and the impact of parenting and teaching styles and of teacher and parent beliefs, values, and perceptions on children's developing self- and task beliefs.

Measures used: Objective measures of the children's competence in math, language arts, and sport/physical skill were obtained. Subjective indicators of the children's competence were obtained from teacher and parent ratings. Detailed information about the school and home social and material context were obtained from parents, children, and teachers.

Web site: http://www.rcgd.isr.umich.edu/cab/home.htm

14. MacArthur School Engagement Project

Ages: First- and third-graders.

Social-emotional constructs assessed: Based on Blumenfeld's model of school engagement, three aspects of school engagement were assessed: (a) affective (e.g., how much children like school), (b) behavioral (e.g., whether children pay attention to the teacher during class), and (c) intellectual (e.g., whether children are actively involved in learning).

Measures used: 22 Likert-type questions followed by 20 open-ended questions. Examples of open-ended questions are "What do you like about school?" and "When your homework is hard, what do you do?"

Web site: http://childhood.isr.umich.edu/current/engage.html

15. MacArthur School Transition Study

Ages: Kindergarten through fifth-graders in Los Angeles; Pittsburgh, PA; and Vermont.

Social-emotional constructs assessed: Effect of age of entry into kindergarten on academic and social outcomes through third grade, young children's feelings about school, effect of instruction on motivation, young children's social competence and relationships with teachers, effects of instruction on student engagement, and parents' beliefs about their role in children's education.

Measures used: Direct assessments of children's math and literacy skills; direct assessments of children's perceptions of their academic competence and their feelings about school; a teacher questionnaire describing aspects of the classroom and curriculum; a teacher questionnaire rating each child on a variety of skills and dispositions, their perceptions and experiences with the child's family, and the school culture; a principal questionnaire on school resources, services, and links to the community, and ratings of the school culture; a school data form on the student population and organization of the school; a summary of information in each child's school record; a direct observation of a math, reading, and writing lesson during a typical school day; and a telephone interview with the child's primary caregiver.

Web site: http://childhood.isr.umich.edu/current/macar.html

16. Children of Immigrants Project

This study focuses on the normative processes and experiences of adjustment and acculturation and the more subjective socioemotional aspects of growing up as the child of an immigrant in the United States.

Ages: 6-12 years.

Social-emotional constructs assessed: The development of ethnic identity, The development of ethnic esteem, The experience of racism and discrimination, Engagement with institutions.

Web site: http://www.childhood.isr.umich.edu/current/children.html

17. California Childhoods Project

Examines how the daily contexts of children's lives influence their experiences and pathways of development in three California communities that vary in social class and ethnic composition and in processes of racialization and histories of immigration.

Ages: Elementary school.

Measures used: Perceived Racial Stress and Coping Apperception Test (Johnson, 1996)

Web site: http://childhood.isr.umich.edu/current/calif.html

OTHER RESOURCES

18. Children, Youth, and Families at Risk Initiative and Evaluation Collaboration Project: Evaluation of the National Outcomes for Children

Ages: Birth to 11.

The National Outcome Work Group for includes individuals affiliated with Cooperative Extension's Children, Youth and Families At Risk Initiative, and specifically with the State Strengthening projects. Provides information regarding suggested outcomes components and suggested indictors/instruments.

Social-emotional constructs assessed: Personal and Social Adjustment (four components): (a) copes effectively with personal challenges, frustrations, and stressors; (b) possesses a good self-image; (c) gets along with other people; and (d) respects cultural and individual differences; Academic and Functional Literacy (two components): (a) demonstrates competence in communication and (b) demonstrates competence in problem solving; Contribution and Citizenship; Responsibility and Independence.

Web site: http://csrees.usda.gov/nea/family/cyfar/cyfar.htm

19. Profile of Student Life: Attitudes and Behaviors

Ages: Grades 6-12.

Social-emotional constructs assessed: The survey focuses on four categories of adolescent experiences (outlined in more detail below): (a) developmental assets, (b) thriving indicators, (c) deficits, and (d) risk behaviors and high-risk behavior patterns.

Developmental Assets. The developmental assets represent the positive relationships, opportunities, skills, and values that promote the positive development of all children and adolescents. The developmental assets are grouped into 20 external assets (i.e., health-promoting features of the environment) and 20 internal assets (i.e., a youth's own commitments, values, and competencies). The 20 external assets are grouped into the four categories of (a) support, (b) empowerment, (c) boundaries and expectations, and (d) constructive use of time. The 20 internal assets are grouped into the four categories of (a) commitment to learning, (b) positive values, (c) social competencies, and (d) positive identity.

The 40 developmental assets (listed by the eight external and internal categories) are as follows:

Support: Family Support, Positive Family Communication, Other Adult Relationships, Caring Neighborhood, Caring School Climate, Parent Involvement in Schooling.

Empowerment: Community Values Youth, Youth as Resources, Service to Others, Safety.

Boundaries and Expectations: Family Boundaries, School Boundaries, Neighborhood Boundaries, Adult Role Models, Positive Peer Influence, High Expectations.

Constructive Use of Time: Creative Activities, Youth Programs, Religious Community, Time at Home.

Commitment to Learning: Achievement Motivation, School Engagement, Homework, Bonding to School, Reading for Pleasure.

Positive Values: Caring, Equality and Social Justice, Integrity, Honesty, Responsibility, Restraint.

Social Competencies: Planning and Decision Making, Interpersonal Competence, Cultural Competence, Resistance Skills, Peaceful Conflict Resolution.

Positive Identity: Personal Power, Self-Esteem, Sense of Purpose, and Positive View of Personal Future.

Thriving Indicators. Healthy development also includes life-enhancing attitudes and behaviors, which in the A&B survey are called *Thriving Indicators*. The eight indicators examined include (a) succeeds in school, (b) helps others, (c) values diversity, (d) maintains good health, (e) exhibits leadership, (f) resists danger, (g) delays gratification, and (h) overcomes adversity. Each of these eight indicators is measured by one survey question.

Web site: http://www.search-institute.org/surveys/abPolicy.html

REFERENCES

Aber, J. L., & Jones, S. M. (1997). Indicators of positive development in early childhood: Improving concepts and measure. In R. M. Hauser, B. V. Brown, & W. R. Prosser (Eds.), *Indicators of children's well-being* (pp. 395–408). New York: Russell Sage Foundation.

Asher, S. R., Hymel, S., & Renshaw, P. D. (1984). Loneliness in children. *Child Development, 55*, 1456–1464.

Asher, S. R., & Wheeler, V. A. (1985). Children's loneliness: A comparison of rejected and neglected peer status. *Journal of Consulting and Clinical Psychology, 53*, 500–505.

Bandura, A. (1976). The self system in reciprocal determinism. *American Psychologist, 33*, 344–358.

Battle, J. (1992). *Culture-free self-esteem inventories* (2nd ed.). Austin, TX: Pro-Ed.

Belmont, M., Skinner, E., Wellborn, J., & Connell, J. (1992). *Teacher as Social Context (TASC): Two measures of teacher provision of involvement, structure, and autonomy support: Student report measure* (Technical report). Rochester, NY: University of Rochester.

Benson, P. (1997). *All kids are our kids*. San Francisco: Jossey-Bass.

Berndt, T. J. (1996). Transitions in friendship and friends' influence. In J. A. Graber, J. Brooks-Gunn, & A. C. Petersen (Eds.), *Transitions through adolescence: Interpersonal domains and context* (pp. 57–84). Mahwah, NJ: Lawrence Erlbaum Associates.

Berndt, T. J. (1997). *Child development* (2nd ed.). Madison, WI: Brown & Benchmark.

Bickham, D. S., Vandewater, E. A., Huston, A. C., Lee, J. H., Caplovitz, A. G., & Wright, J. C. (2003). Predictors of children's media use: An examination of three ethnic groups. *Media Psychology, 5,* 107–137.

Birleson, P. (1981). The validity of depressive disorder in childhood and the development of a self-rating scale. *Journal of Child Psychology & Psychiatry, 22,* 47–53.

Birmaher, B., Brent, D. A., Chiappetta, L., Bridge J., Monga, S., & Baugher, M. (1999). Psychometric properties of the Screen for Child Anxiety Related Emotional Disorders Scale (SCARED): A replication study. *Journal of the American Academy of Child and Adolescent Psychiatry, 38,* 1230–1236.

Bos, J. M., Huston, A. C., Granger, R. C., Duncan, G. J., Brock, T., & McLoyd, V. C. (1999). *New hope for people with low incomes: Two-year results of a program to reduce poverty and reform welfare*. New York: Manpower Demonstration Research Corporation.

Brock, T., Doolittle, F., Fellerath, V., & Wiseman, M. (1997). Creating new hope: *Implementation of a program to reduce poverty and reform welfare*. New York: Manpower Demonstration Research Corporation.

Bryant, B. K. (1982). An index of empathy for children and adolescents. *Child Development, 53,* 413–425.

Bukowski, W. M., & Hoza, B. (1989). Popularity and friendship: Issues in theory, measurement, and outcome. In T. J. Berndt & G. W. Ladd. (Eds.), *Peer relationships and child development* (pp. 15–45). New York: Wiley.

Burnett & Meisells. (2001). *Measures of socio-emotional development in middle childhood*. Working Paper Series, No. 2001-03, National Center for Education Statistics, Washington, DC.

Byrne, B. (1996). *Measuring self-concept across the life span: Issues and instrumentation*. Washington, DC: American Psychological Association.

Canadian Council on Social Development. (2001). *Defining and re-defining poverty: A CCSD perspective*. City, Province: Author.

Capella, E., & Lerner, M. B. (1999). America's schoolchildren: Past, present, and future. *The Future of Children, 9*(2), 21–29.

Carnegie Corporation. (1992). *A matter of time: Risk and opportunity in the out-of-school hours*. New York: Author.

Cartledge, G., & Milburn, J. F. (Eds.). (1995). *Teaching social skills to children and youth: Innovative approaches* (3rd ed.). Boston: Allyn & Bacon.

Cassidy, J., & Asher, S. R. (1992). Loneliness and peer relations in young children. *Child Development, 63,* 350–365.

Catalano, R. F., Berglund, M. L., Ryan, J. A. M., Lonczak, H. S., & Hawkins, J. D. (1999). *Positive youth development in the United States: Research findings on evaluations of positive youth development programs*. Seattle: University of Washington School of Social Work, Social Development Research Group.

Cicirelli, V. G. (1982). Sibling influence throughout the lifespan. In M. E. Lamb & B. Sutton-Smith (Eds.), *Sibling relationships: Their nature and significance across the life span* (pp. 267–284). Hillsdale, NJ: Lawrence Erlbaum Associates.

Coie, J. D., Lochman, J. E., Terry, R., & Hyman, C. (1992). Predicting early adolescent disorder from childhood aggression and peer rejection. *Journal of Consulting and Clinical Psychology, 60*, 783–792.

Cole, D. A. (1991). Preliminary support for a competency-based model of depression in children. *Journal of Abnormal Psychology, 100*, 181–190.

Compas, B. E. (1987). Coping with stress during childhood and adolescence. *Psychological Bulletin, 101*, 393–403.

Cooper, C. R., Denner, J., & Lopez, E. M. (1999). Cultural brokers: Helping Latino children on pathways toward success. *The Future of Children, 9*, 51–57.

Cosby, A. G. (1974). Occupational expectations and the hypothesis of increasing realism of choice. *Journal of Vocational Behavior, 5*, 53–65.

Crick, N. R., & Werner, N. E. (1998). Response decision processes in relational and overt aggression. *Child Development, 69*, 1630–1639.

Daniels, D., Dunn, J., Furstenberg, F. F., & Plomin, R. (1985). Environmental differences within the family and adjustment differences within pairs of adolescent siblings. *Child Development, 56*, 764–774.

Dubow, E. F., Huesmann, L. R., & Eron, L. D. (1987). Childhood correlates of adult ego development. *Child Development, 58*, 859–869.

Dunn, J., & Kendrick, C. (1982). The speech of two- and three-year-olds to infant siblings: "Baby talk" and the context of communication. *Journal of Child Language, 9*, 579–595.

Dunn, J., & Munn, P. (1986). Siblings and the development of prosocial behaviour. *Journal of Behavioral Development, 93*, 265–284.

Dygdon, J., Conger, A. J., Conger, J. D., Wallanda, J. L., & Keane, S. P. (1980). *Behavioral correlates of social competence and dysfunction in early childhood.* Paper presented the Annual Convention of the American Psychological Association, Montreal, Quebec, Canada.

Eccles, J. S. (1999). The development of children ages 6–14. *The Future of Children, 9*, 30–33.

Eccles, J. S., Wigfield, A., Harold, R. D., & Blumenfeld, P. (1993). Age and gender differences in children's self-and task perceptions during elementary school. *Child Development, 64*, 830–847.

Eccles, J. S., Wigfield, A., & Schiefele, U. (1997). Motivation to succeed. In N. Eisenberg (Ed.), *Handbook of child psychology* (5th ed., pp. 1017–1096). New York: Wiley.

Erikson, E. (1950). *Childhood and society.* New York: Norton.

Galambos, N. L., & Maggs, J. L. (1990). Putting mothers' work-related stress in perspective: Mothers and adolescents in dual-earner families. *Journal of Early Adolescence, 10*, 313–328.

Ginzberg, E. (1952). Toward a theory of occupational choice. *Occupations, 30*, 491–494.

Gottfredson, L. S. (1981). Circumscription and compromise: A developmental theory of occupational aspirations. *Journal of Counseling Psychology Monograph, 28*, 545–579.

Gottfried, A. E. (1985). Academic intrinsic motivation in elementary and junior high school students. *Journal of Educational Psychology, 77*, 631–645.

Gottman, J. M., & Parker, J. G. (Eds.). (1987). *Conversations of friends*. New York: Cambridge University Press.

Gresham, F. M., & Elliott, S. N. (1990). *Social Skills Rating System manual*. Circle Pines, MN: American Guidance Service.

Harrison, A. O., Wilson, M. N., Pine, C. P., Chan, S. Q., & Buriel, R. (1990). Family ecologies of ethnic minority children. *Child Development, 61*, 347–362.

Harter, S. (1982). The Perceived Competence Scale for Children. *Child Development, 53*, 87–97.

Harter, S. (1985). *Manual for the Self-Perception Profile for Children*. Denver, CO: University of Denver.

Harter, S., & Pike, R. (1984). The Pictorial Scale of Perceived Competence and Social Acceptance for Young Children. *Child Development, 55*, 1969–1982.

Hartup, W. W., & Stevens, N. (1999). Friendships and adaptation across the life span. *Current Directions in Psychological Science, 8*, 76–79.

Hauser, R. M., Brown, B. V., & Prosser, W. R. (1997). *Indicators of children's well-being*. New York: Russell Sage Foundation.

Henderson, R. W. (1997). Educational and occupational aspirations and expectations among parents of middle school students of Mexican descent: Family resources for academic development and mathematics learning. In R. D. Taylor & M. C. Wang (Eds.), *Social and emotional adjustment and family relations in ethnic minority families* (pp. 99–131). Mahwah, NJ: Lawrence Erlbaum Associates.

Humphrey, L. L. (1982). Children's and teacher's perspective on children's self-control: The development of two rating scales. *Journal of Consulting and Clinical Psychology, 50*, 624–633.

Hymel, S., Rubin, K. H., Rowden, L., & Lemare, L. (1990). Children's peer relationships-Longitudinal prediction of internalizing and externalizing problems from middle to late childhood. *Child Development, 61*, 2004–2021.

Johnson, D. (1996). The Perceived Racial Stress and Coping Apperception Test. In R. Jones (Ed.), *Handbook of tests and measurements for Black populations* (pp. 231–243). Hampton, VA: Cobb and Henry.

Kovacs, M. (1985). The Children's Depression Inventory (CDI). *Psychopharmacological Bulletin, 21*, 995–998.

Kovacs, M. (1992). *Children's Depression Inventory*. Toronto, Ontario, Canada: Multi-Health Systems.

La Greca, A. M., Kraslow-Dandes, S., Wick, P., Shaw, K., & Stone, W. L. (1988). Development of the Social Anxiety Scale for Children: Reliability and concurrent validity. *Journal of Clinical Child Psychology, 17*, 84–91.

La Paro, K. M., & Pianta, R. C. (2001). Predicting children's competence in the early school years: A meta-analytic review. *Review of Educational Research, 70*, 443–484.

Leffert, N., Benson, P. L., & Roehlkepartain, J. L. (1997). Starting out right: Developmental assets for children. Minneapolis, MN: Search Institute.

Lerner, R. M. (1998). Theories of human development: Contemporary perspectives. In W. Damon & R. M. Lerner (Eds.), *Handbook of child psychology: Vol. 1. Theoretical models of human development* (5th ed., pp. 1–24). New York: Wiley.

Lovko, A. M., & Ullman, D. G. (1989). Research on the adjustment of latchkey children: Role of background/demographic and latchkey situation variables. *Journal of Clinical Child Psychology, 18*, 16–24.

Marsh, H. W. (1988). *Self-Description-Questionnaire I. SDQ-I manual and research monograph.* San Antonio, TX: Psychological Corporation.

Marsh, H. W. (1990). A multidimensional, hierarchical model of self-concept: Theoretical and empirical justification. *Educational Psychology Review, 2,* 77–172.

Marshall, N. L., Garcia Coll, C., Marx, F., McCartney, K., Keefe, N., & Ruh, J. (1997). After-school time and children's behavioral adjustment. *Merrill-Palmer Quarterly, 43,* 497–514.

Marshall, H. M., Temple, M., Montes, G., & Russell, R. (1996, June 20-23). *Enhancing young children's social competence: ENHANCE!/SOCIAL COMPETENCE PROGRAM (ESCP)-A field developed program for children, teachers, and parents.* Poster presented at Head Start's Third National Research Conference, Washington, DC.

McLoyd, V. C. (1998). Socioeconomic disadvantage and child development. *American Psychologist, 53,* 185–204.

Midgley, C., Maehr, M., Anderman, L. H., Roeser, R., Urdan, T., Anderman, E., et al. (1996). *Patterns of Adaptive Learning Survey (PALS).* Ann Arbor, MI: Center for Leadership and Learning.

Milburn, T. W. (1972). The management of crisis. In C. F. Hermann (Ed.), *International crisis: Insights from behavioral research* (pp. 259–277). New York: Free Press.

Moore, K. (1997). Criteria for indicators of child well-being. In R. M. Hauser, B. Brown, & W. Prosser (Eds.), *Indicators of children's well-being* (pp. 36–44). New York: Russell Sage Foundation.

Moore, K., Evans, J., Brooks-Gunn, J., & Roth, J. L. (2001). What are good child outcomes? In A. Thornton (Ed.), *The well-being of children and families: Research and data needs* (pp. 59–84). Ann Arbor: University of Michigan Press.

Newman, D. (1994). Computer networks: Opportunities or obstacles? In B. Means (Ed.), *Technology and education reform: The reality behind the promise* (pp. 57–80). San Francisco: Jossey-Bass.

Parkhurst, J. T., & Asher, S. R. (1992). Peer rejection in middle school: Subgroup differences in behavior, loneliness, and interpersonal concerns. *Developmental Psychology, 28,* 231–241.

Pela, O. A., & Reynolds, C. R. (1982). Cross-cultural application of the Revised Children's Manifest Anxiety Scale: Normative and reliability data for Nigerian primary school children. *Psychological Reports, 51,* 1135–1138.

Peterson, J. L., & Zill, N. (1986). Marital disruption, parent-child relationships, and behavior problems in children. *Journal of Marriage and the Family, 48,* 295–307.

Pettit, G. S., Bates, J. E., & Dodge, K. A. (1997). Supportive parenting, ecological context, and children's adjustment: A seven-year longitudinal study. *Child Development, 68,* 908–924.

Pettit, G. S., Bates, J. E., Dodge, K. A., & Meece, D. W. (1999). The impact of after-school peer contact on early adolescent externalizing problems is moderated by parental monitoring, perceived neighborhood safety, and prior adjustment. *Child Development, 70,* 768–778.

Pettit, G. S., Laird, R. D., Bates, J. E., & Dodge, K. A. (1997). Patterns of after-school care in middle childhood: Risk factors and developmental outcomes. *Merrill-Palmer Quarterly, 43,* 515–538.

Piaget, J. (1965). *The moral judgment of the child.* New York: Free Press.

Pianta, R. C. (1992). *The student-teacher relationship scale.* Unpublished manuscript, University of Virginia.

Posner, J. K., & Vandell, D. L. (1994). Low-income children's after-school care: Are there beneficial effects of after-school programs? *Child Development, 65,* 440–456.

Posner, J. K., & Vandell, D. L. (1999). After-school activities and the development of low-income urban children: A longitudinal study. *Developmental Psychology, 35,* 868–879.

Quint, J. C., Bos, H., & Polit, D. F. (1997). *New chance: Final report on a comprehensive program for young mothers in poverty and their children.* New York: MDRC.

Radloff, A. (1997). A longitudinal study of self-regulation of learning in adult university students. Unpublished doctoral dissertation, Murdoch University, Perth.

Radloff, L. S. (1977). The CES-D Scale: A self-report depression scale for research in the general population. *Applied Psychological Measurement, 1,* 385–401.

Reid, M., Landesman, S., Treder, R., & Jaccard, J. (1989). "My family and friends": Six- to twelve-year-old children's perceptions of social support. *Child Development, 60,* 896–910.

Rodman, H., Pratto, D. J., & Nelson, R. S. (1985). Child care arrangements and children's functioning: A comparison of self-care and adult-care children. *Developmental Psychology, 21,* 413–418.

Rosenberg, M. (1965). *Society and the adolescent self-image.* Princeton, NJ: Princeton University Press.

Ryan-Wenger, N. M. (1992). A taxonomy of children's coping strategies: A step toward theory development. *American Journal of Orthopsychiatry, 57,* 316–331.

Sampson, R. J., & Laub, J. H. (1994). Urban poverty and the family context of delinquency: A new look at structure and process in a classic study. *Child Development, 65,* 523–540.

Scarr, S., & McCartney, K. (1983). How people make their own environments: A theory of genotype ? environment effects. *Child Development, 54,* 424–435.

Shaffer, D. R. (1999). *Developmental psychology: Childhood & adolescence* (5th ed.). Pacific Grove, CA: Brooks/Cole.

Steinberg, L. (1986). Latchkey children and susceptibility to peer pressure: An ecological analysis. *Developmental Psychology, 22,* 433–439.

Steinberg, L., Dornbusch, S. M., & Brown, B. B. (1992). Ethnic differences in adolescent achievement: An ecological perspective. *American Psychologist, 47,* 723–729.

U.S. Bureau of the Census. (1995). *Income, poverty, and valuation of non-cash benefits: 1993* (Report No. P60-188). Washington, DC: U.S. Department of Commerce, Bureau of the Census.

U.S. Department of Commerce, Bureau of the Census. (1996). *1990 to 1994 city/ place and metropolitan population estimates.* Washington, DC: U.S. Department of Commerce.

Vandell, D. L., & Corasaniti, M. A. (1988). The relation between third graders' after-school care and social, academic, and emotional functioning. *Child Development, 59,* 868–875.

Wigfield, A., Eccles, J. S., & Rodriguez, D. (1998). The development of children's motivation in school contexts. In P. D. Pearson & A. Iran-Nejad (Eds.), *Review of research in education* (pp. 73–118). Washington, DC: American Educational Research Association.

Chapter 6

Developing Indicators of Confidence, Character, and Caring in Adolescents

Jodie Roth-Herbst
Columbia University

Christina J. Borbely
Columbia University

Jeanne Brooks-Gunn
National Center for Children and Families

Over the past 10 years, the youth development movement's call for a paradigm shift from deterrence to development, captured by the phrase "problem free is not fully prepared," has lad to an "increased acceptance of youth preparation and development, not just problem prevention and deterrence, as broad goals requiring intentional monitoring and strategic action" (Pittman, Irby, & Ferber, 2000). With the maturing of the youth development field, a consensus is emerging on the characteristics of healthy or positive youth development. The goals of positive youth development capture all our hopes and aspirations for a nation of healthy, happy, and competent adolescents on their way to a productive and satisfying adulthood (Roth & Brooks-Gunn, 2000). More concretely, the 5 C's portray the desired outcomes of positive youth development: (a) competence in academic, social, and vocational areas; (b) confidence; (c) connection to community, family, and peers; (d) character; and (5) caring and compassion (Lerner, Fisher, & Weinberg, 2000).

With this shift comes the need for reliable and valid measures of both the outcomes and antecedents of positive development. In this chapter, we explore the definitional and measurement issues involved in delineating indicators for youth's progress towards these goals. As was our charge, we limit our discussion to three of the 5 C's most directly related to youth's psychological and emotional development: (a) confidence, (b) character, and (c) caring.

167

In the first part of this chapter we portray in greater detail these key constructs of adolescents'[1] psychological and emotional development by briefly reviewing the research on how they relate to well-being, drawing on both the research and practice literatures. Keeping Moore's (1997) criteria for indicators of child well-being in mind, we focus on the aspects of these constructs that offer both wide appeal to the public and a sound research base supporting their importance. In the second part of the chapter, we survey how the indicator field related to these constructs has changed and progressed in the past decade. We end the chapter with a discussion of the most important issues for the coming decade of work on indicators of youth psychological and emotional well-being.

KEY CONSTRUCTS OF YOUTH'S PSYCHOLOGICAL AND EMOTIONAL WELL-BEING

Answering the question "Who am I?" is thought to be the fundamental psychological task of adolescence. Adolescents discover who they really are and how they fit into the world in which they live by examining and exploring the psychological characteristics of the self (Harter, 1990). As children enter adolescence, their descriptions of themselves evolve from listings of their physical, behavioral and other external attributes to include traits, values, beliefs, and ideologies, enduring inner qualities (Damon & Hart, 1988). They begin to develop more abstract, differentiated, and better organized concepts of themselves (Steinberg & Morris, 2001). Adolescence, then, is a time to discover and refine the answer to the "Who am I" question. The many physical, cognitive, and social changes of adolescence may lead youth to conclude "I ain't what I ought to be, I ain't what I'm gonna be, but I ain't what I was" (Erikson, 1950, p. 139). Opportunities and supports in young people's lives, within their family, school, and community, provide them with the experiences they need to develop their identity, shape their beliefs, and cultivate their capacities.

CONFIDENCE

Defining Confidence

In a general sense, *confidence* refers to a belief in one's abilities. Psychologists identify several different but related constructs that fall under the general rubric of confidence, including identity, self-concept, self-esteem, and self-efficacy. Together, these constructs address the question of "Who am I?" and "What can I do?" According to Erikson (1963), youth successfully resolve the psychosocial crisis of the teen years (the identity crisis) by establishing an identity, or a firm and coherent sense of who they are, where they are heading, and where they fit in society.

Although most scholars view adolescence as a time of self-exploration, in contemporary society achieving a stable identity typically occurs late in adolescence or even not until young adulthood (Steinberg & Morris, 2001).

Possessing confidence entails an evaluative component of the self as well, referred to as *self-esteem*. Self-esteem conveys satisfaction or dissatisfaction with the self (DuBois, Felner, Brand, Phillips, & Lease, 1996). Youth with high self-esteem recognize their strengths and acknowledge their weaknesses; they are fundamentally satisfied with who they are. Adolescents' self-conceptions contribute to their overall feelings of self-esteem. Adolescents evaluate themselves globally and along several distinct dimensions, such as academics, athletics, and appearance, creating both an overall picture of themselves (global self-esteem) as well as domain-specific self-concepts (Harter, 1990). The link between the domain-specific self-concepts and self-esteem depends on the importance placed on the specific domain and the context. In general, global self-esteem increases slightly during adolescence. Adolescent males have slightly higher self-esteem than adolescent females (Kling, Hyde, Showers, & Buswell, 1999), and African American adolescents show higher self-esteem than White youth (Gray-Little & Hafdahl, 2000).

Confidence also includes a motivational and emotional component. Confidence requires a sense of agency or self-efficacy, a belief not only in one's abilities but also in one's power to accomplish. Self-efficacy theory holds that our beliefs about our abilities influence our behavior by determining what we try to achieve and how much effort we invest (see Bandura, 1982). Self-efficacy governs whether, or how, we put our knowledge into action. Adolescents' success at managing the biological, social, and educational role transitions associated with the teen years depends, in large part, on the strength of their perceived self-efficacy (Bandura, 1997).

To summarize, we believe that adolescents' sense of confidence rests on their view of themselves, their beliefs and abilities. Like self-esteem, youth possess both an overall sense of confidence as well as potentially disparate levels of confidence in different domains and contexts (see Table 6.1).

Table 6.1
The Components of Confidence

Component	Description
Identity	a firm and coherent sense of self
Self-Concept	domain-specific evaluations of the self
Self-Esteem	level of regard one has for the self as a person
Self-Efficacy	belief about one's capability to succeed

Outcomes Associated With Confidence in the Research Literature

Developmental psychologists rarely study confidence per se, but they have investigated, to varying degrees, the effects of identity, self-concept, self-esteem, and self-efficacy on adolescents' thoughts and behavior. Of these constructs, the effects of low versus high self-esteem on youth (as well as adults) receive the greatest attention. Empirical evidence shows that self-esteem correlates with how individuals feel, think, and behave (Kling et al., 1999). In a review of the outcomes of low and high self-esteem, Scales and Leffert (1999) concluded that the evidence typically, although not always, finds that low self-esteem is related to negative outcomes and that high self-esteem is associated with positive outcomes. Self-esteem is an essential component of mental health. Low self-esteem is associated with increased depression, hopelessness, loneliness, adjustment difficulties, and suicidal tendencies. High self-esteem is associated with positive emotionality, relationships, and adjustment and increased satisfaction with life. In regard to behavioral outcomes, high self-esteem is correlated with increased academic achievement and decreased levels of risk-taking behaviors, such as sexual activity and nonmarital childbearing, and drug use. In more sophisticated studies that look at adolescents' self-esteem trajectories over time, high self-esteem emerges as a protective factor (DuBois et al., 2002; Scheier, Botvin, Griffin, & Diaz, 2000; M. A. Zimmerman, Copeland, Shope, & Dielman, 1997).

As noted earlier, there is limited research on stable identity formation in adolescence. Erikson believed that individuals who fail to establish an identity would become depressed or embrace a negative identity (e.g., black sheep, delinquent). Meeus (1996) found a stronger relationship between identity development and positive feelings of psychological well-being than negative feeling of depression. Only at older ages did the failure to develop an identity result in lower levels of well-being and more depression. Youth who were actively exploring their positions on a number of values, interests, ideologies, and careers in search of a stable identity (moratoria) exhibited lower levels of psychological well-being than other youth. This finding is contrary to the results found in other domains, such as social skills, intimate relationships, and school performance. In these domains, moratoria showed an almost equally positive profile as youth who have achieved an identity and a more positive profile than youth who have not begun to question or search for an identity (diffusions) or youth who have prematurely committed themselves to an identity without exploring their options (foreclosures).

Adolescents' beliefs about their agency have been used to explain their contraceptive and drug use (Allen, Leadbeater, & Aber, 1990) and their academic attainments (B. Zimmerman, 1995). In a study of depression in early adolescence, Bandura, Pastorelli, Barbaranelli, and Caprara (1999) found direct and indirect effects for two facets of perceived self-efficacy-academic self-efficacy and social self-efficacy-in both concurrent and subsequent depression. Students' perceived academic self-efficacy, their beliefs in their capabilities to master coursework and regulate their own learning, not their actual performance, predicted depression. Furthermore, youth with high academic efficacy received higher grades, showed more prosocial behaviors, and exhibited lower levels of problem behaviors. Bandura et al. found the same results for youth who reported higher levels of social efficacy, defined as students' beliefs in their abilities to form and maintain social relationships, work cooperatively with others, and manage interpersonal conflicts.

Efforts to Build Confidence

A discussion of how confidence develops is beyond the scope of this chapter. Suffice it to say that, as with other areas of development, individuals' level of confidence results from the interplay between their personal qualities and their experiences in different contexts, including their family, school, and community. Despite only limited empirical research on the outcomes associated with confidence, the general public appears eager to maximize youth's chances of developing confidence. Parents are bombarded with guidance on how to help their children develop high self-esteem and confidence. In the schools, building self-esteem has become paramount (although there is a growing self-esteem backlash). The National Association for Self-Esteem web site (http://www.self-esteem-nase.org) lists many school-based programs that are specifically aimed at enhancing self-esteem. In addition, almost any after-school activity, club, volunteer activity, or community-based program claims to build confidence in its participants (Roth & Brooks-Gunn, 2003).

Empirical evidence from these settings supports the importance of developing a sense of confidence for positive youth development. The vast majority of programs in our reviews of the evaluations of programs that promote positive youth development led to an increase in participants' self-esteem or self-concepts (Roth & Brooks-Gunn, 2003; Roth, Brooks-Gunn, Murray, & Foster, 1998). After a decade of ethnographic research with community-based youth organizations in challenging settings, McLaughlin (2000) found high levels of self-confidence and optimism for the future among the low-income, high-risk urban youth who participated in these organizations, even when compared to typical American teenagers.

These activities can also expose youth to the new experiences, people, and ideas necessary for identity development. Sports, arts, and recreation programs offer youth the opportunity to try out different identities—that of athlete, artist, or performer, for example. Researchers empirically study the effects of one type of activity in particular: volunteer or community service activities. In a study of over 10,000 youth,

Youniss, McLellan, Su, and Yates (1999) found that youths' participation in community service and/or civic affairs roughly doubled the amount of variability accounted for by demographics and part-time work in predicting youths' normative, unconventional, or deviant identities. They concluded that community service exposes youth to socially accepted norms and values that help shape their emerging self-definitions. Reviews of research on quality service learning programs[2] report increases in participants' self-esteem, self-efficacy, and confidence. These programs also promote participants' identity development, in the form of career exploration (Billig, 2001; Stukas, Clary, & Snyder, 1999a).

CHARACTER

Individuals can display their character in everyday actions as well as in the way they act when faced with a dilemma. Deciding between alternative actions requires the capacity for thoughtful inquiry, open-mindedness, information gathering, and reflection (Flanagan & Faison, 2001). Although the roots of character are evident in young children, it is not until adolescence that cognitive abilities and social experiences truly allow for this type of thinking and behavior. Defining and refining an internalized set of commitments that can serve as moral guideposts for thinking and behavior helps youth define who they are and how they relate to others.

Defining Character

Perhaps since the beginning of time-at least documented since the days of the early Greek philosophers-people have been trying to define character, or what qualities, traits, or virtues constitute a good person, a person of character. Character includes both an attitudinal and behavioral component. Thus, a person of character not only holds positive values, or morals, but also acts on them. Values, or morals, are the standards, goals, or principles we hold that guide our thinking and behavior. Particularly in today's pluralistic society, defining a universal list of desired values proves difficult.

Three recent efforts to do so have produced similar lists. A diverse group of ethicists, educators, and youth service professionals brought together by the Josephson Institute of Ethics identified "six pillars of character" (Character Counts, 2001). They defined the pillars in behavioral terms: trustworthiness (being honest), respect (treating others with respect), responsibility (doing what you are supposed to do), fairness (playing by the rules), caring (being kind), and citizenship (doing your share to make your school and community better). The Search Institute's internal asset of "positive values" includes two prosocial values (caring, and equality and social justice) and four behavioral characteristics (integrity, honesty, responsibility, and restraint; Scales & Leffert, 1999). Peterson and Seligman (2002) included six virtues, or core characteristics, valued by moral philosophers and religious thinkers in their list of good character: (a) wisdom, (b) courage, (c) humanity, (d) justice, (e) temperance, and (f) transcendence.

Peterson and Seligman's (2002) efforts are part of the budding interest among psychologists in positive psychology. The list serves as the road map for the Values in Action's (VIA's) *Classification of Strengths Manual*, a "manual of sanities" comparable to the American Psychiatric Association's (1994) influential *Diagnostic and Statistical Manual of Mental Disorders* for psychological conditions. This effort presents the most comprehensive consideration of the concept of character by psychologists we have seen. For our purposes here, it holds the most promise for guidance on developing measurable indicators of character among youth.

The VIA distinguishes among the six virtues, best thought of as *overarching qualities*, and character strengths, how individuals display these virtues, or the behavioral manifestations of the qualities of good character. Their current classification includes 24 character strengths classified under the six virtues (see Table 6.2). The character strengths are ubiquitously recognized and valued, although they rarely are found in one individual. The manual includes the current state of knowledge for each of the character strengths, including how it has been studied; its correlates and outcomes; how it develops and is manifest throughout the life span; factors that encourage or inhibit its development; possible cross-cultural aspects of the strength; and a bibliography of relevant materials.

Table 6.2

The Components of Character Identified in the Values in Action (VIA) Classification (6 Virtues and 24 Character Strengths)

Virtue	Components
Wisdom	creativity; curiosity; judgment/critical thinking; love of learning; perspective
Courage	bravery; industry/perseverance; authenticity; zest
Humanity	kindness; love/intimacy; social intelligence
Justice	citizenship/teamwork; fairness; leadership
Temperance	forgiveness/mercy; modesty/humility; prudence; self-control
Transcendence	awe/appreciation of beauty and excellence; gratitude; hope; playfulness; spirituality

Source: Peterson, C., & Seligman, M. E. P. (2002). The Values in Action (VIA) classification of strengths. Washington, DC: American Psychological Association.

The manual addresses issues of assessment in detail, as well as how the VIA classification can be used in different applied settings.

It is not surprising that the components of character identified in these three recent lists are virtually identical. All include beliefs and actions associated with core values. We propose using the VIA classification scheme for our definition of character for both its breadth and the vast and continuing amount of work being done to delineate and measure each character strength through self-report surveys. Over 1,400 middle and high school students of varying ethnicities and socioeconomic status levels in seven different states have completed a 182-item VIA Inventory of Strengths for Youth thus far (Peterson & Park, 2003). We remind the reader that just as Peterson and Seligman (2002) did not propose that one individual should possess all the character strengths listed, we caution that we do not yet know the degree to which these strengths are evident during the adolescent years. The VIA manual presents a life span approach but relies heavily on research and ideas pertaining to adults. Thus, we draw also on other work pertaining to character to help flesh out our notion of character.

Outcomes Associated With Character in the Research Literature

Developmental psychologists have traditionally limited their research pertaining to character to studies of the development of *moral reasoning*, or the ability to tell right from wrong and to act on this distinction. The concepts in stage theories of moral development (e.g., Gilligan, 1982; Kohlberg, 1976) touch on aspects of wisdom, humanity, and justice in our conceptualization of character. At least for adolescents, there appears to be a weak but fairly consistent positive relationship between moral reasoning and moral conduct. For example, youth at higher stages of moral reasoning are more likely to behave altruistically and conscientiously and are less likely to cheat or engage in delinquent activity (see Rest, 1983).

In their review, Scales and Leffert (1999) found few quantitative studies of the effects of positive values on adolescents. The exception was restraint, which they limited to not being sexually active or using alcohol or other drugs. Restraint, or self-control, falls under the virtue of temperance. Higher levels of restraint are associated with fewer risky behaviors, such as less alcohol and drug use, and fewer delinquent acts and sexual partners, as well as better grades and peer relationships. Methodologically, however, researchers studying restraint have failed to measure values directly. Instead, they tend to take adolescents' behaviors as reflections of their values. Scales and Leffert tentatively concluded that the moderate amount of empirical research, typically conducted with small samples, shows that their six positive values are associated with better mental health, more effective problem-solving and social skills, less risky behavior, and greater academic performance.

These six positive values coincide with four of the virtues in our definition of character: (a) humanity, (b) justice, (c) courage, and (d) temperance.

Another approach to studying character comes from persons interested in promoting civil society. Ensuring the continuation of America's democratic system requires that youth believe in the system and that it works. Youth's values, imparted through families and social institutions, are the foundation for their political views and for the society they will create (Flanagan & Faison, 2001). Self-interest and materialist values are associated with lower levels of tolerance. In a study of adolescents in seven countries, Flanagan and her colleagues found that youth who reported higher altruistic and empathic values were more likely to base their views of resource distribution on people's needs. Similarly, the values of compassion and social responsibility were most consistently correlated with youth involvement in community service (Flanagan & Faison, 2001). The values studied in this line of research fall mainly under the virtues of justice and humanity.

Although religion and spirituality play a role in the lives of adolescents, religion is typically not included in multivariate studies of adolescent development. Evidence from large-scale studies that do include questions of religiosity support the influence of youth's valuing of religion, although not always their actual attendance at religious services, on adolescents' risk behaviors, particularly substance use and sexual activity (Donahue & Benson, 1995; Resnick et al., 1997; C. Smith & Faris, 2002). The importance of religion appears to be a stronger influence on positive outcomes, such as altruism, than on negative (risky) behaviors (Donahue & Benson, 1995). The National Study of Youth and Religion (http://www.youthandreligion.org), a 4-year, large-scale study of the role of religion and spirituality in the lives of American adolescents begun in 2001, addresses the lack of timely and comprehensive research on this dimension of adolescents' lives. Reports from this project should provide greater insight into the outcomes associated with religious beliefs, practices, and commitments.

Efforts to Build Character

Researchers agree that parents play a critical role in shaping children's values, yet, in response to what many see as a decline in civil society and an increase in immoral behavior among youth, over 90% of the public believe that schools should teach character traits to children (Character Education Partnership, 2001). In 2002, 14 states mandated, and 14 more encouraged, character education by law (Character Education Partnership, 2002). Title V of the No Child Left Behind Act of 2001 further promotes character education by designating grants, administered through the U.S. Department of Education's Partnerships in Character Education program (Part D, Subpart 3), to design and implement instruction about aspects of character such as justice, respect, citizenship, responsibility, giving, and caring (U.S. Department of Education, 2003). Today's character education movement differs from the value-free "values clarification" classes of the 1970s. Instead, at their best, character education programs strive to create schools that foster ethical, responsible, and caring youth by modeling and teaching good character through an emphasis on universal values in both the curriculum and school culture (Character Education Partnership, 2001). In this model, character education is not a separate class. Evaluations of efforts to infuse the school culture and inhabitants with character show promise for this holistic approach to developing character in youth. For example, a recent evaluation of the "Resolving Conflict Creatively" program in New York City public schools found that students who received substantial program instruction from their classroom teachers developed more positively: They showed less aggressive thoughts and behavior and significant increases in teacher-rated prosocial behavior and academic achievement (Henrich, Brown, & Aber, 1999). These types of programs are not the norm; instead, many character education programs use a didactic approach to teach students a prescribed set of personal virtues, basically encouraging kids to "be good" (Flanagan & Faison, 2001).

As with confidence, many after-school activities and community youth organizations claim to develop character in their participants. Adults believe that youth participation in sports teaches important lessons about cooperation, commitment, hard work, and the value of fair play. Yet, too often youth sports programs are coached by volunteers, who are untrained and unfamiliar with age-appropriate teaching and motivational strategies, leading to less optimal psychological outcomes for participants (R. E. Smith & Smoll, 1997).

Community service and service learning programs have gained popularity as ways to promote character (as well as increase academic achievement) in youth. Studies of service learning programs have found effects of participation on students' social responsibility, sense of duty to help others, civic involvement, and responsible attitudes toward others (Billig, 2001; Stukas et al., 1999a). The key, it appears, to these effects is the amount of opportunity participants have for reflection about their volunteer experiences.

CARING

Caring is often considered an aspect of character. Because of its importance in development, it is listed as a distinct outcome in the 5 C's of positive development. The development of caring attitudes and behaviors is influenced by adolescents' changing cognitive abilities and social worlds. Adolescents' increased perspective-taking ability allows for an improved cognitive capacity to appreciate the concerns and circumstances of another person. Growing exposure to larger social domains makes adolescence a window of opportunity for the development of caring. Caring is associated with prosocial behavior, moral reasoning, and social responsibility. The extent to which youth develop the capacity to care about others contributes to their social competence and engagement in socially desirable behaviors.

Defining Caring

The concept of caring is at once readily understood and markedly elusive. Regarded as desirable and virtuous across age and culture, definitions of *caring* include mention of kindness, compassion, and support. Closer scrutiny of the construct reveals little consensus on how exactly to define caring. Caring is thought of in limited terms, often as the same as prosocial behavior.

To fully understand the concept, however, all aspects of caring should be considered. Caring requires that individuals develop the ability to recognize and understand others' feelings and actions and to realize and respond to another's point of view. It is a function of social competence and one that has far-reaching implications. Caring involves prioritizing others' needs before one's own and, more broadly, promoting shared or higher community or social goals (Chase-Lansdale, Wakshlag, & Brooks-Gunn, 1995). Instilling the quality of caring in youth is paramount for the positive development of individuals and society in general.

Chase-Lansdale et al.'s (1995) comprehensive review provides a starting point to defining caring in theory, development, and practice. They identified the key elements of caring as attachment and socioemotional competence, prosocial behavior and altruism, moral reasoning, and social responsibility. These same elements of caring comprise Rauner's (2000) theoretical model of caring. Rauner's model organizes caring as a function of three related concepts: (a) *attentiveness*, which involves an awareness of and concern for others' needs, wants, and point of view; (b) *responsiveness*, which relates to one's capacity to act and engage in caring behaviors, regardless of motivation; and (c) *competence*, which refers to the skill of knowing when and how to engage in caring behaviors. Further support for this model comes from research within health and mental health care settings (Smith-Campbell, 1999). We use this conceptualization of caring because it highlights the cognitive and behavioral components of caring and distinguishes caring from other aspects of character.

Attentiveness, known as *empathy* in the research literature, has received the most extensive research attention, but all three concepts are essential ingredients of caring. Empathy includes cognitive and emotional components, such as the ability to imagine another's experiences; relate to his or her point of view; and feel concern, discomfort, and/or anxiety because of that person's circumstance (Feschback, 1975;

Table 6.3
The Components of Caring

Component	Description
Attentiveness	awareness and concern for others' needs, wants, and point of view
Responsiveness	capacity to act and engage in caring behavior, regardless of motivation
Competence	the skill of knowing what and how to engage in caring behaviors

Hoffman, 1977; Hoffner, 1995). These distinctions allow for detailed evaluations of outcomes. The second two components of caring–responsiveness and competence–refer to more general concepts. Responsiveness implies behavior. It requires capacity, motivation, and practice. Competence, doing something right and caring in its most optimal sense, comes from practice in recognizing and responding to the needs of others.

Outcomes Associated With Caring in the Research Literature

Caring is a complex construct, and researchers investigate it using a variety of names. For instance, psychologists study empathy, which is similar to attentiveness in our definition of caring, and prosocial behavior, which is similar to responsiveness. Elements of caring are associated with a variety of positive youth behavioral and attitudinal outcomes. It is not surprising that empathy, or attentiveness, is negatively correlated with aggression in adolescents (Kaukiainen et al., 1999). Data show that empathic children and youth who are exposed to or experience violence are less likely to engage in aggression and noncompliance than their nonempathic peers (LeSure-Lester, 2000). Empathy acts as a protective factor for victims of child abuse and interparental violence.

The association between attentiveness and socially desirable outcomes is strong. Empathy is consistently correlated with youths' prosocial behavior (Eisenberg, Miller, Shell, McNalley, & Shea, 1991), moral reasoning (Humphries, Parker, & Jagers, 2000), and sense of social responsibility (Eberly & Davies, 2001). Empathic concern and attentiveness predict prosocial behavior even when controlling for other aspects of caring, such as altruism, perspective taking, and social responsibility (Eberly & Davies, 2001). Thus, the development of attentiveness represents one step toward becoming a caring individual.

For the most part, caring acts as a protective factor and predicts desirable outcomes. Certain facets of caring, however, may pose a risk to well-being. Girls demonstrate greater amounts of emotional empathy, particularly personal distress, than boys (Davis & Franzoi, 1991;

Karniol, Gabay, Ochion, & Harari, 1998). Consequently, under certain circumstances, caring too much may be detrimental to youth. To the extent that caring results in anxiety or discomfort due to the situation of another, it may have a deleterious effect on, or at least pose a risk to, well-being. Young people experiencing personal distress more often fail to seek comfort from others during a stressful event (Hoffner, 1995). Furthermore, there is some evidence suggesting that highly empathic teens may be at risk of poor school performance because of concern for their peers (Kerley, 1998). For teenagers, balancing the development of personal boundaries and relationships with others is a new and precarious process. Caring too much for others may, in very specific circumstances, result in negative outcomes for young people.

Efforts to Engender Caring

In keeping with the ecological approach to development, Rauner (2000) proposed a hierarchical structure for engendering caring by infusing family, professionals (e.g., teachers, service providers, etc.), organizations (via policies and programs), and society (via individuals advocating policy) with an ethos of caring. This multilevel approach addresses the context-dependent caring exhibited by adolescents (Ferreira & Bosworth, 2000). Adolescents' willingness to care for others varies depending on interpersonal context (e.g., a parent or friend vs. a stranger), and concern about lack of reciprocity and fear of violence were most frequently cited barriers to caring. Because of the barriers reinforced by class, race, gender, and age, efforts to engender caring at all social levels must take into account the respective positions and circumstances in each level to be effective (Webb, Wilson, Corbett, & Mordecai, 1993).

The teachability of caring has yet to be the subject of a substantial body of literature. The limited research suggests that curricular efforts to teach empathy can be effective. Developmental readiness appears to be critical to maximizing the effects of empathy training. In an evaluation of an empathy training curriculum, responsiveness to training increased as a function of age; the college-age students demonstrated stronger gains than high-school students. In addition, despite the gender differences evident before the training, males and females showed equal gains in all dimensions of empathy (Hatcher et al., 1994).

Parents are important educators of their children's caring attitudes and behaviors. Research provides ample information on how parents can foster caring in their adolescent children. Parental warmth and disciplinary styles are associated with aspects of caring in adolescents (see Eisenberg & McNally, 1993). Parents who are responsive to their children (Henry, Sager, & Plunkett, 1996), and mothers who are supportive and warm (Eisenberg & McNally, 1993), have adolescents with higher levels of empathy. Adolescents with parents who used logical reasoning and explanation when disciplining them showed a greater capacity for understanding others' perspectives (Henry et al., 1996). Mothers who were lax or reluctant in disciplining (including nonphysical discipline) had adolescents who were less sensitized to others' emotional states (Eisenberg & McNally, 1993). Empirical studies support the influence of parental affection, responsiveness, and appropriate discipline in promoting the development of caring. There is some evidence that families engender caring in different ways depending on their ethnic background. In one study, the availability of learning materials and variety of experiences provided in the home predicted considerate behavior in Chinese American adolescents, whereas parental responsivity and family conflict predicted the caring behavior of European and African American teens (Bradley & Corwyn, 2000). Universally, however, family-level variables significantly influence attentive and responsive caring.

PROGRESS ON INDICATOR DEVELOPMENT
SINCE THE EARLY 1990S

In the past decade, we have witnessed the growth and acceptance of a paradigm shift in both research and practice away from a focus on primarily preventing problem behaviors and toward a focus on promoting competencies and well-being. It is not a coincidence that during this time there has been progress in the movement to define and measure indicators of well-being as well. These shifts are more evident in our thinking than in our behavior; that is, the national conversation (among both the public and researchers) may be shifting toward a focus on more fully preparing youth for their future, but efforts to understand how to do this and how to measure our progress have lagged behind.

A shift in thinking about the 3 C's of psychological and emotional development is naturally the first step. Psychologists and parents have been concerned with confidence or self-esteem for some time, but in the past decade there has been a rise in the number of programs devoted to increasing youth's self-esteem or confidence. Even within programs not specifically focused on raising self-esteem, measuring improvements in self-esteem is part of most program evaluations (National Research Council, 2002). Perhaps because of the long-time interest in self-esteem among psychologists, brief reliable and valid measures of self-esteem exist and are widely used with adolescents in both basic and applied research.

We are not so lucky when it comes to measuring character. Although concern for the development of good character is not new, discussions of character have mostly been the purview of philosophers and theologians and not prone to quantitative measurement. Current empirical efforts to measure character depend typically on 1-item questions pertaining to a few specific aspects of character, mostly volunteering, civic involvement, and religious activities. With the exception of the VIA inventory and a few smaller efforts with adults (e.g., Cawley, Martin, & Johnson, 2000), we know of little work that has attempted to create a reliable and valid scale to measure the many components implied by the term *character*.

Similarly, measures of caring are typically limited to survey items regarding volunteer activity and/or community service and considerate acts, which capture only the responsive component of caring. Despite some available inventories, measures of attentiveness have been overlooked at the national level and remain restricted to smaller scale projects. Competence of caring has been ignored completely in youth populations. To date, there has been little groundwork laid for developing indicators of caring.

Currently, there are three widely disseminated compilations that include indicators of youth's well-being: (a) KIDS COUNT (Annie E. Casey Foundation, 2003), (b) *America's Children: Key National Indicators of Well-Being* (hereafter *America's Children*; Federal Interagency Forum on Child and Family Statistics, 2003); and (c) *Trends in the Well-Being of America's Children and Youth* (hereafter *Trends*; U.S. Department of Health and Human Services, Office of the Assistant Secretary for Planning and Evaluation, 2002). Our review of these found few indicators of youth's confidence, character, or caring. KIDS COUNT contained none, and *America's Children* listed one—youth participation in volunteer activities—in its special features section in the 2000 report, but not in the most recent report from 2003. The social development section of the *Trends* report contained three: (a) reports of youth's life goals, (b) their religious attendance and religiosity, and (c) their voting behavior (registration and actual voting).

We are not surprised by the scant presence of indicators of confidence, character, and caring in leading indicator reports, for two reasons. First, although there may be general agreement that confidence, character, and caring are desirable goals for youth development, little work has examined what exactly these terms mean and whether the meanings vary for subgroups of youth. Second, given the lack of definitional clarity, methodological issues remain to be resolved before we can reliably measure these characteristics in nationally representative samples of youth.

Despite these limitations, the 1990s brought some promising new approaches. The Search Institute's (2003) Profiles of Student Life: Attitudes and Behaviors (PSL:AB) is perhaps the most relevant. A 156-item self-report survey, the PSL:AB measures the assets, deficits, thriving indicators, and risk behaviors of 6th- through 12th-grade students. Designed to be administered during a class period, the survey uses 92 items to measure 40 developmental assets, or building blocks, that enhance youths' development (see Scales & Leffert, 1999, for more information on the developmental assets). Although many of the assets are measured by widely used standardized and well-validated scales, results are communicated as binary variables-the percentage of youth reporting that they have or do not have the particular asset (Leffert et al., 1998).

The sound theoretical underpinnings of the survey items and the manner in which the results are communicated make the PSL:AB a good source for indicators of well-being. Relevant to our discussion here, the PSL:AB measures aspects of confidence, character, and caring.

Almost 1 million youth completed the PSL:AB during the 1996–97 school year as part of the Search Institute's program to help communities measure how their youth are faring developmentally. During the 1999–2000 school year, another 217,000 6th- through 12th-graders in over 300 communities across the United States completed the survey. Both samples, although large, are not nationally representative. They are self-selected and consist of mostly White youth (86% in the 1996–97 sample and 79% in the 1999–2000 sample), with parents with higher than average formal education and from small- to medium-size towns and cities (only 4% are from major metropolitan areas; Leffert et al., 1998; Search Institute, 2003).

Still, the study provides the greatest detail we have for a large number of youth on their levels of confidence, character, and caring. The Search Institute's internal asset of positive identity maps onto our idea of confidence and includes measures of personal power (similar to self-efficacy), high self-esteem, a sense of purpose, and a positive view of the future. As shown in Table 6.4, fewer than half of the 1996–97 school year survey participants reported feelings of personal power and positive self-esteem. More than half reported a sense of purpose and a positive view of their personal future. There was variation between boys and girls, and between younger (Grades 6–8) and older (Grades 9–12) youth, demonstrated by effect sizes. Older youth expressed higher levels of personal power. Boys reported higher levels of self-esteem and sense of purpose (Leffert et al., 1998). Data from the newer sample, with weights applied to make the sample nationally representative, although not published yet, show similar percentages (A. Sesma, personal communication, July 31, 2003).

Another asset category, called *positive values*, captures beliefs similar to our idea of character but also includes caring. Fewer than half of the survey participants reported placing a high value on helping other people (caring) or on promoting equality and reducing hunger and poverty (equality and social justice). Even fewer demonstrated the value of restraint; less than one quarter believed it is important not to be sexually active or to use alcohol or other drugs. More than half of the students reported holding the positive values of integrity, honesty, and responsibility. Substantially more girls possessed each of these positive values; a majority of the girls reported each of the positive values except for restraint. The percentage of youth who endorsed the restraint value declined sharply between the eighth and ninth grades (Leffert et al., 1998).

Although the Search Institute listed them in other asset categories, we believe service to others, involvement with religious institutions, planning and decision-making skills, cultural competence, and peaceful conflict resolution skills fall under our notion of character. The asset they call *interpersonal competence* provides data on part of our construct

Table 6.4
Findings from Search Institute's Survey of Youths' Assets

Domain	%
Confidence	
Young person feels he or she has control over "things that happen to me"	45%
Young person reports having a high self-esteem	47%
Young person reports that "my life has a purpose"	55%
Young person is optimistic about her or his personal future	70%
Character	
Young person places a high value on promoting equality and reducing hunger and poverty	45%
Young person believes it is important not to be sexually active or to use alcohol or other drugs	24%
Young person acts on convictions and stands up for her or his beliefs	63%
Young person "tells the truth even when it is not easy"	63%
Young person accepts and takes personal responsibility	60%
Young person serves in the community 1 hour or more per week	50%
Young person spends 1 or more hours per week in activities in a religious institution	64%
Young person knows how to plan ahead and make choices	29%
Young person has knowledge of and comfort with people of different cultural/racial/ethnic backgrounds	35%
Young person seeks to resolve conflict nonviolently	44%
Caring	
Young person places a high value on helping other people	43%
Young person has empathy, sensitivity, and friendship skills	43%

Source: Leffert et al., 1998.

of caring. Half of the youth in the survey reported serving in the community 1 hour or more per week, and 64% said they spend 1 or more hours per week in activities in a religious institution. Fewer youth were categorized as knowing how to plan ahead and make choices, as having knowledge of and comfort with people of different cultural-racial-ethnic backgrounds, or as seeking to resolve conflict nonviolently. The percentage of youth who reported competence for caring (measured as having empathy, sensitivity, and friendship skills) was also low. In all these areas, substantially more girls reported having the asset. The difference between boys and girls was particularly large (more than 20 percentage points) for interpersonal competence and peaceful conflict resolution (Leffert et al., 1998).

In the past decade, the addition of four large-scale longitudinal studies of adolescents has increased our sources for indicator data. These new additions include (a) the National Longitudinal Study of Adolescent Health (Add Health), (b) the Panel Study of Income Dynamics Child Development Supplement, (c) the National Longitudinal Survey of Youth (NLSY 97), and (d) the National Educational Longitudinal Study (NELS). Together with the Monitoring the Future (MTF) study, which was initiated in 1975, these studies have the benefit of investigating large, nationally representative samples of youth over time.[3] However, they currently measure only limited aspects of youths' confidence, character, and caring.

Table 6.5 shows whether and how confidence, character, and caring are measured in these five studies. Comparable to our findings in the research and practice literatures, only select aspects of confidence, character, and caring are measured nationally. As we discuss in the next section, these existing efforts allow for only rudimentary indicators of confidence, character, and caring at this point in time. Developing better indicators of character and caring will require substantial theoretical and methodological work, although less so for measuring confidence.

MOST IMPORTANT TASKS FOR THE COMING DECADE

In the first part of this chapter, we sought to build a case for why confidence, character, and caring are aspects of youths' psychological and emotional development worthy of measuring and tracking. In this section, we explore the tasks necessary for constructing indicators to do so. First, we identify, where possible, existing reliable and valid measures of the components of these constructs. Second, we discuss the further methodological work necessary to build and test indicators that capture the multifaceted nature of confidence, character, and caring. Third, we propose ideas for how to further this research.

CONFIDENCE

We believe that developing an indicator of confidence requires only some additional methodological work. As shown in Table 6.5, the five national surveys of youth already measure some aspect of confidence, and all include a measure of global self-esteem. Standard measures of self-esteem exist and are widely used in the psychological and program evaluation literatures, as well as in the national surveys of youth. Kling and colleagues (1999) identified three measures of global self-esteem among the studies included in their meta-analysis of gender differences in self-esteem: (a) the Rosenberg Self-Esteem Scale (Rosenberg, 1965), (b) the Global Self-Worth subscale of Harter's Self-Perception Profile for Chil-

Table 6.5

Measures of Confidence, Character, and Caring Included in Five National Datasets

	Add Health	PSID-CDS	NLSY 97	NELS	MTF
Confidence					
Identity	X^a		X^a	X^a	X^b
Self-Concept		X		X	
Self-Esteem	X	X	X	X	X
Self-Efficacy	X^c			X^d	
Character					
Wisdom	X^e	X^f			
Courage					
Humanity	X^g		X^g	X^h	X^h
Justice		X^f	X^i	$X^{j,k}$	$X^{k,l}$
Temperance	X^m	X^n	X^m	X^m	X^m
Transcendence	$X^{a,o}$		$X^{a,o}$	X^a	X^f
Caring					
Attentiveness		Xf			
Responsiveness	X^f		X^h	X^p	X^p
Competence					

[a]Youth rate their expectations for the future; [b]Youth rate their future goals; [c]Youth rate their efficacy for contraceptive use; [d]Youth rate their locus of control; [e]Youth report how they solve problems; [f]Adult(s) complete the positive behaviors index; [g]Youth rate how much others care for them; [h]Youth report amount of volunteer work/community service; [i]Youth report their views of the criminal justice system; [j]Youth report on views of people of other races; [k]Youth rate their leadership roles in different activities; [l]Youth report on their civic/political involvement; [m]Youth rate their involvement in positive and risky behaviors; [n]Adult(s) complete problem behavior index; [o]Questions pertain to religious beliefs, importance of religion, and religious activities; [p]Youth report their engagement in kind acts towards others.

dren (Harter, 1982), and (c) the General Self subscale of Marsh's (1992) Self-Description Questionnaire. Each has demonstrated reliability. Of these, the Rosenberg Self-Esteem Scale has been used most frequently. Effect sizes for gender differences in self-esteem did not vary by type of measure used.

This finding suggests that although each of the five national studies uses a different measure of self-esteem, they all capture a similar aspect of American youth's self-esteem. Before we can choose which one to track as an indicator of self-esteem, we need to test whether the level of self-esteem among youth from different backgrounds differs depending on the measure. This should be possible with existing data.

Self-esteem is not the same as confidence. A complete picture of the confidence of American youth requires data on their identity development, self-concepts, and self-efficacy. As a field, we are not as far along in measuring these other components of confidence as with self-esteem. Currently, three of the data sets include measures of youths' expectations for the future, which taps into the concept of identity development as well as optimism, part of the character strength of transcendence virtue. We anticipate that future research will help determine whether questions about the future fit better into the confidence or character construct.

As noted earlier, data on identity are already incorporated as an indicator in the *Trends* report with a measure of youths' goals for the future. Drawn from the MTF study, this indicator reports on the number of youth selecting "being successful in my line of work," "having a good marriage and family life," "having lots of money," "making a contribution to society," "working to correct social and economic inequalities," and "being a leader in my community" as extremely important personal goals for the future (U.S. Department of Health and Human Services, Office of the Assistant Secretary for Planning and Evaluation, 2002).

The NELS, NLSY 97, and Add Health surveys include items assessing youths' expectations for the future and offer another way to assess identity and optimism for the future. In the NELS survey, youth rate their chances of graduating from high school, going to college, and having a job that pays well. Similarly, respondents to the NLSY 97 survey rate their percentage chance of being in school, working for pay, getting married, and becoming or getting someone pregnant in the next year and the next 5 years. They also answer questions about the likelihood of experiencing the following risks at least once in the next year and the next 5 years: drinking enough to get seriously drunk; being a victim of a violent crime; and being arrested, rightly or wrongly. In the Add Health study, youth rate their chances of living to age 35, being married by age 25, being killed by age 21, getting HIV or AIDS, graduating from college, and having a middle-class family income by age 30.

In general, research on the relation of these expectations to life outcomes is required before they can be considered for inclusion as indicators. Substantial research linking educational expectations in particular with youths' future educational attainment already exists (e.g., Abu-Hilal, 2000). Thus, we propose developing an indicator of youths' educational expectations based on the data in existing surveys. Such an indicator would provide information on the percentage of youth with a positive scholastic identity-a measure of their confidence in their academic abilities. We recognize, however, that this would provide only a partial view of youths' identity (and thus confidence).

Table 6.5 shows that two of the national studies contain measures of adolescents' self-efficacy. In the Add Health study, however, the measure is specific to contraceptive use, and in the NELS study the measure pertains to students' locus of control. Neither of these capture the full import of self-efficacy for youths' confidence. A newly developed self-efficacy scale, entitled *Things I Can Do If I Try*, does (O'Hagan, 2000). This scale was developed for use in the Project on Human Development in Chicago Neighborhoods, a longitudinal study of approximately 7,000 children and adolescents from diverse backgrounds. Developed in consultation with Susan Harter, an expert on childhood self-competence, this measure consists of 27 items assessing how well students think they can succeed in school, positively affect their home life, safely negotiate their neighborhood, and positively affect their future. Preliminary psychometric data suggest that 24 of the items form four reasonably distinct and reliable scales over time, measuring school, home, neighborhood, and future efficacy (O'Hagan, 2000). We recommend further investigation of the psychometric properties of this scale as well as studying how it relates to positive and negative outcomes for youth. Depending on the findings from these efforts, this scale may be useful for developing an indicator of adolescents' self-efficacy.

Data for developing indicators for the individual components of confidence exist. We do not know yet whether it is possible to combine these components to provide an overall indicator of youths' confidence or one that captures the full range of meaning in the term *confidence* for different domains. Future theoretical and methodological research should investigate this possibility. In our definition of confidence, we addressed the potential for youths' confidence to vary by domain. The additional theoretical and methodological investigations necessary to understand how confidence varies should follow the work done regarding self-concept. Although two of the national data sets include measures of youths' self-concept in several domains, how to incorporate them into an indicator of confidence is still unclear.

CHARACTER

Unlike confidence, charting American youths' character will be substantially more difficult. Despite the public's concern over youths' character, and the seeming agreement on a list of qualities (or character strengths) that constitute character, the details of what exactly to measure, let alone how, are still sketchy. No standard measure of character exists yet. Even theoretically rich studies of aspects of youths' character rely on single items to capture the character component. For example, Flanagan, Bowes, Jonsson, Csapo, and Sheblanova (1998) measure civic commitment by asking students "When you think about your life and your future, how important is it to you personally to (a) contribute to your country and (b) do something to improve your society?" in their study of youths' civic commitment in different countries.

The recent indicator reports include three indicators of youths' character. *Trends* reports on youths' religiosity and voting behavior, whereas *America's Children* reported on community service in 2000, but not in 2003. The indicator of youths' religiosity in the *Trends* report provides information about youths' spirituality, one of the character strengths making up the transcendence virtue. Drawn from the MTF surveys, this indicator reports on the number of youth who attend weekly religious services and the number who say that religion plays a very important role in their lives. We recognize that these two questions do not encompass the full meaning of religiosity and spirituality. Given the vast amount of work to be done on other aspects of character, we feel they will suffice for now.

It is not clear exactly where voting behavior fits in our schema of character. As part of our civic duty, it perhaps best fits under the virtues of justice and courage, and possibly wisdom. Few would argue that voting behavior reflects one's commitment to participating (courage) in the democratic process (justice). Youth, however, cannot vote until they turn 18. Thus, an indicator of voting behavior is more suitable for assessing the character of older adolescents and young adults.

Involvement in community service touches on another part of civic involvement, one that is available to all youth. In addition, community service activities demonstrate the responsiveness component of caring. *America's Children* included an indicator of youth participation in volunteer activities in its special section in 2000 for indicators not collected on a regular basis. Drawn from the National Household Education Survey, this indicator reports the percentage of high school students who participated in any service as well as distinguishing between one-time and regular service. One option would be to continue to include this item in the National Household Education Survey. A second-and, we think, better, option-would be to use data from the NELS study. In NELS, participants not only rate their involvement in volunteer activities but also make a distinction between community service that is strictly voluntary and other types of community service. This distinction is important, particularly as more and more schools institute community service requirements. Existing research suggests that compulsory community service may not result in the same benefits to the volunteer as voluntary service (e.g., Stukas, Snyder, & Clary, 1999b). Thus, we recommend changing the source and exploring the data reported for an indicator of community service.

As shown in Table 6.5, all of the national studies measure different aspects of youths' character. The largest area of overlap pertains to measures that can be used to judge adolescents' levels of self-control, one of the character strengths under the virtue of temperance. This is due mostly to our national concern with the number of youth engaging in risky behavior. It seems feasible that a simple but appealing measure of the self-control of American youth could be developed by summing the number of youth who do not engage in these behaviors. Such an indicator of self-control could be categorical; that is, reports of youths' self-control could include the number of youth with high, moderate, and low levels of self-control depending on the number of risky behaviors in which they engage. What remains to be determined are which behaviors to include in such a list.

The character strength of leadership appears under the justice virtue. Both the NELS and MTF surveys contain straightforward questions about students' involvement in leadership positions in their schools and activities. We recommend creating an indicator of youths' leadership experience with data from one of these studies.

We have identified a number of indicators of youths' character despite the lack of clarity on the qualities that make up the concept of character. With the work currently underway to delineate the character strengths listed in our chart of the components of character through refinement and correlations studies with data from the VIA *Inventory of Strengths for Youth*, we can expect a better understanding of character during adolescence and ideas and means for assessing it in the future. Although this inventory is too long (currently 182 items) to consider for use as an indicator, findings from work on the measure should help efforts to develop indicators of character.

CARING

Caring, as part of positive youth development, requires transitioning from a self-centered reality to one that includes others. In the coming decade, we hope to be able to monitor this transition by expanding the use of current indicators and incorporating new ones.

Responsive caring, the capacity to act and engage in caring, mandates behavioral indicators. As discussed earlier, behavioral indicators of caring dovetail with measures used to assess character. Youth participation in volunteer activity and community service are critical indicators of responsive caring: They reflect the extent to which adolescents engage in this type of caring behavior. It is common for large-scale studies to include one item to measure participation in volunteer or community service activities (see Table 6.5). Singular items and the limited scope of this activity fail to sufficiently reflect the range of caring acts in which teenagers engage.

Participation in caring acts may occur in one or multiple domains. Aside from participation in volunteer or community service activities, youth may engage in caring behaviors at home or school. Helpful, considerate, and affectionate behavior may take the form of caring for younger siblings, comforting a friend in distress, or assisting in the classroom. Substantial methodological work will be necessary to develop measures that capture responsive caring in all spheres of adolescents' lives. Still, we recommend developing indicators of responsive caring that recognize the variety of domains in which a teenager has the opportunity to demonstrate caring behavior.

At present, the Survey of Program Dynamics includes items focused on the degree to which a child is "helpful and cooperative" and "tends to give, lend and share" as part of the Social Competence subscale of the Positive Behaviors Scale completed by the parent. The Canadian

National Longitudinal Survey of Children and Youth includes a similar but condensed item for the parents, teacher, and child to complete. These items measure young people's responsive caring in different domains (family and school). The Considerateness subscale of the Home Behavior Inventory offers another option for tapping into parents' perceptions of their adolescent child's considerate behavior (Bradley & Corwyn, 2000). We recommend that items from the parent and teacher reports be reworded and validated as youth self-report measures. Data generated from these proposed measures complement items on volunteer and community service activity and thus provide a more complete picture of youth engagement in caring behavior. We recommend that, after the necessary methodological work, these measures be incorporated into national studies.

New indicators should be incorporated to monitor attentive caring, or empathy, because it is often a precursor to responsive caring. To date, indicators of attentive caring remain absent from indicator reports. The only attentiveness-specific variable included in a large-scale study asks parents to report on their child's "concern for others" and whether the child is "considerate and thoughtful of other children" (see Table 6.5). The Survey of Program Dynamics incorporates these items from the Social Competence subscale of the Positive Behaviors Scale. Another option for measuring attentive caring is the Interpersonal Reactivity Index, the most commonly used survey measure of empathy (Davis, 1980). This questionnaire includes four seven-item subscales, including the Perspective Taking subscale, the Empathic Concern subscale, the Personal Distress subscale, and the Fantasy subscale. We propose psychometric studies of subscales in order to derive a brief and valid measure of attentive caring. Inclusion of appropriate subscales from the Interpersonal Reactivity Index or the Positive Behaviors Scale would provide opportunity for youth self-report items that reflect adolescent capacity to be aware and concerned with others' needs, wants and point of view.

Indicators of caring depend on measures of empathy and prosocial behaviors demonstrated in one or more contexts. Research that has already incorporated measures of caring adds support to the assertion that caring is an appropriate criterion to include in positive youth development. The lack of research on adolescent competence in caring prohibits proposal of specific measures. Instead, we strongly recommend study devoted to this dimension of caring. For now, measures of attentive and responsive caring represent the heart of quantifying this construct.

The Positive Behaviors Scale effectively captures both attentive and responsive caring, making it a strong candidate for informing indicator reports. We recommend its use within large-scale, regularly administered survey studies. Existing and potential sources of data that reflect dimensions of caring in youth are presented in Table 6.6. The present trend of focusing attention on positive indicators bodes well for continued study and the inclusion of attentive and responsive caring as indicators of adolescent well-being.

Table 6.6
Data Sources for Developing Key Indicators of Confidence, Character, and Caring

Key indicators to develop	Current data sources	Existing studies that can incorporate refined measure
Confidence		
Self-esteem	Add Health, PSID-CDS, NLSY97, NELS, MTF	Add Health, PSID-CDS, NLSY97, NELS, MTF
Identity (scholastic)	Add Health, NELS, MTF	Add Health, PSID-CDS, NLSY97, NELS, MTF
Self-Efficacy	PCHDN	Add Health, NELS
Character		
Volunteering/ community service	NELS, NHES, MTF	Add Health, NLSY97, NELS, MTF
Self-control	Add Health, PSID-CDS, NLSY97, NELS, MTF	Add Health, NLSY97, NELS, MTF
Leadership experience	NELS, MTF	Add Health, NLSY97, NELS, MTF
Caring		
Responsiveness (in 1 or more contexts)	SPD, NLSCY, NELS, NHES, MTF	Add Health, NLSY, NELS, MTF
Attentiveness	SPD, NLSCY	Add Health, NLSCY, NLSY97, NELS, MTF

[1]Add Health is the National Longitudinal Study of Adolescent Health; [2]PSID-CDS is the Panel Study on Income Dynamics – Child Development Supplement; [3]NLSY97 is the National Longitudinal Study of Youth - 1997; [4]NELS is the National Education Longitudinal Study of 1988; [5]MTF is the Monitoring the Future study; [6]PHDCN is the Project on Human Development in Chicago Neighborhoods; [7]NHES is the National Household Education Survey; [8]NLSCY is the Canadian National Longitudinal Survey of Children and Youth; [9]SPD is the Survey of Program Dynamics.

SUMMARY OF RECOMMENDATIONS FOR KEY INDICATORS

We recommend developing and/or refining eight indicators of confidence, character, and caring. Four of these indicators–self-esteem, volunteering, scholastic identity, and leadership-will require minimal effort to develop. Items measuring these four constructs are already in use in national studies. All that needs to be done is some refinement of the items based on their use with subpopulations of youth. The other four—self-efficacy, self-control, responsiveness, and attentiveness—will require more substantial work to develop and test the measures.

We chose these eight indicators to work on in the coming decade because they are representative of the qualities captured by the terms *confidence, character,* and *caring.* In addition, our knowledge about these qualities and ability to measure them are, for the most part, fairly well developed. We hope that as the new millennium progresses, our knowledge of how to more fully measure these constructs will progress as well.

NOTES

1. Throughout this chapter, we use the terms *adolescent* and *youth* interchangeably to refer to roughly the teen years.
2. Service learning programs link community service experiences with classroom instruction.
3. Details about these data sets, including codebooks, are available from the following web sites: http://www.cpc.unc.edu/projects/addhealth for Add Health, http://www.isr.umich.edu/src/child-development/home.html for PSID-CDS, http://stats.bls.gov/nls/nlsy97.htm for NLSY 97, http://nces.ed.gov/surveys/ nels88/ for NELS; and http:// monitoringthefuture.org for MTF.

REFERENCES

Abu-Hilal, M. M. (2000). A structural model of attitudes towards school subjects, academic aspirations and achievement. *Educational Psychology, 20,* 75–84.

Allen, J. P., Leadbeater, B. J., & Aber, J. L. (1990). The relationship of adolescents' expectations and values to delinquency, hard drug use, and unprotected sexual intercourse. *Development & Psychopathology, 2,* 85–98.

American Psychiatric Association. (1994). *Diagnostic and statistical manual of mental disorders* (4th ed.). Washington, DC: Author.

Annie E. Casey Foundation. (2003). *Kids count data book 2003.* Baltimore: Author.

Bandura, A. (1982). Self-efficacy mechanism in human agency. *American Psychologist, 37,* 122–147.

Bandura, A. (1997). *Self-efficacy: The exercise of control.* New York: Freeman.

Bandura, A., Pastorelli, C., Barbaranelli, C., & Caprara, G. V. (1999). Self-efficacy pathways to childhood depression. *Journal of Personality and Social Psychology, 76,* 258–269.

Billig, S. H. (2001). *The impacts of service-learning on youth, schools and communities: Research on K–12 school-based service-learning, 1990-1999.* Retrieved May 2001 from http://www.learningindeed.org/research/slresearch/ slrsrchsy.html

Bradley, R. H., & Corwyn, R. F. (2000). Moderating effect of perceived amount of family conflict on the relation between home environmental processes and the well-being of adolescents. *Journal of Family Psychology, 14,* 349–364.

Cawley, M. J., Martin, J. E., & Johnson, J. A. (2000). A virtues approach to personality. *Personality and Individual Differences, 28,* 997–1013.

Character Counts. (2001). *Six pillars of character.* Marina del Rey, CA: Author. Retrieved May 2001 from http://www.charactercounts.org/backgrnd.htm

Character Education Partnership. (2001). *Questions and answers about CEP and character education.* Retrieved May 2001 from http://www.character.org/resources/qanda.

Character Education Partnership. (2002, June). *State character education activity.* Retrieved July 24, 2003, from http://www.mindoh.com

Chase-Lansdale, P. L., Wakschlag, L. S., & Brooks-Gunn, J. (1995). A psychological perspective on the development of caring in children and youth: The role of the family. *Journal of Adolescence, 18*, 515–556.

Damon, W., & Hart, D. (1988). *Self-understanding in childhood and adolescence.* New York: Cambridge University Press.

Davis, M. H. (1980). A multidimensional approach to individual differences in empathy. *JSAS Catalog of Selected Documents in Psychology, 10*, 85.

Davis, M. H., & Franzoi, S. L. (1991). Stability and change in adolescent self-consciousness and empathy. *Journal of Research in Personality, 25*, 70–87.

Donahue, M. J., & Benson, P. L. (1995). Religion and the well-being of adolescents. *Journal of Social Issues, 51*, 145–160.

DuBois, D. L., Burk-Braxton, C., Swenson, L. P., Tevendale, H. D., Lockerd, E. M., & Moran, B. L. (2002). Getting by with a little help from self and others: Self-esteem and social support as resources during early adolescence. *Developmental Psychology, 38*, 822–839.

DuBois, D. L., Felner, R. D., Brand, S., Phillips, R. S. C., & Lease, A. M. (1996). Early adolescent self-esteem: A developmental-ecological framework and assessment strategy. *Journal of Research on Adolescence, 6*, 543–579.

Eberly, M. B., & Davies, J. (2001, April). *Social responsibility and altruistic behavior: The role of empathy, perspective taking, parental warmth, and prosocial behavior toward parents.* Poster presented at the Biennial Meeting of the Society for Research on Child Development, Minneapolis, MN.

Eisenberg, N., & McNalley, S. (1993). Socialization and mothers' and adolescents' empathy-related characteristics. *Journal of Research on Adolescence, 3*, 171–191.

Eisenberg, N., Miller, P. A., Shell, R., McNalley, S., & Shea, C. (1991). Prosocial development in adolescence: A longitudinal study. *Developmental Psychology, 27*, 849–857.

Erikson, E. H. (1950). Chapter title. In M. J. E. Senn (Ed.), *Growth and crisis of the healthy personality* (pp. 91–146). Oxford, England: Josiah Macy, Jr., Foundation.

Erikson, E. H. (1963). *Childhood and society* (2nd ed.). New York: Norton.

Federal Interagency Forum on Child and Family Statistics. (2003). *America's children: Key national indicators of well-being, 2003.* Washington, DC: Author.

Ferreira, M. M., & Bosworth, K. (2000). Context as a critical factor in young adolescents' concepts of caring. *Journal of Research in Childhood Education, 15*, 117–128.

Feshback, N. D. (1975). Empathy in children: Some theoretical and empirical considerations. *Counseling Psychology, 4*, 25–30.

Flanagan, C. A., Bowes, J., Jonsson, B., Csapo, B., & Sheblanova, E. (1998). Ties that bind: Correlates of male and female adolescents' civic commitments in seven countries. *Journal of Social Issues, 54*, 457–476.

Flanagan, C. A., & Faison, N. (2001). Youth civic development: Implications of research for social policy and programs (Vol. 15, No. 1, pp. 3–14). Social Policy Report.

Gilligan, C. (1982). *In a different voice: Psychological theory and women's development.* Cambridge, MA: Harvard University Press.

Gray-Little, B., & Hafdahl, A. R. (2000). Factors influencing racial comparisons of self-esteem: A quantitative review. *Psychological Bulletin, 126*, 26–54.

Harter, S. (1982). The Perceived Competence Scale for Children. *Child Development, 43*, 87–97.

Harter, S. (1990). Self and identity development. In S. S. Feldman & G. R. Elliott (Eds.), *At the threshold* (pp. 352–387). Cambridge, MA: Harvard University Press.

Hatcher, S. L., Nadeau, M. S., Walsh, L. K., Reynolds, M., Galea, J., & Marz, K. (1994). Teaching of empathy for high school and college students: Testing Rogerian methods with the Interpersonal Reactivity Index. *Adolescence, 29,* 961–974.

Henrich, C. C., Brown, J. L., & Aber, J. L. (1999). *Evaluating the effectiveness of school-based violence prevention: Developmental approaches, 13*(3), 1–16.

Henry, C. S., Sager, D. W., & Plunkett, S. W. (1996). Adolescents' perceptions of family system characteristics, parent–adolescent dyadic behaviors, adolescent qualities, and adolescent empathy. *Family Relations, 45,* 283–292.

Hoffman, M. L. (1977). Empathy: Its development and prosocial implications. In C. B. Keasly (Ed.), *Nebraska Symposium on Motivation* (Vol. 25, pp. 169–218). Lincoln: University of Nebraska Press.

Hoffner, C. (1995). Adolescents' coping with frightening mass media. *Communication Research, 22,* 325–346.

Humphries, M. L., Parker, B. L., & Jagers, R. J. (2000). Predictors of moral reasoning among African American children: A preliminary study. *Journal of Black Psychology, 26,* 51–64.

Karniol, R., Gabay, R., Ochion, Y., & Harari, Y. (1998). Is gender or gender-role orientation a better predictor of empathy in adolescence? *Sex Roles, 39*(1/2), 45–59.

Kaukiainen, A., Bjoerkqvist, K., Lagerspetz, K., Oesterman, K., Salmivalli, C., Rothberg, S., & Ahlbom, A. (1999). The relationships between social intelligence, empathy, and three types of aggression. *Aggressive Behavior, 25,* 81–89.

Kerley, D. C. (1998). The effects of three aspects of social competence on academic performance: A structural equation model. *Dissertation Abstracts International, Section B: Sciences and Engineering, 58*(9-B), 51–92.

Kling, K. C., Hyde, J. S., Showers, C. J., & Buswell, B. N. (1999). Gender differences in self-esteem: A meta-analysis. *Psychological Bulletin, 125,* 470–500.

Kohlberg, L. (1976). Moral stages and moralization: The cognitive developmental approach. In T. Luckona (Ed.), *Moral development and behavior: Theory, research, and social issues* (pp. 31–53). New York: Holt.

Leffert, N., Benson, P. L., Scales, P. C., Sharma, A. R., Drake, D. R., & Blyth, D. A. (1998). Developmental assets: Measurement and prediction of risk behaviors among adolescents. *Applied Developmental Science, 2,* 209–230.

Lerner, R. M., Fisher, C. B., & Weinberg, R. A. (2000). Toward a science for and of the people: Promoting the civil society through the application of developmental science. *Child Development, 71,* 11–20.

LeSure-Lester, G. E. (2000). Relation between empathy and aggression and behavior compliance among abused group home youth. *Child Psychiatry & Human Development, 31,* 153–161.

Marsh, H. W. (1992). *The Self Description Questionnaire I: Manual.* Macarthur, Australia: University of Western Sydney.

McLaughlin, M. W. (2000). *Community counts: How youth organizations matter for youth development.* Washington, DC: Public Education Network.

Meeus, W. (1996). Studies on identity development in adolescence: An overview of research and some new data. *Journal of Youth and Adolescence, 25,* 569–598.

Moore, K. A. (1997). Criteria for indicators of child well-being. In R. M. Hauser, B. V. Brown, & W. R. Prosser (Eds.), *Indicators of children's well-being* (pp. 36–44) New York: Russell Sage Foundation.

National Research Council & Institute of Medicine. (2002). *Community programs to promote youth development* (J. S. Eccles & J. A. Gootman, Eds.). Washington, DC: National Academy Press.

O'Hagan, M. B. (2000). The protective effects of self-efficacy. *The Chicago Project News, 5*(3). Retrieved August 5, 2003, from http://www.hms.harvard.edu/chase/projects/chicago/news/newsletters/fall00/nlfall00.html

Peterson, C., & Park, N. (2003, March). *Assessment of character strengths among youth: Progress report on the values in action inventory for youth.* Paper presented at the Child Trends Conference on Indicators of Positive Youth Development, Washington, DC.

Peterson, C., & Seligman, M. E. P. (2002). *The Values in Action (VIA) classification of strengths.* Washington, DC: American Psychological Association.

Pittman, K., Irby, M., & Ferber, T. (2000). Unfinished business: Further reflections on a decade of promoting youth development. In *Youth development: Issues, challenges, and directions* (pp. 17–64). Philadelphia: Public/Private Ventures.

Rauner, D. M. (2000). *The role of caring in youth development and community life: "They still pick me up when I fall."* New York: Columbia University Press.

Resnick, M. D., Bearman, P. S., Blum, R. W., Bauman, K. E., Harris, K. M., Jones, J., et al. (1997). Protecting adolescents from harm: Findings from the National Longitudinal Study on Adolescent Health. *Journal of the American Medical Association, 278*, 823–832.

Rest, J. (1983). Morality. In P. Mussen (Series Ed.) & J. H. Flavell & E. Markman (Vol. Eds.), *Cognitive development: Vol. 3. Handbook of child psychology* (4th ed., pp. 920–990). New York: Wiley.

Rosenberg, M. (1965). *Society and the adolescent self-image.* Princeton, NJ: Princeton University Press.

Roth, J. L., & Brooks-Gunn, J. (2000). *What do adolescents need for healthy development?: Implications for youth policy* (Vol. 14, No. 1, pp. 3–19). Social Policy Report.

Roth, J. L., & Brooks-Gunn, J. (2003). What is a youth development program? Identifying defining principles. In R. M. Lerner, F. Jacobs, & D. Wertlieb (Eds.), *Promoting positive child, adolescent, and family development: A handbook of program and policy innovations* (Vol. 2, pp. 197–223). Thousand Oaks, CA: Sage.

Roth, J., Brooks-Gunn, J., Murray, L., & Foster, W. (1998). Promoting healthy adolescents: Synthesis of youth development program evaluations. *Journal of Research on Adolescence, 8*, 423–459.

Scales, P. C., & Leffert, N. (1999). *Developmental assets: A synthesis of the scientific research on adolescent development.* Minneapolis, MN: Search Institute.

Scheier, L. M., Botvin, G. J., Griffin, K. W., & Diaz, T. (2000). Dynamic growth models of self-esteem and adolescent alcohol use. *Journal of Early Adolescence, 20*, 178–209.

Search Institute. (2003). *The updated profiles of student life: Attitudes and behaviors dataset.* Retrieved July 2003 from http://www.search-institute.org/research/assets/UpdatedData.html

Smith, C., & Faris, R. (2002). *Religion and American adolescent delinquency, risk behaviors and constructive social activities.* Retrieved July 24, 2003, from http://www.youthandreligion.org/publications/docs/RiskReport1.pdf

Smith, R. E., & Smoll, F. L. (1997). Coaching the coaches: Youth sports as a scientific and applied behavioral setting. *Current Directions in Psychological Science, 6*, 16–21.

Smith-Campbell, B. (1999). A case study on expanding the concept of caring from individuals to communities. *Public Health Nursing, 16*, 405–411.

Steinberg, L., & Morris, A. S. (2001). Adolescent development. *Annual Review of Psychology, 52*, 83–110.

Stukas, A. A., Clary, E. G., & Snyder, M. (1999a). Service learning: Who benefits and why (Vol. 13, No. 4, pp. 1–19). Social Policy Report.

Stukas, A. A., Snyder, M., & Clary, E. G. (1999b). The effects of "mandatory volunteerism" on intentions to volunteer. *Psychological Science, 10*, 59–64.

U.S. Department of Education. (2003). Close-up on No Child Left Behind: Character education. *The Achiever, 2*(3). Retrieved July 24, 2003, from http://www.d.gov/news/newsletters/achiever/2003/080/2003.html

U.S. Department of Health and Human Services, Office of the Assistant Secretary for Planning and Evaluation. (2002). *Trends in the well-being of America's children and youth 2002.* Washington, DC: Author.

Webb, J., Wilson, B., Corbett, D., & Mordecai, R. (1993). Understanding caring in context: Negotiating borders and barriers. *Urban Review, 25*, 25–45.

Youniss, J., McLellan, J. A., Su, Y., & Yates, M. (1999). The role of community service in identity development: Normative, unconventional, and deviant orientations. *Journal of Adolescent Research, 14*, 248–261.

Zimmerman, B. (1995). Self-efficacy and educational development. In A. Bandura (Ed.), *Self-efficacy in changing societies* (pp. 202–231). New York: Cambridge University Press.

Zimmerman, M. A., Copeland, L. A., Shope, J. T., & Dielman, T. E. (1997). A longitudinal study of self-esteem: Implications for adolescent development. *Journal of Youth and Adolescence, 26*, 117–141.

A Developmental Framework for Selecting Indicators of Well-Being During the Adolescent and Young Adult Years

Jacquelynne Eccles
University of Michigan

Brett V. Brown
Child Trends

Janice Templeton
University of Michigan

In this chapter, we have two goals: (a) to suggest a set of psychological and social assets that are important for healthy development during adolescence and young adulthood and (b) to summarize the readily available indicators for these assets. We address the first goal in the first half of our chapter. We address the second goal in the last half of the chapter.

DEVELOPMENT DURING ADOLESCENCE AND YOUNG ADULTHOOD

There is general agreement that the adolescent years are critically important for the successful transition to adulthood. We have included the years from 18 to 25 as well because rapid demographic, sociocultural, and labor market changes have made these years as transitional as the teen years were in previous generations. As recently as the 1960s, the transition into adulthood in most Western industrialized countries (particularly in the United States and Canada) was well defined for most social class groups: adolescents finished high school and either went to college or into the labor market or the military. People generally married and began families in their early 20s. Thus, people were usually launched into adulthood by their early 20s, and there were only a limited number of fairly well-defined pathways from adolescence into adulthood. This is no longer the case for many young people (Arnett, 2000; Corcoran & Matsudaira, 2005; Fussell & Furstenberg, 2005; Mortimer & Larson, 2002; Mouw, 2005; Osgood, Ruth, Eccles, Jacobs, & Barber, 2005). The median age for marriage and childbearing has moved up to the late 20s. Both the length of time and proportion of youth in some form of tertiary education have increased dramatically. Finally, the heterogeneity of passage through this period of life has exploded. There is no longer a small, easily understood set of patterns for the transition to adulthood, making the years between 18 and 25 as challenging a period of life as adolescence. In the United States, the level of challenge is especially high for noncollege youth and for members of several ethnic minority groups, particularly Blacks and Hispanics, for the following two reasons. First unlike many European and Asian industrialized countries, there is very little institutional support for the transition from secondary school to work in the United States, creating what the William T. Grant foundation (1988) labeled a "floundering" period in their important report: *The Forgotten Half*. Second, stereotypes about the competence of Blacks and Hispanics, coupled with lower levels of "soft skills" (Murnane & Levy, 1996) and the loss of employment options in many inner city communities (Wilson, 1997), have made employment of Black and Hispanic youth (particularly males) quite problematic (Corcoran & Matsudaira; 2005; Mollenkopf, Waters, Holdaway, & Kasinitz, 2005).

The years from age 10 to 25 are marked by major changes at all levels. Among the most dramatic are the biological changes associated with puberty. These include dramatic shifts in the shape of the body, major increases in gonadal hormones, and changes in brain architecture. These biological shifts are directly linked to increases in sexual interest and changes in both cognitive and physical capacities. However, there are also major social changes associated with school and work and with the changing roles adolescents and young adults are expected to play by friends, parents, teachers, coaches, and so on. Finally, there are major psychological changes linked to increasing social and cognitive maturity. In fact, very few developmental periods are characterized by so many changes at so many different levels. With rapid change comes a heightened potential for both positive and negative outcomes (Rutter & Garmezy, 1983; Wheaton, 1990). Although most individuals pass through these two developmental periods without excessively high levels of storm and stress, a substantial number of individuals experience difficulty that extends well into young adulthood (Arnett, 1999; Eccles et al., 1993; Osgood et al., 2005).

Adolescence and emerging adulthood are particularly important for life course development because these are times when individuals make many choices and engage in a wide variety of behaviors that have the potential to influence the rest of their lives (see Mortimer, 2003; Mortimer, Zimmer-Gembeck, Holmes, & Shanahan, 2002; Osgood et al., 2005; Settersten, Furstenberg, & Rumbaut, 2005). For example, adolescents pick which high school courses to take, which after-school activities to participate in, and which peer groups to join. They begin to make future educational and occupational plans and to implement these plans through secondary school coursework and out-of-school vocational and volunteer activity choices. Finally, some experiment with quite problematic behaviors linked to drug and alcohol consumption and unprotected sexual intercourse. Similarly, in the emerging adulthood years individuals make choices related to education, vocational training, entry into the labor market, transitions within the labor market, moving out of one's natal family home, spouse selection, and parenthood. Given the power that these choices and behaviors can have over future options and opportunities, it is critical that we understand what influences whether youth stay on a healthy, productive pathways or move onto more problematic, and potentially destructive, pathways as they pass through this important developmental period.

In his theoretical model of life span development, Eric Erikson (1963, 1968) outlined a set of tasks that are particularly salient for individuals between the ages of 10 and 25, namely, developing a sense of mastery, a sense of identity, and a sense of intimacy. Others have expanded these tasks to include establishing increasing autonomy from one's natal family and/or taking on the responsibilities to one's family and community that are identified with adulthood in various ethnic groups, dealing with sexuality and intimacy, finding a niche for oneself in the worlds of education and work, and moving into the roles associated with partnering and parenting (e.g., Havinghurst, 1972; Levinson, 1978). As individuals make the transition into adulthood in this society, they become more and more independent from their natal families. As a consequence, they need to play a much more active role in their own development. This involves taking on and then managing and coordinating multiple demanding life roles; refining the skills necessary to succeed in these roles; finding meaning and purpose in the roles one has selected, or has ended up in for any number of reasons; developing a mature view of one's strengths and limitations; coping with both foreseen and unforeseen events and life changes; making changes in one's life course, if necessary; and then coping with both the planning and implementation of these new choices.

As Erikson (1968) made clear, each of the tasks of adolescence and emerging adulthood is played out in a complex set of social contexts and in both cultural and historical settings (see also Bronfenbrenner, 1979; Eccles et al., 1993; Settersten et al., 2005). For example, the array and severity of risks for adolescents have increased dramatically over the last 30 years as communities have become more transient and less homogeneous, drugs have become more widely available, and social norms have become less rigid and proscribed. Similarly, the passage from 18 to 25 has become increasingly complex during the last 40 years as the transition to adulthood has become more extended in time and less homogeneous in the array of transitional and end-state patterns

(Arnett, 2000; Settersten et al., 2005). These changes have created a situation in which the tasks of emerging adulthood must be carried out in a climate of extreme uncertainty about both one's current options and the implications of one's choices for future options and barriers.

Optimal progress on each of these tasks depends on the psychosocial, physical, and cognitive assets of the individual (Eccles & Gootman, 2002; Erikson, 1963; Wheaton, 1990). Because transition and change are primary characteristics of both of these life periods, personal and social assets that facilitate coping with change will be critical for successful functioning during these periods. Optimal progress also depends on the developmental appropriateness of the social contexts encountered by the individual as he or she passes through these periods of life. Repeated exposure to developmentally inappropriate and unsupportive social contexts during these years can undermine the coping skills of even the most resilient youth (Eccles, Barber, Stone, & Templeton, 2003; Foster & Gifford, 2005; Mortimer, 2003; Rutter, 1988; Setterstein, 2005; Werner & Smith, 1982, 1992). This complexity must be taken into account when one thinks about successful development during this period of life. Equally important is the longer term consequences of well-being during these two periods for the successful transition into adulthood. Failure to deal with these tasks adequately will place restrictions on adult options-restrictions that are very hard to overcome.

PERSONAL ASSETS

Having laid out the major developmental challenges associated with adolescence and emerging adulthood, we now turn to a discussion of the personal and social assets likely to facilitate both optimal passage through these periods of life and optimal transition into the next phase of life-adulthood. In this section, we review what we know about the personal and social assets that predict both concurrent well-being and optimal future life transitions. First, we discuss what theories and practical wisdom tell us about the likely assets, and then we very briefly summarize what empirical studies (particularly longitudinal studies) tell us about these assets.

Theoretical Perspectives

Developmental theoreticians in psychology, sociology, anthropology, and ethology have speculated on the core human needs and how their fulfillment relates to well-being and well-becoming. Freud, the first grand scientific theorist to suggest core human needs, suggested that well-being depended on success in the two broad domains of work and love. More recently, Erikson proposed the following characteristics as key to healthy psychological development: trust (which he linked to positive emotional relationships with caring adults), a strong sense of self-sufficiency, initiative, a strong sense of industry (confidence in one's ability to master the demands of one's world), identity, and intimacy. More recently, theorists ranging from Harter (1990), Bandura (1997), Deci and Ryan (1985), and Connell and Wellborn (1991), in the field of motivation; to Garmezy and Rutter (1983; see also Masten & Coatsworth, 1998) in the arena of risk and resilience; and to Baltes, Lindenberger, and Staudinger (1998), Elder (1998), and Levinson (1986) in the field of life span development have suggested the following: a sense of personal efficacy, intrinsic motivation, a desire for mastery, social connectedness, good emotional coping skills, planfulness, a sense of optimism, and attachment to conventional prosocial institutions.

Practical Wisdom

Over the last 10 or so years, many lists of assets have been proposed by foundations, youth-serving organizations, and practitioners. Lerner, Fisher, and Weinberg (2000) summarized these lists, along with their sense of the empirical literature, in terms of five major psychological assets: (a) competence in academic, social, and vocational arenas; (b) confidence; (c) connection; (d) character; and (e) caring and compassion. The Search Institute (see Scales & Leffert, 1999) has also provided an extensive list of personal assets broken into the following six general areas and has provided extensive research evidence of the importance of each of these assets: (a) commitment to learning; (b) positive values; (c) social, interpersonal, and cultural competencies; (d) positive identity; (e) positive use of time; and (f) autonomy and "mattering."

Empirical Findings

There has been substantial research over the last 50 years aimed at identifying the key characteristics needed for success in the American society. Much of this work has grown out an effort to understand resilience and well-being. By and large, these suggestions coincide quite well with the suggestions made by both theorists and practitioners. For example, in the now-classic study of development of poor children and their families on Kauai, Emmy Werner and her colleagues concluded that the following characteristics are key for resilience: good cognitive skills; good social skills and an engaging personality; self-confidence, self-esteem, and self-efficacy; good self-regulation skills; good coping and adaptation skills; good health; strong social connections to family; strong social connections to prosocial organizations and networks; and spirituality or a sense of meaningfulness. These conclusions were based on a longitudinal study that lasted more than 25 years. Clausen (1993) and Elder (1974) reached similar conclusions based on the classic longitudinal work done on the Berkeley and Oakland Growth Studies, following a sample of children born just before or during the Depression. Clausen added planfulness to the list. Other longitudinal researchers have provided additional support for the importance of various subsets of these characteristics (e.g., Block, 1971; Cairns & Cairns, 1994; Compas, Wagner, Slavin, & Vannatta, 1986; Elder & Conger, 2000; Furstenberg et al., 1987; Furstenberg, Cook, Eccles, Elder, & Sameroff, 1999; Jessor, Donovan, & Costa, 1991; Moritmer, 2003; Sampson & Laub, 1993).

In reviewing this work and related studies of resilience and adolescent development, the National Research Council (NRC) panel on Community-Based Programs for Youth (Eccles & Gootman, 2002) selected the personal assets listed in Table 7.1 (organized around three general categories: intellectual development, psychological and emotional development, and social development). There is quite strong empirical evidence of the link of some of the personal characteristics (assets) to other widely accepted indicators of well-being, such as school success, good mental health, avoidance of involvement in a variety of problem behaviors, and both educational and occupational attainment.[1] The empirical work is much weaker for other assets, and we know very little about how these assets work together to facilitate positive development. For example, very few studies have included more than a couple of the assets and target outcomes. Thus, we have no idea which of these assets are most important for various outcomes, and we have no idea how various patterns of the assets work together to support positive development. It seems quite likely that there are many quite effective profiles of personal assets and that different profiles are more or less effective in different cultural and personal contexts. Nonetheless, the existing literature suggests three major conclusions: (a) it is important to have assets in each of the three general categories; (b) within each general category, one can do quite well with only a subset of the many characteristics listed, and (c) in general, having more assets is better than having only a few.

In addition, much more work is needed to establish the extent to which these assets are equally important in different cultural groups and to extent to which other assets need to be added for other cultural groups. More work is especially needed on the role of constructs linked to culture and ethnicity, including cultural knowledge, ethnic identities, coping skills for dealing with experiences of discrimination and racism, and management skills for living in an ethnically and culturally diverse world. Finally, we know very little about the role of these and possibly other assets for a wide range of subpopulations such as either youth with disabilities or highly gifted youth.

SOCIAL ASSETS

Personal assets do not exist or develop in a vacuum, however. Evidence suggests that these personal assets influence life chances because they both facilitate the engagement of youth in positive social contexts that

Table 7.1

Personal Assets That Facilitate Positive Youth Development

Intellectual development

Knowledge of essential life and vocational skills

Rational habits of mind – critical thinking and reasoning skills

Good decision-making skills

In depth knowledge of more than one culture

Knowledge of skills needed to navigate through multiple cultural contexts

School success

Psychological and emotional development

Good mental health including positive self-regard

Good emotional self-regulation and coping skills

Good conflict resolution skills

Mastery motivation and positive achievement motivation

Confidence in one's personal efficacy

Planfulness

Sense of personal autonomy/responsibility for self

Optimism coupled with realism

Coherent and positive personal and social identity

Prosocial and culturally sensitive values

Spirituality and/or a sense of purpose in life

Strong moral character

Social development

Connectedness – perceived good relationships and trust with parents, peers, and some other adults

Sense of social place/integration – being connected and valued by larger social networks

Attachment to prosocial/conventional institutions such as school, church, out of school youth development centers

Ability to navigate in multiple cultural contexts

Commitment to civic engagement

Source: Box 3-1, Eccles & Gootman, 2002. Content reproduced with permission of the National Academies Press.

support continued positive development and protect youth against the adverse effects of negative life events, difficult social situations, pressure to engage in risky behaviors, and academic failures. So, on the one hand, these personal assets can increase life chances, and on the other hand, excessive and prolonged exposure to negative life events, dangerous contexts, and inadequate schooling are likely to undermine youth's life chances despite personal assets (e.g., X. Cui & Vallant, 1996; Elder, 1998; Jessor et al., 2003; Kim, Conger, Elder, & Lorenz, 2003; Mortimer, 2003). In addition, these personal assets will take youth only so far. They need continued exposure to positive developmental contexts as well as abundant opportunities to refine their life skills so that they have the means to move into jobs that provide living wages. Some youth live in families and neighborhoods that ensure these experiences. Others do not. Given these concerns, the second thing that the NRC panel did was to suggest a set of social assets (characteristics of the contexts in which youth spend their time) that are important for supporting the development of these personal assets. Again the panel relied on theory, practical wisdom, and empirical evidence from work in multiple disciplines. The following contextual characteristics emerged from this review with strong support across studies of families, peer groups, schools, communities, and out-of-school programs for youth:

- adequate provisions for physical and psychological safety, developmentally appropriate levels of structure and adult supervision;
- supportive relationships with adults;
- supportive and respectful relationships among peers;
- opportunities to development a strong sense of belonging;
- opportunities to experience mastery and mattering;
- opportunities to learn the cognitive and noncognitive skills essential for succeeding in school, work, and other prosocial social and institutional settings; and
- strong positive social norms for behavior.

These general assets are elaborated in Table 7.2 along with specific features representative of each asset category. We include these in this chapter because we (like many practitioners and people interested in youth policy, e.g., the Search Institute, public/private ventures, the William T. Grant Foundation) believe it is important to be gathering systematic data on the extent to which communities are providing these contextual experiences for their youth. There are good indicators available for some of these contextual features, particularly with regard to the family context. There are very few such indicators for many of these features for other contexts of development, such as the schools, peer groups, out-of-school programs, and workplace contexts. There are even fewer indicators of these social contextual assets at the community level. The Search Institute has led the way in creating such community-level social asset indicators. Although community asset mapping activities are becoming more common, a great deal of work remains before there will be readily available, high-quality instruments to use as indicators of many of these social assets.

Table 7.2
Features Of Contexts That Promote Youth Development

Context	Descriptors	Opposite poles
Appropriate structure	• Age appropriate monitoring • Limit setting • Clear and consistent rules and expectations • Age appropriate controls and rules continuity • Predictability • Clear boundaries	• Chaotic • Disorganized • Laissez-faire • Rigid • Over-controlled • Autocratic
Physical and Psychological Safety	• Safe and health promoting facilities • Practices that increase safe peer group interaction • Practices that decrease unsafe or confrontational peer interactions	• Physical and health dangers • Fear • Feeling of insecurity • Sexual and physical harassment • Verbal abuse
Emotional and Instrumental Support	• Warmth • Closeness • Connectedness • Good communication • Caring • Support • Guidance • Responsiveness	• Cold • Overcontrolling • Ambiguous support • Untrustworthy • Focus on winning rather than mastery • Inattentive • Unresponsive • Rejecting
Opportunities to Belong	• Opportunities for meaningful inclusion, regardless of one's gender, ethnicity, or disabilities • Social inclusion • Social engagement and integration • Opportunities for social-cultural identity formation • Support for cultural and bicultural competence.	• Exclusion • Marginalization • Intergroup conflict • Tolerance of bullying and discriminative behaviors
Pro-Social Norms	• Prosocial rules of behavior • Strong expectations for prosocial and moral behaviors • Prosocial values and morals • Obligations for service and for helping within program	• Normlessness • Anomie • Tolerance for antisocial and amoral norms and behaviors such as those linked to violence, reckless behavior, bullying, consumerism, and poor health practices • Tolerance of peer pressures to conform.
Opportunity for Efficacy and for Mattering	• Youth based, empowerment practices that support autonomy, mattering, and being taken seriously • Practices that include enabling, responsibility granting, meaningful challenge • Opportunities to demonstrate and acquire mastery in valued activities • Service opportunity • Stress on improvement	• Unchallenging • Overcontrol • Disempowerment • Disabling • Failure experiences without opportunity to improve • Stress on social comparative performance rather than mastery and improvement • Lack of role in governance and program planning

(continued)

Table 7.2 *(continued)*

Context	Descriptors	Opposite poles
Opportunities for Skill Building	• Intentional learning environments • Knowledge-centered environments • Opportunities to learn cultural and media literacies, communication skills, and good habits of mind • Preparation for adult employment • Stress on improvement • Opportunities to develop social and cultural capital	• Practices that promote bad physical habits and habits of mind • Practice that undermine school and learning • Lack of opportunities to learn important life skills • Stress on social comparative performance rather than mastery and improvement
Integration with Family, Schools, and Community	• Concordance, coordination and synergy between family, school, and community • Opportunities to develop social and cultural capital	• Discordance, lack of communication, conflict.

Source: Table 4-1, Eccles and Gootman, 2002. Content reproduced with permission of the National Academies Press.

Although there is strong support for the importance of each of these general social assets, we know very little about how these assets work together across contexts of development. Most of the studies have focused on one context, usually the family. We know little about whether, when, and how assets in one context, like the school or a community-based program for youth, can compensate for the lack of such assets in other contexts, like the family. Studies that do include indicators of multiple contexts (e.g., Cook et al., 2002; Eccles, Early, Frasier, Belansky, & McCarthy, 1997; Elder & Conger, 2000; Furstenberg et al., 1999) suggest that the impact of contexts are additive-meaning they accumulate. These results suggest that exposure to positive social assets in one context can help ameliorate the lack of such exposure in other contexts. These results also indicate that having assets across many contexts is associated with more positive outcomes than having social assets in only one or two contexts.

Another problem hindering our ability to understand the relation of social assets across contexts is the lack of comparable measures for the different contexts. Until quite recently, researchers have tended to focus on one context and have developed measures for only that one context. Consequently, quite different conceptualizations and measures of the social assets of the different contexts have emerged-making comparison across contexts very difficult. Much more work is needed on the development of comparable indicators of social assets across various contexts so that we can actually compare the impact of specific social assets across these contexts.

Finally, as was true for personal assets, the importance of cultural issues is just being acknowledged in both measure development and conceptualization of social assets. As but one example of this problem, consider the role of support for autonomy. Western scholars with a northern European perspective have stressed the importance of independence from one's parents and other adults as a key feature of support for autonomy during adolescence. Scholars with other perspectives have questioned this orientation, suggesting instead that maturity is reflected by a changing form of interdependence between the generations, a form that involves taking on great responsibility for the well-being of one's natal and extended family rather than a form that involves moving away from one's natal and extended family (see Fuligni & Flook, 2005). The types of social opportunities needed for one of these forms of maturity are likely to be different from the opportunities needed for the other. Conceptual and methodological work is needed to further our understanding of such differences.

A second critical example of this problem is the scarcity of indicators of experiences linked to discrimination and racism on the one hand and to experiences linked to learning tolerance and both cultural respect and valuing of diversity on the other. We live in a very diverse society, and yet we have little information about the contextual characteristics and assets that promote well-being in diverse cultural situations. Given the changing demographics in the United States, such work is critical.

EXISTING INDICATORS AND DATA SOURCES

We now turn to a discussion of existing indicators. In the first part of this section, we discuss indicators available at the community level. We then turn to a discussion of various either national or regional survey instruments that have been developed during the last 10 to 20 years. Many of these contain short scales directly related to the assets listed in Tables 7.1 and 7.2. We end this section with a summary of a variety of studies focused on a more limited set of indicators. This section is organized around the assets listed in Tables 7.1 and 7.2. Again we provide information about how to locate these scales.

COMMUNITY-LEVEL INDICATOR DATA

Communities make use of a variety of data sources for monitoring the well-being of their youth. These include census data; administrative sources, such as school records and vital statistics; as well as original surveys using high-quality survey instruments developed for that purpose. Administrative data have the advantage of being available in all communities. However, these data are not always easily accessible outside of the agencies that collect them,[2] and there are many important aspects of youth development and well-being that are not collected through administrative sources. For that reason, some motivated communities will field their own surveys of youth to get a more complete picture of youth well-being and the contextual influences that shape well-being, although the expense keeps many from doing so.

Census Data

Decennial census data have long been available down to the community and even the neighborhood level. Census data focus on basic demographics (i.e., race, age, sex, family structure) and socioeconomic outcomes (educational attainment, income, employment, housing tenure) as well as some data on disability status. These data have been a mainstay of public and private planning for many decades. Their main weakness, however, was the fact that they are collected only once every 10 years, going quickly out of date.

In response to the widely acknowledged need for more current local estimates, the U.S. Census Bureau launched the American Community Survey, which collects virtually all of the same information collected by the decennial census but does so on a continuous basis, interviewing approximately 3 million households each year starting in 2005. As early as 2010, the census bureau will produce annually updated estimates down to the census tract level, generally areas of 2,500 to 8,000 people.[3]

Administrative Data

Examples of administrative data sources include vital statistics birth and death data, school performance assessments, child abuse and neglect records, public assistance data, police records, health surveillance systems, and emergency room admissions records (Child Trends 2006, Tatian 2000; Coulton 1998; Coulton & Hollister 1998).

Every community has access to a variety of youth well-being indicators from administrative data sources. Often, these data are capable of producing estimates down to the neighborhood level, which is very important for many community planning purposes. They also provide information on youth that is not easily collected through surveys such as academic assessments, teen birth data, as well as characteristics of the neighborhoods in which youth live (e.g. poverty rate, crime levels, unemployment rates).

A number of problems are commonly encountered when using administrative data sources.

Data Quality and Consistency

Some sources of administrative data, such as birth and death data, are on the whole quite reliable and consistent over time and across jurisdictions. Other sources, such as child welfare data, have suffered to various degrees from poor or uneven data quality. Even here, though, substantial strides have been made over the last decade through the National Child Abuse and Neglect Data System (Child Trends 2006).

Inconsistent Geographic Units

Administrative data are collected for particular purposes, and collecting agencies will use the geographic units that best suit their needs. For example, the school system will aggregate data by school and school district, others may use census tracts, and some may use health districts. This can make it difficult to produce a rich set of estimates for the same neighborhood, because the boundaries units often cannot be made to match.

Lack of Subgroup Estimates

Administrative data sources tend to collect only the data that are needed for agency work. Background characteristics that would be important for more general purposes (e.g., family income, immigrant status, family structure) are often absent. As a result, separate estimates for important subgroups (poor people, immigrants) may not be available from some administrative sources. For example, vital statistics birth data gathers no information on income, so separate rates for poor and nonpoor people cannot be generated.

Lack of Accessibility

Although administrative data are collected and used in every community, the availability of these data for general planning purposes can vary greatly across communities. Some administrative data that could be of use to many community organizations never make it beyond the walls of the collecting agency. The computerization of administrative records and the growth of the Internet have lowered barriers to sharing such data, but it is still a problem in many communities.

There have been several notable efforts to make community-level administrative data more accessible to the public and across local agencies.

Kids Count

The Annie E. Casey Foundation has for some time funded organizations in every state, the District of Columbia, the Virgin Islands, and Puerto Rico to put out annual reports on the condition of children and youth that feature indicators of child and youth well-being down to the county level. These reports are widely distributed each year in hard copy and over the Internet. In addition, the Casey Foundation has recently made data from all these state reports available in one location in what they call the *CLIKS system*, which stands for *Community Level Information on Kids*.[4] Within states, the data are comparable across counties, allowing for cross-county comparisons. The data presented will vary from state to state according to what data are available.

National Neighborhood Indicators Partnership

Increasingly communities are looking to take administrative data from many sources make them available across agencies and even to the general public by placing them in Geographic Information Systems databases that allow all users to look at data from many sources for particular areas within the community. The National Neighborhood Indicators Partnership was established as a collaboration between The Urban Institute and local data partners to develop and use these neighborhood data systems to support better community planning. As of 2006, groups in 27 cities participated in the partnership. Partners draw from a wide variety of data sources to build their databases. (See Tatian, 2000, for a discussion of commonly available data sources.)

No Child Left Behind

The federal No Child Left Behind (NCLB) initiative to improve student academic performance and close performance gaps across population subgroups mandates regular assessment of all students and holds states accountable for improving student outcomes. The NCLB also mandates that detailed assessment results be made publicly available, down to the school district and individual school level. States have opted to make their data available through a common web portal called *Schoolmatters* (http://www.schoolmatters.com). The data are available in a common format, providing easy access to useful data for individual public schools throughout the country. Assessments are comparable within states, but not between states.

Community-Level Surveys of Youth

Although administrative data are clearly important sources for tracking youth development and well-being, they can also have their limitations in terms of substantive coverage, ability to produce subgroup estimates, quality, and so on. Researchers seeking a more complete picture of youth well-being must turn to surveys. Surveys have their own limitations, of course, principal among them being the expense to collect the data. However, many communities around the country have determined that the additional information provided by surveys is worth the cost. In the following sections, we review three of the most popular and well-designed of these surveys focusing on youth development out-comes and social settings.

Profiles of Student Life: Attitudes and Behaviors

The Profiles of Student Life: Attitudes and Behaviors (PSL:AB) survey was developed by the Search Institute and is grounded in what they call a *developmental assets framework*. They identified 40 assets, both per-sonal and social, that youth need to thrive. The framework is highly compatible with the approach taken by the NRC panel's own frame-work, which guides us here, in that it emphasizes positive developmen-tal outcomes (internal assets) and the positive social settings (external assets). External asset domains (each of which contains multiple assets) include external sources promoting support, empowerment, bound-aries and expectations, and constructive use of time. Internal asset do-mains include commitment to learning, positive values, social competencies, and positive identity. This survey is designed for youth in Grades 6 through 12, although recently they have also developed asset lists for both early and middle childhood.[5]

The 40 assets were derived from a comprehensive review of the youth development literature (Scales & Leffert, 1999), although the research base for some assets is admittedly thin. Most assets are measured using 3- or 4-item scales with Cronbach's alphas (a measure of reliability) ranging between .31 and .82, with most at or above .60 (a common cutoff used in research). Research has demonstrated a strong relationship between the number of assets a youth has and the degree to which he or she is thriving and avoiding risky behaviors (Leffert et al., 1998). The PSL:AB is available through the Search Institute at a modest cost, and they will also process the survey and produce a report for an additional fee.

Because of the comprehensive nature of the assets framework and its compatibility with the NRC model, it is not surprising that the PSL:AB in-cludes measures in every one of the NRC domains, both youth outcome and social setting domains. Most domains in fact include multiple mea-sures. For example, the *social development* domain includes volunteering in the community; friendship skills; capacity for empathy; and respect for cultural diversity; as well as participation in such activities as sports, mu-sic, theater, and art. Measures in the *psychological development* domain in-clude measures of moral character and measures of positive and negative mental health. Measures of social structure within social settings include such things as the presence of clear rules and monitoring activity within the family, the school, and the neighborhood. Not all of the domains have such a generous selection of measures as these, but all are covered.[6]

Communities That Care Youth Survey[7]

This survey was originally developed by research staff at the Social De-velopment Research Group at the University of Washington. The survey is designed for administration at the community level and is based on a risk and protective factors model (Arthur, Hawkins, Pollard, Catalano, & Baglioni, 2002). It is intended for youth in Grades 6 through 12. The risk and protective scales have been shown to have strong reliability and validity across gender and racial-ethnic groups, properly correlated with problem behaviors and with alphas exceeding .65 (Arthur et al., 2002; Mrazek, Biglin, & Hawkins, 2004; Pollard, Catalano, Hawkins, Arthur, & Baglioni, 1999). Many states use or have used this survey, including Arizona, Arkansas, Colorado, Florida, New York, Oklahoma, Oregon, Pennsylvania, Utah, Washington, and Wyoming (Mrazek et al., 2004). The survey and report-generating software area available through the federal government's Substance Abuse and Mental Health Services Administration/Center for Substance Abuse and Prevention.[8]

Like the PSL:AB, the Communities That Care survey includes at least one measure in each of the NRC youth outcome and social setting domains. Unlike the PSL:AB, youth outcomes are overwhelming negative. The survey focuses more on negative outcomes such as drug use, violent behaviors, and delinquency and school suspensions, although a few positive outcomes related to academic achievement are included. For example, questions relating to moral character focus on attitudes toward a host of negative behaviors in which teens may engage rather than positive moral strengths.

Data on the family, peer, and schools environments contain more of a balance of positive and negative influences. There are strong positive measures related to structure (e.g., clear rules; monitoring youth behavior in the family, school, and neighborhood) supportive relationships (e.g., parent-child closeness, teacher attention and praise) opportunities for efficacy (e.g., students help in setting rules at school, parents help youth succeed in school), and positive social norms (parents, peers, and adults in community providing positive role models) as well as measures of safe environments, belonging, and opportunities for skill building.

Youth Risk Behavior Survey

The Youth Risk Behavior Survey (YRBS) was developed by the Centers for Disease Control and Prevention and designed by national experts in the health care field with input from state and city education agencies. The survey, for students in Grades 9 through 12, has been fielded on a regular basis since 1990, and a modified survey for Grades 6 through 8 was fielded in 2005. In 2005, the Grade 9–12 survey was fielded nationally, in 40 states and 21 major cities. In addition, individual counties or school districts have also fielded this survey, and several states have expanded the survey in their states so that separate school district-level estimates can be produced. A detailed, science-based rationale for the inclusion of all measures has been produced and is updated at each redesign.[9]

The YRBS has a much more narrow focus than the PSL:AB and the Communities That Care survey, concentrating on health risk behaviors in six areas: (a) tobacco use, (b) dietary behaviors, (c) physical activity, (d) alcohol and other drug use, (e) sexual behaviors that contribute to unintended pregnancy and sexually transmitted diseases, and (f) behaviors that contribute to injuries and violence. The survey covers important health outcomes and behaviors not covered in the other surveys, including overweight, pregnancy, nutrition, dating violence, and rape, as well as more detailed questions about physical exercise and sexual activity. Information on social settings is nearly nonexistent in this survey, limited to one question each on school safety, driving with a person who has been drinking, and whether the student has ever been taught about AIDS or HIV infection in school. States and communities are, however, allowed to add their own questions to cover other areas of well-being of particular interest.

NATIONAL YOUTH SURVEYS

Like the community surveys, national surveys that focus on youth development offer many high-quality measures across the domains that define the NRC youth development framework. In addition, they have some important advantages. First, whereas the community surveys are designed for middle and high school students, many national surveys follow participants into early adulthood, allowing one to construct and to track indicators of early adult well-being and the transition to adulthood. Second, most of the national surveys include high school dropouts, a critical subgroup that cannot be tapped through the (largely) school-based community surveys. Third, several of the surveys gather data from parents, teachers, and school administrators in addition to youth, providing unique data on the family and school environments in which youth develop.

Most of these surveys are one-time longitudinal surveys. This is a great strength in the sense that they are able to support the development of new indicators based on their relationship to long-term developmental outcomes (see chap. 2, this volume). It is a weakness, though, in the sense that the data generated from these surveys do not allow us to track changes over time for the same age groups, a critical function of social indicators data (Moore, 1997). For that reason, we split our review here into periodic national surveys and one-time surveys.

Periodic National Youth Surveys

These surveys are repeated on a regular basis, which allows users to track changes in youth well-being over time at the national level. In fact, the YRBS, reviewed earlier, also has a national-level survey fielded every 2 years. Two additional periodically collected national youth surveys that include measures of positive youth development and related social settings are summarized next.

Monitoring the Future

Monitoring the Future (MTF) has been surveying national samples of 12th-grade students on an annual basis since 1975, adding 8th- and 10th-graders beginning in 1991. In addition to these annual cross-sectional surveys, a subsample of 12th-graders from each year is periodically reinterviewed into adulthood, allowing one to track early adult outcomes over time. The MTF contains measures that cover every domain within the NRC framework with the exception of the "integration of family, school, and community" domain. Although heavily focused on drug use, it also collects measures of cognitive development (academic achievement, school engagement), social development (civic engagement, connectedness to peers, multicultural understanding), physical activity (hours of sleep, physical activity), and psychological and emotional development (self-worth, religiosity, emotional understanding). Post-high school follow-ups focus on additional issues, including military service and employment, marriage, and parenthood. In the social settings domains there are indicators of structure (clear and fair rules at home and in school), supportive relationships (positive relationship with parents), belonging (opportunities for extracurricular participation), social norms (peer values), support for efficacy (parental expectations), and opportunities for skill building (availability for youth involvement in civic activities).

MTF data are available as raw data files for original analysis, annual compendia of tables that summarize results, and in other regularly released reports. For additional information, visit http://www.monitoringthefuture.org.

National Survey of Children's Health

The National Survey of Children's Health (NSCH) is a survey of over 100,000 families with children ages 0 through 17 and is designed to support separate estimates for each of the 50 states and the District of Columbia. It is the only source of state-level estimates for many measures of positive youth development and youth social settings. It was first fielded in 2003–04 and is scheduled to be repeated every 4 years. Data are collected through telephone interviews with the parent or guardian, but youth are not interviewed. This is a disadvantage of the data in some respects, but it provides an important parental perspective on youth well-being and family and neighborhood context.

Although the major focus of the survey is on health issues, all of the NRC domains of youth outcomes are covered to some extent. Measures related to physical and social development (e.g., sport and club activities, physical exercise, obesity, volunteering, employment, involvement in religious groups) are well represented. In the emotional development domain there are several interesting measures related to the youth's capacity for empathy and his or her ability to engage in conflict resolution with family and friends.

In the social setting domains the NSCH focuses particularly on measures of supportive relationships within the family and in the neighborhood (e.g., parent-child closeness, ability to talk together about things that really matter, family meals, neighborhood cohesion and support). In the social norms domain there are several measures of parental exercise and smoking habits that one does not find in other surveys. Finally, within the "integration" domain, intended to capture the level of integration among the social settings in which youth develop, there is a question of what proportion of the youth's friends the parents know.

Data from the NSCH can be analyzed online at the Data Resource Center for Child and Adolescent Health at http://www.childhealthdata.org/.

Longitudinal Surveys of Youth

There are a number of major national longitudinal surveys that contain rich sets of high-quality measures of positive youth development and related social settings. These surveys are designed to follow a cohort from childhood or adolescence into early adulthood, paying particular attention to the role of family, peers, school, and neighborhood in shaping their development.

Characteristics that set these surveys apart from most of the surveys described above include the following:

- *Multiple respondents.* All of these surveys collect data from both the child/youth and his or her parents, and most also collect data from teachers and school administrators. Many also include data gathered from standardized assessments.
- *More complex measures.* Whereas most of the cross-sectional surveys just discussed are relatively short, longitudinal surveys can last for several hours. This allows for the collection of more complex indexes and scales that will capture a construct more completely than individual items. In addition, these longer scales are often used to guide the construction of optimized short scales that can in turn be used and tracked using periodic cross-sectional surveys (see, e.g., Moore, Halle, Vandivere, & Mariner, 2002).
- *Not repeated periodically.* One of the most important features of an indicators data collection system is the capacity to track changes in the population over time and on a regular basis (e.g., trends in the percentage of teens ages 15–17 who exercise regularly). In longitudinal surveys, however, the children are always getting older, making it

impossible to track changes in well-being over time among the same age group.

• *Follow the same persons over time.* Indicators take their importance both because of their intrinsic worth (e.g., good health is valuable in itself), and because of what they indicate or predict for future well-being (e.g., good health is valuable because it promotes future health and well-being). This dual nature is captured in the notions of well-being versus well-becoming (see Ben-Arieh, Kaufman, Andrews, Goerge, & Lee, 2001). Longitudinal data help us particularly to explore the well-becoming moment of social indicators.

In cases where important measures of well-being do not exist in repeated cross-sectional surveys, then longitudinal surveys can and should be used to produce such estimates, because they still allow us to assess levels of need or strength at a given point in time and to identify differences in well-being across groups, both important functions of social indicators (Brown & Corbett, 2003). Longitudinal data are a necessity in constructing certain types of indicators that are intended to reflect life conditions over time, such as sustained poverty (see Duncan & Moscow, 1997). However, the primary value of these rich data sources is the support of research that can help us to deepen our understanding of existing indicators and to develop new and better indicator measures for the future. Next, we briefly discuss four contemporary longitudinal surveys that are rich with measures reflecting the major well-being domains within the NRC framework.

Panel Study of Income Dynamic Child Development Supplement

The Panel Study of Income Dynamic (PSID) is a nationally representative survey of American families that has been conducted since 1968. In 1997, the PSID added the child development supplement (CDS), gathering data on children ages 0 through 12 within the PSID sample. These children were followed up in 2002–03 and 2005, and an additional follow-up is planned for 2007. The 2005 and 2007 rounds include a special Transition to Adulthood component for respondents ages 18 and older. By 2007, the oldest respondents will be 22.

The PSID-CDS is an extremely rich data set, with data collected from the children through interviews and assessments, from the parents, and from teachers and school administrators. It is also a unique source of data on nonresident fathers. In addition, it uses many detailed, high-quality assessments and scales to capture facets of intellectual, emotional, social, and psychological development. It also collects outcomes of particular relevance for the transition to adulthood, including voter registration, social identity, marriage and children, employment, and postsecondary schooling. In addition to the more common measures related to physical development (obesity, physical activity) there are also detailed questions on nutrition habits. Finally, a unique source of information is the time diary, which is used to collect detailed data on activities and the social context of those activities. Measures of social settings are also broad, covering all of the NRC domains. The PSID-CDS has a particularly rich set of parent and peer characteristics that fall under the "positive social norms" setting domain, including parental volunteering and giving, parent self-efficacy and esteem, peer engagement in school and community, and peer encouragement of positive behaviors.

For more information, and to access PSID-CDS data, visit http://psidonline.isr.umich.edu/CDS/.

National Longitudinal Study of Adolescent Health

The National Longitudinal Study of Adolescent Health (Add Health) study was designed specifically to support research relating social settings (families, friends, schools, neighborhoods, and communities) to the health and health-related behaviors of youth in Grades 7 through 12. These youth were interviewed in 1994, 1996, and 2001, with an additional follow-up planned for 2007, by which time the respondents will be into their mid-20s to early-30s. Sensitive information for youth was gathered using audio computer assisted self-interview techniques. Parent interviews were taken during the initial wave in 1994. Survey data were also collected from siblings and friends of some respondents. In adulthood, partners are also interviewed.

Add Health is the best overall source of longitudinal data on health outcomes and behaviors from youth through adulthood, with detailed information on nutrition, exercise, dieting, sleep patterns, mental health, sexual experience and practices, tobacco and drug use, weapons carrying and violence, sun exposure, and even tattoos. Psychological and emotional development measures tend toward the negative (e.g., depression scale, suicide attempts, deviant behaviors, gambling, risk taking), although there are positive measures related to self-efficacy, self-confidence, and life satisfaction. In early adulthood, marriage, cohabitation, parenthood, and workforce data are gathered in addition to substantial health information.

In addition to the peer-related data gathered from youth respondents, all students in several schools were included in the survey, and for those schools researchers have the means to link the data from friends and romantic partners who were in the same school, offering a unique opportunity to explore peer influences.

Data are available in both public use and restricted forms. The restricted use data are more extensive and sensitive, and require an institutional review board-approved security plan and a confidentiality contract. Restricted use data access requires a nonrefundable fee of $750. Public use data can be purchased through Sociometrics at http://www.socio.com. For additional information on Add Health, visit http://www.cpc.unc.edu/projects/addhealth.

National Longitudinal Survey of Youth 1997

The National Longitudinal Survey of Youth 1997 (NLSY 97) is the latest in a series of longitudinal surveys focusing on schooling and the transition to employment into adulthood. Adolescents ages 12 through 16 were first interviewed in 1997 and have been reinterviewed annually since that time. The annual follow-ups make this a particularly strong data resource for many research purposes, because there are fewer information gaps than in most of the other longitudinal surveys reviewed here. Parents were also interviewed, but in the first year only. Additional information has been collected through standardized testing (ASVAB vocational aptitude battery, PIAT-R math achievement) and through school administrators, including transcripts and elements of the school environment. ZIP code and census tract-level data related to the youth's place of residence are also available, but access is restricted.

As with the other longitudinal surveys covered here, the NLSY 97 contains a set of measures of youth development and related social settings that cover every domain in the NRC framework.[10] It is particularly strong in terms of school and employment-related information. Data and codebooks can be downloaded for free at http://www.nlsinfo.org/ordering/display_db.php3.

Education Longitudinal Survey of Youth 2002

The Education Longitudinal Survey of Youth 2002 is a longitudinal study that follows a nationally representative sample of high school sophomores through high school, postsecondary school, and the transition to the workforce (into their mid- to late 20s). Data are collected from the student, student records, parents, teachers, and school administrators. Survey data are available in several formats at http://nces.ed.gov/surveys/els2002.

Each of the NRC framework domains is covered in the Education Longitudinal Survey of Youth 2002. Measures of supportive relations and opportunities for skill-building are particularly strong, as are measures on the integration of family, peers, school and community. Data on the school environment are particularly rich in this database, with information from the teacher, principal, student, and the youth.

National Longitudinal Survey of Youth, 1979 Cohort: Children and Young Adults Study

The NLSY 79, launched in 1979, is the precursor to the NLSY 97, reviewed earlier. In 1986, a second survey of the children of all NLSY 79 females was started, which substantially expanded the data collected on the children. The detailed longitudinal data on the female parent of these children makes this a unique data set for exploring the relationship between indicators of youth well-being and the well-being of the children of those youth. This allows researchers to explore the fuller meaning of youth indicators as they relate to the well-being of subsequent generations.

Regional and More Local Longitudinal Studies

Studies by Eccles and Colleagues

Eccles and her colleagues are conducting two comprehensive longitudinal studies of development in context that follow youth through adolescence and the transition to adulthood. Each of these studies contain well-validated and quite reliable indicators of many of the personal and social assets discussed earlier. The first, the Michigan Study of Adolescent/Adult Life Transitions (MSALT), began in the mid-1980s with a group of approximately 1,800 working- and middle-class, predominantly White 6th-graders in 12 school districts in southeast Michigan. The participants have been surveyed nine times: twice in the 6th and 7th grades, once in the 10th and 12th grades, and 3 times during their 20s. The study was designed to address the following three general questions: (a) How do social and academic experiences at school, at home, at work, and with one's peers relate to work and educational options and to psychological adjustment during adolescence and the early twenties? (b) How do individual characteristics linked to motivation, psychological adjustment, personal values and both personal and social identities relate to concurrent and subsequent development? (c) How do both the personal and social assets identified in answering the first two questions relate to the successful transition into and through young adulthood? This data set has measures of many of the assets discussed earlier, and the scales have very high face and predictive validity and quite good internal consistency reliabilities. The items and scales are available on the following web site: http://www.rcgd.isr.umich.edu/garp. The data set is archived at the Murray Center. Two good sources of information about this study are the 2001 article by Barber, Eccles, and Stone and the 2005 chapter by Osgood et al.

The second study, the Maryland Study of Adolescent Development in Multiple Contexts (MADICS), focuses on psychosocial development during adolescence and young adulthood within the contexts of family, peer groups, school, and neighborhoods. The sample (65% African American and 30% European American) is a stratified representative sample of youth enrolled in public schools at Grade 7 in Prince Georges County, Maryland. The population is now approximately 28 years of age. The youth and their parents were surveyed when the youth were in the 7th, 8th-9th, and 11th grades. The youth were surveyed 1 year and 3 years after high school. The project had five major goals: (1) provide a comprehensive description of various developmental trajectories through adolescence; (2) test the utility of the Eccles expectancy/value model of choice behavior and of self and identity theories for predicting individual differences in pathways through adolescence; (3) link variations in these trajectories to experiences in four salient social contexts (family, peers, schools, neighborhood) in terms of the following contextual characteristics: (a) structure/control, (b) support for autonomy, (c) emotional support, (d) opportunities and risks, and (e) shared beliefs, values, and expectations, as well as on the developmental fit between changes in both individuals and contexts; (4) investigate the interplay between these social spheres of experience as they influence development; and (5) extend the understanding of Goals 1 through 4 to African American adolescents with a focus on both general developmental processes and the specific dynamics associated with ethnic identity, prejudice, discrimination, and social stratification. The scales developed to study these goals have high face and predictive validity and have internal consistency reliabilities ranging averaging about .70. The scales and questionnaires are available at http://www.rcgd.isr.umich.edu/garp, and the data are archived at the Murray Center. Two good sources of information on this study are 1997 article by Eccles et al. and the 2003 article by Wong, Eccles, and Sameroff.

The Iowa Longitudinal Study

In 1989, Rand Conger and his colleagues at the University of Iowa began a longitudinal study of 451 White families living in eight adjacent counties in Iowa. Farming was the predominant industry in these counties. The study was designed to investigate the impact of the changing farm economy on adolescents and their families. Each family consisted of 2 parents, a seventh-grade youth, and a sibling within 4 years of age of the seventh-grader. These adolescents and their families have been followed several times over the last 15 years—annually from the years 1989 to 1992 and again in 1994. This data set includes many measures of the types of assets outlined earlier and has quite good reliabilities and extensive evidence of construct, discriminant, and predictive validity. One good source of information on this data set is the 2005 article by M. Cui, Conger, and Lorenz. Many measures in this data set have now also been used with a longitudinal sample of African Americans in the Southeast. For a good source of information about this data set, see Conger et al. (2002).

The Carolina Longitudinal Study

In 1981, Robert Cairns and his colleagues launched the Carolina Longitudinal Study of two cohorts of adolescents in eight different public schools in North Carolina. The first cohort included 220 fourth-grade children from four different public elementary schools; the second cohort included 475 adolescents from the seventh grades of four public middle schools. The samples were representative (in terms of race and social class) of the residents in the communities in which the schools were located; 25% were minorities. The participants were followed annually through the end of high school and occasionally through their 20s. Their parents and grandparents were also interviewed at various points. Extensive work went into developing the measures for this study, and there is now extensive information on the reliability and validity of the scales. Many of the scales measure the types of assets discussed earlier. Cairns and Cairns (2002) provided an excellent summary of the study and the quality of the measures. Another excellent source of information about this study is Cairns and Cairns's (1994) book.

Indicators of Measures of Youth Development From Other Sources

The number of useful measures and well-constructed scales tapping into the domains of youth development and social settings reflected in the NRC framework goes well beyond the sources we have reviewed so far. Readers interested in developing their own surveys, and particularly those who would like to focus strongly on particular topical areas, should look beyond to other surveys and small-scale studies in the field. There have been several attempts to catalogue such measures by topical area across surveys and major studies.

The Children, Youth, and Families At-Risk Program is a collaboration of land grant extension services focusing on community-based programs for at-risk children, youth, and their families. The Children, Youth, and Families At-Risk Program Evaluation Collaboration Project worked during the 1990s to catalogue measures of youth, child, family, and community development that could be used for evaluation purposes. Their youth working group catalogued measures relating to youth social competencies and risk behaviors in the following areas: social competency, relationships, conflict resolution, decision making, social responsibility, communication, goals setting, valuing diversity, academic risk, sexual activity, delinquency, and violence. For each area, they supplied an overview of the literature, a detailed bibliography, and a systematic review of available measures. Each review included the measure or scale title, creator, description, availability, cost, psychometrics, and advantages and disadvantages. This information is available at http://www.ag.arizona.edu/fcs/cyfernet/nowg. It appears that these catalogues were last updated around 2000, so measures developed after that time are of course not covered. A separate work group focusing on the family produced a similar set of reviews for measures related to parent and family well-being. Some of the measures they have collected are directly applicable to the families of adolescents.

A second catalogue or compendium of youth development measures was developed by Child Trends in 2001 with funding from the Edna McConnell Clark Foundation. This collection, called the *Youth Develop-*

ment Outcomes Compendium, has a similar format and focuses more on measures from national surveys. Information on each measure includes the name, source, intended respondents, availability, supporting literature, psychometrics, cost, advantages and disadvantages, and the measures themselves. Areas covered overlap substantially the NRC outcomes domains and include Educational Achievement and Cognitive Attainment (educational attainment, grade retention, basic academic/cognitive skills, research–related skills, oral and interpersonal communication skills, language skills, computer skills, arts participation and knowledge, study skills, achievement motivation, and school engagement); Health and Safety (drug and alcohol use, risky sexual behavior, violence, accidents and injuries, good safety habits); Social and Emotional Development (civic engagement), parent–child relationship quality, positive relationships with adults other than parent, behavior problems, productive use of nonschool time, spirituality, and sense of personal identity); and Self–Sufficiency (work). The report is available for free at the Child Trends web site.[11]

Next, we offer some examples of measures and scales of youth development and related social settings as set out in the NRC framework (see Tables 7.1 & 7.2), taken from a variety of sources. It is not intended to be comprehensive but is offered to give readers a sense of the variety of measures that are out there and available.

PERSONAL ASSETS

Intellectual Development

Important aspects of intellectual development for youth include the usual measures, such as standardized assessments, grades, and dropping out, but also include such things as capacity for critical thinking, knowledge of life skills and vocational skills, and knowledge of multiple cultures. Under the NCLB initiative, which seeks to hold all schools accountable for improving the academic performance of all children, every state has adopted its own set of math and reading assessments that are given annually for Grades 3 through 8 and at least once in high school. Assessment results are available online down to the school level.[12] In addition, so that the federal government may track progress using assessments that are consistent across states, every state now participates in the National Assessment for Educational Progress, testing math and reading skills in the fourth and eighth grades.[13]

The Patterns of Adaptive Learning Survey is widely used and contains reliable and valid measures of skills relevant for learning, including personal mastery, performance approach, and performance-avoidance goal orientations (for details, see E. R. Anderman, Urdan, & Roeser, 2005). Finally, Eccles and her colleagues have developed extensive measures of students' academic ability self-perceptions, the value they attach to academic success, causal attributions for academic performance, emotional reactions to success and failure at school, and school engagement in their MSALT and MADICS studies (see http://www.rcgd.isr.umich.edu/garp).

Psychological and Emotional Development

Measures of psychological and emotional development are varied and can include the following: good mental health, including positive self-regard; emotional self-regulation and coping skills; conflict resolution skills; personal efficacy; planfulness; optimism; positive personal and social identity; spirituality; and strong moral character. A common measure of mental health is the Center for Epidemiologic Studies youth depression scale, a 12-item instrument that has been used in NLSY 97, the National Survey of Family Growth, and other national surveys. Psychometrically strong measures of positive attributes such as hope, optimism, spirituality, and strong moral character are more difficult to construct, although this is an area where a lot of interesting work has been done recently. For example, Snyder (2005) recently developed the Children's Hope Scale, which shows good validity and reliability. Similarly, all of the community-based longitudinal studies outlined earlier have extensive high-quality measures of the psychological and emotional assets summarized in Tables 7.1 and 7.2.

Several measures have been developed in recent years to assess issues related to positive ethnic identity. The Multigroup Ethnic Identity Measure (Phinney, 1992) was developed on the basis of ethnic identity components shared across groups. The subscales of the measure include Affirmation and Belonging, Ethnic Identity Achievement, Ethnic Behaviors, Ethnic Self-Identification, Ethnicity, and Parents' Ethnicity. Another measure, the Social Identity Self-Esteem Scale (Luhtanen & Crocker, 1992), was created to assess the positivity of one's social identity. The Multidimensional Inventory of Black Identity (Sellers et al., 1997) includes seven subscales to represent three dimensions of African American racial identity: (a) centrality, (b) ideology, and (c) regard. Finally, Eccles and her colleagues include several measures of racial identity and of perceptions of racial discrimination at school by peers and teachers in the MADICS study (Wong, Eccles, & Sameroff, 2003).

Social Development

Positive social development can include a wide range of activities, including sports, the arts, and after-school youth organizations, as well as peer pressure resistance skills, valuing cultural diversity, and civic engagement.

As an example, Keeter, Jenkins, Zukin, and Andolina (2005) recently developed a scale of youth civic engagement with strong validity and re-

liability whose components include measures of community problem-solving, volunteering, and active group membership. Eccles,
Barber, and colleagues have used data from the MSALT to create composite measures of youth activities sorted into five categories: (a) team
sports, (b) prosocial activities (church attendance, volunteering, service
activities), (c) performing arts, (d) academic clubs, and (e) school involvement (student government, pep club, cheerleading). The measures
were also used to construct indices of participation. (See Barber, Stone,
and Eccles, 2005, for details). The measures showed strong concurrent
and predictive validity.

Delinquency measures are also important measures of social development. The Philadelphia Family Management Study's Attitudes Toward Delinquency & Protective Factor scale focuses on attitudes about
delinquent behavior, including alcohol, stealing, drugs, and skipping
school (for a summary of these measures, see Furstenberg et al., 1999).

SOCIAL SETTINGS THAT PROMOTE POSITIVE DEVELOPMENT

Appropriate Structure

Measures of appropriate structure promoting youth development
would include clear rules setting, age-appropriate monitoring of youth
activities and relationships, and consistent enforcement of rules. This is
important in all social settings, including especially the family, school,
and in youth programs (Eccles & Gootman, 2002, chap. 4).

The Monitoring scale, for example (Barber, 1996; Barber et al., 1994;
Brown et al., 1993), measures parents' awareness of their adolescents'
friends and use of time. Adolescents answer items about how much
their parents know about their lives. Sample items include: who your
friends are? where you go at night? how you spend your money? what
you do with your free time? Even better is Barber, Stolz, and Olsen's
(2005) scale on intrusive parenting as well as Barber's other measures
of parenting that have been validated across many different cultural
and national groups.

The Patterns of Adaptive Learning Survey inventory cited earlier also
includes extensive measures of classroom climate that are appropriate
for assessing structure. Eccles and her colleagues also developed measures of support for autonomy and structure for learning in the MSALT.

Physical and Psychological Safety

Safe family, school, and neighborhood environments are important pre-
requisites for all aspects of positive youth development. For example, as
part of the NCLB initiative, which focuses on raising academic performance, schools are held accountable for taking measures to increase
safety in the schools in order to create an environment in which learning
can flourish.[14]

Family Safety

Although measures related to the physical safety of the family environment are common (e.g., secondary smoke in the house, presence of guns in the house), survey data related to physical violence or psychological abuse are uncommon. Measures are available, but under most circumstances researchers collecting such data are required to report any cases of suspected abuse to authorities. An example of a well-developed measure of home violence is the Conflict Tactics Scale, developed by Strauss and Gelles (1990), which has been administered in several national surveys. It includes scales reflecting parent-child and parent-partner conflict, with subscales covering different modes of violence (Strauss & Gelles, 1990).

Neighborhood Safety

Neighborhood personal safety items from the MacArthur Network ask parents to rate how much of a problem their neighborhood has with sexual assaults or rapes, assaults or muggings, delinquent gangs or drug gangs, and drug use or drug dealing in the open. These measures were included in the Philadelphia Family Management study (see Furstenberg et al., 1999), which also included measures of neighborhood social control that asked parents how likely it would be for someone in the neighborhood to do something if there were problems in the neighborhood, such as fighting, drug selling, or someone breaking into a house.

Supportive Relationships

Parent-Adolescent Relationship

Many aspects of the parent-youth relationship can provide positive support for youth development, including connectedness and attachment, communication, and guidance. (See Hair et al., 2005, for a recent review of measures.)

Parent-Youth Communication. The parent-child communications measures, developed by the MacArthur Adolescent Network, asks parents the frequency their eighth-grader talks with them about topics such as how things are going with his or her friends, problems he or she is having at school, future jobs he or she might have, and what courses he or she should take in school. These items were also used in the MADICS study outlined earlier. Barber et al. (2005) included similar measures in their parenting survey.

Parental Guidance. Parents often find it difficult to provide guidance about sexual activity. Items used by the McArthur Adolescent Network ask parents if they have talked with their child about the biological facts of sex and pregnancy, how to decide whether or not to have sex, different methods of birth control, how to avoid getting a sexually transmitted disease, such as venereal disease or AIDS, and the age at which these issues were discussed with the child. Jaccard, Dittus, and Gordon's (1998) sexual behaviors measure looks at the congruency between parent and adolescent reports of adolescent sexual behavior and the communications about sexual behavior. Specifically, the measure looks at the agreement between mothers' and adolescents' reports of communication about sex, satisfaction with the parent–child relationship, maternal disapproval of adolescent sexual activity, and adolescent sexual behavior.

Parent-Youth Time Together. The Time Use Parenting scale from the MacArthur Adolescent Network collects data on how often the immediate family has dinner together; how much time is spent together on the weekends; and how often the immediate family gets together for birthdays, anniversaries, and other holidays. These items were used in the Philadelphia study (Furstenberg et al., 1999) and the MADICS study discussed earlier.

Support From Peers

As youth mature, they seek more support from their peers. The Friendship Quality Scale (Gauze, Bukowski, Aquan-Assee, & Sippola, 1996) has youth rate their relationship with their best friend on 35 different attributes. The scores for each of four categories (Companionship, Help/Support, Security and Closeness) are used to compute an overall friendship quality score. The Peer Advice Seeking measure (Fuligni & Eccles, 1993) evaluates adolescents' orientation toward their peers.

Support From Teachers

Both the PALS and the studies by Eccles and her colleagues include a variety of measures of perceived social support from teachers. MADICS also includes scales related to lack of social and emotional support from teachers and peers at school. Some of these items focus on experiences of racial and sexual discrimination. Others focus on more general lack of support and low teacher expectations for the students' success.

Connection to Larger Social Networks

In addition to connection to family and friends, attachment to larger prosocial/conventional institutions, such as school, church, and out-of-school youth programs, is believed to be an important part of social development. Measures such as the school/religion/resources items in Add Health's religion scale examine participation in and positive attitudes toward religious activities such as going to church, praying, and attending church-sponsored youth activities. The neighborhood items from the Add Health survey measure the extent to which the respondent perceives him- or herself as being a part of his or her neighborhood.

Opportunities to Belong

Adequate financial resources are necessary to provide opportunities to belong. Mistry and Crosby (1999) measured how often adolescents' activities were restricted because their parents couldn't afford the activity. The items included activities that provide skill-building opportunities, such as sports, as well as activities with somewhat less skill-building utility, such as going to see a movie with friends.

The community also provides opportunities to belong, according the presence or absence of youth activities and organizations such as Boys and Girls Clubs, youth sports associations, and active religious youth groups. A number of surveys, including Add Health and MTF, ask specifically about perceived opportunities to participate in such groups.[15] In addition, some communities are gathering their own data on the availability of such youth resources, using youth to collect the information and offering the results online for public use and program planning. This is called *Community YouthMapping*, and it was developed by the Academy for Educational Development.[16]

A sense of belonging at school is critical to engagement at school (see Wigfield, Eccles, Schefele, Roeser, & Davis-Kean, 2006). MADICS has items that assess this asset. Other such scales are available from L. H. Anderman and Anderman (1999) and Goodenow (1993).

Prosocial Norms

Positive Peer Influence

The Pittsburgh Youth Study gathers information on conventional activities of friends. Youth are asked to think of their friends and then report how involved they have been in activities such as school clubs, special school events, school athletes, community activities such as YMCA or youth clubs, religious activities, and so on. MADICS includes a nice inventory of the perceived beliefs and behaviors of one's friends that can be used to estimate perceived peer social norms.

Parental Influence

Parents who role model unhealthy behaviors can also be a negative influence for youth. Bogenschneider and colleagues (1998) looked at parents' influences on adolescent peer orientation and substance use. The measure they used included items such as how often in the past year the parent used eight substances: (a) tobacco, (b) beer, (c) wine/wine coolers, (d) hard liquor, (e) marijuana, (f) inhalants, (g) hallucinogens, and (h) cocaine/crack.

Parents exert positive influence on their adolescents in many ways. A measure developed by the MacArthur Adolescent Network asked parents how often they encouraged their eighth-graders to get involved in sports and other school activities, to be good to others, to get ahead in life, to work hard, to show respect to others, to have faith in God, and so on. In other words, the items indicated whether parents encouraged their adolescents to accept prosocial values. These are available through the MADICS and Iowa studies.

Opportunity for Efficacy and for Mattering

Overcontrolling parents do not provide optimal support for youth. The Perceived Parent Overprotectiveness scale of Philadelphia Family Management Study may give some indication of inadequacy in the number of opportunities youth are given to achieve a sense of efficacy and mattering. The measure asks youth how often their parent tells them what to do or how to act and whether their parent tries to protect them too much, lets them make their own mistakes, has too many rules, and often treats them like a baby. Item responses may indicate that the youth is feeling unchallenged, overcontrolled, and disempowered. Barber et al. (2005) provided similar measures.

However, there are very few such measures related to the critical nonfamilial contexts where opportunities are most likely to be available. For the most part, evaluations of service learning type programs provide single-item indicators of the opportunities to engage in meaningful social service. We need scales that assess youth's perceptions of these opportunities and of their sense that they are actually making a difference in these programs.

Opportunities for Skill Building

The transition to adulthood requires youth to gain knowledge and skills in many areas, including intellectual, social, practical, and life skills. In schools, for example, such opportunities depend in part on elements of school quality, such as teacher skills and experience, course design, and class size (see chap. 10, this volume, for related measures).

CONCLUSION

Existing research has amply demonstrated the importance supportive social settings in promoting positive youth development and the importance of positive youth outcomes for making a smooth transition to adulthood. Areas of opportunity for pushing the field forward include the extent to which a lack of assets in one context (e.g., the family) can be compensated for with assets in another context (e.g., after-school programs), the extent to which personal and social assets may have different effects on development across different social groups (e.g., male and female, Black and Hispanic; rich and poor), the extent to which the effects of assets are additive, and the extent to which certain assets may be culture specific (e.g., the importance of independence from the family as a defining characteristic of adulthood). Exploration of these questions will lead us to more effective and targeted intervention strategies for helping youth and to the development of better measures for tracking progress.

Our review of available data sources indicates that a great deal of data are available for tracking the well-being of adolescents and those transitioning to adulthood, although many important measures are not tracked on a regular basis or at all levels of geography. The measures available in one-time national longitudinal studies and in community survey instruments like the Communities That Care survey and the Search Institute's youth assets survey are far richer than those in existing national and state surveys that are repeated on a regular basis. We believe that greater efforts should be made to migrate measures of positive development and positive social settings into these periodically fielded surveys, particularly as research from the longitudinal studies enriches our understanding of these measures.

Finally, although there are many high-quality measures of positive youth development and positive social settings strewn across the many sources we have reviewed, they are often buried in data archives or in other nooks and crannies of the Internet, when they are publicly available at all. Several attempts have been made to collect and organize these measures into compendia, but they have not been kept up to date. Researchers and professionals in the field need ready access to such measures in developing their own research and tracking efforts. We believe it would be a boon to research and practice if there were a single online source, consistently updated, that offered such access.

ACKNOWLEDGMENT

Some sections of this chapter draw heavily from the National Research Council report *Community Programs to Promote Youth Development* (Eccles & Goodman, 2002).

NOTES

1. Concurrent indicators of well-being include good mental health, good school performance, good peer relations, good problem-solving skills, and low levels (or the absence) of involvement in a variety of problematic behaviors such as gang membership, drug and alcohol use, school failure, school

dropout, delinquency, and early pregnancy. Longitudinal indicators of more adult well-being include completing high school, completing tertiary education, adequate transition into the labor market (obtaining and keeping a job that pays at least a living wage), staying out of prison, avoiding drug and alcohol abuse, turning around a problematic adolescent trajectory, and entering a stable and supportive intimate relationship (usually assessed in terms of one's marital partner). Some recent studies have included involvement in civic and community activities as an indicator of positive adult outcomes.

2. There are an increasing cities putting their administrative data into community Geographic Information Systems databases that are accessible to the public. For additional information, see the National Neighborhood Indicators Partnership, at http://www2.urban.org/nnip/. See also databooks produced by state KIDS COUNT organizations in each state, at http://www.aecf.org/kidscount/

3. For additional information, visit http://www.census.gov/acs/www/index.html

4. See the CLIKS data system at http://www.aecf.org/cgi-bin/cliks.cgi

5. For additional information on the Search Institute's assets approach, visit http://www.search-institute.org/assets/

6. For a detailed crosswalk of PSL:AB indicators and the NRC framework, see Eccles and Gootman (2002, Table 8-1).

7. This survey is also known as the *Student Survey of Risk and Protective Factors*.

8. For additional information, visit http://www.preventionplatform.samhsa.gov/

9. For the most recent version of the rationale, and for a copy of the instrument, visit http://www.cdc.gov/HealthyYouth/yrbs/index.htm

10. For a more detailed breakdown by domain, see Tables 8-2 and 8-3 in Eccles and Gootman (2002).

11. Because of its size, the compendium must be downloaded in sections:
http://www.childtrends.org/files/Compendium_Phase1_Intro.pdf
http://www.childtrends.org/files/Compendium_Phase1_DivA.pdf
http://www.childtrends.org/files/Compendium_Phase1_DivB.pdf
http://www.childtrends.org/files/Compendium_Phase1_DivC.pdf
http://www.childtrends.org/files/Compendium_Phase1_DivD.pdf

12. To see NCLB state assessment results, visit http://www.schoolmatters.com

13. For additional information on the National Assessment of Educational Progress, visit http://nationsreportcard.gov

14. For additional information on school violence and NCLB, visit http://www.ed.gov/nclb/freedom/safety/keeping_kids_safe.pdf

15. For additional information on the NSCH visit http://www.cdc.gov/nchs/about/major/slaits/nsch.htm

16. For additional information on Community YouthMapping, visit http://www.aed.org/Projects/cym.cfm

REFERENCES

Anderman, E. R., Urdan, T., & Roeser, R. (2005). The Patterns of Adaptive Learning Survey. In K. A. Moore & L. H. Lippman (Eds.), *What do children need to flourish? Conceptualizing and measuring indicators of positive development* (pp. 223–236). New York: Springer.

Anderman, L. H., & Anderman, E. M. (1999). Social predictors of changes in students' goal orientation. *Contemporary Educational Psychology, 25*, 21–37.

Arnett, J. J. (1999). Adolescent storm and stress, reconsidered. *American Psychologist, 54*, 317–326.

Arnett, J. J. (2000). Emerging adulthood: A theory of development from the late teens through the twenties. *American Psychologist, 55*, 469–480.

Arthur, M. W., Hawkins, J. D., Catalana, R. F., & Pollard, J. A. (1995). *Item construct dictionary for the student survey of risk and protective factors and prevalence of alcohol, tobacco, and other drug use.* Seattle: University of Washington, Social Development Research Group.

Arthur, M. W., Hawkins, J. D., Pollard, J. A., Catalano, R. F., & Baglioni, A. J. (2002). Measuring risk and protective factors for substance use, delinquency, and other adolescent problem behaviors: The Communities That Care Youth Survey. *Evaluation Review, 26*, 575–601.

Baltes, P. B., Lindenberger, U., & Staudinger, U. M. (1998). Life-span theory in developmental psychology. In W. Damon & R. M. Lerner (Eds.), *Handbook of child psychology (5th ed.): Vol. 1. Theoretical models of human development* (pp. 1029–1144). New York: Wiley.

Bandura, A. (1994). *Self-efficacy: The exercise of control.* New York: Freeman.

Barber, B. L., Eccles, J. S., & Stone, M. R. (2001). Whatever happened to the Jock, the Brain, and the Princess?: Young adult pathways linked to adolescent activity involvement and social identity. *Journal of Adolescent Research, 16*, 429–455.

Barber, B. K., Stolz, H. E., & Olsen. J. A. (2005). Parental support, psychological control, and behavioral control: Assessing relevance across time, culture, and method. *Monographs for the Society for Research on Child Development, 70*, 1–137.

Barber, B., Stone, M. R., & Eccles, J. S. (2005). Adolescent participation in organized activities. In K. A. Moore & L. H. Lippman (Eds.), *What do children need to flourish? Conceptualizing and measuring indicators of positive development* (pp. 133–146). New York: Springer.

Ben-Arieh, A., Kaufman, N., Andrews, A., Goerge, R., & Lee, B. (2001). *Measuring and monitoring children's well-being.* New York: Springer.

Block, J. (1971). *Lives through time.* Berkeley, CA: Bancroft.

Bronfenbrenner, U. (1979). *The ecology of human development: Experiments by nature and design.* Cambridge, MA: Harvard University Press.

Brown, B., & Corbett, T. (2003). Social indicators as tools of public policy. In R. Weissberg, H. Walberg, M. U. O'Brien, & C. B. Kuster (Eds.), *Long-term trends in the well-being of children and families* (pp. 27–49). Washington, DC: Child Welfare League of America.

Call, K. T., & Mortimer, J. T. (2001). *Arenas of comfort in adolescence: A study of adjustment in context.* Mahwah, NJ: Lawrence Erlbaum Associates.

Cairns, R. B., & Cairns, B. D. (1994). *Lifelines and risks: Pathways of youth in our time.* New York: Cambridge University Press.

Cairns, R. B., & Cairns, B. D. (2002). Plotting developmental pathways: Methods, models, and madness. In E. Phelps, F. F. Furstenberg, & A. Colby (Eds.), *Looking at lives: American longitudinal studies of the twentieth century* (pp. 267–296). New York: Russell Sage Foundation.

Castro, F. G., Boyer, G. R., & Balcazar, H. G. (2000). Healthy adjustment in Mexican American and other Hispanic adolescents. In R. Montemayor, G. R. Adams, & T. P. Gullotta (Eds.), *Adolescent diversity in ethnic, economic, and cultural contexts* (pp. 141–178). Thousand Oaks, CA: Sage.

Child Trends. (2006). *An assessment of state-level data on child maltreatment and foster care: Summary of meeting of experts* (Kids Count Working Paper Series). Baltimore: Annie E. Casey Foundation.

Clausen, J. A. (1993). *American lives: Looking back at the children of the Great Depression.* New York: Free Press.

Compas, B. E., Wagner, B. M., Slavin, L. A., & Vannatta, K. (1986). A prospective study of life events, social support, and psychological symptomatology during the transition from high school to college. *American Journal of Community Psychology, 14,* 241–257.

Conger, R. D., Wallace, L. E., Sun, Y., Simons, R. L., McLoyd, V. C., & Brody, G. H. (2002). Economic pressure in African American families: A replication and extension of the family stress model. *Developmental Psychology, 38,* 179–193.

Connell, J. P., & Wellborn, J. G. (1991). Competence, autonomy, and relatedness: A motivational analysis of self-system processes. In R. Gunnar & L. A. Sroufe (Eds.), *Minnesota Symposia on Child Psychology* (Vol. 23, pp. 43–77). Hillsdale, NJ: Lawrence Erlbaum Associates.

Cook, T. D., Herman, M. R., Phillips, M., & Settersten, R. A., Jr. (2005). Some ways in which neighborhoods, nuclear families, friendship groups, and schools jointly affect changes in early adolescent development. *Child Development, 73,* 1283–1309.

Corcoran, M., & Matsudaira, J. (2005). Is it getting harder to get ahead? Economic attainment in early adulthood for two cohorts. In R. A. Settersten, Jr., F. F. Furstenberg, & R. G. Rumbaut (Eds.), *On the frontier of adulthood: Theory, research, and public policy* (pp. 356–395). Chicago: University of Chicago Press.

Coulton, C. (1998). Using community-level indicators of child's well-being in comprehensive community initiatives. In J. Connell, A. Kubisch, L. Schorr, & C. Weiss (Eds.), *New approaches to evaluating community initiatives: concepts, methods, and contexts* (pp. 173–200). Washington, DC: Aspen Institute.

Coulton. C. & Hollister, R. (1998). Measuring comprehensive community initiative outcomes using data available for small areas. In K. Fullbright-Anderson, A. Kubisch, & J. P. Connell (Eds.), *New approaches to evaluating community initiatives: Vol. 2. Theory measurement, and analysis* (pp. 165–220). Washington, DC: Aspen Institute.

Cross, W. E. (1991). *Shades of black: Diversity in African-American identity.* Philadelphia: Temple University Press.

Cui, M., Conger, R. D., & Lorenz, F. O. (2005). Predicting change in adolescent adjustment from change in marital problems. *Developmental Psychology, 41,* 812–823.

Cui, X., & Vaillant, G. E. (1996). Antecedents and consequences of negative life events in adulthood: A longitudinal study. *American Journal of Psychiatry, 153,* 21–26.

Deci, E. L., & Ryan, R. M. (1985). *Intrinsic motivation and self-determination in human behavior.* New York: Plenum.

Duncan, G., & Moscow, L. (1997). Longitudinal indicators of children's poverty and dependence. In R. Hauser, B. Brown, & W. Prosser (Eds.), Indicators of children's well-being (pp. 258–278). New York: Russell Sage Foundation.

Eccles, J. S., Barber, B., Stone, M., & Templeton, J. (2003). Adolescence and emerging adulthood: The critical passage ways to adulthood. In M. H. Bornstein, L. Davidson, C. L. M. Keyes, K. A. Moore, & The Center for Child Well-Being (Eds.), *Well-being: Positive development across the life span* (pp. 383–406). Mahwah, NJ: Lawrence Erlbaum Associates.

Eccles, J. S., Early, D., Frasier, K., Belansky, E., & McCarthy, K. (1997). The relation of connection, regulation, and support for autonomy in the context of family, school, and peer group to successful adolescent development. *Journal of Adolescent Research, 12,* 263–286.

Eccles, J. S., & Gootman, J. (2002). *Community programs to promote youth development.* Washington, DC: National Research Council Institute of Medicine, National Academy Press.

Eccles, J. S., Midgley, C., Buchanan, C. M., Wigfield, A., Reuman, D., & Mac Iver, D. (1993). Developmental during adolescence: The impact of stage/environment fit. *American Psychologist, 48,* 90–101.

Eccles, J. S., Wigfield, A., & Schiefele, U. (1998). Motivation to succeed. In N. Eisenberg (Ed.), *Handbook of child psychology* (5th ed., Vol. 3, pp. 1017–1095). New York.

Elder, G. H. (1974). *Children of the Great Depression.* Chicago: University of Chicago Press.

Elder, G. H. (1998). The life course and human development. In W. Damon & R. M. Lerner (Eds.), *Handbook of child psychology: Theoretical model of human development* (Vol. 1, pp. 939–992). New York: Wiley.

Elder, G. H., & Conger, R. (2000). *Children of the land.* Chicago: University of Chicago Press.

Erikson, E. H. (1963). *Childhood and society.* New York: Norton.

Erikson, E. H. (1968). *Identity, youth and crisis.* New York: Norton.

Ford, D. Y., & Harris, J. J. (1996). Perceptions and attitudes of Black students toward school: School, achievement, and other educational variables. *Child Development, 67,* 1144–1152.

Foster, E. M., & Gifford, E. J. (2005). The transition to adulthood for youth leaving public systems: Challenges to polices and research. In R. A. Settersten, Jr., F. F. Furstenberg, & R. G. Rumbaut (Eds.), *On the frontier of adulthood: Theory, research, and public policy* (pp. 501–533). Chicago: University of Chicago Press.

Fuligni, A. J. (2001). Family obligation and the academic motivation of adolescents from Asian and Latin American, and European backgrounds. In A. Fuligni (Ed.), *Family obligation and assistance during adolescence: contextual variations and developmental implications* (pp. 61–76). San Francisco: Jossey-Bass.

Fuligni, A. J., Witkow, M., & Garcia, C. (2004). Ethnic identity and the academic adjustment of adolescents from Mexican, Chinese, and European backgrounds. *Developmental Psychology, 41,* 799–811.

Fuligni, A. J., & Zheng, W. (2005). Attitudes toward family obligation among adolescents in contemporary urban and rural China. *Child Development, 75,* 180–192.

Furstenberg, F., Cook, T., Eccles, J., Elder, G., & Sameroff, A. (1999). *Managing to make it.* Chicago: University of Chicago Press.

Fussell, E., & Furstenberg, F. F. (2005). The transition to adulthood during the twentieth century: Race, nativity, and gender. In R. A. Settersten, Jr., F. F. Furstenberg, & R. G. Rumbaut (Eds.), *On the frontier of adulthood: theory, research, and public policy* (pp. 29–75). Chicago: University of Chicago Press.

Goodenow, C. (1993). Classroom belonging among early adolescent students: Relationships to motivation and achievement. *Journal of Early Adolescence, 13,* 21–43.

Hair, E. C., Moore, K. A., Garrett, S. B., Kinukawa, A., Lippman, L. H. & Michelson, E. (2005). The Parent-Adolescent Relationship Scale. In K. A.

Moore & L. H. Lippman (Eds.), *What do children need to flourish? Conceptualizing and measuring indicators of positive development* (pp. 183–202). New York: Springer.

Harter, S. (1990). Causes, correlates and the functional role of self-worth: A life-span perspective. In R. J. Sternberg & J. Kolligian (Eds.), *Competence considered* (pp. 67–97). New Haven, CT: Yale University Press.

Havighurst, R. J. (1972). *Developmental tasks and education* (3rd ed.). New York: McKay.

Jessor, R., Donovan, J. E., & Costa, F. M. (1991). *Beyond adolescence: Problem behavior and young adult development*. New York: Cambridge University Press.

Jessor, R., Turbin, M. S., Costa, F. M., Dong, Q., Zhang, H., & Wang, C. (2003). Adolescent problem behavior in China and the United States: A cross-national study of psychosocial protective factors. *Journal of Research on Adolescence, 13,* 329–360.

Kee, J. K., Conger, R. D., Elder, G. H., & Lorenz, F. O. (2003). Reciprocal influences between stressful life events and adolescent internalizing and externalizing Problems. *Child Development, 74,* 127–143.

Keeter, S., Jenkins, K., Zukin, C., & Andolina, M. (2005). Community-based civic engagement. In K. A. Moore & L. H. Lippman (Eds.), *What do children need to flourish? Conceptualizing and measuring indicators of positive development* (pp. 325–338). New York: Springer.

Larson, R. W. (2000). Toward a psychology of positive youth development. *American Psychologist, 55,* 170–183.

Leffert, N., Benson, P. L., Scales, P. C., Sharma, A. R., Drake, D. R., & Blyth, D. A. (1998). Developmental assets: measurement and prediction of risk behaviors among adolescents. *Applied Developmental Science, 2,* 209–230.

Leong, F. T. L., Chao, R. K., & Hardin, E. E. (2000). Asian American adolescents: A research review to dispel the model minority myth. In R. Montemayor, G. R. Adams, & T. P. Gullotta (Eds.), *Adolescent diversity in ethnic, economic, and cultural contexts* (pp. 179–209). Thousand Oaks, CA: Sage

Lerner, R. M., Fisher, C. B., & Weinberg, R. A. (2000). Toward a science for and of the people: Promoting civil society through the application of developmental science. *Child Development, 71,* 11–20.

Levinson, D. J. (1978). *The seasons of a man's life.* New York: Ballantine.

Masten, A. S., & Coatsworth, J. D. (1998). The development of competence in favorable and unfavorable environments: Lessons from research on successful children. *American Psychologist, 53,* 205–220.

Mollenkopf, J., Waters, M. C., Holdaway, J., & Kasinitz, P. (2005). The ever-winding path: Ethnic and racial diversity in the transition to adulthood. In R. A. Settersten, Jr., F. F. Furstenberg, & R. G. Rumbaut (Eds.), *On the frontier of adulthood: theory, research, and public policy* (pp. 454–500). Chicago: University of Chicago Press.

Moore, K. (1997). Criteria for indicators of child well-being. In R. Hauser, B. Brown, & W. Prosser (Eds.), *Indicators of children's well-being* (pp.36–44). New York: Russell Sage Foundation.

Moore, K. A., Halle, T., Vandivere, S., & Mariner, C. (2002). Scaling back survey scales: How short is too short? *Sociological Methods & Research, 30,* 530–567.

Mortimer, J. T. (2003). *Working and growing up in American.* Cambridge, MA: Harvard University Press.

Mortimer, J. T., & Larson, R. W. (2002). *The changing adolescent experience: Societal trends and the transition to adulthood.* New York: Cambridge University Press.

Mortimer, J. T., Zimmer-Gembeck, M. J., Holmes, M., & Shanahan, M. J. (2002). The process of occupational decision making: Patterns during the transition to adulthood. *Journal of Vocational Behavior, 61*, 439–465.

Mouw, T. (2005). Sequences of early adult transitions: A look at variability and consequences. In R. A. Settersten, Jr., F. F. Furstenberg, & R. G. Rumbaut (Eds.), *On the frontier of adulthood: theory, research, and public policy* (pp. 256–291). Chicago: University of Chicago Press.

Mrazek, P., Biglan, A., & Hawkins, J. D. (2004). *Community monitoring systems: tracking and improving the well-being of America's children and adolescents.* Fairfax, VA: Society for Prevention Research

Murnane, R. J., & Levy, F. (1996). *Teaching the new basic skills: Principles for educating children to thrive in a changing economy.* New York: Free Press.

Office of Educational Research and Improvement. (1988). *Youth indicators 1988.* Washington, DC: U.S. Government Printing Office.

Osgood, D. W., Ruth, G., Eccles, J. S., Jacobs, J. E., & Barber, B. L. (2005). Six paths to adulthood: Fast starters, parents without careers, educated partners, educated singles, working singles, and slow starters. In R. A. Settersten, Jr., F. F. Furstenberg, & R. G. Rumbaut (Eds.), *On the frontier of adulthood: theory, research, and public policy* (pp. 320–355). Chicago: University of Chicago Press.

Phelan, P., & Davidson, A. L. (Eds.). (1993). *Renegotiating cultural diversity in American schools.* New York: Teachers College Press.

Phinney, J. S. (1990). Ethnic identity in adolescents and adults: A review of research. *Psychological Bulletin, 108*, 499–514.

Pollard, J. A., Catalano, R. F., Hawkins, J. D., Arthur, M. W., & Baglioni, Jr., A. J. (1999). *Measuring risk and protective factors for substance abuse, delinquency, and other problem behaviors in adolescent populations* (Technical Report No. 198). Seattle, WA: Social Development Research Group.

Rutter, M. (Ed.). (1988). *Studies of psychosocial risk: The power of longitudinal data.* New York: Cambridge University Press.

Rutter M., & Garmezy, N. (1983). Developmental psychopathology. In P. H. Mussen & E. M. Hetherington (Eds.), *Handbook of child psychology: Vol. 4. Socialization, personality, and social development* (pp. 775–911). New York: Wiley.

Sampson, R. J., & Laub, J. H. (1993). *Crime in the making: Pathways and turning points through life.* Cambridge, MA: Harvard University Press.

Scales, P. C., & Leffert, N. (1999). *Developmental assets: A synthesis of the scientific research on adolescent development.* Minneapolis, MN: Search Institute.

Settersten, Jr., R. A. (2005). Social policy and the transition to adulthood: Towards stronger institutional and individual capacities. In R. A. Settersten, Jr., F. F. Furstenberg, & R. G. Rumbaut (Eds.), *On the frontier of adulthood: theory, research, and public policy* (pp. 534–560). Chicago: University of Chicago Press.

Settersten, Jr., R. A., Furstenberg, F. F., & Rumbaut, R. G. (2005). *On the frontier of adulthood: theory, research, and public policy.* Chicago: University of Chicago Press.

Snyder, C. R. (2005). Measuring hope in children. In K. A. Moore & L. H. Lippman (Eds.), *What do children need to flourish? Conceptualizing and measuring indicators of positive development* (pp. 61–74). New York: Springer.

Spencer, M. B. (1995). Old issues and new theorizing about African-American youth: A phenomenological variant of the ecological systems theory. In R. L. Taylor (Ed.), *Black youth: Perspectives on their status in the United States* (pp. 37–70). New York: Praeger.

Strauss, M. A., & Gelles, R. J. (1990). The Conflict Tactics Scales and its critics: An evaluation and new data on validity and reliability. In M. A. Straus & R. J. Gelles (Eds.), *Physical violence in American families: Risk factors and adaptations to violence* (pp. 49–73). New Brunswick, NJ: Transaction.

Tatian, P. (2000). *Indispensable information–Data collection and information management for healthier communities.* Washington, DC: The Urban Institute.

Werner, E. E., & Smith, R. S. (1982). *Vulnerable but invincible: A study of resilient children.* New York: McGraw-Hill.

Werner, E. E., & Smith, R. S. (1992). *Overcoming the odds.* Ithaca, NY: Cornell University Press.

Wheaton, B. (1990). Life transitions, role histories, and mental health. *American Sociological Review, 55,* 209–223.

William T. Grant Foundation. (1988). *The forgotten half: Pathways to success for America's youth and young families.* Washington, DC: The William T. Grant Commission on Work, Family, and Citizenship.

Wilson, W. J. (1987). *The truly disadvantaged: The inner city, the underclass, and public policy.* Chicago: University of Chicago Press.

Wong, C. A., Eccles, J. S., & Sameroff, A. (2003). The influence of ethnic discrimination and ethnic identification on African-Americans adolescents' school and socio-emotional adjustment. *Journal of Personality, 71,* 1197–1232.

Part IV

Social Context of
Development Indicators

Chapter 8

The Family Environment: Structure, Material Resources and Child Care

Gary D. Sandefur
University of Wisconsin at Madison
Ann Meier
University of Minnesota at Twin Cities

Behavioral and social scientists have long considered the family material and social environment to be among the most important influences on one's life during childhood and adolescence. An exhaustive body of research in several disciplines has demonstrated how important this environment is for social and cognitive development, educational attainment, and other outcomes. Developmental psychologists and developmental pediatricians, for example, have explored the role of the family in many aspects of social and cognitive development. The recent National Research Council report, *Neurons to Neighborhoods*, states that

> virtually every aspect of early human development, from the brain's evolving circuitry to the child's capacity for empathy, is affected by the environments and experiences that are encountered in a cumulative fashion, beginning early in the prenatal period and extending throughout the early childhood years. (Shonkoff & Phillips, 2000, p. 6)

The family constitutes perhaps the most critical environment among those encountered by children early in life.

Sociologists, as well as other scientists, have shown how couple relationships and parenting quality affect child well-being. Amato and Booth (1997) used data from an extensive multiyear study to show that family conflict and divorce have persisting effects on young people. In their analyses, family conflict seemed to be as important or more important than an actual divorce, suggesting that the critical aspects of the social environment of the family include much more than whether two parents are present or how many siblings are in the household. Family conflict is but one of many forms of family processes that are key components of the family social environment (Day, Gavazzi, & Acock, 2001).

The material aspects of the family environment are also central influences on child well-being. The studies summarized in *Consequences of Growing Up Poor* (Duncan & Brooks-Gunn, 1997) show that poverty affects children even before they are born; for example, it limits the ability of mothers to receive prenatal care. These effects continue during infancy; for example, infants from poor families are less likely to receive immunizations. Children from poor families are also less likely to receive adequate health care during early childhood. Some research suggests that family income during early and middle childhood may be more important than family income during adolescence in shaping ability and achievement (Duncan & Brooks-Gunn, 1997).

Until recently, most social scientists did not question whether family income, family size, or the presence of parents in the household affected children's short- and long-term well-being. The question was how large these effects were. In the last few years, however, behavioral geneticists have asked whether the family material and social environment is really important in influencing child and adolescent well-being (see, e.g., Rowe, 1994). Judith Harris (1998) argued in *The Nurture Assumption* that many aspects of the family environment, especially the social relationship between parents and children, had almost no effect on how children turned out; instead, in her view, inherited traits and the effects of peers and others outside the home were what were important in understanding the formative factors in children's lives.

The views of David Rowe, Judith Harris, and others remain a less accepted alternative to the pervasive social science view of the importance of the material and social environment of the home. On the other hand, most social scientists know that no one component of the family social and material environment in and of itself is the most important influence on child and adolescent development. A large body of research has shown that the individual effects of low income, residing in a single-parent family, family size, and the quality of out-of-home child care, for example, on cognitive development and educational attainment are modest (Duncan & Brooks-Gunn, 1997; Mayer, 1997b; McLanahan & Sandefur, 1994). Yet even modest effects are very important, especially in combination with one another, as often occurs in the lives of children (e.g., a single-parent family, poverty, low quality of out-of-home care, etc.). The presence of even modest effects points to the critical significance of identifying and measuring key aspects of the family material and social environment. Furthermore, these effects provide support for social policies designed to improve the social and economic environment for children, especially very disadvantaged children. However, social scientists and policymakers have realized that the relatively modest changes in family material and social environments that are possible through changes in social policy are likely to have only modest effects on child outcomes.

This chapter is divided into three major sections. First, we review what we know about measuring family structure, material resources, and child care and their effects on child outcomes. This is a very cursory review given space limitations, but it establishes a context within which to understand why these factors are important and why certain indicators have been emphasized in the notable publications on child and family well-being. Second, we examine what the papers presented at the 1994 conference, the precursor to this conference on which the present volume is based, recommended about the development and use of indicators of the family environment (Hauser, Brown, & Prosser, 1997). We then examine the extent to which these recommendations have been implemented. Several papers at that conference and chapters in the subsequent volume dealt with different aspects of this environment. Among the major relevant reports that have begun publication since the 1994 conference are *America's Children: Key Indicators of Well-Being, Trends in the Well-Being of America's Children and Youth*, and *KIDS COUNT*. Third, we discuss some key indicators of the family environment that are in need of further development. Although we have made significant progress in developing and disseminating indicators of family and child well-being since 1994, there still are significant gaps in our understanding of, and ability to adequately measure, the family and child care environment. Most important, we still do not have adequate measures of the child's social environment over the course of childhood, and our most widely used measure of poverty misses some key resources and needs during childhood. Fortunately, the National Children's Survey, currently in the pilot study stage, provides a new opportunity to investigate key components of the family environment and how these change for children over time.

WHAT WE KNOW ABOUT INDICATORS OF THE FAMILY MATERIAL AND SOCIAL ENVIRONMENT

We begin by delimiting what we mean by the *family environment*. No widely accepted definition of this exists within or across disciplines. We limit our consideration of the family environment to characteristics of the family and household within which an individual resides and to a parent who may reside outside the home. Given the critical importance of child care outside the home and its connection to the activities of the parents, we also look at child care. We consider family material environment, family structure, and child care. By the *family material environment* we mean income and consumption of goods of particular importance to children. By *family structure* we mean family living arrangements, the stability of these arrangements, and family size.

Why the Family Material Environment Is Important

Most social scientists agree that whether a family is poor is an important indicator of the opportunities and risks facing a child. A vast body of research has shown that poor children do worse on almost all developmental and achievement outcomes than do nonpoor children, when other factors are held constant (Duncan & Brooks-Gunn, 1997; Shonkoff & Phillips, 2000). Yet such a statement misses much of the subtlety in the relationship between income and/or poverty and child outcomes. Being poor for a short period of time has different effects than being poor for a long period of time. Being poor at different points in childhood has different effects on different outcomes (Duncan & Brooks-Gunn, 1997). Also, it is important to look at consumption among families with children as well as at income (Mayer, 1997a), because families with the same income have differential access to health care and housing of acceptable quality. In general, the percentage of children covered by health insurance increases with income. In 2001, 95% of children with annual family incomes of $75,000 or more were covered by health insurance, compared with 81% of children whose families earned $25,000 or less annually (Current Population Survey, 2001). Yet Medicaid covers only some of the poor families and children in the United States while others of similar means have no health care coverage.

Susan Mayer concluded her discussion of the indicators of children's economic well-being at the 1994 conference with the following assessment: "No single measure can provide reliable evidence about changes in children's economic well-being, if by economic well-being we mean the material resources available to families" (Mayer, 1997a, p. 249). Her review covered several indicators of the family material environment, including the poverty rate for children, mean income, consumption, housing problems, access to selected consumer durables, and visits to doctors. She pointed out that all of the measures showed the same general pattern over the past two decades: Income increased over those two decades, as did consumption and living conditions. She suggested that we should look not only at measures of income and/or poverty but also at consumption, because trends over time in these different measures suggested somewhat different stories.

Mayer's (1997a) discussion of parental employment focused mostly on the trade-off between working and spending time with children. She pointed out that some research suggested that the greater work effort of married and single mothers was not necessarily associated with less time with their children, because leisure time has increased rather than decreased even as time working increased. She focused primarily on labor force participation and hours worked as key indicators of parental employment.

Another subtlety in the relationship between the family material environment and child outcomes is that it may take significant changes in the family material environment that go well beyond those envisioned by most mainstream social policy proposals in order to have a socially significant impact on any given child outcome. The association between family income and cognitive development and educational attainment provides numerous illustrations of both the importance of income and the size of changes necessary to bring about substantial changes in outcomes. Avoiding the experience of deep and persistent poverty during early childhood would substantially improve cognitive development (Duncan & Brooks-Gunn, 1997). Fortunately, relatively few children experience deep and persistent poverty; however, ensuring that all children avoid this experience is not a likely outcome of any current anti-poverty policies or most alternative policies being considered. Other research suggests that family income in late adolescence is significantly associated with the likelihood of completing college (Haveman, Sandefur, Wolfe, Campbell, & Voyer, 2003). However, differences in family income that are associated with substantial differences in college graduation are in the tens of thousands of dollars. Again, none of our existing policies are designed to bring about these kinds of major changes in family income.

Why Family Structure Is Important

Relative to how scholars view the effects of family material resources, there is more controversy and debate over the importance of family structure and over how to measure the family social environment. Social scientists agree less, for example, about the effects of the presence or absence of two parents on child outcomes than they do about the effects of income on child outcomes. The American family has experienced tremendous change over the past 50 years, and much of this change comes from changing family structure. Over the past decade, various researchers have established that living in any family form other than a biological two-parent family brings negative consequences for children. These consequences are beyond the economic consequences associated with a nonintact family structure (McLanahan & Sandefur, 1994). McLanahan (1997) reviewed findings from 12 studies compiled in the volume *Consequences of Growing Up Poor* (Duncan & Brooks-Gunn, 1997) to determine the importance of parent absence relative to poverty for children's well-being. In this volume, authors examined multiple aspects of well-being that span the course of youth, adolescence, and early adulthood, including test scores, behavior problems, psychological problems, educational attainment, jobs and income, and health outcomes. Negative effects of parental absence have been established for nearly all of these measures. McLanahan reported that, in general, family income explains roughly half of the negative effects associated with parent absence. The rest is accounted for by differences in parental supervision and social capital for different family structures.

The most recent data indicate that 69% of all children currently live with two parents (biological, adopted, or step), 23% live with their mother only, 4% live with their father only, and 5% live with neither parent (Child Trends DataBank, 2003; U.S. Bureau of the Census, 2002). Official statistics do not separately account for children who live in cohabiting unions with their biological mother and her partner or their biological father and his partner. Children in these types of households are counted as living with their mother only or their father only. Bumpass and Lu (2000) estimated that nearly 40% of all nonmarital births in the 1990s were within cohabiting unions, so the true proportion of children born to single parents is much lower than what is represented in official statistics. However, recent efforts to encourage official accounting of cohabitation, as evinced by the 2001 *Counting Couples* report, suggests that the counting of these couples in federal data may not be far off (Federal Interagency Forum on Child and Family Statistics, 2001).

There is a good deal of racial and ethnic heterogeneity underneath the global numbers representing the distribution of family structure. Asian American and non-Hispanic White children are much more likely to grow up in a two-parent family than are Black or Hispanic children. Hispanic children, and especially Black children, are much more likely to live in mother-only households. In addition, Black children are more than twice as likely as Whites to reside with neither parent. However, this does not mean nonfamily members are raising these children. Black children are five times as likely as Hispanic and White children to be raised by grandparents—5% versus 1.4% and 1.1%, respectively (Child Trends DataBank, 2003).

There are three pathways to single parenthood: (a) nonmarital childbearing, (b) divorce, and (c) the death of one parent. Rendall (1999) showed that most Black single mothers enter single parenthood through nonmarital childbearing, whereas most White single mothers enter through divorce. These different pathways have consequences for father involvement and financial stability, both of which have positive impacts on child well-being (Amato & Gilbreth, 1999). Fathers who were once married to their child's mother are more involved and contribute more financially to their children (Seltzer, 1991). Contact between never-married (to the mother) nonresidential fathers and their children is frequent soon after birth but declines significantly by the time the child is of school age (Child Trends DataBank, 2002). Regular nonresident father involvement has been linked to positive development and life satisfaction of the child. However, children of widowed parents do as well as those from two-parent families after the initial shock of a parent's death (Biblarz & Gottainer, 2000).

As family patterns changed through the 1990s, a considerable amount of research interest around the topic of stepfamilies began. Most research shows that children from stepfamilies do not do as well as those from original two-parent families; instead, they are similar to children from single-parent families (McLanahan, 1997; McLanahan &

Sandefur, 1994). Downey (1995) found that children in stepparent families receive fewer parental resources—economic, interpersonal, and cultural—than children in intact families, and this accounts for their lower academic achievement. Perhaps this difference is due to obligations that stepparents have to children from previous marriages. Stepparents may also divert some of the biological parent's attention away from the child and to themselves instead. Another possibility is that the stepparent-stepchild relationship may be strained, at least initially. This may cause the stepparent to withhold resources or the stepchild to resist resources being offered. These possible explanations are not yet well established in the literature on stepfamilies.

Family Stability. Yet another dimension of the impact of family structure on child well-being is that of changes in family structure. Changes in family structure occur with divorce or separation, marriage for previously never-married parents, remarriage for divorced individuals, and change in extended family residential patterns and relationships (Sandefur & Mosley, 1997). Most of the research on family structure changes examines the effects of divorce. Although some researchers claim that the event of divorce has direct negative consequences for children (Wallerstein, Lewis, & Blakeslee, 2000), others argue that perhaps these negative effects are really effects of parental conflict that precedes divorce (Hanson, 1999; Jeklielek, 1998).

Residential changes often accompany family structure changes. Several researchers have established the importance of residential stability for child well-being (Coleman, 1988; Hagan, MacMillan, & Wheaton, 1996; Pribesh & Downey, 1999; Tucker, Marx, & Long, 1998). Pribesh and Downey (1999) found that moving lowers a child's academic performance because of ruptured social relationships experienced by students who move. However, Hagan and colleagues (1996) found that the negative effects of moving are not inevitable. They found that negative effects of family migration are particularly pronounced in families with uninvolved fathers and unsupportive mothers. When families are strong, the enhanced social capital provided by parents compensates for the loss of community social capital due to moving.

Oftentimes, the media, the general public, policymakers, family practitioners, and even researchers exaggerate the negative effects of growing up without both parents. To be true to the experiences of most children who experience family disruption or who have always lived with only one parent, it is important to temper this fervor with the realization that most children of these experiences do just fine (Amato, 2000; Cherlin, 1999; Demo & Cox, 2000). In fact, when negative consequences of parent absence are found, some of these effects may be temporary (Amato, 2000; McLanahan, 1997). McLanahan's (1997) review found that recentness of disruption has a significant and negative impact on child well-being. As the amount of time since disruption increases, some negative effects may dissipate. However, it is also important not to underestimate the effects of family structure. Although most children are fairly resilient to family change, overall, those in nonintact families do not fare as well as those who grow up with both parents. The basic message, then, is that family structure matters for many outcomes, but child well-being does not hinge on family structure alone.

Family Size. There is a long-running debate regarding the effects of family size on child well-being. Most of the existing literature has used intellectual development or educational achievement as a measure of well-being. The consistent finding that children from larger families have lower intellectual development is among the most robust findings in family stratification research. However, the process by which this finding results is one of considerable debate. Blake (1981) used a *resource dilution* model to argue that couples can have higher achieving or smarter children by having fewer of them. This argument is rooted in the idea that a larger family size stretches resources—money, food, or affection—so that each member gets less. Zajonc (1976) proposed a similar model, the *confluence model*, which suggests that additional children lead to lower IQ for all children in the family, but especially those at later birth orders (second-, third-, fourth-born, etc.). Page and colleagues (Page & Grandon, 1979; Velandia, Grandon, & Page, 1978) have suggested a different model to explain the family size-intellectual development finding: the *admixture model*, which suggests that birth order or family size do not cause lower intellectual development but that parents of lower intelligence tend to have larger families.

Several recent empirical tests indicate that perhaps the admixture model is closer to the true story about family size and intelligence. Guo and VanWey (1999) used within-family sibling data from the National Longitudinal Survey of Youth to show that when characteristics that are shared between siblings (e.g., parental intelligence) are controlled, the negative relationship between family size and intellectual development disappears (see also Rodgers, Cleveland, van den Oord, & Rowe, 2000). A recent article by Conley and Glauber (2006) used an instrumental variable approach to estimate the effect of family size on education attainment. They used the fact that families with two same-sex children are about 7 percentage points more likely to have a third child than families with two opposite-sex children. This fact provides a source of randomized variation in the propensity to have three children as opposed to two. Conley and Glauber's instrumental variable estimates indicate that the impact of family size is smaller than the traditional estimates of the earlier studies, but larger than zero, as estimated by Guo and VanWey (1999). The fact that children from larger families have lower intellectual development remains, while the debate about the source of this difference continues.

A key component not yet addressed with regard to family size here is number of parents. With regard to the resource dilution model, two parents (compared to one) can provide more resources to children. Family size measures that fail to consider the number of adults in the household misrepresent the theoretical arguments proposed in the literature. Hogan and Eggebeen (1997) wisely suggested that adult:child or parent:child ratios should be used to measure family size in addition to the traditional count of the number of dependent children living in the household.

As families have been changing in parental living arrangements, they have also been changing in size. Fertility patterns in the United States have resulted in smaller average family sizes and less variation in family size across the population. Fewer women are having four or more children, and more women are remaining childless (Office of the Assistant Secretary for Planning and Evaluation, 2001). The current total fertility rate (TFR) for all women in the United States was 2.0 in 2001 (Hamilton, Martin, & Sutton, 2002).[1] This means that women today are having two children in their lifetime. By contrast, the TFR for cohorts in the 1920s was just over 3.0, and in the late 1950s and early 1960s the TFR was around 3.5 (Morgan, 1996). Family size differs significantly across racial-ethnic groups. The birth rates for Blacks, Hispanics, and Native Americans are higher than for Whites and Asian Americans, but differences are smaller than they once were and are projected to converge even more in the future (Morgan, 1996).[2]

Why Child Care Is Important

With changes in family structure and women entering the labor force in large numbers, child care has increasingly become a priority for families with children. With approximately two thirds of children under 6 years of age in nonparental care on a regular basis, some of the attention that was once focused on the family as the environment of early childhood development is now extended to nonparental care providers and facilities (Vandell & Wolfe, 2000). The effects of parental employment are in part dependent on the extent and quality of care provided to children in the absence of their parents. Therefore, we need indicators of what children do or what they are exposed to while in nonparental care arrangements. In this section, we discuss the effects of receiving nonparental care on child outcomes, different types of child care and who uses them, and several key policy issues.

Effects of Nonparental Care on Child Outcomes.   The increase in nonparental care raises questions of how such care may promote or deter child development. In the research literature on child care effects, the debate centers primarily on two aspects of care: (a) quantity and (b) quality. Vandell and Wolfe (2000) critically examined the research evidence on the importance of child care quality. Two standard aspects of quality are typically addressed: (a) process quality and (b) structural characteristics. *Process quality* refers to the kinds of experiences children have with caregivers and other children, social stimulation, and exposure to various materials. *Structural characteristics* are factors such as child:adult ratio, the size of the group of children under care, and the training and credentials of caregivers. Vandell and Wolfe reported that process quality and cognitive and language skills are strongly associated. Another review of the child care effects literature commissioned by the National Research Council (NRC) and the Institute of Medicine (2003) concurs with Vandell and Wolfe. This study reported three consistent findings with regard to the importance of quality of care: (a) structural characteristics predict process quality; (b) process quality predicts children's cognitive, language, and social competencies both in the short and longer term; and (c) structural characteristics predict children's cognitive, language, and social competencies. The findings are in the expected direction-when quality is higher, children do better in these areas, and when it is lower, they do worse.

With regard to quantity of care, the literature bears some consistency in the finding that children who are in care more hours per week are more likely to exhibit behavioral problems than those in care fewer hours. However, substantial behavior problems outside of the "normal" range are evinced only for children who average 45 or more hours per week in care up to age 4½ years (National Institute of Child Health and Human Development Early Child Care Research Network 2003, see also NRC & Institute of Medicine, 2003). In addition, there is some evidence that children who were in child care 30 or more hours a week during their infancy (by 9 months) had lower pre-academic skills at 3 years of age (Brooks-Gunn, Han, & Waldfogel, 2002).

Understanding the effects of nonmaternal childcare on children is complicated by several factors. Most important, family decisions concerning nonmaternal care may be affected by maternal, child, and familial characteristics already in place before care begins. Although it is difficult to capture all possible preceding characteristics in empirical analysis, the above-cited studies do a fairly good job of considering these selection factors.

Types of Child Care.   There are three general settings for nonparental child care: (a) home-based care provided by a relative, (b) home-based care provided by a nonrelative, and (c) center-based care. According to a report by the Federal Interagency Forum on Child and Family Statistics (2002), the largest setting for nonparental care among infants and toddlers (birth to age 2) was in some type of home-based care. For children ages 3 to 6 but not yet in kindergarten, the predominant care setting was center-based care, and for children in kindergarten through third grade the predominant setting was home-based care, possibly because parents could work at least part time while children were in school. About 22% of 3- to 6-year-olds had multiple types of arrangements, compared with 6% of the other age groups. So, it seems that parents address the issue of nonparental child care most intensely during the noninfant and nonschool ages, when they are likely to be trying to balance careers with full-time child care needs.

Among children under the age of 6 and not yet in kindergarten in 2001, the predominant nonparental care setting for White and Black children was center-based care, followed by in-home care by another relative. The reverse is true for Hispanic children: If they are not cared for by their parents, Hispanic children are more likely to be in in-home care provided by a relative than in center-based care (Federal Interagency Forum on Child and Family Statistics, 2002). The least likely care arrangement for all groups is in-home care by a nonrelative, although Whites are more likely than those in other race groups to receive this kind of care.

Socioeconomic status also plays a role in determining the child care setting. Children under 6 with mothers who work full time are most likely to be in center-based care, followed by in-home care by a relative, in-home care by a nonrelative, and parental care. Children with mothers who do not work are most likely to be in parental care, followed by center-based care and in-home care by relatives and nonrelatives. Furthermore, mothers with higher levels of education have children in center-based care or nonrelative home-based care more often than those with lower levels of education, who tend to rely on relatives for some or all of their child care needs. Similarly, higher income parents have children in center-based care more often, while lower income parents use home-based care provided by relatives (Federal Interagency Forum on Child and Family Statistics, 2002).

CURRENT INDICATORS OF THE FAMILY MATERIAL ENVIRONMENT

The volume of papers from the 1994 conference contained a separate section on economic security, with three papers, and a separate section on population, family, and neighborhood containing two papers that dealt with components of the family social environment. Other papers in the volume that were focused primarily on child and adolescent outcomes also contained material on some aspects of the family material and social environment. Some of the papers on health indicators, for example, discussed health insurance coverage for children and families with children.

These papers contained a variety of recommendations for improving the collection and dissemination of indicators of the family material and social environment.

Among the most concrete sets of suggestions were those in the chapter by Duncan and Moscow (1997). They were primarily concerned with looking at longitudinal indicators of children's poverty and dependence. Among their suggestions were time series indicators of the following:

- The number and characteristics of the "point-in-time" population of poor or dependent children or families with children.
- The number and characteristics of children experiencing first and subsequent transitions into and out of poverty or dependence and the events associated with these transitions.
- The number and characteristics of long-term poor or dependent children.
- Intergenerational correlations of poverty and welfare receipt.

Around the time that authors were preparing their chapters for the 1997 *Indicators* volume, a National Research Council panel was examining the way in which poverty was measured in the United States (Citro & Michael, 1995). This panel summarized a number of concerns with the official measure of poverty that had been identified by researchers over the years. Many of these concerns are especially relevant for measuring poverty among families and children. One of these is that the official poverty definition did not distinguish between families in which parents worked and had to pay for child care and those where child care was not needed. A second was that the official measure did not take into account whether a family had health insurance; neither did it take into account possible differences in out-of-pocket medical expenses. A third critical problem with the official poverty measure was that it did not take into account the impact of the Social Security payroll tax or participation in the food stamps and other noncash assistance programs on family well-being. The panel recommended an improved poverty measure, and we include this as one of our recommendations, presented later.

The final chapter on the family material environment focused on parental employment and children (Smith, Brooks-Gunn, & Jackson, 1997). The authors concluded with the final recommendations about measures to be included in future data collection efforts:

- Mother's job characteristics should include: employment history prior to child-birth, length of maternity/parenting leave, hours of employment in each year of the child's life including summer hours and number of job changes, a subjective measure of mother's satisfaction with her employment schedule, mother's salary, fringe benefits, and social security coverage.
- Father's job characteristics should include hours of work for each year of the child's life including summer hours and number of job changes and unemployment; length of parenting leave, a subjective measure of father's satisfaction with his employment schedule; father's salary, fringe benefits, social security coverage, and whether or not he pays child support. (Smith et al., 1997, p. 299)

All in all, these sets of recommendations would involve a lot of information, some of which is readily available, but some of which is very difficult to obtain with existing data. Consequently, it is not surprising that only some of these recommendations have been followed in the major compilations of indicators that have appeared since the 1994 conference. More specifically, *America's Children: Key National Indicators of Well-Being* (Federal Interagency Forum on Child and Family Statistics, 2003) includes the following indicators:

- Percentage of related children under age 18 in poverty: 16% in 2001.
- Percentage of related children under age 18 by family income relative to the poverty line: 7% of children lived in families with incomes below one half of the poverty line in 2001.
- Percentage of children under age 18 living with parents with at least one parent employed full-time all year: 79% in 2001.
- Percentage of households with children under age 18 that reported any of three housing problems (physically inadequate housing, crowded housing, or housing that cost more than 30% of household income): 36% in 2001.
- Percentage of children under age 18 in households experiencing food insecurity with hunger: 4.1% in 2001.
- Percentage of children ages 2 to 6 with a good diet: 20% in 1999-2000.
- Percentage of children under age 18 covered by health insurance: 88% in 2001.
- Percentage of children under age 18 with no usual source of health care: 6% in 2001.

The *America's Children 2003* section on economic security concludes with recommendations that reflect some of those in papers at the 1994 conference, including a call for richer measures of family material resources, for measures of long-term poverty over the course of childhood, and for measures of homelessness.

CURRENT INDICATORS OF THE FAMILY SOCIAL ENVIRONMENT

Much of the work on the family social environment has concentrated on what we might think of as classic measures, such as the presence of parents in the household and family size. More recently, researchers have turned their attention to work on other indicators, such as the amount of time spent with children; the quantity and quality of nonparental child care received by children; and the involvement of noncustodial parents, generally divorced or never-married fathers, with their children.

Among the recommendations to come from the 1994 conference were the following:

- Distinguish a minimum of five race and ethnic groups in studies of child well-being: (a) non-Hispanic White, (b) Black, (c) Latino (non-Black), (d) Asian and Pacific Islander, and (e) Native American (Hogan & Eggebeen, 1997).

• Ideally, distinguish among three groups of children-foreign born, native born of foreign-born parents, native born of native-born parents-but an adequate distinction would be *immigrant children* (defined as foreign born or native born of foreign-born parents) and *native children* (Hogan & Eggebeen, 1997).

• Identify blended families (containing stepparents, stepsiblings, and half-siblings) and children living with unmarried but cohabiting parents (Sandefur & Mosley, 1997).

• Measure the geographical proximity and frequency of contact with noncustodial parents (Sandefur & Mosley, 1997; Smith et al., 1997).

• Measure family size in two ways: as (a) the number of dependent children under age 18 living in the household and (b) adult:child or parent:child ratios (Hogan & Eggebeen, 1997).

• Measure the amount of time the mother and the father spend with a child on a typical weekday (Smith et al., 1997).

• Report on foster care, abuse, and neglect (Sandefur & Mosley, 1997).

• Measure a variety of child care indicators, including type of care, caregiver's training, and changes in care across time (Smith et al., 1997).

All of these measures are available in at least some of the national data sets used to study families and children, and several of them have found their way into the major publications of indicators of family and child well-being. *America's Children 2003* (Federal Interagency Forum on Child and Family Statistics, 2003) provided the following information:

• The race-ethnicity of children: In 2000, 64% of children were non-Hispanic White, 15% were non-Hispanic Black, 16% were Hispanic, 4% were Asian/Pacific Islander, and 1% were Native American/Alaska Native.

• Nativity: In 2002, 16% of children were native children with at least one foreign-born parent, and 4% were foreign-born children with at least one foreign-born parent.

• Family structure: In 2002, 69% of American children lived with two parents, 23% lived with only their mothers, 5% lived with only their fathers, and 4% lived with neither parent.

America's Children 2003 contains no indicators of living with cohabiting parents, contact with noncustodial parents, family size or the ratio of children to adults, time spent with parents, or the quantity or quality of child care. It does contain information on births to unmarried women and measures of child care. The report calls for regularly collected measures of family structure that include cohabitation and nonresident parents. It also calls for the development of measures of time use by children and adults and for better measures of the exposure to contaminants in drinking water and food.

Trends in the Well-Being of America's Children and Youth: 2001 contains several additional measures of the family social environment. These include information on immigrant children and children of immigrants, family size, number of parents in the household, child care arrangements, children living in foster care, reported abuse and neglect, closeness with parents, and parents' activities with children.

NEXT STEPS

We have made substantial progress since the 1994 conference on developing, collecting, and disseminating information on key indicators of the family material and social environment. *America's Children, KIDS COUNT*, and *Trends in the Well-Being of America's Children and Youth* are available in print and on the web. They contain a number of important indicators of family income, poverty status, consumption of housing and health care, and the social characteristics of families. These publications and related efforts make it possible to quickly gain a picture of how families and children are doing. Such a picture was much more difficult to obtain 10 years ago. Although it is difficult to document systematically the impact of these publications on the public discussion of family and child issues and on the development of public policies and local area programs, anecdotal evidence suggests that the impact has been significant and is well worth the costs involved in these efforts.

Nonetheless, much remains to be done in terms of developing a useful set of indicators. Our suggestions for four indicators that are most needed in the area of the material and social environment are the following:

1. *Modify the measurement of poverty among families with children to follow the procedures suggested in the NRC report on poverty and its measurement.*
   The NRC issued a report calling for a revision in the measurement of poverty around the same time as the interest in indicators of family and child well-being became pronounced. The NRC recommendations have some profound implications for understanding and measuring child poverty in that they consider differences in the cost of living across locations, taxes, noncash benefits, the cost of health care, and other factors that are very important for families with children. We would have a better picture of the material environment of families with children if we adopted and used these recommendations in our national data collection efforts.

2. *Measure and report measures of consumption by families with children that extend beyond housing, health insurance, and food security.*

Because trends in income and trends in consumption do not necessarily correspond with one another, it is important to look at both. Fortunately, we now have regular reports on the percentage of children with acceptable housing, health insurance coverage, and food security. Two other items that seem particularly important are a telephone and a family car. These items open up opportunities for children that are not otherwise available.

3. *Bring the measurement of family structure into the 21st century by reporting on cohabitation, blended families, same-sex parents, and other family forms that are becoming increasingly prevalent.*

The federal statistical system is gradually catching up with the major transformations that have taken place over the past several years in the kinds of families in which children live. The complexity of current family forms makes this difficult, but we need to have more information than the common typology of two parents, single mother, single father, no parents.

4. *Develop and report measures of the involvement of residential and nonresidential fathers in the lives of their children.*

Fatherhood and the role of fathers have received a good deal of attention from the media and politicians recently and have also attracted social scientists to the study of fatherhood. Unfortunately, we have few regularly collected measures of the involvement of residential or nonresidential fathers in the lives of their children. This involvement is a key component of the social environment of the family, and in the case of nonresidential fathers is also related to a key component of the material environment of the family: the formal or informal financial support provided to the mother and children by the nonresidential father. A recent report titled *Charting Parenthood: A Statistical Portrait of Fathers and Mothers in America* (Child Trends, 2002) represents a step in the right direction. This report contains information on resident father involvement (amount and type) and non-resident father contact (existence and frequency of contact).

CONCLUSIONS

We have reviewed selectively the literature on the importance of the family material and social environment. We then examined the development and dissemination of information on indicators of this environment that have occurred since the 1994 conference. Finally, we discussed our top recommendations for improving the information that is available.

We have come a long way in the past decade in improving the measures of the family social and material environment that are available for people who want or need to understand how families with children are doing. The major reports prepared by the Federal Interagency Forum on Family and Child Statistics, by the Assistant Secretary for Planning and Evaluation at the U.S. Department of Health and Human Services, and by the Annie E. Casey Foundation and its grantees have gone a long way to improving the quality, quantity, and timeliness of the information we have available about families with children. In addition, researchers have explored more and more carefully how the relationship between parents, in the home, or between residential and nonresidential parents, is associated with the social, emotional, and cognitive development of children. The National Institute of Child Health and Human Development Early Childcare Research Network has published a number of studies documenting the ways in which out-of-home child care is associated with child development and well-being. The research described by Duncan and Brooks-Gunn (1997) has significantly advanced our understanding of the child outcomes that are and are not affected by family income. In sum, the federal statistical community and the research community are continuing to take advantage of the opportunities provided by existing data and data collection efforts to advance our understanding of the role of the family material and social environment in promoting child well-being.

Nonetheless, yearly reports such as *Indicators of Child Well-Being*, volumes such as *The Well-Being of Children and Families* (Thornton, 2001), and conferences such as "Counting Couples I" and the planned "Counting Couples II," continue to call attention to the need for data to provide the basis for time series measures of additional family attributes. Also, researchers continue to ask for additional measures and improved measures of family structure, family processes, and family material and nonmaterial resources. Fortunately, new efforts to gather improved measures are afoot. The National Children's Study, for example, which currently is in the pilot study stage, provides an opportunity to implement some of these recommendations. One of the major goals of the study is to measure the environments within which children are born and raised and the effects of these environments on their well-being. This study provides the opportunity for the federal statistical community and researchers to develop better measures that can be collected and tracked over time. We hope that a new volume of papers in the not-too-distant future will be able to include within its chapters discussion of how the National Children's Study has improved our ability to understand the role of the family material and social environment in promoting child well-being.

ACKNOWLEDGMENTS

Work on this chapter was supported by a grant (HD37566) to Gary D. Sandefur as part of the National Institute of Child Health and Human Development Family and Child Well-Being Research Network. We thank Brett Brown for his helpful comments and suggestions.

NOTES

1. TFR is defined as the average number of children that would be born alive to a woman if she were to live up to and through her childbearing years subject to the age-specific fertility rates of a given year.
2. If family size influences intellectual development, then the trend toward smaller families portends a higher level of intellectual development in American society. Still, differentials in family size by race and other socioeconomic factors may suggest continued stratification on academic outcomes.

REFERENCES

Amato, P. R. (2000). The consequences of divorce for adults and children. *Journal of Marriage and the Family, 62,* 1269–1287.

Amato, P. R., & Booth, A. (1997). *A generation at risk: Growing up in an era of family upheaval.* Cambridge, MA: Harvard University Press.

Amato, P. R., & Gilbreth, J. G. (1999). Nonresident fathers and children's well-being: A meta-analysis. *Journal of Marriage and the Family, 61,* 557–573.

Annie E. Casey Foundation. (2001). *Kids count data book.* Baltimore: Author.

Biblarz, T. J., & Gottainer, G. (2000). Family structure and children's success: A comparison of widowed and divorced single-mother families. *Journal of Marriage and the Family, 62,* 533–548.

Blake, J. (1981). Family size and the quality of children. *Demography, 18,* 421–442.

Blake, J. (1989). *Family size and achievement.* Berkeley: University of California Press.

Brooks-Gunn, J., Han, W., & Waldfogel, J. (2002). Maternal employment and child cognitive outcomes in the first three years of life: The NICHD Study of Early Child Care. *Child Development, 73,* 1052–1072.

Bumpass, L., & Lu, H. H. (2000). Trends in cohabitation and implications for children's family contexts in the United States. *Population Studies, 54,* 29–41.

Cherlin, A. J. (1999). Going to extremes: Family structure, children's well-being and social science. *Demography, 36,* 421–428.

Child Trends. (2002). *Charting parenthood: A statistical portrait of fathers and mothers in America.* Washington, DC: Author.

Child Trends DataBank. (2003). Calculations using Fields, J. (2003). *Children's living arrangements and characteristics: March 2002* (Current Population Reports, P20-547). Washington, DC: U.S. Census Bureau.

Citro, C. F., & Michael, R. T. (1995). *Measuring poverty: A new approach.* Washington, DC: National Academy Press.

Coleman, J. (1988). Social capital in the creation of human capital. *American Journal of Sociology, 94*(Suppl.), S95–S120.

Conley, D., & Glauber, R. (2006). Parental Educational Investment and Children's Academic Risk: Estimates of the Impact of Sibship Size and Birth Order from Exogenous Variation in Fertility. *Journal of Human Resources, 41*(4), 722–737.

Current Population Survey. (2001). Annual demographic survey, March supplement. Retrieved September 8, 2002 from http://bls.census.gov/cps/ads/sdata.htm

Day, R. D., Gavazzi, S., & Acock, A. (2001). Compelling family processes. In A. Thornton (Ed.), *The well-being of children and families: Research and data needs* (pp. 103–126). Ann Arbor: University of Michigan Press.

Demo, D. H., & Cox, M. J. (2000). Families with young children: A review of re-search in the 1990s. *Journal of Marriage and the Family, 62*, 876–895.

Downey, D. B. (1995a). Understanding academic achievement among children in step households: The role of parental resources, sex of stepparent, and sex of child. *Social Forces, 73*, 875–894.

Downey, D. B. (1995b). When bigger is not better: Family size, parental re-sources, and children's educational performance. *American Sociological Review, 60*, 746–761.

Duncan, G. J., & Brooks-Gunn, J. (Eds.). (1997). *Consequences of growing up poor.* New York: Russell Sage Foundation.

Duncan, G. J., & Moscow, L. (1997). Longitudinal indicators of children's poverty and dependence. In R. M. Hauser, B. V. Brown, & W. R. Prosser (Eds.), *Indicators of child well-being* (pp. 258–278). New York: Russell Sage Foundation.

Federal Interagency Forum on Child and Family Statistics. (2003). *America's children: Key national indicators of well-being 2003.* Washington, DC: U.S. Government Printing Office.

Federal Interagency Forum on Child and Family Statistics. (2001). *Counting cou-ples: Improving marriage, divorce, remarriage and cohabitation data in the fed-eral statistical system.* Washington, DC: U.S. Government Printing Office.

Guo, G., & VanWey, L. (1999). Sibship size and intellectual development: Is the relationship causal? *American Sociological Review, 64*, 169–187.

Hagan, J., MacMillan, R., & Wheaton, B. (1996). New kid in town: Social capital and the life course effects of family migration on children. *American Sociologi-cal Review, 61*, 368–385.

Hamilton, B. E., Martin, J. A., & Sutton, P. D. (2003). Births: Preliminary data for 2002. *National Vital Statistics Report, 51*(11).

Hanson, T. L. (1999). Does parental conflict explain why divorce is negatively associated with child welfare? *Social Forces, 77*, 1283–1315.

Harris, J. R. (1998). *The nurture assumption: Why children turn out the way they do.* New York: Free Press.

Hauser, R. M., Brown, B. V., & Prosser, W. R. (Eds.). (1997). *Indicators of child well-being.* New York: Russell Sage Foundation.

Haveman, R., Sandefur, G., Wolfe, B., Campbell, M. E., & Voyer, A. (2002, June). *What does increased economic inequality imply about the future level and disper-sion of human capital?* Paper presented at the 2002 Institute for Research on Poverty Annual Workshop on Problems of the Low Income Population, Mad-ison, WI. (Revised version presented at the Russell Sage Workshop on Family Inequality, New York City, April 2003.)

Hogan, D. P., & Eggebeen, D. J. (1997). Demographic change and the population of children: Race/ethnicity, immigration, and family size. In R. M. Hauser, B. V. Brown, & W. R. Prosser (Eds.), *Indicators of children's well-being* (pp. 311–327). New York: Russell Sage Foundation.

Jekielek, S. M. (1998). Parental conflict, marital disruption and children's emo-tional well-being. *Social Forces, 76*, 905–935.

Mayer, S. E. (1997a). Indicators of children's economic well-being and parental employment. In R. M. Hauser, B. V. Brown, & W. R. Prosser (Eds.), *Indicators of child well-being* (pp. 237–257). New York: Russell Sage Foundation.

Mayer, S. E. (1997b). *What money can't buy: Family income and children's life chances.* Cambridge, MA: Harvard University Press.

McLanahan, S. S. (1997). Parent absence or poverty, which matters more? In G. J. Duncan & J. Brooks-Gunn (Eds.), *Consequences of growing up poor* (pp. 35–48). New York, Russell Sage Foundation.

McLanahan, S. S., & Sandefur, G. D. (1994). *Growing up with a single parent: What hurts, what helps?* Cambridge, MA: Harvard University Press.

Morgan, S. P. (1996). Characteristic features of modern American fertility. In J. B. Casterline, R. D. Lee, & K. A. Foote (Eds.), *Fertility in the United States: New patterns, new theories* (pp. 19–63). New York: Population Council.

National Research Council & Institute of Medicine. (2003). *Working families in America: Challenges, opportunities, and options* (E. Smolensky & J. A. Gootman, Eds.). Washington, DC: National Academy Press.

National Institute of Child Health and Human Development Childcare Research Network. (2003). Does amount of time spent in child care predict socio-emotional adjustment during the transition to kindergarten? *Child Development, 74*, 976–1005.

Office of the Assistant Secretary for Planning and Evaluation. (2001). *Trends in the well-being of America's children and youth 2001.* Washington, DC: U.S. Department of Health and Human Services.

Page, E. B., & Grandon, G. (1979). Family configuration and mental ability: Two theories contrasted with U.S. data. *American Educational Research Journal, 16*, 257–272.

Phillips, M. (1999). Sibship size and academic achievement: What we now know and what we still need to know. *American Sociological Review, 64*, 188–192.

Pribesh, S., & Downey, D. B. (1999). Why are residential and school moves associated with poor school performance? *Demography, 36*, 521–534.

Rendall, M. S. (1999). Entry or exit? A transition-probability approach to explaining the high prevalence of single motherhood among Black women. *Demography, 36*, 369–376.

Rodgers, J. L., Clevelenad, H. H., van den Oord, E., & Rowe, D. C. (2000). Resolving the debate over birth order, family size and intelligence. *American Psychologist, 55*, 599–612.

Rowe, D. C. (1994). *The limits of family influence: Genes, experience, and behavior.* New York: Guilford.

Sandefur, G. D., & Mosley, J. (1997). Family structure, stability, and the well-being of children. In R. M. Hauser, B. V. Brown, & W. R. Prosser (Eds.), *Indicators of children's well-being* (pp. 325–345). New York: Russell Sage Foundation.

Seltzer, J. A. (1991). Relationships between fathers and children who live apart: The father's role after separation. *Journal of Marriage and the Family, 53*, 79–101.

Shonkoff, J. P., & Phillips, D. A. (Eds.). (2000). *From neurons to neighborhoods: The science of early child development.* Washington, DC: National Academy Press.

Smith, J. R., Brooks-Gunn, J., & Jackson, A. (1997). Parental employment and children. In R. M. Hauser, B. V. Brown, & W. R. Prosser (Eds.), *Indicators of child well-being* (pp. 279–309). New York: Russell Sage Foundation.

Stolberg, S. G. (2001, April 19). *Link found between behavioral problems and time in child care.* New York Times.

Thornton, A. (2001). *The well-being of children and families: Research and data needs.* Ann Arbor: University of Michigan Press.

Tucker, C., Marx, J. J., & Long, L. (1998). Moving on: Residential mobility and children's school lives. *Sociology of Education, 71*, 111–129.

U.S. Bureau of the Census. (2002). *Living arrangements of children under 18 years old: 1960 to present.* Retrieved March 14, 2007 from http://www.census.gov/population/www/socdemo/hh-fam.html

Vandell, D. L., & Wolfe, B. (2000). *Child care quality: Does it matter and does it need to be improved?* Institute for Research on Poverty Special Report No. 78, University of Wisconsin-Madison.

Velandia, W., Grandon, G., & Page, E. B. (1978). Family size, birth order and intelligence in a large South American sample. *American Educational Research Journal, 15,* 399–416.

Wallerstein, J. S., Lewis, J. M., & Blakeslee, S. (2000). *The unexpected legacy of divorce.* New York: Hyperion.

Zajonc, R. B. (1976). Family configuration and intelligence. *Science, 192,* 227–236.

Chapter 9

Indicators of the Peer Environment in Adolescence

Kathleen Mullan Harris
University of North Carolina at Chapel Hill

Shannon E. Cavanagh
University of Texas at Austin

Social scientists, educators, and parents have long been interested in youth friendships and the peer environment as an important context for the social and psychological development of adolescents. As adolescents strive for autonomy and independence, they loosen their bonds with parents and enjoy the equality and reciprocity achieved in relationships with people their own age. The peer group becomes a resource that helps young people master age-graded tasks. Teenagers attach increasing importance to friendships and peer group relationships, especially during early adolescence, and grow more receptive to peer influence. Peers may provide crucial information or contacts to help youth negotiate the social world, reinforce values and norms of behavior, and promote trustworthiness and obligations in reciprocal relations.

To understand the developmental significance of the peer environment, several layers of indicators are needed. The majority of developmental research portrays friendships as positive, indicating one's ability to get along with others and be liked by others. Studies have found that young people with friends are more confident, cooperative, altruistic, and less aggressive and demonstrate greater social competence, school involvement, and work orientation than those without friends (Fletcher, Darling, Steinberg, & Dornbusch, 1995; Hartup & Stevens, 1997). Despite these findings of friendships as beneficial, the large majority of research on peer influence is focused on negative influence and antisocial behavior (Jessor & Jessor, 1977; Miller, Norton, Curtis, Hill, Schvaneveldt, & Young, 1997). This contradiction highlights the distinctions we will draw in the indicators we propose: Having friends is crucial to youth development, but who one's friends are and the quality

259

of friendship relations further define how the peer environment is related to developmental outcomes (Hartup & Stevens, 1997).

In this chapter, we consider indicators of the peer environment that are most salient to youth development and well-being. We first review the literature on why and how peers matter and the theoretical types of peer influence identified in previous scholarship. We then describe the different methodological approaches to obtaining data with which to measure peer indicators. Next, we define a set of indicators according to three dimensions of the peer context. We then discuss the structure of peer relationships, detailing how indicators can be constructed at different levels of peer structure. We end with our recommendations for the development of peer indicators and research on peers in the future.

WHY AND HOW ARE PEERS IMPORTANT?

The peer group is a key arena in which adolescence development occurs (Bronfenbrenner, 1979; Brown, 1990; Furman, Brown, & Feiring, 1999). Although peers groups exist well before adolescence, changes to the character of peer groups in adolescence make them a more prominent context for development. Brown (1990) highlighted three key changes. First, youth spend more time with friends in adolescence than they do with parents; nearly one third of their waking hours is spent with friends (Larson & Bradney, 1988). Adolescent peer groups also function under less adult supervision than do groups in childhood. Friendships are less likely to be neighborhood based, granting youth more freedom to engage in activities outside the view of adults. Finally, the peer group comes to include more cross-sex friendships. Although peer groups are mostly single sex well into adolescence, the degree of gender segregation that defines childhood friendships becomes less pronounced in this phase of the life course (Brown, 1990; Thorne & Luria, 1986). Together, these structural changes help to set the parameters for the kinds of experiences in which a young person can engage and, therefore, affect developmental processes.

It is important to clarify what we mean by the terms *peers* and *peer group*, because they are often used rather loosely in the research literature. A very broad concept of peers is the set of similar-aged individuals who share some social context (e.g., birth cohort, school, classroom). However, a peer group is an interaction-based entity, comprising a limited number of adolescents identified as a group because they "hang around" together and develop close relationships. These close relationships are *friendships*. *Friends* are individuals who are attracted to each other, with equality governing the social exchanges between the individuals involved (Hartup & Stevens, 1997). Friendships with those considered *best* friends are marked by greater intensity, with these friendships based on higher levels of emotional support, loyalty, trust, intimacy, and fun compared with other ties. Not everyone has friendships, but these relationships are sought after and valued, especially during the adolescent stage of the life course.

Developmental research views friendships as crucial to socialization. Peer socialization occurs as peers serve as credible sources of information, role models of new social behaviors, sources of social reinforcement, and bridges to alternative lifestyles.

The development of one's romantic identity is an example of how peer socialize one another (Brown, 1999). Adolescents are expected to understand themselves as sexual actors and learn the rules of heterosexual behavior (Eder, 1985; Simon, Eder, & Evans, 1992). Youth learn these behaviors through *sexual scripts*, the rules that define who does what in a romantic context, with whom, when, how, and what it means (Thorne & Luria, 1986). Although parents and the media play an important role in teaching youth these scripts, friends play a key role in facilitating this process by assisting each by setting standards about dating, guiding and judging potential mates, sanctioning behaviors viewed as inappropriate, and accepting dating partners into the group.

Friendships also serve as a source of social capital from which youth can draw throughout adolescence. According to James Coleman (1988), *social capital* refers to the resources inherent in relationships between and among individuals, resources that are created and maintained by commitment and trust. Social capital exists not only in the presence or absence of ties but also in the values and behaviors that each individual brings to the relationship.

Much of the research spurred by Coleman's (1988) thesis has considered the family (e.g., McLanahan & Sandefur, 1994; Parcel & Dufur, 2001; Teachman, Paasch, & Carver, 1996) and, to a lesser extent, the school community (e.g., Coleman, Kilgore, & Hoffer, 1982; Parcel & Dufur, 2001; Sampson, Morenoff, & Earls, 1999), as primary sources of social capital affecting youth adjustment. Another set of relations that might matter to youth is relationships with friends. Although most friendships are not as long lasting as relations with family members, these associations are based on trust and commitment and do channel of information to youth and serve as a source of emotional support (McLanahan & Sandefur, 1994). They are also a space where youth come to develop day-to-day attitudes and habits that affect their academic and career aspirations. The extent to which youth develop these attitudes and behaviors might be linked to social capital of friends.

Mechanisms of Peer Influence

Scholars have identified four theoretical types of peer influence: (a) peer pressure, (b) modeling, (c) norm setting, and (d) providing opportunities (see Brown & Theobald, 1999, for a review). The most commonly discussed form of influence is *peer pressure*; this type of influence is manifest through direct or explicit statements that urge a youth to behave in a certain way. A second type of influence is *peer modeling*, which occurs when an individual's behavior or attitude serves as a model or example on which a friend bases his or her own behavior or attitude. Unlike peer pressure, where the influence is direct, this form of influence is more subtle (Billy & Udry, 1985).

Third, peer groups set and enforce group norms that have a bearing on members' attitudes and behavior. A group's normative climate is defined by the enforced norms that mark the boundaries of acceptable behaviors for its members (Billy, Rodgers, & Udry, 1984). Youth may be embedded in a group where members are expected to make the honor roll each semester or be part of a crowd where members are expected to get drunk on weekends. Moreover, the setting and enforcing of group norms is an ongoing process within friendship groups. Regardless of the nature of the norms, an adolescent will likely follow them in an effort to confirm group membership and avoid reprisals and remonstrations from other members.

A final way the friendship group may matter to its members is by structuring opportunities to participate in behaviors and express attitudes. These opportunities result as members behave in accordance with group norms. For example, a girl embedded in a friendship group that encourages dating and sexual activity is more likely to find herself in situations with the opportunity to engage in sexual intercourse, such as an unsupervised party, and this opportunity may lead to sexual activity. Similarly, a boy involved in a crowd that praises high academic achievement may be more likely to participate in academic clubs that increase his opportunity to come into contact with teachers (Brown & Theobald, 1999; Crosnoe, Cavanagh, & Elder, 2003).

Selection

Although most of us believe in the power of "peer influence" in adolescence, measuring and estimating this influence has been problematic. A cursory look at the attitudes and behaviors of a typical American peer group suggests that social influence goes a long way in explaining why kids in the same circle of friends often talk alike, dress alike, and share similar aspirations and behaviors. However, this similarity does not result from influence alone; it also results from social structural forces that bring like people together and the selection that occurs within those contexts.

The social organization of the school, which sorts youth into classes of same-aged peers, makes it likely that adolescent friendships will develop among individuals who meet in school, in general, and in the classroom, in particular. It is important to note that the social composition of a school reflects the community in which it is embedded. Where kids go to school and with whom they interact is not a random process: Parents choose where their family will live and which schools their children will attend, thus, parents' play a role in the selecting their children's peers. In addition, similar parents make similar decisions about where to send their kids and, because kids are similar to their parents, youth in the same school and neighborhood are often similar to each other at the start (Bearman & Bruckner, 1999). For example, individuals are more likely to initiate friendships with those who match them on sociodemographic characteristics such as race, social class, gender, and age (Hallinan & Tuma, 1978; Joyner & Kao, 2000; Kandel, 1978). These processes intersect because residence and schooling in the United States are related to socioeconomic class and race (Zhou, 1997). Thus, the way communities and schools are structured in the United States maximizes the opportunities for youth to interact with similar peers at the same time that it minimizes the likelihood that youth interact with dissimilar peers.

Within these contexts, selection continues to operate as individuals tend to choose friends on the basis of similar interests, special abilities and personality traits. Often referred to as the *reflection problem*, similarity in peers and peer outcomes simply represent these selective choices of people who are most alike along multiple dimensions (Manski, 1993). As a result, it remains a major challenge for social scientists to disentangle the *influence* of peers from the *selection* of peers. Research that attempts to untangle the effect of selection from influence has found that both processes contribute to the similarity of developmental outcomes in peer groups and work together in maintaining friendships (e.g., Kandel, 1978, 1996; Matsueda & Anderson, 1998).

Moreover, peer influence is inherently reciprocal, further complicating its estimation. Often referred to as the *simultaneity problem*, adolescents influence their friends at exactly the same time that their friends influence them. Peer relations are founded on the principles of equality and reciprocity rather than on the power differentials that characterize adult–adolescent relationships (Youniss, 1980). To date, it remains a methodological challenge to separate out influence from selection effects or to capture reciprocal patterns of influence (Manski, 1993).

INDICATORS OF THE PEER ENVIRONMENT

There are two general ways to obtain data about friends and peer groups with which to create indicators of the peer environment: (a) ask individuals about their friends or (b) collect data directly from the friends of individuals. The large majority of social science research on peer effects uses the former method. These data typically are obtained using a survey method in which respondents are asked to report on their friends' attitudes, aspirations, expectations, or behaviors. For example, in the Monitoring the Future Survey, respondents are asked to indicate the level of disapproval they would receive from their peers for taking one to two drinks nearly every day, smoking marijuana even occasionally (as opposed to trying it once), taking cocaine even occasionally (as opposed to trying it once), and smoking one or more packs of cigarettes per day (U.S. Department of Health and Human Services, 1999). This same instrument asks respondents the level of importance that getting good grades has to their peers as an indicator of peer approval. This approach relies on the accuracy of the respondents' perceptions of friends' attitudes and values.

A similar approach is used to assess youth's perception of friends' behavior. A common topic in the peer literature is peer influence on adolescent sexual behavior (Billy & Udry, 1985; Cavanagh, 2003; Hayes, 1987; Rodgers, 1996), focusing on whether adolescents are more likely to exhibit sexual behavior if their friends are also sexually active. This line of inquiry typically relies on survey questions that ask a respondent whether his or her friends are sexually active. In the National Survey of Children, negative peer influence reflected by behavioral norms of the peer group was assessed by the question "When you were 16, how many of your friends (1) had become parents; (2) were supported by welfare; or (3) had dropped out of school?" (see http://www.socio.com/afdacat.htm for more information about the National Survey of Children). This measure contains less measurement error because many of these events are discrete and observable, but it still relies on the adolescents' accounting or second-hand knowledge of friends' behavior.

These measures of peer attitudes or behavior are therefore based on the respondent's perception of the group norms, and although norms and the opportunities that arise from compliance to them are considered important to group members' behaviors and attitudes, relying on the respondent's perception introduces the possibility that his or her perception has no relationship to actual norms. Research has indicated that individuals' behavior and attitudes more closely mirror what they think their friends do and believe rather than what is really going on (Hayes, 1987). Also, an individual might overestimate the friend effect by attributing to friends a set of behaviors or attitudes in which only he or she engages. By indicating that friends do it as well, the respondent can rationalize his or her behaviors or attitudes (Billy & Udry, 1984). In addition, one reason why individuals choose one another as friends is because they share similar values, and although this reflection of oneself is inherent in all peer measures, measures based on perceptions of peer attitudes and behavior may overstate this reflection to the extent that perceptions of similarity are exaggerated.

Finally, most survey instruments that ask about the attitudes or behavior of friends do not preface such questions by first asking respondents whether they have friends. Thus, respondents who do not have friends (a fundamental indicator of the peer context in its own right) may indicate no peer influence (e.g., no friends are sexually active),1 and their response will be confounded with the responses of adolescents who have friends who are not sexually active. In sum, there are considerable problems with the reliability and validity of peer indicators using this first approach of asking respondents their perceptions of peer norms. A second approach, obtaining data directly from respondents' friends, requires a specific study design; namely, respondents' friends need be part of the study sample. School-based designs in which all members of a school are interviewed, or snowball samples, where respondents provide names of friends who are then interviewed, are examples of designs that allow one to use friends' reports of their own behavior to construct measures of the peer group.

A handful of studies have used school-based designs to assess the nature of peer friendships. For example, the Biosocial Factors in Adolescent Behavior project, a study of biological and social factors affecting adolescent sexuality, attempted to interview all students in two junior high schools: one in North Carolina and the other in Florida (Billy & Udry, 1985). Students were asked to nominate their three best male and female friends; most of these friends also attended this school and were interviewed as well. That both the adolescent and his or her friends were interviewed allowed researchers to construct more accurate measures of youth friendships.

A more recent example of this method is found in the National Longitudinal Study of Adolescent Health (Add Health). Unlike the Biosocial Factors in Adolescent Behavior project, a study limited to two schools in two communities, Add Health is nationally representative of American school-going adolescents in Grades 7 through 12. This study was designed to assess the health status and explore the causes of health-related behaviors of adolescents, paying special attention to the multiple contexts in which adolescents are embedded (Harns et al., 2003). One context considered is the peer group. The initial wave of Add Health data collection-the in-school questionnaire-attempted to interview all youth in each sampled school. From this saturated pool, friends' reports of their own attitudes and behavior can be used to construct aggregate measures reflecting the norms and behaviors of peer groups.

Between September 1994 and April 1995, students in each sampled school[1] completed the in-school questionnaire. This instrument provides measures of social and demographic characteristics of respondents, reports of parents' education and occupation status, household structure, risk behaviors, self-esteem, grade point average (GPA), school-year extracurricular activities, and health status. In addition, each youth was asked to nominate up to five of his or her closest female and male friends, beginning with a best friend and then next best friend and so on (for a maximum of 10 students). Students were given a roster on which all schoolmates' identification numbers (defined by Add Health) were listed. Students then transferred friends' identification numbers onto their questionnaires. Those who had close friends who did not attend their school entered a generic code. A total of 90,118 questionnaires were completed.

Given that the in-school sample was a saturated sample, with nearly all kids in the school interviewed, the identification numbers of nominated friends can be linked back to their own in-school questionnaire. Once a link is made, each friend's self-reports of school achievement, sexual behavior, or violence, for example, as well as demographic characteristics, are identified and indexed across the group, resulting in peer group level indicators.

This method represents a significant improvement in the way we capture youth friendships. By using friends' own reports of attitudes, life circumstances, and behavior, we are better measuring the social context of friendships. Although this approach does not avoid measuring friendship selection as well as peer influence, it greatly reduces measurement error associated with perceptions of peer group norms and behaviors. In the following section, we propose what we consider to be the most important indicators of the peer environment, and we use data from Add Health to illustrate their construction.

DIMENSIONS OF PEER INDICATORS

To understand how peer indicators relate to developmental outcomes for youth, three dimensions of peer context are required: (a) presence of friendships, (b) the composition of friendships, and (c) the quality of friendships. At the most basic level is the presence or number of friendships. Having friends suggests that an adolescent is other oriented, has egalitarian attitudes toward emotional exchange, and can manage conflict. Research also suggest that having friends increases one's social skills and well-being (Hartup & Stevens, 1997).

Add Health provides data with which to construct fundamental indicators of whether one has any friends and the number of friends. In addition, Add Health allows us to determine whether youth have any school-based friends and whether they have a "best" friend. The nationally representative (i.e., weighted) estimates indicate that 10% of youth report no friends. An additional 4% report that they have no school-based friends but do have at least one friend outside of school. Just under three quarters of youth (72%) report having a best friend, suggesting that some youth have friends but do not consider these friendships as a best friend. In terms of number, the size of an average peer group is 6.9 friends, ranging from 0 to 10.

The likelihood that an adolescent reports having friends differs by gender. For example, boys are twice as likely to be friendless than are girls, with 14% of boys reporting no friends compared with 7% of girls. Girls are also more likely to report having a best friend, a finding consistent with the literature that highlights the more intimate nature of girls' friendships compared with boys (Maccoby, 1998). Finally, girls report more friends than do boys.

The presence of friends, however, tells us nothing about the salience of those friendships for developmental outcomes. Friendships can have both positive and negative influences on youth, and thus a second dimension of the peer group must consider who these friends are. Friends and peer groups can be characterized in several ways: according to attitudes, behaviors, and demographic characteristics.

The saturated nature of the Add Health in-school sample allows investigators to identify respondents' nominated friends; pull friends' own reports of achievement, attitudes, and behaviors from their in-school survey; and link friends' responses, representing the peer context, with each respondent. These reports are then indexed across the peer group and measures are constructed to represent the normative climate of the friendship group. As mentioned earlier, youth report on GPA, self-esteem, and engagement in extracurricular activities as well as prosocial and problem behaviors.

In Table 9.1 we present some illustrative indicators that characterize the peer group. The first set of indicators show the peer group level measures of GPA, school attachment, and problem behaviors separately for girls and boys. The average GPA of the friendship group is based on the youth reports of grades in the current school year. We capture the degree of school attachment within the peer group by indexing how close youth felt to people at school, how much they felt a part of their school, and whether they were happy to be at their school in the past year. Responses, ranging from 1 to 5, were reverse coded so that higher values

Table 9.1

Indicators of the Social and Behavioral Context of Girls' and Boys'
Peer Groups, Add Health 1994-95

Peer Indicator	Girls	Boys
Mean GPA in friendship group	2.67	2.62
Mean school attachment	3.45	3.41
Mean problem behaviors	0.90	0.97
Proportion friends who are same-gender	0.64	0.64
Proportion of friends who are other-gender	0.36	0.36
Proportion of friends who are older	0.25	0.21
Proportion of friends who are same-aged or younger	0.75	0.79
Proportion friends who are white	0.61	0.64
Proportion of friends who are Black	0.15	0.11
Proportion of friends who are Hispanic	0.11	0.10
Proportion of friends who are Asian	0.03	0.03
Proportion of friends of other or missing	0.10	0.12

Note. Data based on the sample of in-school friends who also completed an in-school survey.

indicate higher levels of attachment. Responses to these items are averaged among those who had valid responses on at least two of the items. The last index measures participation in problem behaviors that make up certain elements of youth culture. These behaviors include drinking, getting drunk, skipping school, getting into fights, having trouble with teachers, having trouble with other students, and doing dangerous things because someone dared you in the past year. The index ranges from 0 to 4.8, with an average of 0.85. Peer group level indicators are calculated by simply averaging the friends' GPAs or indexes; those who did not have valid responses were coded at 0. Because these indicators come from friends' in-school questionnaires, the sample is necessarily restricted to youth whose friends also completed the in-school questionnaire.

Overall, the average GPA for peer groups is 2.64, a value that does not vary significantly for boys and girls. The average level of school attachment among the peer group is 3.43, with girls' peer groups reporting somewhat higher levels of attachment than do boys. The problem behavior index also varies little by gender but is slightly higher for boys than girls, suggesting that these behaviors are gendered.

Another important characterization of the peer context is its social composition. Structural factors, ranging from the ethnic composition of a town to the age-graded nature of U.S. classrooms, affect the demographic composition of peer groups well before an individual youth selects a friend. Consequently, peer groups tend to be highly segregated by age and race. Similarly, gender segregation continues to mark friendships in adolescence, with youth embedded in peer groups that are mostly single sexed.

However, friendship groups that are more heterogeneous in terms of gender and age might have important developmental consequences for youth, because dissimilar youth bring different values, information, attitudes, and behaviors to the group. For instance, the norms surrounding romantic relationships, drinking, and part-time employment are age-graded in that they are prohibited for younger adolescents but are somewhat more acceptable for older youth. Thus, the norms and opportunities structures for an adolescent embedded in a friendship group that includes both older and younger peers might be different than those in a same-aged friendship group. Similarly, the norms governing behaviors described earlier tend to be different for boys and girls, with boys less sanctioned for engaging in sexual relationships or drinking than are girls. Therefore, the age and gender compositions of the peer group are important indicators of the peer context.

These indicators are shown in the second set of measures in Table 9.1. The gender composition of peer groups is similar for boys and girls, with the majority of close friends the same sex as the respondent. We see that one fifth to one quarter of friends in a peer group are older, with girls tending to have more older friends than boys. The balance of friends includes both same-aged and younger friends.

The racial and ethnic composition of the peer group is another important contextual feature. Again, we expect that peer groups that are more heterogeneous in terms of race and ethnicity might expose youth to different cultural norms and attitudes, more diverse models of behavior, and more varied opportunities, which in turn may influence developmental outcomes. These indicators are shown in the last set of measures in Table 9.1 and reveal that the racial composition of peer groups reflects the overall racial and ethnic composition of adolescents in the United States. The substantive significance of the racial and ethnic composition of the peer group lies in its relation to the individual's race and ethnicity, which we explore in the next section.

We now add a layer of complexity, as most researchers will want to do, to understand the significance of these peer indicators by examining how they vary by the gender and race and ethnicity of youth. These data are shown in Table 9.2. The differences we observe in the peer context across groups suggest possible peer mechanisms that may mediate the effects of race and ethnicity with respect to developmental outcomes. Because of limited space, we highlight only some of the more interesting differences in Table 9.2. First, we see that Asian youth are embedded in a peer context marked by a higher than average GPA and school attachment and lower than average engagement in problem behavior. Taken together, these factors likely play a role in the overall academic success of Asian youth. Conversely, the peer groups of Hispanic youth have lower than average GPAs and school attachment reports and higher than average participation in problem behavior. The peer groups of non-Hispanic White and Black youth fall in the middle of these two groups, with the peer groups of Whites more closely resembling Asians and the peer groups of African Americans more closely resembling Hispanic youth. Gender differences within race mirror differences for all youth.

The salience of racial homophily in peer groups is evident once the sample is broken down by race. Across the board, most adolescents are embedded in a friendship group composed of coethnics, with non-Hispanic White and Black youth in the most homogeneous peer groups. For both Hispanic and Asian American youth, coethnics remain the modal ethnicity group, but non-Hispanic Whites make up about 30% of both groups. Minor gender differences exists by race in the racial composition of peer groups, with girls in more homogeneous groups than boys.

We show the immigrant composition of peer groups as an especially interesting and illuminating characteristic around which youth select friends. Although less salient for a non-Hispanic White and Black youth, the average Asian and Hispanic adolescent is embedded in a peer group where about one half of friends are first- or second-generation immigrants to the United States. Given what we are learning about differential health and health behavior outcomes among immigrant youth (e.g., J. R. Harris, 1999), this feature of the peer group may have increasing significance for the outcomes of native ethnic youth in America

Table 9.2
Indicators of the Peer Context by Gender and Race and Ethnicity, Add Health 1994–95

Race and indicator	Girls	Boys
Non-Hispanic White		
Number of in-school friends	5.75	5.45
Mean GPA in friendship group	2.91	2.89
Mean school attachment	3.74	3.74
Mean problem behaviors	0.95	1.03
Proportion friends who are same-gender	0.64	0.63
Proportion of friends who are other-gender	0.36	0.37
Proportion of friends who are older	0.24	0.21
Proportion friends who are white	0.85	0.86
Proportion of friends who are Black	0.03	0.02
Proportion of friends who are Hispanic	0.06	0.05
Proportion of friends who are Asian	0.01	0.01
Proportion of friends who are 1st generation	0.02	0.02
Proportion of friends who are 2nd generation	0.05	0.05
Non-Hispanic Black		
Number of in-school friends	4.96	4.99
Mean GPA in friendship group	2.58	2.49
Mean school attachment	3.45	3.46
Mean problem behaviors	0.98	1.09
Proportion friends who are same-gender	0.64	0.63
Proportion of friends who are other-gender	0.36	0.37
Proportion of friends who are older	0.28	0.23
Proportion friends who are white	0.09	0.12
Proportion of friends who are Black	0.77	0.71
Proportion of friends who are Hispanic	0.09	0.11
Proportion of friends who are Asian	0.005	0.01
Proportion of friends who are 1st generation	0.03	0.03
Proportion of friends who are 2nd generation	0.05	0.03
Asian		
Number of in-school friends	4.98	5.03
Mean GPA in friendship group	3.10	3.00
Mean school attachment	3.66	3.63
Mean problem behaviors	0.83	0.96

Race and indicator	Girls	Boys
Proportion friends who are same-gender	0.65	0.64
Proportion of friends who are other-gender	0.35	0.36
Proportion of friends who are older	0.25	0.20
Proportion friends who are white	0.29	0.33
Proportion of friends who are Black	0.06	0.06
Proportion of friends who are Hispanic	0.14	0.15
Proportion of friends who are Asian	0.42	0.38
Proportion of friends who are 1st generation	0.26	0.23
Proportion of friends who are 2nd generation	0.24	0.26
Hispanic		
Number of in-school friends	4.60	4.73
Mean GPA in friendship group	2.61	2.61
Mean school attachment	3.46	3.47
Mean problem behaviors	1.01	1.11
Proportion friends who are same-gender	0.64	0.63
Proportion of friends who are other-gender	0.36	0.37
Proportion of friends who are older	0.26	0.23
Proportion friends who are white	0.28	0.33
Proportion of friends who are Black	0.07	0.08
Proportion of friends who are Hispanic	0.56	0.51
Proportion of friends who are Asian	0.04	0.05
Proportion of friends who are 1st generation	0.22	0.19
Proportion of friends who are 2nd generation	0.26	0.24

Note. Data based on the sample of in-school friends who also completed an in-school survey.

and might serve as a mechanism explaining the positive health behaviors reported by immigrant youth.

Finally, to assess the degree to which friends influence one another, the quality or intensity of friendships should be considered as a third dimension of the peer context. For a given youth, her level of intimacy, closeness, and reciprocity with friends in her peer group is not likely equivalent. Consequently, the impact these friends have on her behavior, attitudes, and values will also vary in important ways. Thus, to get at a more nuanced understanding of the mechanisms by which friends come to matter, we need to consider the quality of these relationships.

Add Health lends itself to addressing such questions. In the in-school questionnaire, youth were asked to describe their level of involvement with nominated peers. After naming each friend, youth reported the following five activities: (a) whether they went to this friend's house, (b) met this friend after school to hang out or go somewhere, (c) spent time with this friend last weekend, (d) talked with this friend about a problem, and (e) talked with this friend on the phone. All interactions are based on the "past seven days" except for (c), which asks about last weekend. Understanding how the quality and intensity of friendships are related to variation in developmental outcomes has not received as much research attention, at least not with representative samples of youth. Although unique study designs are required, and the data demands fairly high, more refined measures of peer context beyond the crude indicators of the presence of friends are needed to explore the dynamics of peer relations and its significance in adolescence.

STRUCTURE OF PEER RELATIONSHIPS

The indicators that we described in the previous section primarily relate to individual friends or peer groups, because these are the peer contexts in which relations are most intimate and influence is thought to be the strongest. However, peer indicators can be measured at several levels of association. In general, peer relations can occur at four different levels: (a) a dyad (two persons), (b) a small group or *clique*, (c) a crowd, and (d) the adolescent cohort or youth culture as a whole (Brown, 1999). Figure 9.1 depicts these levels of peer interaction.

The dyadic relationship includes individual friendships and romantic and sexual relationships. Researchers often focus on relationships at this

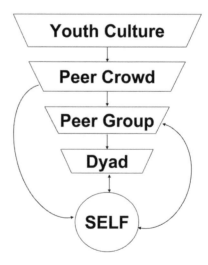

Figure 9.1. Levels of peer interaction.

level because they expect adolescents to be highly invested in them and more susceptible to peer influence. Adolescents typically spend a lot of time with their best friends and exchange feelings and ideas about the world in which they live. A second level of peer interaction involves small groups of friends, or cliques. The peer group is regarded as the locus of teenagers' social interaction and a major source of peer influence. Friendship groups can vary in size, intimacy, and openness to outsiders, but they typically remain small enough to allow for regular interaction of all members and serve as the primary base of interaction with groups of age mates. Most research on peers has focused on best friends and the peer group.

A third level of peer interaction occurs in the peer crowd, which first emerges in this stage of the life course. Crowds are reputation-based groups that are associated with some image or identity that adolescents have established among peers. They may be based on location (e.g., neighborhood, gangs), ethnicity (e.g., Asians, Mexicans), social status (e.g., populars, geeks) or individual abilities and interests (e.g., jocks, brains, nerds, druggies). Whereas peer group norms develop from within the group, crowd norms are imposed from outside the group and reflect the stereotypic image that peers have of crowd members. Because crowd labels theoretically group together individuals with similar characteristics, peer group members often share the same crowd affiliation. Social scientists rarely have sufficient data to measure this larger peer context.

A fourth level of peer interaction is the general youth culture, either in a specific institutional context, such as a school or religion, or the overall age cohort or generation (e.g., Baby Boomers, Generation X). Influence from this rather amorphous peer group is thought to occur largely through mass media mechanisms in advertising, popular music, and contemporary slogans or symbols.

An excellent example of peer indicators measured at multiple levels of peer relations is contained in a study by Bearman and Bruckner (1999), who used Add Health data to analyze peer effects on adolescent sexual debut and pregnancy. They characterized peers according to their school orientation and performance and problem behavior (e.g., use of alcohol, fighting, getting in trouble in school) and constructed these peer measures at five levels of peer relations: (a) best friends, (b) the peer group of close friends, (c) the clique represented by friends of friends, (d) the leading crowd represented by the most popular adolescents in the school, and (e) the school as a whole. They therefore further refined the second level of peer relations of the peer group into the network of close friends, and a larger network of teenagers who are connected to each other by having mutual friends (which they call the *clique*). This highly textured design permitted them to examine the level at which peer relations and interaction peer influence on sexual behavior is most salient. They found that the level social scientists on which have spent the most time—best friends—is the least important. The circle of close friends and the larger peer group of friends of friends in which adolescents are embedded are far more influential. Having data to create indicators at multiple levels of peer contexts will extend the frontiers of our knowledge about the developmental significance of the peer environment, with important implications for peer intervention programs.

FUTURE RESEARCH ON INDICATORS
OF THE PEER ENVIRONMENT

Social scientists have long thought that the peer environment is a crucial development context that becomes increasingly important in adolescence as young people explore adult roles and behaviors, try on new identities, and learn to negotiate and forge close intimate bonds with same-aged peers. This comes about as relationships with parents are redefined, with friends filling the "gap" as young people attempt to reduce dependence on parents (Erickson, 1968). Indeed, a theme in the peer literature is the waning influence of parents during adolescence and the increasing influence of peers who socialize youth according to peer norms, attitudes, and values and who shape adolescents' behaviors (J. R. Harris, 1998).

Despite this long-standing scholarly interest, the lack of appropriate data, measures, and methods has constrained our understanding of the role of the peer context in youth development and the interrelationships between the peer environment and other contexts in which adolescents are embedded, such as institutions, neighborhoods, communities, and the family. Most research on peers has relied on survey data in which a respondent reports his or her perceptions of friends' attitudes, values, and behavior. Such questions are not conditioned by whether the individual has friends, a fundamental and developmentally significant indicator of adolescent well-being. Even the term *friends* is ambiguous, left up to the respondents to formulate their own specific concept of "friends" in referencing their perception of behavior or attitudes. Finally, the issue of confounding selection with influence in research on peer influence is virtually ignored in the literature. Most research acknowledges this confounding, but usually proceeds to talk about "influence" and "effects" of peers despite the fact that causal interpretation is inappropriate.

Study designs that directly obtain data from individuals' friends have improved the quality of peer indicators. Because of the difficulty of fielding such a study design, most of these studies are based on local samples or on nonrandom, nonrepresentative samples. The Add Health study, which obtains peer data based on friends' own reports and is a nationally representative sample, is an exception.

To understand the developmental significance of the peer environment requires peer indicators from three dimensions: (a) the presence of friendships, (b) the social and behavioral composition of peer groups, and (c) the quality of these ties within them. Add Health provides the data with which to construct indicators of these three dimensions and permits the researcher to then explore the different levels of understanding obtained from each dimension in relation to developmental outcomes. We recommend that research on peers rely on data obtained directly from friends rather than on individuals' perceptions about friends to measure these three dimensions of indicators. If only perceptions data are available, we recommend using only indicators of the first dimension-those that measure the presence or number of friends. Indicators of the social and behavioral characteristics of peers and the quality of friendships are subject to substantial measurement error and confound the reflection problem with perceptions data on friends.

Last, a richer understanding of where the strongest associations lie between the peer environment and developmental outcomes can be achieved if indicators can be constructed at different levels of peer interactions. It is clear that the mechanisms of norm setting, modeling, providing opportunities, and peer pressure operate differently in the close and intimate dyad of best friends than in the more indirect interactions among peers in a clique.

Finally, we expect that a more nuanced view of peer groups, one that considers these three dimensions, will highlight how peer groups magnify the differential opportunities and constraints of young people in the United States. Such analysis might also point to the peer group as a source of social capital in its own right, because the characteristics of friends affect the day-to-day attitudes and habits of youth, which in turn might affect their own developmental trajectories. The nature of peer groups for Asian and Hispanic American youth described earlier illustrates this point. In both cases, the behaviors of peer group members mirror those of the target youth, and this similarity goes a long way in explaining why these friendships exist. However, these friendships and the values, attitudes, and behaviors youth bring to their friendship groups might also enhance or constrain the academic or behavioral disposition of youth. Viewed from this perspective, peers can both positively and negatively affect youth development. Future research should focus more on the positive associations between the peer environment and youth development.

In addition to these recommendations about indicators, we want to emphasize that research on "peer influence" can speak only to associations between the peer context and developmental outcomes. At present, our methods do not enable us to make causal statements about how peers influence individuals, only about similarities among peers and associations between the nature of the peer environment and developmental outcomes.

ACKNOWLEDGMENTS

We gratefully acknowledge support from the National Institute of Child Health and Human Development through the Family and Child Well-being Research Network, Grant U01 HD37558. This research uses data from Add Health, a program project designed by J. Richard Udry, Peter S. Bearman, and Kathleen Mullan Harris, and funded by grant P01-HD31921 from the National Institute of Child Health and Human Development, with co-operative funding from 17 other agencies. Special acknowledgment is due Ronald R. Rindfuss and Barbara Entwisle for assistance in the original design. Persons interested in obtaining data files from Add Health should contact Add Health, Carolina Population Center, 123 W. Franklin Street, Chapel Hill, NC 27516-2524 (www.cpc.unc.edu/addhealth/contract.html).

NOTES

1. Most schools that agreed to participate in the study permitted the adminis-tration of the in-school survey. However, about one quarter of students in the in-home sample attended schools that did not allow the in-school survey to be given. This, combined with slippage due to student absence, resulted in 27% of the full Add Health sample without friendship group data.

REFERENCES

Bearman, P., & Bruckner, H. (1999). Peer effects on adolescent sexual debut and pregnancy: An analysis of a national survey of adolescent girls. In *Peer poten-tial: Making the most out of how teens influence each other* (pp. 7–26). Washing-ton, DC: National Campaign to Prevent Teen Pregnancy.

Berndt, T. (1996). Transition in friendship and friends' influence. In J. A. Graber, J. Brooks-Gunn, & A. C. Petersen (Eds.), *Transitions through adolescence: Interper-sonal domains and context* (pp. 57–84). Mahwah, NJ: Lawrence Erlbaum Asso-ciates.

Billy, J. O. G., Rodgers, J., & Udry, J. R. (1984). Adolescent sexual behavior and friendship choice. *Social Forces, 62,* 653–678.

Billy, J. O. G, & Udry, J. R. (1985). The influence of male and female best friends on adolescent and sexual behavior. *Adolescence, 20,* 21–31.

Bronfenbrenner, U. (1979). *The ecology of human development.* Cambridge, MA: Harvard University Press.

Brown, B. B. (1990). Peer groups and peer cultures. In S. S. Feldman & G. R. Elliot (Eds.), *At the threshold: The developing adolescent* (pp. 16–53). Cambridge, MA: Harvard University Press.

Brown, B. B. (1999). You're going out with who?: Peer group influences on ado-lescent romantic relationships. In W. Furman, B. B. Brown, & C. Feiring (Eds.), *The development of romantic relationships in adolescence* (pp. 291–329). Cambridge, MA: Harvard University Press.

Brown, B. B., & Theobald, W. (1999). How peers matter: A research synthesis of peer influences on adolescent pregnancy. In *Peer potential: Making the most out of how teens influence each other* (pp. 27–80). Washington, DC: National Campaign to Prevent Teen Pregnancy.

Cavanagh, S. E. (2003). *The sexual debut of girls in early adolescence: The intersec-tion of pubertal timing and friendship group dynamics.* Unpublished manu-script, University of North Carolina at Chapel Hill.

Coleman, J. C. (1980). *Friendship and the peer group in adolescence. In Adelson (Ed.), Handbook of adolescent psychology* (pp. 408–431). New York: Wiley.

Coleman, J. (1988). Social capital and the creation of human capital. *American Journal of Sociology, 94,* 596–319.

Coleman, J. S., Kilgore, S. B., & Hoffer, T. (1982). Public and private schools. *Society, 19,* 4–9.

Crosnoe, R. (2000). Friendships in childhood and adolescence: The life course and new directions. *Social Psychology Quarterly, 63,* 377–391.

Crosnoe, R., Cavanagh, S. E., & Elder, G. H., Jr. (2003). Adolescent friendships as academic resources: The intersection of social relationships, social structure, and institutional context. *Sociological Perspectives, 46,* 331–352.

Eder, D. (1985). The cycle of popularity: Interpersonal relations among female adolescents. *Sociology of Education, 58,* 154–165.

Erickson, E. (1968). *Identity: Youth and crisis.* New York: Norton.

Feld, S. (1981). The focused organization of social ties. *American Journal of Sociology, 86,* 1015–1035.

Fletcher, A. C., Darling, N. E., Steinberg, L., & Dornbusch, S. C. (1995). The company they keep: Relation of adolescents' adjustment and behavior to their friends' perceptions of authoritative parenting in the social network. *Developmental Psychology, 61,* 599–610.

Furman, W., Brown, B. B., & Feiring, C. (1999). *The development of romantic relationships in adolescence.* Cambridge, MA: Harvard University Press.

Hallinan, M. T., & Tuma, N. B. (1978). Classroom effects on change in children's friendships. *Sociology of Education, 51,* 270–282.

Harris, K. M. (1999). The health status and risk behavior of adolescents in immigrant families. In D. J. Hernandez (Ed.), *Children of immigrants: Health, adjustment, and public assistance* (pp. 286–347). Washington, DC: National Academy Press.

Harris, K. M., Florey, F., Tabor, J., Bearman, P. S., Jones, J., & Udry, J. R. (2003). *The National Longitudinal Study of Adolescent Health: Research Design.* The Carolina Population Center, University of North Carolina at Chapel Hill. Retrieved March 19, 2007 from http://www.cpc.unc.edu/projects/ addhealth/design

Harris, J. R. (1998). *The nurture assumption: Why children turn out the way they do.* New York: Free Press.

Hartup, W. W., & Stevens, N. (1997). Friendships and adaptation in the life course. *Psychological Bulletin, 121,* 355–357.

Hayes, C. D. (Ed.). (1987). *Risking the future: Adolescent sexuality, pregnancy, and childbearing* (Vol. 1). Washington, DC: National Academy Press.

Jessor, R., & Jessor, S. (1979). *Problem behavior and psychosocial development: A longitudinal study of youth.* New York: Academic.

Joyner, K., & Kao, G. (2000). School racial composition and adolescent racial homophily. *Social Science Quarterly, 81,* 810–825

Kahn, R. L., & Antonucci, T. (1981). Convoys of social support: A life-course approach. In S. B. Kiesler, J. N. Morgan, & V. K . Oppenheimer (Eds.), *Aging: Social change* (pp. 383–405). New York: Academic.

Kandel, D. B. (1978). Homophily, selection and socialization in adolescent friendship. *American Journal of Sociology, 84,* 427–312.

Kandel, D. B. (1996). The parental and peer contexts of adolescent deviance: An algebra of interpersonal influences. *Journal of Drug Issues, 26,* 289–315.

Larson, R., & Bradney, N. (1988). Precious moments with family members and friends. In R. M. Milardo (Ed.), *Families and social networks* (pp. 107–126). Newbury Park, CA: Sage.

Maccoby, E. E. (1998). *The two sexes: Growing up apart, coming together.* Cambridge, MA: Harvard University Press.

Manski, C. (1993). Identification of endogenous social effects: The reflection problem. *Review of Economic Studies, 60,* 531–542.

Matsueda, R., & Anderson, K. (1998). The dynamics of delinquent peers, and delinquent behavior. *Criminology, 36,* 269–398.

McLanahan, S., & Sandefur, G. (1994). *Growing up with a single parent: What hurts, what helps.* Cambridge, MA: Harvard University Press.

Parcel, T., & Dufur, M. (2001). Capital at home and at school: Effects of child social adjustment. *Journal of Marriage and the Family, 63,* 32–47.

Rodgers, J. L. (1996). Sexual transitions in adolescence. In J. A. Graber, J. Brooks-Gunn, & A. C. Petersen (Eds.), *Transitions through adolescence: Interpersonal domains and context* (pp. 85–110). Mahwah, NJ: Lawrence Erlbaum Associates.

Sampson, R. J., Morenoff, J. D., & Earls, F. (1999). Spatial dynamics of collective efficacy for children. *American Sociological Review, 64,* 633–660.

Simons, R., Eder, D., & Evans, C. (1992). The development of feeling norms underlying romantic love among adolescent females. *Social Psychology Quarterly, 55,* 29–46.

Steinberg, L., Sandford, D. M., & Brown, B. B. (1992). Ethnic differences in adolescent achievement. *American Psychologist, 47,* 723–729.

Teachman, J. D., Paasch, K., & Carver, K. (1996). Social capital and dropping out of school early. *Journal of Marriage and the Family, 58,* 773–783.

Thorne, B., & Luria, Z. (1986). Sexuality and gender in children's daily worlds. *Social Problems, 33,* 176–190.

U.S. Department of Health and Human Services. (2002). *Trends in the well-being of America's children and youth 2001.* Washington, DC: U.S. Government Printing Office.

Youniss, J. (1980). *Parents and peers in social development: A Sullivan-Piaget perspective.* Chicago: University of Chicago Press.

Zhou, M. (1997). Growing up American: The challenge confronting immigrant children and children of immigrants. *Annual Review of Sociology, 23,* 63–95.

Chapter 10

Key Indicators of School Quality

Daniel Mayer
Maynard Public Schools
John Ralph
National Center for Education Statistics

WHY COLLECT INDICATORS ON SCHOOLS?

The current policy debate in education is primarily focused on standards and accountability and not on why some schools facing the same set of standards and accountability measures as other schools will do better in meeting them. As noted in the Action Statement from the 1999 National Education Summit, however, "Raising standards and developing tests may have been the easiest part of the journey; the more daunting task is ensuring that all students reach these standards" ("Action Statement," 1999).

Because some schools do perform better than others, it is important to look at the components that have been found to be linked to student learning and that may influence whether schools are successful in helping their students meet state and local standards. To ensure the existence of quality schools, school quality needs to be defined, assessed, and monitored.

Student learning is, in part, a function of various characteristics of the schools and the process of schooling. Examining the characteristics of schools that are related to learning illuminates some of the reasons why students are or are not learning at optimum levels. In its 1991 report "Education Counts: An Indicator System to Monitor the Nation's Educational Health" (U.S. Department of Education, National Center for Education Statistics [NCES], Special Study Panel on Education Indicators for the NCES, 1991), the NCES panel called for reports that discuss indicators of the health of the U.S. education system. Although it is less common to use indicators to measure the quality of schools than to gauge the health of the economy, there are compelling reasons to do so. For example, inflation, unemployment, growth rates, imports and ex-

279

ports, and wage growth are indicators that are looked at both separately and together to gauge the economy's strength. Unemployment might be low while inflation may be high. Each indicator reveals some important information about the economy, and none alone tells the whole story. Similarly, school quality is simultaneously related to several characteristics of schools. It is a function of the training and talent of the teaching force, what goes on in the classrooms (including the size of the classes, the topics covered in them, and the pedagogical approaches used in them), and the overall culture and atmosphere within a school.

Defining *school quality* is the first step toward measuring and monitoring it. Both social and academic dimensions might be considered. The social dimension includes the attitudes, ambitions, and mental well-being of students, whereas the academic dimension pertains to student learning. Both are important, but this chapter responds to the current national concern about academic quality by focusing solely on the school characteristics that have been shown to improve student learning.

In this chapter, we have three goals: (a) to highlight which characteristics of school research suggests are related to student learning, (b) to identify where national indicator data are currently available and reliable, and (c) to assess the current status of our schools by examining and critiquing these national indicator data.

REFINING THE INDICATORS WE COLLECT

When thinking about what researchers have learned about school quality, it is useful to go back to the debate started by the "Equality of Educational Opportunity" report (Coleman et al., 1966), better known as the *Coleman Report*. This large national study sent shock waves through the education community when it concluded that measurable characteristics of teachers and schools are not significantly related to student achievement. Protracted debate has surrounded these findings, and numerous subsequent studies both support and refute the Coleman finding. The most comprehensive support, and the most widely cited, is Hanushek's (1986) review of the findings from 38 quantitative studies of the determinants of student achievement. These studies assessed the impact of the teacher:pupil ratio, teacher education, teacher experience, teacher salary, expenditures per pupil, administrative inputs, and facilities. Hanushek (1986) concluded that, among these studies, "There appears to be no strong or systematic relationship between school expenditures and student performance" (pp. 1,162).

Many researchers do not accept Hanushek's (1986) conclusions. For example, Hedges, Laine, and Greenwald (1994) claimed that his findings rest on inappropriate statistical methods and poor data. They conducted two separate studies to support their claim. In the first study, they reanalyzed the studies Hanushek (1986) used and found a "positive relationship between dollars spent on education and output" that "is large enough to be of practical importance" (Hedges et al., 1994, p. 5).[1] To address the data quality limitations that they argue exist in Hanushek's (1986) work, Greenwald, Hedges, and Laine (1996) replicated the 1994 analysis using a more refined set of studies. The findings from this study bolster those from their earlier work.

Although Hanushek (1986) and Hedges et al. (1994) came to different conclusions, even Hanushek (1986) agreed that the data show that "teachers and schools differ dramatically in their effectiveness" (pp. 1,159). In more than 30 years of research and study on schooling and the educational process since the Coleman Report, a conclusive understanding of the definitive features of quality schools has yet to be found. However, it is apparent that no single factor guarantees school quality. School quality depends on multiple, interdependent elements. Furthermore, as we discuss in this chapter, research also suggests that one of the main reasons some studies have failed to detect why schools differ in their effectiveness is because they use poor measures of school quality, and/or they entirely exclude certain elements essential to quality. In the following sections, we identify where more precise measures are needed and which phenomena have not been adequately addressed.

Using More Precise Measures

The need for more precise measures is evident when considering teacher qualifications. Numerous studies have examined the relationship between teacher qualifications and student learning, but they usually measure whether teachers are certified, whether they have master's degrees, and how long they have taught. When teacher qualifications are measured in these ways, the evidence that they make a difference in school quality is inconsistent. This may be because these measures lack specificity. For example, knowing whether a teacher is certified or whether a teacher has a master's degree does not reveal whether a teacher is smart and academically able. In addition, with the exception of brand-new teachers, knowing how many years a teacher has taught tells us little about the teacher's skills. On average, researchers have not found a discernible difference between teachers with 5, 10, 15, or 20 years of experience. Recent research suggests that more precise measures of teacher training, experience, and academic skills are stronger predictors of student learning and school quality.

Using New Measures

Different aspects of the schooling process that may also be related to quality have traditionally been understudied in national data collection efforts. Specifically, differences in student performance may well have to do with content coverage and instructional practice (how teachers deliver the content) but, until very recently, data on classroom practices were in short supply, in part because policymakers and researchers emphasized an input-output model when studying schools and because these attributes of the schooling process are harder to measure than traditional input indicators.

Within the classroom, the curriculum is the cornerstone of the academic experience. According to researchers who worked on the Second International Mathematics Study, the curriculum has three levels (McKnight et al., 1987):

1. The *intended* curriculum, which is defined by officials at the state and local levels;
2. The *implemented* curriculum, which is how teachers translate the intended curriculum into practice; and
3. The *attained* curriculum, which is what students learn as represented by their scores on standardized tests.

Inadequate data, however, make it difficult to measure the impact of the implemented curriculum on student learning. Before the mid-1980s, nationally representative studies (e.g., High School and Beyond and the National Assessment of Educational Progress) limited their data collection to elements of the intended curriculum and other inputs, such as per-pupil spending, course titles, and teacher salaries. Then, several reports highlighted the importance of determining what happens in classrooms by studying elements of the implemented curriculum, such as curricular content, instructional strategies, and organization (McKnight et al., 1987; Powell, Farrar, & Cohen, 1985; U.S. Department of Education, National Commission on Excellence in Education, 1983). Therefore, in the late 1980s researchers and policymakers began for the first time to push for the regular collection of data that provide information on the schooling process (Murnane & Raizen, 1988; Shavelson, McDonnell, Oakes, & Carey, 1987; U.S. Department of Education, Office of Educational Research and Improvement, State Accountability Study Group, 1988).

In response, studies have been launched to ascertain how to develop more precise curriculum content indicators that measure the intellectual rigor and cognitive demand of the implemented curriculum (Burkam, Lee, & Smerdon, 1997; Burstein et al., 1995; Porter, Kirst, Osthoff, Smithson, & Schneider, 1993). Similarly, NCES has recognized the need for data that are more specific. National surveys (e.g., the National Assessment of Educational Progress and the National Education Longitudinal Study of 1988) now ask teachers if they cover various topics, but they have started to collect information on the implemented curriculum that goes far beyond the surface views of intended curriculum provided by course credits and titles.

THIRTEEN INDICATORS TO WATCH

Research indicates that school quality affects student learning through the training and talent of the teaching force, what goes on in the classrooms, and the overall culture and atmosphere of the school. Within these three areas are 13 indicators of school quality that recent research suggests are related to student learning. These indicators are summarized in Figure 10.1.

Teachers

Substantial research suggests that school quality is enhanced when teachers have high academic skills, teach in the field in which they are trained, have more than a few years of experience, and participate in high-quality induction and professional development programs. Students learn more from teachers with strong academic skills and classroom teaching experience than they do from teachers with weak academic skills and less experience. Teachers are less effective in terms of student outcomes when they teach courses they were not trained to teach. Teachers are thought to be more effective when they have participated in quality professional development activities, but there is no statistical evidence to evaluate this relationship.

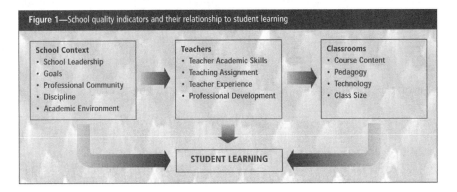

Figure 10.1.   School quality indicators and their relationship to student learning. The figure illustrates that these school quality factors can affect student learning both directly and indirectly. For example, school context characteristics, such as school leadership, can have an impact on teachers and what they are able to accomplish in the classroom, and this in turn may influence student learning. In addition, various teacher-level attributes can affect the quality of the classroom and, in turn, student learning. Traits at each of these levels can also directly affect student learning.

Classrooms

To understand the effectiveness of classrooms, research suggests that it is necessary to understand the content of the curriculum: the pedagogy, materials, and equipment used. Students appear to benefit when course content is focused and has a high level of intellectual rigor and cognitive challenge. Younger students, especially disadvantaged and minority students, appear to learn better in smaller classes. Nationally representative data on the process of schooling, now becoming available for the first time, will further our understanding of the role of these factors in determining school quality.

School Context

How schools approach educational leadership and school goals, develop a professional community, and establish a climate that minimizes discipline problems and encourages academic excellence clearly affects school quality and student learning. For three reasons, however, the effect of school-level characteristics is more difficult to ascertain than the effect of teachers and classrooms. First, even though they are integral to a school, these characteristics are difficult to define and measure. Second, their effect on student learning is likely to be exerted indirectly through teachers and classrooms, compounding the measurement problem. Last, with some exceptions, reliable, school representative information about these indicators of quality is minimal. These difficulties should not overshadow the importance of collecting such data to learn more about how these characteristics operate and affect student learning through teachers and classrooms. The preponderance of national, regional, and local efforts to develop quality schools heightens the benefits that would be derived from additional refined and reliable school-representative measures of school characteristics.

FIVE KEY INDICATORS

Although each of the 13 indicators are important, 5 should be given special attention: (a) teacher academic skills, (b) teacher experience, (c) class size, (d) course content, and (e) technology. As we show in the following sections, research suggests that each has strong, meaningful links to student learning.

1. The Academic Skills of Teachers

Many studies have shown that students learn more from teachers with strong academic skills than they do from teachers with weak academic skills (Ballou, 1996; Ehrenberg & Brewer, 1994, 1995; Ferguson, 1991; Ferguson & Ladd, 1996; Hanushek, 1996; Hedges et al., 1994; Mosteller

& Moynihan, 1972). This is not to say that academic skills perfectly predict how well a person will teach. Some educators argue that teacher quality has less to do with how well teachers perform on standardized tests than with how they perform in the classroom (Darling-Hammond, 1998). In fact, classroom observation is the traditional way of assessing teacher quality. Obviously, several other traits not measured on standardized tests (e.g., interpersonal skills, public speaking skills, and enthusiasm for working with children) influence whether someone will be an effective teacher, but to date the only way these traits are systematically assessed is through formal classroom observation. Because these data are hard to quantify, most studies that have examined the link between teacher skills and student learning limit their definition of *teacher skills* to academic skills. We will look at the findings from three of the most recent studies in this area.

Ehrenberg and Brewer (1994) investigated whether the quality of a teacher's undergraduate institution is related to student learning. Controlling for student and teacher background characteristics, such as race-ethnicity and socioeconomic status, they found that the higher the quality of the institution a teacher attended, as measured by admission selectivity, the more students learned over the course of 2 years.[2] To the extent that the quality of a teacher's undergraduate institution is correlated with the academic skills of the teacher, this finding suggests that the more able teachers have students with higher scores.

Ferguson (1998) and Ferguson and Ladd (1996) have used a more direct measure of the academic skills of teachers: their scores on standardized tests. These studies used state-specific data sets and, after controlling for several community and teacher characteristics such as race-ethnicity, found that higher teacher test scores are positively correlated with higher student test scores. Ferguson (1998) used Texas district-level data (from about 900 school districts) to measure the relationship between the average basic literacy skills of the teachers in a district and student learning gains over 2 years on mathematics tests and reported that a 1-*SD* change in the literacy skills of teachers would be associated with a 0.16-*SD* increase in high school students' learning and a 0.18-*SD* increase in elementary school students' learning.

In Alabama, Ferguson and Ladd (1996) obtained test scores from the teachers of almost 30,000 fourth-grade students in 690 schools. The scores were from the American College Test exams the teachers took when they applied for college. Over the course of 1 year, Ferguson and Ladd found that a 1-*SD* difference in a school's distribution of teacher American College Test scores was associated with a 0.10-*SD* change in the distribution of that school's fourth-grade reading test scores.

What cumulative impact will raising the overall academic caliber of teachers have on student learning from Grades 1 through 12? Unfortunately, this is currently unknown. Even though the effect sizes reported in these two studies are modest, they show impacts only over a 1- and 2-year period. Do students who are annually taught by higher caliber teachers receive persistent advantages (beyond 2 years) compared with their counterparts in lower caliber teachers' classrooms? Are these gains of the same magnitude year after year? If there are annual gains, the effect sizes presented earlier may greatly underestimate the benefit students would receive throughout their schooling from being taught by more academically able teachers.

Given that students learn more from teachers with strong academic skills than they do from teachers with weak academic skills, it would be useful to monitor the academic strength of the teaching force. How do the academic skills of teachers compare with those of other professionals? Is the academic talent of teachers distributed evenly among different types of schools?

Several studies have shown that over the past three decades, teachers with low academic skills have been entering the profession in much higher numbers than teachers with high academic skills (Ballou, 1996; Gitomer, Latham, & Ziomek, 1999; Henke, Chen, & Geis, 2000; Henke, Geis, & Giambattista, 1996; Murname, Singer, Willett, Kemple, & Olson, 1991; Vance & Schlechty, 1982).[3]

Recent studies, using data from the 1993 Baccalaureate and Beyond Longitudinal Study, provide a comprehensive picture of the pipeline from preparation to employment (Henke et al., 2000; Henke et al., 1996). These studies found that the college entrance examination scores of the 1992-93 college graduates in the teaching pipeline (defined by NCES as students who had prepared to teach, who were teaching, or who were considering teaching) were lower than those students who were not in the pipeline. "At each step toward a long-term career in teaching, those who were more inclined to teach scored less well than those less inclined to teach" (1996, p. 21).

For example, as shown in Figure 10.2, by 1997, the 1992–93 college graduates in Baccalaureate and Beyond Longitudinal Study with the highest college entrance examination scores were consistently less likely than their peers with lower scores to prepare to teach and, when they did teach, they were less likely to teach students from disadvantaged backgrounds:

- Graduates whose college entrance examination scores were in the top quartile were half as likely as those in the bottom quartile to prepare to teach (9% vs. 18%).
- Teachers in the top quartile were more than twice as likely as teachers in the bottom quartile to teach in private schools (26% vs. 10%).
- Teachers in the top quartile were at least one third as likely as teachers in the bottom quartile to teach in high-poverty schools (10% vs. 31%).
- Graduates in the top quartile who did teach were twice as likely as those in the bottom quartile to leave the profession within less than 4 years (32% vs. 16%; Henke et al., 2000).

These studies show a consistent trend and suggest that there is a need to monitor closely the supply and distribution of teacher academic skills. Unfortunately, the national data on teacher academic skills currently available are limited by their lack of specificity, timeliness, generalizability, and ability to link to student performance. The Survey of Recent College Graduates ascertains the academic quality of the undergraduate institution a person attended, but it does not reveal whether the person was in the top or bottom of the academic distribution at that institution. The National Adult Literacy Study and the Baccalaureate and Beyond Longitudinal Study provide information about how teachers' academic skills compare to those of other professionals, but neither study allows for a link to student performance. Although some currently available data give a more direct measure of an individual teacher's academic ability and can be linked to student test scores , the data are not collected routinely and are limited to a few states. Better nationally representative data are needed to gauge several aspects: how the academic caliber of teachers compares with that of other professionals, how the existing teaching talent is distributed throughout the country, and how teachers' academic skills have a cumulative impact on student academic performance.

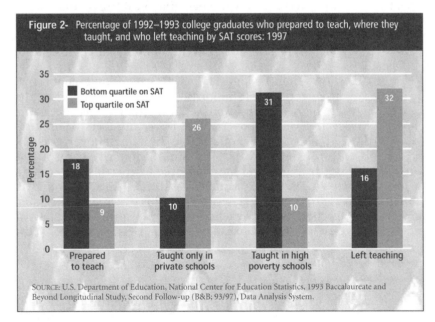

Figure 2- Percentage of 1992–1993 college graduates who prepared to teach, where they taught, and who left teaching by SAT scores: 1997

SOURCE: U.S. Department of Education, National Center for Education Statistics, 1993 Baccalaureate and Beyond Longitudinal Study, Second Follow-up (B&B; 93/97), Data Analysis System.

Figure 10.2. Percentage of 1992-93 college graduates who prepared to teach, where they taught, and who left teaching by Scholastic Aptitude Test scores: 1997. Source: U.S. Department of Education, National Center for Education Statistics, 1993 Baccalaureate and Beyond Longitudinal Study, Second Follow-up (B&B; 93/97), Data Analysis System.

2. Teacher Experience

Studies suggest that students learn more from experienced teachers than they do from less experienced teachers. Murnane and Phillips (1981) reported that in a large city in the Midwest, after controlling for other student and teacher characteristics, such as race-ethnicity and socioeconomic status, children taught by a teacher with 5 years of experience make 3 to 4 months' more progress in reading skills during a school year than do children taught by a first-year teacher. A more recent study conducted by Rivkin, Hanushek and Kain (1998) found that fourth-, fifth-, and sixth-grade students in more experienced teachers' classrooms in Texas over the course of 1 year gained about 0.10 SD in reading and math compared with their peers in classrooms where teachers had less than 2 years of experience. The benefits of experience, however, appear to level off after 5 years, and there are no noticeable differences, for example, in the effectiveness of a teacher with 5 years of experience versus a teacher with 10 years of experience (Darling-Hammond, 2000). However, teachers with 5 or 10 years of experience are more effective than new teachers.

Although it is impossible to limit the teaching force only to experienced teachers, the effects of new teachers may be diffused and reduced if new teachers are evenly distributed among the schools and if proper assistance is given to new teachers. As of 1998, teachers with 3 or fewer years of experience were not spread evenly among different types of schools.

Figure 10.3 shows that the highest poverty schools and schools with the highest concentrations of minority students (those in the top quartile) have a higher proportion of inexperienced teachers than schools with lower levels of poverty and lower numbers of minority students (those in the three other quartiles). The highest poverty schools and schools with the highest concentrations of minority students had nearly double the proportion of inexperienced teachers as schools with the lowest poverty (20% vs. 11%) and lowest concentration of minority students (21% vs. 10%). One likely cause for this overrepresentation of inexperienced teachers is that teacher attrition disproportionately affects high-poverty schools (Henke, Choy, Chen, Geis, & Alt, 1997).

3. Course Content

Research shows that students learn more from courses offering demanding content than from courses that expect little of students. Gamoran, Porter, Smithson, and White (1997) found that over the course of 1 year the standardized math scores for students in low level math courses could be raised by 0.10 SD if they received the type of content coverage offered in higher level courses.

Concerns about curriculum content and how a lack of focus in the U.S. curriculum affects student achievement have appeared in influen-

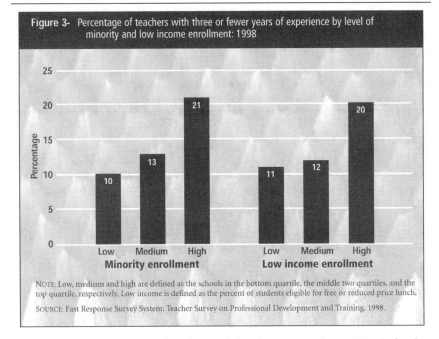

Figure 3- Percentage of teachers with three or fewer years of experience by level of minority and low income enrollment: 1998

NOTE: Low, medium and high are defined as the schools in the bottom quartile, the middle two quartiles, and the top quartile, respectively. Low income is defined as the percent of students eligible for free or reduced price lunch.

SOURCE: Fast Response Survey System: Teacher Survey on Professional Development and Training. 1998.

Figure 10.3.   Percentage of teachers with 3 or fewer years of experience by level of minority and low-income enrollment: 1998. *Low, medium,* and *high* are defined as the schools in the bottom quartile, the middle two quartiles, and the top quartile, respectively. *Low income* is defined as the percentage of students eligible for free or reduced-price lunch. *Source*: Fast Response Survey System: Teacher Survey on Professional Development and Training, 1998.

tial studies since the early 1980s. In 1983, the National Commission on Excellence in Education (NCEE) made the following conclusion:

> Secondary school curricula have been homogenized, diluted, and diffused to the point that they no longer have a central purpose. In effect, we have a cafeteria-style curriculum in which the appetizers and desserts can easily be mistaken for the main courses. Students have migrated from vocational and college preparatory programs to "general track" courses in large numbers. The proportion of students taking a general program of study has increased from 12 percent in 1964 to 42 percent in 1979. This curricular smorgasbord, combined with extensive student choice, explains a great deal about where we find ourselves today. (U.S. Department of Education, NCEE, 1983, p. 18)

The NCEE recommended that the curriculum be brought under control by requiring high school students to take the "Five New Basics:" 4 years of English, 3 years of mathematics, 3 years of science, 3 years of social studies, and a half year of computer science. Although these recommendations were advanced for the times, they were stated only in terms of numbers of courses, not about particular courses or the rigor or topics within a course. The authors of *The Shopping Mall High School* seemed to note this distinction:

> High schools seem unlikely to make marked improvement, especially for the many students and teachers now drifting around … until there is a much clearer sense of what is most important to teach and learn, and why, and how it can best be done. (Powell, Farrar, & Cohen, 1985, p. 306)

Does a lack of content focus result in poor performance? Yes, according to an analysis of results from the Second International Mathematics Study (SIMS) in the early 1980s. An analysis of the curriculum guides from the Third International Mathematics and Science Study (TIMSS) countries in the early 1990s also provides some useful data, although links to achievement are not clear cut. In both studies, U.S. 8th- and 12th-graders scored low on international comparisons in math and science.[4] In 1987, McKnight et al. directed the blame at a diffuse curriculum, and a decade later TIMSS researchers confirmed the curriculum guides' lack of focus in U.S. mathematics and science curricula. This is a critical finding. Standards documents serve as official education policy both in the United States and abroad; they signal educators about what they are expected to do in their classrooms.

Compounding the lack of focus in the intended U.S. curriculum, the implemented curriculum varies tremendously from classroom to classroom in this country. For example, SIMS researchers found that 13-year-olds in the United States received very uneven exposure to a range of curriculum topics relative to the other countries (McKnight et al., 1987). This might be explained by the fact that during the time of the SIMS data collection, more than 82% of the U.S. students in this age group were in schools offering two or more differently titled mathematics classes (Schmidt, McKnight, Cogan, Jakwerth, & Houang, 1999). In contrast, many of the countries that scored high on the SIMS mathematics tests (France, Hong Kong, and Japan) offered the same mathematics course to all students.

Student enrollment patterns show the percentage of high school graduates who studied each subject. Figures 10.4 and 10.5 reveal trends in the mathematics and science enrollment patterns of high school students. From 1982 to 1998, there was an increase in the percentage of students enrolling in higher level mathematics and science courses (Wirt et al., 2000). High school graduates in 1998 were more likely than their 1982 counterparts to have taken the most advanced mathematics courses, such as trigonometry, precalculus, and calculus. For example, 5% and 6% of 1982 high school graduates took these types of advanced academics: Level II and III courses, respectively (as defined in Wirt et al., 2000) and, in 1998, the percentage of students taking these courses rose to 15 and 12, respectively.

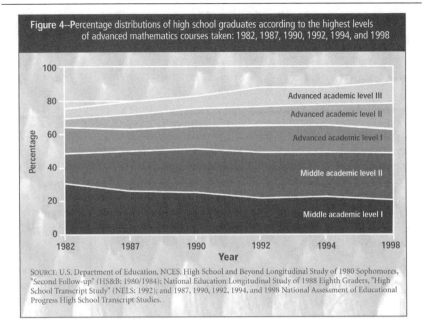

Figure 4--Percentage distributions of high school graduates according to the highest levels of advanced mathematics courses taken: 1982, 1987, 1990, 1992, 1994, and 1998

SOURCE: U.S. Department of Education, NCES. High School and Beyond Longitudinal Study of 1980 Sophomores, "Second Follow-up" (HS&B: 1980/1984); National Education Longitudinal Study of 1988 Eighth Graders, "High School Transcript Study" (NELS: 1992); and 1987, 1990, 1992, 1994, and 1998 National Assessment of Educational Progress High School Transcript Studies.

Figure 10.4.   Percentage distributions of high school graduates according to the highest levels of advanced mathematics courses taken: 1982, 1987, 1990, 1992, 1994, and 1998. *Source*: U.S. Department of Education, NCES, High School and Beyond Longitudinal Study of 1980 Sophomores, "Second Follow-up" (HS&B: 1980/1984); National Education Longitudinal Study of 1988 Eighth Graders, "High School Transcript Study" (NELS: 1992); and 1987, 1990, 1992, and 1998 National Assessment of Educational Progress High School Transcript Studies.

Furthermore, in the middle academic level, a larger percentage of high school graduates took Level II courses (such as Algebra II) as their highest level mathematics course in 1998 than in 1982 (increasing from 18% to 28%), and a lower percentage took Level I courses (such as Algebra I and plane geometry) as their highest level mathematics course (decreasing from 31% to 20%; Wirt et al., 2000).

In science, the trend is similar. For example, 5% of high school graduates completed Chemistry II or Physics II in 1982, but 7% completed these courses in 1998. Furthermore, during the same period, the percentage of graduates who completed Physics I increased from 18 to 34, and the percentage of graduates who completed Chemistry I increased from 7 to 19 (Wirt et al., 2000).

Despite these encouraging signs, the experience is not reflected equally among racial-ethnic and income groups. In 1998, White and Asian/Pacific Islander high school graduates were usually more likely than Black, Hispanic, and Native American/Alaskan Native graduates to complete advanced academic-level mathematics and the highest level

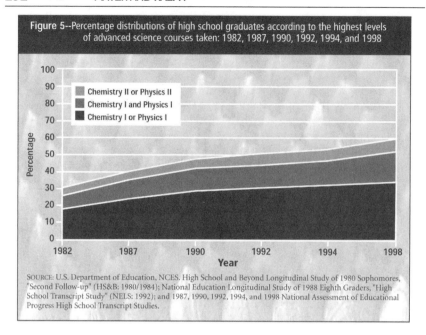

Figure 10.5. Percentage distributions of high school graduates according to the highest levels of advanced science courses taken: 1982, 1987, 1990, 1992, 1994, and 1998. *Source*: U.S. Department of Education, NCES, High School and Beyond Longitudinal Study of 1980 Sophomores, "Second Follow-up" (HS&B: 1980/1984); National Education Longitudinal Study of 1988 Eighth Graders, "High School Transcript Study" (NELS: 1992); and 1987, 1990, 1992, and 1998 National Assessment of Educational Progress High School Transcript Studies.

science courses (Wirt et al., 2000). For example, whereas 45% of White and 56% of Asian/Pacific Islander high school graduates took at least one advanced mathematics course in 1998, 30% of Blacks, 26% of Hispanics, and 27% of Native American/Alaskan Natives took courses at this level (Wirt et al., 2000). Finally, students from low-income families were less likely to be enrolled in a college preparatory track through which they would be more likely to take such courses (U.S. Department of Education, NCES, Office of Educational Research and Improvement, 1995).

All of the available data have limitations, however. The TIMSS approach of examining standards documents reveals the intended curriculum: what states, districts, and schools are asking teachers to cover in their classrooms, not what actually gets covered. NCEE standards that rely only on course titles, with no guidance on the topics that should be taught or mastered within those courses, do not directly address the SIMS/TIMSS concerns that topic coverage is not uniform across classrooms and that the U.S. curriculum lacks focus. The NCES data on enrollment patterns attempt to address the issue at a lower, more revealing level, but they are also limited because they depend heavily on course titles that may incorrectly assume identical course content,[5] and they are not applicable to primary grades.[6]

4. Technology

Former Education Secretary Richard Riley's statement that "over the last decade, the use of technology in American life has exploded" (U.S. Department of Education, 1996, p. 1) characterizes the inevitable: Computers and the Internet play a role in classrooms, and although the explosion has yet to reverberate within schools to the same degree it has in other sectors of American society, technology and computers are rapidly appearing in schools and redefining the perception of a quality school. Computers and Internet access are used in a variety of ways in schools, and each use may have an independent impact on student learning. Very little research on the effect of technology on learning looks at the uses and effect of Internet access; most examines the instructional power of the computer to teach discrete skills. Numerous studies conducted in the elementary and secondary grades have concluded that student learning is enhanced by computers when the computer is used to teach discrete skills in the style referred to as "drill and practice."[7] Four separate meta-analyses support this conclusion, and so far none have refuted it (President's Committee of Advisers on Science and Technology, Panel on Educational Technology, 1997). The magnitude of the effect is considerable, ranging in these four studies from 0.25 to 0.40 *SD*. The benefits appeared to be strongest for students of lower socioeconomic status, low achievers, and those with certain learning problems (President's Committee of Advisers on Science and Technology, Panel on Educational Technology, 1997).

In the past decade, education reformers have seized on research about how students learn and on research about what skills are demanded in today's economy (e.g., Murnane & Levy, 1996) to conclude that students need to be taught differently. Research on the application of computers for developing higher order thinking skills, problem solving, group work, and hands-on learning activities, however, is less extensive and less conclusive. Two studies have shown positive effects (Glennan & Melmed, 1996; Wenglinsky, 1998), and a third concludes it is not known whether computers can be used for this type of teaching in a cost-effective manner with any "degree of certainty that would be desirable from a public policy viewpoint" (President's Committee of Advisers on Science and Technology, Panel on Educational Technology, 1997). It may be that these studies are less conclusive because teachers are less adept at teaching in this new way. This suggests that the challenge of using computers to develop higher order thinking skills may be closely tied to the challenge of improving professional development for teachers.

Because computer technology is expensive, researchers and administrators want to assess its availability, equity, use, and effect on student learning. Recognizing both the growing use of technology in schools and the limited amount of applicable research and data collection, former President Clinton's Panel on Educational Technology identified a "pressing need for large-scale, federally sponsored research and evaluation on school technology" (President's Committee of Advisers on Science and Technology, Panel on Educational Technology, 1997, p. 51).[8] Secretary Riley echoed that concern when speaking to the 1999 National Conference on Educational Technology.

Thus, large-scale data collection on technology in the classroom should address four issues: (a) the availability of quality computers and Internet access, (b) whether computers and access are equitably distributed among schools and students within schools, (c) how the technology is used, and (d) how it affects student learning.

The available national information on classroom technology currently is skewed: We have ample data on the availability of computers, and some information about their distribution among schools and students, but we know little about how computers or the Internet are used. The country would benefit from more and better information on the instructional role that computers play in classrooms and their effectiveness in achieving student learning.

5. Class Size

How teachers implement the course content, instructional pedagogy, and technology use in the classroom may all be influenced by the number of students in the class. Manipulating class size as a way to improve student learning is now at the forefront of the education policy debate, because some evidence suggests that students may achieve more in smaller classes, particularly primary-grade students who are minorities or who come from economically disadvantaged backgrounds (Grissmer, Flanagan, & Williamson, 1998; Krueger, 1998; Mosteller, 1995; Mosteller, Light, & Sachs, 1996; U.S. Department of Education, 1998). Why does class size matter, and how might it affect student learning? With fewer students, teachers may be able to use a different pedagogical approach and implement the curriculum in a more effective manner.

The number of studies that have examined the relationship between class size and teaching quality are limited, and a better understanding is needed of the effects of class size on instructional practice and the quality of the classroom environment. From the limited research available, there is evidence that teachers in smaller classrooms deal with fewer disciplinary problems, spend more time on instruction and enrichment activities, and offer more opportunities for student participation (Achilles, 1996; Finn, 1998; Shapson, Wright, Eason, & Fitzgerald, 1980; U.S. Department of Education, 1998). Teachers also express greater satisfaction and report better morale when working with smaller classes (Shapson et al., 1980; U.S. Department of Education, 1998).

Do smaller classes also lead to greater learning? Hundreds of studies have focused on the relationship between class size and student achievement, and several researchers have compiled and analyzed these studies. Most of these meta-analyses have concluded that smaller classes do raise student test scores (Finn, 1998; Glass & Smith, 1979; Robinson & Wittebols, 1986; Slavin, 1989; U.S. Department of Education, 1998).

Others disagree. Their views are represented in this summary statement by Hanushek (1998):

> Extensive statistical investigation of the relationship between class size and student performance shows as many positive as negative estimates. With close to 300 separate estimates of the effect of class size, there is no reason to expect performance improvements from lowering class sizes. (p. iii)

However, in a reanalysis of Hanushek's (1989) synthesis of education production function studies, Hedges et al. (1994) concluded that class size made a difference in student learning. In addition, in a subsequent study that examined a larger-and, according to the authors, more comprehensive-group of studies, Greenwald et al. (1996) again found a positive, statistically significant relationship between small classes and student performance.

These findings are supported by a recent and widely cited study on class size, a randomized experiment conducted by the state of Tennessee (Krueger, 1998; Mosteller, 1995; Sanders & Rivers, 1996). Because randomized studies are considered to be among the most valid study designs and because they are so rare in the field of education research, the results from this study have received a tremendous amount of attention from researchers, policymakers, and the general public.[9] The first phase of the study, called *Project STAR* (Student-Teacher Achievement Ratio), compared the achievement of elementary students in small classes with those in regular-sized classes with and without a full-time teacher's aide.[10] By the end of first grade, after 2 years of intervention, students attending smaller classes benefited by approximately 0.25 *SD*. The effect sizes for the Stanford Achievement Test were 0.23 for reading and 0.27 for math.[11] This means that an average student achieving at the 50th percentile rank would see a boost in achievement of 10 percentage points (Mosteller, 1995). These effect sizes show the advantage of small classes over regular-sized classes in standard deviation units.

When analyzed by race-ethnicity, the results showed that Black students experienced a greater boost in achievement than White students in the early years. The effect size for Black students was double the effect size for White students when standardized achievement test results were averaged over the first 2 years (Mosteller, 1995). Further examination of the Tennessee data confirmed the finding that Black and disadvantaged students benefited disproportionately in the early grades

(Achilles, 1996; Finn, 1998; Grissmer et al., 1998; Hanushek, 1998; Krueger, 1998; Mosteller, 1995; Mosteller et al., 1996; U.S. Department of Education, 1998). This finding also coincides with a recent analysis of data from the National Assessment of Educational Progress that shows the trend toward smaller classes may have contributed to the decrease in the achievement gap between 9-year-old Blacks and Whites (Grissmer et al., 1998). However, in which grade Tennessee students experienced the greatest gains and how long those gains have persisted continue to be debated (Achilles, 1996; Hanushek, 1998; Krueger, 1998; Mosteller, 1995).

What is the optimal class size in the primary grades, or the threshold at which gains in student achievement are realized? Glass and Smith (1979) and Slavin (1989) have suggested that the threshold lies somewhere between 15 and 20 students; the Tennessee study compared classes of 13 to 17 students with classes of 22 to 26 students. How do these class size numbers compare with classrooms across the country? In 1994, more than 47% of elementary classes in the United States had 25 or more students ("Quality Counts," 1998), and in 1998 the average public elementary school class consisted of 23 students (Lewis et al., 1999). Thus, the majority of elementary classrooms is far from being in the 13- to 20-student range that these researchers identify as desirable.

Nationally representative data show that the pupil:teacher ratio across all public elementary and secondary schools was 27 pupils to 1 teacher in 1955 and 17 to 1 in 1991 (see Figure 10.6).

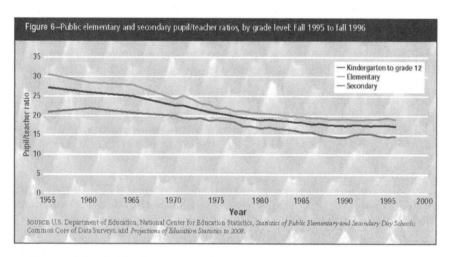

Figure 10.6.   Public elementary and secondary pupil:teacher ratios, by grade level: fall 1995 to fall 1996. *Source:* U.S. Department of Education, National Center for Education Statistics, *Statistics of Public Elementary and Secondary Day Schools*; Common Core of Data Surveys; and *Projections of Education Statistics to 2008.*

Pupil:teacher ratios, however, are an imprecise indicator of class size, because they do not account for frequently intense teaching resources targeted toward Title I, special education, or bilingual services in some schools. When schools use those resources to attain low ratios for those targeted populations, they mask much higher ratios for the remaining classes. This is especially true for poor and urban districts, because they enroll higher numbers of students needing specialized instruction (Finn, 1998; Hanushek, 1998).

The better indicator of class size is the average number of students in regular classrooms. Unfortunately, national class size estimates (distinct from pupil:teacher ratios) date back only to the late 1980s. The average class size in public elementary and secondary schools was similar in the 1987-88, 1990-91, and 1993-94 school years (Smith, Young, Bae, Choy, & Alsalam, 1997). In 1993-94, the average public elementary class consisted of 24.1 students, whereas the average secondary class consisted of 23.6 students. As of 1998, the average class size for public school general elementary classrooms was down to 23 (Lewis et al., 1999).[12] Class size data for secondary schools in 1998 are not available.

QUALITY OF THE CURRENT DATA

The quality of data on these five indicators varies in predictable ways. Where the dimension being measured is straightforward (teacher experience, and class size) or has been measured for an extended period of time (the standardized tests used to gauge teacher academic skills), the data are high quality. Where little information exists about a particularly important facet of an indicator (course content, technology), the quality of the data is somewhat compromised.

The indicators of teacher experience and class size each represent straightforward concepts and are easy to measure, and the data are of high quality. In addition, data on teacher experience and class size have been collected for several decades, further ensuring the quality of the data. Data on teacher academic skills are also high quality, but less straightforward. Although the academic skills of teachers constitute only one aspect of teaching ability, standardized tests that measure the academic skills of future teachers are quite advanced and have consistently shown links to student learning.

Data on indicators of course content and technology are of moderate quality. The national data collection efforts of these specific measures are relatively new compared with the efforts to collect data on high-quality indicators, and the indicators are more complex than the data currently collected. National data on indicators of course content and academic environment are based primarily on course titles, and consequently their usefulness is hampered because of their vagueness. Similarly, current data on technology primarily measure the availability of hardware and access to the Internet and provide too little information on the instructional role of technology in the classroom.

However, even the high-quality measures are compromised by not being kept up to date. There are no regularly scheduled efforts to use standardized tests to measure the academic skills of prospective teachers or to monitor the course-taking patterns of students.

CONCLUSION

A review of the national data pertaining to the five key indicators reveals the following: Teacher indicators show that the teaching profession attracts teachers with low academic skills who have been entering the profession in much higher numbers than teachers with high academic skills (Henke et al., 2000). Inexperienced teachers and those with low academic skills are more likely to teach in high-poverty schools and schools with high concentrations of minority students (Henke et al., 2000). The classroom indicators show more positive trends. Students are taking more rigorous academic courses in high school, and more computers are available and are used more frequently (Smith et al., 1997; Wirt et al., 2000). However, minority high school graduates were usually less likely than Asian/Pacific Islander or non-Hispanic White students to enroll in these classes (Wirt et al., 2000). Although the average public elementary school class in 1998 had 23 students, the strongest gains in student achievement seem to occur in classes with 13 to 20 students, especially for disadvantaged and minority students (Krueger, 1998; Mosteller et al., 1996; Robinson & Wittebols, 1986).

As we continue to collect indicator data on these dimensions of schools, there are at least three challenges of which policymakers should be aware. The first challenge pertains to building higher quality indicators. As noted earlier, national data on course content and technology usage are currently lacking in specificity. This is due in part to this being a relatively new area for data collection, but it is also due to the complexity of the instructional process. Research and development efforts should continue to support the development of measures pertaining to course content and technology usage.

A second challenge is for policymakers to anticipate unintended outcomes that can arise if policy is based on these indicators in isolation. For example, large-scale efforts to reduce class size may set in motion unintended negative consequences. Two years after California's initiative for smaller classes in kindergarten through third grade greatly increased the demand for a limited supply of qualified teachers, more than 12% of California K-3 classroom teachers do not meet minimum qualifications, compared with less than 1% before the initiative (Bohrnstedt & Stecher, 1999). In addition, those underqualified teachers are more likely to teach minority and disadvantaged students. In fact, third-grade students in the bottom quartile of reading achievement in California are five times as likely to have an underqualified teacher as are students in the top quartile (Shields et al., 1999). These studies suggest that lowering class size by itself may not enhance student learning if unqualified teachers are used to reduce class size.

A third challenge is for policymakers to find a way to collect data pertaining to the academic quality of the existing teaching force. There currently are no standardized tests administered to teachers. Current data on teacher academic quality come from college entrance scores of perspective or new teachers, but a more complete picture of the academic talent of the entire teaching force (veterans as well as novices) could be obtained by administering an achievement test to a nationally representative sample of the existing teaching corps. Such a testing effort will meet stiff resistance from the teacher unions, but the potential benefits may outweigh the costs of fighting such a battle.

These challenges should be met in order to improve our nation's schools. The research cited in this chapter makes the case that not all schools facing the same sets of standards and accountability measures will perform equally well on high-stakes standardized tests because the training and talent of the teaching force, what goes on in classrooms, and the overall culture and atmosphere within a school are linked to student learning. Consequently, a meaningful system for gauging the health of the nation's education system should include up-to-date measures of each of these components. Monitoring the indicators of school quality outlined in this chapter will help policymakers account for why some schools are failing while others are succeeding. In turn, the indicators can then be used to help policymakers determine how to create policies that can help remedy this inequity.

ACKNOWLEDGMENTS

This chapter represents the views of the authors and does not necessarily represent the views of the federal government. This chapter was adapted from a National Center for Education Statistics report titled *Monitoring School Quality: An Indicators Report* (Mayer, Mullins, & Moore, 2000). We thank John E. Mullens, Mary T. Moore, and all others acknowledged in that report for their assistance in laying the foundations for this chapter.

NOTES

1. The authors report that some of the studies used by Hanushek were excluded because they did not provide enough information to use in their analysis. The excluded studies were those that reported nonsignificant resource effects and did not report the sign of the coefficient.
2. The data come from the High School and Beyond study's 1984 supplementary teacher and administrative survey. This survey contains information about the undergraduate institutions teachers attended. The authors then

linked these institutions to an admissions selectivity scale presented in *Barron's* (1984) and ranked the teachers' undergraduate institutions on a 6-point scale ranging from most selective to least selective.

3. Two studies (Bruschi & Coley, 1999; Rollefson & Smith, 1997) using one data source, the National Adult Literacy Survey, found that in 1992 the teachers in U.S. schools had literacy skills similar to those of professionals in several other occupations for which a bachelor's degree is a prerequisite. These professionals included physicians, engineers, postsecondary teachers, writers, and artists. The National Adult Literacy Survey data differ from the data used in these other studies in that they pertain to literacy skills, as opposed to a more general set of academic skills, and to the skills of existing teachers, not the skills of new entrants.

4. Research scientists suggest there are clear limitations in using SIMS and TIMSS data to make international comparisons because neither study design adequately controlled for substantial differences in student selectivity, curriculum emphasis, and the proportion of low-income students in the test-taking populations (Rotberg, 1998).

5. Do all Algebra I classes cover the same material for the same duration? In fact, findings from SIMS and TIMSS suggest that they do not. And to what extent have course titles, but not substance, changed to better "meet" external standards?

6. Course titles are virtually useless as indicators of the curriculum in the primary grades, because students at this level do not have electives and the course titles are generally no more specific than *reading, mathematics, science,* and *social studies.*

7. This was defined by the President's Committee of Advisors on Science and Technology, Panel on Educational Technology (1997) as "practice sessions often focused on the acquisition of basic skills" in which "the student [is] exposed to successive blocks of textual material and [answers] a series of questions posed by the computer."

8. Almost all data inventorying the computer hardware in the nation's schools come from two private companies: Quality Education Data and Market Data Retrieval. Data from the former company have been used in several major reports (see, e.g., Coley, Cradler, & Engel, 1997; Glennan & Melmed, 1996; President's Committee of Advisors on Science and Technology, Panel on Educational Technology, 1997; U.S. Department of Education, 1996). These companies survey schools to assess their equipment inventories and future buying plans. They attempt to get data from every school, because their main objective is to create marketing lists and reports for technology companies. Because schools are under no obligation to complete the surveys, many schools choose not to, and therefore the inventory data present a conservative picture-a limitation that is generally overlooked because of heightened policy interest in these areas.

9. In an experimental study, the researchers are able to allocate each student to a control or treatment group, typically through random assignment whereby each student has an equal chance of being in either group. This produces two statistically equivalent groups, allowing researchers to attribute any differences in outcomes to the intervention. In an observational study, the researchers have no control over how people choose from among various options, a phenomenon called *self-selection.* When self-selection occurs, it is not possible to determine whether groups differ in outcomes because of the intervention or because of other characteristics that come about as a result of

self-selection. Experimental studies are therefore thought to be superior to observational studies for understanding causation.
10. Over 4 years, about 80 schools and 11,600 students participated in Project STAR. A small class had 13 to 17 students per teacher, and a regular class had 22 to 26 students. Students and teachers were assigned to each type of class at random, and researchers made sure that a school with at least one small class also had a regular-sized class with or without an aide in an attempt to rule out the effects of school characteristics when analyzing results.
11. Effect sizes were calculated by subtracting the average achievement score for regular classes from the mean score for small classes in standard deviation units. The average achievement score for regular classes was obtained by taking the average of the mean score for regular classes with aides and without aides (Finn, 1998). The Stanford Achievement Test is a standardized instrument that was administered to all students in the study at the end of each school year.
12. General elementary classrooms are classrooms that are self-contained for most of the day and in which one teacher is responsible for instructing in all core subjects, including reading/language arts, mathematics, social studies, and science (but not necessarily art, music, and physical education). General elementary classrooms are distinct from departmentalized settings in which a teacher's main teaching assignment is in one particular subject area (Lewis et al., 1999).

REFERENCES

Action statement, 1999 National Education Summit. (1999). Retrieved June 1, 2001 from main summit site at http://www.achieve.org/ node/301

Achilles, C. M. (1996). Response to Eric Hanushek: Students achieve more in smaller classes. *Educational Leadership, 76–77.*

Ballou, D. (1996). Do public schools hire the best applicants? *Quarterly Journal of Economics, 97–133.*

Bohrnstedt, G. W., & Stecher, B. M. (1999). *Class size reduction in California: Early evaluation findings, 1996–1998* (CSR Research Consortium, Year 1 evaluation report). Palo Alto, CA: American Institutes for Research.

Bruschi, B. A., & Coley, R. J. (1999). *How teachers compare: The prose, document, and quantitative skills of America's teachers.* Princeton, NJ: Educational Testing Service, Policy Information Center.

Burkam, D. T., Lee, V. E., & Smerdon, B. A. (1997). *Mathematics, foreign language, and science course taking and the NELS: 88 transcript data.* Ann Arbor: University of Michigan.

Burstein, L., McDonnell, L. M., Van Winkle, J., Ormseth, T., Mirocha, J., & Guitton, G. (1995). *Validating national curriculum indicators.* Santa Monica, CA: RAND.

Coleman, J. S., Campbell, E. Q., Hobson, C. J., McPartland, J., Mood, A. M., Weinfeld, F. D., & York, R. L. (1966). *Equality of educational opportunity.* Washington, DC: U.S. Government Printing Office.

Coley, R. J., Cradler, J., & Engel, P. K. (1997). *Computers and classrooms: The status of technology in U.S. schools.* Princeton, NJ: Educational Testing Service, Policy Information Center.

◁▦▷ MAYER AND RALPH

Darling-Hammond, L. (1998). Teachers and teaching: Testing policy hypotheses from a national commission report. *Educational Researcher, 27*(1), 5–15.

Darling-Hammond, L. (2000). Teacher quality and student achievement: A review of state policy evidence. *Education Policy Analysis Archives, 8*(1). Retrieved June 1, 2001 from http://olam.ed.asu.edu/epaa/v8n1/

Ehrenberg, R. G., & Brewer, D. (1994). Do school and teacher characteristics matter? Evidence from high school and beyond. *Economics of Education Review, 13*, 1–17.

Ehrenberg, R. G., & Brewer, D. (1995). Did teachers' verbal ability and race matter in the 1960s? Coleman revisited. *Economics of Education Review, 14*, 1–21.

Ferguson, R. F. (1991). Paying for public education: New evidence on how and why money matters. *Harvard Journal on Legislation, 28*, 465–499.

Ferguson, R. F. (1998). Can schools narrow the Black-White test score gap? In C. Jencks & M. Phillips (Eds.), *The Black-White test score gap* (pp. 318–374). Washington, DC: Brookings Institution.

Ferguson, R. F., & Ladd, H. (1996). How and why money matters: An analysis of Alabama schools. In H. F. Ladd (Ed.), *Holding schools accountable: Performance-based reform in education* (pp. 265–298). Washington, DC: Brookings Institution.

Finn, J. D. (1998). *Class size and students at risk: What is known? What is next?* Washington, DC: U.S. Department of Education, Office of Educational Research and Improvement.

Gamoran, A., Porter, A. C., Smithson, J. L., & White, P. A. (1997). Upgrading high school mathematics instruction: Improving learning opportunities for low-achieving, low-income youth. *Educational Evaluation and Policy Analysis, 19*, 325–338.

Gitomer, D. H., Latham, A. S., & Ziomek, R. (1999). The academic quality of prospective teachers: The impact of admissions and licensure testing. Princeton, NJ: Educational Testing Service, Teaching and Learning Division.

Glass, G. V., & Smith, M. L. (1979). Meta-analysis of research on class size and achievement. *Education Evaluation and Policy Analysis, 1*, 2–16.

Glennan, T. K., & Melmed, A. (1996). *Fostering the use of educational technology: Elements of a national strategy*. Santa Monica, CA: RAND.

Greenwald, R., Hedges, L. V., & Laine, R. D. (1996). The effect of school resources on student achievement. *Review of Educational Research, 66*, 361–396.

Grissmer, D., Flanagan, A., & Williamson, S. (1998). Why did the Black White score gap narrow in the 1970s and 1980s? In C. Jencks & M. Phillips (Eds.), *The Black-White test score gap* (pp. 182–226). Washington, DC: Brookings Institution.

Hanushek, E. A. (1986). The economics of schooling: Production and efficiency in public schools. *Journal of Economic Literature, 24*, 1141–1177.

Hanushek, E. A. (1989). The impact of differential expenditures on school performance. *Educational Researcher, 18*(4), 45–51.

Hanushek, E. A. (1996). A more complete picture of school resource policies. *Review of Educational Research, 66*, 397–409.

Hanushek, E. A. (1998). *The evidence on class size*. Rochester, NY: University of Rochester, W. Allen Wallis Institute of Political Economy.

Hedges, L. V., Laine, R. D., & Greenwald, R. (1994). Does money matter? A meta-analysis of studies of the effects of differential school inputs on student outcomes. *Educational Researcher, 23*(3), 5–14.

Henke, R. R., Chen, X., & Geis, S. (2000). *Progress through the teacher pipeline: 1992–93 college graduates and elementary/secondary school teaching as of*

1997 (NCES 2000-152). Washington, DC: U.S. Department of Education, National Center for Education Statistics, Office of Educational Research and Improvement.

Henke, R. R., Choy, S. P., Chen, X., Geis, S., & Alt, M. N. (1997). *America's teachers: Profile of a profession, 1993–94* (NCES 97–460). Washington, DC: U.S. Government Printing Office.

Henke, R. R., Geis, S., & Giambattista, J. (1996). *Out of the lecture hall and into the classroom: 1992–93 college graduates and elementary/secondary school teaching* (NCES 96-899). Washington, DC: U.S. Government Printing Office.

Krueger, A. B. (1998). *Experimental estimates of education production functions.* Princeton, NJ: Princeton University Industrial Relations Section.

Lewis, L., Parsad, B., Carey, N., Bartfai, N., Farris, E., & Smerdon, B. (1999). *Teacher quality: A report on the preparation and qualifications of public school teachers* (NCES 1999-080). Washington, DC: U.S. Government Printing Office.

Mayer, D. P., Mullens, J. E., & Moore, M. T. (2000). *Monitoring school quality: An indicators report.* Washington, DC: U.S. Department of Education.

McKnight, C. C., Crosswhite, F. J., Dossey, J. A., Kifer, E., Swafford, J. O., Travers, K. J., & Cooney, T. J. (1987). *The underachieving curriculum: Assessing U.S. school mathematics from an international perspective.* Champaign, IL: Stipes.

Mosteller, F. (1995). The Tennessee study of class size in the early grades. *The Future of Children, 5*(2), 113–127.

Mosteller, F., Light, R. J., & Sachs, J. A. (1996). Sustained inquiry in education: Lessons from skill grouping and class size. *Harvard Education Review, 66*, 797–842.

Mosteller, F., & Moynihan, D. P. (Eds.). (1972). *On equality of educational opportunity.* New York: Random House.

Murnane, R. J., & Levy, R. (1996). *Teaching the new basic skills: Principles for educating children to thrive in a changing economy.* New York: Free Press.

Murnane, R. J., & Phillips, B. R. (1981). Learning by doing, vintage, and selection: Three pieces of the puzzle relating teaching experience and teaching performance. *Economics of Education Review, 1*, 453–465.

Murnane, R. J., & Raizen, S. A. (Eds.). (1988). *Improving indicators of the quality of science and mathematics education in grades K–12.* Washington, DC: National Academy Press.

Murnane, R. J., Singer, J. D., Willett, J. B., Kemple, J. J., & Olson, R. J. (1991). *Who will teach? Policies that matter.* Cambridge, MA: Harvard University Press.

Porter, A. C., Kirst, M. W., Osthoff, E. J., Smithson, J. L., & Schneider, S. A. (1993). *Reform up close: An analysis of high school mathematics and science classrooms.* Madison: University of Wisconsin-Madison School of Education, Center on Organization and Restructuring of Schools, and Wisconsin Center for Education Research.

Powell, A. G., Farrar, E., & Cohen, D. K. (1985). *The shopping mall high school: Winners and losers in the educational marketplace.* Boston: Houghton-Mifflin.

President's Committee of Advisors on Science and Technology, Panel on Educational Technology. (1997). *Report to the President on the use of technology to strengthen K–12 education in the United States.* Washington, DC: The White House.

Quality counts. (1998). *Education Week, 17*(Suppl.).

Rivkin, S. G., Hanushek, E. A., & Kain, J. F. (1998). *Teachers, schools and academic achievement.* Paper presented to the Association for Public Policy Analysis and Management, New York City.

Robinson, G. E., & Wittebols, J. H. (1986). *Class size research: A related cluster analysis for decision making.* Arlington, VA: Education Research Service.

Rollefson, M. R., & Smith, T. M. (1997). Do low salaries really draw the least able into the teaching profession? In D. M. Byrd & D. J. McIntyre (Eds.), *Research on the education of our nation's teachers: Teacher education yearbook V* (pp. 43–58). Thousand Oaks, CA: Corwin.

Rotberg, I. C. (1998). Interpretation of international test score comparisons. *Science, 280,* 1030-1031.

Sanders, W. L., & Rivers, J. C. (1996). *Cumulative and residual effects of teachers on future student academic achievement.* Knoxville: University of Tennessee, Value-Added Research and Assessment Center.

Schmidt, W. H., McKnight, C. C., Cogan, L. S., Jakwerth, P. M., & Houang, R. T. (1999). *Facing the consequences: Using TIMSS for a closer look at U.S. mathematics and science education.* Dordrecht, The Netherlands: Kluwer Academic.

Shapson, S. M., Wright, E. N., Eason, G., & Fitzgerald, J. (1980). An experimental study of effects of class size. *American Educational Research Journal, 17,* 141–152.

Shavelson, R., McDonnell, L., Oakes, J., & Carey, N. (1987). *Indicator systems for monitoring mathematics and science education.* Santa Monica, CA: RAND.

Shields, P. M., Esch, C. E., Humphrey, D. C., Young, V. M., Gaston, M., & Hunt, H. (1999). *The status of the teaching profession: Research findings and policy recommendations.* Santa Cruz, CA: Center for the Future of Teaching and Learning.

Slavin, R. E. (Ed.). (1989). *School and classroom organization.* Hillsdale, NJ: Lawrence Erlbaum Associates.

Smerdon, B., & Cronen, S. (2000). *Teachers' tools for the 21st century: A report on teachers' use of technology* (NCES 2000-102). Washington, DC: U.S. Department of Education, National Center for Education Statistics.

Smith, T. M., Young, B. A., Bae, Y., Choy, S. P., & Alsalam, N. (1997). *The condition of education 1997* (NCES 97-388). Washington, DC: U.S. Government Printing Office.

U.S. Department of Education. (1996). *Getting America's students ready for the 21st century: Meeting the technology literacy challenge.* Washington, DC: National Center for Education Statistics.

U.S. Department of Education. (1998). *Reducing class size: What do we know?* Washington, DC: National Center for Education Statistics.

U.S. Department of Education. (2000). *Internet access in public schools and classrooms: 1994–99* (NCES 2000-086). Washington, DC: National Center for Education Statistics.

U.S. Department of Education, National Center for Education Statistics, Office of Educational Research and Improvement. (1995). *A profile of the American high school senior in 1992* (NCES 95-384). Washington, DC: U.S. Government Printing Office.

U.S. Department of Education, National Center for Education Statistics, Special Study Panel on Education Indicators for the National Center for Education Statistics. (1991). *Education counts* (NCES 91-634). Washington, DC: U.S. Government Printing Office.

U.S. Department of Education, National Commission on Excellence in Education. (1983). *A nation at risk: The imperative for educational reform.* Washington, DC: U.S. Government Printing Office.

U.S. Department of Education, Office of Educational Research and Improvement, State Accountability Study Group. (1988). *Creating responsible and responsive accountability systems.* Washington, DC.

Vance, V. S., & Schlechty, P. C. (1982). The distribution of academic ability in the teaching force: Policy implications. *Phi Delta Kappan*, 22–27.

Wenglinsky, H. (1998). *Does it compute? The relationship between educational technology and student achievement in mathematics*. Princeton, NJ: Educational Testing Service.

Wirt, J. G., Choy, S., Gruner, A., Sable, J., Tobin, R., Bae, Y., et al. (2000). *The condition of education, 2000* (NCES 2000-062). Washington, DC: National Center for Education Statistics.

Chapter 11

Constructing Community Indicators Of Child Well-Being

Jeffrey D. Morenoff
University of Michigan

Robert J. Sampson
Harvard University

At the outset of the 1990s, Jencks and Mayer (1990) argued that if "neighborhood effects" exist, presumably they are constituted from social processes that involve collective aspects of community life (e.g., contagion, socialization, and institutions). Their assessment was ultimately pessimistic, however, for few studies could be found that measured and identified neighborhood social processes. The reason is that the data sources on which neighborhood researchers have traditionally relied most heavily—the U.S. Census and other government or administrative statistics—provide information on the sociodemographic composition of statistical neighborhoods (e.g., census tracts or ZIP codes) but do not tell us what is actually happening within these places that might affect child and adolescent well-being. Jencks and Mayer's challenge was formidable.

The good news is that the 1990s marked a period of major advances in both the scope and the quality of neighborhood data, as researchers began to explore new methods for measuring what makes places more or less healthy for children. A number of new studies and approaches were launched, so much so that the study of neighborhood effects, for better or worse, has become something of a cottage industry. In this chapter, we review some of these developments, identify recent community-level indicators of social and institutional processes related to children's well-being, highlight new directions in community research and their implications for constructing indicators, and conclude with recommendations for developing community indicators of child well-being. We begin with a discussion of how researchers typically define local communities. Our consideration of community indicators then follows, beginning with the measurement of structural differentiation and continuing with more recent advances in the measurement of neighborhood mechanisms (i.e., social and institutional processes). We conclude by proposing new directions for research on the community context of child well-being and suggest a strategy for collecting benchmark data on social environments that can be compared across communities.

DEFINING *LOCAL COMMUNITY*

Long ago, Robert Park and Ernest Burgess laid the foundation for urban sociology by defining communities as "natural areas" that develop as a result of competition between businesses for land use and between population groups for affordable housing. A neighborhood, according to this view, is a subsection of a larger community—a collection of both people and institutions occupying a spatially defined area that is conditioned by a set of ecological, cultural, and political forces (Park, 1916, pp. 147–154). Suttles (1972) later refined this view by recognizing that communities often do not voluntarily form their identities as the result of free market competition. Instead, some communities have their identity and boundaries imposed on them by outsiders. Suttles also argued that the local community (a term we use interchangeably with *neighborhood*) is best thought of not as a single entity but rather as a hierarchy of progressively more inclusive residential groupings. In this sense, we can think of neighborhoods as ecological units nested within successively larger communities. There is no one neighborhood, but many neighborhoods that vary in size and complexity depending on the social phenomenon of interest and the ecological structure of the larger community.

In practice, most social scientists rely on statistical neighborhoods in their analyses, which means that geographic boundaries are defined by the census or other administrative agencies (e.g., school districts, police districts, or ZIP codes). In many cities there exist *local community* or *city planning* areas that have reasonable ecological integrity. Although large, these areas often have well-known names and borders, such as freeways, parks, and major streets. For example, Chicago has 77 local community areas averaging about 40,000 persons that were designed to correspond to socially meaningful and natural geographic boundaries. Some boundaries have undergone change over time, but these areas are widely recognized by administrative agencies and local institutions. *Census tracts* are smaller and more socially homogeneous areas of roughly 3,000 to 5,000 residents on average; their boundaries are usually drawn to take into account major streets, parks, and other geographical features. A third and even smaller area approximating the layperson's concept of neighborhood is the *block group*—a set of blocks averaging approximately 1,000 residents.

It should be obvious that ecological units such as planning areas, census tracts, and block groups offer imperfect operational definitions for research and policy. On the other hand, geographical units such as census tracts and block groups are reasonably consonant with the notion of overlapping and nested ecological structures, and for the most part there are few practical alternatives. Most of the research on which we draw in our discussion of community indicators is thus based on census geography, but increasingly researchers have become interested in new methods that might help define neighborhoods in such a way that is more respectful of the logic of street patterns and possibly more reflective of the social networks of "neighboring" behavior (Grannis 1998). We discuss some of these developments later, but first we consider two broad classes of community indicators: (a) structural characteristics and (b) neighborhood mechanisms.

STRUCTURAL DIFFERENTIATION

Although there is a long history of sociological research on urban communities (Sampson & Morenoff 1997), the study of neighborhood effects gained prominence throughout the social sciences during the 1990s, especially with respect to child and adolescent development. Spurred by Wilson's (1987) seminal book, *The Truly Disadvantaged*, neighborhood research has focused primarily on the effects of concentrated urban poverty and related dimensions of structural economic disadvantage, such as racial and ethnic exclusion (Jargowsky 1996, 1997; Massey & Denton, 1993). The range of child and adolescent outcomes associated with multiple forms of concentrated disadvantage is quite wide and includes infant mortality, low birthweight, teenage childbearing, dropping out of high school, low measured IQ, child maltreatment, and adolescent delinquency (see Brooks-Gunn, Duncan, & Aber, 1997a, 1997b). Moreover, there is an unfortunate parallel to the concentration of disadvantage with regard to health outcomes: the ecological concentration of multiple adverse outcomes, such as homicide, infant mortality, low birthweight, accidental injury, and suicide (Morenoff, 2003; Almgren, Guest, Imerwahr, & Spittel, 1998; Sampson, 1999; Wallace & Wallace 1990). Thus, there may be geographic hot spots for a number of unhealthy outcomes.

Economic resources and sociostructural differentiation in the United States are spatially organized in ways that are often overlooked. Physical capital and human capital (e.g., income, education, housing stock) are unevenly distributed across neighborhoods–often in association with ascribed characteristics such as racial or ethnic composition (Massey & Denton, 1993). One major component of spatial inequality stems from socioeconomic disadvantage and racial and ethnic segregation. Wilson (1987) argued that the geographical concentration of low-income residents, especially of African Americans and female-headed families, stems from macroeconomic changes related to the deindustrialization of central cities and the outmigration of middle-class residents. Massey and Denton (1993) argued that when economic shocks occur in metropolitan areas with high levels of residential segregation, they are more likely to increase the geographic concentration of poverty.

Sampson, Raudenbush, and Earls (1997) argued that such extreme resource deprivation combined with racial exclusion acts as a centrifugal force that hinders collective efficacy (discussed in greater detail shortly). Economic stratification by race and residence thus fuels the neighborhood concentration of cumulative forms of disadvantage, intensifying the social isolation of low-income, minority, and single-parent residents from resources that could support collective social control. The continuing significance of spatial inequality is fundamental to a full understanding of what communities supply for children.

At the other end of the spectrum, it is important to consider the conceptually distinct factor of concentrated *affluence* (Brooks-Gunn, Duncan, Kato, & Sealand, 1993; Massey, 1996). Focusing on the pernicious effects of concentrated disadvantage, although obviously important, may obscure the potential protective effects of affluent neighborhoods. After all, concentrated affluence may be more than just the absence of disadvantage. Recent years have seen the increasing separation of affluent residents from middle-class areas (Massey, 1996), a phenomenon not captured by traditional measures of poverty. Brooks-Gunn et al. (1993), for example, argued that it is the positive influence of concentrated socioeconomic resources, rather than the presence of low-income neighbors, that enhances adolescent outcomes. The resources that affluent neighborhoods can mobilize are theoretically relevant to understanding the activation of social control, regardless of dense social ties and other elements of social capital that might be present. Yet research on child and adolescent development has tended to focus on poverty, neglecting the growing phenomenon of concentrated wealth.[1]

Another such set of structural indicators relates to the continuity or stability of community structure. By *stability* we do not mean lack of change but rather the social reproduction of neighborhood residential structure, typically when population gains offset losses and home values appreciate. A high rate of residential turnover, especially excessive population loss, may foster institutional disruption and weaken interpersonal ties. Not only does residential instability hinder the formation of new social networks, but also the severing of existing ties initiates a disruptive process that affects the entire system of social networks (Coleman, 1990, p. 316). Homeowners also have a shared financial interest in supporting neighborhood life. Thus, residential tenure coupled with home ownership has been argued to promote collective efforts to maintain neighborhood exchange values (Logan & Molotch, 1987) and social control (Sampson et al., 1997; Sampson, Morenoff, & Earls, 1999).

To be sure, other characteristics affect the ability of local communities to engage effectively in collective aspects of childrearing. For example, the density of adults relative to children indicates the child-centered nature of neighborhood life. Although the constraints imposed by group size are often overlooked (Blau, 1994), some neighborhoods may generate little social capital for children simply because of the relative absence of adults. Another factor is the sheer concentration of the overall population. High population density and its accompanying anonymity form a structural limit to what can be achieved through relational ties.

In short, empirical research on community differentiation and spatial inequality has established a reasonably consistent set of four neighborhood facts relevant to children and adolescents.

1. There is considerable race-linked social inequality between neighborhoods and local communities, evidenced by the clustering of indicators of socioeconomic status (both advantage and disadvantage) with racial isolation. Even in areas of racial-ethnic homogeneity, however, economic segregation is common.

2. Myriad social problems tend to come bundled together at the neighborhood level, including but not limited to crime, adolescent delinquency, social and physical disorder, low birthweight, infant mortality, school dropout and child maltreatment.

3. These two sets of clusters are themselves related-neighborhood predictors common to many child/adolescent outcomes include concentrated poverty, racial isolation, family disruption, and residential instability.

4. Empirical results have not varied much with the operational unit of analysis. The ecological stratification of local communities in American society by factors such as social class, race, family status, and crime is a robust phenomenon that emerges at multiple levels of geography, whether local community areas, census tracts, or other neighborhood units.

Neighborhoods and residential differentiation thus remain persistent in American society. As any real estate agent or homeowner (especially those with children) will attest, location does seem to matter. The next logical question is: Why does neighborhood matter, and for what? Taken together, the facts on neighborhood differentiation yield a potentially important clue in thinking about this question. If numerous and seemingly disparate child outcomes are linked together empirically across neighborhoods and are predicted by similar structural characteristics, there may be a common underlying cause or mediating mechanism. Before we turn to these mechanisms, however, we consider how to construct indicators of neighborhood socioeconomic structure.

Measuring Neighborhood Structure

There are two different perspectives on how to construct community indicators for children, which Coulton (1995) referred to as an *outcome orientation* and a *contextual orientation*. The outcome orientation views community indicators as aggregates (typically expressed as rates) of individual-level outcomes relating to health and safety (e.g., infant mortality, low birthweight, child abuse, child homicide), social behavior (e.g., teen childbearing, delinquency), cognitive development and achievement (e.g., educational attainment and school performance), and economic well-being (e.g., child poverty). Such indicators, which are crucial measures of child well-being, have been well covered in a previous review (Coulton, 1995-see her Table 1). Our perspective on constructing community indicators focuses more on explicitly contextual characteristics of communities rather than on aggregates of individual-level outcomes. In this section we focus on indicators of community structure (and in the next section on indicators of social process/institutions) that previous research has shown to be associated with positive and negative child outcomes.

Previous research on structural differentiation and child well-being suggests that there are at least four key components of neighborhood structure: (a) population structure, (b) resource deprivation/affluence, (c) residential stability, and (d) immigration/ethnicity. We draw the first two components from Land, McCall, and Cohen's (1990) research on the structural covariates of homicide, which is arguably still the most comprehensive study of structural differentiation. Land and colleagues analyzed the relationships among the following structural indicators represented in 21 previous macrolevel studies of homicide: population size, population density, percentage of the population that is Black, percentage youth (i.e., percentage of the population aged 15-29), percentage of divorced males, percentage of children not living with both parents, median family income, percentage of families living in poverty, the Gini index of income inequality (a statistical index that measures the degree to which the total income of a population is concentrated among a small fraction of its total families), and the unemployment rate. Using principal-components analysis, the authors found that two clusters of variables consistently "hang together" over time (i.e., for 1960, 1970, and 1980) and space (i.e., for cities, standard metropolitan areas, and states): (a) population size and population density, which combine to form what they called a *population structure component*, and (b) median income, percentage of families below the poverty line, the Gini index of income inequality, percentage Black, and percentage of children not living with both parents, which comprise what they called a *resource deprivation/affluence component*.[2]

There are additional structural variables that Land and colleagues (1990) did not include in their study but that have been shown to cluster together and to correlate with measures of child health and well-being. For example, many researchers have constructed indices of residential stability from census indicators of the proportion of residents who have moved within the past 5 years, the proportion of owner-occupied houses, and the rate of population change between census years (Sampson et al., 1997, 1999). A final cluster of structural variables, which have taken on increasing importance as waves of immigration fueled urban change in the 1990s, are the proportion of residents who are Hispanic and the proportion who are foreign born. This component has been referred to as *concentrated immigration* (Sampson et al., 1997).

In short, there are no widely accepted conventions for constructing indicators of neighborhood structure. Some researchers take a theoretical approach to measuring structural differentiation and either use single-item measures or construct indexes out of the variables they feel are most salient to the outcome in question. Others take a more analytical approach and distinguish structural dimensions on the basis of factor analyses. In either case, we caution here that one widespread tendency is to conflate the concentration of disadvantage with the concentration of affluence, both of which were subsumed by Land et al. (1990) under the resource deprivation/affluence component. In practice, this occurs because indicators of disadvantage (e.g., of families in poverty or receiving welfare, or the proportion of unemployed men in the labor force) and affluence (e.g., the proportion of college-educated residents or the proportion in managerial/professional occupations) are highly correlated across geographical units. It is possible, however, to reflect both tails of the income distribution in one index. We thus extend our focus to a measure that simultaneously captures the concentration of poverty and affluence. The *index of concentration at the extremes* (ICE; Massey, 2001) is defined for a given neighborhood as: [(number of affluent families – number of poor families) / total number of families], where *affluent* is defined as families with income above a certain threshold (e.g., $75,000), and *poor* is defined as families below the poverty line. The ICE index ranges from a theoretical value of –1 (which represents extreme poverty, viz., that all families are poor) to +1 (which signals extreme affluence, viz., that all families are affluent). A value of zero indicates that there is an equal share of poor and affluent families. ICE is therefore an inequality measure that taps both ends of the income distribution, or, as Massey (2001, p. 44) argued, the proportional imbalance between affluence and poverty within a neighborhood.

NEIGHBORHOOD MECHANISMS

One of the major advances in neighborhood research during the 1990s is that scholars began to theorize and measure how neighborhood mechanisms like informal social control bear on the well-being of children (Elliott et al., 1996; Furstenberg, Cook, Eccles, Elder, & Sameroff, 1999; Sampson et al. 1999). In their review of the literature on neighborhoods and child outcomes, Leventhal and Brooks-Gunn (2000) distinguished among three interrelated mechanisms, or pathways through which neighborhood effects are transmitted to children and adolescents: (a) institutional resources, (b) relationships, and (c) norms/collective efficacy.

Institutional Resources

Institutional resources refers to the quality, quantity, and diversity of institutions in the community that address the needs of children, such as schools and other learning centers, libraries, child care, organized social and recreational activities, medical facilities, family support centers, and employment opportunities. For example, a large body of research shows that access to high-quality child care and early intervention programs is associated with positive cognitive and socioemotional outcomes but that lower quality child care can be associated with negative outcomes, such as increased tolerance for aggressive behavior and potential injuries (Leventhal & Brooks-Gunn, 2000). Above and beyond the benefits or detriments associated with specific institutions, however, the overall institutional presence in a community may have more diffuse effects on the social environment for children. Children and adults may form connections with one another through institutions, and those connections may then spill over into other realms of neighborhood life. Moreover, the way institutions relate to one another within a community can determine their effectiveness in bringing extra-local resources into the community. One can imagine a community with a large number of dispirited and isolated institutions, perhaps even in conflict with one another. This is hardly a recipe for social organization, suggesting that it not just dense institutional ties that matter but the ways in which institutions are connected and work together on behalf of the community.

Relationships

Theoretically, one of the driving forces behind much of the research on neighborhood mechanisms has been the idea of *social capital*. Although definitions of the concept vary, social capital is generally conceptualized as a resource that is realized through relationships, as opposed to *physical capital*, which takes observable material form, and *human capital*, which is embodied in the skills and knowledge acquired by an individual. Consider, for example, Coleman's (1990) notion of *intergenerational closure*, which occurs when parents know the parents of their children's friends. When parents have these relationships with other parents, they can observe their children's actions in different circumstances, talk with other parents about their child, and establish norms (Furstenburg et al., 1999). The idea of intergenerational closure can also be generalized to include any local adult—a teacher, religious leader, businesses person, agent of juvenile justice, or concerned resident.

Another important way in which relationships can translate into social capital is through *social support networks* and *reciprocated exchange*. For example, what is the intensity of interfamily and adult interaction with respect to childbearing? An adult may know other parents and

children by face or name in a community but rarely exchange information or otherwise interact. Social capital is reinforced by interactions
such as the exchange of advice, material goods, and information about
child rearing. Reciprocated (or relatively equal) exchange leads to social
support (Portes & Sensenbrenner, 1993) that can be drawn on not just
by parents but also by children themselves as they develop.

Norms/Collective Efficacy

In previous work, Sampson et al. (1997, 1999) have argued that when
neighbors form mutual expectations that they can and will intervene on
behalf of public order and child well-being, they generate *collective efficacy* for children. In our view, social capital for children refers more to
the potential resources represented by personal and organizational networks, whereas collective efficacy adds the element of *mutual trust* and
the *social control* of children through the active engagement of adults in
the community. Using neighborhood-level data from Chicago, we have
shown that collective efficacy is associated with neighborhood structural characteristics (concentrated disadvantage, residential instability,
and immigrant concentration) and that collective efficacy mediates a
substantial part of the association between neighborhood structural
factors and rates of community violence (perceived violence, violent victimization, and homicide rates; see Sampson et al., 1997). In related
work, Sampson (1997) found that a measure of informal social control
of children was associated with neighborhood rates of adolescent delinquency, accounting for approximately 50% of the effect of neighborhood structural characteristics (residential stability) on adolescent
delinquency. Collective efficacy also predicts future rates of violence,
controlling for prior violence and a host of structural characteristics
(Morenoff, Sampson, & Raudenbush, 2001).

Measuring Neighborhood Mechanisms

The 1990s witnessed a number of new efforts to directly measure neighborhood mechanisms. With respect to children, some of the more important include studies in Philadelphia; Denver, Colorado; and Prince
Georges County, Maryland, sponsored by the MacArthur Network on
Successful Adolescence (Cook, Shagle, & Degirmencioglu, 1997; Elliott
et al., 1997; Furstenberg et al., 1999). Furstenberg et al. (1999) in particular designed their study to simultaneously focus on social processes
at the family and neighborhood level. Similarly, Cook et al. (1997) examined family and neighborhood social processes along with key structural factors. The indicators that Cook et al. used, most of which are
directly relevant to the present discussion, are reproduced in Table 11.1.
This table also presents the proportion of variance in each measure that
lies between neighborhoods.

Table 11.1

Intraclass Correlations for Demographic, Process, and Outcome Measures in Philadelphia and Prince George's County, Maryland

Measure	Philadelphia	Prince George's County
Family SES resources	.18	.43
Household education	.14	.16
Household income	.13	.34
Household assets	.18	.44
Neighborhood climate	.22	.25
Social control	.11	.06
Probability of child's success	.20	.26
Social cohesion	.10	.13
Lack of problems	.19	.05
Neighborhood organizations	.13	.17
Availability of organizations	.06	–
Quality of teen programs	.06	–
Quality of schools		
Parenting		
Parent-child communication	.04	.03
Discipline effectiveness	.11	.10
Autonomy	.03	.00
Parent psychological resources	.05	.00
Family Management		
Institutional connections	.03	.04
Parent investment	.08	.07
Positive social networks	.11	–
Parent restrictiveness	.13	–
Attending private school	.08	–
Child/adolescent outcomes		
Academic		
Academic competence	.07	–
Achievement tests	–	.08
Grades	–	.06
Algebra enrollment	–	.08
Absenteeism	–	.06
Activities		
Activity involvement	.04	.02

Measure	Philadelphia	Prince George's County
Problem behavior	.04	.00
Soft drug use	–	.02
Psychological well-being		
Emotional problems	.00	–
Positive feelings about the self	–	.01
Negative feelings about the self	–	.00
Global success	–	.05

Source: Cook et al., 1997, p. 106.

Another effort on which we have labored is the Project on Human Development in Chicago Neighborhoods (PHDCN), a multilevel, longitudinal study of children that is designed to elucidate the role of contextual factors (family, neighborhood, and school) on individual development (Earls & Buka, 1997). Part of this project included a clustered community survey of 8,782 individuals 18 years or older who were interviewed in their homes in 1995, with an average of 25 individuals in each of 343 Chicago neighborhoods (Sampson et al., 1997). A second community survey was conducted in 2002 in the same 343 neighborhoods but with a new sample of 3,105 individuals 18 or older, for an average of 9 respondents per neighborhood. On both surveys, participants rated their neighborhoods on a number of dimensions, including social and physical disorder, violence and victimization, social cohesion, informal social control, danger, and availability of resources (Sampson, 1997; Sampson et al., 1997). We highlight here several child-relevant measures that are reliable and have been validated empirically.

Norms and Collective Efficacy. *Collective efficacy* was operationalized by combining measures of social cohesion and social control (Sampson et al., 1997). Social cohesion is constructed from a cluster of five conceptually related items measuring respondent's level of agreement (on a 5-point Likert scale) with statements such as "People around here are willing to help their neighbors" and "People in this neighborhood do not share the same values" (reverse coded). Informal social control is constructed from respondent assessments of the likelihood (on a 5-point Likert scale) that their neighbors could be counted on to intervene in five situations, such as children skipping school, fighting, and a "fire station closest to their home was threatened with budget cuts." A 3-item Likert scale was also disaggregated from the collective efficacy scale used by Sampson et al. (1997). Specifically, we separated child-centered social control from more general aspects of social cohesion and neighborhood control (e.g., mutual trust, mobilization to keep open a local fire station). Residents were asked about the likelihood ("Would you say it is *very likely, likely, neither likely nor unlikely, unlikely,* or *very unlikely?*") that their neighbors could be counted on to "do something" if children were skipping school and hanging out on a street corner, children were spray-painting graffiti on a local building, and children were showing disrespect to an adult. We took the average of these items as our measure. Norms and tolerance of deviance were tapped by a previously validated scale in which respondents were asked "How wrong is it for teenagers around 13 years of age to (1) smoke cigarettes, (2) use marijuana, (3) drink alcohol, and (4) get into fist fights?" These items were measured on a 5-point Likert scale that ranged from 1 (*not wrong at all*) to 5 (*extremely wrong*). Four corresponding questions asked how wrong the same acts were for "teenagers around 19 years of age" (Sampson & Bartusch, 1998). Tolerance of deviance varies significantly and systematically across neighborhood context.

Relationships and Ties. Five items were used to measure intergenerational closure for children. Each respondent was asked whether: "Parents in this neighborhood know their children's friends," "Adults in this neighborhood know who the local children are," "There are adults in this neighborhood that children can look up to," "Parents in this neighborhood generally know each other," and "You can count on adults in this neighborhood to watch out that children are safe and don't get in trouble." Coded on a 5-point scale that ranged from *strongly disagree* to *strongly agree*, these questions tap the possibility for intergenerational connections and active support of neighborhood children by adults—whether or not the adults are parents. *Reciprocated exchange* was measured by a 5-item scale tapping the relative frequency of social exchange within the neighborhood on issues of consequence for children. The items were "About how often do you and people in your neighborhood do favors for each other? By favors we mean such things as watching each other's children, helping with shopping, lending garden or house tools, and other small acts of kindness?" (*never, rarely, sometimes,* or *often*); "How often do you and people in this neighborhood have parties or other get-togethers where other people in the neighborhood are invited?"; "When a neighbor is not at home, how often do you and other neighbors watch over their property?"; "How often do you and other people in this neighborhood visit in each other's homes or on the street?"; "How often do you and other people in the neighborhood ask each other advice about personal things such as childrearing or job openings?" *Friend/kinship ties* measures the number and relative proportion of friends and relatives that respondents in the survey reported living in their neighborhood.

Institutional Resources. *Organizations/services* was a 9-item index of reported local organizations and programs (e.g., presence of a block group, tenant association, crime prevention program, family health service) combined with a 5-item inventory of youth services (youth center, recreational programs, after-school programs, mentoring/counseling services, mental health services, and crisis intervention). *Voluntary associations* taps involvement by residents in local religious organizations; neighborhood watch programs; block groups, tenant associations, or community councils; business or civic groups; ethnic or nationality clubs; and local political organizations. *Neighborhood activism* summarizes responses to five questions on whether respondents had contacted local officials (e.g., politician, church leader) or otherwise taken action "to take care of a local problem, or to make the neighborhood a better place to live." Other resource measures are available as well.

We caution that the measures just discussed are illustrative only of the types of child-related social indicators that can be derived from a clustered survey approach. Nonetheless, the good news is that a fair number of studies are now underway or completed that use similar measures of social processes. We envision a day not too far off where greater standardization will emerge, allowing for even greater comparison and comparability across community studies in different cities. A promising example of a recently launched effort is the Los Angeles Family and Neighborhood Study (see http://www.lasurvey.rand.org/index.htm).

NEW DIRECTIONS IN COMMUNITY INDICATORS

Along with the advances made in the previous decade in conceptualizing and measuring neighborhood mechanisms come new questions and problems that lead the field in exciting directions. We highlight three new directions in research on the community context of child well-being: (a) redefining neighborhood boundaries in ways that are more consonant with children's experiences, (b) collecting data on the physical and social properties of neighborhood environments through systematic social observations, and (c) taking account of the spatial relations between neighborhoods in constructing community indicators. All three of these issues bear on decisions and recommendations for creating community indicators of child well-being.

Neighborhood Boundaries

Although predominant in the neighborhood effects literature, the strategy of defining neighborhoods on the basis of census geography and using tracts or higher geographical aggregations as proxies for neighborhoods is especially problematic from the standpoint of studying young children and their emotional health (Leventhal & Brooks-Gunn; Sampson, 1992). The microdimensions of neighborhood life may be particularly important for child well-being because of the spatial constraints on young children's patterns of daily activities. A new approach to defining neighborhoods, as seen in Grannis's (1998, 2001) recent studies of Los Angeles; San Francisco; Pasadena, California; and Ithaca, New York, delineates ecological contexts based on the geography of street patterns. Using a Geographic Information System (GIS), Grannis's (1998, 2001) defines residential units that he called *tertiary communities* by delineating aggregations of street blocks that are "reachable" by pedestrian access—meaning that pedestrians can walk through the area without having to cross over a major thoroughfare. In his research, Grannis compared these communities defined by residential street patterns to data on the social networks of neighbors and found that neighborhood residents generally seem to interact more with people living within their tertiary communities than with people who live nearby but across a major thoroughfare.

This micro-ecology of pedestrian streets bears directly on patterns of interaction that involve children and families. Parents are generally concerned with demarcating territory outside of which their children should not wander unaccompanied by an adult, to ensure that their children stay in areas that are safe for play and conducive to adult monitoring. To the extent that these limited spaces of children's daily activities usually do not cross major thoroughfares, Grannis' (1998, 2001) approach to defining tertiary communities may provide a foundation for constructing community indicators of child well-being. However, at present, this research is still in its infancy, and a great deal remains to be learned about how generalizable the idea of a tertiary community is across cities, suburbs, and rural areas.

Systematic Social Observation

Another trend in neighborhood research is to collect data that more directly reflect the sights, sounds, and feel of the streets. The motivation behind collecting observational data is that there are physical and social features of neighborhood environments that cannot be captured in surveys but that provide very tangible contexts for child development. Consider the example of using systematic social observation of street blocks. The PHDCN research team conducted such an exercise in Chicago neighborhoods. Between June and October 1995, observers trained at the National Opinion Research Center drove a sport utility vehicle (SUV) at a rate of 3 to 5 miles per hour down every street within the stratified probability sample of 80 Chicago neighborhoods. To observe each block face (one side of a street within a block), the National Opinion Research Center team fielded a driver, a videographer, and two observers. As the SUV was driven down the street, a pair of videorecorders, one located on each side of SUV, captured social activities and physical features of both block faces simultaneously. At the same time, two trained observers, one on each side of SUV, recorded their observations onto an observer log for each block face. The observers added audio commentary onto the videotape when relevant (e.g., about unusual events such as an accident or drug bust). Block faces were observed and videotaped between the hours of 7:00 a.m. and 7:00 p.m. Applying these procedures, we produced Hi-8 videotapes, observer logs, and audiotapes for every block face in each of the 80 sampled neighborhoods-yielding a total of 23,816 block faces that were observed and videorecorded. Given the geographical structure of observing block faces, data can be aggregated to any level of analysis desired (block, block group, housing project, school, and neighborhood) to characterize social and physical characteristics. Such data can be exploited to build new measures of micro-neighborhood contexts.

Sampson and Raudenbush (1999; Raudenbush & Sampson, 1999a, 1999b) have developed a method for constructing observational measures of neighborhoods from these data and used the resulting scales to analyze neighborhood crime rates. In previous research and other ongoing analyses, we have constructed several neighborhood indicators that bear on child well-being, including the following four:

1. *Physical disorder* is a scale composed of items coded from videotape including, in declining order of observed frequency, the presence or absence of cigarettes or cigars in street or gutter, garbage or litter on street or sidewalk, empty beer bottles visible in street, tagging graffiti, graffiti painted over, gang graffiti, abandoned cars, condoms on sidewalk, needles/syringes on sidewalk, and political message graffiti.

2. *Social disorder* includes items coded for the presence or absence of adults loitering or congregating,[3] drinking alcohol in public, peer group with gang indicators present, public intoxication, adults fighting or arguing in a hostile manner, prostitutes on the street, and selling drugs.

3. *Physical condition of housing* is defined by items tapping vacant houses, dilapidated houses, burned-out houses, dilapidated parks, poorly maintained commercial buildings, and burned out commercial buildings.

4. *Alcohol and tobacco advertising* is measured by the presence of alcohol signs and tobacco signs on a block. A related variable is *alcohol sales*, defined by the presence of bars and liquor stores on block.

One limitation of systematic social observation as a method is that it is relatively expensive and tedious to videotape neighborhood block faces and then code the resulting tapes. However, in a collaborative project between PHDCN and other researchers at the Institute for Social Research (at the University of Michigan), we are currently implementing this method on a wider scale by having interviewers observe and rate city blocks on foot while they are out in the field conducting interviews. If this method, which is substantially cheaper than using videotapes, yields comparably reliable measures, it could serve as a model for more widely implementing systematic social observation as a tool for constructing indicators of child well-being.

Spatial Dynamics of Child Well-Being

A third trend in neighborhood research is to expand the idea of community context to include nearby areas of the city outside of the formal boundaries of a given neighborhood, however it is defined. The general idea is that a child's well-being is influenced by not only what happens in the child's immediate neighborhood but also by what happens in surrounding neighborhoods. For example, the benefits of collective efficacy may accrue not just to the residents of a particular neighborhood but potentially to residents in adjacent areas. Parents who send their child to play with friends in a nearby neighborhood where residents tend to engage in collective supervision and monitoring of children derive a spatial advantage from living next to a place that is collectively efficacious, much in the way that they would benefit from living next to a park or a good school. By contrast, neighborhoods with minimal expectations for social control and sparse interfamily exchange produce spatial disadvantages for parents and children who live in adjoining areas. This framework highlights the implications of residential segregation for child well-being. As a consequence of segregation, many African American neighborhoods are surrounded by areas of high crime and low social control. Parents who live in neighborhoods that are collectively efficacious but where the surrounding areas offer much less social control of children may need to exercise more constant monitoring and supervision of their children than parents who live in areas of the city where collective efficacy is more spatially concentrated.

One implication of these spatial dynamics for the study of child well-being is that community indicators that focus on processes or outcomes internal to a given neighborhood are getting only part of the story. To construct indicators that tap into the wider spatial dynamics of child well-being, we have applied descriptive techniques from spatial statistics (Morenoff et al., 2001; Sampson et al., 1999). For example, it is possible to categorize neighborhoods by their values of an indicator, y, and the weighted average of y in spatially contiguous neighborhoods, Wy.[4] Cross-classifying neighborhoods on the basis of whether they are above or below the mean on both y and Wy results in what is called a *Moran Scatter plot* (Anselin 1995a, 1995b). Using our scale of child-centered social control (described earlier) as an example, if neighborhoods that are above the mean on y are considered to have high values of control, whereas neighborhoods that are below the mean are classified as low, and if the same distinction is made with respect to values of Wy, we get the following four categories: (a) low-low, for neighborhoods that have low levels of control and are near other neighborhoods with low levels of control; (b) low-high, for neighborhoods that have low levels of control but are near others with high levels; (c) high-low, for neighborhoods that have high levels of child control but are near others with low levels; and (d) high–high, for neighborhoods with high levels of control that are also near others with high levels of control. Anselin (1995a, 1995b) has developed a statistic called the *Local Moran indicator*, which builds on this typology but also adds a test of the statistical significance of spatial clustering in each neighborhood (see Sampson et al., 1999).

In Figure 11.1, we reproduce a map from previous work (Sampson et al., 1999) that shows the spatial typology of child-centered social con-

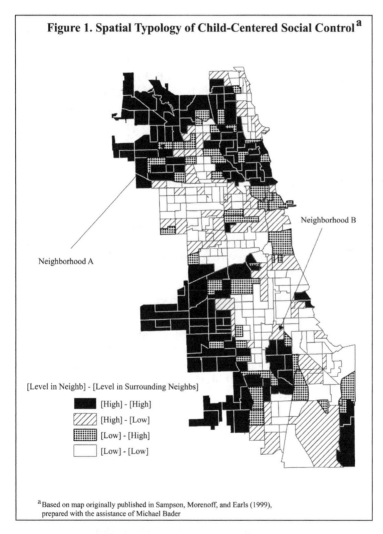

Figure 1. Spatial Typology of Child-Centered Social Control [a]

Neighborhood B

Neighborhood A

[Level in Neighb] - [Level in Surrounding Neighbs]

■ [High] - [High]
▨ [High] - [Low]
▩ [Low] - [High]
□ [Low] - [Low]

[a] Based on map originally published in Sampson, Morenoff, and Earls (1999), prepared with the assistance of Michael Bader

Figure 11.1.   Spatial typology of child-centered social control. Based on a map originally published in Sampson, Morenoff, and Earls (1999), prepared with the assistance of Michael Bader.

trol in Chicago neighborhood clusters (aggregates of census tracts).[5] Most neighborhoods in this map fall into either the high-high (red) or low-low (blue) category, meaning that the level of child control in that area is congruent with the level in surrounding areas. However, neighborhoods in which the level of child control is at variance with that in surrounding areas are important theoretically because they display patterns of spatial advantage and disadvantage. For example, in Figure 11.1, Neighborhood A has low shared expectations of child social control but adjoins a cluster of neighborhoods in which expectations are significantly higher. This type of neighborhood, despite lacking a crucial element of collective efficacy, is likely to derive a spatial advantage from the spillover of child control in surrounding areas. On the other hand, Neighborhood B illustrates the potential operation of spatial disadvantage: Despite having high expectations of child control, this neighborhood is located near areas in which there is significantly less shared willingness to intervene on behalf of children. The predicament faced by this type of neighborhood is similar to one Pattillo-McCoy (1998) described from her ethnography of a middle-class African American neighborhood at spatial risk-one surrounded by concentrated poverty and high crime.

Indicators of spatial association such as the Local Moran statistic could be easily applied to the study of child well-being given aggregate data in which the units of analysis (e.g., census tracts) completely cover a geographic area. Such an approach does not make sense, however, when data are drawn from samples that are distributed over a wide region and cannot be aggregated to form meaningful ecological units that are geographically contiguous.

IMPLICATIONS

Consideration of the structural properties and social mechanisms linked to community environments promises a deeper understanding of the etiology of child outcomes and the development of community-based monitoring strategies. An important step in fostering further progress would be to support the systematic collection of benchmark data on social environments that can be compared across communities (Singer & Ryff, 2001, chap. 6). The goal would be to develop a standardized approach to the collection and dissemination of data that individual communities could use to evaluate where they stand in regard to national and/or regional norms. Similar to school report cards that track the progress of educational reform, a standardized approach to assessing collective properties would eventually allow local communities to gauge how well or poorly they are doing on a variety of child-related dimensions.

Several cities already have in place systematic efforts to collect data on neighborhood indicators. One example is the "Sustainable Seattle" project, where some 40 indicators have been collected for use as a benchmark to gauge the progress of Seattle in meeting various goals of public and civic health. An innovative combination of archival records, census data, and surveys have been used to compile sustainability trends across five basic areas: (a) environment (e.g., air quality), (b) population and resources (e.g., fuel consumption), (c) economy (e.g., housing afford-ability, poverty), (d) youth and education (e.g., high school graduation, literacy), and (e) community health (e.g., low birthweight, neighborliness). The Leaders Roundtable in Portland, Oregon, has undertaken a similarly ambitious initiative ("The Caring Community") that has collected data on community health using a combination of focus groups, surveys, key stakeholder interviews, and document reviews. In an effort to develop and coordinate such data collection activities in cities across the country, the Urban Institute has partnered with affiliates in 21 cities to form the National Neighborhood Indicators Partnership (http://www.urban.org/nnip/), which builds neighborhood-level information systems to be used in local policymaking and community-building efforts (Kingsley, 1999; Pettit, Kingsley, & Coulton, 2003). More recently, Robert Putnam has launched a benchmark survey both nationwide and in about 40 American communities, with the goal of assessing baseline levels of social capital (see http://www.cfsv.org/communitysurvey/). We also noted earlier some strategies for new data collection involving systematic social observation. If measurement standards and systematic procedures at the national level could be developed, communities could then use benchmark data to develop early warning signs with respect to changes in the quality of child environments.

Alongside such data collection there is a need for strategic investment in methods that are central to building an infrastructure capable of supporting the assessment and analysis of community social capital on a systematic and flexible scale. In addition to multilevel spatial methods and ecometrics that take seriously the community as a unit of measurement and analysis (see Raudenbush & Sampson, 1999), a practical move is to invest in GIS and support the geographical linkage of ongoing data collection efforts. For instance, data on child outcomes can now be linked virtually in real time to address-level databases on density of liquor stores, mixed land use, and building code violations. Such *geocoding* would support the ability to use existing records to construct community health profiles for children, thereby aiding in the development of benchmark standards. A principal advantage of GIS is the ability to overlay multiple phenomena in time and space.

When combined with the advances emphasized earlier in this chapter on directly measuring social processes, defining microneighborhood contexts on the basis of street patterns, systematically observing public spaces, and detecting and displaying spatial dynamics, the future looks bright for constructing community-level indicators that reflect both the outcomes and contextual sources of child development.

CONCLUSION

The idea of condensing the complexity of community life down to a limited set of indicators is daunting. In this chapter, we organized our discussion around two broad classes of indicators–neighborhood structure and neighborhood social processes–to highlight an important trend in the field toward identifying and studying social and institutional processes and to emphasize that policymakers and child advocates, who have tended to focus exclusively on structure (mainly for practical reasons), should also consider constructing indicators of process. With this in mind, we tentatively suggest that the following community indicators of child well-being are critical to develop over the coming decade (a summary of our recommended indicators is presented in Table 11.2):

• *Consider the ICE as a primary indicator of neighborhood structure*: Although it is not widely used in research, it is a convenient summary index of the relative levels of both affluence and poverty in a given location. It also has the advantages of being easy to implement from census data and of having a consistent interpretation across time and space because it does not rely on changing empirical correlations between various dimensions of disadvantage and affluence, as do other more commonly used structural measures.

• *Consider adapting scales of social cohesion and child-centered social control as primary indicators of neighborhood mechanisms*: Selecting indicators of neighborhood mechanisms is especially difficult because they cannot be neatly classified as either positive or negative features of neighborhood context. One of the basic points of the emerging literature on negative social capital is that not all of the processes we consider to be neighborhood mechanisms have uniform positive effects (see Portes, 1999). For example, we would not consider racial exclusion, such as practiced in "defended" neighborhoods (Suttles, 1972), a desirable form of social capital. With this caveat in mind, we nonetheless recommend that the measures we have developed for social cohesion and child-centered social control have displayed strong empirical correlations across a range of neighborhood outcomes, including crime, physical and social disorder, and low birthweight. Although there is currently no national data set that contains such measures, the ideal arrangement would be to append them to an ongoing national survey, such as the General Social Survey, which has a clustered sampling design necessary to derive aggregate measures of social context.

• *Consider systematic observational measures, especially as linked to surveys.* We have specifically listed indicators of disorder, housing quality, and alcohol advertising and sales, all of which can be recorded using observational instruments. These measures have been shown to have high reliability at the block group level, and they bear

Table 11.2
Recommended Community Indicators

I. From census data

Index of Concentrated Extremes

$$\frac{(\text{\# Affluent Families} - \text{\# Poor Families})}{\text{\# Families}}$$

II. From community survey

Social Cohesion: Agreement (on scale of 1–4) with following statements:

This is a close-knit neighborhood.

People around here are willing to help their neighbors

People in this neighborhood generally get along with each other

People in this neighborhood can be trusted

People in this neighborhood share the same values

Child-Centered Social Control: For each of the following scenarios, respondents were asked, "how likely is it that your neighbors would do something about it" (on scale of 1–4):

If a group of neighborhood children were skipping school and hanging out on a street corner, how likely is it that your neighbors would do something about it?

If some children were spray-painting graffiti on a local building, how likely is it that your neighbors would do something about it?

If a child was showing disrespect to an adult, how likely is it that people in your neighborhood would scold that child?

If there was a fight in front of your house and someone was being beaten or threatened, how likely is it that your neighbors would break it up?

III. From Systematic Social Observation

Physical Disorder: Observe the presence/absence of the following on a block face:

Garbage/litter/broken glass (scale from 1–4)

Cigarette/cigar butts

Beer/Liquor bottles

Needles/syringes/drug-related paraphernalia

Condoms

Abandoned cars

Gang graffiti

Tagging graffiti

Graffiti painted over

directly on the lives of children in American cities. We specifically recommend the measure of physical disorder, which has been shown to be highly reliable in previous research (Raudenbush & Sampson 1999b).

ACKNOWLEDGMENT

Parts of this chapter were previously published in Sampson, Morenoff, and Gannon-Rowley (2002). Reprinted by permission.

NOTES

1. Pebley and Sastry's (2003) study on the effects of neighborhood poverty and affluence on children's reading-related and math-related achievement found that neighborhood-level median income accounts for more variation in children's achievement than their measures of either concentrated poverty or concentrated affluence. They concluded that the overall income level in a neighborhood may be a more important contextual indicator for children's achievement than either the proportion of very poor or affluent people/families in a neighborhood.
2. Although the variables in the resource deprivation/affluence component seem to tap somewhat different concepts, Land and colleagues found they could not be separated empirically.
3. Because children and teenagers commonly play in public spaces, the coding rules limited the observation of loitering to groups of 3 or more adults not waiting for scheduled activities or businesses. For example, groups of adults waiting for public transportation or in line for a store would not be included. Coders were trained to a high degree of interrater agreement across all types of neighborhoods. Still, we acknowledge some residual ambiguity in the meaning of *loitering*.
4. More formally, Wy for a given observation i is defined as $\Sigma_i w_{ij} y_i$. In this case, the spatial weights matrix, w_{ij}, is defined as a binary contiguity matrix, meaning that $w_{ij} = 1$ if i and j are contiguous, 0 if not.
5. In this map we do not display the statistical significance of each category on the Moran Scatter plot spatial typology. For map displaying statistical significance, see Sampson et al. (1999, Fig. 2).

REFERENCES

Almgrem, G., Guest, A. Imerwahr, G., & Spittel, M. (1998). Joblessness, family disruption, and violent death in Chicago, 1970-1990. *Social Forces, 76*, 1465–1493.

Anselin, L. (1995b). *SpaceStat Version 1.80: User's guide*. Morgantown: West Virginia University.

Anselin, L. (1995a). Local indicators of spatial association-LISA. *Geographical Analysis, 27*, 93–115.

Blau, P. (1994). *Structural contexts of opportunities*. Chicago: University of Chicago Press.

Brooks-Gunn, J., Duncan, G., Kato, P., & Sealand, N. (1993). Do neighborhoods influence child and adolescent behavior? *American Journal of Sociology, 99,* 353–395.

Brooks-Gunn, J., Duncan, G. J., & Aber, L. (Eds.). (1997a). *Consequences of growing up poor.* New York: Russell Sage Foundation.

Brooks-Gunn, J., Duncan, G. J., & Aber, L. (1997b). *Neighborhood poverty: Policy implications in studying neighborhoods.* New York: Russell Sage Foundation.

Coleman, J. S. (1990). *Foundations of social theory.* Cambridge, MA: Harvard University Press.

Cook, T., Shagle, S., & Degirmencioglu, S. (1997). Capturing social process for testing mediational models of neighborhood effects. In J. Brooks-Gunn, G. Duncan, & L. Aber (Eds.), *Neighborhood poverty: Policy implications in studying neighborhoods* (pp. 94–119). New York: Russell Sage Foundation.

Coulton, C. J. (1995). Using community-level indicators of children's well-being in comprehensive community initiatives. In *New approaches to evaluating community initiatives* (pp. 173–199. Washington, DC: Aspen Institute.

Elliott, D., Wilson, W. J., Huizinga, D., Sampson, R. J., Elliott, A., & Rankin, B. (1996). Effects of neighborhood disadvantage on adolescent development. *Journal of Research in Crime and Delinquency, 33,* 389–426.

Felton, E., & Buka, S. (1997). *Project on human development in Chicago neighborhoods: Technical report.* Rockville, MD: National Institute of Justice.

Furstenberg, F. F., Cook, T. D., Eccles, J., Elder, G. H., Jr. & Sameroff, A. (1999). *Managing to make it: Urban families and adolescent success.* Chicago: University of Chicago Press.

Grannis, R. (1998). The importance of trivial streets: Residential streets and residential segregation. *American Journal of Sociology, 103,* 1530–1564.

Jargowsky, P. (1996). Take the money and run: Economic segregation in U.S. metropolitan areas. *American Sociological Review, 61,* 984–998.

Jargowsky, P. (1997). *Poverty and place: Ghettos, barrios, and the American city.* New York: Russell Sage Foundation.

Jencks, C., & Mayer, S. (1990). The social consequences of growing up in a poor neighborhood. In L. E. Lynn & M. F. H. McGeary (Eds.), *Inner-city poverty in the United States* (pp. 111–186). Washington, DC: National Academy Press.

Kingsley, G. T. (Ed.). (1999). *Building and operating neighborhood indicator systems: A guidebook* (National Neighborhood Indicators Partnership Report). Washington, DC: Urban Institute.

Land, K., McCall, P., & Cohen, L. (1990). Structural covariates of homicide rates: Are there any invariances across time and space? *American Journal of Sociology, 95,* 922–963.

Leventhal, T., & Brooks-Gunn, J. (2000). The neighborhoods they live in: The effects of neighborhood residence on child and adolescent outcomes. *Psychological Bulletin, 126,* 309–337.

Logan, J., & Molotch, H. (1987). *Urban fortunes: The political economy of place.* Berkeley: University of California Press.

Massey, D. S. (1996). The age of extremes: Concentrated affluence and poverty in the twenty-first century. *Demography, 33,* 395–412.

Massey, D. S. (2001). The prodigal paradigm returns: Ecology comes back to sociology. In A. Booth & A. Crouter (Eds.), *Does it take a village? Community effects on children, adolescents, and families* (pp. 41–48). Mahwah, NJ: Lawrence Erlbaum Associates.

Massey, D. S., & Denton, N. (1993). *American apartheid: Segregation and the making of the underclass.* Cambridge, MA: Harvard University Press.

Morenoff, J. (2003). Neighborhood mechanisms and the spatial dynamics of birth weight. *American Journal of Sociology*, 108, 976–1017.

Morenoff, J., & Sampson, R. J. (1997). Violent crime and the spatial dynamics of neighborhood transition: Chicago, 1970–1990. *Social Forces*, 76, 31–64.

Morenoff, J., Sampson, R. J., & Raudenbush, S. (2001). Neighborhood inequality, collective efficacy, and the spatial dynamics of homicide. *Criminology*.

Park, R. (1916). The city: Suggestions for the investigations of human behavior in the urban environment. *American Journal of Sociology*, 20, 577–612.

Pattillo-McCoy, M. E. (1998). *Black picket fences: Privilege and peril among the Black middle class*. Chicago: University of Chicago Press.

Pebley, A., & Sastry, N. (2003). Concentrated poverty vs. concentrated affluence: Effects on neighborhood social environments and children's outcomes (RAND Labor and Population Working Paper Series 03-24). Santa Monica, CA: RAND.

Pettit, K. L. S., Kingsley, G. T., & Coulton, C. J. (2003). *Neighborhoods and health: Building evidence for local policy*. Washington, DC: Urban Institute.

Portes, A. (1998). Social capital: Its origins and applications in modern sociology. *Annual Review of Sociology*, 24, 1–24.

Portes, A., & Sensenbrenner, J. (1993). Embeddedness and immigration: Notes on the social determinants of economic action. *American Journal of Sociology*, 98, 1320–1350.

Raudenbush, S., & Sampson, R. J. (1999a). Assessing direct and indirect effects in multilevel designs with latent variables. *Sociological Methods and Research*, 28, 123–153.

Raudenbush, S., & Sampson, R. J. (1999b). "Ecometrics": Toward a science of assessing ecological settings, with application to the systematic social observation of neighborhoods. *Sociological Methodology*, 29, 1–41.

Sampson, R. J. (2001). How do communities undergird or undermine human development? Relevant contexts and social mechanisms. In A. Booth & N. Crouter (Eds.), *Does it take a village? Community effects on children, adolescents, and families* (pp. 3–30). Mahwah, NJ: Lawrence Erlbaum Associates.

Sampson, R. J., & Morenoff, J. D. (1997). Ecological perspectives on the neighborhood context of urban poverty: Past and present. In J. Brooks-Gunn, G. J. Duncan, & J. L. Aber (Eds.), *Neighborhood poverty: Volume 2. Policy implications in studying neighborhoods* (pp. 1–22). New York: Russell Sage Foundation.

Sampson, R. J., Morenoff, J. D., & Earls, F. (1999). Beyond social capital: Spatial dynamics of collective efficacy for children. *American Sociological Review, 64,* 633–660.

Sampson, R. J., Morenoff, J. D., & Gannon-Rowley, T. (2002). Assessing "neighborhood effects": Social processes and new directions in research. *Annual Review of Sociology*, 28, 443–478.

Sampson, R. J., & Bartusch, D. J. (1998). Legal cynicism and (subcultural?) tolerance of deviance: The neighborhood context of racial differences. *Law and Society Review*, 32, 777–804.

Sampson, R. J., & Raudenbush, S. (1999). Systematic social observation of public spaces: A new look at disorder in urban neighborhoods. *American Journal of Sociology*, 105, 603–651.

Sampson, R. J., Raudenbush, S., & Earls, F. (1997). Neighborhoods and violent crime: A multilevel study of collective efficacy. *Science*, 277, 918–924.

Singer, B., & Ryff, C. (Eds.). (2001). *New horizons in health: An integrative report.* Washington, DC: National Academy Press.

Suttles, G. (1972). *The social construction of communities.* Chicago: University of Chicago Press.

Wilson, W. J. (1987). *The truly disadvantaged: The inner city, the underclass, and public policy.* Chicago: University of Chicago Press.

Part V

Child and Youth Indicators in Practice

Chapter 12

Social Indicators as a Policy Tool: Welfare Reform as a Case Study

Thomas J. Corbett
University of Wisconsin at Madison

Developing and implementing a system of social indicators that can instrumentally shape public policies has emerged as a critical challenge in recent years. Driving this challenge are the public sector *devolution* and *reinvention* movements, two of the more powerful themes now shaping U.S. social policy. Devolution constitutes a shift in program authority from more inclusive levels of government to levels closer to the problems intended to be addressed (e.g., from the national government to local communities). Similarly, the reinvention movement shifts public sector management from a focus on process and inputs (what programs and policies do or invest) to a focus on outcomes (what policies and programs accomplish).

This focus on results has inevitably driven state and local governments to rethink how they organize what they do for vulnerable families and communities. It demands that services be organized and delivered along lines shaped by the problems and challenges addressed rather than by the arbitrary way programs are structured and funded at state or federal levels. In short, this focus on results, public accountability, and new forms of organizing social assistance increasingly demands a much more sophisticated use of what we broadly think of as *social indicators* (see Koshel, 1997).

The two governance themes of devolution and reinvention, proponents argue, give policy officials and program managers greater freedom to restructure the ways they deliver services. Taken together, these themes could well alter policy making and management by facilitating the emergence of outcome-based accountability strategies, of systemwide coordination and integration efforts, of performance-based competitive service models, and of public sector privatization and democratization schemes. It is not surprising, then, that extraordinary at-

333

tention has been paid to the development and use of indicators as a critical instrument for advancing these management strategies over the course of the past two decades or so.

Simply put, an *indicator* can be thought of as a measure of some phenomenon or attribute that taps something of importance to society. In the economic realm, we have well-developed indicators whose importance is fully reflected in the frequency with which they are reported and the eagerness with which they are anticipated. The most recent inflation and unemployment data are reported as soon as they become available. The nuances and consequences of the numbers are vetted immediately and endlessly, in part because they might well influence a host of policy levers and decisions made by the Federal Reserve Board, private investment decisions by individuals and firms, and policy in a score of other public agencies.

Some indicators—for example, the various equity market indicators—have been around for more than a century and have always received considerable attention. Today, however, these purported measures of economic vitality and health are ubiquitous. In real time, one can access data in airports, on cable television channels, on electronic billboards, and elsewhere. There is a sense of immediacy and consequence attached to these numbers. For many, being out of touch, even for the briefest period, evokes anxiety and uncertainty.

Social indicators, on the other hand, quantitatively measure key attributes that reflect how society, or seminal populations of interest, are doing. In one sense, virtually all indicators are social in that they reflect, even if indirectly, the well-being of individuals and families. Unemployment rates are a direct measure of social hurt if you are the one without a job, and they are a measure of community health if you are working in a jurisdiction where the rate is unacceptably high. Measures of poverty can certainly be thought of as both an economic and a social indicator. The poverty measure is considered a reflection of the economic and social health of the larger community because an insufficient command over resources is seen as a proxy for a host of other difficulties affecting families and communities.

As we move from the economic realm to the social realm, our investment in the quality and timeliness of our important indicators diminishes. It is true enough that we annually report the national poverty rate as well as rates for important subgroups, and the publicity and attention surrounding the publication of this indicator can be significant. Still, immediate policy responses to problems reflected in the data are rare. More remarkable is that there has been no serious attempt to improve the official poverty measure despite the widespread acknowledgment that the current measure is seriously deficient (see "Revising the Poverty Measure," 1998). In addition, we invest little in the data infrastructure that would enable us to monitor poverty trends in real time at substate levels of aggregation and among many populations of interest, for example, minority children. It is hard to imagine that indicators used to track the business cycle would be permitted to languish in such a fashion.

The quality of what might be considered purely social indicators and their application to public and private sector policy challenges evidences a complex and ambiguous track record. As detailed further later in this chapter, some attention has been paid to indicators tapping community, family, and children's well-being. For example, the comprehensive publication of the U.S. Department of Health and Human Services (DHHS) titled *Trends in the Well-Being of America's Children and Youth* is an excellent example of a well-meaning effort to bring policy attention to some of the nation's most vulnerable members (Office of the Assistant Secretary of Planning and Evaluation [ASPE], 2003). The report presents recent and reliable estimates on more than 80 indicators of child well-being, covering five broad domains: (a) population, family, and neighborhood; (b) economic security; (c) Health conditions and health care; (d) social development, behavioral health, and teen fertility; and (e) education and achievement.

Trends in the Well-Being of America's Children and Youth, which incorporates data from all the major executive agencies as well as research organizations, is intended to "provide the policy community, the media, and all interested citizens with an accessible overview of data describing the condition of children in the United States" (ASPE, 2003). The publication of these data, however, typically elicits little of the excitement surrounding the availability of new economic data.

With few exceptions, these indicators are treated more as resource information than as input into the policy debate about the meaning of the good society and how to achieve it. Social indicators are used and occasionally can capture public and political attention, but they do not routinely drive policy agendas.

This chapter examines the potential of social indicators and how they might be better used as policy tools. Particular attention is paid to the conceptual and practical challenges of realizing their practical potential. In doing so, several questions are posed. Can social indicators, particularly those reflecting the circumstances of children and youth, shape and inform social policy to the extent that labor market and economic indicators do? Will the observed transformations in public policy and governance in fact motivate us to improve the quality and timeliness of child, family, and community indicators, or will our failure to do so short circuit these broader societal transformations?

BACKGROUND AND CONTEXT

The use of social and community indicators goes back a long way. Early progressives and social reformers, along with scholars from the early days of sociology, attempted to document community health and the status of vulnerable groups, particularly immigrants, at the beginning of the 20th century. Progressive reformers, sometimes associated with settlement houses (e.g., Hull House in Chicago) and newly formed university-based sociology departments, tried to map out the situation of urban slums using crude measures of community health. The devastation of the Great Depression prompted continuing interest in economic measures of societal health, and the late 1960s witnessed another wave of serious interest in using social indicators, more broadly defined (see Patterson, 1986).

Starting in the 1980s, the social indicator movement has reemerged. For example, in 1989 the state of Oregon launched its ambitious Oregon Benchmarks project, an effort to use a broad array of social indicators as a basis for increasing local accountability. In response to this renewed interest in performance and government efficiency and effectiveness, the development of social indicators has become an issue in Washington, DC, and the states as well as among academics and others in the policy world.

Interest in developing social indicators as policy monitoring and management tools accelerated in the early 1990s. The Annie E. Casey Foundation's KIDS COUNT project began routinely publishing national indicators on the status of children and eventually supported similar efforts in each of the states. In short order, the number of organizations actively involved in the indicator movement grew, as did the intensity of their involvement.[1] Despite this growing interest, it quickly became clear that there exists a fine and ever-shifting line between informing society about social conditions and influencing current and future policy discussions, the latter demanding quality and believable information. Data on indicators are expensive and can be difficult to obtain, however, so we often rely on what is available rather than what is needed. Some domains, or areas of interest, are well covered, whereas indicators in other domains, for all practical purposes, do not exist. There are many pitfalls in the collection and interpretation of indicators. Every step in the process of using social indicators—selection, collection, mode of presentation, choice of baseline or comparative data—is partly subjective and thus open to second guessing. It became clear early on that developing a good set of social indicators and actually using them for policy purposes would be a marathon effort.

Recognizing these challenges, the Institute for Research on Poverty (IRP), Child Trends, and the ASPE sponsored a 1-day planning workshop in 1993. From that event emerged plans for a national conference on child and family indicators, held in November 1994. The papers from that national conference were subsequently updated and revised and published in 1997 in book form as *Indicators of Children's Well-Being* (Hauser, Brown, & Prosser, 1997). Initially, a third event was to have taken place, one that would translate the more academic work of the 1994 conference into a plan of action, but the conservative mood in Congress in the mid-1990s did not encourage an aggressive social policy agenda.

Still, some momentum remained in the indicators agenda outlined and articulated at the 1994 conference. The Federal Interagency Forum on Child and Family Statistics began to function in the mid-1990s. It fostered the coordination and integration of data collection for children and the reporting of children's conditions among nine federal agencies. It filled gaps in the federal statistical system that limit our capacity to monitor the condition of children even in the midst of profound social policy transformations. The Forum's first report, *America's Children: Key National Indicators of Well-Being*, was published in 1997 and has been published annually since then.[2]

Another key development was the initial shift in policy attention to the states and counties as they began to flex their policy muscles in the early stages of the devolution revolution. Such changes would surely increase the need to monitor child and family well-being and to use those data for policy purposes, at the state and local levels. In response, IRP brought together a number of states in 1995 in perhaps the first forum where state-level initiatives on policy use of social indicators were reported to a federal audience (see *Focus*, *18*[1], for a full description of this workshop).

The Family and Child Well-Being Research Network of the National Institute of Child Health and Human Development also contributed to continuing work on indicators of children's well-being. Researchers affiliated with the network continued to explore areas of children's life that require better measurement, developing new sets of questions for federal surveys that will better capture the status of children, and they continued to examine ways to use existing data sources to report on the condition of children.

Momentum toward improving social indicators continued in the latter part of the decade. In April 1997, then-President Clinton signed Executive Order No. 13045, which formally established the Federal Interagency Forum and required an annual report to the nation on the status of children. With support from the Pew Charitable Trusts, Child Trends organized a workshop in May 1997, "Social Indicators of Child and Family Well-Being in the Age of Devolution: Defining Next Steps." The workshop focused on the growing use of social indicators at the state and local levels.[3]

DHHS continued its interest in the development of social indicators during the latter part of the 1990s. The Administration for Children and Families, in concert with Child Trends and ASPE, attempted to develop a set of child outcomes that could be used to evaluate the effects of welfare reform. Although this effort was not strictly an initiative to create indicators of child well-being, because most of the measures were to be used as dependent variables in conventional experimental evaluations, the effort was crucial to the ongoing effort to conceptualize and measure critical child outcomes.

Through Chapin Hall at the University of Chicago, DHHS also worked with a number of states in a project titled "Advancing State Child

Indicators" that addressed the technical, conceptual, and political barriers to advancing the child indicator movement. Several important questions were how can administrative data be improved and integrated to enable the well-being of children and families to be effectively tracked? and how can one effectively use data in the policy process to work across program and jurisdictional lines and to overcome normative and partisan rigidities?

CONCEPTUAL, DEFINITIONAL, AND APPLICATION CHALLENGES

Despite this concerted effort and attention, progress toward developing and implementing social indicators that would influence public policy making has been modest. There undoubtedly are many reasons for this, not all of which can be explored here. In this section, the conceptual ambiguity surrounding indicators and how they are used is examined, on the assumption that some of the reasons for any failure to advance the social indicator agenda lies in this conceptual and definitional confusion. Achieving greater clarity, or some form of a consensus on a basic vocabulary for social indicators, might well be a good place to start. So, what are some of the steps that anyone interested in using social indicators in the real world should consider?

1. We Must Sort Out Populations of Concern

Analysts often struggle to define the appropriate level of analysis. Welfare analysts and policymakers alternate their focus among several targets: the individual adult caretaker, the child(ren), the family as a whole (or household, which may be larger than the related family), or even the community. These different levels of analysis can be affected by welfare reform in quite different ways, and the desired outcomes for each will differ. Labor market outcomes obviously are appropriate for the adult caretaker but make less sense for children, at least in the intermediate term. For adults, the outcomes may be employment, human capital improvements, or measures of family stability and quality of parenting. For a child, the outcomes may be health, school attendance, and academic achievement. For families, they may be reduced homelessness and reduced intrafamily tensions and violence. For neighborhoods, the indicators may include lower crime rates, higher civic participation, and an improved economic climate.

Analysts also make distinctions among larger groups of people. The outcomes most typically measured are those related to welfare clients and their families, who are the direct and obvious concern for reform initiatives. Within this broad population there may also be an interest in determining the differential results for subpopulations of welfare families, such as those who live in rural areas compared to urban areas or members of different minority or disability groups. In addition, there are reasons for tracking outcomes for groups that might be affected only indirectly by specific reforms, or where the connection is tenuous at best. For example, potential welfare clients (low-income heads of families) could be tracked to determine entry rates or (conversely) deterrent effects, and those who were former welfare recipients could be followed to ascertain changes in the rates of reentry into the system.

2. We Must Think Through the Types of Measures That Can Be Used

Three different types of measures are often used interchangeably when discussing population attributes: (a) indicators, (b) outcomes, and (c) impacts. These are very different measures and are not fungible in all cases.

Indicators. Indicators typically track the behaviors or situations of broad population groups. These measures can be tracked over time, across groups, or across geographic units. Tracking the progress of broad population indicators, such as out-of-wedlock births or poverty rates, is useful, but it is important to realize that changes (or differences across population groups) in these indicator data may be the result of many factors. It is typically inappropriate to attribute differences to specific policies or programs. In effect, social indicators are not normally used to establish causality.

Outcomes. Outcomes are numerical measures of behaviors or events that are generally believed to be a result of a policy or program of interest. Outcomes typically are positive and relate to goals that the program or policy hopes to achieve. Some actual outcomes, however, may be unanticipated, negative, or undesired. In welfare reform, an example of a positive outcome would be an increase in the number of welfare recipients leaving cash assistance and getting jobs. However, outcome data are not always collected in ways that make it possible to say that reforms have definitely caused the positive or negative change in the indicator. Absent a rigorous (often experimental) method for collecting and analyzing data, it may not be possible to determine whether falling caseloads are due to reforms or to changes in the economy, at least to everyone's satisfaction.

Impacts. An outcome becomes an impact only if the indicator of interest is collected in such a way that one can confidently assert that it was caused by the program or policy intervention. Researchers generally agree that establishing an "impact" in any scientific sense requires a rigorous evaluation design. The most reliable evaluation is the classic experiment with random assignment of participants to an experimental group (i.e., those who experience the program or policy) or to a control group (i.e., those who do not). For a number of reasons, some of which are growing in importance, it is not always possible or feasible to conduct such an experiment to determine overall program impacts, especially where the intervention is complex, comprehensive, and continuously evolving.

The inappropriate use of indicators, however unintentional, can undermine the credibility placed in data and those who use the data.

3. We Must Select Measures That Meet Acceptable Standards

Just because something can be measured does not mean it would be is a good social indicator. Kris Moore, former executive director of Child Trends, developed a list of criteria of what constituted a good social indicator in 1997 (see Moore, 1997) Below is my slightly modified version of her list.

- *Comprehensive coverage.* Indicators should assess well-being across a broad array of outcomes, behavior, and processes.
- *Clear and comprehensible.* Indicators should be readily and easily understood by the public and users.
- *Both positive and negative indicators.* Indicators should assess positive as well as negative indicators.
- *Depth, breadth, and duration.* Indicators are needed that assess dispersion across a given measure of well-being, children's duration in a status, and cumulative risk factors experienced by children.
- *Common interpretation.* Indicators should have common interpretation in various subgroups, or across different jurisdictions, or over time.
- *Forward looking and predictive.* Indicators collected in the present should be able to be used to anticipate the future by providing appropriate baseline information against which to judge trends.
- *Rigorous methods.* Coverage of the population or event being monitored should be complete or very high, and data collection methods should be of high quality and consistent over time.
- *Geographically detailed and covering populations of interest.* Indicators must be developed at the state and local levels as well as the national level. They must also cover important groups, such as various age cohorts of children.
- *Cost efficient and feasible.* Strategies to expand and improve the data infrastructure need to be thoughtful, well planned, and cost efficient.
- *Reflective of broader social goals.* At least some indicators should allow us to track salient societal goals at the national, state, and local levels.

Too often, indicators are used because they are available. However, all numbers are not equal in relevance or quality. Prudence dictates that great care be taken in the selection of indicators.

4. We Must Carefully Think About How We Want to Use Any Social Indicators Actually Chosen

The forms of social assistance that have emerged over the last few years have made distinct demands on the characteristics of the social indicators used and on the expertise of those who use them, with different consequences for the policy process. It is important for policymakers to understand the unique features of these uses and how each relates to the others. Furthermore, it is essential that policymakers develop a common understanding and a common language regarding social indicators, both of which are still not fully developed. The goal of this section is to lay a foundation for this common understanding and common language.

Purpose drives how we think about the data that make up basic indicators. Brown and Corbett (2003) identified five purposes:

1. *Descriptive functions.* Here, we merely track an indicator for the sake of knowledge. *Trends in the Well-Being of America's Children and Youth*, which reports 80 indicators, is an example of indicators used for descriptive purposes.[4] Little attempt has been made to identify the more important measures, selection being driven more by availability and the quality of data rather than societal importance.

2. *Monitoring functions.* Here, we ratchet up the importance of the indicators chosen. An implicit choice is made on the basis of how well the measures reflect important societal goals. These are indicators to which we should pay more attention.

3. *Goal-oriented functions.* Again, we ratchet up the importance of the indicator. Here we actually set performance expectations, numerical aspirations for performance, sometimes between higher and lower levels level of government and between public and private groups at all levels of government.

4. *Accountability functions.* Now we really get serious. Accountability adds a new dimension to the goal-setting function by attaching rewards and punishments to performance. When incentives are attached, the stakes are made substantially higher. Stakeholders are more likely to question the indicators chosen, the standards set, and the rigor of data collection and interpretation. In short, every aspect of the process of indicator development and use is open to question.

5. *Evaluative functions.* The end of this function is to determine which programs and policies are effective (or destructive) and, where possible, to shed light on the reasons for success or failure. Here, the objective of establishing new theoretical knowledge and practical understanding of what works demands even more rigorous technical consideration of how data are used and interpreted. Scientific rigor demands that the data are collected in accordance with those proto-

cols and interpreted according to acceptable analytic standards, if causal conclusions are to be accepted.

These purposes are organized into a typology, structured around progressively exacting demands on each use, that Brown and Corbett (2003) likened to a Russian doll image: description forms the outermost shell, evaluation the core, and the three intermediate levels share some characteristics of those outside in addition to their own particular characteristics.

When there is active interest in some dimension of social well-being, one that might require a governmental response, the task of description becomes one of monitoring. When social indicators become associated with active policies intended specifically to improve social well-being, monitoring becomes goal setting. When there are consequences associated with success or failure in meeting specified goals, goal setting becomes outcomes-based accountability. Finally, when those held accountable are asked to demonstrate scientifically the relation between their activities and the social outcomes they are intended to affect, accountability becomes evaluation. Any single indicator—child poverty, for example—can be used for each and every one of these functions. It all depends on how the data are used.

Moving from level to level-from describing to monitoring to setting goals-increases the importance of actual numbers or rates under observation (in this case, child poverty) to the policy-making and public management processes. It is not surprising that the need for high-quality numbers, or indicators, is critical. If child poverty, for example, is used merely in a descriptive sense, then flaws in the way it is conceptualized and measured may be of interest but not of great social importance. However, when we use an indicator to hold entities responsible and to decide whether programs are useful, we had better know what we are measuring and be confident that it is what we think it is.[5]

USING SOCIAL INDICATORS IN THE REAL WORLD: WELFARE REFORM AS A CASE STUDY

Another way to think about the use of social indicators is to examine a real life application. In doing so, both the potential and the challenges of the method are clarified.

Welfare Reform

One push for usable indicators comes from the evolution of policies designed to help low-income families with children. The welfare reform story is seemingly clear. The passage of the Family Support Act in 1988 was followed by increasing activity at the state level in the form of waiver-based, or incremental reform. The confidence of states, emboldened by their success in introducing increasingly ambitious reform concepts through the liberal application of waiver authority, paved the way for structural reform in the form of the Personal Responsibility and Work Opportunity Reconciliation Act (PRWORA) of 1996.

The rudiments of PRWORA are straightforward. PRWORA eliminates welfare as an entitlement and places a 60-month lifetime limit on the receipt of federal benefits. It requires that recipients engage in work or work-related activities within 24 months of the receipt of benefits. States face nationally set goals for recipients' participation in work-related activities, increasing the single-parent caseload engaged in work activities to 50% in 2002, 90% for two-parent families.[6] Whereas earlier welfare policy (the Family Support Act of 1988) had required participation in welfare-to-work activities for mothers with children 3 years and older (younger at state option), and had defined such activities more broadly to include education and training activities as well as work activities, PRWORA applies the participation requirement to mothers with infants 12 months and up as well as to older children and defines the permissible work activities more narrowly. Mothers previously exempted from participation in the Family Support Act (those caring for a child who is severely ill or disabled; those with a mental health or physical problem) are no longer specifically exempted under the new federal legislation. Under PRWORA, states have made widespread use of sanctions (reductions in or withdrawal of benefits) for noncompliance with program benefits.

When rigorously applying indicators or outcomes of interest to a policy area such as welfare reform, one first must identify program goals and choose feasible measures that are clearly related to those goals. Some goals may be explicitly stated in law and statute, but the sophisticated part of this exercise is to articulate goals that may not be widely recognized or appreciated. The exercise of identifying and clarifying

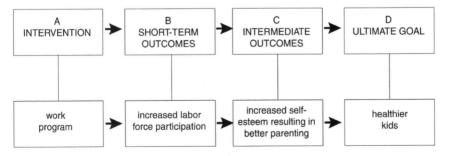

Figure 12.1. Connecting interventions to outcomes.

goals can often reveal areas of normative conflict, conceptual confusion, and simple misunderstanding of what is going on.

The first step in developing a system of social indicators is to articulate a complete and coherent narrative, or story line, about what is happening as a consequence of reform. In effect, this story-building process represents a strategy for acknowledging the broader context of reform. Too often, welfare experts focus on a narrow set of core outcomes that are related to specific policies or programs. Welfare reform initiatives cannot, however, be viewed in isolation. At the least, one must operate within the broader framework of values, goals, and principles that underlie the history and meaning of a variety of social assistance programs. This often requires thinking outside the box, or working across various systems and services available to the target population, as well as incorporating changes in private markets and systems.

The key step is to actually to connect those goals to the policy and program innovations being introduced. This primarily means specifying a series of plausible, causal links between the planned intervention and the measures tapping the phenomenon of interest that we hope to change or affect. In effect, the outcomes chosen must be logically related to the intervention itself. It does no good to measure a particular outcome unless a series of stepping stones can be laid out showing how policy actually links to the indicators, outcomes, or impacts of interest.

Developing a clear path for behavioral change through welfare reform can seem complex. Some measures represent short-term or intermediate outcomes-those things that first must be affected before the actual goals are reached. These benchmarks create stepping stones in the path to the ultimate goal. One way to approach this process is to think through the intervention (policies and programs) as if they were part of a plot line in a story in which A is supposed to affect B in a way that then affects C, and so forth. If the narrative does not link actions and events in a sufficiently compelling and plausible fashion, then the mere attempt to articulate the plot line can reveal important (if shaky) logical flaws.

Finally, one must take into account pragmatic issues of feasibility and cost. Some outcomes are easier to measure than others, and some outcome data—such as caseload rates, entrances and exits to the caseload, job entries, and so on—are routinely collected by welfare agencies. Other outcome data, such as marital status or educational attainment, are not collected across all agencies in a routine or standardized manner. Additional effort and cost would be incurred. Still other data, such as the quality of child care, are much more difficult and expensive to collect, not to mention steeped in controversy. Using indicators in this area would require political will, management effort, and additional public or private resources.

Getting the Question Right

Taken at face value, welfare reform might be considered welfare with liberal doses of tough love attached. If this is the case, developing measures of success would be relatively straightforward. In fact, we might well set up an outcomes-based system that defines a rather limited population of interest that is little different than those participating in the Temporary Assistance to Needy Families (TANF) program. The outcomes of interest, and thus the indicators or measures of interest, would focus on traditional work and welfare factors. In effect, we would have a rather straightforward performance-measurement system, like the JobStat system used in New York City.

But what if welfare reform had spawned something radically different? What would that mean for the development of a system of social indicators, and what would the existence of that system mean for the future viability of this larger vision of reform? The individuals charged with understanding the nature of change in the world of welfare, either assessing effects or simply describing what is happening, have struggled to understand the magnitude and meaning of the changes taking place. It sometimes seems as if the operational world of welfare is changing so fast that one might at least fear that the evaluation community was no longer asking the right questions. The rate of change has been unexpected and unprecedented, as a report by the National Research Council (Moffitt & Ver Ploeg, 2001) suggested:

> Welfare reform is a moving target for evaluation because the strategies and policies practiced by states are still evolving. There is some evidence that states, having largely accomplished their caseload-reducing goals, are now turning their attention to the provision of services to poor families, in general, and to women and families who are not receiving welfare. Provision of work supports, such as childcare, as well as services meant to address other problems and barriers women experience in attempting to reach self-sufficiency are widely discussed. Welfare reform is a continuing, dynamic process as states gradually confront new problems and face new challenges. The energy in this evolution is an indication of a system that is constantly trying to improve itself, which is clearly desirable, but it makes the problem of evaluation quite difficult. Estimates of the effect of welfare reform to date are not necessarily applicable to the future, when the nature of the reform may have changed. Moreover, from an evaluation point of view, it can be argued that the highest priority now should be to set up data and evaluation mechanisms that are capable of monitoring relevant populations and evaluating the impact of the new and ongoing strategies constantly being adopted.

This rapidly evolving welfare world, the so-called moving target, has been called the "new face" of welfare.

The New Face of Welfare

The notion of a "new face of welfare" emerges from an ongoing dialogue among senior welfare officials from the states in the upper Midwest, members of the Welfare Peer Assistance Network or WELPAN. Meeting quarterly, since passage of PRWORA in 1996, the network shares challenges and solutions and has arrived at some interesting insights about the emerging nature of what we used to call welfare. Some of these changes may have significant implications for the knowledge-building and policy communities.[7]

Two major transformations may suggest that the reality of social assistance for low-income families with children may radically differ from the accepted reality of welfare, that is, TANF. First, the character of TANF, what the program does, has changed radically since PRWORA was passed in 1996. It is widely appreciated that the cash assistance caseloads dropped by more than half between 1994 and 2001-at an even higher rate if the child—only cases are excluded—and was surprisingly stable in response to a subsequent economic downturn. In consequence, the character of the population served by welfare programs has changed and, for awhile at least, resources were freed up that could be invested in new service strategies.

One reflection of the transformed character of the program is that many states have radically altered the investments they are making with TANF dollars. Implicitly recognizing this, the WELPAN network examined the patterns of TANF and matching state expenditures in fiscal years 1996 and 2000. An analysis of expenditure data in the seven WELPAN states clearly showed that the income support function, the dominant function of traditional welfare, had rapidly declined. In 1996, an average of 72% of all TANF resources were devoted to the traditional welfare function: cash assistance. Just 4 years later, that proportion had fallen to about 30% of all expenditures on average (Members of the WELPAN Network, 2002).

If states are not spending the majority of resources on cash assistance, where is the money going? Among the WELPAN states, child care has become the major expenditure item, outranking even cash assistance in importance. Spending on efforts to move recipients into the labor force has also increased, but perhaps less than anticipated. Spending on what the states call *family formation and stability initiatives* has evidenced the most dramatic increase, from 6% of all TANF spending in the WELPAN states to about 18%. This spending category includes a variety of initiatives, ranging from home visits to newborns in low-income families through housing stabilization programs to efforts to reduce intrafamily violence and conflict, to initiatives to reattach fathers to their children, to teen pregnancy programs and efforts to help youth achieve more in school. The emerging principle appears to be that strong families produce better workers and that work helps stabilize families. Some states now invest as much on family-related activities and goals as they do on income assistance.

Second, much of the real action may be outside TANF. Supports for the working poor, at the federal level alone, multiplied some seven- or eightfold in real terms between 1984 and 2000. Although cash welfare reaches fewer families, the EITC, the increased minimum wage, and greatly increased support for child care suggest that the cash transfer functions of TANF per se may not be the best place to look to assess the effects of reform. For example, the minimum wage increased in real terms by 15% between 1989 and 1999; the federal EITC for families with two or more children jumped by more than 200%.[8]

Interpreting This New Face of Welfare

The pace, scope, and even locus of change suggests that there no longer is a set-piece policy apparatus by which important decisions are made in Washington, or through which Washington controls the pace and direction of change. In many instances, state capitols are no longer the key arenas, but rather local agencies and the networks of nonprofits and for-profits through which they deliver services.

The primary purposes and goals of social assistance appear to be shifting as fast as observed expenditure patterns. The transition from income support functions to job placement functions under TANF exceeded the expectations of all but the most optimistic. Now, many states are engaged in work support functions, job stability, and career advancement, where the need is to think about how to serve the working poor, as opposed to the nonworking poor. And with smaller and more challenging caseloads, states are doing more to provide direct services to challenged families either directly or through networks of local providers including faith-based organizations. At the same time, they are widening their lens to implement preventive services to broader segments of the low-income community.

All of these changes, happening to different extents and at different speeds among the various states and substate jurisdictions, raise serious issues for the evaluation community. We have shifting purposes, shifting program technologies (i.e., core program functions), ever-confusing and porous organizational boundaries (where is the welfare agency?), and confusion about the target population. The Wisconsin Department of Workforce Development commissioned a white paper simply to explore the definition of a *case* as the new face of welfare unfolds.[9]

When the WELPAN group first began to meet, one of their first agenda items was to define success: How would they know whether what they were about to do in the name of reform would work? Intuitively, this return to basics was a response to the rapid changes taking place. For several meetings, they struggled with this question, eventually publishing their first consensus document in January 1998, *Welfare Reform: How Will We Know If It Works?* The report borrowed many of the concepts and much of the vocabulary that was developing as part of the national movement to advance the use of indicators described earlier. However, one aspect of the WELPAN deliberations was quite prescient. Members noted that there were really two kinds of outcomes. One group consisted of measures that the major stakeholders (e.g., their legislators) would expect them to meet. Those they called *interim measures* (see Figure 12.2).

INTERIM:

WELFARE DEPENDENCY
SELF-SUFFICIENCY
ECONOMIC WELL-BEING
PARENTAL RESPONSIBILITY

ULTIMATE:

CHILD WELL-BEING
ADULT/PARENT WELL-BEING
FAMILY WELL-BEING
COMMUNITY INVOLVEMENT
ECONOMIC DEVELOPMENT
FAMILY FORMATION

Figure 12.2.   Welfare Peer Assistance Network measures of success.

A second group of measures were more forward looking. The network sensed early on that welfare reform would not merely be about getting people off the rolls, or simply getting them into the labor market; ultimately, reform would be about transforming the lives of individuals, families, and communities.

Achieving these ends meant going well beyond adding on a few conditions-work requirements and time limits-to the basic function of getting a check out the door. It meant transforming fundamental purposes and institutional cultures. This transformation is reflected in the following themes (see Figure 12.2).[10] First, the central mission of cutting-edge programs is not to get a check out the door but to transform individual, family, and community behaviors. Second, the locus of real, as opposed to nominal, program authority shifted first to the states and then to local authorities and (increasingly) to the front lines. This radical devolution is, in part, due to the third major theme, *reprofessionalization*.[11] Service programs that attempt to transform behaviors, as opposed to those that rely on changing economic incentives, have their own technological imperative: They are less rule driven and demand more autonomy and judgment by front-line workers.

Given the other themes, the last, reinvention, follows by necessity. You can run an income transfer program from a state capitol or from Washington, DC. Service-oriented programs attempting to alter behaviors must be locally driven and managed. In this regard, it is much more difficult to monitor rules and process and much more likely that accountability will be governed by outcomes and products.

The WELPAN network noted the rapidity of program change, as reflected in the shifting expenditure patterns described earlier. In just a few years, the driving purposes of at least some (former) welfare agencies have gone through several transitions (see Figure 12.3). They have gone from check-writing institutions to job placement institutions to agencies increasingly concerned about serving the working poor. As case-loads plummet, some find themselves adjusting their focal lens to meet two emerging demands. The first is to deal with the very challenged families that remain on their caseloads. Many agencies now have teams of workers, drawing on multiple disciplines (mental health, substance abuse, domestic violence specialists, law, etc.) to work with these families. At the same time, they are widening their focal lens to work with broader segments of the low-income community, sometimes by offering selected services for families up to 200% of poverty or even higher, particularly for services that are preventive in nature. In some instances, there are efforts to effect community-wide systems change.

Changing purposes demand new institutional forms, new agency cultures. Again, the WELPAN group has thought hard about this. In Figure 12.3, I lay out a set of changes in program purpose we see occurring in the welfare arena. It should be noted that these are not transformations that have taken place in all agencies in all states. That is not true by any stretch of the imagination. These are perceived trends, shifts from one way of doing business to another. Neither are these shifts unidirectional and linear. It is not the case that the future will witness a full transformation in the directions indicated. Many factors, such as resource constraints, the vagaries of politics during the recent reauthorization debate, or the severe economic downturn of the last few years, might well channel change in unanticipated directions.

A Transformational Process

The benefits-oriented era of cash assistance was in many respects simple, and program purposes were fairly limited: Get checks out to eligible fami-

PRIMARY PROGRAM PURPOSES

INCOME SUPPORT
↘
JOB PLACEMENT
↘
WORK SUPPORT
↘
FAMILY SUPPORT
↘
COMMUNITY SUPPORT
↘
PREVENTION

Figure 12.3.   Primary program purposes.

lies accurately and, in some jurisdictions, at least, efficiently. The time horizon for managing cases was short. Each month was a new accounting period where assets and income were, in theory at least, recalculated to determine whether a resource shortfall existed. The target groups of interest were similarly limited—mainly the adult recipients, only on occasion the children. The worker-client interaction tended to be uniform, episodic, and routine. Typically, no one asked applicant families what their problems were, or where their strengths lay, or how best to move them into society's mainstream. The gatekeeping function was to separate the eligible from the ineligible. Even if applicants were asked about problems, they were provided with a laundry list of programmed responses.

In such a system, horizontal equity was to be assured by treating apparently similar families in the same way. Conformity to bureaucratic norms emerged as an institutional virtue, which in turn encouraged vertical, top-down, communication patterns. At the extreme, local agency and worker discretion was severely constrained and discouraged. If the situation is A, you must do X; if it is B, you must do Y. This paradigm had the virtue of clarity. Everyone knew what a case was and where the welfare agency was located. Organizational and program boundaries were clear; professional roles were fixed. Most workers functioned autonomously to carry out a narrow range of responsibilities for their own caseloads.

In the emerging paradigm, the program challenge is to encourage behaviors that are positive and, if possible, to discourage those that are counterproductive. The new programs have varied and multiple goals (work, marriage, parenting) encompassing multiple targets (parent, child, community). Complex, behavior-focused programs tend to be dynamic and longitudinal, based on change over time. They tend to be so multidimensional that many workers must adopt professional norms that eschew bureaucratic rules.

In turn, the organizational forms in which the workers function are transformed, becoming flatter and less hierarchical. Horizontal communications replace vertical patterns. Agency boundaries become porous as interagency agreements and one-stop models emerge. Entrepreneurship and outcome-based institutional philosophies begin to supplant risk-aversive public monopolies. Discretion at the operational level is replacing traditional command-and-control organizational strategies. Malleable and plastic institutional forms that can respond quickly to new challenges are supplanting traditional set welfare systems.

The new culture may well require a different kind of worker. In the past, welfare managers wanted "left-brain" dominant workers, those who excelled at routinized, detail work and operated well at linear, unvarying tasks. Suddenly, the need is for "right-brain" dominant workers who can see the big picture and are creative at problem solving. The new management challenge is to continually motivate staff to forget the rules and work on finding solutions to complex family and community problems.

The welfare world has been turned upside down. Individual workers, teams of workers, and institutional partnerships will be tackling society's most difficult problems. They will no longer be functionaries executing policies but professionals creating policies. They will no longer dwell on symptoms but address fundamental cures and, rather than ignoring the most difficult cases, the most troubled families, they will be trying to engage them in creative ways. At least, that is one vision of the future.

The implications of all this change for monitoring, managing, and evaluating the emerging forms of social assistance are profound. Single programs cannot possibly deal with the challenges being taken on by former welfare agencies and their collaborators. Instead, state and local officials are trying to develop coherent systems of service delivery (one-stop and "no wrong door" strategies) so that broad segments of the community can access a range of services. In the future, it may even be difficult to know what a case is. The situation is so complex that thinking in traditional silos, the separate programmatic and funding streams that emanate from Washington, is seen by some states and localities as totally dysfunctional.

Increasingly, state and local officials are attracted to the strategy of using social indicators, particularly those tapping family and child well-being, for a variety of purposes and reasons.

- States are devolving more control to local agencies and communities. Some states are hoping that the local planning process can be improved immeasurably by first developing goals and measures of those goals. Then the narrative development process can begin.
- This is the only way of monitoring performance given the growing ambiguities surrounding caseloads, target populations of interest, systems and program boundaries, and the like. It is likely that a wider net must be cast if one wants to appropriately implement the traditional "canary-in-the-mineshaft" function.
- This is one of the best ways of ensuring accountability (the Brown-Corbett [2003] function ladder, or Russian doll). Many states want to move in the direction of performance-based and/or competitive strategies for governing state-local relations, but because the new forms of social assistance are so varied, again, developing good indicators is a key.
- Some states want to use social indicators as a way to drive further toward the type of cross-systems collaboration they see as necessary if their service systems can seriously tackle the difficult family and community problems that reforms are beginning to take on.
- Because caseloads and actual service delivery systems are so ambiguous and complex, this is the best way of measuring effects-look-

ing for population-level changes. Here we are spilling over into higher level functions, using nonexperimental methods to begin teasing out potential causal impacts.

In short, the evolution of policy and program forms unleashed by PRWORA have brought about changes that make social indicators far more critical to the planning, implementation, monitoring, and understanding of social assistance at both the federal and local levels. We see this growing importance at all the levels along the Brown-Corbett (2003) functional scale, from the descriptive use of indicators (useful for program planning at the very least) through what we normally think of as higher level uses of outcomes of interest: net outcomes or impacts associated with analytic uses of indicators.

The classic experiment can no longer be relied on as the only analytic strategy for determining whether welfare reform is working, and why.[12] Experiments worked very well under set-piece policy regimes where the federal government controlled the scope and pace of change. This is no longer the case as officials seek to transform the culture of agencies that serve the poor and to radically alter how individual systems and programs relate to one another. It may no longer be possible to causally link particular policies and programs to defined target populations.

The new face of welfare is not one that is easily defined or understood. It probably should not be thought of as a specific set of programs and policies; instead, it might better be defined as a set of attributes or, better still, challenges:

- *Pace of change*. Whereas the old welfare rules were static and relatively fixed, change is now endemic and constant.
- *Scope of change*. Many still believe that TANF is merely welfare with some "tough love" conditions attached-time limits, stricter work requirements, and a more liberal use of sanctions. However, there is evidence that, in some jurisdictions at least, welfare is a qualitatively different experience for both the persons running the programs and the customers who access the programs.
- *Locus of change*. Devolution is thought of as a transfer of authority from the federal government to the states. However, state decisions, as well as shifts in decision making inherent in any service-based program as opposed to an income-transfer technology, have pushed devolution further toward the front lines.
- *Core technology ambiguities*. What is the core function, or technology, of the new welfare agency? If it is not to issue checks, then what is it? The drift appears to be toward changing individual, family, and community behavior, thus requiring a service orientation. Social service programs cannot be run effectively with detailed procedures. Instead, they demand a professional orientation where judgment, discretion, and expertise are prized.

• *Porous institutional and program boundaries.* Traditional program and institutional boundaries seem less defined. Where is the welfare agency? Where does welfare end and community services or tax policies begin, at least if we are to attribute cause to observed changes in the well-being of children and families?

• *Population uncertainties.* On whom are we focusing our policies and programs? Is it those whom we actually serve as "official cases?" Is it those whom we touch even indirectly through programs, whether directly funded and run by welfare agencies and programs or supported by TANF resources? Perhaps the target population is all the people whose decision making might be influenced by the changing signals embedded in the new set of expectations associated with social assistance.

• *Shifting program purposes.* New policy purposes suggest a different set of evaluative questions, perhaps even a new framework for thinking about research and management questions. For example, under the old regime we wondered about the effects on children of mothers' increased labor market participation. The effects were somewhat indirect; we asked: How did the shift of mothers from full-time, in-home caretakers to working mothers affect the well-being of various age cohorts of children? Under the new regime some of the questions are more direct. What is the best form of child care, and which early child intervention initiatives hold the best promise for child well-being?

All of this change and uncertainty suggest the need for dramatic reformulations in how we think about basic monitoring, management, and evaluative functions. We must take more pains to get basic research and evaluation questions right. Probably everything—populations of interest, outcomes of interest, appropriate methods, and such basic questions as what is a case and what is the real nature of the policy set under investigation—should be placed on the table for review. We need more complex narratives for talking about the new forms of social assistance and how they are likely to affect low-income families. Also, not surprisingly, we will need a wider range of methods and disciplinary partners (not just the usual suspects), including those who can make sense of the organizational transformations taking place. Basically, we need a very flexible lens, sometimes a wide-angle lens, to look at the broad influences that emerging policies and programs are having on vulnerable families and children. At the same time, we need a tight focus on particular subgroups that face disproportionate risk. Most of all, however, we need to look toward where we are going rather than examine where we have been.

Management Consequences of Reform, and Some Federal Responses

At the federal level there have been concerted efforts to push new forms of governance that implicitly recognize the types of changes in social welfare programs that I have just reviewed and that advance the social indicator agenda. For example, there have been a number of initiatives directed toward performance-based management of federal and state programs.[13] The National Partnership for Reinvention; the Office of Management and Budget requirements for performance information to accompany budget requests (1992); Executive Order No. 12862, which encouraged surveys of consumers of federal programs; the Government Performance and Results Act of 1993; the Government Management and Reform Act of 1994, and the Federal Financial Management and Improvement Act of 1996 are just a few of the federal initiatives that have tried to move governance from the traditional focus on inputs and process toward products and outcomes.

PRWORA also contained provisions that were designed to encourage states to adopt a more explicit focus on performance, which has prompted the Office of the Secretary in the DHHS to remain very active in the area of indicator development and performance management.

Welfare programs traditionally have been monitored by assessing process measures. The Quality Control system assessed the accuracy of eligibility and payment calculations, and not the effects of such transfers on family well-being or functioning.[14] The PRWORA legislation introduced at least three types of performance measures.

1. *Rule conformance measures.* This category encompasses measures of whether states are spending sufficient resources on "maintenance of effort," whether certain data reporting provisions are being complied with, and whether states have implemented the time limit provisions of the federal law correctly.

2. *Process measures.* There are work participation measures, separate standards for one-parent and two-parent families. I consider these to be process measures, because the purpose seems to be to push states toward serious tough love strategies.

3. *Outcome measures.* Several of the original measures seem to be moving in the direction of true outcome measures. These include job entry rates, job retention rates, wage or earnings increases, and paternity establishment.

In general, the rule conformance and process measures are enforced through sanctions or penalties for states that do not meet established standards. The outcome measures involve bonuses to the top producers. Unfortunately, discussions among state officials suggest that rankings on performance measures strike both winners and losers as arbitrary and capricious. There seems to be little connection between what states do and where they are ranked. Neither are the rankings very stable from year to year, leading officials to think of this as a lottery. Sometimes you win, and sometimes you lose, but you never really know why.

Those committed to the performance measures agenda and the larger social indicators agenda believe the early challenges are no reason for dismay. Instead, the prevailing tack is to keep at it.

Some State Examples: Iowa, Ohio, and Wisconsin

Some of the most exciting advances in the use of indicators and performance measures are taking place at the state level. It is here, of course, that the new face of welfare is best appreciated and where efforts to transform the culture of welfare as well as the structure of the social safety net are most advanced. The following are three examples from the WELPAN network.

1. *Iowa*. In recent years, the Iowa Department of Human Services has worked hard to develop a set of broad social indicators both to measure local performance and to drive cross-systems change (see DHHS, 2003). Iowa, even though a state-administered welfare system, has long been interested in fostering local innovation and in de-categorizing (i.e., breaking down the silos) that keep local agencies from dealing with families holistically and from delivering a seamless set of services. To accentuate local control, systems integration, and accountability, the state has engaged in a serious process of indicator development that fully incorporates the perspective of all key stakeholders. State officials have looked for indicators that were compelling, measurable, and that would help structure critical processes. As a result of this planning process, four domains were identified as being particularly important: (a) individual and family safety, (b) healthy adults and children, (c) individual and family stability, and (d) self-sufficient individuals and families.

A number of specific indicators or measures have been developed under each domain. It is hoped that no single program or agency can meet these broad goals, thus driving the kind of coherent, integrated community effort necessary to achieve such ambitious ends.

2. *Ohio*. The Ohio Department of Jobs and Family Services is a reflection of the state's interest in integrating its traditional welfare and workforce development institutional cultures.[15] The state also has had a long-standing tradition of strong local control. Strategically, the state had adopted what is facetiously termed the "Wendy's franchise approach" to state-local governance. Account managers work with local officials on developing uniquely tailored community plans for dealing with low-income families. A great deal of TANF resources are distributed through what are called *prevention, retention, and contingency funds*. Each community then comes up with a plan to deliver preventive services; to help working families stay in the workplace and advance; and to help families deal with emergencies that might, in the past, have brought them onto the welfare rolls.

In the context of this "secondary devolution" strategy, Ohio uses social indicators as an explicit tool for framing the local planning process and for ensuring local accountability. The state has developed a sophisticated conceptual framework and vocabulary. The overall process incorporates five steps in which performance measures become a vehicle for thinking through each procedure from envisioning a plan to reviewing results and making appropriate adjustments: (a) community plan visioning and revisioning, (b) developing action plans to be incorporated into community plan implementation, (c) tracking performance on a routine basis, (d) controlling and using outcomes and reports, and (e) making recommendations and adjustments.

Each of these steps is viewed in terms of process, technical focus, product, and people.

3. *Wisconsin.* Wisconsin also has undertaken a vigorous process of developing and using indicators as a basis for structuring state-local relations and for organizing strategies for making resource investments. The Wisconsin effort is unique in some respects. From the onset of "Wisconsin Works" (W-2), there was an interest in pushing performance measures further along the Brown-Corbett (2003) functional continuum. This would not just be a monitoring or even a goal-setting exercise. Instead, performance would be used in the classic accountability sense, where failure to meet acceptable standards might jeopardize an agency's role as a W-2 provider. In Wisconsin, public, nonprofit, and for-profit firms theoretically can compete to be the W-2 provider. In truth, those agencies meeting minimal standards can exercise a *right of first refusal* clause. The guiding principle has been that competition will make the agencies work more efficiently and effectively. It certainly has raised the stakes in how performance measures are developed and used.

It has been clear that the use of performance indicators has been an evolutionary process. Early on, caseload reduction was the basis for determining who would run W-2 in most areas of the state. Without the decisive reduction in caseload, the reallocation of dollars to child care, workforce development, and intensive family services would not have been possible. In the second, and now the third, round of W-2 contracts (each contract period runs 2 years), thinking about performance measures has become more expansive. A more balanced set of measures has been put in place, reflecting a shift from mere caseload reduction to several measures of success in the labor market.

In all of these examples, and many more can be found around the country, we see state and local officials actively working to use indicators to achieve several of the functions on the Brown-Corbett (2003) scale. What is the prospect for success this time around? After all, states have been actively engaged in using indicators as a way of thinking about the status of children and families since Chapin Hall began producing status-of-children reports for the state of Illinois in the mid-1980s. Ambitious state agendas for using indicators as a way of structuring state and local resources on behalf of children and families have been around nearly as long, particularly in states such as Oregon, Minnesota, Georgia, and Vermont.

Some Challenges From the Real World

The challenges to effective development and use of indicators for more advanced purposes along the Brown-Corbett (2003) scale remain daunting. Some challenges are clearly political in character. As the stakes go up, people will pay much more attention to each phase in the process: selection, measurement, interpretation, and incentive use. Think how complex the task of selecting domains and measures within domains becomes when there is something at stake.

The political character of indicator use cannot be ignored. Let us take one issue as an example: Who should be in charge? If you were holding local communities accountable for improving the well-being of children and families, and basing that assessment on tracking measurable indicators over time or across jurisdictions, a fundamental issue about ultimate responsibility would arise immediately. Ensuring that any population would evidence an improvement in well-being demands imaginative systems cross-walking. Child poverty, for example, is neither the fault of any particular program or system; neither can any single authority or institution be expected to solve the problem. Then to whom does one assign responsibility: the TANF agency, the one-stop human service or workforce development center, if one exists? Or does one issue the challenge to the community at large and let the community decide?

There are also number of technical challenges, most of which have long been known to those who wish to advance the indicator agenda. We want measures that actually tap what we believe they tap, that do it the same way over time and across jurisdictions, that are available when we want them and for the populations of interest, and so forth.

Consider what we think of as important to society. Take child poverty, for example. This measure would be on any list of important indicators of child well-being, yet we cannot measure this in most states with confidence, and certainly not for subgroups of interest in smaller states, except during the decennial census. The reality is that our data infrastructure for social indicators is woefully lacking, unlike the capacity we have for economic indicators critical for labor market and business decision making.

CONCLUSION

The story of child and family indicators, or social indicators in general, is long and frustrating. Still, the last decade or so has witnessed a concerted effort to incorporate the use of social indicators into national, state, and local policy making. These efforts, although they do not match the expectations of child advocates and the purveyors of improved public management, have no doubt made considerable progress. This success has been added, in part, by the broader government reinvention movements at the federal level and work toward breaking down the program silos at the state and local levels. These movements demand new forms of public accountability.

This chapter did not attempt to cover all aspects of the social indicator movement. It has looked specifically at the welfare reform drama and the attendant devolution revolution. That drama highlights strong and purposeful efforts to crosswalk systems at the local level and to create a seamless set of opportunities for low-income families, in some cases moving toward prevention strategies. This drama, as it plays out, clearly moves the traditional welfare system in new directions where product, not process, counts.

Despite all the promises, the challenges remain daunting; political, technical, and capacity issues are no more easily solved than a decade ago. However, the call for more, and better, use of indicators comes from those actually operating the programs, those actually trying to improve public and private responses to social challenges.

It is clear that we have entered a period of policy reform and government reinvention. Whether children fare well or poorly in the context of all the changes taking place is an empirical, not a normative, question, but it will be normative, partisan, and probably inconclusive if we do not have the data with which to decide, or the will to use those data dispassionately. A generation or so ago, during the War on Poverty, a litmus test by which new policies were judged had a certain currency: What does it do for the poor? Today, a new litmus test may be emerging: What does it do for children?

AFTERWORD

This chapter was originally written in 2001. At that time, states for the most part enjoyed a positive fiscal picture that permitted many of them to invest in the new initiatives that were described as belonging to the new face of welfare described earlier. Since then, the fiscal picture has changed dramatically. When the data become available, we very likely will see a substantial cutback in investments for children and family functioning purposes in the current fiscal year. Moreover, although these state examples are now dated, there has been, if anything, increased interest and commitment to the concept of social indicators and outcome or performance measures at the state level.

At the same time, interest in developing integrated service models and cross-systems innovations remains high. In 2002, the WELPAN network published a report called *Eliminating the Silos: Or, Its Not Just Welfare Any More* (WELPAN, 2002a).[16] The report called for greater flexibility so that states could develop and introduce new visions of social assistance that operated across the traditional federal program silos. Within a few months, the administration included the so-called "Superwaiver provision" in its first attempt to reauthorize the TANF program. This would have permitted states to seek waivers of federal rules and regulations that crossed traditional federal programs and executive agencies. This has proven to be a very controversial provision, with opponents fearing that states would use this added flexibility to further erode federal protections for the disadvantaged.

Nevertheless, interest in developing systems of social assistance that integrate and coordinate traditionally separate service systems remains very high. In July 2003, representatives from a number of innovative sites that were successfully developing integrated human service systems met in St. Paul, Minnesota, to share successful strategies and examine remaining challenges. Resource constraints have not diminished the growing realization that the old program silos no longer suffice. The Institute for Research on Poverty, and the National Governors Association Center for Best Practices, in partnership with other national organizations, have developed a broad-based agenda for advancing state and local capacity to mount and manage integrated service models (see *Focus*, 2003, 22[3], p. 57).

At the same time, those working on integrated service models fully appreciate the fact that vulnerable populations must be carefully monitored in such systems. Ensuring accountability requires that officials think about how target populations are doing, not just those who participate in individual programs. The best one-stop and integrated-service models serve communities, not program participants. The services and assistance they provide cannot be reduced to the numbers receiving a check or the numbers actually getting subsidized child care. What these systems offer is too broad and individualized to be reduced to program inputs or processes.

We are moving from an old concept of welfare to a new vision of social assistance (see Corbett, 2002). This transformation will succeed only if we can transform our systems of accountability from those focusing on inputs and effort to those focusing on results and the well-being of the people we wish to help. The old litmus test of "What does it do for the poor?" is even more relevant today, if a bit narrow. Perhaps today's question is "What does it do for the child, the family, and the community?"

NOTES

1. Some of the key organizations include Child Trends; the Institute for Research on Poverty at the University of Wisconsin; the National Institute of Child Health and Human Development; the Office of the ASPE and the Administration for Children and Families, both in the U.S. DHHS; the Board on Children at the National Research Council; Chapin Hall, University of Chicago; The Joint Center for Poverty Research (University of Chicago and Northwestern University); the federal Interagency Forum on Child and Family Statistics; several state collaboratives, including WELPAN; and many others.

2. The forum's official web site is http://childstats.gov/

3. The papers for this workshop are compiled in special reports available from the Institute for Research on Poverty, University of Wisconsin-Madison; they are Brown and Corbett (1997); Brown, Kirby, and Botsko, (1997);and Koshel (1997).

4. For example, DHHS/ASPE, *Trends*.

5. The poverty measure has been widely criticized for some time (see Citro & Michael, 1995).

6. States can meet these requirements by lowering their caseloads as well as by increasing the proportion of the caseload working.

7. The WELPAN network includes officials from Illinois, Indiana, Iowa, Michigan, Minnesota, Ohio, and Wisconsin. A senior official from Oregon has attended several meetings, and a West coast group, called WESTPAN, is being organized on the basis of the Midwest model. For a good reference to many of the points made in this part of the paper, see WELPAN (2000).

8. See Scholz and Levine (2000), for an overview of spending trends.

9. The white papers are published in full on the web site of the Wisconsin Department of Workforce Development: http://www.dwd.state.wi.us/dws/w2/w2whitepapers.htm

10. See WELPAN (2000) for a more complete description of the changes in the purposes of social assistance and institutional functioning as perceived by the WELPAN network.

11. I call it *reprofessionalization* because the early ADC and Aid to Families with Dependent Children programs, up through the late 1960s, involved a great deal of service intervention and permitted front-line workers a good deal of discretion.

12. There is a more extensive discussion of this issue in an article Corbett and Noyes (2003).

13. This section is based in part on comments by Kathryn Newcomer at the ASPE Conference on "Using Performance Measures to Improve Management of State Programs," March 2001, at George Washington University in Washington, DC. Of course, performance-based approaches at the federal level go back a long way; the Management by Objectives movement and the Program Performance and Budgeting Systems that emerged in the 1960s promised to revolutionize governance in the public sector.

14. Of course, some of the related work programs (e.g., the Jobs Training Partnership Act) had a history of using performance measures that goes back several decades.

15. See http://jfs.ohio.gov/ for more information.

16. See http://www.irp.wisc.edu/initiatives/outreach/welpan/finalsilo.pdf for the report and other WELPAN reports on the topic.

REFERENCES

Brown, B., & Corbett, T. (1997). *Social indicators and public policy in the age of devolution* (Special Report 71). Madison: University of Wisconsin, Institute for the Research on Poverty.

Brown, B., & Corbett, T. (2003). Social indicators as tools of public policy. In R. Weissberg, H. Walberg, M. U. O'Brien, & C. B. Kuster (Eds.), *Long-term trends in the well-being of children and families* (pp. 27–49). Washington DC: Child Welfare League of America.

Brown, B., Kirby, G., & Botsko, C. (1997). *Social indicators of child and family well-being: A profile of six state systems* (Special Report 72). Madison: University of Wisconsin, Institute for the Research on Poverty.

Citro, C., & Michael, R. (1995). *Measuring poverty: A new approach*. Washington, DC: National Academy Press.

Corbett, T. (2002). The new face of welfare: From income transfers to social assistance, *Focus, 22*(1), 3–10.

Corbett, T., & Noyes, J. L. (2003). The service integration issue: Political, conceptual, and methodological challenges. *Focus, 22*(3), 50–57.

Department of Human Services. (2003). *Better results for kids: State of Iowa*. Retrieved October 14, 2005 from http://www.irp.wisc.edu/publications/focus/pdfs/foc223.pdf

Federal Interagency Forum on Child and Family Statistics. (n.d.). *America's children: Key national indicators of child well-being*. Washington, DC: U.S. Government Printing Office.

Hauser, R., Brown, B., & Prosser, W. (Eds.). (1997). *Indicators of children's well-being*. New York: Russell Sage Foundation.

Institute for Research on Poverty. (1998). Revising the Poverty Measure [Special Issue]. *Focus, 19*(2): Spring 1998. Retrieved October 14, 2005 from http://www.irp.wisc.edu/publications/focus.htm#F19:2

Koshel, J. (1997). *Indicators as tools for managing and evaluating programs at the national, state, and local levels of government-Practical and theoretical issues*. IRP Special Report No. 73, Madison, WI.

Moffitt, R., & Ver Ploeg, M. (2001). *Evaluating welfare reform in an era of transition*. Washington, DC: National Academy Press.

Moore, K. (1997). Criteria for indicators of child well-being. In R. Hauser, B. Brown, & W. Hauser (Eds.), *Indicators of children's well-being* (p. 37). New York: Russell Sage Foundation.

Newcomer, K. (2001, March). Comments at the ASPE Conference on Using Performance Measures to Improve Management of State Programs, George Washington University, Washington, DC.

Office of the Assistant Secretary for Planning and Development. (2003). *Trends in the well-being of America's children & youth, 2002*. Washington, DC: U.S. Department of Health and Human Services, Office of the Assistant Secretary for Planning and Evaluation.

Patterson, J. T. (1986). *America's struggle against poverty: 1900–1985*. Cambridge MA: Harvard University Press.

Scholz, J. K., & Levine, K. (2000). The evolution of income support policy in recent decades. *Focus, 21*(2), 9–15.

Swartz, R. J. (2001). *What is a "case" in post-reform Wisconsin? Reconciling caseload with workload.* White paper, Wisconsin Department of Workforce Development. Retrieved October 15, 2005 from http://www.dwd.state.wi.us/dws/w2/pdf/swartz_paper.pdf

Trends in the well-being of America's children and youth, 2003. (2003). Retrieved 2000 - put out Oct. 2000; 2002a - put out Jan. 2002, from http://aspe.hhs.gov/hsp/03trends

WELPAN. (2000). *The new face of welfare: Perspectives of the WELPAN Network.* Retrieved October 17, 2005 from http://www.irp.wisc.edu/initiatives/outreach/oct00intro.pdf

WELPAN. (2002a). *Eliminating the silos, or its not just welfare anymore.* Retrieved October 17, 2005 from http://www.irp.wisc.edu/initiatives/outreach/welplan/final/silo.pdf

WELPAN. (2002b). Welfare then, welfare now: Expenditures in some Midwestern states. *Focus, 22*(1), 11–15.

Wisconsin Department of Work Force Development. (2002). *Wisconsin works (W2): "Where do we go from here?"* (W2 white papers). Retrieved October 12, 2005 from http://www.dwd.state.wi.us/dws/w2/w2whitepapers.htm

Chapter 13

Creating Community Capacity to Use Social Indicators

David Murphey
Vermont Agency of Human Services

The use of social indicators (and, indeed, of other types of indicators-environmental, economic, etc.) at a community level is increasing rapidly. In many cases, communities themselves, rather than regional or state government entities, are at the leading edge of this work. These communities see the value of using carefully chosen measures that reflect their core concerns, including those having to do with children and families. As part of this work, these communities embrace a much broader concept of accountability for long-term results, holding both traditional programs and a variety of other community actors, including ordinary citizens, responsible for measurable progress toward well-being as they define it.

However, to be effective in this work, and to sustain it over time (and social indicators demand a longer term perspective), communities need to acquire a set of tools that in many cases are unfamiliar to them. These include sorting through data; making comparative judgments that are based, in part, on those data; and using indicators to leverage action to improve well-being. This chapter summarizes some of the knowledge and tools that communities need to pursue this agenda. It draws on some first-hand experience working with communities in Vermont as well as on conversations with a number of people involved in this work across the United States.

USING INDICATORS WITHIN AN OUTCOMES/RESULTS FRAMEWORK

Lists of indicators acquire much greater power when they are integrated within a conceptual framework that focuses on desired outcomes or results.[1] These are statements that describe desired states or conditions, for individuals, for families, or for communities. Indicators, after all, are only means. The ends, presumably, have to do with the well-being of children, families, and their communities. The outcomes identified will help determine the indicators that are selected.

Although many communities have organized their indicators under traditional categories, such as "health," "education," "economics," and so on, many who do this work believe that such an organization is ultimately less effective than one that uses outcomes. First, the categorical approach tends to reinforce the unfortunate separations between service systems, which traditionally each take a "piece" of well-being (economic security, child protection, substance abuse treatment, etc.) and try to fix that piece rather than treating people as whole human beings with interrelated concerns. Second, the outcomes approach explicitly, if subtly, makes reference to values, to what is desired. Framing the indicators this way introduces a powerful motivational element that is missing in the typical categorical framework.

A community group should take the time to develop, through a consensus process, these outcomes statements.[2,3] They should express in clear, simple language what it is they would like to see for children and families. These typically are short (a single phrase or sentence) statements that ring true for, and create buy-in from, many stakeholders (i.e., they are noncontroversial). Examples are "all babies are born healthy," "young people make wise choices," and "families are economically self-sufficient." The process of gaining a broad-based consensus on the outcomes is critical. By their nature, outcomes are achieved not by single programs, or even by groups of programs, but by the combined efforts of individual residents, voluntary associations, and environmental strategies such as new policies or renewed enforcement, in addition to formal programmatic efforts.

If the outcomes are in fact to enlist such allies, they must speak to all of these constituents, and they should not reflect, through language or otherwise, parochial concerns of particular agencies or organizations. In one of Vermont's outcomes-based regional partnerships, more than 250 people came together to envision the values for their community that would be embodied in their outcome statements. Vermont has also paid for professional facilitation when some community groups have expressed a need for this kind of assistance (Champlain Initiative, n.d.).

DEFINING *COMMUNITY*

Deciding on the level(s) of geography on which an indicator system will report is a critical decision. It should reflect both what is locally meaningful and important practical considerations. For example, in some regions the county may represent a natural commonality of interest; in others, it may be a parish, a metropolitan region, or even a particular neighborhood. The decision usually will reflect a number of compromises among these issues. An additional consideration is whether the geographic unit conforms to a political division (e.g., one managed by a city council, school board, etc.) that controls significant resources. That may prove important when it comes time to think about moving from data to action.

As important as the foregoing issues are, there are a number of practical constraints that will probably bear on this decision. What is the smallest geographic level at which most of the contemplated indicators are available? How consistent (or inconsistent) is this across the various data sources? How reliable will these divisions be over time? (ZIP code areas are commonly proposed as unit of analysis; however, these are frequently reassigned.) What is the group's capacity to produce indicator reports on multiple areas? What audiences does the group hope to influence by the report(s)?

IDENTIFICATION AND SELECTION OF INDICATORS

Data Sources

Communities need to begin with what's available. A common mistake community groups[4] often make is to come up with lists of indicators and then discover that the data for those indicators are not available. Some will argue that it is preferable to identify what they would like to measure, rather than to be constrained by what is measured. Undoubtedly, existing data systems do not provide everything that we would like. They may focus on the wrong populations; they may not be able to break down the data at the level of geography we would like; they may, in fact, collect the wrong data—typically focused on illness, deficits, and risk factors. However, indicators without existing data lack teeth: They become wish lists rather than functional tools. Developing new data sources/systems should be a priority, but that need not delay reporting on what we do know, while noting the limitations of our current systems.

Vermont provides an example of a case in which a relatively small investment in new data yielded impressive returns. Seeking to address the particular lack of positive indicators describing adolescents, in 1997 Vermont offered to school districts, on a voluntary basis, the survey of developmental assets produced by the Search Institute. More than two thirds of the districts participated, demonstrating communities' keen interest in having positive indicators. These data now have become part of youth-related planning efforts in many of these communities (see Development of Positive Indicators section; Alliance for Building Community, 2002; Champlain Initiative, 1999).

Another common mistake is to think that the community members have to dig up the existing data themselves. Sometimes this is true, but increasingly indicator data (or data that can be readily turned into indicator data) are easily available. The World Wide Web; libraries; government offices; and community agencies, such as chambers of commerce, regional planning commissions, schools, and police departments are all likely sources for indicator data. State KIDS COUNT organizations, in particular, are generally an excellent source for county-level information. As this work has progressed, a number of community-level data-banks have grown up, sometimes overseen by U.S. Census Bureau-designated state data centers or by universities. For example, the Cleveland Area Network for Organizing and Data, housed at the Center on Urban Poverty and Social Change at Case Western Reserve University, is a particularly comprehensive collection of geocoded neighborhood data, including everything from public transportation routes, to child care facilities, to juvenile crime, and more, and going back up to 20 years (Sabol, n.d.).

Types of Indicator Data

Data for indicators fall generally into one of three types, often confused but important to distinguish, because each has some special characteristics.

Census Data

These are data collected on an area's total population. These include the vital statistics of births, deaths, marriages, and so on, that each state collects. Census data are those in which everyone is counted, as opposed to just a sample or a special population. Population figures, and some other information collected by the U.S. Census Bureau, are census data.[5] These efforts usually are mandated by law; thus, the data tend to be as accurate as possible as well as being maximally inclusive. However, they often suffer from not being particularly timely: The published data can lag several years (or more) behind the present.

Administrative Records

Administrative records are data dealing with particular client populations, ranging from public school students, to food stamp recipients, to hospital patients, and prison inmates. On these subpopulations, the data may include much information; however, they only include clients. Thus, it would be a mistake to draw conclusions about health or health care solely on the basis of hospital admissions records, or even to make assumptions about young people based on school records (a number of youth are not in school). Moreover, participation in most programs (apart from schools) is voluntary. Therefore, even though food stamp program administrative data may be useful in estimating the extent of poverty, they are not ideal, because not all eligible families or individuals sign up. Nevertheless, administrative data are often an underused resource for indicators. They are collected and maintained by professionals, so the data quality is generally high; however, there may be issues of confidentiality that need to be dealt with before they can be shared.

Sample Survey Data

Any data that are not census data, or administrative data, are probably sample survey data. In this case, information was gathered from something less than a whole population-a sample-either a random sample or a convenience sample. A *random sample* is the only sample that we can be reasonably sure is representative of a larger group (e.g., all eighth-graders in a community). A *convenience sample* is, as the name suggests, composed of people who happened to participate in the data collection effort, either because they were chosen or because they chose themselves. With any convenience sample, there is a (strong) possibility that the sample is biased in one way or another. However, for practical reasons this type of sample is often used (think of the typical newspaper poll). Communities interested in constructing social indicators will want to avoid biased samples whenever possible, because they undermine the validity (and credibility) of that effort. An indicator based on biased data does not really indicate what it purports to and can mislead any interventions that may rely on it. This is a case where bad data are worse than no data at all.

Another consideration with sample survey data is whether the individuals responding are identifiable. Many sample surveys (e.g., the Youth Risk Behavior Survey, or the Search Institute's Profiles of Student Life: Attitudes and Behaviors survey) are anonymous, often to encourage people to participate. However, the less personally identifying information is collected, the fewer the possibilities are for linking the survey information with any other data on the same individuals.

Communities will have a significant new resource available to them, starting in the next few years, with the Census Bureau's American Community Survey (ACS). The ACS is essentially the long form of detailed questions that has been used every 10 years in the census, but it will be fielded on a rotating sample, on a continuous basis. When fully functional, the ACS will provide annual community-level data (down to the census block level), including racial-ethnicity data, income and poverty data, information on family composition, educational attainment, immigration, and so on. In particular, the data on income and poverty will be very important tools for evaluating child and family well-being.

It is difficult to overstate the importance of the ACS for community planning efforts. Instead of waiting up to 10 years for more current sub-state-level data, these will be available annually, approximately 6 months following the end of the year. Beginning in 2003, for geographic areas with populations greater than 250,000, the ACS will provide single-year estimates; for places of 65,000 or more, these will be available beginning in 2006. For smaller localities down to 20,000, beginning in 2008, it will provide annually updated 3-year averages; for the smallest population areas there will be annually updated 5-year averages, beginning in 2010 (U.S. Census Bureau, 2003). With the ACS, communities will have access to greatly improved indicators as well as a new resource for evaluation of broad-based community efforts, such as those associated with welfare reform. However, accompanying these more frequent data will be increased community need for capacity in accessing, interpreting, and using this information.

Collecting New Data

At some point, communities run up against the limitations of off-the-shelf data and decide that they need new kinds of information. A number of well-established data-gathering techniques are available: structured observations, surveys, interviews with key informants, focus groups, and community forums. However, communities often need help deciding on the most appropriate and cost-effective of these methods and with interpreting results.

Choosing Indicators

It is not the case that the more indicators, the better. In fact, a shorter, well-selected list will usually prove to be a more powerful tool than a laundry list of indicators. However, it can be difficult to make these selections, particularly because it is likely that every proposed indicator has its supporters who are ready to advocate for its inclusion in any final list.

Fortunately, there are a number of helpful suggestions of objective criteria for choosing indicators. For example, Mark Friedman (n.d.) suggested the considerations of communication power, data power, and proxy power. *Communication power* refers to the "public square" test: If you stood there with the aim of rallying public support for this work, could you define an indicator such that the man on the street would be readily convinced of its importance? *Data power* refers to the quality of the data: Are they reliable, consistently reported, frequently reported? *Proxy power* refers to the notion that indicators often move in groups: when one rises (or falls), others follow. Therefore, we may be able to identify a smaller set of indicators that, in effect, stand for a larger set. A community group can rank candidate indicators against all three criteria (e.g., high, medium, or low on each), and use such a process to whittle down the list.[6]

Kristin Moore of Child Trends has outlined a number of ideal criteria for child indicators, in particular. These include comprehensiveness (reflecting multiple dimensions of well-being); a multi-age scope (covering the life span up to adulthood); and clarity and comprehensibility (Friedman's [n.d.] communication power). Indicators also should cover positive as well as negative aspects of well-being; should be multidimensional (e.g., breaking out subgroups, dealing with spans of time as well as snapshots of time); and should be accurate, complete, and consistent, and have sufficient geographic detail. Finally, indicators should be cost efficient, should reflect social goals as well as anticipate future trends, and be capable of adjustment to reflect population changes over time (Moore, 1994; also see chap. 12, this volume, for details).

KIDS COUNT has a similar list of criteria for the child indicators it uses (Annie E. Casey Foundation, 2003). Other useful frameworks for indicators in general have been suggested by Jacksonville (FL) Community Council (n.d.), Maureen Hart (n.d.), and Redefining Progress (1997).

Without minimizing the importance of applying a rational process to the task of indicator selection, to some extent the final cut will always represent some subjective judgments. In particular, it will (or should) reflect a community's values–just as the outcomes or results do. For example, in Vermont, the Champlain Initiative in Chittenden County tracks, in addition to many of the indicators the state makes available to all communities, indicators having to do with recreational opportunities, housing affordability, and solid waste generation (Champlain Initiative, 2001).

USING INDICATORS

Data Fundamentals (Estimates, Rates, Adjustments, Presentation, etc.)

Community groups concerned with child well-being indicators need to develop a certain comfort level with data. Many people have negative reactions to dealing with numbers, either because they feel they dehumanize human services work, or because they are uncomfortable with numbers, or both. In Vermont, the human services agency made training and technical assistance vouchers available to each of its community partners and provided a menu of training topics, including how to understand and use community-level data. Training deals with where to find existing data as well as techniques for collecting additional, community data. Other topics include interpreting rates and trends, making comparisons, using indicators to help set priorities for action, and developing logic models as planning and evaluation tools. New York (Izzo, Rich, Dozier, & DeMasi, 2001), Georgia (Georgia Department of Community Affairs, 2006), and many KIDS COUNT organizations also have developed curricula on this topic.

Fortunately, the mathematical concepts needed to use indicators effectively are relatively simple. The following are some examples.

Estimates

The first concept is *estimation*. There is error involved in any measurement, so communities must learn to live with something other than exactitude. Even the best data (generally census data, e.g., birth records) are prone to errors of accuracy (e.g., data misentry), completeness (e.g., maybe we missed some home births), and other human (and computer!) errors. Population data, essential for calculating rates present special problems because they comprise such a moving target. Not only are people being born and dying all the time, but they also are moving in and out of a region. Data that derive from a sample (e.g., most survey data) are transparently estimates, because they purport to describe a whole population on the basis of characteristics of a portion of it. In general, the larger the sample, the better the estimate, but the margin of error, which should be included in any reporting of sample data, is also sensitive to a number of other issues, such as the rarity of the phenomenon being studied, the tendency of respondents to be candid about the subject, and how the sample was selected.

Rates

One of the first issues a community group working with data encounters is the many ways the same information can be reported: raw numbers, percentages, rates per 100,000, parts per milliliter, and so on. For most purposes, it is helpful to use not raw numbers but rates. Rates standardize a measurement so that a user can compare two different measurements (e.g., at an earlier time and a later time, or between one community and another). Without rates, these kinds of comparisons would be difficult (and misleading).

In practice, most of this is figured out ahead of time, because there are certain conventionally used rates to report on particular indicators. Unfortunately, they are not as consistent as one might like. So, whereas crimes are measured "per 100,000 population," school dropouts are typically reported as "percentage of enrolled students," births to teens as "births per 1,000 female teens," and so on.

The "Rare Event" Problem

A major issue raised by using indicators at a community level is that numbers (or, more specifically, rates) behave differently when they are small. To illustrate, let us suppose there are 400 infants with low birthweight born this year in the state. In one community, there are 4. We can calculate rates of low birthweight for each division (state, community), by dividing those numbers by the number of total births for that year (that have valid, nonmissing weight information). So far, so good. Suppose, simply for purposes of this example, that next year there are the same numbers of total births at each level, but the state total of low birthweight infants this time is 413, and the community number is 6. The state rate of low birthweight will have gone up incrementally (around 3% higher than the previous year's), but the community rate will have gone up 50%!

Can this be right? Of course! The math is impeccable. The problem is that when numbers are as small as these, "normal" year-to-year variation can result in huge changes in rates. If we chart these (say, on a trend line), we would see wild upward and downward spikes. A community could easily overreact to such a picture one year, and underreact the next; or should they react at all?

Presumably, their goal is to gain a clearer picture of the real proportions of low birthweight in their community. The reason that's difficult in this scenario is that, in addition to the real drivers of a condition such as low birthweight (e.g., perhaps smoking during pregnancy, inadequate prenatal care, other factors associated with poverty) there is some degree of random fluctuation from year to year. The greater the numbers, the smaller proportion is due to these random factors, and the greater proportion we can feel confident attributing it to real factors.

To consider a simpler example, if my community has one high school dropout this year, and two the next, that's a 100% increase; if the neighboring community has 10 dropouts this year, and 11 the next, that's a 10% increase. But both communities gained only 1 dropout.

Fortunately, there are some techniques available to reduce the erratic nature of small numbers. One often-recommended approach is to compute multiyear averages. By averaging rates over several years, extremes tend to get smoothed out on the trend line. Of course, the trade-off in doing this is that you lose some specificity. This can be partly mitigated by using *moving averages*: for example, 1995–97, 1996–98, 1997–99, and so on. This technique accomplishes the smoothing while preserving a degree of the annual variation. Three-year moving averages are typically used, but in some cases one may want to consider 2-year, or 5-year, averages (U.S. Maternal and Child Health Bureau, 1998).

There are no hard and fast rules about when to use multiyear averages instead of single-year data. A community coalition might try presenting the data in question several ways and judge which seems to provide a more helpful picture. Another commonly followed practice is not to compute rates at all, when the number of events is below a certain threshold (some use 100, others use 30, or 5). It can be argued that simply presenting the unvarnished numbers is a more honest approach than any alternative. Of course, then the ability to make comparisons with other regions (or to adjust for population changes in one's own region) is sacrificed.

Another technique is to calculate *confidence intervals* around rates. A close relative to the concept of confidence intervals is the more familiar idea of margin of error. In brief, the idea here is that any given year's rate is an approximation (an estimate) of the true or underlying rate. The true rate could be lower or higher than the reported rate-a range captured by the confidence interval. When making comparisons between two rates, one can examine their respective confidence intervals; if these overlap (i.e., their ranges include some of the same values), then the two rates are not statistically significantly different, which means any difference could very well be due to chance rather than signifying a real difference. There are mathematical formulas to calculate confidence intervals, based on the size of the rate denominators and numerators; several different methods have been recommended.[7]

In general, there is a vast unmet need at a community level for practical expertise in understanding indicator data. High schools, community colleges, and businesses could all presumably play a role in promoting greater data literacy among average citizens.

Presentation

In communicating data, as in fine dining, presentation is everything. Many communities have in mind the preparation of a report card on the indicators. Others include indicator data within the context of a broader annual report to the community that includes updates on the strategies that are ongoing to have an impact on the indicators. Still others supplement printed reports with online resources, which can include databases, mapping capabilities, and links to related information. Data can be hard enough for people to understand under optimum circumstances; the presentation should clarify rather than further obscure. Usually, this means that simpler is better. Although charts and other graphics are powerful communication tools, it is best to resist the temptation to overdo these, in either quantity or elaborateness.[8]

A few well-chosen indicator charts (ideally, trended over time), presented in a consistent format, are easier on the eye and mind than a hodge-podge of data, some in tabular form, others in charts (pie graph, bar graph, line graph, etc.). Vermont's Community Profiles aim in this direction, although the indicators are probably too many (Vermont Agency of Human Services, multiple years). Sometimes, it is helpful to give the data a headline; for example, one might label a chart "One in 6 Vermont Children Lives in Poverty" instead of simply "Rate of Child Poverty in Vermont." That way, a reader gets some up-front help with interpretation. Another strategy to help people see beyond the data is to present, alongside the data, concrete illustrations that motivate deeper thinking. These could have to do with factors driving the data, with possible interventions to "turn the curve," or anecdotes that help bring the cold numbers to life. Of course, explicitly localizing the data is often enough to gain people's attention, because people are generally unused to thinking that data are actually relevant to their own community.

Distinguishing Between *Community Indicators* and *Program Indicators*

As programs increasingly collect performance measures on the populations they serve, including measures of client outcomes, it is important to keep clear the distinction between such *program* indicators and *community* indicators. In general, for community-based organizations whose focus is on the well-being of all children and families in the community, indicators that refer to the entire population of children and families are preferable. However, in some cases it may be important to report on special populations, such as "children in families receiving public assistance." In those examples, administrative data (i.e., data on clients) will be essential.

In general, though, program indicators (although essential for program managers and other stakeholders) are less useful for a community. Often, the number of community members participating in a particular program is quite small; thus, indicators for the program will not represent the population at large. In addition, even among the subpopulation the program is designed to serve, not all eligible persons will participate, so program indicators will be imperfect measures even of that subpopulation.

In theory, community indicators are a reflection of a number of program efforts (reflected in program indicators), as well as efforts and influences that fall outside of programs as we typically think of them. Thus, there may be efforts of individual citizens or voluntary associations that in fact make significant contributions to the well-being of families and children but do not show up in any program's accounting. In addition, local, state, and federal policy changes; economic downturns or upswings; and other unpredictable events, including natural disasters or catalytic incentives to community mobilization (e.g., a large employer leaves, a freeway moves in) can all influence community indicators. This makes the job of attributing change on the indicators to specific, single causes (such as single programs) difficult (see CREATING A THEORY OF CHANGE section).

Prioritizing Indicators

Having even the best indicators is only a beginning. The idea is to make use of indicators in the context of making community change. Before that can happen, there needs to be some rational process of review of the indicator data. What do they tell a community? How can the information be organized? Assuming a community cannot address everything right away, where does it make sense to start?

Making Comparisons, Using Multiple Contexts

The process of choosing which indicators on which to focus efforts usually requires making comparisons of one kind or another. The beginning questions for a community coalition might be: Where are our biggest problems? Where are we doing well? However, those simple questions each imply another question: Compared to what?

In essence, one can compare oneself to a standard, or one can make relative comparisons. Standards (sometimes called *benchmarks*, *goals*, or *targets*) may be set at a national level (e.g., the Healthy People 2010 goals; U.S. Department of Health and Human Services, n.d.) or at state or local levels. Some standards may seem self-evident; for example, a community may decide that its target is zero child abuse. In most cases, however, setting a standard is a difficult exercise, ideally taking into account what is known about past trends, current and anticipated prospects for progress, and specific demographic considerations, among other things. It is common to set targets that are either too easily reached or too unrealistic. Either way, the results can be demotivating. A community might want to ask itself why it needs a target other than "continuous improvement."

Turning to relative comparisons, a community can compare its performance on one or more indicators to that of its county or its state. This can reveal whether the community's record is in the same ballpark as the wider communities of which it is part or, conversely, if it is seriously out of line. There are several reasons why a community may not be satisfied with such comparisons, however. It may feel, in fact, that it wants to hold itself to a higher standard than just average. Or, it may know that its characteristics (e.g., of socioeconomic status, of ethnic mix, or other features) make it quite different from the state or the county. In that case, it may prefer to compare itself with like communities—those that share its characteristics. In practice, though, this may be hard to do—that is, to specify just what characteristics to use to identify peer communities. Most communities believe there is enough about them that is unique to defy an easy match making. However, this approach is worth considering. This is also an area where communities could benefit from the expertise of officials in higher education or government. As one example, Vermont's Department of Education has an interactive web site that allows users to compare their school's student assessment data with data from similar schools, which were identified on the basis of grade configuration, enrollment, poverty rank, and the educational attainment level of adults in the community (Vermont Department of Education, n.d.).

The most useful comparisons to make will involve a community's own data, over time. On this indicator, is the community getting better, getting worse, or staying about the same? Is it consistently above or below, say, the state average? In short, is the community satisfied with what it sees? How satisfied or dissatisfied? To answer these sorts of questions, of course, requires having data over a sufficient period of time-at least 5 years, if not 10. Thus, for an indicator system to be useful right away (i.e., without waiting 5–10 years), communities are well advised to collect not only the most current data but (if possible) data that go back a number of years. This will also serve to mitigate to some degree the small-numbers issues referred to earlier.

Other factors to consider are the absolute magnitude represented by an indicator, natural clusters of indicators, the state of knowledge about the dynamics behind an indicator, and issues of community will. Although rates are generally preferred over raw numbers for most purposes, it is helpful for the community group to know what the numbers are that underlie the rates. For example, a community's rate of teen pregnancy might seem high relative to another's but may be based on three or four pregnancies per year. Depending on the circumstances (which may in fact warrant attention to this indicator), the group may decide to focus on an indicator that may be less of an outlier, within some comparative context, but that is tied to greater numbers of people. For instance, the data may indicate that 40% of the community's high school students drink alcohol regularly. If there are 800 students in the high school, that is 320 students who are certainly at risk for a number of bad outcomes. It may be that 40% is not an unusual figure, but this is an area where the raw numbers are considerable.

Another way of reviewing indicators is to note clusters of related indicators. These may be organized around a particular age group (e.g., young children or adolescents), or they may be related in other ways: for example, having to do with education, or poverty, or health. Such clusters may suggest where attention to an indicator may naturally lead to impacts on others.

An important reality test for a community to apply to a review of indicators is: Do we know enough about an indicator to suggest that our efforts will be successful? The state of the art around prevention, and even when it comes to intervention strategies, is in some cases poorly developed. We simply may not understand enough yet about the best ways to reduce the incidence of childhood asthma, for example, even though we would agree that it is a major concern. In that case, it will be more productive to address an indicator where, in fact, we know a good deal about effective strategies.

Finally, the group will want to recognize where there is community will to deal with the issues related to an indicator. Will is not always based on rational analysis, but failure to acknowledge where it does and does not exist can doom a group's efforts. Will is sometimes galvanized by high-profile (i.e., heavily covered in the media) events—a child's death, a crime involving a local celebrity, a school shooting that may have occurred thousands of miles from this community. On the other hand, community will may have been building slowly but steadily over many years, as a problem became increasingly difficult to deny. In any event, the group would be smart to capitalize on this energy, although it should not let its agenda be driven solely by these factors.

Collecting Additional Information

Because all indicators are imperfect (in terms of data quality, timeliness, construction, etc.), identifying from the data those indicators that are most compelling should be seen as a preliminary stage, to be followed up by further investigation. This, as Mark Friedman (n.d.) referred to it, is "getting the story behind the baseline [data]." This usually involves talking with those people who are in a position to shed some light on the numbers—either to corroborate them or to suggest where they may have missed the mark.

Community group members should talk with the agencies that supplied the data-ideally, their representatives with responsibility and/or knowledge of the community's area. They should also speak with others who may not have objective data but can provide valuable perspective on the reasons why the data look as they do. There may be reporting issues, for example, or other anomalies in local practices that suggest that the data either under- or overestimate reality; perhaps there were locally significant events that influenced the data in 1 or more years. In Vermont, rates of injuries to children resulting in hospitalization showed declines from the late 1980s through the 1990s in all regions and across all age groups (Vermont Agency of Human Services, multiple years). Could this reflect the effects of injury prevention programs, including new seat belt laws? Could it also reflect changing practices around hospitalization versus outpatient treatment? Perhaps the data are just plain wrong; sometimes the only way to catch such errors is to have people close to the source review the numbers.

CREATING A THEORY OF CHANGE

The purpose of indicators is to support change efforts. Collecting additional information on the indicators often leads naturally to considerations of underlying causes and, by implication, of what it will take for one or more indicators to show improvement. Having a theory of change provides an essential framework for community efforts, which will typically include multiple points of focus.

Each of us has a sense, sometimes intuitive, sometimes informed by special study or experience, of the reasons why children and families do poorly and, conversely, of what characteristics, supports, or conditions are likely to lead to success. A theory of change starts with a simple articulation of these beliefs and assumptions. Among a community group there is likely to be diversity of views. The idea is not necessarily to come to consensus on a single theory of change but to consider these different maps of reality, to press for further details, further rationales. Most theories of change rest on a number of "if-then" assumptions, many of which are rarely examined objectively. By laying these out in detail, stakeholders can then subject to test the theories such assumptions embody. Of course, through a give-and-take process, some theories may be rejected or withdrawn from further consideration, as participants realize they either do not make sense or contain assumptions that are too many or too difficult to test.

A community group wanting to understand what drives an indicator can refer to the now-extensive literature on risk and protective factors as well as to authoritative material on program evaluation, or accumulated best practices wisdom (see, e.g., Child Trends, n.d.; Gambone, Klem, & Connell, 2002; Hawkins, Catalano, Kosterman, Abbott, & Hill, 1999; National Research Council & Institute of Medicine, 2002; Scales & Leffert, 1999). Reinventing wheels is not the goal here. However, this is also the place for the group to consider the particular characteristics of its community. For example, there may be local sources of both risk and protection (or assets) that will be important to take into account. The idea is to think strategically, not choosing programs or strategies because they sound great or because they already have a constituency. The bottom-line test should be: What do we think will work, based on the best thinking available to us? In essence, a theory of change is a conceptual map that often includes a number of indicators, linked in some causal chain. Unfortunately, as I note at the end of this chapter, the science here is still largely undeveloped. Communities can, however, advance the current state of knowledge by advancing well-articulated models and collecting the data that can test those models.[9]

In Vermont, the Essex Community Wellness Committee developed a theory of change for the outcome "Youth Choose Healthy Behaviors." Their model included some research-validated contributors to positive youth development, such as "opportunity for interaction with caring adults outside school and home," "opportunities for involvement in extra-curricular activities," and "opportunity for youth leadership development." The model also included some testable hypotheses around other strategy components: "emphasis on all students experiencing success," a "health curriculum," and "media use." Perhaps most significant, the model identified elements of a comprehensive approach linking schools, the local teen center, the police department, the wider community, and the Wellness Committee itself.

"Turn the Curve" Work Groups, and Strategic Plans

After identifying key indicators, and developing a (provisional) theory of indicator change, the next step for a community group is to implement activities intended to turn the curve on an indicator. "Turning the curve" refers to the (recent) historical trend on an indicator. Preferably, the group has historical data (5 years' worth is good; 10 is better) sufficient to discern a pattern of direction-improving, declining, staying about the same (or erratic). The goal, presumably, is to see improvement. Sometimes improvement can be simply slowing the rate of worsening performance on an indicator; in other cases, it may mean quickening the pace of improvement; in still other cases, it may mean actually bending a deteriorating curve into a positive direction.

As mentioned earlier, setting targets is a problematic exercise. A coalition should ask itself: Do we really need a specific target, or can we say our goal is continuous improvement? In some situations, the group may decide that, drawbacks aside, having one or more indicator targets is an important motivating tool. However, it must then be prepared to deal with any fallout if targets are not met.

Work groups (task forces, committees) can be formed around one or more of the indicators. These should include representatives of all groups in the community who have something to contribute to a turning the curve." Their function is not only regularly to review the data but also to coordinate the local (and sometimes regional and state) efforts. They are responsible for aligning efforts with the theory of change. What is already in place? What is missing? What's working well, and what's not working well? Which populations are being served, and which ones are not being served?

The work group can create a *community logic model*, or theory of change, as well as assist those programs with a stake in the indicator in creating their own, program-specific logic models.[10] There should be regular feedback from programs on outcome indicators for the populations they serve given to the work group that will oversee how those separate efforts, together with nonprogram contributors, are making a difference in turning the curve. In an ideal situation, the work group meets regularly to review and refine the coordinated strategy as it unfolds. The group may consider new research findings that bear on their efforts, as well as local data (programmatic or otherwise) that indicate progress or the lack of it. New information may lead to modification of the community logic model—for example, perhaps "We've learned that Program X is particularly effective, while Program Y has fallen flat; let's redirect resources to have more of Program X and less of Y."

Communities are just beginning to do this kind of important work. It clearly requires a high level of collaboration and a willingness to stay focused over a long term.

FOLLOW-THROUGH

Revisiting the Outcomes and Indicators

It is important for the community group members frequently to remind themselves that indicators are at best imperfect measures of the outcomes/results that are desired. The group is the "keeper of the flame"; no one else is likely to keep the big picture in mind. Thus, it would be a mistake to get too bogged down in indicator analysis at the expense of losing sight of the bigger picture. This is one of those periodic reality checks needed in this type of work.

Along these lines, indicators themselves need to be reexamined from time to time to make sure they continue to provide useful information. New sources of data may become available, permitting better indicators. Conversely, previously relied-on sources may change or disappear. Community priorities may shift, requiring more detailed attention in a particular area. Opportunities may present themselves for the coalition to align its indicators with those of other related indicator efforts, either within the same community or on a wider (regional, state, national, or international) stage.

Notwithstanding the importance of keeping the indicator process dynamic, there are also advantages to maintaining a degree of continuity. In particular, indicators should not be abandoned simply because they have not changed (or because they have). In the first place, indicator change is almost always a slow process; in the second place, it would be a mistake to remove an indicator from the radar screen because a community felt it had taken care of that one. Experience suggests that when attention to an indicator lapses, progress can be undone.

Communicating With Stakeholders

The most important audience for information on the indicators is the community group that originally devised the outcomes-and-indicators framework. The format used to present the indicator data is a critical factor in determining its broad usefulness to the group (see the earlier discussion on presentation of data).

Getting feedback from the data on a regular schedule is important for letting the group members know whether their efforts are on track. If the coalition can get frequent updates (say, quarterly or even monthly) on at least some of the indicators, that is ideal. In most cases, however, data will be updateable only annually. Depending on the resources of the group, it may not be feasible to produce an indicators report every year; every other year is a reasonable cycle, but intervals longer than that risk having the group lose focus.

Communicating with the Media

Local media are important partners to engage in this work. They need to be informed of the big picture in which the indicators fit-that is, the outcomes/vision/values they reflect and the nature of the stakeholder group.

Once the media are on board with the overall concept, the group can suggest that they feature an "indicator of the month/week." This is an opportunity to present the rationale behind the selection of the indicator, as well as current trends, appropriate comparisons with other jurisdictions, and so on. Depending on the indicator, this could also be the place to list local organizations that are most directly involved with issues connected to the indicator, and ways for interested citizens to contribute-for instance, in their families and other relationships, through their work or volunteer activities, and through other personal choices (e.g., consumption, exercise, diet) they make.

In Vermont's Lamoille County, the community group produced a series of full-page advertisements that appeared over a 3-year period (1998–2001) in their monthly newspaper. Each display in the series, called "The State of Our Youth," highlighted an issue (substance abuse, high school dropout, positive youth development, etc.) with local data (including well-chosen comparisons both with state data and among the region's several communities). The format was informal, with cartoon drawings and conversational language. Ideas for "what you can do" were listed, as was contact information for local resources.

ADDITIONAL TOOLS/ISSUES

Sooner or later, as this work progresses, communities will encounter new challenges and opportunities. This section deals with a few of these; there are doubtless others to be met as work in this area matures.

Disaggregation

Any *aggregate* data (i.e., any data not broken down to individual cases) have the disadvantage of masking what may be important differences among certain subgroups. On the same indicator, data for boys may be quite different from the same data for girls. There may be wide differences between racial or ethnic groups and significant differences according to income level. Moreover, there may be major differences by geography within a particular community, however *community* has been defined. How should all of these be addressed?

Of course, in some cases the data will not permit disaggregation. Perhaps the data as originally collected did not include gender, race, or other such stratifying factors, or, at any rate, that is not how they were made available to the community group. In other cases, decisions to disaggregate the data by one or more of these factors will be easily made on the basis of knowledge of the community. For example, not all communities have sufficient numbers of particular racial or ethnic groups to warrant breaking out the data along these lines. However, the question of what numbers are sufficient is ultimately a judgment call.

Ideally, the group would examine the data, broken out along one or more of these dimensions, and determine from that examination what kinds of disaggregation was warranted for the final report. The group members would need to keep in mind, too, the readability implications of their decisions-too many subgroup analyses could make a report difficult to follow.

Probably the disaggregation issue most likely to loom large in such projects is that of geography. If county-level reports are prepared, the data will mask any number of within-county differences that reflect spatial patterns of income level or race-ethnicity. If the reports are city level, they will likely mask some important between-neighborhood differences. To a great extent this is a no-win issue: No matter what level of geography is chosen for the community, it is likely to contain heterogeneous groupings of one or more kinds. The best that can be done is to acknowledge the compromises that all such decisions represent and to encourage users of the data to consider the results in light of their knowledge of within-community differences.

Geographic Information Systems.   One tool that directly addresses the geographic disaggregation issue is the mapping of indicator data–a function of a set of computer applications referred to as Geographic Information Systems (GIS). The idea behind GIS is to tag each piece of data with a place label (commonly referred to as *geocoding*). The label can be as specific as a street address or precise coordinates of latitude and longitude, or it can be as global as a town, county, or state. Of course, the more finely grained the label, the easier it is to aggregate the original data up to larger units. For social indicator data, street address is the ideal smallest unit. Practically, however, census block or tract information is generally the smallest unit available, because of privacy concerns.

Once the data have been tagged with one or more geocodes, GIS software can create maps that display features of the data. For instance, where are problems concentrated? What areas are doing well? What areas have seen the greatest recent change (positive or negative)? Multiple layers of data can be drawn, either as overlays or in a series, to show relationships among several indicators.

For example, the National Neighborhood Indicators Partnership (NNIP) of the Urban Institute has highlighted examples where communities have used GIS to show relationships between vacancy rates and crime, to illustrate neighborhoods' needs for child care, to depict the spatial distribution of lead poisoning, or show the location of institutional assets (NNIP, 1999). The maps reveal areas where outreach efforts should be focused. Recently, NNIP has partnered with a GIS vendor on the Neighborhood Change Database. This can produce, for any of the 65,232 U.S. census tracts, a standard set of census-based indicators, in some cases going back to 1970 (Urban Institute, n.d.).

Another example of this work can be found at the web site "Vermont Children's Well-Being On-Line" (http://www.maps.vcgi.org/cwb/).

This work, in the areas of land use planning, natural resource management, pollution control, and crime prevention, is much more advanced than its application to date for social indicators. Therefore, there is much potential here. At the simplest level, creating maps of the data provides an aid for visual learners, who may find tables of numbers particularly uninspiring. Moreover, this kind of visual display can reveal patterns that may not be obvious any other way, particularly when dealing with large numbers of geographic units. Maps also communicate well with diverse audiences and so can be useful in bringing additional partners to the indicators discussion.

One promising application of GIS to the field of social indicators is its ability to display the relationships between resources and outcomes. In Baltimore, Maryland, the Family League and the City Data Collaborative prepared maps showing the location throughout the metro area of youth-serving organizations; early childhood and school-age child care slots; and a composite "after-school risk index" that includes student performance, school attendance, juvenile arrest rate, and teen pregnancy rate (Bruns, n.d.).

However, one shouldn't invest mapping with too much "magic." It is a tool that permits one to look at the data in new ways, and thereby it often raises a number of interesting questions: Why are these areas doing well/poorly? Why do certain areas scoring low on this indicator also do poorly on that indicator? Although mapping will help identify such questions, it will not answer them. For answers, the community will still have to turn to other sources for the story. In addition, communities will need considerable technical expertise to create and maintain GIS applications, and currently many who have the technological skills for GIS lack familiarity with issues of social well-being.

Development of Positive Indicators

One of the current frontiers of indicators work has to do with conceptualizing, developing, and using measures that focus on "what's right" with people and communities. As communities know too well, the typical indicators focus on the bad news story, cataloging the myriad ills to which individuals, families, and communities are prone. There are good reasons why things developed this way. In general, bad news gets attention, and indicators have often been used by advocates whose first challenge is to get broader public attention to an issue.

Over time, however, we have learned the limits of framing indicators to measure problems, needs, deficits, risks, and disease. First, such a frame can be very unmotivating, even disempowering, because it implicitly casts people and communities as victims who, at best, can only remove or reduce various threats to well-being. Second, we know that health, or well-being, is more than the absence of disease, more than the prevention of rotten outcomes. The reduce-the-negative agenda does not really tell us how to promote our desired ends. It does not, so to speak, offer us specific building blocks to strengthen, points of leverage on which to capitalize.

In recent years, the tide has begun to shift, although there is still a long way to go. Working within a community-development model (McKnight & Kretzmann, 1993), or a youth development model (e.g., Scales & Leffert, 1999), researchers and practitioners have begun to articulate the assets (or strengths) that contribute to well-being. Some of these are individual qualities of competence and character; others are interrelational, such as connections with significant others; and still others are institutional, such as the number of community associations, public green spaces, and so on.

The Search Institute, based in Minneapolis, has over the past decade or so been creating a national movement around "developmental assets of youth." Explicitly focused on communities (instead of the academic or government arenas), the Search Institute promotes the idea that communities need to mobilize to support all youth by building assets. *Assets* are described as the building blocks of healthy youth development; the Search Institute has identified 40 such assets and grouped them into eight categories: (a) support, (b) empowerment, (c) boundaries and expectations, (d) constructive use of time, (e) commitment to learning, (f) positive values, (g) social competencies, and (h) positive identity. The Search Institute is clear about the fact that some of the 40 assets have better support in the scientific literature than others (Scales & Leffert, 1999); however, they have begun to publish their findings in peer-reviewed journals, which will probably lead to some refinement of their original framework (Leffert et al., 1998).

The centerpiece of the Search's Institute's work is a survey, Profiles of Student Life: Attitudes and Behaviors, which measures the 40 assets and has been administered (including earlier survey versions) to more than 300,000 sixth- through twelfth-graders across the country. Initially taken up by individual communities contracting with the Search Institute, in recent years several states have taken an interest in using the assets survey statewide.[11]

In Vermont, the assets work clearly struck a chord with communities who were anxious to adopt a strengths-based perspective on working with young people. After several people in state government were also introduced to this framework, interest grew still further. Key leaders saw not only the links with allied research on protective factors and resiliency but also the potential of this approach for tapping new sources of energy at a community level. The state provided funds to offer the assets survey to any school district that was interested, and more than two thirds volunteered. Data were collected from nearly 20,000 students (Search Institute, 1998). Each participating community received its own report on the data; in addition, selected assets were included in Vermont's *Community Profiles*, annual compilations of community-level social indicators.[12] Communities have used the data in a number of ways, including for school-wide and community-wide forums, for grant applications, and in state-required action plans to improve school performance. Recently, several assets questions were incorporated into Vermont's biannual Youth Risk Behavior Survey, in which more than 95% of schools participate, so the state will have some ongoing (albeit limited) data on assets (Vermont Departments of Health and Education, 2001).

Developing new indicators that are broadly accepted as valid and reliable is an uphill struggle, but in this case it is work that simply needs to be done. It will be critical to getting the kind of sustained community commitment to an indicators framework that is necessary for the overall success of this work.

Using Indicators to Negotiate for Funding Flexibility

In general, it is not appropriate to use community (as distinct from program) indicators in a high-stakes accountability system. There are simply too many factors—some of which are beyond the control of the community itself—that influence community indicators. However, sooner or later, as outcomes-and-indicators work matures, it should come to have an impact on funding decisions; otherwise, it will be seen by some as a dispensable exercise. The aim should be to do this with more "carrots" than "sticks" and to proceed cautiously.

In one example, in 1996 a Vermont regional coalition focused on child welfare issues made the following proposal to the state child welfare department: If we can use our indicators to show that, over a period of several years, we are succeeding in reducing the number of out-of-home placements (without increasing our child abuse and neglect rates), can we keep some of the savings that would accrue to the state and reinvest those in the family preservation activities we believe are at least partly responsible for our progress? The agreement reached was one of mutual gain: The state department retained 50% of the savings, and the regional coalition got the rest.

Such an arrangement is far short of redesigning entire funding streams to align more closely with the outcomes. Although superficially attractive, in practice this idea runs into a number of obstacles, aside from the usual institutional resistance to change. In the first place, it is difficult, if not impossible, to tag many funding streams to a single outcome; frequently, they should properly be assigned to multiple outcomes (e.g., ready for school, and succeeding in school). It is a poor use of time and energy to haggle over, or somehow portion out, which dollars go with which outcome. Second, even if this could be done, how is this ultimately to be used? If outcomes are poor (and/or declining), do we reward a region with extra funding, or chasten it by docking funds? Conversely, if a region is doing well (and/or improving), is that reason to withdraw funding, or to increase it? There are no universally correct answers, of course.

At this point in the development of social indicators, it makes more sense to have the data enter funding decisions in meaningful but not predetermined ways. In other words, the indicators can be a part of, but not the sole basis for, negotiations between who is funding and who is funded.

Con Hogan (quoted in Hogan & Murphey, 2002), former Vermont human services secretary, made the distinction between *accountability*, which is appropriate for programs, and *responsibility*, which is a more appropriate concept at a community level. Where community indicators are concerned, responsibility (i.e., credit as well as "blame") should be widely shared. Not only is it difficult from a practical standpoint to attribute to discrete programs improvement or decline on particular indicators, but it also is a bad idea politically, when presumably the aim is to engage and sustain broad community involvement. Each year, when Vermont's *Community Profiles* are published, the human services secretary sends a personal letter to coordinators in each of the state's human services districts, highlighting both good news and not-so-good news as indicated by the profile data. The letters serve as gentle reminders that the state pays attention, recognizes progress, and offers assistance; there is no "gotcha" agenda here.

Cost-of-Bad-Outcomes Analyses

Mark Friedman (1995) wrote about the value of preparing estimates of the costs of bad outcomes-in essence, the current public spending that exists because we have not achieved the well-being outcomes we have identified. Under this notion, then, spending for education, for example, would not be included, and probably some other programs, such as immunizations, well-child pediatric care, and so on, also would not be included.

The point of this exercise is to begin to link current indicator trends with some fiscal correlates and, ultimately, to begin to shift dollars from ameliorative programs (e.g., child foster care, dropout recovery, substance abuse treatment) to strategies that are preventive in emphasis.

At a community level, such a task requires the capacity to identify dollars coming into the community from multiple sources (local, state, federal), as well as (perhaps) an ability to tag programs as relating primarily to particular outcomes, such as "healthy births," or "youth making positive choices." In addition, this kind of work should include a review of what practices are known to be effective (or ineffective), and an analysis of where current funds could be shifted to support more effective strategies, particularly those that emphasize prevention. In communities than have the capability to do this, it would certainly be a powerful tool for leveraging change.

Outcomes-Based Budgeting

Some would view this as the Holy Grail of outcomes-and-indicators work, because, as we all know, money talks. The vision implied by outcomes-based budgeting is to organize all line-item spending by outcome ("children are ready for school," "youth successfully transition to adulthood," etc.), and to make the indicators (as measures of progress toward the outcomes) at least one tool to judge program effectiveness and thus the appropriateness of current spending priorities.

Although a number of jurisdictions have adopted children's budgets or children and families' budgets, and used these to identify apparent gaps or imbalances in spending, in general they have not achieved a major overhaul of budgeting practices. One obvious challenge to this work is that, as long as communities are dependent on nonlocal sources of revenue, they are to a degree bound by categorical funding systems devised elsewhere.

TASKS OF PRIORITY FOR THE COMING DECADE

Within the last 5 or so years, many communities have made real strides in developing indicator tools to take stock of conditions for children and families. Indeed, there is sufficient evidence to suggest some common recommendations for moving this work forward to what might be termed the *second generation* of community indicators work. The following are a few suggestions.

Development of Positive Indicators

As noted earlier, this is an area ripe for both conceptual and applied work. Because indicator development at the national level inevitably faces a greater number of barriers, communities are likely to lead the way here, developing and testing positive indicators that may in time see broader adoption.

Continued Development of Tools for Small-Area Analysis

Although there is much basic groundwork to be laid in the area of social indicators, many are eager to see how social indicators can be used in more rigorous, hypothesis-testing paradigms. The challenges here are many (the obvious one being accounting for complex causality), but there are some specific obstacles presented by community-level data. These are the small-numbers issues raised earlier. In brief, can we tell from the kinds of unstable rates to which small populations are prone what is really going on? Of course, any analyses that include community-level indicators as part of a model also encounter this challenge. To my knowledge, the literature on this topic is still slim, with most examples from the field of health care (Diehr, Cain, Connell, & Volinn, 1990; Haggard, Shah, & Rolfs, 1998).

Looking at Linkages Among Indicators

Another area waiting for examination is the study of relationships among indicators, both cross-sectionally and longitudinally. What indicators typically tend to move together (and why)? Presumably, one application could be to identify particular "bellwether" indicators that are proxies for changes in a number of other indicators. Temporally, are there leading and lagging indicators? Are there typical progressions at a community level, where certain indicators improve first, leading to later improvements on other indicators and still later improvements on yet another group? All of these questions are properly part a community's theory of change, and it should be possible to test at least some of them, given adequate specification.

Dealing With the Ecological Fallacy

Largely ignored in discussions of social indicators, but potentially looming large in its implications for this work, is a problem, first pointed out by Robinson (1950) over 50 years ago, that has been called the *ecological fallacy*. In brief, this is the error of assuming that correlations that hold true on a population level necessarily hold true on an individual level. Unfortunately, many of us implicitly make this assumption, which can lead to strategies that are ultimately misguided, because most of our strategies target individual, and not community, behavior.

The implication of this for community indicators work is that there must be the capacity to analyze both aggregate and individual-level data if we are to understand how particular aspects of well-being are inter-related. Given that individual-level data are generally more difficult to obtain (because of privacy considerations), as well as more cumbersome to work with, this raises an additional barrier to be overcome if work in this area is to proceed.

Developing Indicator-Forecasting Techniques

Forecasting, whether it concerns the weather or the NASDAQ, seems to be something of a voodoo science. Do we dare apply it to social indicators, particularly at a community level? Presumably, communities are interested not simply in tracking what has been but in understanding how to influence the future. Considerations of priority setting, attracting public support, and resource management all would argue for having credible forecasting tools, yet there is a slim literature to provide guidance on this point.

Contemporary systems theory would suggest that communities (of whatever geographic scope) are examples of complex systems, where even small perturbations can have outsized effects.[13] As a first step, we need to begin to specify the elements of such systems and how we believe they are connected in some developmental or causal sense. Only then can we begin to build plausible forecast models.

Theories of Indicator Change That Incorporate Program and Nonprogram Influences

Communities can begin by articulating theories of change around particular indicators. In general, these should incorporate both the formal programs that are intentionally aimed at, say, teen pregnancy, or youth substance abuse, and whatever additional, nonprogram factors are believed to be accounting for the current trend. These may include community norms or values; access to services; changes in policies and laws; and ecological factors, such as the health of the local/global economy, the impact of local/global media, and so on.

Any theory of change is provisional, subject to revision when new data or new understandings emerge. However, most theories are testable (or at least falsifiable), at least to a degree. If X changes, does Indicator Y change in the expected direction? What is the impact on Y if X, F, and G all change in a coordinated direction?

Communities are "where the rubber meets the road," in terms of social indicators. For indicators to be of more than academic interest, it is essential for communities themselves to continue to develop new kinds of expertise (as well as new ways of working together and with government and other funders). It is likely that communities will in fact be important testbeds for new indicator development, new theories of change, and new knowledge about what works. Thus, it behooves all of us to help them get the right tools for the job.

ACKNOWLEDGMENT

The views expressed in this chapter are the those of the author and do not necessarily represent the position of the Vermont Agency of Human Services.

NOTES

1. The terms *outcomes, results, goals,* and some others are variously used to reference desired ends. For simplicity's sake, here they will be referred to as *outcomes*. Likewise, indicators are sometimes called *benchmarks, milestones,* and so on.
2. In some cases, there may be lists of outcomes and associated indicators that have been adopted at regional, state, or national levels. A community should certainly consider aligning its work along these lines, for example, by adopting a core set of outcomes and indicators aligned with the region's or state's, supplemented by additions that reflect unique community concerns.
3. Useful resources in this context include Samuels, Ahsan, and Garcia (1995); Redefining Progress (1997); and Sofaer (2003).
4. I use the term *community group* to refer to any broadly representative group of stakeholders in the outcomes. Sometimes, these are highly organized councils, often with formal relationships with municipal, regional, or state governments; other times, these are relatively new, informal grassroots groups still building legitimacy with the powers that be. In any case, they should have broad representation across agencies and across sectors (human services, education, business, faith community, etc.) and include ordinary residents as well as professionals.
5. Most U.S. Census data are actually not census data but are based on a random sample. These include most questions on the long form (e.g., on income, education, household characteristics) that is distributed to about 1 in 6 households. Only the short form, which includes basic questions on household size and age of members, and race-ethnicity data, is distributed to every person and household. For more information, see U.S. Census Bureau (2002).

6. Friedman has extensive materials designed for use by community groups. These are available on two web sites: http://www.resultsaccountability.com and http://www.raguide.org
7. Helpful resources for communities on many of these data interpretation topics include Simons and Jablonski (1990), Voices for Illinois Children (n.d.), and The Access Project (1999).
8. One of the best treatments of this subject (though a bit technical) is Tufte (2001).
9. One of the best treatments of theories of change at the community level is provided by two publications from The Aspen Institute: Connell, Kubisch, Schorr, and Weiss (1995) and Fulbright-Anderson, Kubisch, and Connell (1998).
10. The United Way of America (1996) has promoted a logic model framework for use by programs. However, it focuses (naturally) not on community indicators but on indicators for the particular participants of programs.
11. For further information, see the Search Institute's web site: http://www.search-institute.org.
12. This is available at http://humanservices.vermont.gov/publications/community-profiles/2005-community-profiles
13. See, for example, "tipping point" theory (Gladwell, 2002).

REFERENCES

The Access Project. (1999). *Using data: A guide for community health activists.* Retrieved May 3, 2007 from http://www.accessproject.org/downloads/data.pdf

Alliance for Building Community. (2002). *Outcomes, indicators, & strategies: An update on turning the curve.* East Dummerston, VT: Author.

Annie E. Casey Foundation. (2003). *2003 Kids Count data book.* Baltimore: Author.

Bruns, E. (n.d.). *Baltimore after-school strategy roundtable: Selected resource and risk maps.* Baltimore: Author.

Champlain Initiative. (1999). *Youth and developmental assets: A framework for success.* Burlington, VT: United Way of Chittenden County.

Champlain Initiative. (2001). *Champlain Counts: A report on the health of our Chittenden County community.* Burlington, VT: United Way of Chittenden County.

Champlain Initiative. (n.d.). *How it all began.* Retrieved May 3, 2007 from http://www.unitedwaycc.org/cihistory.htm.

Child Trends. (n.d.). *What works: A tool for improving services to children and youth.* Retrieved May 3, 2007 from http://www.childtrends.org/_docdisp_page.cfm?LID=82530A0F-03A4-4CC7-ACBF36EBFC4668B8

Connell J. P., Kubisch, A. C., Schorr, L. B., & Weiss, C. H. (Eds.). (1995). *New approaches to evaluating community initiatives: Concepts, methods, and contexts.* Washington, DC: Aspen Institute.

Diehr, P., Cain, K., Connell, F., & Volinn, E. (1990). What is too much variation: The null hypothesis in small-area analysis. *Health Services Research, 24,* 741–771.

Friedman, M. (1995). *From outcomes to budgets: An approach to outcome-based budgeting for families and children's services.* Washington, DC: Center for the Study of Social Policy.

Friedman, M. (n.d.). *Results based decision making and budgeting*. Baltimore: Fiscal Policy Studies Institute.

Fulbright-Anderson, K., Kubisch, A. C., & Connell, J. P. (Eds.). (1998). *New approaches to evaluating community initiatives: Vol. 2. Theory, measurement and analysis*. Washington, DC: Aspen Institute.

Gambone, M. A., Klem, A. M., & Connell, J. P. (2002). *Finding out what matters for youth: Testing key links in a community action framework for youth development*. Philadelphia: Youth Development Strategies, Inc., and Institute for Reform in Education.

Georgia Department of Community Affairs. (2006). *Georgia community indicators: User guide*. Retrieved May 3, 2007 from http://www.dca.state.ga.us/commind/guide.asp

Gladwell, M. (2002). *The tipping point: How little things can make a big difference*. Boston: Back Bay Books.

Haggard, L. M., Shah, G., & Rolfs, R. T. (1998). Assessing community health status: Establishing geographic areas for small area analysis in Utah. In *Utah's health: An annual review* (pp. 18–35). Salt Lake City, UT: Governor Scott M. Matheson Center for Health Care Studies.

Hart, M. (n.d.). *Characteristics of effective indicators*. Retrieved May 3, 2007 from http://www.sustainablemeasures.com/Indicators/ Characteristics.html

Hawkins, J. D., Catalano, R. F., Kosterman, R., Abbott, R., & Hill, K. G. (1999). Preventing adolescent health-risk behaviors by strengthening protection during childhood. *Archives of Pediatric and Adolescent Medicine, 153*, 226–234.

Jacksonville (FL) Community Council, Inc. (2002). *Quality of life in Jacksonville: Indicators for progress: 2002*. Retrieved May 3, 2007 from http:// www.jcci.org/statistics/documents/2006_quality_of_life_progress_report.pdf

Leffert, N., Benson, P. L., Scales, P. C., Sharma, A. R., Drake, D. R., & Blyth, D. A. (1998). Developmental assets: Measurement and prediction of risk behaviors among adolescents. *Applied Developmental Science, 2*, 209–230.

McKnight, J. P., & Kretzmann, J. L. (1993). *Building communities from the inside out: A path toward finding and mobilizing a community's assets*. Evanston, IL: Institute for Policy Research.

Moore, K. A. (1994). *Criteria for indicators of child well-being*. Paper prepared for the Conference on Indicators of Children's Well-Being, Bethesda, MD.

National Neighborhood Indicators Partnership. (1999). *Stories: Using information in community building and local policy*. Washington, DC: Urban Institute.

National Neighborhood Indicators Partnership. (2003). *The NCDB: An overview*. Retrieved May 3, 2007 from http://www2.urban.org/nnip/index.htm

National Research Council and Institute of Medicine. (2002). Community programs to promote youth development. In J. Eccles & J. A. Gootman (Eds.), *Board on Children, Youth, and Families, Division of Behavioral and Social Sciences and Education* (pp. 1–411). Washington, DC: National Academy Press.

Redefining Progress. (1997). *The community indicators handbook: Measuring progress toward healthy and sustainable communities*. San Francisco: Author.

Robinson, W. S. (1950). Ecological correlations and the behavior of individuals. *American Sociological Review, 15*, 351–357.

Sabol, W. J. (n.d.). *Creating and using indicators to measure program performance: The CANDO case*. Cleveland, OH: Case Western Reserve University, Center on Urban Poverty and Social Change.

Samuels, B., Ahsan, N., & Garcia, J. (1995). *Know your community: A step-by-step guide to community needs and resources assessment*. Chicago: Family Resource Coalition of America.

Scales, P. C., & Leffert, N. (1999). *Developmental assets: A synthesis of the scientific research on adolescent development*. Minneapolis, MN: Search Institute.

Search Institute. (1998). *Vermont statewide aggregate data*. Minneapolis: Author.

Simons, J., & Jablonski, D. M. (1990). *An advocate's guide to using data*. Washington, DC: Children's Defense Fund.

Sofaer, S. (2003). *Working together, moving ahead: A manual to support effective community health coalitions*. New York: Baruch College, City University of New York.

Tufte, E. (2001). *The visual display of quantitative information* (2nd ed.). Cheshire, CT: Graphics Press.

United Way of America. (1996). *Measuring program outcomes: A practical approach*. Alexandria, VA: Author.

U.S. Census Bureau. (2003). *Census 2000 basics*. Retrieved May 3, 2007 from http://www.census.gov/acs/www/Downloads/ACS04H5LO.pdf

U.S. Census Bureau. (2003). *American community survey operations plan*. Washington, DC: Author.

U.S. Department of Health and Human Services. (n.d.). *Healthy People 2010: Understanding and Improving Health* (2nd ed.) Washington, DC: U.S. Government Printing Office, November 2000. Retrieved May 3, 2007 from http://www.healthypeople.gov/Document/HTML/uih/uih_4.htm

U.S. Maternal and Child Health Bureau. (1998). *Analytic methods in maternal and child health*. Vienna, VA: National Maternal and Child Health Clearinghouse.

Vermont Agency of Human Services. (multiple years). *Community profiles*. Waterbury, VT: Author. Also available at http://humanservices.vermont.gov/publications/community-profiles/2005-community-profiles

Vermont Department of Education. (n.d.). *School improvement support guide*. Retrieved May 3, 2007 from http://education.vermont.gov/new/pdf.doc/pubs/apg/apg_03_analyze.pdf

Voices for Illinois Children. (n.d.). *Information is power! A child advocate's guide to fear-free fact finding*. Chicago: Author.

Part VI

Social Indexes
of Child Well-Being

Child and Youth Well-Being in the United States, 1975–1998: Some Findings From a New Index

Kenneth C. Land
Vicki L. Lamb
Sarah Kahler Mustillo
Duke University

Every generation of adults is concerned about the conditions of its children and youth (Moore, 1999). From the stagflation and socially turbulent days of the 1970s through the decline of the rust belt industries and transition to the information age in the 1980s, to the relatively prosperous e-economy and multicultural years of the late 1990s, Americans have fretted over the material circumstances of the nation's children, their health and safety, their educational progress, and their moral development. Are their fears and concerns warranted? How do we know whether circumstances of life for children in the United States are bad and getting worse, or good and improving? On what basis can the public and its leaders form opinions and draw conclusions?

Since the 1960s, researchers in social indicators/quality-of-life measurement have argued that well-measured and consistently collected social indicators provide a way to monitor the condition of groups in society, including children and families, today and over time (Land, 2000). The information thus provided can be strategic in forming the ways we think about important issues in our personal lives and the life of the nation. Indicators of child and youth well-being, in particular, are used by child advocacy groups, policymakers, researchers, the media, and service providers to serve a number of purposes. In three instances—(a) to describe the condition of children, (b) to monitor or track child outcomes, and (c) to set goals—the use of indicators is well within the long-established "public enlightenment" function of social indicators. And although there are notable gaps and inadequacies in existing child and family well-being indicators in the United States (Ben-Arieh, 2000; Moore, 1999), there also literally are dozens of data series and indicators from which to form opinions and draw conclusions (see, e.g., Brown, 1997).

In face of this surfeit of data, we address in this chapter a crucial part of the public enlightenment function, namely, the summarization question: Overall or on average, how well are children and youth in the America doing? Focusing on the last quarter of the 20th century in particular, did overall child and youth well-being-defined in terms of averages of social conditions encountered by children and youth-in the United States improve or deteriorate? Did it improve or decline in various domains or areas of social life? For specific age groups? For particular racial-ethnic groups? Did racial-ethnic groups' disparities increase or decrease?

We address these questions by engaging in a measurement exercise. Specifically, we construct a new Index of Child and Youth Well-Being based on numerous specific indicators in seven domains of life: (a) material well-being, (b) social relationships (with family and peers), (c) health, (d) safety/behavioral concerns, (e) productive activity (educational attainments), (f) place in community (participation in schooling or work institutions), and (g) emotional/spiritual well-being. In the next section, we commence with a discussion on how child and youth well-being can be conceptualized and review the methods and data we used to construct our basic Index of Child and Youth Well-Being. In subsequent sections, we discuss trends in this basic index and several variations thereon. In the final section, we summarize the main conclusions that can be drawn from the index, discuss its limitations, and cite ways in which it could be improved with a better system of child and family indicators. (A note on terminology: Throughout this article, we generally refer to "child and youth well-being" and to our summary index as the "Index of Child and Youth Well-Being." Sometimes, however, for purposes of simplicity of the grammar, we use terms like *child well-being* or the *well-being of children* as shorthand expressions. In such cases, the references should be understood as inclusive of child and youth well-being, unless the context suggests otherwise.)

CONCEPTS, DATA, AND METHODS OF INDEX CONSTRUCTION

Conceptualization of Child and Youth Well-Being, Sources of Data, and Basic Indicators

How should the child and youth well-being construct be conceptualized? We seek to measure the circumstances of children's lives-to assess their quality of life-and track changes therein over time. Fortunately, we do not have to reinvent the wheel here, as the subject of quality-of-life assessment has been studied by many social scientists during the past three decades. Reviews by Cummins (1996, 1997) of empirical studies of the quality of life are particularly helpful. Cummins (1996, p. 118) reviewed 27 definitions that have attempted to identify domains or subject areas of the quality of life and drew three conclusions:

1. The term *quality of life* refers to both the objective and subjective axes of human existence.

2. The objective axis incorporates norm-referenced measures of well-being (i.e., measures of life circumstances on which there is a consensus among the general public that they are significant components of better or worse life circumstances). Usually, objective measures of well-being are based on observable facts (e.g., infant deaths) or reports on behavior (e.g., victimization of a sample survey respondent in a violent crime incident within the last year).

3. The subjective axis incorporates measures of perceived or subjective well-being based on individuals' personal values, views, and assessments of the circumstances of their lives.

The norm-referenced approach mentioned in the second point dates back to the definition put forward by Mancur Olson. As the principal author of *Toward a Social Report*, published on the last day of the Lyndon B. Johnson Administration, Olson wrote "A social indicator is a statistic of direct normative interest which facilitates concise, comprehensive and balanced judgements about the condition of major aspects of a society" (U.S. Department of Health, Education, and Welfare, 1969, p. 97). The perceived or subjective well-being approach to quality-of-life measurement was initially explored in great methodological detail by Andrews and Withey (1976) and Campbell, Converse, and Rodgers (1976).

Both of the latter works also applied the two major approaches to quality of life measurement that have dominated the research literature. These are the measurement of assessments of life quality by individuals (a) as a single, unitary entity or (b) as being composed of discrete domains or areas of life. The former approach is tapped by the prototypical single, sample survey question "How do you feel about your life as a whole?," with responses typically obtained on a Likert rating scale of life satisfaction/dissatisfaction. The latter approach is typified by sample survey questions requesting satisfaction/dissatisfaction responses concerning a number of domain or subject area aspects of life, such as work, income, family, friends, and so on.

The literature reviews by Cummins (1996, 1997) of 27 subjective well-being studies offering definitions of the quality of life that identify specific domains suggests that there is a relatively small number of domains that comprise most of the subject areas that have been studied. Specifically, Cummins found that about 68% of the 173 different domain names, and 83% of the total reported data found in the studies reviewed, can be grouped into the following seven domains of life:

1. Material well-being (e.g., command over material and financial resources and consumption)
2. Health (e.g., health functioning, personal health)
3. Safety (e.g., security from violence, personal control)
4. Productive activity (e.g., employment, job, work, schooling)
5. Place in community (e.g., socioeconomic (education and job) status, community involvement, self-esteem, and empowerment)
6. Intimacy (e.g., relationships with family and friends)
7. Emotional well-being (e.g., mental health, morale, spiritual well-being)

Cummins (1996) stated that the weight of the empirical literature indicates that all of these seven dimensions are very relevant to subjective well-being. Therefore, indexes of the quality of life, whether based on objective or subjective data, should attempt to tap into as many of these domains as possible. Of course, it is the case that these seven domains of well-being are derived from subjective assessments in focus groups, case studies, clinical studies, and sample surveys that cannot, by definition, be replicated in studies of the quality of life that use objective data. Nonetheless, as recommended in a recent comprehensive review of numerous quality-of-life indexes (Hagerty et al., 2001), the domains identified by Cummins (1996) can and should be used to guide the selection and classification of indexes of the quality of life that are based on objective data, as we illustrate for the case of child and youth well-being later in this chapter.

There are, however, some considerable challenges to the application of these domain areas to the measurement of the quality of life, and changes therein, of children and youths in the United States. To begin with, most extant studies of subjective well-being have included as participants (in focus groups and respondents in sample surveys) only individuals who are 18 years and older. This raises the question of how applicable the domains of quality of life identified in existing empirical studies are to the quality of life of children and youth. Fortunately, the samples used in existing studies of subjective well-being have been quite diverse—ranging from general samples of adult populations to college students to various clinical populations. This variety of sampling frames suggests that the seven domains identified by Cummins have at least a fair level of robustness and applicability across different populations.

In addition, comparisons can be made with a few recent studies of subjective well-being that have focused on children and adolescent samples. For instance, Gilman, Huebner, and Laughlin (2000) found that the following domains of life related to general life satisfaction in a sample of American adolescents enrolled in Grades 9 through 12 (ordered from greatest to lowest association with general life satisfaction): family (relationships), self (image), living environment (material well-being), friends (relationships), and school. Although the survey questionnaires used by Gilman et al. do not contain questions on all of the domains identified by Cummins (1996) and cited earlier, it nonetheless is the case that several of these domains have similar content.

In brief, we proceed on the presumption that the seven domains of well-being identified earlier are applicable-with some adaptations-to the measurement of the quality of life of children and youth. It is clear, for instance, that the main "productive activity" of most children up to age 18 is schooling or education rather than work. It also is evident that the principal way in which the command of children and youth over economic and material resources is measured in national data sources through the income status of their parents or guardians.

Even with conceptual adaptations of this kind, the number of data sources available for the operationalization and measurement of child and youth well-being in the United States are limited. Basic demographic data on family structures and incomes for households with children under age 18 present are available on an annual basis from the Annual Demographic Supplements to the March Current Population Surveys. Additional annual data on selected mortality and other vital statistics also are available from the sample surveys and vital statistics compiled by the National Center for Health Statistics. In addition, there are three data sources based on replications of annual sample surveys that were developed in response to the Social Indicators Movement of the 1960s and that date back to the mid-1970s:

1. The *National Crime Victimization Survey*, which provides data on violent crime victimization from sample household members down to age 12 as well as data on the perceived ages of offenders as reported by victims in sample households.

2. The High School Senior Survey-which evolved into the Monitoring the Future (MTF) study as it also began surveying samples of 8th- and 10th-graders in 1991-provides data on illicit drug use (including cigarettes, alcohol, marijuana, cocaine, and heroin).

3. The *National Assessment of Educational Progress* (NAEP), which provides reading and mathematics test scores that are comparable over time from samples of children/youth at ages 9, 13, and 17.

Since 1997, about 20 national time series of child and youth well-being from these various data sources have been compiled as *Key National Indicators of Child Well-Being* and published annually by the Federal Interagency Forum on Child and Family Statistics (1999, 2000). The purpose of these annual reports is to provide the American public with a broad annual review of data on child and youth well-being and to monitor changes in the key indicators over time. The key indicators were chosen on the basis of five criteria (Federal Interagency Forum on Child and Family Statistics, 1999, p. viii); they must be:

1. Easy to understand by broad audiences.
2. Objectively based on substantial research connecting them to child well-being and based on reliable data.
3. Balanced so that no single area of children's lives dominates the reports.
4. Measured regularly so that they can be updated and show trends over time.
5. Representative of large segments of the population rather than one particular group.

A related data source that contains a larger set of indicators for selected years is the series of annual volumes, *Trends in the Well-Being of America's Children & Youth*, compiled by staff members at Child Trends and the Urban Institute and published by the U.S. Department of Health and Human Services, Office of the Assistant Secretary for Planning and Evaluation (2000).

Using the *Key National Indicators* ... and *Trends* ... data sources accessing and/or computing additional data to place all of the time series on an annual basis, we have compiled some 28 basic indicators of child and youth well-being, which are identified in Table 14.1. They are grouped in Table 14.1 as much as possible according to the domains of well-being identified by Cummins (1996), reviewed earlier.[1] In some cases, we have identified some of the basic indicator series as jointly indicative of two domains of well-being. Note that the indicators listed in Table 14.1 generally refer to broad age groups across the entire infant to youth age ranges. However, many are available for specific age groups, such as children and teenagers, as we show later when temporal trends in the indicators are described. This also facilitates the construction and comparison of summary indicators of trends by age categories, as also is described later herein.

Of the 28 indicator series identified in Table 14.1, 25 are available at least back to the mid-1970s, whereas 3 (health insurance coverage, subjective health assessments, and reports of activity limitations) begin only in the mid-1980s. Furthermore, most of the series in Table 14.1 are reported annually. The exceptions are the reading and test scores (from the NAEP), the obesity prevalence rates (from the National Health and Nutrition Examination Surveys [NHANES]), and the voting in Presidential election years percentages (which necessarily occur on 4-year cycles). The NAEP test scores originally began on a 5-year cycle in 1975, changed to a 2-year cycle in 1985, and then changed to a 2-year cycle in 1999. Because these time series change quite smoothly, however, they quite easily can be interpolated to an annual basis. The obesity data from the NHANES studies were collected in cycles spanning the years 1971-74, 1976-80, and 1988-94. To fit with the annual spacing of the other time series in Table 14.1, these data also have been interpolated for the intervening years. Similarly, the voting percentages were interpolated to an annual basis from the 4-year cycles of Presidential elections.

TABLE 14.1

Twenty-Eight National Indicators of Child Well-Being in the United States

Domain	Indicators
Material well-being	1. Poverty rate—All families with children
	2. Secure Parental Employment Rate
	3. Median Annual Income—All Families with Children
Material Well-Being* and Health	4. Rate of Children with Health Insurance Coverage
Material Well-Being and Social Relationships*	1. Rate of Children in Families Headed by a Single Parent
Social Relationships	2. Rate of Children Who Have Moved Within the Last Year
Health	1. Infant Mortality Rate
	2. Low Birth Weight Rate
	3. Mortality Rate, Ages 1–19
	4. Rate of Children with Very Good or Excellent Heath (as reported by their parents)
	5. Rate of Children with Activity Limitations (as reported by their Parents)
	6. Rate of Overweight Children and Adolescents, Ages 6–17
Health and Behavioral Concerns	1. Teenage Birth Rate, Ages 10–17
Safety/Behavioral Concerns	2. Rate of Violent Crime Victimization, Ages 12–17
	3. Rate of Violent Crime Offenders, Ages 12–17
	4. Rate of Cigarette Smoking, Grade 12
	5. Rate of Alcoholic Drinking, Grade 12
	6. Rate of Illicit Drug Use, Grade 12
Productivity (Educational Attainments)	1. Reading Test Scores, Average of Ages 9, 13, 17
	2. Mathematics Test Scores, Average of Ages 9, 13, 17
Place in Community* and Educational	1. Rate of Preschool Enrollment, Ages 3–4
	2. Rate of Persons Who Have Received a High School Diploma, Ages 18–24
	3. Rate of Youths Not Working and Not in School, Ages 16–19
	4. Rate of Persons Who Have Received a Bachelor's Degree, Ages 25–29
	5. Rate of Voting in Presidential Elections, Ages 18–20
Emotional/Spiritual Well-Being	1. Suicide Rate, Ages 10–19
	2. Rate of Weekly Religious Attendance, Grade 12
	3. Percent who Report Religion as Being Very Important, Grade 12

Note 1: A few basic indicators can be assigned to two domains. For these, the * denotes the domain-specific index to which the indicators are assigned for computation purposes. Explanations for the domain assignments are given in the text.

Note 2: Unless otherwise noted, indicators refer to children ages 0–17.

All of the indicator series, with the exception of the test scores, are reported in either of two forms. Many of the series are based on data on the prevalence of some identifiable characteristic or property. These are reported as prevalence rates (usually computed as the percentage of persons or the number per 1,000 with a given characteristic, e.g., good or excellent health, per year). However, some of the series are based on numbers of events that occur in a year. These are reported as incidence rates (usually computed as the number of events of some type, e.g., infant deaths, per population unit exposed to the risk of the incident, e.g., per 1,000 births, per year).

With respect to the seven domains of the quality of life identified by Cummins (1996) and summarized earlier, one can see that the child and youth well-being indicator series identified in Table 14.1 are most adequate with respect to the first five domains: (a) material well-being, (b) health, (c) safety/behavioral concerns, (d) productive activity/educational attainments (as measured by NAEP test scores), and (e) place in community (as measured by indicators of participation in school and work organizations). Only two indicators in Table 14.1—(a) the rate of children in families headed by a single parent and (b) the rate of children who have moved residences in the last year—can be construed as tapping the intimacy domain identified by Cummins. In fact, these two indicators can be construed only as imperfect measures (more commentary on this later) of the "relationships with family" and "relationships with peers" parts of Cummins's intimacy domain, respectively. Thus, we henceforth refer to these indicators as measures of a *social relationships* domain.

In addition, the single-parent indicator also measures, in part, the ability of families to command material resources. Hence, we separately identify the rate of children in families headed by a single parent as measuring both of these domains. Similarly, we separately identify the rate of children with health insurance coverage as measuring both the material well-being and health domains and the teenage birth rates as indicative of both the health and behavioral concerns domains. We also separately identify four of the schooling/work indicators as indicative of both the productive activity (educational attainments) and place in community domains. Thus, a few basic indicators can be assigned to two domains. However, as noted in Table 14.1 for purposes of index calculations, they are included in only one domain. Explanations for the domain assignments are given later in the text.

Another limitation of the list of indicators in Table 14.1 is that there are none that directly measure the emotional and spiritual well-being domain. Instead, we are limited to indirect indicators—suicide rates and MTF study questions on religious attendance and the importance of religion. Suicide is viewed in the mental health literature as indicative of extreme emotional stress (American Psychiatric Association, 1994). Thus, an increase in suicide rates in the late childhood/adolescence and teenage years may be indicative of a greater prevalence of persons in these age groups who are suffering from very high levels of stress and, inversely, low levels of emotional well-being. Similarly, the rate of weekly attendance at religious ceremonies from the MTF study is, at best, an indirect indicator of spiritual well-being. However, the indicator identified in Table 14.1 pertains to teenagers who are enrolled in Grade 12 and hence are about 17 years of age. It may thus be presumed that there is at least some volitional component of the religious attendance indicator. Accordingly, fluctuations up and down in the religious attendance time series may be indicative of trends in the spiritual well-being of American teenagers, especially when used in combination with responses to the MTF question on the importance of religion in the lives of 12th-graders.

Note, finally, that only 2 of the 28 indicators in Table 14.1 are based on subjective well-being responses (the very good/excellent health and activity limitations indicators), and these are based on survey responses from parents of the children rather than the children themselves. In sum, although the selection of indicators identified in Table 14.1 is guided by the recent statement on key domains of the quality of life by Cummins (1996), it also is highly constrained by available national data series, is almost exclusively based on objective indicators, and has relatively poor indicators to measure the intimacy and emotional well-being domains. Some implications of these measurement gaps are discussed in the DISCUSSION AND CONCLUSIONS section.

Methods of Index Construction

After describing levels and trends in each of the individual indicator series cited in Table 14.1 in the next section of the chapter, we report on our efforts to construct summary indexes of well-being therefrom. In its broadest sense, an *index number* is a measure of the magnitude of a variable at one point (say, a specific year that is termed the *current year*) relative to its value at another point (called the *reference base* or *base year*). The index number problem occurs when the magnitude of the variable under consideration is nonobservable (Jazairi, 1983). In economics, where index numbers are widely used, this is the case, for example, when the variable to be compared over time is the general price level, or its reciprocal, the purchasing power of money.

In the present case, the variable to be compared over time is the overall well-being of children in the United States—defined in terms of averages of social conditions encountered by children and youths. As noted, for example, by Ruist (1978), the index number problem arises in measuring the general price level because there are multiple prices to be compared. In the case of overall child and youth well-being, there are multiple indicators of well-being to be compared. Over any given historical period, the prices of some economic goods will have risen, and some will have fallen. Similarly, over any period of years, some indicators of child and youth well-being likely will have risen, and some will have fallen.

In the case of the general price level, the problem that arises is how to combine the relative changes in the prices of various goods into a single number that can meaningfully be interpreted as a measure of the relative change in the general price level of economic goods. In the case of child and youth well-being, the problem similarly is how to combine the relative changes in many rates of behaviors pertaining to child and youth well-being into a single number that can meaningfully be interpreted as a measure of the relative change over time in a fairly comprehensive selection of social conditions encountered by children and youths. A key point is that in any given year no single consumer is likely to purchase all of the items that comprise the market basket of goods used in constructing the consumer price index. On the other hand, fluctuations over time in the consumer price index signal changes in general price levels that generally are encountered by consumers, and most consumers are interested in how the general price level is changing. Similarly, in any given year no single child encounters all of the social conditions that enter into the overall Index of Child and Youth Well-Being that is developed in this chapter. Fluctuations over time in the Index of Child and Youth Well-Being can be taken, however, as signaling changes in the overall context of social conditions encountered by children and youths. And many policymakers, officials, adults, and parents (and some children and youths as well) are interested in how the general level of social conditions faced by children and youths in a recent year, such as 1998, compares to the corresponding level in a previous year, such as 1985.

The statistical theory of index numbers deals with the development and assessment of functional forms or aggregation functions for the construction of indexes. Because efforts to construct summary indexes of child and youth well-being are in their infancy, there is virtue in the application of the simplest possible aggregation function. We therefore have applied index formulas of the following type:

$$\text{Index of Child and Youth Well-Being in Year } t = (1/N) \, \Sigma_i \, \{100 + [(R_{it} / R_{ir}) \times 100]\}, \quad (14.1)$$

where N denotes the number of basic indicators on which the index is based, R_{it} denotes the ith child and youth well-being indicator rate in the year $t > r$, R_{ir} denotes the i^{it} rate in the reference or base year r, R_{it} and R_{ir} are called *rate relatives*, and the summation is taken over N indicator rates.[2] In Equation 14.1, $R_{it} = R_{it} - R_{ir}$ denotes the numerical value of the *finite difference* or *change* in indicator i from the base year r to year t. Therefore, by standard rules of differential calculus (see, e.g., Chiang, 1974, p. 307), each change rate ratio R_{it}/R_{ir} is a finite approximation to the time derivative of the logarithm of the rate R_i, with the accuracy of the approximation deteriorating as time increases from the base year.

Each change rate ratio in Equation 14.1 is multiplied by 100 to measure the percentage change in the rate from the base year value. Values of the change ratios years subsequent to the base year then either are greater (equal to or lesser than) than 100, indicating an improvement (no change or a deterioration) in the time series relative to its base year value. These values in subsequent years then are added to, or subtracted from, the base year index of 100. Mean values of all percentage change rate ratios then are computed. In index number terminology (Jazairi, 1983, p. 56), the formula in Equation 14.1 is a mean of *percentage change rate ratios index*, is additive, and applies equal weights to all component rates.[3]

In the analyses described next, we apply Equation 14.1 in two ways. First, we group the basic child and youth well-being indicators cited in Table 14.1 by the domain categories in the table and apply Equation 14.1 to each indicator series within the well-being domains.[4] Then we calculate the arithmetic average of the domain-specific well-being indexes to obtain an overall summary child and youth well-being index. We term this the *equally weighted domain-specific average index*. Second, to ascertain the effects of the groupings by well-being domains, we also apply Equation 14.1 to calculate an *equally weighted components-specific average index*. This second approach to index construction gives more weight to those domains for which we have a larger number of well-being indicator series.

RESULTS

Times Series Graphs of Basic Well-Being Indicators

Before reporting the results of our index construction efforts, we first review the levels and trends over time in the 28 child and youth well-being indicator series cited in Table 14.1. Commencing with the component indicators of the material well-being domain, Figure 14.1 reports the trends, 1975–98, of two of these indicators, namely, the poverty prevalence rate and the secure parental employment rate.[5] The former is measured as the percentage of children ages 0 through 17 living in families whose incomes in a given year fall below the official poverty line calculated for each family type by the Census Bureau. The latter is defined as the percentage of children ages 0 through 17 living in families with at least one parent employed full time all year. Children living in families below the poverty line and with parents who do not have stable jobs from which to earn income clearly have limited command over material resources and may indeed be severely deprived in terms of basic necessities of food, housing, and clothing (see, e.g., Bianchi, 1999; Duncan & Brooks-Gunn, 1997). In brief, the relevance of each of these indicators to the material well-being of children is clear.

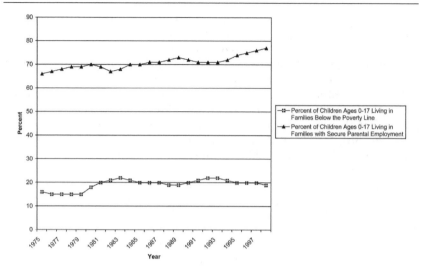

Figure 14.1.   Poverty and secure parental employment rates, 1975–98.

With respect to levels and trends in Figure 14.1, it can be seen that the child poverty prevalence rate was at its lowest levels (in the 15%–16% range) in the 1970s, rose above 20% with economic recession and changing family structures in the 1970s and 1980s (toward more single parent-headed families; see Figures 14.2 & 14.5), declined to about 19% with the economic expansion of the late 1980s, rose again with the recession of the early 1990s, and began declining to 20% or below again with the long economic expansion period of the mid- to late-1990s. However, it is significant that the rate of children living in families below the poverty line in the late 1990s has yet to match the low points of the 1970s. The secure parental employment rate shows an over-time pattern that is the inverse of the poverty rate, namely, falling during economic recessions and rising during expansions. Noteworthy in Figure 14.1 is the long-term rise in the rate of secure parental employment as the economy has restructured across the three decades to more than 75% in recent years.

Figure 14.2 shows the corresponding poverty prevalence rates for single-parent families with children, a subpopulation at particular risk of having incomes below the poverty line.[6] This is verified in Figure 14.2 by rates that generally are higher than those in Figure 14.1. One also can see that the trends stated earlier for the overall poverty rate in Figure 14.1 generally apply to the three subpopulations identified in Figure 14.2. The exception is that female-headed single-parent families were less likely to have incomes below the poverty line in the late 1990s than was the case in the 1970s. This may be due to a change over the decades in the composition of the population of female heads of families with

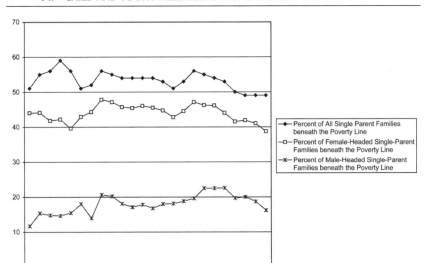

Figure 14.2. Poverty rates for single-parent families with children, 1975–98.

children to include more females with higher educational attainments who are more likely to be employed in jobs with higher incomes and, therefore, at lower risk of poverty.[7]

Figure 14.3 displays levels and trends in another basic indicator of child material well-being: median annual family income of families with related children under the age of 18 (in constant 1998 dollars), both overall for all families with children and for female- and male-headed families. As in the case of the poverty and secure parental employment indicator series, these time series show downturns corresponding to economic recessions in the late 1970s/early 1980s and in the early 1990s and an upturn in the mid- to late-1990s. Overall, the trend over the 23 years shown in the figure is up from about $46,600 in 1975 to about $57,000 in the most recent years.

Figure 14.4 reports levels and trends in indicators that have bearings on both the material well-being of children as well as their health—namely, prevalence rates of children living in families with health insurance—in total and with private and public sources of the insurance.[8] These indicators are based on questions that were added to the March Current Population Surveys beginning in 1987; thus, the length of the series in the figure (1987–98) is shorter than those displayed previously. With respect to levels and trends, it can be seen that the overall health insurance rate has varied little (between 87% and 85%) over the 12 years shown in the figure. However, the impact of the restructuring of family welfare in 1996 from the old Aid to Families with Dependent Children to the Temporary Assistance to Needy Families in 1996 shows up in the

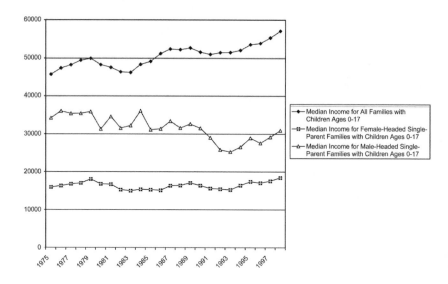

Figure 14.3. Median family income in families with children in 1998 dollars, 1975–98.

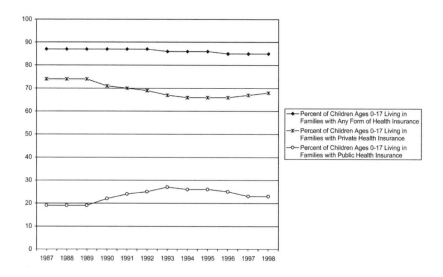

Figure 14.4. Rates of children living in families with health insurance, 1987–98.

406

drop in the percentage of families with public health insurance in the late 1990s (see also Chavkin, Romero, & Wise, 2000).

As final indicators of circumstances that bear on material well-being as well as on the social relationships domain of the quality of life, the graphs in Figure 14.5 exhibit levels and trends in prevalence rates for children ages 0 through 17:

- living in single-parent families for the years 1975 to 1998, both overall and for children in female-headed and male-headed single-parent households, and
- children who have moved residences in the past year (residential mobility), for the years 1975 to 1998.

We include the overall single-parent time series in our summary indexes of child and youth well-being for two reasons. First, as we noted in the discussion of Figure 14.2, children in single-parent families are at greater risk (than two-parent families) of poverty (see also Bianchi, 1999; Hernandez, 1997). Second, much social science research has found that children in single-parent families are less likely, on average, to have full, open, and pleasant connections and associations with members of both sides of their biological parents than are children in families with both parents present.[9] They thus are likely to experience a loss with respect to the intimacy or social relationships quality-of-life domain identified by Cummins (1996) as reviewed earlier. In our efforts to construct domain-specific and overall child and youth well-being in-

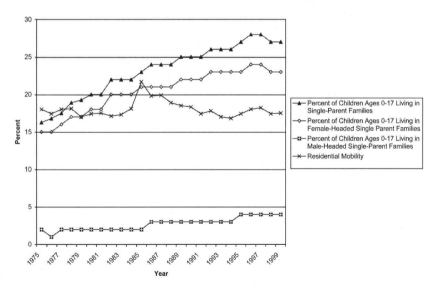

Figure 14.5.   Percentage of all children ages 0 through 17 living in single-parent families and residential mobility, 1975–99.

dicators later, we accordingly treat the single-parent prevalence rate as an indicator of trends in the social relationships domain of well-being.

Some research also has found that, because of the economic hardships, especially of female custodial parents whose incomes decline after separations or divorce, family disruptions often are associated with residential relocations (London, 2000). These, in turn, are negatively associated with the maintenance of stable peer relationships (McLanahan & Sandefur, 1994). As an indicator of the extent to which the peer relationships of children and youth may be affected by changes in residential locations overall (i.e., not just due to divorce or separation of parents), Figure 14.5 thus also reports the overall residential mobility series.

To provide information about trends in children living in single-parent families overall as well as in different types, we report in Figure 14.5 both the overall single-parent prevalence rate as well as the separate female- and male-headed household rates. It can be seen that the trends in the three prevalence rates for single parenthood in Figure 14.5 generally are consistent over time.[10] The overall single-parent prevalence rate starts at about 16% in 1975, rises to a peak of 28% in 1995 and 1996, and shows a slight drop in 1997 and 1998. It is clear, however, that the overall conclusion from Figure 14.5 is that single-parenthood has been at much higher levels—with the implications of this for increased child poverty risk and decreases in family relationships—in the last decade or so than was the case in the 1970s. However, the dramatic increases of this indicator series experienced from 1975 through about 1985 appear to have slowed in the 1990s, with even slight reverses in recent years.

By comparison, the general trend shown by the residential mobility indicator time series in Figure 14.5 is flatter—with significant peaks in the mid-1980s and mid- to late 1990s—than that of the series on children living in single-parent families. In brief, the trend in the single-parent time series generally has been up, especially in the 1975–86 time period, thus leading in many cases to residential relocations. The single-parent series also shows periods of increases in the mid-1980s and mid-1990s that appear to be associated with peaks in the residential relocations series. However, there evidently has been a decreasing relocation trend among children living in two-parent families in such a way that the overall residential relocation trend from 1975 to 1998 was relatively flat.

Social capital theories (see, e.g., Coleman, 1988, and McNeal, 1999) may be relevant to the interpretation of these trends. These theories have articulated the pathways by which parental involvement and peer ties affect children's academic, social, and economic achievements. From such a theoretical perspective, the implications of the indicator time series in Figure 14.5 are that children's social capital in the United States has declined in recent decades more through decreased noncustodial parental contact than through disruptions of peer relationships.

Moving on to the health' domain indicators identified in Table 14.1, Figure 14.6 shows the levels and trends in six child health series for the

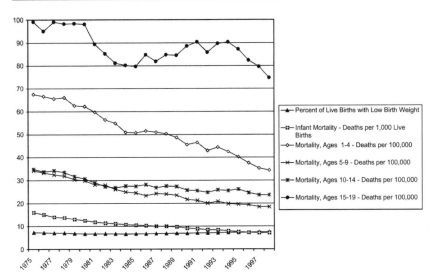

Figure 14.6.   Mortality and low birthweight rates, 1975–98.

years 1975 to 1998. Infant mortality rates (the number of deaths before age 1 per 1,000 live births) are given in the figure. In addition, mortality (incidence) rates per 100,000 population units are reported for ages 1 through 4, 5 through 9, 10 through 14, and 15 through 19.[11] In general, these mortality indicator series show downward trends across the years for the first four of these age groups. In the case of the oldest age group, ages 15 through 19, the biggest drop occurred in the early 1980s, followed by increases through the mid-1990s and then another decline in the late 1990s.

The sixth indicator series in Figure 14.6, the percentage of live births with low birthweight (infants weighing less than 2500 g at birth), is a measure that is indicative of the prevalence of premature births. Although the scale of the figure is not sufficiently refined to show this, there has been a tendency since the mid-1980s for an increase in this series to be correlated with decreases in the infant mortality rate series. Thus, the infant mortality rate series in the United States may now be in a range such that declines in this series are due to the presence of hospital care technology that rescues and saves from early death some of the premature, low-birthweight babies who would have died in earlier decades (Buehler, Kleinman, Hogue, Strauss, & Smith, 1987; Hack et al., 1995).[12] Another reason for the increase in low-birthweight infants over this period is that the number of twin, triplet, and higher order multiple births has increased (Federal Interagency Forum on Child and Family Statistics, 1999, p. 25). Twins and other multiple births are much more likely than singleton infants to be of low birthweight (Martin & Taffel, 1995).

Two subjective health prevalence indicators—(a) the percentage of children ages 0 through 17 with very good or excellent health and (b) the percentage of children ages 0 through 17 with activity limitations (both as reported by their parents)—are displayed in Figure 14.7. These indicators are based on questions that were added to the National Health Interview Survey beginning in 1984; thus, the length of the series in the figure (1984–97) is shorter than most of the others displayed previously. Both of these basic indicator series show slight changes over the years–with the percentage of children with very good/excellent health increasing from 78 in 1984 to 81 in 1997. This increasing trend is counterbalanced somewhat, however, by an increase in the percentage of children with activity limitations, from 5% in 1984 to 6.5% in 1997.

Figure 14.8 reports prevalence rates and trends therein for overweight children (ages 6–11) and adolescents (ages 12–17).[13] Overweight prevalence among children and adolescents has become an important social concern in recent years, because persons who are overweight in childhood and adolescence are at greater risk of being overweight as adults, and adults who are overweight are at higher risk of numerous health problems. Among these are hypertension, coronary heart disease, gall bladder disease, type II (non insulin dependent) diabetes, and some cancers (Troiano, Flegal, Kuczmarski, Campbell, & Johnson, 1995). The graphs for the overweight series in Figure 14.8 show that both overweight time series have generally increased over the years 1975 to 1998. The overweight series for children has nearly tripled in value—from 6% in 1975 to 17.6% in 1998. The corresponding values for adolescents range from 6% in 1975 to a projected 14.6% in 1998.

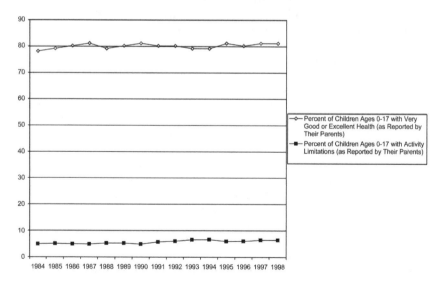

Figure 14.7.   Subjective health indicators, 1984–98.

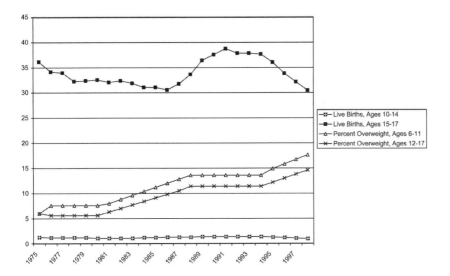

Figure 14.8.   Teenage birth rates and overweight percentages, 197–98.

Figure 14.8 also reports incidence rates for two additional basic indicator series that, as noted in Table 14.1, tap into both the health and the
behavior concerns domains for the years 1975 to 1998-incidence rates
for births to teenagers aged 10 through 14 and 15 through 17. Births to
teenagers have relevance to health concerns for both the infants and
their young mothers (Klerman, 1993), but they also are indicative of
non-normative, and sometimes rebellious, behavior patterns and thus
also are indicative of teenage behaviors about which there is much public concern. With respect to our efforts to construct domain-specific indexes reported later, however, we group the two teenage birth rate time
series into the safety/behavioral concerns domain. The reason for this
grouping is that the over-time behavior patterns of teenage birth rate
series are more similar to those of the other safety/behavioral indicators
than they are to the health indicators. It can be seen, in particular, from
Figure 14.8 that the most dramatic changes in the teenage birth rate
time series occur for the 15- to 17-year-old age group.[14] This series
shows a substantial upturn from the mid-1980s to the mid-1990s followed by a decrease in recent years. Indeed, the ages 15–17 birth rate in
1998 (32.1) is lower than that of 1975 (36.1). Although at much lower
levels, the time series for the 10- to 14-year-old age group shows the
same over time pattern.

Considering next the safety/behavioral concerns domain indicators
identified in Table 14.1, Figure 14.9 displays levels and trends for the
years 1975 to 1998 in two prevalence rate indicator time series of the
physical safety of children. The first is the rate per 1,000 population

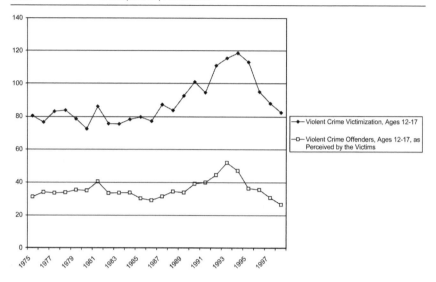

Figure 14.9.   Violent crime victimization and offender rates, 1975–98.

unit of children/youth aged 12 through 17 who are victims of violent crimes. The second is the rate per 1,000 children in this age group who are offenders (as perceived and estimated by victims in the National Crime Victimization Survey). It can be seen that the victimization rate generally runs over twice as high as the offender rate, which is consistent with a number of violent events experienced by children in these ages wherein the offender is of an older age. In terms of levels and trends, both time series show substantial stability from 1975 through the mid-1980s followed by a rise to peak levels in the late 1980s to mid-1990s and declines in the most recent years.

Complementing the violent crime safety indicators in Figure 14.9, Figure 14.10 shows prevalence levels (percentage of sample survey respondents) and trends in self-reported teenage illicit cigarette smoking, alcohol drinking, and psychoactive drug (e.g., marijuana, cocaine, heroin) use in the previous 30 days at the time of the survey. Trends are displayed in the figure for children enrolled in all three grades—8th, 10th, and 12th—included in the MTF study. For the 8th- and 10th-graders, MTF data collection began in 1991, whereas the 12th-grade data date back to 1975. We include the graphs for the lower grades in Figure 14.10, however, so that readers can see that the trends in the 1990s are highly correlated across all three grades. Thus, even though we include only the 12th-grade data in our summary well-being indexes, they capture the major trends in the other two age groups as well. In terms of the levels and trends shown in Figure 14.10, one can see that the smoking, drinking, and drug use prevalence rates generally were at their highest levels in the late 1970s and early 1980s. This was followed by declines to

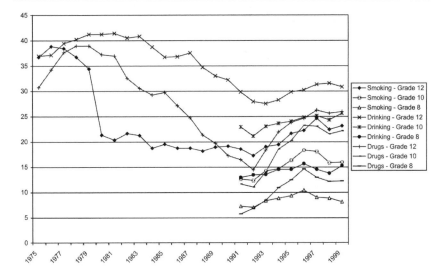

Figure 14.10.   Teenage illicit smoking, drinking, and drug use, 1975 (or 1991) to 1999.

about 1992 and then increases to the late 1990s. The last 2 years show some leveling and/or declines in these rates.

Consider next the productive activity (educational attainments) domain of indicators in Table 14.1. We use this terminology because, as noted earlier, the primary *productive activity* (the domain label used by Cummins, 1996, 1997) circumstance of children's lives is schooling rather than work. In particular, Figure 14.11 focuses on indicators of children's achievements with respect to their schooling activities. It displays levels and trends in average test scores in the reading and mathematics tests administered as part of the continuing NAEP series for children ages 9, 13, and 17 (we noted earlier the years for which the time series in Figure 14.11 are interpolated). In general, these time series show more consistent increases since the mid-1980s at all three ages in the average test scores for the mathematics tests than for the reading tests. The latter scores either are stable or slightly declining (ages 9 and 17) or show very small increases (age 13) since 1985.

In Figure 14.12, we group the graphs of levels and trends in five basic indicator series that are indicative of attachments of children to such productive activities as schooling and work and to participation in the electoral process through voting in Presidential elections. These series also are indicative of Cummins's (1996, 1997) concept of a *place in community* domain related to socioeconomic status as well as indicators of participation in the activities of one's local community. In fact, for purposes of construction of the domain-specific and summary well-being indexes reported later, we group these five indicators into a place-in-

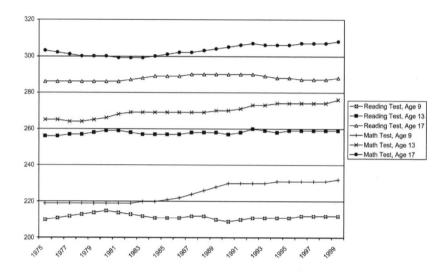

Figure 14.11. National Assessment of Educational Progress test scores for reading and mathematics skills (with interpolated values for missing years), 1975–99.

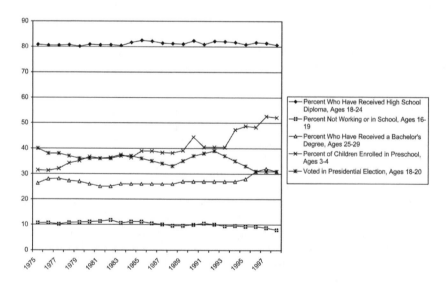

Figure 14.12. Enrollment, schooling attainment rates, and voting, 1975–98.

community domain set. Figure 14.12 specifically shows levels and trends from 1975 to 1998 in prevalence rates of enrollments or attainments in four categories: (a) percentage of children ages 3 through 4 enrolled in preschool, (b) percentage of youth ages 18 through 24 who have received a high school diploma or its equivalent, (c) percentage of young adults ages 25 through 29 who have received a bachelor's degree, and (d) percentage of youth ages 16 through 19 who are not enrolled in school and not employed and thus detached from either of the educational or work institutions. Figure 14.12 also contains a prevalence rate time series defined by the percentage of youths, ages 18 to 20, who reported voting in Presidential elections.[15]

With respect to levels and trends of the time series shown in Figure 14.12, one can seen that the percentage of children enrolled in preschool has generally trended upward over the entire period, with particularly dramatic increases in the mid- to late 1990s. The percentage of young adults who have received a bachelor's degree by ages 25 to 29 also has trended upward in recent years, but this series also shows an initial downturn in the late 1970s and early 1980s. The other two schooling/work-related time series are more stable over the years. Nonetheless, the percentage of 18- to 24-year-olds who had received a high school diploma is higher in 1998 than in the first several years of the time series, and the percentage of youths ages 16 to 19 who were not working and not enrolled in school showed a slight decline in the 1990s. By comparison, the time series on the percentage of 18- to 20-year-olds who voted in Presidential elections showed a general decline from 1975 to 1996—with, however, a clear upturn (to a level comparable to the 1976 percentage) associated with the 1992 election. Evidently, a tightly contested popular Presidential election can raise substantially the level of electoral participation among 18- to 20-year-olds.

Finally, Figure 14.13 shows levels and trends in the four indicator series we have for the emotional and spiritual well-being quality-of-life domain. These are the suicide rates for ages 10 through 14 and 15 through 19, measured by incident rates per 100,000 population[16] and the prevalence rates (percentages) of religious attendance at Grade 12 and of students in Grade 12 who reported that religion plays a very important role in their lives from the MTF study. It can be seen that both suicide rates moved upward at a slow pace from 1975 to the mid-1980s. Beginning in 1984, both series then exhibited more rapid increases, with the increase in the younger age group lasting only a couple of years while the suicide rate for the 15- to 19-year-old group increased until 1988. The latter series then remained near 11 per 100,000 until 1995, whereupon it declined through 1998.

By comparison, the percentage of 12th-grade students who reported weekly attendance at religious ceremonies in the MTF study generally declined from the 39% to 42% level in the period 1975 through 1981 to about 30% in 1991. Since 1991, this series has stayed in the 31%-to-32% range. The companion indicator on the importance of religion in the

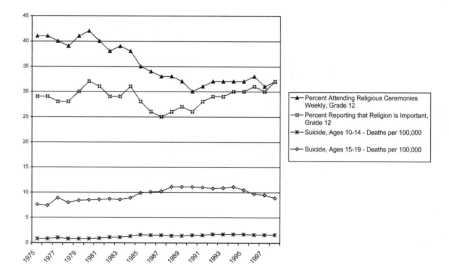

Figure 14.13.   Religious attendance, beliefs, and suicide rates, 1975–98.

lives of 12th-graders shows more stability-it stayed around 30% through the mid-1980s, dropped toward the 25% level in the late 1980s, and then increased to the 30% level or slightly above in the mid- to late 1990s. Two points are noteworthy. First, the greater declines observed from 1975 to the late 1980s in the percentage of 12th graders attending religious ceremonies weekly than in the percentage reporting that religion is very important in their lives is consistent with an "individualization" trend in American religious observance in the last quarter of the 20th century (Roof & McKinney, 1987). Second, note the slight inverse correlation between the decrease in the religious importance time series below the 30% level in the mid-1980s through the early 1990s with the increases in the suicide rate for teenagers aged 15 to 19 in the same period. This suggests that these series share a commonality.

Basic Summary Well-Being Indexes and Best-Practice Computations

We applied the mean of change rate ratios index construction formula of Equation 14.1 to the 28 basic indicators of child and youth well-being identified in Table 14.1, for which we have just reviewed levels and trends over time. Because 25 of the 28 time series date back to 1975, we used 1975 as one base year for application of Equation 14.1, and because all 28 basic indicator time series are available by the mid-1980s, we used 1985 as a second base year. To compute the indices, we used 100 as the reference point for each base year and measured the values of the indexes for subsequent years as a percentage value of this base year value. Thus, an index value that is greater than 100 for a subsequent year indicates improvement compared to 1975 (or 1985), and a value less than 100 indicates a deterioration compared to the base year. Figures 14.14 and 14.15 display the graphs for the resulting domain-specific indexes of child and youth well-being, for 1975 to 1998, and 1985 to 1998, respectively.

Consider first the seven domain-specific indexes with 1975 as the base year in Figure 14.14. One can see that the emotional/spiritual well-being, social relationships, and health domains show the most deterioration among the seven indexes over the 23 years from 1975 to 1998. The social relationships index fell rapidly from 1975 to 1985. The social relationships index then remained at about 70% of its 1975 base value through the mid-1990s, whereupon it showed a slight dip and then an increase. The emotional/spiritual well-being index stayed within 10% of its 1975 level until 1985. It then declined by 1990 to about 70% of the base 1975 level, followed by a rise to near the 90% level in the late-1990s. By comparison, the health domain index increased to levels above the 1975 base year until the mid-1980s. It then fell below the 1975 level and stayed there through 1998. Although several of the components of the health domain index show improvements compared to 1975, the percentage-overweight component began a period of deterioration in the early 1980s and early 1990s. This is a major factor in the declines observed in the health index.

Another domain-specific index in Figure 14.14 that had a difficult time rising above the 1975 base year values is the material well-being index. It fell to its lowest levels in the early 1980s and early 1990s in association with economic recessions. It did, however, increase by 1997

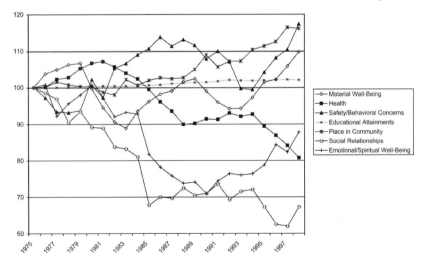

Figure 14.14.   Domain-specific indexes of child well-being, 1975–98.

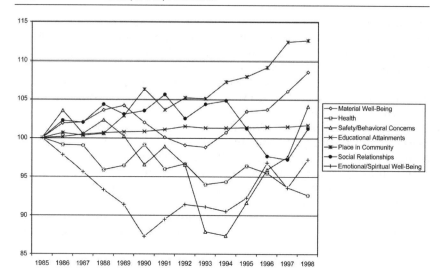

Figure 14.15.   Domain-specific indexes of child well-being, 1985–98.

and 1998 to the 105%-to-110% level (compared with the 1975 base year value). A fifth domain index in Figure 14.14 that shows substantial waves of increases and declines over the years is safety/behavioral concerns. This index declines to below 100% (of base year 1975 levels) in the late 1970s as well as in the early 1990s. The latter low point corresponds to a decline that began in the late 1980s. The series then begins to increase again only in the late 1990s.

One of the other three domain indexes of Figure 14.14—place in community (attachments to school, work, and political institutions)—shows a pattern of stability around the 1975 level until the late 1980s followed by relatively steady increases to 1998. By comparison, the index of productive activity (educational attainments), is the most stable of all of the domain indexes in Figure 14.14. Average test scores in the 1990s were just slightly higher than their 1975 base year values.

What happens to inferences about changes in domain-specific child and youth well-being if the base year is changed? Figure 14.15, which shows the domain-specific summary indexes with 1985 as the base year, provides the information to address this question. In general, the seven indexes in Figure 14.15 show trends similar to those observed for Figure 14.14. When 1985 levels of the component indicator time series are used as base year values, however, only one domain-specific index—health—has values in the late 1990s that are below its 1985 level. Again, this is due to the increasing prevalence of overweight children and adolescents, which pulls down an otherwise-improving health domain.

What do these domain-specific trends imply for changes in overall child and youth well-being from the 1970s to the 1990s? Figure 14.16, which shows graphs of two overall summary well-being indexes with 1975 as the base year, addresses this question. One of the indexes in Figure 14.16—the equally weighted domain-specific average index—is computed by applying the rate ratios formula of Equation 14.1 a second time to average the seven domain-specific indexes of child and youth well-being illustrated in Figure 14.14. The second index in Figure 14.16, the equally weighted component time series average index, applies Equation 14.1 directly to all 25 basic indicator time series that date back to 1975. The first index weights the seven domain-specific indexes equally, whereas the second weights the 25 component time series equally. Thus, the second index gives more weight to those domains for which we have more component time series, whereas the former treats the seven domains equally. A comparison of the two indexes helps to ascertain the effects of the domain groupings on the overall summary well-being indexes. Quality-of-life researchers (see, e.g., Hagerty et al., 2001) generally prefer to interpret domain-specific indexes, arguing that they yield a more balanced representation of well-being.

On can see in Figure 14.16 that the two 1975 base year summary indexes show broadly similar over-time trends but diverging levels beginning in the mid-1980s. Using the equally weighted component time series index, there is a slight decline in the value of the index in the late-1970s followed by a recovery to 1975 levels by 1980. The index then fluctuates but generally declines through the 1980s and early 1990s, reaching a low point of just above 94% of 1975 levels in 1993.

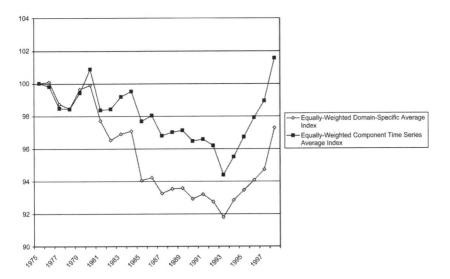

Figure 14.16.   Summary indexes of child well-being, 1975–98.

The index then climbed steadily to near 102% of 1975 levels in 1998. By comparison, the behavior of the equally weighted domain-specific index is similar up to 1981. It then fell more or less steadily in value through the 1980s and early 1990s. This index also reached its lowest levels in 1992 through 1994 and then showed increases through 1998 to a level of about 97% of its 1975 base.

It also is noteworthy in Figure 14.16 that the increases in the two summary well-being indexes in the late 1990s are considerably above the levels observed as late as 1993. In part, this is due to the downturn of the material well-being and safety/behavioral domain-specific components in the late 1980s and early 1990s, as noted earlier. However, the rapid increases in the overall summary well-being indexes over the years 1993 to 1998 shown in Figure 14.16 also are due to the fact that the trends in the mid- to late 1990s in six of the seven domain-specific indexes (and most of their component time series) have been in concert and pointed upward-for the first time in the 23 years since 1975.

Again, we can ask what effect, if any, the choice of base year for computing the summary indexes has on conclusions about trends over time. Figure 14.17, which shows the two summary well-being indexes with the 1985 base year, addresses this question. It can be seen that, over most years of this time period, the domain-average index yields values somewhat higher than the component-average index. On the whole, however, the over-time pattern displayed in Figure 14.17 is consistent with that from Figure 14.16, namely, a plateau in the mid-1980s followed by a decline in the late 1980s to early 1990s, and then a sustained rise since 1993. In the most recent years, the two summary indexes suggest that overall child and youth well-being in the late 1990s has increased to just above—by 2% to 3%—the 1985 base year levels.

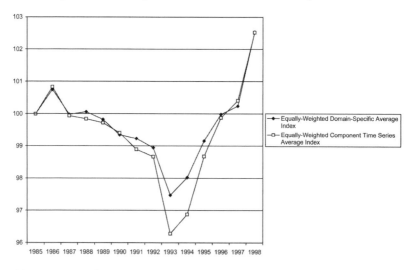

Figure 14.17.   Summary indexes of child well-being, 1985–98.

In brief, on the basis of the domain-average summary child and youth well-being indexes just reported, one can inferred that, on average and overall, the quality of life of children/youth in the United States has been stable or declined slightly compared to 1975 and has increased very slightly compared to 1985. In addition, there have been some important periodic downturns associated with economic recessions and with a wave of behavioral problems in the late 1980s and early 1990s.

In the absence of a suitable gold standard or yardstick for scale values of the overall summary well-being index, however, it is difficult to assess the meaning of these numerical values with respect to possibilities for improvements in child and youth well-being in the United States. One possible yardstick is summarized in Table 14.2, in which we report our efforts to compute a best practice numerical value for our domain- average summary well-being index, using 1975 as the base year. This best practice value is computed by using as a yardstick for each component indicator rate either: the best value of this indicator ever recorded historically in the United States or the best value observed internationally in any other country for which there are comparable indicators and for which the performance of the United States is inferior.[17] Accordingly, the first column of Table 14.2 identifies the component indicators, the second identifies the best practice standard for the United States, and the third gives corresponding international best practice values (when these are available). In the bottom of the table, we report the numerical values of both the domain-specific indexes and the overall summary child and youth well-being index, based on both sets of best practice indicators.

It can be seen in Table 14.2 that the numerical value of the domestic domain-average best practice summary index is about 123. To interpret this numerical value, recall that the domain-average summary Index of Child and Youth Well-Being in the late 1990s (see Figure 14.16) was at about 97% of its 1975 value, indicating a deterioration of about 3% compared to 1975. By contrast, the domestic best practice value of the index in Table 14.2 implies that—if the United States had been at or near its best historically observed values on the component indicators of the seven domains of child and youth well-being—the index could have improved by about 23% compared to 1975 levels. The numerical value of the corresponding international best practice summary index in Table 14.2 is 138.21. Again, this implies that if the United States had achieved levels on the component social indicators comparable to the best values observed internationally in the late 1990s, then the Index of Child and Youth Well-Being would have improved by about 38% compared to 1975 levels. From this perspective on the overall domain-average summary well-being index charted in Figure 14.16, one can infer that although the social conditions of children and youth in the United States were rapidly improving in the late 1990s as compared to the mid-1970s, there nonetheless are large improvements that yet can be

Table 14.2
Historically-Based United States and International Comparative Best Practice for Child Well-Being Indicators

Indicator	United States Historical Best Values	International Best Values
Material Well-Being		
1. Poverty	15, 1976–1979	3.5, Sweden 1995
2. Secure Employ	77, 1998	
3. Health Insurance	87, 1987,1992	100, Australia 1996
4. Median Income	$57,022, 1998	
Health		
1. Very Good Health	81, 1987,1990,1995-96	
2. Activity Limitation	4.9, 1987,1990	
3. LBW	5, Health 2000 Target	2.9, Iceland 1992
4. Infant Mort	7.2, 1998	3.5, Sweden 1996
5. Mort, 1–19	37.28, 1998	18.73, Sweden, 1995
6. Obesity, 6–17	5.6, 1976–80	
Safety/Behavioral Concerns		
1. Victim	72.5, 1980	
2. Crime	26.5, 1998	
3. Smoke	6, Healthy People 2000 Target (12–17)	9, Israel 1993–4 (age 15)
4. Drink	12.6, Healthy People 2000 Target (12–17)	
5. Drugs	3.2, Healthy People 2000 Target (12–17)*	0, Romania 1999 (age 16)*
6. Birth, 10–17	15.75, 1997–1998	3.9, Japan 1997 (ages 15–19)
Educational Attainments		
1. Reading, 9–17	282, U.S. Regional Score, 1996–1998	
2. Math, 9–17	275, U.S. Regional Score, 1996	
Place In Community		
1. Preschool	52.6, 1997	82.4, Belgium 1998
2. High School	82.4, 1985	98.3, Japan, 1995
3. No Work or School	8, 1998	
4. College	32, 1999	34.9, Australia, 1995
5. Voting	48, 1972	55.1, Germany 1979 (ages 18–21)
Emotional Well-Being		
1. Suicide,10–19	4.1, 1976	1.7, Greece 1996 (ages 15–24)
2. Spiritual Attitude, Gr 12	32, 1998	
3. Church Attendance, Gr 12	42, 1980	
Social Relationships		
1. Single Parent	7, 1950	4.5, Japan 1980
2. Residential Mobility	16.8, 1994	

Implied Best Practice (using 1975 as base year)

International (except when unavailable) Domain Specific Indices		United States Domain Specific Indices	
Material	133.69	Material	111.98
Health	152.37	Health	131.38
Behavior	159.36	Behavior	152.12
Education	102.88	Education	102.88
Place in Community	155.79	Place in Community	127.17
Emotional/Spiritual	124.10	Emotional/ Spiritual	105.05
Social Relationships	139.28	Social Relationships	131.46
Summary Index	138.21	Summary Index	123.15

*For Marijuana

made. Of course, it should be noted that no single nation-state has numerical values on all of the component indicators that are at the international best practice level. Thus, by using the international best practice value of our summary index in Table 14.2 as a comparative standard by which to judge the recent performance of the United States with respect to conditions of life for its children and youth, we are indeed using a very tough evaluative standard.

Age-Specific/Developmental Summary Well-Being Indexes

To further probe the meaning of the levels and trends in our summary child and youth well-being indexes it is helpful to disaggregate, as best as we can, the component indicators of our overall summary indexes of child and youth well-being according to the ages of the children and youth to which they refer. Of the 25 basic social indicator time series in Table 14.1 that date back to 1975, a moderate number are available for specific age groups. In Table 14.3 we report our allocation of these series into three age-specific/developmental categories: (a) infancy/preschool (ages < 6), (b) childhood (ages 6–11), and (c) adolescence/teenage years (ages 12–19).[18] Of these three categories in Table 14.3, the adolescence/teenager grouping has the largest number of indicators—21—and domains of well-being represented—5. The infancy/preschool and childhood groupings each have 6 indicators from three domains of well-being.

For a summary index of well-being for the adolescence/teenage groups, we include the violent crime indicator time series from the National Crime Victimization Survey for ages 12 through 17 (see Figure

TABLE 14.3

Infancy/Preschool

1. Poverty, Ages 0–5
2. Health Insurance, Ages 0–5*
3. Infant Mortality
4. Low Birth Weight
5. Mortality, Ages 1–4
6. Preschool Attendance, Ages 3–4

Childhood

1. Poverty, Ages 6–17
2. Health Insurance, Ages 6–11*
3. Mortality, Ages 5–9
4. Overweight, Ages 6–11
5. Reading, Age 9
6. Math, Age 9

Adolescence/Teenage Years

1. Poverty, Ages 6–17
2. Health Insurance, Ages 12–17*
3. Mortality, Ages 10–14
4. Mortality, Ages 15–19
5. Overweight, Ages 12–17
6. Births, Ages 10–14
7. Births, Ages 15–17
8. Crime Offenders
9. Crime Victimzation
10. Drinking, Grade 12
11. Drugs, Grade 12
12. Smoking, Grade 12
13. Reading, Age 13
14. Math, Age 13
15. Reading, Age 17
16. Math, Age 17
17. Not Working or in School, Ages16–19
18. Suicides, Ages 10–15
19. Suicides, Ages 12–17
20. Religious Attendance, Grade 12
21. Religion Importance, Grade 12

*The health insurance time series enter into the calculation of the age-group indices beginning in 1987, the first year these series are available.

14.9) and the high school seniors (ages 17–18) time series data on smoking, drinking, and illicit drug use time series from the MTF study (see Figure 14.10). The age ranges of these violent crime and illicit drug use time series are concentrated in certain areas of the adolescence/teenage grouping. However, trends over time in violent crime victimization and offending and illicit substance use tend to be correlated across the teenage years, as can be seen in Figure 14.10 for substance use among 8th-, 10th-, and 12th-graders. Unfortunately, only the time series for the 12th-graders dates back to 1975. In the case of the violent crime time series, the age range of the data does not include the first 2 and the last 2 years of the ages 10- to 19-year-olds category. Again, however, it no doubt is the case that trends in the violent crime indicator series for the ages 12-through-17 group are quite highly correlated with trends at both ends of the ages 10-to-19 grouping.

Figure 14.18 displays the resulting age-specific summary indicators of child and youth well-being. Do they yield meaningful information about levels and trends over time? Focusing first on the infancy/preschool index, it can be seen in the figure that this index showed fairly steady increases in the entire period from 1975 to 1998. It does, however, have a slight acceleration above the overall time trend in the late 1970s and a slight deceleration below the overall trend line in the early 1990s. After 1993, the infancy/preschool index then resumed increasing in the most recent years, reaching a level about 25% above the 1975 base year values by 1998. This last period of increases in the in-

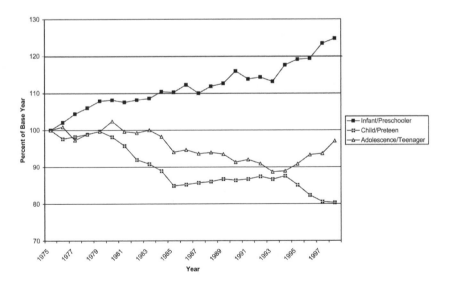

Figure 14.18.   Age-specific summary indicators of child well-being, 1975–98.

fancy/preschool index is associated with decreases in poverty and mortality rates for these ages in the mid- to late 1990s as well as increases in preschool attendance.

By comparison, the childhood and adolescence/teenage indexes in Figure 14.18 exhibit a plateau near their 1975 levels through about 1980. Both indexes then show declines to 1985. After 1985, the childhood/preteen index shows a plateau through about 1993 to 1994. By comparison, the adolescence/teenage index declines at a slow rate through 1993 to 1994. After 1994, the two indexes diverge, with the adolescence/teenage index showing increases to levels near the 1975 base values by 1998 while the childhood index declined to about 80% of the 1975 base year. The declines in the childhood and adolescence/teenage indexes are very much influenced by the increases in the prevalence of overweight children and youth noted in Figure 14.8. In the most recent period, the adolescence/teenage group has a sufficient number of indicators that are improving so that its overall summary index increases in the 1993-to-1998 period. This is not the case for the childhood index, however, for which we have only six indicator series and for which the overweight increases pull the overall index downward.

On the whole, the trends displayed in the age-specific summary indicators of well-being in Figure 14.18 are meaningful and consistent with the trends noted earlier in the corresponding component social indicator series. In particular, they point to the following themes as the primary age-specific patterns of change in well-being over the past three decades:

- a deceleration in the 1980s in the rate of improvement of the circumstances of lives of infant/preschool children followed by a resumption of improvements in the mid- to late 1990s, and
- a deterioration in the circumstances of the lives of school-aged children, adolescents, and teenagers in the period from the mid-1980s to the mid-1990s followed by evident improvements for the latter, but not the former, group since 1994.

Clearly, it would be desirable to have a better and larger selection of age-specific indicators from which to form the summary indexes in Figure 14.18, especially for the two younger age groups.

Racial-Ethnic Group-Specific Indexes and Disparity Indexes

As another means for disaggregating our overall domain-specific and summary indexes of child and youth well-being, we now examine the effects of classification by membership in three major racial-ethnic groups as recorded in the census, vital statistics, and sample survey data sources from which our basic indicator have been compiled: Whites,

Blacks, and Hispanics.[19] As the United States has become an increasingly multiracial and multiethnic society in recent decades, major concerns about child and youth well-being have focused both on improvements in the circumstances of children's lives within specific racial-ethnic groups and on levels of disparity among these groups. In brief, parents, members of public interest groups, policymakers, and public and private agency administrators and personnel would like to see improvements in the circumstances of all children within racial-ethnic groups as compared to past levels of child and youth well-being within their own groups. In addition, however, levels of disparity in well-being among racial-ethnic groups also are a concern, because Black and Hispanic populations historically have experienced discrimination in American society and disadvantages, on average, in life circumstances. Accordingly, growing disparities in child and youth well-being for Black and Hispanic populations are a matter of public concern and for which social indicators researchers should engage in monitoring and social reporting.

Consider first the question of levels and trends in racial-ethnic group- specific versions of our domain-specific indexes of child and youth well- being.[20] Figures 14.19, 14.20, and 14.21 show graphs of six of seven domain-specific indexes for children who are White, Black, and Hispanic, respectively. These graphs, as well as others discussed later, use 1985 as the base year for index construction, because the Hispanic classification has been commonly available in the data sources for the basic social indicators in Table 14.1 only since about 1980.

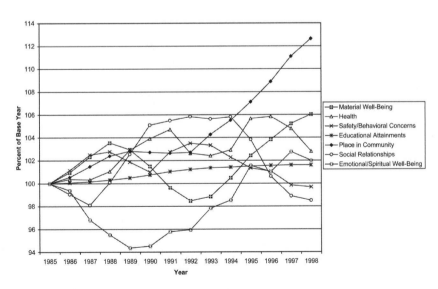

Figure 14.19. Domain-specific indexes of child well-being for Whites, 1985–98.

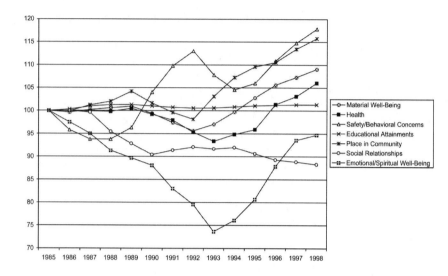

Figure 14.20. Domain-specific indexes of child well-being for Blacks, 1985–98.

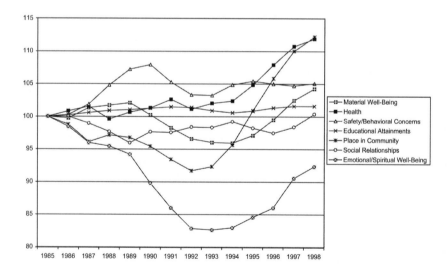

Figure 14.21. Domain-specific indexes of child well-being for Hispanics, 1985–98.

428

It might be expected that the domain-specific indexes for White children/youths would show levels and trends that are similar to those of the overall domain-specific indexes reported earlier, because White children are a majority of the population of children in the United States over the period analyzed. The graphs in Figure 14.19 show that this indeed is the case; that is, compared to levels in 1985 for White children/youth, the following are observed:

- The place-in-community and health indexes showed relatively consistent increases across the period, although increases in the health domain index are tempered by the upward trend in the prevalence of overweight children and youth.
- The material well-being index showed a decline in the late 1980s and early 1990s followed by a return in the late 1990s to levels above those of 1985.
- The productive activity (educational attainments) domain index is very stable and showed slight increases over time.
- The safety/behavioral concerns index showed a decline in the late 1980s, an increase in the early 1990s, and another decline to 1985 levels in the late 1990s.
- The social relationships domain index showed increases in the early 1990s followed by a decline to just below 1985 levels in the late 1990s.
- The emotional/spiritual well-being domain index fell in the late 1980s and early 1990s and then increased to slightly above 1985 levels by the late 1990s.

The levels and trends in the domain-specific indices for Black children/youth shown in Figure 14.20 are quite different.[21] Although downturns below 1985 base year levels can be seen in several of the indexes in the early to mid-1990s, they show that, for Black children:

- Five of the seven domain indexes were above 1985 levels by the late 1990s; in particular,
- The safety/behavioral concerns, place-in-community, material well-being, and health indexes had improved to between 7% and 20% above 1985 levels by 1998;
- The productive activity (educational attainments) index was slightly above 1985 levels in the late 1990s;
- The social relationships domain index fell about 10% below 1985 base year levels in the late-1980s and stayed at about that level through the late 1990s; and
- The emotional/spiritual well-being index fell to about 75% of its 1985 level by 1993 and then recovered to about the 95% level by 1998.

The levels and trends in the domain-specific indexes for Hispanic children/youth displayed in Figure 14.21 take on yet another pattern from 1985 to 1998. Again, although several of the domain-specific indexes showed substantial downturns in the late 1980s to mid-1990s, the following points are evident:

- Indexes for four of the domains-place in community, health, safety/behavioral concerns, and material well-being-showed 4% to 10% improvements over 1985 base year values for Hispanic children/youth by 1998;
- The place-in community-index, in particular, showed rapid increases since 1992 after falling for several years;
- The productive activity (educational attainments) index showed slow changes over time and was just 2 percentage point above 1985 levels by the late 1990s; and
- The emotional/spiritual well-being domain index fell in the late 1980s and early 1990s to about 83% of its 1985 value by 1992–94 and then began to rise to about 92% by 1998.

Averaging across these trends in the domain-specific indices, the levels and trends in the overall racial-ethnic group-specific summary indexes of child and youth well-being for the 1985-to-1998 period are reported in Figure 14.22. Across this entire period one can seen, first of all, that the summary well-being indexes of the Black and Hispanic groups show the impacts of the declines in the mid-1980s to early 1990s in the domain-specific indexes noted earlier. Since the mid-1990s,

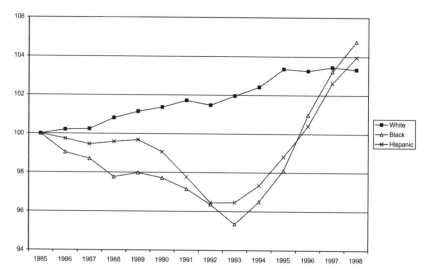

Figure 14.22. Racial-ethnic group-specific summary indexes of child well-being, 1985–98.

the overall well-being indexes for Black and Hispanic children/youth have increased quite rapidly to about 4% to 5% above 1985 levels. By comparison, the overtime trend in the summary well-being index for White children/youth shows a more steady increase to about 3% above 1985 levels, although the index is flat for the years 1995 through 1998.

In brief, children from all three of the racial-ethnic groups showed overall increases in well-being from 1985 to the late-1990s. What about racial-ethnic group disparities in child and youth well-being? Have these increased or decreased over these years? Figures 14.23 and 14.24 contain graphs that provide a means for addressing this question. These figures show graphs of trends in domain-specific disparity indexes for the same six domains of well-being as in Figures 14.20 through 14.22. For each comparison of a racial-ethnic group with Whites, these are computed by taking the disparity or gap in the levels of each social indicator series that was recorded in 1985 as defining a base of 100%. Absolute values of the disparities in each subsequent year then are calculated and computed as percentages of the disparity levels in the base year. The indicator-specific disparity indexes for each year then are averaged across the components in each domain to arrive at the domain-specific indexes reported in Figures 14.23 and 14.24.[22] Note that by calculating the disparity indexes in this way, the interpretation of levels reported in these figures differs from the interpretation of graphs of indexes discussed earlier; that is, in Figures 14.23 and 14.24 a value of the domain-specific indexes above (below) 100 in years subsequent to 1985 means that the absolute value of the disparity or gap between the groups being

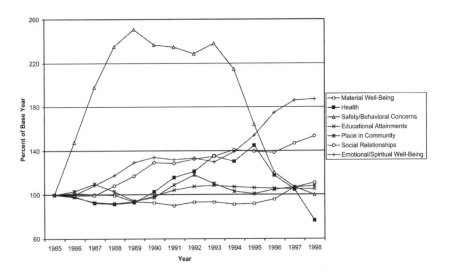

Figure 14.23.   Domain-specific disparity indexes of child well-being for Blacks as compared to Whites, 1985–98.

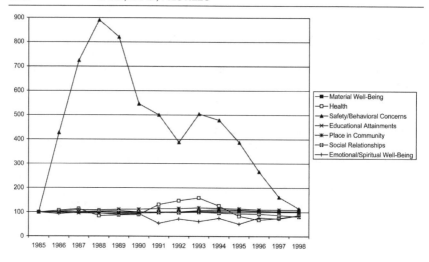

Figure 14.24. Domain-specific disparity indexes of child well-being for Hispanics as compared to Whites, 1985–98.

compared has grown (declined) relative to the size of the gap in 1985. In short, these disparity indexes measure just that-absolute levels of disparity or gap in conditions of child and youth well-being between racial-ethnic groups. One should not inferred from the disparity indexes, for example, that White children consistently have circumstances of life that are better than Black or Hispanic children. In fact, there are indicators for which this is not true. For example, in the health domain in recent years, the prevalence rate for low-birthweight births and the infant mortality rate for Hispanic children are lower in some years than those for White children.

Given the foregoing statement on the calculation of the disparity indexes, what do the levels and trends shown in Figures 14.23 and 14.24 tell us? Examining Figure 14.23 first, it can be seen that the safety/behavioral concerns domain index shows a large increase in Black-White disparity in the late 1980s to early 1990s. By the late 1990s, however, this disparity had declined to below 1985 base year values. The health domain index shows a similar, but muted, pattern of increase to a high point in the mid-1990s followed by a decline to below 1985 levels. By contrast, disparity in the social relationships domain (affected by disparities in the single-parenthood rate) increased fairly steadily across the years to about 50% above 1985 levels by 1998. Finally, the emotional/spiritual domain disparity shows an increase to a peak in 1990 followed by a 3-year decline and then a rise to over 400% of the 1985 level by 1998. It should be noted that the Black-White disparity index in the emotional/spiritual well-being domain is a disparity in favor of higher well-being for Black children/youth—due to lower suicide rates and higher rates of religious attendance and religious importance. This disparity remained high and/or grew over the 1985-to-1998 period for these indicators. The disparity in weekly religious attendance grew especially large—in 1985, 35% of White 12th-graders reported attending religious services weekly, compared to 36% of Black 12th-graders—by 1998, the corresponding percentages are 31 and 42. Disparity indexes for the other three domains (material well-being, educational attainments, and place in community) showed some increases by the late 1990s but generally on the order of 10% or less.

On can see in Figure 14.24 that the story for the domain-specific disparity indexes for Hispanic children/youth as compared to their White counterparts is that most disparity indexes remained relatively close to their 1985 levels across the years. The exception is that the safety/behavioral concerns domain-specific index showed a large divergence (to levels about nine times the 1985 base year values by 1988) followed by a decline to near 1985 levels by 1998.

Averaging across these trends in the domain-specific racial-ethnic disparity indexes, Figure 14.25 reports the levels and trends in the overall racial-ethnic group-specific disparity indexes of child and youth well-being for the 1985-to-1998 period. Note first that the overall well-being disparity index for Black children compared to White children increased to more than 20% above the level in the base year 1985 by 1988. It then increased to about 35% above the base year level by 1993, followed by a decline to about 20 percent% above base level by 1998. Much of the 20 percentage point difference in the overall Black-White disparity in 1998 (compared to 1985 levels) is due to disparities in social relationships (wherein White children/youth have an

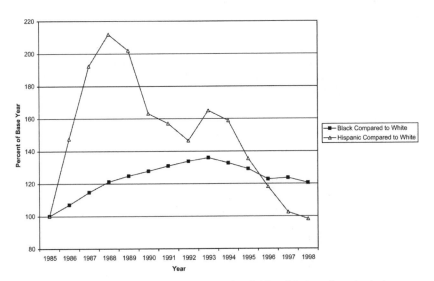

Figure 14.25.   Racial-ethnic group-specific child well-being disparity indexes, 1985–98.

advantage due to lower rates of living in single-parent families) and in emotional/spiritual well-being (wherein Black children/youths have an advantage due to lower rates of suicide and higher rates of religious attendance and importance). By comparison, the overall well-being disparity index for Hispanic children compared to White children showed more variability over the years. This index of disparity grew to levels greater than 160% of 1985 base year values in the years 1988 to 1991. In the most recent years, however, the disparity index has declined—reaching levels at or below 1985 values in the 2 most recent years. The overall conclusion from Figure 14.25 is that well-being disparities for Black and Hispanic children/youth relative to White children/youth increased from 1985 levels, dramatically so for Hispanics, during the late 1980s through the early 1990s. The period 1994 to 1998 saw declines of these disparities—to levels near those in 1985 for Hispanic children/youth and to about 20% above 1985 levels for Black children/youth.

DISCUSSION AND CONCLUSIONS

In the foregoing sections, we have described levels and trends in some 28 separate time series of basic indicators of child and youth well-being. We also have reported on a number of aspects of our efforts to construct an Index of Child and Youth Well-Being for assessing trends in the circumstances of the lives of children and youth in the United States over the last quarter of the 20th century. What overall conclusions can be drawn from these explorations in social measurement? We think the following points are among the most important conclusions from our study.

- Conclusions about trends in child and youth well-being in the United States in the last quarter of the 20th century depend on both the base year and the formula by which the summary indices are calculated. Findings about child and youth well-being also are dependent on the specific indicators and domains used in the composition of the summary indexes.
- Using 1975 as the base year and our overall summary index as the metric for measuring changes over time, we conclude that conditions of life for children and youth in the United States deteriorated fairly steadily for a number of years in the 1980s and reached low points in the 1992-to-1994 period. They then began an upturn that continued through 1998 toward, but still below, 1975 levels. In other words, whereas some domains and conditions of life for children/youth improved by 1998 as compared to 1975, others deteriorated. Averaging across all of the domains of life and conditions included in our summary indexes, the basic finding is that, overall, the quality of life of children/youth in the United States was not better in 1998 than in 1975.

• Using 1985 as a base year, overall quality of life for children and youth showed a similar pattern of decline through the early 1990s followed by an improvement through 1998 to levels slightly above those of the 1985 base year. In other words, compared to 1985 base levels, overall conditions of well-being for children/youth in the United States had slightly improved by the late 1990s.

• Numerically, with 1975 as the base year, we estimate that overall child and youth well-being was on the order of 2% to 3% lower in 1998 than in 1975 when our index is computed by averaging across the seven domains of well-being that we have studied. By comparison, when the index is computed by averaging across the individual component time series, we estimate a slight improvement—on the order of 1% or 2%—in child and youth well-being for the same years. Because the latter form of the index gives more weight to those domains of well-being for which we have more indicator time series, quality-of-life researchers generally prefer to interpret the former version. Using 1985 as the base year, we estimate corresponding increases by 1998 of 2% to 3% in these two forms of the index.

• Among the seven domains of well-being studied, the largest and most steady increases have been in the place-in-community domain. The improvements in this domain are due primarily to increased rates of participation in schooling and work institutions from early childhood through young adulthood.

• The material well-being and safety/behavioral concerns domains showed some improvements (compared to base year levels) by the late 1990s. However, both domains have had waves of increases and decreases. In the case of material well-being, these waves were associated with economic recessions and expansions and periods of restructuring of economic institutions. In the case of the safety/behavioral concerns domain, the waves were associated with trends in youth behaviors in the areas of teenage childbearing, crime and violence, and the use of psychoactive substances (cigarettes, alcohol, illicit drugs).

• There has been a slight increase in the productive activity (educational attainments on standardized tests) domain across the years studied.

• The health domain index shows improvements in its components pertaining to infant, child, and adolescent/teenage mortality. It has been pulled down since the mid-1980s by increases in the prevalence of low-birthweight births and especially by increases in the prevalence of overweight children and youth.

• Indexes for the social relationships and emotional/spiritual well-being domains show long-term declines across the three decades studied. These indexes reached historically low levels in the mid-1980s through mid-1990s but have shown some increases in recent years.

• The period from about 1993 to 1998, in particular, has been noteworthy for sustained and substantial increases in six of seven do-main-specific indexes of child and youth well-being-all but health (which, again, has been pulled down by the overweight-prevalence indicator). This sustained upturn has been coincident with the long-term economic expansion of the mid- to late-1990s. We also noted downturns in several of the domain-specific indexes associated with past economic recessions. This suggests that this recent sus-tained period of increases in several domains of child and youth well-being could well be interrupted and reversed by a new economic re-cession. An economic recession negatively affects not only the mate-rial well-being of children but also the health, place-in-community, and safety/behavioral concerns domains. However, there also are other aggregate social forces that affect trends in child and youth well-being. For instance, a substantial deterioration in the public health system and in access to health care for children could nega-tively impact the health domain index, and a new episode of a broad-scale youth involvement in drug use, sex/pregnancy, and violence (as in the late 1980s through the mid-1990s) no doubt would substan-tially depress our safety/behavioral concerns index.

• Compared to best practice values of the various indicators stud-ied (based either on the best historically observed values for the United States or on the best contemporary values of other advanced industrial societies), there is much room for improvement. We found that-if the United States were performing at the best levels on the component indicators of the Index of Child and Youth Well-Being that it had ever achieved historically—then, in the late 1990s, the index would have been about 23 percentage points higher than in the 1975 base year. Correspondingly, if the United States had achieved levels on the component indicators comparable to that of the best performance internationally, then it could have achieved a level of the index about 38% higher in the late 1990s than that of the 1975 base year. These are tough yardsticks by which to assess recent conditions in child and youth well-being in the United States, but they give us an idea of how much these conditions can be improved.

• On the basis of our age-specific index calculations, we found in-creases of about 25% by the late 1990s (compared to 1975 values) in child well-being for the infancy/preschool years. By comparison, our childhood/preteen index of well-being showed a decline of about 10% (compared to 1975 levels) through much of the 1980s and 1990s. Our adolescence/teenager index of well-being showed a similar de-cline of 10% to 20% through much of the same period.

• Our overall summary indexes of child and youth well-being showed improvements of 4% to 5% by the late-1990s for the Black and Hispanic racial-ethnic groups compared to within-group 1985 base year levels. By comparison, White children/youth showed in-creases of about 3% in overall well-being compared to their 1985 base year levels. Substantial declines in overall well-being in the mid-1980s to mid-1990s were experienced by the Black and Hispanic children/youth.

• Our analyses of levels of disparity in child and youth well-being (compared to the levels that existed in the 1985 base year) suggest that disparities of Hispanic children compared to White children increased during the 1980s and early 1990s more than those of Black children compared to White children. However, by 1998 the overall intergroup disparities had declined again to near 1985 base year levels for Hispanic children compared to White children. For Black children compared to White children, overall disparities were about 20% greater than 1985 levels. As noted earlier, much of the 20 percentage point difference in the overall Black–White disparity in 1998 (compared to 1985 levels) is due to disparities in social relationships (wherein White children/youth have a well-being advantage due to lower rates of living in single-parent families) and in emotional/spiritual well-being (wherein Black children/youth have a well-being advantage due to lower rates of suicide and higher rates of religious attendance and importance).

It must be emphasized that specific numerical values associated with these conclusions are dependent both on the methods of index construction and on the specific domains and component time series indicators of child and youth well-being that we have studied. For instance, suppose that we dropped the health, social relationships, and emotional/spiritual well-being domain indexes from our summary Index of Child and Youth Well-Being, that is, that we computed a summary index based only on the material well-being, safety/behavioral concerns, place-in-community, and educational attainments domain indexes. Then we would conclude that there was a 10% to 20% improvement in overall child and youth well-being by 1998 as compared to 1975. Even if we retained the health domain in the summary index, we still would conclude that overall child and youth well-being improved by 5% to 6% from 1975 to 1998. As noted earlier in the section on conceptualization of child and youth well-being, however, numerous studies of subjective well-being over the past three decades have found that all seven of the domains of well-being studied here are important in determining the overall quality of life. Therefore, we believe that a comprehensive summary index should be based on all seven of the domains with which we have worked.

Note also that the domain indexes themselves are sensitive to their components. For example, as we have noted, most of the component indicators in the health domain index generally improved by the late 1990s as compared to 1975, but our summary index for the health domain decreased over this time period because of the inclusion of indicator time series on the percentage of children and youths who are overweight. Given the serious health complications associated with being overweight noted earlier, it does not seem reasonable to leave this health indicator time series out of our health domain summary index.

Because of these and related limitations of the indicators with which to measure the seven domains of well-being on which our summary index is based, the methods of index construction that we have used have been deliberately chosen to be as straightforward and transparent as possible. We also have used component time series that generally are considered among the best available indicators for assessing child and youth well-being. Accordingly, it likely is the case that the general qualitative conclusions (e.g., that there was a deterioration in the 1980s followed by an upturn in the 1990s) from our index work, but not the specific numerical values, are relatively robust to the use of different methods of index calculation and component indicators.

Our index work also provides a basis from which additional efforts to assess trends in child and youth well-being can be designed. In particular, the construction and analysis of our Index of Child and Youth Well-Being helps to identify major inadequacies and lacunae in the current indicator system for child and youth well-being in the United States. Most obvious is the relative lack of reliable time series data with which to measure trends in the emotional well-being of children, especially adolescents and teenagers. Similarly, our index would benefit greatly from additional indicators for the social relationships domain of well-being, that is, of the relationships of children to family and friends. Also, many of the conditions of child and youth well-being tapped by the component indicators of the index (e.g., the percentage of children enrolled in preschool at ages 3–4) give no indication of levels or variations in the quality of the condition measured (e.g., levels and variations in the quality of preschool programs to which young children are subjected). Social indicator analysts and social scientists and statisticians need to begin planning now for building an improved indicator system for child and youth well-being that will, in turn, facilitate improvements in our Index of Child and Youth Well-Being in years to come.

ACKNOWLEDGMENTS

This chapter was originally published in *Social Indicators Research*, December 2001. Reprinted by permission. The research reported in this chapter was supported by a grant from the Foundation for Child Development. We thank Don Hernandez, Vonnie McLoyd, Kristen Moore, Ruby Takanishi, and Fasaha Traylor for comments and suggestions on this project as it developed. We also extend thanks for comments and suggestions received from participants in the "Conference on Key Indicators of Child and Youth Well-Being: Completing the Picture," sponsored by Child Trends at the National Institutes of Health, Bethesda, Maryland, June 2001.

NOTES

1. Detailed descriptions of the indicators and graphs of their trends over time are given in the RESULTS section. An appendix table cites the sources for all of the data series on which the indicators are based.

2. With the exception of the time series on median family income and average test scores from the NAEP, all of the basic indicators identified in Table 14.1 are measured either as prevalence rates or as incidence rates. Hence, we refer to the components of Equation 14.1 as *rates*.

3. We also have experimented with the application of other formulas for index construction (e.g., a geometric rather than an arithmetic mean). In general, these other formulas show patterns of over-time changes in overall child and youth well-being that are similar to those reported in the chapter from the application of Equation 14.1; that is, in general, alternative formulas show patterns of stable or declining child and youth well-being through the late 1980s or early 1990s, followed by increases. These patterns could, of course, be changed by the application of an unequally weighted index formula to the seven domains of well-being identified in the text. The only general guidance available on weighting from empirical studies of the quality of life (see, e.g., Haggerty et al., 2001) suggests that the emotional well-being and social relationships domains are of primary importance. Given the trends in the basic indicators described later in the chapter, the application of an index formula that gives additional weight to these domains would result in greater declines in the index values through the early 1990s.

4. Before Equation 14.1 is applied to the component time series, each series is reflected so that an increase indicates an improvement and a decrease indicates a deterioration in the condition measured by the indicator. For instance, consider the case of the percentage of children living in families with secure parental employment (see Table 14.1). For this time series, an increase in the indicator series is indicative of an improvement in the material well-being circumstances of children's lives, which the indicators in the material well-being domain are intended to measure. By contrast, a decrease in the infant mortality rate (see Table 14.1) is indicative of an improvement in the health circumstances of children's lives that the indicators in the health domain are intended to measure. Thus, for those time series for which a decline is indicative of an improvement in the series, we first subtract the value observed for the rate in a current year from the value in the base year. Then we compute the ratio of this difference to the value of the rate in the base year and add this ratio to 100 to obtain the percentage improvement in the time series relative to the base year.

5. Observed values for most of the basic social indicator time series identified in Table 14.1 are available from the base years through 1998. In a few cases, however, this is not the case. To compute the values of our summary indexes through 1998, we therefore assumed no changes from the observed values of the most recent year available for those time series. Specifically, we used the 1997 observed values for the single-parent poverty rate, the child mortality rates for ages 5 through 9 and 10 through 14, the percentage of children with very good or excellent health, and the percentage of children with activity limitations. As the observed values of these indicator time series become available, they will be used in the calculation of our summary indexes rather than these estimated values. Finally, because the time series for the rate of children with health insurance coverage commenced only in 1987, we did not include this indicator in the calculation of the summary indexes until 1987.

6. We use only the overall child poverty rate in our summary well-being indexes; however, the family structure specific time series shown in Figure 14.2 are displayed to provide further information and to verify that trends exhibited in the population-specific time series are similar to those in the overall poverty rate series.

7. Bianchi (1996) found that, by the mid-1990s, more unmarried women with dependent children were working than in previous decades. Also, because 1980 nonmarital childbearing rates have increased more rapidly for nonteen women compared to that of teens, and, in the 1990s, birth rates for older women have continued to rise whereas teen rates have been falling (Ventura, Martin, Curtin, Mathews, & Park, 2000). Research using data from the Panel Study in Income Dynamics indicates that older, single, childbearing women are more likely to work before and after giving birth (Foster, Jones, & Hoffman, 1998).

8. For purposes of our efforts to construct domain-specific summary indexes, however, we include the prevalence rate of children with some form of health insurance coverage in the material well-being index, as indicated in Table 14.1. In brief, we treat this basic indicator primarily as an index of the command a child's family has over material resources.

9. There is a large research literature documenting that many nonresident fathers and their relatives have little or no contact with their children (e.g., Furstenberg & Nord, 1985; King, 1994; Mott, 1990; Seltzer & Brandreth, 1994).

10. Again, only the overall single-parent prevalence rate time series is used in our summary indexes of child and youth well-being; however, the female- and male-specific rates are included in Figure 14.5 to provide evidence of consistency of the trends over time in these rates.

11. Recall that many of the basic indicator time series identified in Table 14.1 are available in age-disaggregated form, as, for example, the mortality series exhibited in Figure 14.6. In the construction of our domain-specific and overall summary indexes of child and youth well-being, however, we aggregate the mortality series across all ages 1 to 19 in order not to give extra weight to age specificity for these series as compared to other series that are available only for broad age groups. Similar comments apply to other basic indicators for which age-specific data are available.

12. The relationship of the availability of such medical technology to socioeconomic status was documented by Gortmaker and Wise (1997).

13. The overweight time series in Figure 14.8 follow the definition give in the *Trends* volume (U.S. Department of Health and Human Services, Office of the Assistant Secretary for Planning and Evaluation, 2000); that is, *overweight* is defined as a body mass index at or above the sex- and race-specific 95th percentile. Body mass index cutoff points were calculated at 6-month intervals for children ages 6 through 11 from the 1963–65 National Health Examination Survey (NHES) and for adolescents ages 12 through 17 from the 1966–70 NHES. Age is at time of examination at mobile examination centers in the NHES. The overweight time series in Figure 14.8 were linearly interpolated for intervening years from the waves of the NHANES I (1971–74), II (1976–80), and III (1988-94) and projected from the most recent wave through 1998.

14. Even taking into account the fact that the scale of the graph does not show the fine detail of changes in the birth rate for the 10-to-14 age group, the changes are smaller than those for the ages 15-to-17 group.

15. Because Presidential elections occur on a 4-year cycle, the time series in Figure 14.12 is interpolated for the intervening years in order to be consistent with the annual time series format of the other indicators in our index. For the most recent years beyond the 1996 Presidential election (1997 and 1998), we fixed the voting percentage at the level of the last observation: the 1996 election.

16. The suicide deaths counted in the incident rates of Figure 14.13 have been subtracted out of the general mortality rates for the corresponding age groups reported in Figure 14.6 so that these deaths are not counted twice.

17. To compute numerical values of the international best practice summary index, we use the best practice U.S. values for those indicators in Table 14.2 for which comparable data cannot be found for other countries.

18. We have not been able to disaggregate one indicator: the rate of children and adolescents living in families with incomes below the poverty line, by age below the ages 6-to-17 range. Therefore, to capture trends in the poverty rate over time (which likely are quite similar for the childhood and adolescence/teenage categories), we include this indicator in both the childhood and adolescence/teenage groups of indicators in Table 14.3.

19. Data limitations prevent us from including two other racial-ethnic groups, namely, Native Americans and Asian Americans, in the analyses reported in this section. Almost none of the basic social indicator time series used in constructing our indexes are available in annual time series form for these two groups.

20. The racial-ethnic group-specific domain indexes of child and youth well-being are based on 26 of the 28 basic indicator series identified in Table 14.1. Two of the basic indicators are not included because of a lack of racial-ethnic specificity. One of these is a subjective health prevalence rate: the prevalence rate of children with very good or excellent health. For violent crime, we include only the offender time series, for which we have rates for Blacks and Whites; for Hispanics, we use the overall rate.

21. Graphs of the unadjusted domain-specific indexes of well-being for both Black and Hispanic children/youth exhibit more over-time variability than found in the graphs for White children/youth. This is consistent with the presence of more statistical variability in the databases (often sample surveys) from these smaller populations. To reduce the year-to-year variability in these indexes so that trends can be more easily deciphered, we applied 3-year moving averages to the domain-specific and summary indexes for Black and Hispanic children/youth. The resulting smoothed time series are plotted in Figures 14.20 through 14.22.

22. The data for the disparity indexes shown Figures 14.23 through 14.25 were smoothed by 3-point moving averages (see note 18) to reduce erratic fluctuations and enable the analysis of trends over time. In addition, because of its exceptional year-to-year variability, we smoothed one individual component time series for these computations: the residential mobility Black-White disparity series. Finally, we smoothed the disparity index for Black-White religious attendance by taking a 4-year moving average for the 1985 and 1998 years and a 5-year average for all of the intervening years. The reason for this is that rate ratio indexes are very sensitive to small values for base year rates, which are arbitrary when the choice of base years is arbitrary. In the case of religious attendance, the Black-White numerical difference in 1985 is 1%. This difference seemed artificially small compared to differences in other years. Accordingly, we applied the moving average procedure indicated.

REFERENCES

American Psychiatric Association. (1994). *Diagnostic and statistical manual of mental disorders* (4th ed.). Washington, DC: Author.

Andrews, F. M., & Withey, S. B. (1976). *Social Indicators of Well-Being: Americans' Perceptions of Life Quality.* New York: Plenum.

Ben-Arieh, A. (2000). Beyond welfare: Measuring and monitoring the state of children-New trends and domains. *Social Indicators Research, 52,* 235–257.

Bianchi, S. M. (1996). Women, work and family in America. *Population Bulletin, 51,* 1–48.

Bianchi, S. M. (1999). Feminization and juvenilization of poverty: Trends, relative risks, causes, and consequences. *Annual Review of Sociology, 25,* 307–333.

Brown, B. V. (1997). Indicators of children's well-being: A review of current indicators based on data from the Federal Statistical System. In R. M. Hauser, B. V. Brown, & W. R. Prosser (Eds.), *Indicators of children's well-being* (pp. 3–35). New York: Russell Sage Foundation.

Buehler, J. W., Kleinman, J. C., Hogue, C. J. E., Strauss, L. T., & Smith, J. C. (1987). Birth weight-specific infant mortality, United States, 1960 and 1980. *Public Health Reports, 102,* 151–161.

Campbell, A., Converse, P. E., & Rodgers, W. L. (1976). *The quality of American life.* New York: Russell Sage Foundation.

Chavkin, W., Romero, D., & Wise, P. H. (2000). State welfare reform policies and declines in health insurance. *American Journal of Public Health, 90,* 900–908.

Chiang, A. C. (1974). *Fundamental methods of mathematical economics.* New York: McGraw-Hill.

Coleman, J. S. (1988). Social capital in the creation of human capital. *American Journal of Sociology, 94,* S95–S120.

Cummins, R. A. (1996). The domains of life satisfaction: An attempt to order chaos. *Social Indicators Research, 38,* 303–328.

Cummins, R. A. (1997). Assessing quality of life. In R. I. Brown (Ed.), *Quality of life for handicapped people* (pp. 116–150). London: Chapman & Hall.

Duncan, G. J., & Brooks-Gunn, J. (Eds.). (1997). *Consequences of growing up poor.* New York: Russell Sage Foundation.

Federal Interagency Forum on Child and Family Statistics. (1999). *America's children: Key national indicators of well-being.* Washington, DC: U.S. Government Printing Office.

Federal Interagency Forum on Child and Family Statistics. (2000). *America's children: Key national indicators of well-being.* Washington, DC: U.S. Government Printing Office.

Foster, E. M., Jones, D., & Hoffman, S. D. (1998). The economic impact on nonmarital childbearing: How are older, single mothers faring? *Journal of Marriage and the Family, 60,* 163–174.

Furstenberg, F. F., & Nord, C. W. (1991). *Divided families: What happens to children when parents part.* Cambridge, MA: Harvard University Press.

Gilman, R., Huebner, E. S., & Laughlin, J. E. (2000). A first study of the multidimensional students' life satisfaction scale with adolescents. *Social Indicators Research, 52,* 135–160.

Gortmaker, S. L., & Wise, H. P. (1997). The first injustice: Socioeconomic disparities, health services technology, and infant mortality. *Annual Review of Sociology, 23,* 147–170.

Hack, M., Wright, L., Shankaran, S., Tyson, J. E., Horbar, J. D., Bauer, C. R., & Younes, N. (1995). Very low-birthweight outcomes of the National Institute of

Child Health and Human Development Neonatal Network, November 1989 to October 1990. *American Journal of Obstetrics and Gynecology, 172,* 457–464.

Hagerty, M. R., Cummins, R. A., Ferriss, A. L., Land, K., Michalos, A. C., Peterson, M., et al. (2001). Quality of life indexes for national policy: Review and agenda for research. *Social Indicators Research, 55,* 1–96.

Hernandez, D. J. (1997). Poverty trends. In G. J. Duncan & J. Brooks-Gunn (Eds.), *Consequences of growing up poor* (pp. 18–24). New York: Russell Sage Foundation.

Jazairi, N. T. (1983). Index numbers. In S. Kotz, N. L. Johnson, & C. B. Read (Eds.), *Encyclopedia of statistical sciences* (Vol. 4, pp. 54–62). New York: Wiley-Interscience.

King, V. (1994). Nonresident father involvement and child well-being: Can dads make a difference? *Journal of Family Issues, 15,* 78–96.

Klerman, L. V. (1993). Adolescent pregnancy and parenting: Controversies of the past and lessons for the future. *Journal of Adolescent Health, 14,* 553–561.

Land, K. C. (2000). Social indicators. In E. F. Borgatta & R. V. Montgomery (Eds.), *Encyclopedia of sociology* (rev. ed., pp. 2682–2690). New York: Macmillan.

London, R. A. (2000). The dynamics of single mothers' living arrangements. *Population Research and Policy Review, 19,* 73–96.

Martin, J. A., & Taffel, S. M. (1995). *Current and future impact of rising multiple birth ratios on low birthweight* (Statistical Bulletin 76). New York: Metropolitan Life Insurance Company.

McLanahan, S., & Sandefur, G. (1994). *Growing up with a single parent: What hurts, what helps.* Cambridge, MA: Harvard University Press.

McNeal, R. B., Jr. (1999). Parental involvement as social capital: Differential effectiveness on science achievement, truancy, and dropping out. *Social Forces, 78,* 117–144.

Moore, K. A. (1999). *Indicators of child and family well-being: The good, the bad, and the ugly* (1999 Seminar Series). Bethesda, MD: National Institutes of Health, Office of Behavioral and Social Sciences.

Mott, F. L. (1990). When is father really gone? Paternal-child contact in father-absent homes. *Demography, 27,* 499–517.

Roof, W. C., & McKinney, W. (1987). *American mainline religion: Its changing shape and future.* New Brunswick, NJ: Rutgers University Press.

Ruist, E. (1978). Index numbers: Theoretical aspects. In W. H. Kruskal & J. M. Tanur (Eds.), *International encyclopedia of statistics* (Vol. 1, pp. 451–456). New York: Free Press.

Seltzer, J. A. (1994). What fathers say about involvement with children after separation. *Journal of Family Issues, 15,* 49–77.

Troiano, R. P., Flegal, K. M., Kuczmarski, R. J., Campbell, S. M., & Johnson, C. L. (1995). Overweight prevalence and trends for children and adolescents: The National Health and Nutrition Examination Surveys, 1963–1991. *Archives of Pediatrics and Adolescent Medicine, 149,* 1085–1091.

U.S. Department of Health, Education, and Welfare. (1969). *Toward a social report.* Washington, DC: U.S. Government Printing Office.

U.S. Department of Health and Human Services, Office of the Assistant Secretary for Planning and Evaluation. (2000). *Trends in the well-being of America's children & youth 1999.* Washington, DC: U.S. Government Printing Office.

Ventura, S. J., Martin, J. A., Curtin, S. C., Mathews, T. J., & Park, M. M. (2000, March 28). Births: Final data for 1998. *National Vital Statistics Reports, 48.*

Methodological Issues Surrounding the Construction of an Index of Child Well-Being

Neil G. Bennett
Baruch College

Hsien-Hen Lu
Columbia University

In the effort to monitor the improvement or deterioration of child well-being over time, there is a tension between researchers and policymakers with respect to the nature of the measure that is desired. If one were to generalize, advocates and policymakers tend to prefer a measure that is simple and readily accessible by the public, in the hope that such a measure can help them achieve their goals. In contrast, researchers often balk at simple measures, believing that the quest for simplicity comes at too great a cost and simple unfortunately translates into simplistic. The creation of a single index, they might argue, has the potential of misleading those whom they hope to inform. It is a difficult challenge to satisfy both constituencies without having either one feel that they have sacrificed too much.

In recent years, there have been many efforts to create indexes of well-being. They tend to be methodologically simple, which has its benefits and drawbacks. The indicators incorporated into each index typically are weighted equally and the indexes are not adjusted for demographic compositional differences in the units, usually states, that are being compared. In this chapter, we examine the extent to which such a simplification is problematic and potentially misleading. Other possibly confounding issues with these measures include the value of objective versus subjective assessments of health and which array of variables one should incorporate into an overall index of child well-being. We will conduct an empirical examination of these last two matters in future work.

A few of the more notable efforts at index construction are those by Kenneth Land, Vicki Lamb, and Sarah Mustillo, discussed in chapter 14 of this volume; by Marc Miringoff, Marque-Luisa Miringoff, and Sandra Opdycke (see, e.g., Miringoff, Miringoff, & Opdycke, 1996); and by the Annie E. Casey Foundation (see, e.g., Annie E. Casey Foundation, 2003).

The breadth of the Land et al. work is impressive; they review many of the important issues concerning indicator selection and index construction and examine in depth the time trends in a wide-ranging set of 28 indicators and a small set of domains within which all of the indicators are grouped. As a consequence, we get some sense of the ebb and flow of child well-being in the United States.

Miringoff et al. (1996) constructed an index of social health in which they created a single index that synthesizes some 16 variables they believe to relate to this larger notion of social health. These variables include (a) infant mortality, (b) child abuse, (c) child poverty, (d) teenage suicide, (e) drug abuse, (f) dropping out of high school, (g) unemployment, (h) mean weekly earnings, (i) health insurance coverage, (j) poverty of the elderly, (k) out-of-pocket health costs among the elderly, (l) homicide, (m) alcohol-related traffic fatalities, (n) food stamp coverage, (o) access to affordable housing, and (p) the gap between the rich and poor.

A major purpose of the index of child well-being that is published by the Annie E. Casey Foundation in a volume called *KIDS COUNT* is to rank the states according to their overall performance on 10 dimensions of child well-being, namely: (a) infant mortality; (b) child (ages 1–14) mortality; (c) low-birthweight births; (d) child (under age 18) poverty; (e) children living without a parent employed full-time year-round; (f) children living in single-parent families; (g) low-income children without health insurance; (h) teens (ages 16–19) dropping out of high school; (i) teen deaths (ages 15–19) by accident, homicide, and suicide; and (j) teen (ages 15–17) birth rate.

One critically important issue in index construction of this sort is how one might develop a best set of indicators on which to base a single index. We suffer under no illusion that we are able to select an assortment of indicators superior to that chosen by others, and thus we make no attempt here to come up with a definitive array of indicators on which to base a single index.

There is, of course, considerable debate-as evidenced by the discussions offered in this compendium-over the domains of indicators that would be appropriate to include in the construction of a child well-being index and, further, the particular indicators adopted within each of those domains.

One might argue, for example, that self-perceived morbidity measures would be ideal for this purpose. However appealing they may be, though, reliance on them would present significant problems. Murray and Chen (1992) and others have brought to light, for example, the following dramatic comparisons:

- Self-reported acute morbidity is approximately six times as high in the United States as in India.
- Kenyan and Mexican adults in the range of age groups between 15 and 55 reported only 0.4 to 2.0 days of bedridden morbidity annually. In stark contrast, the corresponding group of Americans reported 2.6 to 9.3 bed days.

In this vein, it is useful to compare the prevalence of conditions reported in interviews with that indicated by clinical examination. Such a comparison is bound to give us pause. In Ghana, as discussed by Belcher, Neumann, Wurapa, and Lourie (1976), we see extraordinary differences between the two. Illustrative of the problem are the statistics on the following three conditions:

- Only 8.1 individuals per 1,000 indicated that they suffered from malnutrition; examination revealed the true rate to be 321.0 per 1,000, or 40 times as high.
- Self-reports showed that 1.9 per 1,000 had intestinal parasites, in contrast to a clinically observed rate almost 300 times as high, 550.0 per 1,000.
- Last, and most striking, was the fact that only 0.3 per 1,000 reported missing an extremity, whereas clinical examination revealed a prevalence rate almost 20 times as high, 5.3 per 1,000. The most logical explanation for the underreporting of missing extremities is that these individuals had adapted over time to their situation and no longer felt handicapped in any meaningful way.

Few would contend that we would encounter as vast differentials—that is, between self-reports and clinical examination—in the United States as we do in India, Ghana, or elsewhere outside of the industrialized world. Indeed, Rogers, Hummer, and Nam (2000) provided evidence that self-reported health is an important predictor of the probability of survival. However, one can make the larger point that this phenomenon serves to show that, although there are obviously objective elements to morbidity, it is undeniably subjective, as well.

Any self-report of not only physical well-being, but also of psychological well-being, is based on both the notions of *relative* and *absolute* levels of sickness. If we choose to compare subgroups within the United States, then it is clearly possible that one such group will have a cultural perspective that gives rise to different reported levels of well-being than those reported by another group with an alternative cultural perspective. Does one group truly suffer more than another, or does that group simply have more exacting health standards?

Sorting this out—the objective, versus the subjective, meanings of well-being—is a challenge to us all, indeed to the extent that sorting out is necessary, for subjective notions of well-being may in some instances be precisely what we seek. We do not attempt here to resolve this issue of subjective versus objective measures of well-being. Instead, we raise the matter to highlight the fact that too little attention has been devoted to a topic of considerable importance.

It is also worth mentioning that the selection of some variables found in various existing indexes may be viewed as opportunistic. For example, as one of their 28 indicators, Land et al. include rate of weekly religious attendance among 12th-graders. The desire to incorporate in their index some measure of spiritual well-being is commendable but, as they note, it is certainly an imperfect measure. We may hope that at the age of 17 or 18 that religious attendance is largely volitional, but the fact remains that there may be other forms of spiritual well-being that are not manifested in religious attendance. That said, the indicator is included because it does offer relevant information contributing to overall child well-being and, obviously, simply because the data are available. One must forgive opportunism such as this because a significant obstacle to index creation in this area is the paucity of relevant and well-measured data that relate to well-being. As data collection expands and improves over time, we will see a concomitant improvement in the selection of variables that comprise indexes of well-being.

In this chapter, we adopt a state-specific perspective. Certainly, in this era of devolution and welfare reform, the states have become that much more relevant as units of analysis. Consequently, we concentrate our efforts on creating an index that allows us to rank the states (plus the District of Columbia).

Of the many methodological issues we could address, here we concentrate on but a few. All but ignored in much of the research to date focusing on developing indexes of well-being are the weights that one attributes to each of the indicators that comprise the overall index. All of the indices mentioned earlier—those by Land et al. (chap. 14, this volume), by Miringoff et al. (1996), and by the Annie E. Casey Foundation (2003)—assume that each variable comprising their respective indexes merits equal weight. That is, each variable—whether, for example, infant mortality, being raised by a single parent, or child poverty—should be deemed to have equal impact with respect to the notion of overall child well-being.

Along these same lines, some dimensions of well-being are overweighted, although theoretical considerations would not seem to warrant that. Implicit "double-counting" occurs in Land et al.'s formulation of their child well-being index, for example, where both the poverty rate of families with children and median income among families with children are included in the index's construction. Although these indicators by no means measure the same thing, they are certainly correlated. The question, then, is should two such indicators receive as much weight as two other indicators that are wholly uncorrelated with each other? Indeed, the 2000 Census reveals that, at the state level, the correlation between these two variables is as great as –.73. We may conclude, then, that these two variables do not represent two variables' worth of independent information, in contrast, let us say, to the amount of independent information contributed by the two variables infant mortality and the high school dropout rate. The characteristic of either uniform weighting or double-counting is inherent in many other indexes that have been developed over the years. Consequently, we first examine the impact of allowing weights to be freely determined, rather than having them be constrained to be uniform. Second, we explore the importance of controlling for compositional differences among the states in determining state rankings.

Among other areas of consideration that we do not address is the notion that statistically derived weights are not all that are of concern to us. We recognize that-regardless of how uncorrelated an indicator is with all others-it may still be of minor substantive relevance to the larger picture of child well-being. Ideally, then, we have to somehow layer weights indicative of substantive significance on top of those indicative of statistical significance.

ANALYTIC APPROACH

A typical application of uniform weights would be to standardize the values within each indicator and then simply add up the standardized scores across all of the indicators. States would then be ranked by this sum of scores. As an alternative, we relax the assumption of uniform weights by taking a latent class analysis approach (Heinen, 1996; Vermunt & Magidson, 2000).

This is an exercise on which we will elaborate more rigorously in the future. To illustrate the benefits of this approach, we set out here to create an index composed of just three variables, as shown in Table 15.1: (a) timely progress in school, (b) self-reported health status, and (c) poverty status

The schooling and health variables have two categories each: whether a child is progressing on time or faster, and whether he or she is in very good health or better,. However, poverty status has categories. We redefine poverty status using four levels: (a) under 50%, (b) 50% to 100%, (c) 100% to 200%, and (d) above 200% of the official poverty line. We also define self-reported health status, using a four-level scale that ranges from *fair/bad* to *excellent*.

The data are obtained from the March 1996, 1998, and 2000 Current Population Surveys (CPSs), from which we randomly select one child between the ages of 15 and 18 from each family. We use every other year of CPS data to avoid the problem of including the same children in adjacent years, which occurs due to the sampling scheme the Census Bureau uses. To avoid correlation due to including children from same family, as noted we also randomly selected only one qualified child from each family.

Method

To measure the well-being of teenage children, we use two strategies to define our indicators. First of all, we use three observed indicator vari-

Table 15.1

Distributions of indicators of child well-being and key control variables
comprising overall index of well-being

Variable	Percentage of teens (weighted) in each Category
Indicators of child wellbeing	
Poverty status	< 50% (4.6)
	50–100% (8.4)
	100–200% (18.7)
	> 200% (68.4)
Parent- reported health status	Excellent (47.6)
	Very good (30.7)
	Good (19.0)
	Fair / bad (2.7)
Timely progress in school	Delayed (8.6)
	Not delayed (91.4)
Key control variables	
Race/ethnicity	Non-Hispanic white (67.5)
	Non-Hispanic black (14.7)
	Hispanic (12.7)
	Others (5.2)
Immigration status	Kids w/native-born parents (85.5)
	Kids w/any parent foreign-born (14.5)

ables (y_m): levels of income-to-needs ratio (y_1), whether the highest grade the teenage child attended is delayed for more than 2 years compared with the mean of all children of the same age (y_2), and a subjective evaluation of health (y_3). In order to compare a strategy weighing these indicators equally and a strategy allowing the weight for each indicator varies, we also define a combined well-being measure by using a combined measure y', which is defined as $y' = \sum_{m=1}^{M=3} y_m$. For a detailed definition of these indicator variables and their distributions, see Table 15.1.

For analyses allowing unequal weights for different indicators, the following model is defined to estimate state ranking, discounting for the impact of control variables (Vermunt & Magidson, 2000):[1]

$$\pi(Y|Z) = \sum_x \pi(x|Z) \prod_{m=1}^{M=3} \pi(y_m|x). \qquad (15.1)$$

$\pi(.)$ is an underlying distribution of child well-being, $Y = \{y_1, y_2, y_3\}$ is as we defined above; x is a latent class-ordered factor (the well-being of teenage children) with only two categories, which can be interpreted as disadvantaged and not disadvantaged children; and $Z = \{z_1, z_2, \ldots, z_L\}$ refers to L exogenous variables (i.e., race-ethnicity, etc.), including various control variables and state dummies, which allow us to rank states. These variables are shown in Table 15.1. In this model, we assume that the Z variables do not have any direct effect on the Y variables but that the Z variables are determinants of the latent variable, x, that is, an unobserved composite well-being measure for teenage children. The analyses, assuming equal weights, can be defined in a similar way:

$$\pi(Y'|Z) = \sum_x \pi(x|Z)(y'|x). \tag{15.2}$$

Logit models are used to estimate the relationships between the latent factor (x) and the observed indicators (Y), and the impacts of the Z variables, including state rankings. Two logit models are specified in Equations 15.3 and 15.4 and estimated simultaneously (Agresti, 1990; Moustaki, 2002; Vermunt & Magidson, 2000):

$$\log\left[\frac{\pi(x_{\leq t}|Z)}{1 - \pi(x_{\leq t}|Z)}\right] = t - \sum_{l=1}^{L} \sum_{j=1}^{J_l} \gamma_{xz_{jl}}. \tag{15.3}$$

Equation 15.3 is used to estimate γ, that is, the impacts of the various Z variables, and the threshold of the underlying distribution of well-being, namely, τ_t. As mentioned earlier, we define $t = \{1, 2\}$, for the sake of simplicity, and $\sum_{t=1}^{T=2} \tau_t = 0$. We discuss the content of the Z vector, and the J_l and L constants in more detail later. Equation 15.4 is used to estimate the relationships between the latent factor (the well-being of teenage children) and the observed indicators, which are indicated by y_m, for analyses that allow the impacts of the latent factor on the indicators to vary:

$$\log\left[\frac{\pi(y_m \leq s_m|x_{\leq t})}{1 - \pi(y_m \leq s_m|x_{\leq t})}\right] = \tau_{s_m} - \beta_{y_m x} x_{\leq t} \tag{15.4}$$

where b reflects the impacts of the latent factor on the observed indicators. For each indicator, τ_{s_m} is used to define the threshold. As in Equation 15.3, we also define $\sum_{s_1=1}^{s_1=4} \tau_{s_1} = \sum_{s_2=1}^{s_2=2} \tau_{s_2} = \sum_{s_3=1}^{s_3=4} \tau_{s_3} = 0$. To estimate the state ranking based on equally weighted indicators, we can rewrite Equation 15.4 as the following:

$$\log\left[\frac{\pi\left(y' \le s'|x_{\le t}\right)}{1 - \pi\left(y' \le s'|x_{\le t}\right)}\right] = \tau_{s'} - \beta_{y'x}x_{\le t} \qquad (15.5)$$

where $\sum_{s'=8}^{S'=8}\tau_{s'} = 0$. There are eight observed categories for $y' = \sum_{m=1}^{M=3}y_m$, since, and the minimum values for the y_m's all equal zero.

Definition of Z

We estimate the following models using specifications based on Equation 15.3 to define models with different control variables.

***Model* 1** – $\pi\left(y'|x, Z\right)=$ *f(year, age, state)*   Using Equation 15.5, Model 1 assumes an equal impact of the latent factor on all indicators. There are three determinants in Model 1. In addition to state dummies that allow us to produce state rankings, the model also controls for year and age. By incorporating year dummies, unobserved factors associated with year, such as business cycles and variations in data quality by year, are controlled for. Indicators of child well-being may also vary by age group. For example, the educational delay for children at college age may not be as important as the delay for younger children. In this model, L reflects three variables—J_1, J_2, and J_3—included in the array Z. There are 51 (J_1) dummy variables indicating the level of well-being of teenage children in the 50 states and Washington, DC, in contrast to the grand mean of the United States. There are three CPS survey years (J_2): 1996, 1998, and 2000. Finally, there are four dummy variables (J_3) used to control for age variations in the measure of well-being:

$$\log\left[\frac{\pi\left(x_{\le t}|Z\right)}{1 - \pi\left(x_{\le t}|Z\right)}\right] = \tau_t - \left[\sum_{j_1=1}^{J_1=51}\gamma_{xz_{j_1}} + \sum_{j_2=1}^{J_2=3}\gamma_{xz_{j_2}} + \sum_{j_3=1}^{J_3=4}\gamma_{xz_{j_3}}\right] \cdot (15.6)$$

***Model* 2** – $\pi\left(y'|x, Z\right)=$ *f(year, age, state)*   There are three determinants in Model 2. The determinant structure of Model 2 is identical to that of Model 1, but we allow the weight of each observed indicator to vary. In Model 2, we estimate Equations 15.4 and 15.6 simultaneously.

***Model* 3** – $\pi\left(y'|x, Z\right)=$ *f(year, age, state, immigration, race-ethnicity)* Model 3 is defined in the same way as Model 2 but has more control variables. It has five determinants that include all of the variables in Model 2 and two variables for individual characteristics, immigration status and race-ethnicity, which may affect the distribution of the well-being of teenage children but may not be affected by state policies.

J_4 is used to indicate the nativity status of the children–either both parents being native born or at least one being foreign born. An array of dummies (J_5) is used to identify non-Hispanic White, non-Hispanic Black, Hispanic children, and children of any other race/ethnicity.

$$\log\left[\frac{\pi\left(x_{\leq t}|Z\right)}{1-\pi\left(x_{\leq t}|Z\right)}\right] = \tau_t - \left[\sum_{j_1=1}^{J_1=51}\gamma_{xz_{j_1}} + \sum_{j_2=1}^{J_2=3}\gamma_{xz_{j_2}} + \sum_{j_3=1}^{J_3=4}\gamma_{xz_{j_3}} + \sum_{j_4=1}^{J_4=2}\gamma_{xz_{j_4}} + \sum_{j_5=1}^{J_5=4}\gamma_{xz_{j_5}}\right]$$

(15.7)

Findings

What difference do unconstrained weights make? In Figure 15.1 we display the state rankings stemming from uniform weights (Model 1) versus those resulting from unconstrained weights (Model 2). Regardless of method, one sees those states typically found at the bottom of these sorts of rankings—such as Mississippi, New Mexico, and the District of Columbia—and those usually found at the top, as well-such as Utah,

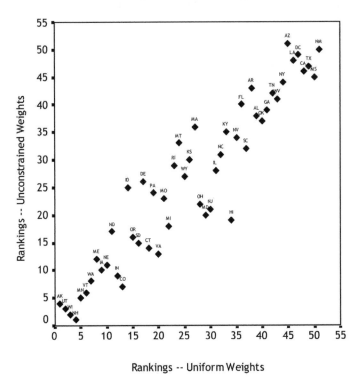

Figure 15.1.   Rankings resulting from using uniform weights (Model 1) versus using unconstrained weights (Model 2).

Wisconsin, and New Hampshire. If there were no differences resulting from the two methods, then rankings would be identical, and we would see all states falling along the 45-degree line. The rankings are strongly correlated, with a rank correlation coefficient of .943. We see in Figure 15.2 that movement in rankings is not great for many states. However, a number of states do experience what some may view as significant slippage or gain in rankings as a result of allowing weights to vary. For example, nine states fall in the rankings by at least five spots, including Massachusetts, Montana, Delaware, and Idaho, which slip by nine or more positions. In contrast, eight states improve their rankings by at least five spots, with Maryland, New Jersey, and Hawaii rising by nine or more positions.

Next, we determine the degree to which racial and ethnic composition and immigrant status affect state rankings. In other words, what would the rankings look like if all states were on equal footing with respect to these important demographic characteristics (Model 3)?

We know that racial and ethnic composition differs dramatically across the 50 states and the District of Columbia. Among our sample of teenagers, state minority proportions are 5% or less in Vermont, Maine, Iowa, and West Virginia. In contrast, so-called minorities constitute the majority in the District of Columbia and the states of Texas, California,

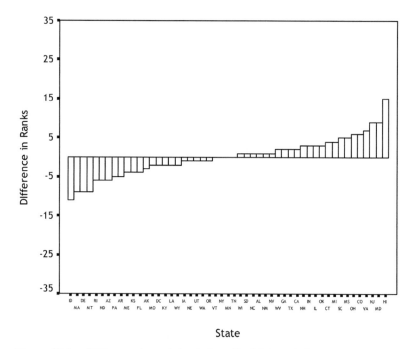

Figure 15.2. Difference in rank (rank from Model 1- rank from Model 2): uniform weights versus unconstrained weights.

New Mexico, and Hawaii. So, too, is there dramatic variation in the proportion of immigrants across states. The proportion of children who have at least one parent who is an immigrant ranges from under 1% in South Dakota, West Virginia, and Montana to greater than 25% in New York (26%), Florida (27%), and California (40%). To the extent that disparities exist with respect to racial-ethnic and immigrant/native groups in each of our indicators, as they certainly do, we would expect to find significant changes in rankings if we appropriately account for these compositional differences.

When one examines our next graph, in Figure 15.3, the impact of such an adjustment is immediately apparent. The scatter plot exhibits much more variation about the 45-degree line. Indeed, the rank correlation is only .392. Again, in more practical terms, what does this mean? The following graph, in Figure 15.4, shows clearly the very substantial changes in rankings resulting from netting out the effects of differential racial composition among the states.

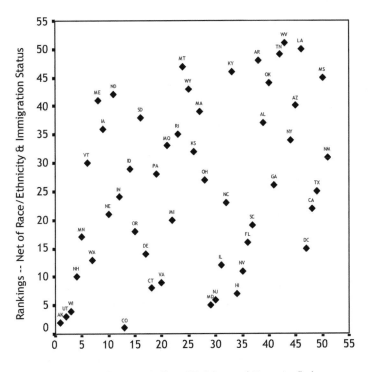

Figure 15.3. Rankings resulting from using uniform weights with no controls (Model 1) versus using unconstrained weights with controls for race, ethnic, and immigrant composition (Model 3).

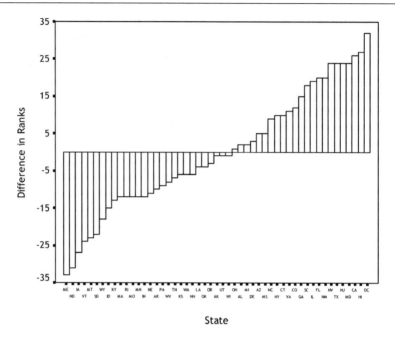

Figure 15.4.   Difference in rank (rank from Model 1 - rank from Model 3): uniform weights with no controls versus unconstrained weights and controls for race-ethnicity and immigration status.

At one end of the spectrum, we find that the District of Columbia improves its ranking by 32 spots, from 47th to 15th. California and Hawaii also rose in the rankings by more than 25 spots. In all, nine states improved by 20 or more positions. States such as Hawaii, California, Nevada, and Texas also rise quite a bit in the rankings. On the other hand, we see that Maine fell by 33 spots, from 8th to 41st. North Dakota and Iowa also dropped by over 25 spots. Half a dozen states fell by at least 20 positions. These are all states with small minority populations. Such dramatic differences in rankings would surely be of much concern to state policymakers.

It should be noted, however, that rankings may give a false impression of precision with respect to how states compare to one another. For example, one cannot tell whether a state ranked 1st in child well-being is significantly different from a state ranked 10th. It may be more statistically honest, so to speak, to avoid the temptation of ranking states and to rely instead on a summary of which states are performing either significantly better or worse than the overall national mean, although the latter approach may not be as appealing or, indeed, as effective for policymakers, the general public, or the media as the former. Such a categorization is displayed in Table 15.2. At the .10 level, child well-being in

Table 15.2
States That are Significantly Better or Worse
With Respect to Child Well-Being Than the National Mean

Better	Worse
Alaska	Arizona
Colorado	Arkansas
Connecticut	Kentucky
Hawaii	Louisiana
Illinois	Massachusetts
Maryland	Mississippi
Nevada	Montana
New Jersey	New York
Utah	Oklahoma
Virginia	Tennessee
Wisconsin	West Virginia
	Wyoming

11 states—such as Utah and Wisconsin, but also New Jersey and Illinois —is significantly superior to the national mean, whereas that in 12 states—including Mississippi and Louisiana, but also Wyoming and Montana—is significantly worse.[2]

DISCUSSION

By finding such large differences in ranking between the models that do and do not control for race and ethnic composition, as well as differences in immigrant status across the states, a next important step is to explore the nature of disparities in indicator levels among these demographic groups. The fact that many states moved up dramatically in the rankings once we controlled for different aspects of composition does not imply that these states may rest easy in their efforts to improve child well-being. It simply means that we have a better understanding of the characteristics associated with child well-being. It is still necessary to examine why such discrepancies exist among different demographic groups and for policymakers to explore factors that are directly amenable to public policy intervention.

We have tried here to show the robustness or lack of robustness of index construction to a pair of methodological concerns. In short, we found that composition effects play a large role in currently existing indexes of child well-being but that weights play a lesser role in influencing rankings. We are convinced that any sort of index, however statistically sophisticated, will engender heated debate. That notwithstanding, we hope that our effort sheds at least a faint ray of light so that we can find a path toward consensus on what is necessary to create both a readily accessible and statistically defensible index of child well-being.

ACKNOWLEDGMENTS

We are grateful to Brett Brown and Kenneth Land for their suggestions and comments. We also thank Mei-Chen Hu for her valuable input.

NOTES

1. The latent class factor model is equivalent to a latent class cluster model with two clusters (Magidson & Vermunt, 2001). We choose to present it as a factor model rather than a cluster model because the parameterization of the factor model, as specified, is easier to interpret in the context of our research. For the purpose of illustration, we discuss only the case with one factor with two latent categories instead of three or more categories. With our sample and indicators, we also found that models assuming more than one factor or models with one factor but assuming more than two categories do not fit as well as the model discussed here (a model with only one factor with two latent categories).
2. A by-product of allowing weights to vary from uniformity is that the precision of our estimates of the level of child well-being by state improves. Thus, we are better able to determine whether state levels of child well-being fall significantly above or below the national mean.

REFERENCES

Agresti, A. (1990). *Categorical data analysis.* New York: Wiley.
Annie E. Casey Foundation. (2003). *2003 Kids Count data book: State profiles of child well-being.* Baltimore.
Belcher, D. W., Neumann, A. K., Wurapa, F. K., & Lourie, I. M. (1976). Comparison of morbidity interviews with a health examination survey in rural Africa. *American Journal of Tropical Medicine and Hygiene, 25,* 751–758.
Heinen, T. (1996). *Latent class and discrete latent trait models: Similarities and differences.* Thousand Oaks, CA: Sage.
Land, K. C., Lamb, V. L., & Mostillo, S. K. (2007). Child well-being in the United States, 1975–1998. *Some findings from a new index* (pp. 393–444). Boca Raton, FL: Taylor & Francis Group.
Magidson, J., & Vermunt, J. K. (2001). Latent class factor and cluster models, bi-plots, and related graphical displays. *Sociological Methodology, 31,* 223–264.
Miringoff, M. L., Miringoff, M., & Opdycke, S. (1996). Monitoring the nation's social performance: The index of social health. In E. F. Zigler, S. L. Kagan, & N. W. Hall (Eds.), *Children, families, and government: Preparing for the twenty-first century* (pp. 10–30). New York: Cambridge University Press.

Moustaki, I. (2002). *A general class of latent variable models for ordinal manifest variables with covariate effects on the manifest and latent variables.* Unpublished manuscript, Athens University of Economics and Business, Athens, Greece.

Murray, C. J. L., & Chen, L. C. (1992). Understanding morbidity change. *Population and Development Review, 18,* 481–503.

Rogers, R., Hummer, R. A., & Nam, C. B. (2000). Living and dying in the USA. San Diego, CA: Academic Press.

Vermunt, J. K., & Magidson, J. (2000). *Latent gold: User's guide.* Belmont, MA: Statistical Innovations.

Author Index

Subject Index